creating
3-D

Harry N. Abrams, Inc., Publishers

REVISED EDITION

creating 3-D animation

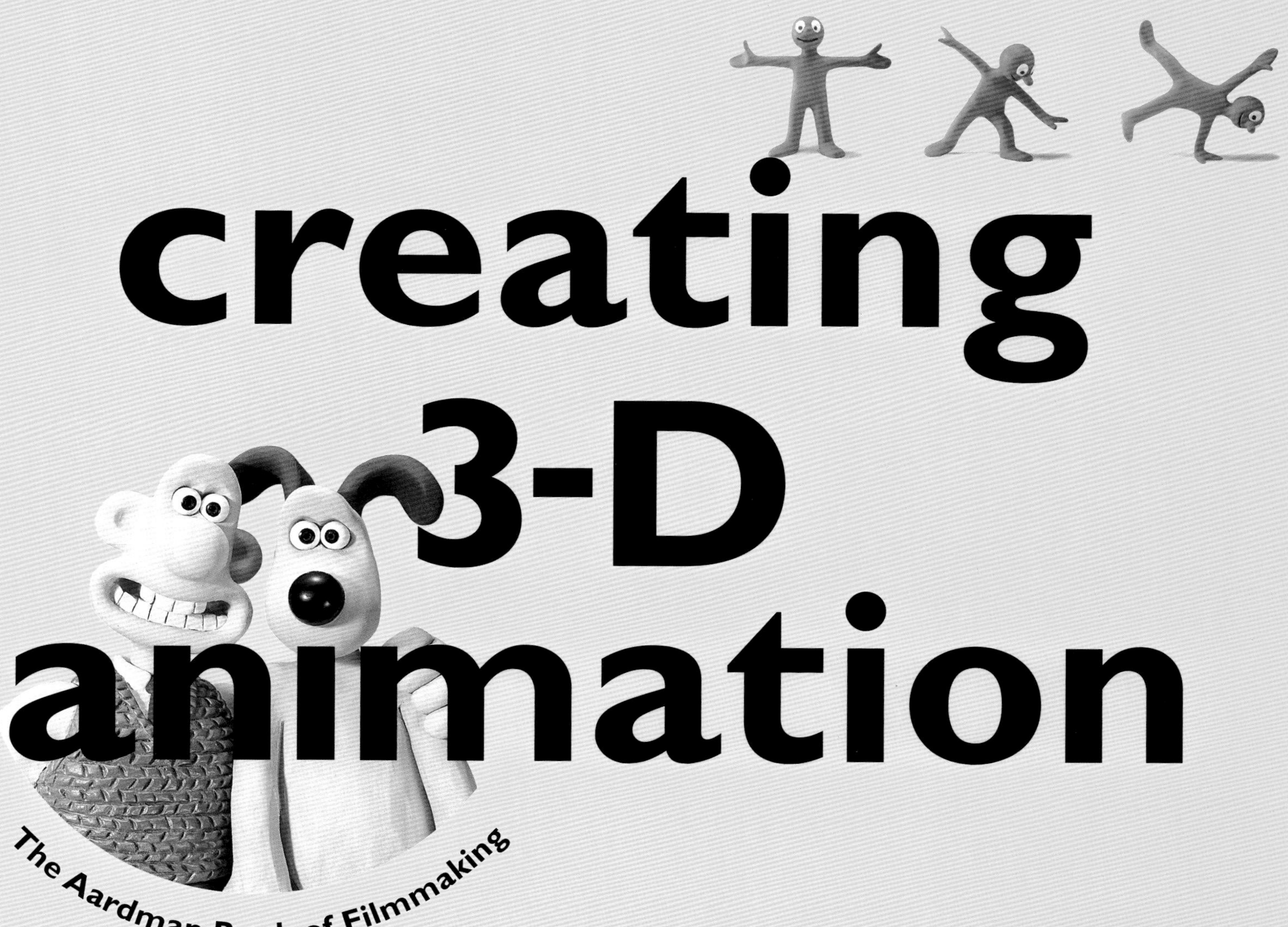

The Aardman Book of Filmmaking

Peter Lord & Brian Sibley

Foreword by Nick Park

contents

6 **foreword** Nick Park

8 **introduction** Peter Lord

16 **the medium** Brian Sibley

66 **practical animation** Peter Lord

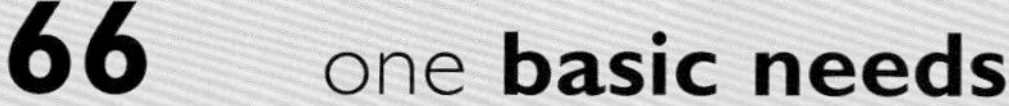

66 one **basic needs**

The Camera
Video Cameras and Computers
A Simple Studio
A Complex Studio
The Power of Lighting

80 two **simple techniques**

Simple Clay Animation
Simple Object Animation
Other Animation Techniques

92 three **models and modelmaking**

Basic Principles
Making a Sheep
Gromit Construction
Wat Construction
Rex Construction

110 four **set design and making**

Planning a Set
A Straightforward Set
Matching Sets to Products
A Complex Set
Ingenuity and Props
Special Effects
Advanced Special Effects

132 five **animation and performance**

Movement
Walk Cycles
Making Movement Believable
Acceleration and Deceleration
Action and Reaction
Special Movement Effects
Expressions and Gestures
Speech and Lip-sync

158 six **making a film**

Thinking About a Script
Creating a Storyboard for *Adam*
Creating a Storyboard for *The Wrong Trousers*
Creating a Storyboard for *A Close Shave*
Chicken Run - the Challenge
Shooting *Chicken Run* - the Technical Side
CGI Computer Generated Imagery
Chop Socky Chooks
Using Flash Animation - *Big Jeff*
Creating *Angry Kid*
Characterisation
New Directions for Animators
Editing
Sound and Music
A Career in Animation

220 **filmography & bibliography**

222 **index**

foreword Nick Park

Gromit reacts in terror at his first sighting of the mysterious Techno Trousers in *The Wrong Trousers* (1993), directed by Nick Park.

I wish this book had been written in the Seventies when I was a teenager and started experimenting with animation and making my first movies. I did not meet another animator, or even anyone with a vague knowledge of the technique, for years. My early experience in animation was therefore a solitary one; a case of guesswork and trial and error. I felt that everyone else must be 'doing it right', and there must be something very obvious that everyone else knew about that I was not doing. I scoured old library books and movie magazines for any scraps of information, but found very little.

Later I met Peter Lord and David Sproxton whose work I had long admired. Through them and Aardman Animations I met more of our species, and was surprised to find that they had all felt similarly isolated and had worked through experimentation either at college or on the kitchen table.

Although there is now a great deal more information available about animation, especially now that computer animation has become so prominent, this book still holds a wealth of valuable hints, tips and insights. In the past few years it has actually become much easier to make animated films using small video cameras and simple computer systems, but the performance skills and story-telling aspects of the craft never change. I hope this edition fills you with enthusiasm for the world of 3-D animation.

introduction

Peter Lord

Peter Lord with his character Adam. Released in 1991, *Adam* won Aardman an Oscar® nomination.

I began animating as a hobby, when I was a teenager, over thirty years ago. And though it has now become my career, it has never stopped being a hobby. Other boys of my age were spending their leisure time building model aircraft, or recording train numbers, or sitting on riverbanks awaiting the appearance of fish. But Fate led me to animation. Fate in the shape of my best friend's Dad, who owned a cine camera.

I met Dave Sproxton, my partner at Aardman, when we were both twelve. We sat at adjoining desks at Woking Grammar School for Boys. His father worked for the BBC as a producer of religious programmes and was also a keen photographer. Like many a producer in those days, and probably to the despair of the Film Union, Vernon Sproxton was not averse to shooting some of his own material if he could get away with it. So he owned a cine camera, a clockwork 16mm Bolex, which was the key factor in our decision to become animators. Along with access to the camera, Dave picked up his father's enthusiasm for photography and an understanding of how films are made. It is significant that Nick Park grew up in a similar environment. His father was a professional photographer who had also dabbled in film-making. He had even done a little bit of animation. So in Nick's family too there was always a cine camera about the place. In both households, film-making was made to seem possible and accessible, even normal.

So we had access to the camera; and one rainy day, probably encouraged by his father, Dave and I experimented with animation. In the great tradition of British amateurism our first film was made on the kitchen table. Only later, after we had served our apprenticeship, and got in the way of everybody's mealtimes, did we advance to the spare room. Our camera was mounted on a developing stand pointing straight downwards at the table, and our first piece of animation was achieved by drawing a chalk figure on a blackboard, shooting a frame, then rubbing out part of the figure, redrawing it in a new position and shooting another frame. And so on. At the time it seemed painstaking, but compared to some of our subsequent experiences in animation, that first film was a high-speed, spontaneous affair.

We did not launch into animation entirely unprepared. We had seen documentaries about the world of cartoons, and heard how Disney and Hanna Barbera made films with thousands of separate drawings on acetate sheets, but we had no access to the techniques or the materials to shoot this sort of 'traditional' animation. We made up the chalk technique quite independently, to suit our circumstances, though I now know that like so much else in the world of animation it had all been done before – much of it ninety years ago or more!

The original Aardman, a cel sequence featuring an inept figure with a costume based on Superman.

In a matter of hours we became bored with chalk animation, and tried a different technique: cut-outs. We cut pictures out of magazines, crudely cutting off their limbs so they could be animated as separate elements. We had discovered one of the quicker and simpler forms of animation. Our first 'film' consisted of several experiments like this. It was simply a string of animated events, lasting for a couple of minutes. We had no story to tell, no ideas to convey, it was strictly stream of consciousness. We called it *Trash* - not knowing that Andy Warhol had already used the name. It took only a couple of days to complete – although at the time that seemed a pretty mammoth effort – and for the first but not the last time we observed that animation was a slow process. When the developed film came back from the laboratory, we showed it in the living room to our assembled families, with a record on the hi-fi as an accompaniment. And we loved it. We thought it was great. We experienced that sense of magic which happily you never lose, and which I believe is unique to animation. The day-to-day business of animation is usually slow, repetitive and painstaking – and seldom particularly funny. But when it is all over, when the performance is finished, and the hard work mostly forgotten, then you see the result and bingo! – it's alive!

We followed *Trash* with a film called *Godzilla*. Naturally it had no giant lizards in it. It was a similar mix of techniques: cut-outs, chalky, swirly transformations which used the properties of chalk to blur and soften and drag out a line, and a couple of 3-D objects, like toy cars, thrown in for good measure. Though I have not seen either film for twenty years, I assume it was an improvement on *Trash*. When you are just starting out in animation, you learn really fast. Every new completed piece is a revelation. Only when your film is returned from the lab can you see what you have done, for better or worse. Only then can you find out how bad your timing is, how clumsily your drawings move, how insignificant one-twelfth of a second can be.

The studio during the early years - when the entire modelmaking department was confined to a single table.

Shortly after this, Dave's Dad arranged for us to show our work to a producer at the BBC. Patrick Dowling produced the 'Vision On' series, which was

'Cracking toast, Gromit!' Wallace and Gromit at the breakfast table in *A Grand Day Out* (1989).

specifically designed for deaf children. It was a great programme – imaginative, brave, technically innovative and stimulating for those with hearing as well as the deaf because it presented visual information in an intelligent and surprising way. The outcome of our first meeting was that PD, as we called him – everyone knew that TV execs were known by their initials – gave us a 100ft roll of film to experiment with. In the late 1960s this precious roll of unexposed negative probably represented the BBC's total investment in new animation talent.

We filled that roll with tests and experiments – some chalk animation, a cel sequence (the original Aardman film), some pixillation (where human beings are treated as animation puppets), and a couple of sequences where we experimented with Plasticine (modelling clay). In one of these, we made a low-relief Plasticine model of a cottage – a crude, childlike thing, I recall. As before, the camera was directly above, looking down on to the model. Under the camera it metamorphosed, as only Plasticine can, into a low-relief model of an elephant. Not the world's greatest storyline, I agree. The BBC showed no inclination to buy this piece, or to commission more, but for me a seed was sown. I had tried this new malleable medium and found it strangely attractive. It took another couple of years for the technique and the storylines to evolve, but our animation future was going to be in three dimensions.

In fact what the BBC did buy was the Aardman sequence. It was a piece of conventional cel animation, and I remember it as the most 'professional' piece on the roll. Aardman is a character that I originally drew in a strip cartoon. He

Today the Aardman studio plays host to a growing number of talented film-makers. Here Jeff Newitt acts out the facial expressions of his character while animating him for *Loves Me ... Loves Me Not* (1992).

was based on Superman – in costume, at any rate – with a jutting chin, a cape and a large letter 'A' on his chest. He became the star of our first cel animation, though we left the letter 'A' off his chest, because it took too long to draw.

In his first animated appearance Aardman is walking past, as I recall, a background of brown wrapping paper. He has a goofy walk: legs bent, leaning well back, his arms not swinging but hanging straight by his sides. As he walks, he approaches a cartoon 'hole' – the classic black ellipse on the ground. He stops, sticks out a foot and taps the ellipse. It seems solid. He walks on, right over the 'hole', quite unharmed. One step later, he falls through the ground, down an invisible hole. After a pause, his hand emerges from the ground, feels around, finds the ellipse and pulls it over himself. Then he climbs out and walks off.

That may not be a gripping read, but it was good enough to get bought – and for £15 or so. This was the moment when, faced with a 'purchased programme' agreement and a cheque from the BBC, we opened a bank account in the name of Aardman Animations. I remember discussing the merits of 'Dave and Pete Productions', 'Lord Sproxton Films' and numerous other possibilities - but 'Aardman' it was.

Two teenagers picked a name, little dreaming that it would hang around so long. Now, all those years later, the name no longer stands for a couple of enthusiastic schoolboy animators; now it stands for a diverse group of film-makers and producers – a studio, in fact. We've produced children's series, TV commercials, teasers for the internet, Academy Award winning shorts and even a feature film. But the impulse that drives us is still the same. We want to tell stories and we love making films, Initially, it was terribly simple: two young men making short animated films to amuse themselves, for the pleasure of creation, for the pleasure of communication, to show off, to do something a little different, to get a laugh, to affect people we had never met. Later, as Aardman got bigger and more established, we discovered that we were not just individuals whistling in the dark but part of a scattered and formless community of film-makers in Britain and worldwide.

Scene from Peter Lord's medieval fantasy *Wat's Pig* (1996).

Then the approval of our peers became important. Suddenly a film was more than just a story told for a few friends, or broadcast to a large invisible TV audience. It became like a public statement, or a brick in the wall of something much larger and oddly noble: 'The World of Animation'. Later on the game changed again as we started to employ people, who made their own films which did not come from Dave and me but were Aardman films. Nick Park is the most famous of the film-makers who have joined us in this way. Then the source of pleasure changed slightly. From being entirely selfish, it became broader: from look-at-me to look-at-us. It was rather like becoming a parent. Before you become a parent, life is more or less selfish. Then, when you have kids, you start to live through them to some extent – for good or ill – enjoying their triumphs and sharing their defeats.

When we were just a two-man partnership, life - or at any rate business - was simple. But now we are a studio, often employing hundreds of people, and our operation has become very complex and fascinating – not to mention bewildering. The last seven or eight years have seen huge changes as we've embarked on feature films and entered the world of computer animation.

Chicken Run, our first full-length feature film, was a challenge we couldn't resist. There's not much point in making films if you don't show them to other people; and while a large TV audience is a very satisfying thing, there's nothing to beat the excitement of showing your work to hundreds of people in a cinema. With a live audience, the film itself comes to life in a way which never happens on the small screen. Anyway, for whatever reason, we were determined to 'crack' Hollywood, and I can report that it was a massive effort. Though *Chicken Run* was only three times as long as *The Wrong Trousers*, the whole scale of the shoot seemed to be about twenty times bigger. We had to train new animators, convert a warehouse into a customised stop-frame studio and build hundreds of chickens. Yet despite the scale, and the mountains of work we heaped up for ourselves, *Chicken Run* is still a typical Aardman film. It was made by a team of hundreds of talented people - animators, modelmakers and film-makers of every description – people who love what they're doing and do it especially well.

At about the same time as we were embarking on feature films, we started seriously developing our CG department, and every year we produce more and more computer animation alongside our traditional work. Of course these

Computer-generated Bookworm ident for BBC Television's 'Big Read', plugging the virtues of George Orwell's *Nineteen Eighty-Four.*

days, when most people in the film industry talk about 3-D animation, it's CG animation they're talking about. So I'm happy to claim that we're involved in the best 3-D animation whether it's actual or virtual. Within Aardman, there are some of us who cross over from the hands-on world of the studio floor, with its cameras, lights and Plasticine models, to the world of computers and monitors. Others stay firmly on one side of the fence or the other and show no desire to move. There's no doubt in my mind that in our traditional hand-made animation we produce something unique and increasingly rare. But to me, the essential point is the similarities between the techniques: both require an expressive use of camera angles, lenses and lighting. Both depend on acting, movement and the expressive use of the body, the hands, the face and especially the eyes. All the really important things apply to either medium: storytelling, editing, composition, design, and performance.

So Aardman is still growing, and changing as it has done ever since 1976 when we officially decided to go Professional. Today we employ all the skills and the crafts of a busy film studio. There are animators, of course, but we also employ engineers and electricians. Lighting grids need to be rigged, films edited, and scripts developed, but the year-end accounts also have to be prepared on time. As well as people who make models we need people who strike deals. We need to be profitable to continue to do what we love, but making money is not what interests or motivates us. It is certainly not why we make films.

The big pleasure for me at this stage in Aardman's evolution is the feeling I sometimes get – not every day, it is true – of being in a community of artists. I love being among dozens of creative people, under one roof, generating ideas, discussing them, interacting, being influenced and affected by each other. The

Scene from *Chicken Run,* Aardman's first feature-length film. Star chicken Ginger is flanked by Babs (right) and Mac, the bespectacled Scottish chicken.

studios too are an exciting place, the product of twenty years of growth and change. Ever since the old days of the kitchen table, we have steadily invested in people and equipment; and as we have met other specialists in our tiny field we have learnt new techniques, tricks and practices which have changed our way of working. Some of the ways we work are standard film-industry practice, some we have learned from other animation studios, some are derived from the theatre and many have simply evolved on site. Technology, culture and working practice have slowly accumulated like a coral reef, or like a junk pile, if you prefer. All that knowledge has been built up by trial and error and by word of mouth over the last twenty years. How often we wished in the early days that some predecessor of ours had written a book like this, to pass on the precious information.

the medium

Brian Sibley

Steve Box animates the fleeing Penguin in the staircase sequence of *The Wrong Trousers* (1993).

Animation is a form of movie magic that has its origins in a tradition that is longer and older than might, at first, be supposed. The aim of this opening section is to provide an independent view of the history of animated films, both drawn (2-D) and model (3-D) animation, and to place the work of Aardman Animations within the broader context of a film-making technique that began in the 1890s.

One of the earliest films by Peter Lord and Dave Sproxton shows a human hand flattening and shaping a ball of clay that then takes on animated life. A tiny hand and arm reach up out of the clay, then another hand and arm emerge, followed by the head and torso of a little man, struggling to haul himself free. Then the human hand reappears, seizes the man and wrenches him - fully formed - out of the clay. This little being, made from the very stuff of the earth itself, looks towards his creator, sits down and assumes the position of Rodin's sculpture, *The Thinker* ...

The creation myth is very old and is found, with variations, in many different cultures and faiths. As a symbolic picture, explaining not just the origin of man but also the source of man's creativity, it has provided a recurrent image for artists down the centuries and, in particular, for the work of the three-dimensional animator. Peter Lord, for example, returned to the idea in his 1991 Oscar-nominated film *Adam*, in which the relationship between an animator and his clay became an amusing analogy for the relationship between God and Man.

But first things first: what is 3-D animation? Most forms of animated film-making achieve their effect through essentially flat images usually drawn on cels (transparent sheets which can be overlaid on background paintings and then photographed), but occasionally painted on glass or even directly onto the film itself. A three-dimensional animator, however, works with articulated puppets or with models built around a metal, moveable 'skeleton' called an armature, and made of Plasticine (modelling clay), fabric or latex. Occasionally, the 3-D animator will work with cut-outs, and he often uses his skills to give animated life to a bizarre range of inanimate objects from a bra to a burger.

The power of animation lies in the fact that, like all film, it plays with an optical illusion known as 'persistence of vision'. The human eye retains an image for a fraction of a second after it has been seen. If, in that brief time-space, one image can be substituted for another, slightly different, image, then the illusion of movement is created. What we are really seeing when we look at a cinema screen is not a 'moving picture' at all, but a series of still pictures - 24 every second - shown in such rapid succession that our eyes are deceived.

Capturing the dynamics of action: a Greek image of chariot racing from the 6th century BC.

The essential difference between making a live-action and an animated film is that the live-action camera captures a scene moving in *real* time, automatically 'freezing' it into separate still pictures, which can then be projected onto a screen. For the animator, however, nothing exists to be filmed until it is created and put in front of the camera. Using drawings, models or, increasingly nowadays, computer imagery, the animator creates every single frame of film from scratch. In a live-action film, there is nothing hidden between one frame and the next, whereas the space between every frame of an animated film represents a complex series of creative actions which, if the film is well made, will be undetectable to the audience.

Not only must characters and settings be designed, but decisions must also be taken about what movement will be involved in a scene and the kind of shot - such as a close-up or a long-shot - that will be used. So, whilst animation is a highly creative medium, it is weighed down by time-consuming processes that require the successful animator to have vision, vast quantities of patience and a sustained belief in the film that is being made.

There is also a major difference between drawn and model animation, as Peter Lord explains: 'Drawn animation is a process that develops in a very controlled, measurable way. When your character is walking (or jumping or flying) from A to B, you start by drawing position A and position B, the key positions, and then you systematically draw all the positions in between - the animation. But in puppet animation, when you set off from position A you do not know where B is, because you have not got there yet (like real life, come to think of it). So

every single stage of a movement is an experiment, or even an adventure. You have this idea of where you are heading, but no certainty of getting there ...'

The desire to animate is as old as art itself. The early man who drew pictures on his cave wall depicting spear-waving hunters in pursuit of a wild boar attempted to convey the illusion of movement by showing the beast with multiple legs. The vases of ancient Greece with their gods and heroes, and the friezes of Rome with their battling warriors and galloping steeds, also sought to capture, in static images, the dynamics of action. Stories of pictures that came to life can be found in folklore and fairy-tale, but it was not until the 19th century - in the years leading up to the invention of the motion picture - that animated pictures became a real possibility.

Muybridge's baseball hitter, who served as a model for the animated sequence shown on pages 142-143.

Among the many pioneers in Europe and America who explored ways of capturing images of real life, and attempted to analyse and replicate movement, were Britain's William Henry Fox Talbot, who devised a photographic method for recording the images of the 'camera obscura', and English-born American, Eadweard Muybridge, who, in 1872, began producing a series of studies of human and animal life, photographed in front of a plain, calibrated backdrop. The photographs, shot every few seconds, revealed what the human eye cannot register: the true complexity involved in the mechanics of physical locomotion.

A photographic sequence by Eadweard Muybridge, whose 19th-century experiments have been of priceless help to later generations of animators.

The Phenakistiscope, invented in 1832 by Joseph Plateau. When the picture disc is spun, a viewer looking through the slots sees continuous movement. In other versions the slots and pictures are combined on a single disc, and viewed in conjunction with a mirror.

In 1880, Muybridge conducted one of his most sophisticated experiments when he photographed a running horse using 24 still cameras set up alongside a race track and triggered by a series of trip-wires. Muybridge's photographs of horses, dogs and the naked human form would become an indispensable aid to later generations of animators. Indeed, while Peter Lord was working on some of the models shown in this book, such as the baseball player on page 142, Muybridge's book was a constant source of reference.

Experimentation with photographic and optical techniques led to various devices such as the Stereoscope, which used two slightly different photographic images to create the illusion of 3-D pictures, and sophisticated magic-lantern slides on which parts of the picture could be made to move: a ship tossing on a stormy sea, a rat running into the open mouth of a sleeping man.

There were also a number of popular optical toys, designed to recreate the illusion of life. The earliest, and simplest, devised in 1825 by Dr John Ayrton Paris, was the Thaumatrope: a disc of card with a picture of a bird on one side and a bird-cage on the other. Strings attached to either side of the disc were twisted tight and held taut; then, when the tension on the strings was released, the disc spun so fast that the bird appeared to be inside the bird-cage.

Seven years later, Joseph Plateau, a physicist from Belgium, invented the Phenakistiscope, a disc fixed to a handle (rather like a child's windmill toy) so that it could spin freely. Around its perimeter the disc had a series of drawn figures in various stages of movement, separated by slots. The disc was held up to a mirror and spun, while the viewer looked through the slots and saw - reflected in the mirror - a running horse, a leaping acrobat or some other moving miracle.

William George Horner of Britain was the first to attempt to create moving images for more than one viewer. He devised the Zoetrope, in which spectators looked through slots in a fast-moving drum at a continuous strip of drawings arranged around the inside. The speed with which the drum revolved blurred the slots into a 'window' and gave life to the static pictures. For variety, the strips of drawings could be changed, but the sequences were limited and repetitious such as a dog jumping through a hoop, or a clown's nose endlessly growing and shrinking.

The Praxinoscope, a drum viewer. The images on the perimeter of the drum are reflected in a mirror as they flash past the viewer's eyes.

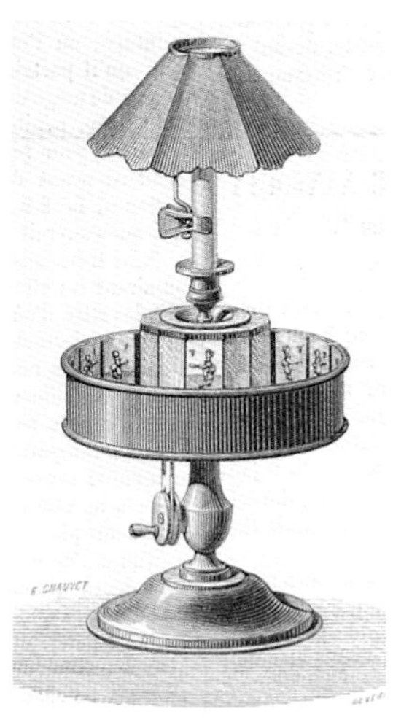

Emile Reynaud and his Théâtre Optique, which projected 'moving pictures' and backgrounds on to the same screen.

It was due to a visionary Frenchman, Emile Reynaud, that the evolution of the animated film took two major steps forward. The first of these, invented in 1877, was the Praxinoscope, a sophisticated development of the Zoetrope, which enabled viewers to watch the moving pictures as they turned past the eye on a rotating drum.

Reynaud, who was a painter of lantern-slides, spent the next fifteen years improving his device until he found a method of combining the illusion created by the Zoetrope with the projected images seen at the magic-lantern show. The Théâtre Praxinoscope, as it was called, used light and mirrors to show a limited cycle of moving figures against a projected background on what looked like the stage of a toy theatre. Reynaud then further refined his device into the Théâtre Optique, first demonstrated at the Musée Grévin, Paris, in 1892. This elaborate machine simultaneously projected 'moving pictures' and backgrounds onto the same screen. The shows, entitled 'Pantomimes Lumineuses', were not limited to the short cycles of action seen on a Praxinoscope but lasted up to fifteen minutes and comprised some 500 pictures on a transparent strip of gelatin. Although the mechanism had to be turned by hand (a laborious process for the operator), Reynaud's equipment anticipated various cinematic devices including the film-spool and sprocket-holes for moving the pictures on while, at the same time, keeping them in focus. Interestingly, Reynaud used drawings rather than photographic images, and every subsequent animated film using line animation - from Felix the Cat and Mickey Mouse to the Rugrats and the Simpsons - is a successor to the moving pictures that he created.

Reynaud's 'films' were simple - sometimes mildly saucy - tales mainly concerned with love and rivalry: a young lady at a seaside resort goes into a beach hut to change into her bathing costume, unaware that a peeping tom is watching her through the door. The cad is eventually given the boot by a young man who, as a reward for his gallantry, is allowed to accompany the young lady on a swim. Audiences were amazed and delighted by these moving drawings, but rapid developments quickly provided new entertainments that were to upstage Reynaud's Théâtre Optique.

Experiments by Etienne-Jules Marey in France, Thomas Edison in America and William Friese-Greene and Mortimer Evans in Britain resulted in coin-in-the-slot 'box-projectors' showing acrobatics, ballet and boxing matches, slapstick

The rocket lands on the eye of the Moon, from Georges Méliès's fantasy film *Voyage to the Moon* (1902).Many of the visual tricks employed in this film were achieved by stopping the film, altering the image and photographing the new scene.This later becameone of the basic techniques of 3-D animation films.

comedy routines or saucy fan dancers. The popularity of such entertainments was eventually eclipsed by the invention of a device that was, for ever, to change the culture of the world - the Cinématographe.

It was in 1895, just three years after Emile Reynaud showed his Théâtre Optique, that two French brothers, Auguste and Louis Lumière, presented the first authentic demonstration of what we now think of as cinema. There was nothing particularly sophisticated about the Lumières' first films - workers leaving a factory, a baby being spoon-fed, a train entering a station - but to those early audiences they were nothing short of miraculous. Indeed, when the railway engine rushed towards the camera, billowing clouds of smoke and steam, some patrons were so startled by the realism that they fled the theatre before the engine could run them down!

Emile Reynaud's presentations of moving drawings had been superseded. The Lumière brothers were offering audiences not characters from a toy-theatre, but images of real people. However, since the appeal of mere novelty tends to be short-lived, the time soon came when audiences ceased to be astonished at the moving picture's ability to hold a mirror up to life and began to demand stories. The fledgling cinematographers responded not just with dramas, comedies and romances but also with fantasies. And there was one fantasy film-maker in particular who made a discovery of vital importance to the technique of animation.

The films of Georges Méliès grew out of his childhood love of marionettes and toy theatres combined with an adult fascination with conjuring. Describing himself as 'a great amateur of the magical art', Méliès was an accomplished stage-illusionist who saw the new medium of cinema as a natural extension of his magical arts with their transformations, metamorphoses and mysterious appearances and disappearances. The sources for his fantastical films were fairy stories, popular tales and the science-fiction sagas of fellow-Frenchman Jules Verne. He also recreated various classics of magic in which the conventional skills of the magician were replaced by trick photography.

Curiously, the technique enabling Méliès to transform a girl into a butterfly, or make a woman vanish and replace her with a skeleton, was discovered by accident: 'The camera I was using in the beginning (a rudimentary affair in which the film would tear or would often refuse to move) produced an unexpected effect one day [in 1896] when I was photographing very prosaically the Place de l'Opéra. It took a minute to release the film and get the camera going again. During this minute, the people, buses and vehicles had, of course, moved. Projecting the film, having joined the break, I suddenly saw a Madeleine-Bastille omnibus changed into a hearse and men into women. The trick of substitution, called stop action, was discovered, and two days later I made the first metamorphoses of men into women and the first sudden disappearances which had a big success ...'

Although this camera trick had first been used a year earlier in America to create a compelling illusion in the Edison Kinetoscope film, *The Execution of Mary Queen of Scots* (in which, just before the executioner's axe fell, a dummy was substituted for the actress playing the Queen), Méliès was unquestionably the first European film-maker independently to discover this technique and to then use it to great effect.

Stop action (or stop motion) enabled Méliès to create astonishing visual illusions in such trick-film masterpieces as *Voyage to the Moon* (1902), and it subsequently became the standard technique by which, over the decades, many cinema special effects were achieved. 'I do not hesitate to say,' wrote Méliès in 1907, 'that in cinematography it is today possible to realise the most impossible and the most improbable things.' Whilst the basic film technique of animation is universal - film an image, stop the camera, alter the image, film it, stop the camera and alter the image again - the animated film has employed a diversity

Chalk animation by J Stuart Blackton in *Humorous Phases of Funny Faces* (1906). Blackton drew his image on a blackboard, photographed it, then erased it, or at least took out the 'moving' part, then drew in the next phase.

of media with which to create its illusions of life. The most popular has been drawn animation, probably because of the important link between storytelling and illustration, the heritage of cartoonists and caricaturists and the visual impact of graphic design in advertising.

The history of line animation is fascinating but, in this book, must be briefly told. In 1906, J Stuart Blackton, a Briton who settled in America and who was to make trick-films with various media (including, as we shall see, puppets and clay models), produced a film entitled *Humorous Phases of Funny Faces*, inspired by a then-popular stage entertainment. One of the speciality acts seen at turn-of-the-century vaudeville shows was the 'Lightning Sketch' artist who created rapid pictures and portraits, sometimes undergoing a comic metamorphosis. Blackton recreated this effect on film with faces drawn on a chalkboard which were then brought to life with amusing results, as when smoke from a gentleman's cigar billows across the smiling face of a lady and leaves her scowling. Blackton's process of drawing a picture, photographing it, rubbing part of it out and then redrawing it was the most basic use of the stop-motion technique.

A similar process was used, in 1908, by the Parisian caricaturist and film-maker Emile Cohl in *Fantasmagorie*. The adventures of a little clown, drawn as a rudimentary stick figure, used some two thousand drawings and ran for under two minutes. What made *Fantasmagorie* memorable were the bizarre, dreamlike transformations: a champagne bottle changing into a pineapple which then becomes a tree, while an elephant turns into a house. There were many artists who advanced animation such as the brilliant American cartoonist, Winsor McCay, whose comic newspaper strip 'Little Nemo in Slumberland' (which frequently had the appearance of being a series of film frames) became an animated picture in 1911 and was followed, three years later, by *Gertie the Trained Dinosaur*. This interactive entertainment allowed the real Winsor McCay to 'converse' with the on-screen Gertie. At the end of the show, McCay would walk off-stage and reappear as a diminutive animated figure in his own cartoon.

Raoul Barre, whose film series 'The Animated Grouch Chasers' featured a caricature album that came to life, was responsible for several significant technical developments such as registration holes in animation paper, to stop the drawings from wobbling when filmed. Barre also devised a simple method for cutting down the time-consuming process in which not just the characters but also the backgrounds had to be redrawn for every single frame of film. Barre's solution was to draw a single background picture and then animate on pieces of paper that had been carefully cut so as not to obscure the setting.

It was J R Bray (creator of the comic character Colonel Heeza Liar) who came up with the idea of drawing the backgrounds on sheets of celluloid and placing them on top of the animation drawings. This served until Earl Hurd refined the process by animating his characters on sheets of celluloid that were positioned over painted backgrounds. This technique, pioneered in Hurd's 'Bobby Bump' series, remained (until the recent introduction of computer technology) the standard procedure throughout the industry.

The scene was now set for the emerging talents of a group of artists who would dominate the early years of film animation. They included Pat Sullivan (creator of Felix the Cat) and his collaborator Otto Mesmer; Dave Fleischer (responsible for the 'Out of the Inkwell' series); Paul Terry ('Aesop's Fables'); Walter Lantz (Dinky Doodle and, later, Woody Woodpecker), and the man who created Mickey Mouse, introduced sound and then colour to the animated film, pioneered feature animation and whose name eventually became a synonym for the cartoon film - Walt Disney.

The development of three-dimensional animation is less easily charted since it employed two distinct techniques - one using puppets, the other clay models - each of which went through a particular evolutionary process. In outlining the history of these two traditions, it should be understood that many of the animators whose films will be discussed worked in more than one medium.

Scene from *Gertie the Trained Dinosaur* (1914) by Winsor McCay, an interactive show in which the artist appeared live on stage and as an animated character in the film.

One such was J Stuart Blackton who, with his partner Albert E Smith, had used stop-motion photography to create startling effects in his 1907 live-action film *The Haunted Hotel* and, the following year, produced what is claimed as the first stop-motion puppet film, *The Humpty Dumpty Circus*. This film, now lost, used jointed wood toys of animals and circus performers belonging to Smith's daughter, which were posed and then photographed. Looking back, years later, on the making of this film, Smith recalled: 'It was a tedious process in as much as the movement could be achieved only by photographing separately each position. I suggested we obtain a patent on the process. Blackton felt it wasn't important enough. However, others quickly borrowed the technique, improving upon it greatly.'

A rival claimant for having made the first puppet animated film is the British film-maker Arthur

Melbourne Cooper. Among Cooper's earliest experiments with stop-motion photography was *Matches: An Appeal*, a film of 'moving matchsticks' made in 1899 for the match manufacturer Bryant & May, and probably the world's first animated commercial. For his entertainment films, Arthur Cooper looked for inspiration to the nursery toy cupboard, producing such titles as *Noah's Ark* (1906) and *Dreams of Toyland* (1908), in which a child is given various toys, including a teddy bear and a little wooden horse, and then falls asleep and dreams that the toys come to life. Although Cooper's method of filming outdoors with sunlight had its drawbacks - the combination of the stop-motion process and the earth's rotation produced strange, flickering shadows - he went on to make other successful films on similar themes, including *Cinderella* and *Wooden Athletes* (both 1912) and *The Toymaker's Dream* (1913).

The 'toys come to life' was a recurrent scenario with early animators partly because toys (particularly ones with jointed limbs) made good actors and because the idea connected with a strong European literary tradition of stories about living toys. A typical example - which also incorporated the popular dream device - is Italian film-maker Giovanni Pastrone's film *The War and the Dream of Momi* (1913), in which an old man tells his young grandson, Momi, tales of war. Falling asleep, Momi dreams of a dramatic battle between puppets, during which he gets spiked by one of the soldiers' bayonets. The boy wakes to discover that the weapon was in fact only a rose-thorn.

Children's dreams and animated toys figure prominently in the films of the pioneering puppet animator, Wladyslaw Starewicz. In *The Magic Clock* (1928), automata figures of kings, princesses, knights and dragons, decorating a fantastical clock, come alive and embark on an adventure which is not controlled by clockwork. Another, *Love in Black and White* (1927), concerns an accident-prone travelling showman whose puppet performers include likenesses of Hollywood stars Tom Mix, Mary Pickford and Charlie Chaplin.

A child's toys come to life in *Dreams of Toyland* (1908) by Arthur Melbourne Cooper.

Born to a Polish-Lithuanian family in 1882, Starewicz had a passion for drawing and sculpture and was interested in photography, magic lanterns and early attempts at film animation such as Emile Cohl's 1908 film *The Animated Matches*, which he saw when it was screened in Russia. Starewicz was also fascinated by entomology and it was while studying (and attempting to photograph) insect life that he decided to adopt the stop-motion technique used in Emil Cohl's film: 'In the mating

Charlie Chaplin is one of several Hollywood-inspired performers in *Love in Black and White* (1927) by Ladislas Starevich, the pioneering puppet animator.

season, beetles fight. Their jaws remind one of deers' horns. I wished to film them but, since their fighting is nocturnal, the light I used would freeze them into total immobility. By using embalmed beetles, I reconstructed the different phases of that fight, frame by frame, with progressive changes; more than five hundred frames for thirty seconds of projection. The results surpassed my hopes: *Lucanus Cervus* (1910, 10 metres long), the first three-dimensional animated film ...'

Within a year, Starewicz had produced a more ambitious film. Entitled *The Beautiful Leukanida*, it was 250 metres long and told how the beautiful beetle, Elena, became the subject of a duel between two rival insect suitors. The film was widely acclaimed and audiences were astonished, and mystified, by Starewicz's photography. Many people found the film totally inexplicable, and journalists in London confidently revealed that Starewicz had filmed living insects that had been carefully trained by a Russian scientist! It is small wonder that such theories were put forward, since Starewicz's animation of his spindly-limbed characters was extraordinarily accomplished.

Starewicz's cast of insect characters appeared in a series of modern fables, among them *The Cameraman's Revenge* (1911) that featured such tiny miracles as a grasshopper on a bicycle and a dragonfly ballet dancer. Perhaps because they take the viewer into a secret world, these films are as amusing and ingenious as when they were made eighty years ago. In 1919, Starewicz moved to Paris, adopted a French spelling of his name - Ladislas Starevitch - and, for a

The country lad and the sophisticated urbanite in one of Ladislas Starevich's animal fables, *Town Rat, Country Rat* (1926).

time, occupied a studio formerly used by Georges Méliès. Recognising that the characters in his insect films were limited by their lack of facial expressions, Starevitch began making puppets of mammal characters for such films as *Town Rat, Country Rat* (1926) and his elaborate feature-length film, *The Tale of the Fox*, which he began working on in 1925 and completed five years later, but which was not released until 1938.

The Tale of the Fox, an episodic story based on the fables of La Fontaine, features the exploits of a cunning Fox who is forever tricking the other animals - particularly a slow-witted Wolf. There is also a Lion King and his Lioness Queen as well as a wily Badger who acts as defence counsel when charges are brought against the Fox by assorted chickens, ravens, and rabbits. Although the animals in Starevitch's films wear human clothes, in the style of a thousand book illustrations, they seem more like human characters in animal masks. Starevitch crams every scene with characters and activity: frogs sing, mice dance and birds flutter among the trees. The physical animation is exceptional: when the fox schemes, his eyes narrow and his lip curls in a sinister sneer, and when a feline troubadour serenades the Queen, Her Majesty closes her eyes in ecstasy and we see the royal breast heaving with emotion.

In *The Mascot* (1934), Starevitch returned to toys with a live-action story about a poor toy-maker whose daughter is feverish and asking for the impossible - a cool, juicy orange. Duffy, a toy puppy-dog, hears and notes her request. The following day, the toys stage an escape from the van that is taking them to market and Duffy sets off to find an orange. Duffy succeeds in his mission, but among his adventures in the real world - represented by inter-cutting with live-action - is a nightmarish episode in which he finds himself in a sinister backstreet underworld ruled by a Devil doll and inhabited by goblins, insects and reptiles, anthropomorphic turnips, carrots and hair-brushes, a moth-eaten stuffed monkey, a gruesome mummified character with trailing bandages and the animated skeletons of chickens and fish. At the conclusion of this scary sequence, the Devil bursts open and collapses into a heap of sawdust.

An eccentric restaging of Lewis Carroll's mad tea-party in Jan Svankmajer's *Alice* (1987).

Homunculus figure in Jan Svankmajer's treatment of Faust (1994). Svankmajer achieves haunting effects in his films with his mixtures of live action and animation.

In its more bizarre and beastly moments, *The Mascot* foreshadows the films, three decades later, of Czech animator Jan Svankmajer. In his film *Alice* (1987), a skeletal fish and a small animal skull with doll's eyes and tiny human legs travel in a coach pulled by white cockerels with skulls instead of heads.

From his first film, *The Last Trick* (1964), Svankmajer brought to the cinema the theatrical skills of masks and puppets, combining them with film animation techniques using clay, models, cut-outs and inanimate objects conjured into life with a sharply focused surreal imagination that is endlessly startling. Svankmajer's films play on universal phobias: dark cellars and empty houses; dead things - such as an ox's tongue - that look uncomfortably human; and dangerous things such as nails, scissors and broken glass. His subject matter flies in the face of social taboos, linking food, death and sex, pain and pleasure in shocking, unforgettable imagery.

Film titles such as *Jabberwocky* (1971), *The Fall of the House of Usher* (1981) and

The Brothers Quay, Stephen and Timothy, on the set of *Street of Crocodiles* (1986). The original films of these two Americans bear the influence of both Jan Svankmajer and the Eastern European puppet tradition.

The Pit and the Pendulum (1983) reveal two of the major influences on Svankmajer - Lewis Carroll and Edgar Allan Poe - and reflect his fascination with dream states: those uncertain regions where reality and unreality are excitingly, and often frighteningly, blurred; states of mind where a pile of old shoes, their soles coming adrift from the uppers, become a pack of snapping dogs, or where a stuffed rabbit can sew up a gaping seam to prevent the sawdust from spilling out.

Svankmajer's films often combine animation with live action, as in *Alice* and his other feature *Faust* (1994), but whether pixillating live actors or manipulating china dolls, joints of uncooked meat or, in *Dimensions of Dialogue* (1982), two lumps of deathly-grey clay which form themselves into heads and then eat and regurgitate one another, Svankmajer is an undaunted renegade of animation art.

A compelling animated documentary on Svankmajer's work, The *Cabinet of Jan Svankmajer: Prague's Alchemist of Film*, was made in 1984 by Stephen and Timothy Quay, twin brothers born in Philadelphia, USA, but working primarily in Britain. The Brothers Quay, as they are known, owe much to Svankmajer's inspiration and their films, which include *Nocturna artificialia* (1979) and *Street of Crocodiles* (1986), present a complex vision of a dusty, decaying world where the overpowering feeling is one of claustrophobia and Kafkaesque confusion. For all their originality, the Quay brothers' films acknowledge the Eastern European heritage of puppet film-making, a tradition which itself springs from the long and distinguished heritage of the puppet theatre.

Soldiers parade next to the bound body of their captive, from *The New Gulliver* (1935) by Alexander Ptushko.

That heritage was the motivating force behind many of the earliest puppet films which - although now virtually unknown or seldom seen - were hailed in their day as being innovative cinema. *The New Gulliver* (1935) by the Russian animator, Alexander Ptushko, features another dream story in which a boy falls asleep over a copy of *Gulliver's Travels*. Ptushko's film includes scenes filmed in the camera (as opposed to being created through optical techniques in processing), incorporating a live actor and some 3000 puppets. Ptushko went on to produce a number of feature-length films combining animation and live-action including *The*

Fisherman and the Little Fish (1937) and *The Little Golden Key* (1939), based on a Russian version of *Pinocchio* by Alexander Tolstoi in which an organ-grinder, Papa Karlo, transforms an amazing talking log into a little wooden boy named Buratino.

A ship made from blown glass in George Pal's exquisite film *The Ship of the Ether* (1935).

In 1935, the same year that Ptushko released *The New Gulliver*, the Hungarian-born animator George Pal produced an exquisite film, *The Ship of the Ether*, featuring the voyage of a ship made from blown glass. Pal's earliest films were made in Germany, where he used stop-motion photography to produce an animated commercial for a cigarette company in Cologne: 'They liked it so much that they ordered other films where the cigarettes spoke. So we put little mouths on them - no faces yet, just mouths. And then we put faces on them, and put hats on them, and put arms and legs on them - wire legs with buttons for feet...'

With the rise of Nazism in 1933, Pal moved to Eindhoven in Holland where he produced a series of fairy-tale subjects such as *The Magic Lamp* and *Sinbad the Sailor*. At what was soon the biggest puppet-animation studio in Europe, Pal was making short entertainment films for commercial sponsors such as Phillips Radio, Unilever and Horlicks. Then, in 1939, George Pal moved to America and set up studio in Hollywood where, assisted by some of the finest puppet animators from Europe, he began producing a series of theatrical shorts called 'Puppetoons'.

George Pal's musical fantasy *Tubby the Tuba* (1947), using techniques developed in his short puppet films which he called 'Puppetoons'

Pal's early puppets were very basic: heads and hands tended to be wooden balls, bodies were blocks of wood and limbs were made of bendy covered wire. Although they would become more sophisticated, they remained highly stylised with movements that have an almost mechanical precision producing a look not unlike that achieved, decades later, with early computer animation. Pal's films required the use of a great many models or part-models: for a Puppetoon to walk through a scene might require the use of as many as 24 sets of legs, while up to 100 replacement heads could be used for a character in one of his more elaborate films such as *Tubby the Tuba* (1947).

George Pal surrounded by some of the army of puppets he used to film by the substitution method (see also pages 90-91).

Based on a story by Paul Trip and music by George Kleinsinger, *Tubby the Tuba* was a tale about a tuba in an orchestra who (much to the amusement of the other instruments) wanted to play a 'tune' as opposed to just oompah-ing away in the background. With the help of a genial bull-frog, Tubby learns a tune and, in turn, teaches it to the rest of the orchestra. This simple fable about accepting others for what they are (and, indeed, learning to accept yourself) is a good example of Pal's film-making: funny, touching and deftly animated.

Pal was, however, capable of darker visions such as *Tulips Shall Grow* (1942), a powerful anti-Nazi film in which an idyllic picture-book portrayal of Holland - tulips, windmills and a pair of cute, clog-wearing lovers - is suddenly overrun by a marauding army of goose-stepping mechanical men. Made from nuts, bolts and washers, the robotic soldiers carry banners bearing the name 'Screwballs'. Bombs rain down from metal, bat-shaped planes until the windmills are broken skeletons against a blood-red sky. Only when it rains do the armies finally grind to a halt in a sea of rust.

One of the most popular of Pal's characters was a little black boy named Jasper who appeared in almost twenty films with such titles as *Jasper Goes Fishing* (1943), *Jasper and the Beanstalk* (1945) and *Jasper in a Jam* (1946). Also in 1946 Pal made *John Henry and the Inky Poo* (1946), a powerful little film based on the American folk tale of the black railroad ganger who competed with a track-laying machine called the Inky Poo. John Henry, depicted in a naturalistic style that is far removed from that of the Jasper films, wins his spike-driving contest and, though he dies in the effort, proves that 'there ain't a machine made that can beat a man once a man's got a mind he can beat that machine'.

There have been several animated films of Hansel and Gretel; this one, based on the Humperdinck opera, was made in 1954 by Michael Myerburg using stop-motion techniques or, as the publicity called them, "electronic puppetry".

George Pal's Puppetoons won an affectionate audience in America and a number of model animators who worked on the films went on to successful careers of their own, including Joop Geesink who produced his own series of puppet films under the generic title 'Dollywood', and Ray Harryhausen who, in 1945, began producing a short series of films with fairy-tale subjects.

Laurence Harvey as the Shoemaker with George Pal's elves in *The Wonderful World of the Brothers Grimm* (1962).

The first of these films, *Mother Goose Stories*, featured highly detailed sets and charming 'cartoon-style' puppets of Humpty Dumpty, Little Miss Muffet, Old Mother Hubbard and others. Harryhausen then made *Little Red Riding Hood*, *Hansel and Gretel*, *The Story of Rapunzel* and *The Story of King Midas* before concentrating on stop-motion special effects. Harryhausen's fairy-tale films show the skill of an exceptional puppet-maker. His slavering wolves, bald-headed demons and warty-nosed hags foreshadow the fiends and monsters which he was later to create for the live-action cinema.

As for George Pal, he went on to produce and direct a memorable string of science-fiction and fantasy films such as *Destination Moon* (1950), *When Worlds Collide* (1951) and his unforgettable versions of HG Wells's *The War of the Worlds* (1953) and *The Time Machine* (1960). Many of these films

The hand of dictatorship in Jiri Trnka's last film *The Hand* (1965).

included brilliant special effects using model work and stop-motion photography, and some of them - *Tom Thumb* (1958) and *The Wonderful World of the Brothers Grimm* (1963) - featured superbly crafted puppet sequences with animated toys, elves and dragons.

Pal's doll-like puppets have a strong affinity with those of another significant animator, Jiri Trnka, who was born in the former Czechoslovakia, worked with various puppet theatres and went into film-making after the Second World War when he set up the animation division of the nationalised Czech cinema and became its first head of production. Trnka was also an illustrator, working with an assured and elegant line and delicate palette of pastel colours with which he decorated various books of legends and fairy-stories including those by Hans Christian Andersen and the Brothers Grimm. It was natural, therefore, for Trnka to turn to an illustrative form and work in conventional cel animation, creating what critics described as 'Disneyfied' characters in such filmed folk-tales as *Grandpa Planted a Beet* (1945) and, the following year, *The Animals and the Brigands*. Also in 1946 he made a biting satire in stark black and white, *The Devil on Springs* (also known as *The Chimney Sweep*), reflecting on the German occupation of his country and the role of the SS collaborator.

Eventually, Trnka tired of cel animation, feeling that too many processes intervened between the concept and the finished film and that this way of working required the talents of too many other artists to bring his ideas to life. He turned instead to the puppet film, drawing on his years of experience as a maker and operator of marionettes. His earliest experiments were made with the help of the Czech animator Bretislav Pojar: 'We animated one of my oldest wooden puppets, a ballerina. It moved well, but gave an abstract impression. The effect was nice, but did not mean anything. Thus we understood that a puppet film needs concrete situations, or a "story".'

Trnka's later films varied in subject matter - a Hans Andersen fairy-tale, *The Emperor's Nightingale* (1948); a Western parody, *Song of the Prairie* (1949) and a three-part serialisation of Jarolev Hasek's comic novel, *The Good Soldier Schweik* (1954-5) - but his style remained virtually unchanged for almost a decade, his films peopled with squat, chunky characters who lacked the gracefulness found in his book illustrations. However, in two films, *Old Czech Legends* (1953) and *A Midsummer Night's Dream* (1955), Trnka showed himself capable of evoking moods of mystery and rare beauty, demonstrating the truth of his philosophy of film-making: 'Puppet films stand on their own feet only when they are outside the scope of live-action films - when the stylisation of the scenery, the artificially heroic look of the human actors and the lyrical content of the theme might easily produce an effect both unconvincing and ludicrous or even painful ...'

In Jiri Trnka's last film, *The Hand* (1965), the central character has a typical impassive face, and although he is presented to us as a sculptor, he is dressed and has the look of a pierrot. With an outsized head, a beaky nose and two large, soulful eyes, he is clearly the comic tragedian. A gigantic Hand (symbolising dictatorship) demands that this innocent little artist carve a likeness of him for a monument. When the sculptor refuses, the Hand imprisons him in a cage and forces him to carry out the commission. Having reluctantly completed the work, the sculptor escapes, but Trnka concludes his allegory on the freedom of art with the Hand pursuing and destroying the sculptor and then celebrating his work with a grand funeral.

Following Trnka's retirement, Bretislav Pojar continued the puppet film tradition with films such as *The Gingerbread Cottage* (1951), *One Too Many* (1953), a piece of anti-drink propaganda in which a motorcyclist takes the fatal decision to have 'one more for the road', and *The Lion and the Song* (1958), in which a lion encounters a musician singing in the desert and shows his bestial taste in music by eating the singer.

Floating, Chagall-like image of Ariel with Prospero in Stanislav Sokolov's *The Tempest* (1992). This was one of a series of films called 'Shakespeare, the Animated Tales' made as a co-production by S4C/BBC/Christmas Films, Moscow.

Another of Trnka's creative heirs is the Japanese puppet animator Kihachiro Kawamoto. Born in Sedagaya in 1925, Kawamoto saw Jiri Trnka's *The Emperor's Nightingale* and travelled to Europe to study with the Czech film-maker before working in Hungary, Poland, Rumania and Russia and then returning to Japan. Kawamoto's films, which include *Demon* (1972), *A Poet's Life* (1974), *Dojoji* (1976) and *House of Flame* (1979), unite the European approach to puppet film-making with the long tradition of puppetry in Japan which dates back to the Bunraku puppet plays first presented in the 17th century.

Drawing his inspiration from the masks of the Noh drama, Kawamoto's puppets are not only animated with precision, they are also painstakingly made: 'The creation of a single puppet takes ten days. The head requires particular care. First I prepare a plaster mould with which I fashion the head from an agglomerate of Japanese paper, which is then covered with a fine, supple leather and subsequently painted; thus it is light but solid. Eyes, mouth and eyebrows are moveable, and the ears, in plastic, are made from moulds ... Teeth are fashioned from a type of paraffin, the chests from rigid paper; the hands, in supple rubber, are easily moved. For ten minutes of animation, one year of preparation is required.'

Scene from Galina Beda's *Ruth* (1996), one of the 'Testament' series made by S4C/BBC/Christmas Films, Moscow.

Where some puppet-film animators have followed the aesthetic principles of Jiri Trnka, including Polish-born Yoram Gross, whose *Joseph the Dreamer* (1961) was the first such film to be animated in Israel, others, such as Norway's Ivo Caprino, have returned to the realistic style of Ladislaw Starewich. Caprino's masterpiece, *The Pinchcliffe Grand Prix* (1975), is a fast-paced action-comedy about a remarkable car called 'Il Tempo Gigante', and contains scenes that are literally crowded to overflowing with charming and eccentric characters.

Some of the finest puppet animation in recent years has emerged from a collaboration between the British television company S4C, the BBC and the Moscow-based group of animators, Christmas Films. Three series (using a variety of animation media) have been made: 'Shakespeare, The Animated Tales', 'Operavox' and 'Testament' including, among many fine pieces of animation, Stanislav Sokolov's elemental visualisation of *The Tempest* (1992); Maria Muat's *Twelfth Night* (1992) which captures the romance, confusion and buffoonery of Shakespeare's comedy, and Galina Beda's *Ruth* (1996) which retells the moving Old Testament story of love and loyalty with a precision and delicacy that recalls the work of Trnka.

These films received great acclaim in Britain and America, two countries that - whilst slow to embrace the puppet film - have had a long fascination with automata, marionettes, glove-puppets and ventriloquists' dolls. Unlikely though it may seem, two of the greatest stars in the early days of American radio were ventriloquist Edgar Bergen's dummies Charlie McCarthy and Mortimer Snerd. Similarly, in Britain, Peter Brough and his cheeky companion, Archie Andrews, were hugely successful on both radio and television.

One of the top-rated TV shows in America in the 1950s featured the string-puppet Howdy Doody, while, for a later generation, Jim Henson's glove-puppets achieved national, and then international stardom with 'Sesame Street' and 'The Muppet Show'. In Britain, where puppet plays featuring the characters Punch and Judy have been a centuries-long part of the nation's popular culture, many of the earliest television shows for children featured marionettes. Rather than use expensive and time-consuming stop-motion photography, the puppets were manipulated 'live' before the camera and appeared, strings and all! Nevertheless, characters such as Andy Pandy, Muffin the Mule, The Woodentops and Bill and

CLARABELL

Puppeteers on the set for Bob Smith's 'Howdy Doody' show, which had a great success on American TV in the 1950s.

Right: Bob Smith with his puppet characters Howdy Doody and Heidi Doody.

Ben, the Flowerpot Men (all between 1950 and 1955) quickly established themselves as children's favourites.

By the end of the 1950s, puppet shows on television were becoming more elaborate with Gerry Anderson's 'The Adventures of Twizzle' and 'Torchy the Battery Boy', both of which featured fantastic child heroes: Twizzle, with endlessly extending arms and legs, and Torchy, a human battery with a light in his hat that had magical properties. Anderson also made a puppet Western series, 'Four Feather Falls', featuring Sheriff Tex Tucker, Rocky his horse and Dusty his dog. This was a revolutionary series that aimed at satisfying the expectations of an increasingly sophisticated audience. New techniques enabled Anderson to manipulate his puppets with extra fine wires that, at 1/5000th of an inch thick, were scarcely visible. A further development, electronically sychronising lip-movements, added a sense of realism not usually associated with puppet characters.

Anderson's pioneering television puppet films continued with 'Supercar' (1961), 'Fireball XL5' (1963), 'Stingray' (1964), and the phenomenally successful 'Thunderbirds' (1965), filmed in what Anderson called 'Supermarionation'. But, despite strong characters, dramatic plots and the endlessly fascinating sci-fi gadgets and gizmos with which the cars, boats and planes were fitted, Anderson's puppets still had strings attached.

Scene from Serge Danot's series 'The Magic Roundabout' which enjoyed a long career on BBC Television from 1965.

One film-maker who found the confidence to cut the strings and turn to stop-motion photography was Gordon Murray who, at the beginning of the Sixties, was producing elaborate puppet plays about the bewigged inhabitants of a Ruritanian principality named Rubovia, but who within only a few years was producing stop-motion films about the small-town dramas in idealised rural communities (represented by model-village settings and characters in 1930s costumes) called 'Camberwick Green' (1966) and 'Trumpton' (1967) .

In 1964, modelmaker Oliver Postgate and writer Peter Firmin created one of the earliest stop-motion puppet series on British television with their forest fantasies about the lives of the folk in 'Pogles' Wood'. Postgate and Firmin's company - modestly named Smallfilms - went on to produce such series as 'The Clangers' (1969), about a race of small pink knitted creatures (vaguely resembling aardvarks) who lived in holes - covered by dustbin-lids - on a small blue planet; and 'Pingwings', about a race of black-and-white knitted creatures (something like penguins) who lived in a barn on Berrydown Farm.

In France, Serge Danot created 'The Magic Roundabout' (from 1965) with its cast of memorable eccentrics, including a dog that looked like an animated floor mop, a pink cow and a moustachioed character on a spring. This series was greatly loved in France and - thanks to a free-wheeling translation - in Britain, and later inspired a feature-length film, *Dougal and the Blue Cat* (1970). One of Danot's animators was British-born Ivor Wood, who later joined Filmfair, a stop-motion animation studio founded by Graham Clutterbuck and responsible for such series as 'The Wombles' (1973), about a race of shaggy-haired, long-nosed litter-gatherers who live on Wimbledon Common. Ivor Wood went on to create his own enchanting series, 'Postman Pat' (1981), about the daily exploits - and occasional daring adventures - of a genial, bespectacled country postman and Jess, his black-and-white cat.

All these series - regardless of whether their characters were made out of wood, fabric or knitting-wool - had a Trnka-like simplicity of shape and fixed expressions. In contrast, many of the films produced by Cosgrove Hall (a partnership of two British artists, Brian Cosgrove and Mark Hall) have preferred the detailed realism and moving features pioneered by Ladislaw Starewich.

Cosgrove Hall's full-length film of *The Wind in the Willows* (1983), and the series

The characters' mobile features and subtle eye and lip movements were widely praised in the Cosgrove Hall films inspired by *The Wind in the Willows* (1983).

which followed it, featured finely crafted puppets meticulously brought to life with movements which suggest a combination of animal behaviour and human nature ideally suited to Kenneth Grahame's original characters, who sometimes seem to be animals in human clothes and at other times appear more like humans wearing animal masks.

Lou Bunin with a character from his *Alice in Wonderland* (1948), which included live and puppet players.

Working with rubber moulded heads, Cosgrove Hall have shown that it is possible to achieve the most subtle eye and lip movements. However, because latex always has a rubbery look, it is far more suited to modelling animals with skin, such as Toad, than furry creatures like Mole and Rat. Additionally, all moulded rubber puppets run the risk of showing tell-tale traces of the joins on the plaster moulds from which they are cast.

Despite these drawbacks, Cosgrove Hall's numerous films - in various animation media - have been extremely successful. Their later puppet film series include a superb three-dimensional recreation of the Toyland home of Enid Blyton's 'Noddy' (1992) and 'Oakie Doke' (1995) which introduced the title-character - an engaging tree-sprite with an acorn head and oak-leaf 'ears' - who helps the woodland creatures to solve their various

In Tim Burton's *Vincent*, the eponymous hero is a seven-year-old boy who models his life on the movie career of horror star Vincent Price, whose voice is heard on the soundtrack.

problems. In 1991, Cosgrove Hall also made a feature-length puppet film, based on *Truckers*, Terry Pratchett's novel about a diminutive - and fast-diminishing - race of 'Nomes' who survive by travelling the motorways of Britain in 'borrowed' trucks. Most recently, their sensitivity in creating small, utterly convincing imaginary worlds has been demonstrated in the film versions of Jill Barklem's stories about 'Brambley Hedge'.

In America, Lou Bunin made a version of *Alice in Wonderland* (1948) which used live and puppet players, and Jules Bass produced a series of Christmas specials, such as *Rudolph the Red Nosed Reindeer* (1964), and a feature-length film, *Mad Monster Party* (1968), in which Dr Frankenstein summons a convention of movie monsters. Apart from these films, however, and the work of George Pal, American puppet animated films have been a rarity. Even the powerful Disney studio only ever flirted with the medium a couple of times making *Noah's Ark* (1959) and *A Symposium on Popular Songs* (1962). Both films were nominated for Academy Awards and featured animated characters made from fabric and assorted household objects including an Arkload of kitchen-utensil animals. Then, in 1982, a young artist at the Disney studio came up with a bizarre idea for a short puppet horror film aimed at children!

Tim Burton's *Vincent* told the story of a strange little boy who modelled his life on the movie career of his idol, the horror star Vincent Price. Burton's stylised puppets - uncomfortably sharp and angular - were animated by Stephen Chiodo and shot in black and white with a lot of atmospheric shadow. The hero's unnatural preferences for the dark, for reading books by Edgar Allan Poe and conducting Frankenstein-like experiments on his dog, were wittily presented and perfectly complemented by the voice of the real Vincent Price on the soundtrack. But, at the time, the film was decidedly not a Disney picture.

Burton made one more attempt to exercise his macabre imagination at the Disney studio with *Frankenweenie* (1984), a live-action pastiche of Universal's *Frankenstein*, after which he left to become a Hollywood legend in his own right with such grotesque films as *Beetlejuice*, *Edward Scissorhands* and the first two of the new dark breed of Batman movies.

While pursuing his live-action film-making career, Tim Burton still had in mind a scenario which he had developed while he was with Disney, but which had never been put into production. Eventually, at what was by now a very different Disney studio, work began on *A Nightmare Before Christmas*. Directed by a talented animator, Henry Selick, Burton's *Nightmare* told the saga of Jack Skellington, the Pumpkin King, who rules the darkly sinister world of Halloween but who would much rather have the job of being Father Christmas. The elaborate film featured 227 puppets - vampires, werewolves, ghosts, gargoyles, mummies and freaks - many of which could be fitted with an extensive range of heads or faces in an animation process that, though superbly executed, was merely a sophisticated version of the methods used, years before, by George Pal.

A Nightmare Before Christmas (1993) was the first stop-motion feature film to receive worldwide distribution. Some of the finest model animators in the world brought the creepy characters eerily to life on elaborate sets with grotesque anthropomorphic buildings, crumbling masonry, rusting railings and dank cobbled streets, all of which were textured to have the look of the scratchy, cross-hatched pen-work found in Tim Burton's original drawings.

The mischievous Lock, Shock and Barrel in Tim Burton's *A Nightmare Before Christmas* (1993).

Many of the figures were a triumph of modelmaking and animation, for example the cadaverous Jack - a black-suited figure, all skull and bones - whose arms and legs had no more thickness than a pipe-cleaner, yet who moved with an elegant gracefulness without a hint of a shimmer or a shake.

The popular and critical success of *Nightmare* prompted the Disney studio to make, again under

the direction of Henry Selick, a puppet animated film based on Roald Dahl's best-selling children's book, *James and the Giant Peach* (1996). Despite a strong narrative and original characters - including a cigar-chomping Centipede from Brooklyn, an aristocratic, violin-playing Grasshopper with a monocle, and a seductive French Spider - *James and the Giant Peach* was weighed down by musical numbers and, for all its charms, failed to capture the imagination as Burton's darkly disturbing *Nightmare* had done.

Puppet film-makers have, over the years, used all manner of materials: wood, metal, rubber, fabric, leather, paper and plastic. Then there is a material called Plasticine, invented as long ago as the 1890s, which offers a different kind of potential to the animator. Film-makers began using clay-like substances to create animated effects from the earliest days of the movies and, as with line animation, their efforts owed a debt to the theatre.

An early experimenter with clay animation was an American teenager named Willis O'Brien, who in 1915 was working in a small decorator's shop in San Francisco. O'Brien was keen on boxing and one day, when work was slack, he modelled a small boxer out of a piece of clay. When a colleague did the same, the two lads staged a mock boxing-match by posing and reposing the little figures. For O'Brien, it was the beginning of a thought process that carried him to the idea of making motion-picture cartoons with clay instead of drawings. He made a one-minute film featuring a miniature caveman and a model dinosaur made with clay built around a wooden skeleton. On the strength of this experiment, a San Francisco producer advanced the money for a five-minute comedy entitled *The Dinosaur and the Missing Link* (1915). For this film, O'Brien refined his animation process by constructing prehistoric creatures from jointed metal skeletons covered in sheet rubber.

O'Brien continued making short prehistoric comedies such as *Curious Pets of our Ancestors* and *The Birth of a Flivver* (both 1917) in which two early inventors create a dinosaur-pulled form of transport that ends in disaster. In 1919, he made a two-reel dinosaur drama, *The Ghost of Slumber Mountain*, which led to a full-length film version of Arthur Conan Doyle's *The Lost World* (1925). The animation, by today's standards, was crude but to an audience in the mid-Twenties it appeared so authentic that when Conan Doyle showed advance footage from the film to the Society of American Magicians (without declaring its origin) many observers were convinced they were looking at authentic film of prehistoric wildlife.

The success of Willis O'Brien's early animations and a public fascination with dinosaurs in the 1920s - spurred on by several notable fossil finds - inspired other model animators. Buster Keaton's film, *The Three Ages* (1923), opened

Tim Burton's elaborate film *A Nightmare Before Christmas* (1993) which used 227 puppets and was the first stop-motion feature film to receive worldwide distribution.

KING
KONG
FAY WRAY
ROB'T ARMSTRONG
BRUCE CABOT
A PERSONALLY DIRECTED
MERIAN C·
COOPER
ERNEST B·
SCHOEDSACK
PRODUCTION
FROM THE STORY BY MERIAN C·COOPER and EDGAR
CHIEF TECHNICIAN·WILLIS J.O'BRIEN DAVID O. SELZNICK·

with a model of the deadpan comic riding on the back of a clay dinosaur. Later, in 1928, animator Virginia May made *Monsters of the Past*, which featured a battle between those ever-popular prehistoric combatants, the Triceratops and the Tyrannosaurus Rex.

Eight years after *The Lost World* (and having failed to complete another prehistoric project, *Creation*), Willis O'Brien created the special effects for Merian C Cooper's classic fantasy, *King Kong*: a film which so powerfully created its illusions that, more than fifty years on, it still haunts the imagination. *King Kong* is full of stunning animation sequences, many of which incorporate footage of the film's live-action stars. Among its most memorable scenes are those in which Kong battles with various prehistoric creatures, including a Tyrannosaurus Rex and a Pteranodon, and the unforgettable climax on the top of the Empire State Building when Kong attempts to fight off the attacking aircraft.

O'Brien's animation, in which he was assisted by long-time associates E B Gibson and Marcel Delgardo, was exceptional and even minor imperfections - the fluttering effect on Kong's fur caused by the animator's handling of the puppet - cannot detract from its towering achievement. The success of *King Kong* led to a sequel, *Son of Kong* (1933), and several other monster and fantasy films to which O'Brien contributed effects. His work has been the inspiration for many, including his protégé, Ray Harryhausen, whose animation techniques were to surpass even those of the Master.

Left: Poster for Merian C Cooper's classic fantasy *King Kong*, with special effects by Willis O'Brien.

Kong and the Pteranodon battle over Fay Wray, one of the film's many animation sequences incorporating live action.

Harryhausen worked as O'Brien's assistant on a further ape picture, *Mighty Joe Young* (1949), and was responsible for the greater part of the film's animation effects. He also animated O'Brien's dinosaur models in the prehistoric sequences of *The Animal World* (1956) and, in his own right, went on to create some of the most memorable stop-motion monsters in the history of the cinema: *The Beast from 20,000 Fathoms* (1953); the giant octopus in *It Came from Beneath the Sea* (1955); the Ymir, duelling with an elephant in the Colosseum in *20 Million Miles to Earth* (1957), and yet more dinosaurs in *One Million Years BC* (1966) and *The Valley of Gwangi* (1969).

In fantasy films that range from *The 7th Voyage of Sinbad* (1958) to *The Clash of the Titans* (1981), Ray Harryhausen brought to life a troupe of terrifying mythological creatures - sirens, dragons, centaurs, griffins, a two-headed roc and a one-eyed Cyclops. Ray Bradbury once referred to these alarming and alluring creatures of Harryhausen's genius as 'the delicious monsters that moved in his head and out of his fingers and into our eternal dreams'. In what is probably Ray Harryhausen's finest film, *Jason and the Argonauts* (1963), there is a stunning episode in which live-action star Todd Armstrong fights a skeletal army, born from the scattered teeth of a Hydra. It is a breathtaking sequence of screen magic which has inspired many animators, including Aardman's Peter Lord and Dave Sproxton.

Although, in the earliest days of cinema, clay animation had featured prominently, its use declined as a reaction to the increasing sophistication in cel-animation techniques. A curiosity from this transitional period is *Modeling* (1921), a film in the 'Out of the Inkwell' series in which live-action footage showed animator Max Fleischer drawing his cartoon character Ko Ko the clown, who would then embark on some escapade both on, and off, the drawing-board. In one episode, Max's fellow animator, Roland Crandall, is seen sculpting a bust of a gentleman with a grotesquely large nose. The sitter arrives and is not best pleased with the likeness. Meanwhile, on paper, Ko Ko is having fun in a winter landscape, building a snowman which also has a huge nose. To stop Ko Ko's antics, Max throws a lump of real clay on to the line-animated image. The clown throws the clay back, escapes from the drawing and runs amok in the studio. Before being returned to the inkwell, Ko Ko climbs on to the sculpture of the large-nosed gentleman and hides in one of the cavernous nostrils.

Drawing by Ray Harryhausen for one of the animation sequences in *Jason and the Argonauts* (1963).

The dynamic on-screen realisation of the skeleton battle in *Jason and the Argonauts*.

Following the release, in 1927, of Walt Disney's *Steamboat Willie*, the first cartoon with synchronised sound, the public appetite for cel animation left little room for any other medium. Apart from one or two highly stylised experimental films, such as Leonard Tregillus's and Ralph Luce's *No Credit* (1948) and *Proem* (1949), clay animation had all but been abandoned.

The medium was not revived until 1955, when Art Clokey created a character who has been described as 'almost irritating in his utter cuteness', but who became an American institution - Gumby. Art Clokey produced 127 six-minute films featuring Gumby and his little horse, Pokey, each of which was a combination of ingenious animation effects (frequently achieved on a shoestring budget) and scenarios that reflected their creator's strongly held beliefs in fairness, tolerance and goodness. The innocence in Gumby's personality is reflected in his look: an arrangement of geometric shapes making the character easy to construct and animate. Gumby is essentially a flat, upended rectangle of greenish-blue clay, divided at the bottom into two splayed, footless legs.

Art Clokey's character Gumby, with his faithful steed Pokey, whose success in the mid-1950s revived interest in clay animation films.

Gumby's tubular arms end in mitten-shaped hands and his facial features are limited to those simple circles and semi-circles that you find on the face of a gingerbread man. His most sophisticated feature is a 'bump' on the left side of his head, intended to suggest (though it is not entirely obvious) a quiff of combed-back hair.

The Gumby 'look' has a child-like naiveté, although most children would probably be more likely to model a man using conventional round and sausage shapes, closer in appearance to Peter Lord's Morph. Although Gumby could scarcely be described as cuddly, his characteristic kindheartedness and upbeat attitude to life endeared him to a generation and, following the revival of interest in clay animation in the 1980s, gave him the chance of a comeback. The new Gumby series, which began in 1987, had greater sophistication than had been possible with the earlier series, which had been made with great economy and had used doll's house furniture as props along with occasional toy cars and space-rockets. The mix of clay people with objects that are recognisably from the 'real' world never bothered Art Clokey, but other animators have adopted the purist attitude that stories told in clay should not include anything that is not made of clay. One such artist is the man who did much to revive an interest in clay animation, Will Vinton.

It was in 1974 that Will Vinton and his then-partner, Bob Gardiner, came to prominence with *Closed Mondays*, a film about a drunk who gets into an art gallery where - to his inebriated gaze - the pictures appear to come to life. *Closed Mondays* won an Academy Award in the category previously called 'Best Short Subject - Cartoon' but now renamed 'Best Short Subject - Animated Film'. Although Vinton's early models were relatively unsophisticated, his technical aims were ambitious, with painstaking attempts to achieve lip sync by studying the film footage of actors reading the lines of dialogue. Vinton's films also involved complex camera moves including pans, zooms and tracks - all of which had to be created frame by frame.

Vinton eventually coined the term Claymation to describe his work and, like many animators before him, turned to folk- and fairy-tales for his inspiration. A film version of Leo Tolstoy's *Martin the Cobbler* (1976) was followed by Washington Irving's *Rip Van Winkle* (1978) and Antoine de Saint-Exupéry's *The Little Prince* (1979), which included innovative sequences by Joan Gatz, an animator who 'paints' on glass using a palette-knife and a mix of clay and oil. Gatz, whose work with Vinton includes *Creation* (1981) and *A Claymation Christmas Celebration* (1987), went on to win the 1992 Academy Award for her film *Mona Lisa Descending a Staircase*.

Vinton's films show a meticulous attention to detail in creating worlds in which everything, being made of clay, has a uniformity of vision. There are, however, limitations to the Claymation technique: some objects and aspects of the settings have a soft, squashy, chunky look that draws undue attention to incidental background detail, while the predominantly human characters tend to have a heavy, leaden look that is a world away from the fluid human animation created on cel by Disney and others.

Short films such as *Dinosaur* and *A Christmas Gift* (both 1980) and *The Great Cognito* (1982) led to Vinton making the first feature animated in clay, *The Adventures of Mark Twain* (1985). Also known as *Comet Quest*, this is an ingenious but episodic tale in which the great American writer and wit sets out on a wild journey to meet Halley's comet on a vessel that is an amalgam of hot-air balloon and Mississippi paddle-steamer. Twain is joined by three of his fictional characters - Tom Sawyer, Huck Finn and Becky Thatcher - for whom some of the author's less well-known stories are inventively brought to life. The film contains exceptional animation, especially in the creation and manipulation

Characters in one of Will Vinton's adventurous advertising films made for the California Raisin Advisory Board.

of the title character with his mane of white hair, walrus moustache, twinkling eyes and ever-present cigar. Will Vinton's Twain is an incomparable example of human animation in a style that subtly combines naturalism with caricature. The film also contains numerous stunning special effects as when one of the books in Mark Twain's airborne library snaps open and a river of multi-coloured clay flows and splashes out. *The Adventures of Mark Twain* received a limited critical success as did the Disney live-action feature film, *Return to Oz* (1985), to which Will Vinton contributed amazing animated effects. This sombre, songless sequel to the happy-go-lucky MGM classic returns Dorothy to a now ruined Emerald City and, among various scary encounters, she visits the underworld domain of the Nome King who, in an ingenious Claymation sequence, is gradually transformed from an animated rockface into the actor Nicol Williamson.

The weird and wonderful vessel in Will Vinton's *The Adventures of Mark Twain* (1985), also known as *Comet Quest*, the first clay animated feature film.

In America, Will Vinton's pioneering work has since been overshadowed by the phenomenal success of his clever series of advertising films for the California Raisin Advisory Board. Designed to make raisins appealing to a young audience, Vinton created a group of anthropomorphic raisins who sing and play rock-and-roll music. Beginning with Marvin Gaye's song, 'I Heard It through the Grapevine', the series went on to feature the music of Michael Jackson and Ray Charles, performed by raisin caricatures of those musicians. Although Will Vinton took the art of clay animation to new heights of invention and

Morph, with his friend and alter-ego Chas, was an early creation of Peter Lord and Dave Sproxton, and first appeared in the BBC 'Vision On' series in 1976.

sophistication, the medium failed successfully to challenge the supremacy of cel animation, particularly with the revival of animation talent at the Disney studio, beginning in 1989 with *The Little Mermaid*.

The present renaissance in clay animation had its origins in 1960s Britain with the work of Peter Lord and Dave Sproxton. Whilst still at school, and then university, Lord and Sproxton began contributing short animated films to a BBC television programme for deaf children called 'Vision On'. They were influenced in their ambition to animate by the films of Ray Harryhausen (especially *Jason and the Argonauts*) and by Terry Gilliam's work for the avant-garde television comedy series, 'Monty Python's Flying Circus'. They also aspired to equal the quality of animation seen in some of the puppet-film series then being shown on British TV, such as 'The Wombles' and 'The Magic Roundabout'. The fact that Serge Danot's 'Roundabout' had also established a large adult following suggested to them that the appeal of animation might not simply be limited to 'kid's stuff'.

Lord and Sproxton eventually focused on developing their skills with Plasticine/clay animation, mainly because nobody else in Britain appeared to be working in the medium (which gave it a saleable uniqueness) and because it offered a flexibility denied to the most sophisticated puppet. An early example of a clay film sequence for 'Vision On' featured a real table with a real plate on which clay food - sausages, peas and potatoes - moved around before merging into what Peter Lord describes as 'a muddy brown quadruped like a bear or a wombat', which then walked off the plate.

The success of these short pieces led to the creation, in 1976, of Morph, the small terracotta man who interacted with the programme's artist Tony Hart, and who had a propensity for 'morphing' into animals, objects or sometimes just a ball of the raw material of which he was made. Viewers responded to Morph's simple shape, friendly features and warm colour; he quickly became a star of the small screen and secured Lord and Sproxton's reputation. His regular appearances on 'Vision On' were followed by a series, 'The Adventures of Morph' (1981-3), in which he was joined by an ever-expanding family of delightful and quirky characters.

In 1978, Aardman Animations' work took a quantum leap when they were commissioned to make two short films, called 'Animated Conversations', for

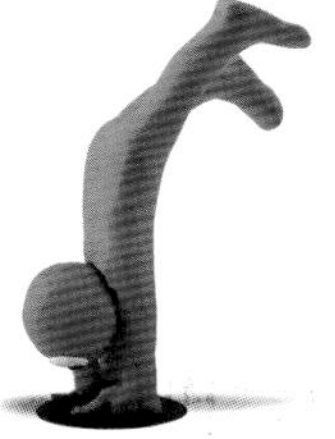

late-night screening by BBC Bristol. Taking the skills mastered in animating Morph, Lord and Sproxton applied them to realistic human figures acting out small, intimate dramas based on true-life situations.

The soundtracks for 'Animated Conversations' used voices of 'real people', recorded in various day-to-day situations. For example, in the first film, *Confessions of a Foyer Girl*, two usherettes in a cinema foyer talk about boys and boredom and what they are going to do when they get home from work. The concept of 'Animated Conversations' was developed into a series of five 'Conversation Pieces' (1982-3) for Channel 4, using increasingly sophisticated animation to depict ways in which people succeed - but more often fail - at communication. *On Probation* depicts a group meeting where a tortuous exchange takes place between a young man who needs to visit a member of his family and a probation officer who is trying to negotiate the terms of the visit - with various unhelpful interjections from the other members of the group. The resulting drama is filled with brilliant observation - people tapping pencils, taking off their spectacles, looking edgily at one another - and is ultimately funnier, sadder and far more memorable than if the same small scenario had been presented in live-action.

A scene from *On Probation*, one of five ground-breaking films in the Aardman series 'Conversation Pieces' (1982-3). For these films, Peter Lord and Dave Sproxton built their stories around real-life taped interviews, but they themselves never met the people involved.

With their overlapping dialogue, false starts and unfinished sentences, these films have all the hallmarks of fly-on-the-wall TV reportage. This, however, is quite misleading: they are, as Peter Lord puts it, 'almost a documentary but complete fiction!'

There has long been a difference of opinion between animators about what can and cannot be achieved in the medium. There are those who share the view expressed by Halas and Manvell in *The Technique of Film Animation*: 'In all animation, there should never be any doubt that what is being achieved on the screen could only be achieved by this means.' Others hold that any subject matter can be dealt with in animation and, indeed, the Disney studio's move towards making animated films of live-action stories, such as *Pocahontas* and *The Hunchback of Notre Dame*, suggests that audiences are not worried by the distinction. Kihachiro Kawamoto probably spoke for many in the animation business when he remarked: 'What interests me most in the production of animated film is that the person who creates it is the only one who can express what he feels, like a painter.'

That is certainly what Lord and Sproxton achieved in 'Animated Conversations' and 'Conversation Pieces'. Although the audio-track suggests that the characters on screen have been accurately drawn from life, the truth is more complex since the animation is, in fact, an imaginative interpretation of what is heard. By hearing the dialogue 'performed' by a realistic puppet - who may not bear any resemblance to the real owner of the voice - the words seems more sharply focused and the passing banalities of life take on a new significance.

The quiet desperation of the door-to-door salesman in the Lord and Sproxton film *Sales Pitch*, another in the 'Conversation Pieces' series.

For example, in *Sales Pitch*, an ever-hopeful door-to-door salesman gets into conversation with an elderly couple who are quite happy to chat, but who have clearly no intention of buying his mops and brushes. The desperation of the salesman - covered though it is by his easy, laughing manner - is painful to watch, and when he packs up his case and turns to go there is a moment where the audience glimpses the unnamed burdens that are weighing on his shoulders. At the same time, *Sales Pitch* is full of delightful comic character animation: the wife, saying little, deferring to the husband who abstractedly cleans out his pipe while the salesman relentlessly continues his pitch; the neighbour in an adjacent house, eavesdropping on the conversation, then accidentally banging her head on the open window; or the dog, seen at the end of the film chewing a sample brush.

One of the other films in this series was a significant departure. *Palmy Days* animated a rambling over-the-tea-cups conversation between several elderly people repeating oft-told tales and laughing politely at unfunny anecdotes. Peter Lord and Dave Sproxton could not, at first, see any value in this material, until they took a leap of the imagination, dressed the old folks in tattered clothes and palm-leaf skirts and placed them in a hut on a tropical island with a crashed plane in the background. By juxtaposing the surreal with the commonplace, *Palmy Days* gained a disturbing subtext that is not a part of the original recording.

The success of these series began to generate commercial work that, in turn, required the employment of more animators. Among those who joined the

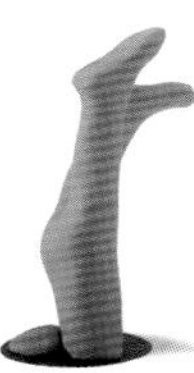

Wallace tastes Moon cheese in *A Grand Day Out* (1989), the first Wallace and Gromit film which Nick Park completed after joining the Aardman studio.

studio were Barry Purves, who came from Cosgrove Hall where he had been a director and the character animator for Toad in *The Wind in the Willows*; graphic artist Richard Goleszowski, who joined the studio in 1983, and Nick Park, who was invited to join Aardman in 1985 in order to complete *A Grand Day Out*, a film he had started while a student at the National Film and Television School. Nominated for an Academy Award, *A Grand Day Out* (1989) introduced the world to Wallace, the eccentric, cheese-loving inventor and his faithful dog, Gromit. The story was pure comic-book adventure - building a space rocket and blasting-off to the moon in search of cheese. The characters, however, were strongly delineated: the naive, somewhat inept Wallace (voiced by Peter Sallis) and the real brains behind the partnership, Gromit, whose facial expressions - wide, slightly mournful eyes - quickly register his despair, frustration or total incredulity.

The success of *A Grand Day Out* demanded a sequel, and in 1993 Wallace and Gromit returned in *The Wrong Trousers*, followed two years later by *A Close Shave*, all three films having been commissioned by Colin Rose of the BBC. The later films, both of which won Oscars, have tightly constructed plots involving a villainous penguin disguised as a chicken and a psychopathic mechanical dog. They are packed with visual jokes (Gromit reading a paper carrying the headline 'Dog Reads Paper') and visual puns (Gromit's collection of records by 'Bach'), and there is a proliferation of wacky gadgetry, ranging from the ex-NASA Techno-Trousers to Wallace's Knit-O-Matic machine via a porridge gun and a device that catapults dollops of jam on to a piece of toast as it springs out of a pop-up toaster. Park's films work on many levels. Children respond to the broad character comedy, adults to the more sophisticated elements including the affectionate spoofing of movie genres such as horror films, thrillers, heist pictures, action movies and the deep shadows and crazy camera angles of *film noir*. The richness of characterisation and the relentlessly paced animation (the model train chase in *The Wrong Trousers* and the motorbike pursuit in *A Close Shave*) have carried clay animation to unprecedented heights.

Below: A sketch of Gromit for the chase sequence in *A Close Shave* (1995)

Between completing *A Grand Day Out* and beginning work on *The Wrong Trousers*, Park contributed to a series of five diverse animated

Compilation of images from Barry Purves's films *Next*, *Screen Play*, *Rigoletto* and *Achilles*

films, produced in 1989-90 under the title 'Lip Synch'. The project was devised to give Peter Lord and three of Aardman's growing staff of animators an opportunity to experiment with the idea of imaginatively animating real conversations. 'Lip Synch' was a wry choice of title since, although the dialogue would be synchronised to the characters' lip movements, the accompanying images would not necessarily be 'in sync' with the personalities, moods or settings in the recordings. It was complicated by the fact that two of the directors took a slightly divergent view and produced films where 'lip syncing' turned out to be of minimal importance!

A soundtrack of grunts and guttural gabblings accompanied Richard Goleszowski's *Ident*. As the title suggests, the film is about identity: a grotesque, phallus-shaped character - pink, bald and naked - is attempting to escape from a claustrophobic maze where he is constantly expected to conform and wear a mask. Eventually he finds a way into another world only to discover that, once more, people attempt to reshape his identity.

Equally idiosyncratic was Barry Purves's film, *Next*, made with puppets (as opposed to clay) and containing hardly any dialogue apart from the word 'Next!', bellowed from the stalls of a theatre by a bored director who is holding auditions. The hopeful player who enters the spotlight is William Shakespeare who, in a *tour de force* of animation, mimes the Complete Works and proves that 'one man in his time plays many parts'. From a wicker prop-basket, the

Grotesques converse in *Ident*, the contribution of Richard Goleszowski to the Aardman series 'Lip Synch'.

Bard produces masks, crowns, swords, items of costuming and a stuffed dummy which he manipulates as a supporting cast of lovers and corpses. At the conclusion of the performance, the director (a caricature of Sir Peter Hall) looks up from a book - having missed the entire audition - and shouts 'Next!'.

Full of surprises, this witty film established Barry Purves's elegant style, seen in the puppet film which he has made since leaving Aardman Animations: *Screen Play* (1992), an Oscar-nominated presentation of a Japanese Kabuki-style drama, performed by ornately clothed puppet-actors on a stage-set which is constantly being transformed by a complex arrangement of sliding and revolving screens.

Purves went on to produce a darkly sinister visualisation of *Rigoletto* (1993) for the S4C/BBC series 'Operavox', and in 1995 a homoerotic retelling of the legend of *Achilles*, a powerful and passionate film with a cast of characters modelled to look like sculpted figures and enacted in a highly stylised dramatic form evoking the theatrical conventions of Ancient Greece.

The remaining films in the 'Lip Synch' series followed the convention of the earlier 'Animated Conversations' and 'Conversation Pieces'. From Peter Lord came two vastly different films: a charmingly dotty piece of humorous storytelling, *War Story*, and *Going Equipped*, an intensely focused monologue on a sombre theme. The fifth film in the series was Nick Park's *Creature Comforts*

(1990), in which zoo animals confess to feelings of depression, claustrophobia and boredom. This film won Nick Park his first Academy Award. The following year saw the start of a series of Heat Electric commercials featuring Frank the Tortoise and Carol the Cat, who became cult figures with British television audiences. The commercials were later released on video, and Frank, Carol and other animal characters also appeared on various items of merchandise. Almost fifteen years later, another collection of *Creature Comforts* would return to the small screen to delight a new generation.

Meanwhile in 1996, the format was adapted for a series of American TV commercials for Chevron. Featuring talking cars, moaning about being tired, having dents in their doors and hearing strange knocking and pinging sounds, these commercials are crammed with visual gags and funny incidental detail.

A talking car in a TV commercial for the American company Chevron, as it was visualised in sketch form, above, and in the finished film, below left.

Aardman Animations had begun making TV commercials in 1984 with an advertising film for Enterprise Computers, in which various competing computers were depicted as clattering fossils given rickety life. More bony animation followed with the Scotch Videotape Skeleton, a jokey character who recalls the skeletal warriors in Ray Harryhausen's *Jason and the Argonauts*. Over the years, Aardman's commercials have given animated life to all manner of inanimate objects from a bottle of Domestos bleach guarding a bathroom to a bottle of Perrier with a pair of dancing straws.

The studio has also specialised in giving human form to a variety of edible products: a singing sausage-man for Bowyers; a *pas de deux* danced by two figures made from Jordan's Crunchy and Chewy bars; a fruit-and-vegetable man for a healthy-eating campaign and - perhaps most memorably - the Lurpak Butterman. Emerging, Morph-like, from a block of butter, 'Douglas' (as he was eventually named) has various adventures - such as snorkeling, rowing, hang-gliding and motorcycling - on a food-laden table. Other ingenious metamorphoses include the bulbous-nosed, porridge-coloured man advertising

Readybrek, who in quick succession becomes a train, an alarm clock and a pop-singer; and, in the commercials for Crunchie, chocolate bars which undergo a rapid series of transformations into chocolate submarines, dancing girls, performing seals, roller-coasters, rocket-ships and rodeo cowboys.

Other innovative commercial work includes the wooden man advocating the use of Cuprinol wood preservative; the Chewits Monster, styled after the popular monstrous-beast-on-the-rampage-movies of the 1940s (with a nod towards Harryhausen's various behemoths); the Polo commercials with their spoof revelations of such inside information as the way in which the mints get their characteristic hole, and a series of stunning Lego advertisements in which heaps of Lego bricks assemble themselves into a pirate and a spaceman who then take on fully animated life.

All this commercial work has developed alongside the studio's broadcast films in a creative harmony that has allowed each discipline to benefit from the other. The lessons learned in making the 'Lip Synch' series, for example, have been exploited in commercials for a variety of products from Walkers Crisps to the Britannia Building Society. In an expensive medium, it is often the commercial work which not only funds less remunerative ventures, but provides opportunities to develop and experiment.

In 1986 Aardman completed work on *Babylon*, a chilling 15-minute film for Channel 4, set in the sumptuous surroundings of a grand hotel where a conference of arms-dealers is taking place. As a speaker refers to the dark view the world has of their trade - seeing them as 'the vultures of society' living 'off the honest gains of the people' - the dinner-suited guests become increasingly bestial and one grows to gargantuan size before bursting in a torrent of blood and bullets.

Douglas the Butterman, who has become something of a star in his own right in the commercials Aardman have made for Lurpak.

In the same year - and in striking contrast - the studio produced a pop video for Peter Gabriel's single, *Sledgehammer*, directed by Steve Johnson. This tirelessly inventive film created a series of lip-synced images using the singer's real head alternated with likenesses in clay, ice and - courtesy of the Brothers Quay who contributed to the film - bleached wood, rusting metal and assorted fruit and vegetables, animated in the style of Jan Svankmajer.

One of the benefits of having a seemingly inexplicable company name like Aardman Animations is that it provides more opportunities

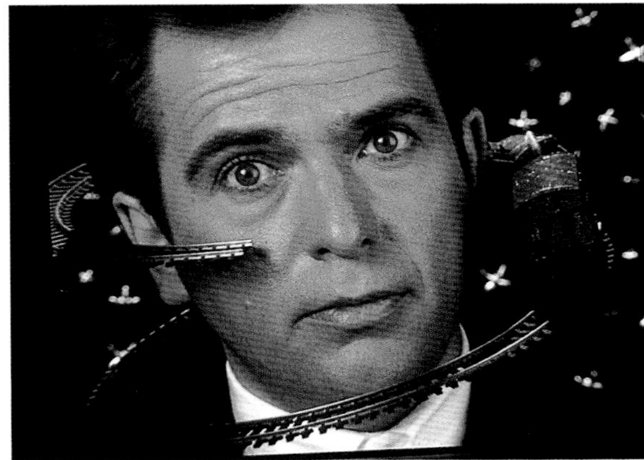

Frames from the Aardman pop video made for Peter Gabriel's single release, *Sledgehammer* (1986). The video was directed by Steve Johnson.

for individual artistic expression and lessens the tendency to associate the studio with one 'name' - such as Walt Disney or Will Vinton - which narrows audience expectations and limits commercial and creative commissions. In addition to Nick Park, several Aardman animators have been encouraged to produce films which carry their own individual stamp, such as Peter Peake who produced *Pib and Pog* (1996), a spoof on a television programme for small children, featuring the voice of an enthusiastic lady storyteller and two anarchic characters who relentlessly attempt to destroy one another.

In 1991, Richard Goleszowski took a flat Plasticine dog who had appeared in his film *Ident*, called him Rex the Runt and made two short films - *Dinosaurs* and *Dreams*. Joined by his doggy chums Wendy, Bad Bob and Vince, Rex has various adventures which sway between the surreal and the banal. The BBC subsequently commissioned an entire series of bizarre 'Rex the Runt' stories, beginning with *A Holiday in Vince* in which the gang miniaturise a submarine and go on a fantastic journey through Vince's brain.

Rex was part of a late-Nineties genre that might be described as bizarre-meets-grunge and which included such anarchic and grotesque series as Sarah Ann Kennedy's 'Crapston Villas' (a spoof, fly-on-the-wall, docu-drama about a group of repellent residents of what has been called 'the happy house from Hell') and Deiniol Morris and Michael Mort's BAFTA Award-winning 'Gogs', featuring an obnoxious family of cave-dwellers struggling to coexist with the ubiquitous dinosaur population.

Steve Box, who joined Aardman in 1992 and animated with Nick Park on *The Wrong Trousers* and *A Close Shave*, directed his first film, *Stage Fright*, in 1997. A black comedy, set in a decaying theatre at a time when music hall was giving way to cinema, the film tells how Tiny - a diminutive, dog-juggling freak - wreaks a terrible revenge on the villainous Arnold Hugh who uses Tiny's trained dogs to help establish his own career as a film actor. The time-scale in *Stage Fright* shifts constantly between the present and flash-back just as, visually, it alternates between scratched and grainy black-and-white film images and the world of the

A Burger King commercial, in which realistic-looking model versions of the product were combined with customers from the fantasy world of clay.

theatre, filmed in sombre colours and lit with harsh stage lighting that surrounds the actors with deep shadows.

In marked contrast to the theatricality of *Stage Fright* are Dave Riddett's and Luis Cook's *Knobs in Space* (1994), made for the Terrence Higgins Trust, and Sam Fell's *Pop* (1996), in which a quirky little character hopes to relieve his boredom with a can of fizzy drink which goes into orbit and finally blows his head off, leaving his vacated neck to be occupied by a singing goldfish.

As the company has grown, David Sproxton has increasingly taken on a supervisory role, overseeing much of the production work undertaken, particularly the commercials, though this means he has become less involved in a hands-on way with individual productions. The rapid growth of the company has also required it to assume a more formal structure, and a great deal of David's time is now spent in managing its affairs.

Meanwhile, Peter Lord has continued directing his own films, such as *Wat's Pig* (1996), a medieval fable - told with hardly any dialogue - about two brothers who are parted at birth. One brother becomes a king, the other a pig-keeper and their contrasting fortunes are shown in a unique split-screen format until a war with a neighbouring country unites their lives and their stories. *Wat's Pig* was nominated for an Academy Award, as was Lord's earlier film *Adam* (1991), in which a human (but also God-like) hand creates and then controls the existence of a little man whom Lord describes as being 'Morph with genitalia'. Having no dialogue, *Adam* works in the universal language of mime, and the film shows the subtlety of acting with clay that is Aardman's particular contribution to this form of animation.

In 1998 Peter Lord and Nick Park embarked on what was, at the time, the studio's most ambitious project - its first feature-length film, *Chicken Run,* released in 2000: an endlessly inventive pastiche of classic prisoner-of-war escape movies, enacted by chickens.

The film boasted incomparable model-making, a cunningly contrived plot and a cast of strong, memorable characterisations: from the plucky Ginger, leader of the rebel chickens, and Rocky the American rooster who helps her hatch an escape plan, to the sinister Mrs Tweedy, gripped by a vision of saving her failing farm by switching from egg-production to the manufacture of chicken pies. The supporting players: dizzy hens; an elderly, disgruntled cockerel with the manner of a veteran RAF flyer, and a pair of wise-cracking rats added to the richness of the film. The scope of the film, ranging from the comic and absurd to the moving and dramatic, showed Aardman as capable of sustaining and advancing character emotions and fully meeting the demands of a feature-length film.

Whilst having all the appearance (and appeal) of traditional Aardman model-animation, *Chicken Run* also made significant use of computer animation techniques at a time when the industry, driven on by an intense public interest, was increasingly embracing 'computer generated imagery' or, as it is usually abbreviated, CGI.

'Rex the Runt', Richard Goleszowski's 13-part series, was launched on BBC Television in 1998.

The progress of computer animation can be tracked across a series of groundbreaking movies from early experiments such as *Tron* (1982), through the various 'Terminator' and 'Jurassic Park' movies to *Starship Troopers* (1997) and *Star Wars: Episodes I and II: The Phantom Menace* (1999) and *Attack of the Clones* (2002). The rise of CGI, both in the field of animated films and as a special effects tool for the live-action movie industry is a fascinating by-product of a rapidly increasing sophistication in computer technology.

Film-makers who once would have made use of stop-motion effects artists (such as Phil Tippett, creator of the memorable long-legged AT-AT walkers in *Star Wars: The Empire Strikes Back* (1980) and the robots in the 'Robocop' movies) increasingly began turning to the computer.

This rapid transition took place within little more than a decade so that only three years after Phil Tippett had supervised the stop-motion dinosaurs in *Jurassic Park* (1993), the animator's alien invaders created for Tim Burton's *Mars Attacks!* were abandoned in favour of computer generated extra-terrestrials. Ironically, what is now seen as providing the most effective three-dimensional animation effects is actually a two-dimensional medium.

With films such as *The Matrix* (1999), *Spider-man* (2002) and *The Hulk* (2003), CGI animation reached an astonishing sophistication, particularly as showcased in Peter Jackson's *The Lord of the Rings Trilogy* (beginning in 2001 with *The Fellowship of the Ring*) which not only demonstrated that the computer can create compelling scenes peopled by thousands of digital extras, but can also simulate the likenesses of real actors and use them to enact impossible scenarios.

The computer's challenge to traditional feature animation was heralded by the instantaneous success of Pixar Animation Studio's *Toy Story* (1995), followed by *A Bug's Life* (1998). Rival studio, Dreamworks, was soon in direct competition, releasing its own insect movie, *Antz*, in the same year as Pixar's bugs appeared. The phenomenal success subsequently achieved by Pixar's *Toy Story 2* (1999) and Dreamworks' *Shrek* (2001), and the record-breaking Pixar hit, *Finding Nemo* (2003), seemed to many to be sounding a death-knell for traditional cel-animation techniques.

The antics of Angry Kid, the obnoxious boy created by Darren Walsh, are performed by a live actor wearing a succession of face masks to show his changing moods and expressions.

Aardman Animations' response to this trend has been to seek ways of harnessing the potential offered by the computer, whilst maintaining the unique individuality and artistry that secured its reputation. As a result they are constantly seeking ways in which the computer can enhance their stop-motion film-making while collaborating with Dreamworks to develop *Flushed Away*, an ambitious CGI feature film concept by Peter Lord and Sam Fell starring rats, that will be devised and designed in Bristol but animated in Hollywood. The studio will also be working with other partners in the creation of a television series with a kung-fu theme, entitled 'Chop Socky Chooks'.

Aardman continues to push at the boundaries of animation both in terms of story-telling and technique as well as in exploring new ways of reaching audiences. Hence the arrival of 'Angry Kid', featuring a typically obnoxious adolescent with red hair and a fiery temperament, whose one-minute adventures (or, rather, *misadventures*) made their début on the internet.

Angry Kid (written, directed and spoken for by Darren Walsh) uses pixillation, a technique in which a model-animated head is superimposed on a human body and produces an intriguing sense of dislocated reality when a seemingly animated character is seen in live-action environments: cycling down a street, riding in the back of a car or cleaning his teeth in front of a bathroom mirror.

Angry Kid's sixty-second scenarios were a bold departure for the studio: watching a sex education programme on TV with a mixture of fascination and repulsion, falling off his bike and grappling with a dog that goes after an exposed bone in his arm or using swear words that would never been heard from the lips of Wallace or from the beaks of chickens on Tweedy's Farm.

Even as they explore new areas of entertainment, Aardman have consistently held onto the hallmark qualities that have set them apart from other animation studios

Performing bears from the second series of ***Creature Comforts***, **directed by Richard Goleszowski.**

and refused to turn their back on the creations that first brought them international acclaim.

In 2002, the studio revisited the successful *Creature Comforts*, launching a new series in 2003 that followed the premise of Nick Park's Oscar-winning film from 1989. Despite the intervening fourteen years, the new 'Creature Comforts', created by Nick and directed with wit and flair by Richard Goleszowski, recaptured the essence of the original with ease: putting the thoughts and opinions of 'The Great British Public' into the mouths of Plasticine animals 'interviewed' beside the seaside,

at the vet's clinic, back-stage at the circus, down on the farm, in pet store, garden and home.

Christmas 2003 saw Nick Park's man-and-dog double act enjoying a long-awaited revival with a series of short, three-minute films featuring 'Wallace and Gromit's Cracking Contraptions', more zany, havoc-wreaking machines, the names of which ('Snoozatron', 'Christmas Cardomatic', 'Snowmanatron') tell all any seasoned Wallace-watcher needs to know about the inevitable chaos to come. The series provided a prelude to their much anticipated forthcoming feature film, *The Great Vegetable Plot*.

'I always describe puppet animation,' says Peter Lord, 'as being instinctive. You go through it as you go through life: reasonably well-informed about what you've just done, with a plan for what you intend to do, but prepared also for an unpleasant surprise at any moment. You hold the puppet in your two hands, and maybe your left hand is holding the shoulders while your thumb lies commandingly on the spine. Your right hand is on the pelvis, ready to move either leg or both at once. So you've got the whole figure under your hand, ready to respond to your instruction. You can feel the movement in it, and the logic as it twists and bends. Often the puppet leads you, you can feel its inner life ...'

It is all very like those ancient creation myths in which some god or demi-god takes up a fistful of mud and shapes it into a thing that can hold, within its fragile form, all the passions, ambitions, dreams and despairs that are the lot of humankind - though without any certainty about how that creation will direct its own destiny.

Nick's

basic needs

The Camera

Standard 8 cine camera, superseded by the Super 8 and now by video.

When you watch a film, or a television programme, or a video, what are you actually looking at? Everyone knows the answer: freeze-frame the video and you get a still picture. The moving pictures that we see on our screens are basically made up of a series of still images in sequence. When these still images are played back at sufficient speed - normally at the rate of 25 frames per second (fps) on TV, or 24 in the cinema - our brains stop seeing these images as separate and static, and instead perceive movement.

This is because of a phenomenon known as persistence of vision which was first properly identified in 1825, shortly before the invention of photography. It means that our brain holds onto an image for about one-tenth of a second after the image has been removed from our sight. This delay in our rate of perception is enough to allow quickly changing static images (the photographed frames) to be merged into one another, creating smooth, flowing moving images.

Compared with ordinary film-makers, who just point their camera at something moving and shoot it, animators have made life extremely difficult for themselves, inventing incredibly elaborate and tortuous ways to create moving images. Instead of capturing something that is already moving, we painstakingly create each one of the still pictures needed to imitate movement in real life. Unless we go for a shortcut - for example, by shooting in 'double-frame' (see below) - we have to create 24-25 separate pictures for every second of finished film or tape.

Whichever way the still pictures are generated, the same basic equipment is required: a camera with a lens to focus the image, a system to record and retain it, and a steady tripod for the camera.

When they started out, most of our animators got themselves Standard 8 or Super 8 cine cameras, with some, like us, even having their own 16mm film cameras (see illustration). These film formats have been largely superseded with the advent of video, although 16mm cameras (the Bolex) provide very high-quality images if one has the resources to buy film and process it through a professional film laboratory.

Most of Aardman's work is done with 35mm Mitchell cine cameras, equipped with electric motors. These provide the high quality needed for films which will be shown in cinemas on the big screen. The cost, however, is in the thousands, and not worth considering for most amateur film-makers. In the professional environment, there are various other aids to accuracy and consistency, but these too are expensive and not at all essential in the early years of a film-making career. There are many more basic skills to be mastered

16mm cine camera

before a 35mm camera has to go to the head of the shopping list. Video cameras are now widely used for stop-frame animation even in professional studios, with Mini DV cameras being perfectly suitable for amateur use when linked to an appropriate computer programme.

If you are purchasing a video camera, ask whether it has a single-frame facility. Many cameras will take 'still frames' but they actually record 4–6 frames or more at a time and not true single frames. If you are using a computer programme like Adobe Premier, Stop Motion Pro or I-Stop Motion, you won't need the camera to record your images as such: that will be done on the computer. In this case the video camera can be very simple, and even some web-cams will provide a cheap and practical method of capturing digital images.

Single-and double-frame Animating in single-frame means you have to animate your model 24 times for one second of completed film. If you do it well, the results are gorgeous. It is, however, a pretty time-consuming method. Fortunately, there is a standard and very acceptable shortcut, which is to take two frames every time you move the model. This is called double-frame, and means you only need to create 12 different images for every second of film. Common sense may tell you that double-frame must look jerkier than single-frame. For now I will only say that we used double-frame for most of Wallace and Gromit's adventures, and they don't look bad. In fact, I prefer to use double-frame whenever possible. Also, you would be crazy to start your animation career working in single-frame. Finally, some further jargon. Single-frame animation is also called 'singles' and 'ones', and double-frame (surprisingly) is called 'doubles' or 'twos'. Work these terms into your conversation, as in: 'Blimey! You mean they shot the whole thing on twos?'

FIXING THE TRIPOD

Make sure your tripod is firmly fixed and does not move while the camera is in use. You can weight a tripod by putting weights on the legs and/or suspending a weight from the midpoint beneath the camera. You can fix the legs to the floor or plant them in a triangular spreader which has holes for the legs and stops them slipping sideways. To help prevent the spreader from shifting if someone accidentally knocks against it, weigh down each of its arms with sandbags.

35mm camera with control box.

Video camera.

Video Cameras and Computer Animation

For the amateur, video has many advantages over cine film. These include low light exposure, auto exposure, reusable tape (making it cheaper to run), good picture quality, no need for a projector (you just watch it on TV), and instant replay. The disadvantage is that most of the cameras available in the high street do not have true single-frame recording facilites. They shoot 4–6 frames (1/4 of a second) at a time. As this is too long an interval for smooth animation, the best solution is to link the camera to a computer software programme which can import single frames and replay them at full speed (25 fps).

As computers have become more popular, it has become much easier to find suitable programmes for animation. Stop Motion Pro for the PC and I-Stop Motion for the Macintosh are two well-known programmes, while Adobe's Premier is a sophisticated video editing programme which can take in still images and play them out as video. Every year more systems come on the market, so take a look at the relevant web-sites or visit your local computer store to see what is available.

At Aardman we use a system called 'Lunchbox Sync' (made by Animation Toolworks in the USA) for tests and simple set-ups. A video picture signal is fed into the system, and sound can be loaded in so that animators can work to a voice or music track. It's a great system for practising making characters speak (lip-sync) and gives very high-quality results. Being reasonably priced, it is a very popular system for schools and colleges.

It is also possible to make animated films entirely on computers. At Aardman we have a computer animation department that uses software called 'Maya'. This very sophisticated package allows an animator to construct virtual puppets, clothe them, animate them and light them very much as we do for conventional filming. The technique is completely different but the animation skills needed are the same. Such systems are often used on special-effects movies and entire films such as *Toy Story*, *Shrek* and *Finding Nemo*. As ever with tools like these, you still have to have a good story to tell!

★ To calculate how far the camera should move during a pan or tilt, fix a pointer to the back of the camera head which follows an arc on a piece of cardboard. Basically, you divide the distance the camera has to move by the number of frames the move runs for. The move needs to accelerate to its full speed and then slow to a stop at the end. On the arc, mark off gradually increasing and decreasing increments for the first and last quarters of the move.

35mm camera with connection for video assist (see page 74) mounted on top of the camera body.

MOTION CONTROL

The most common camera moves are pans, where the camera rotates horizontally, and tilts, where it pivots up and down. You can also track a camera, moving the whole thing to one side, or forwards and backwards.

Any movement of the camera must be done smoothly, and there are various devices for controlling the camera as it moves. At the top end of the motion-control field is the Milo, right, a massive rail-mounted electrically driven computer-operated crane, with a boom arm that swivels on a revolving pedestal. This super-versatile rig allows the camera to be moved with optimum smoothness in just about any conceivable direction, its operation controlled by computer. It also repeats movements with extreme accuracy.

With a small, light video camera buy a lightweight geared head which fits on top of the tripod. The head is equipped with handles which you turn to make a pan or tilt. To track a camera sideways or on a curve, you only need some kind of wheeled support on to which you can fix the camera. For straight line movements, try a skateboard, guided along between planks. For greater variety you could use a wagon from a model train set, which you then push along a section of rail.

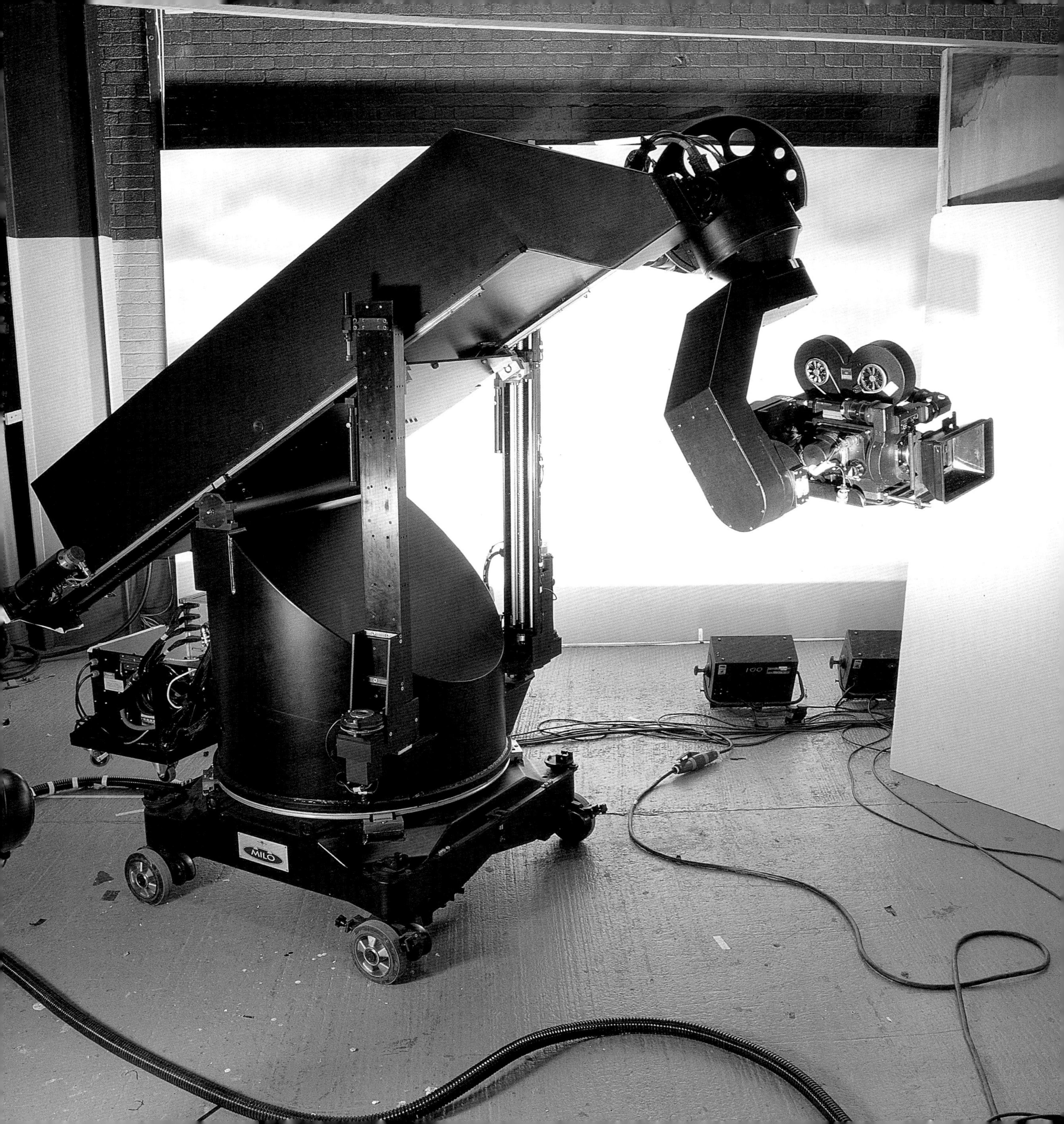
MILO

A Simple Studio

Our first studio was the kitchen in Dave's parents' house. Our stage was the kitchen table and our tripod was an old enlarging stand. In later years we moved up-market, first to the spare bedroom and later to his sister's room in the attic (which, I hasten to add, she had vacated). As this suggests, the basic requirements for a model-animation studio are very simple. You need your camera - film or video - and a computer (if that is your chosen method of storing the images). You need a tripod, to support the camera, a flat surface to act as a stage or set, and some lighting to ensure an unchanging level of light while you are animating. And, of course, your character, puppet or whatever.

There is one simple golden rule in the model-animation studio. Nothing should move unless you want it to. When most people start experimenting with animation - and that certainly includes us - the most common fault is that either the set, the shadows from the lights, the camera or the environment itself moves about almost as much as the animated puppet. Any part of your studio which is not firmly fixed down is liable to get knocked or jogged during the hours that you are animating, and every such movement becomes an irritating distraction in your finished film. To avoid this happening, everything possible needs to be fixed down, or otherwise rendered idiot-proof.

Morph and his mate Chas, deep in some squabble of huge unimportance. When Morph first appeared on BBC's 'Vision On', our brief was to provide a small blob-like character who would change into various shapes, charge around the table-top, and interact with presenter Tony Hart.

Of course, you have to be careful too. No camera, however sturdily fixed, is going to stay still if you clout it with the full force of your body. I notice that animators, even big clumsy ones, acquire in time great spatial awareness. They become instinctively aware of all the things they must not bump into and manage to avoid them - often without looking - with balletic elegance. Even so, we have to make sure that everything is fixed down.

You should be able to tighten your tripod so that the camera cannot slip, even over days. If, as we have already said, you can tape or otherwise fix the tripod legs to the floor, great. If not, try to weight it down so that a glancing blow will not shift it. Sometimes at Aardman we erect barriers - which could simply be ribbon or string - around the tripod, just to keep the animator at a safe distance from it.

Similarly, you do not want your table to start shifting. A succession of gentle nudges will appear like an earthquake in your finished film. The answer is to use

This is how we used to shoot Morph, on 16mm film. These days we use video. Essentials of the scene are: tripod legs firmly secured; camera set well back so the animator has plenty of room; storyboard close by and other props ready to hand - so no need to rummage around later.

the most solid base you can. The table-top is your stage, and the surface should be appropriate. We will see later how models can be fixed to the table to hold their position, and some of these methods are fairly intrusive, involving pins or screws. It may be best not to use the actual table-top but to fix another surface to it. If you decide to do this, thick fibreboard is a good choice. If you follow the Aardman career path and start with clay models, you should be aware that oil and sometimes pigment can seep out of the clay and stain unvarnished wood. You may imagine that clay would stick well to a textured surface, but I found with Morph that he actually stuck best to something smooth and hard, like varnished wood, melamine or formica. If your chosen surface is a board laid on top of an existing table, make sure it is firmly clamped to the table.

Right, top: To give a sense of place in *Limoland,* we built a big panoramic view of a non-specific American city, measuring about 40ft x 30ft (12m x 9m), with the dwindling perspective you would get from an aerial shot of a real city. Because the set was so large, we were able to crane the camera down over the scene, though we did not have space to track across it.

A Complex Studio

As you can see, we have moved off the kitchen table. I love the studios at Aardman. I love the fact that they look, and sometimes feel, totally chaotic, though actually they are spaces which have evolved to be the way they are, and this includes being very efficient and businesslike. Even so, I hesitate to show them off to aspiring animators, in case they are discouraged by the complexity and technical sophistication.

In fact, however, the heart of a studio, no matter how complex it may seem, is the same as ever: model, set, camera and lights. We still use 35mm film cameras, though now we use them in conjunction with sophisticated devices that give us precise motion control (see page 66), allow us to plan a character's movements on-screen (video assist) and mix between one frame and the next one before shooting (digital frame store).

The main characters in *Limoland* are singers Tina Turner, above, and Barry White, and because they appear in sets of different sizes we had to make them in two different versions. One set was the ordinary size for puppets, which is about 9in (23cm) high, and the other was double that.

Video Assist When shooting on film, as we do for our feature films, the only way to see the camera's view of a scene is by looking through the camera viewfinder. Video assist is a system for showing the same scene on a TV monitor. The big advantage is that it simplifies the real 3-D world into a two-dimensional world on the TV screen. To help ensure that your puppet is moving smoothly and evenly through the shot, you can draw on the screen with a water-soluble pen. If you trace, for example, the line of the character's back, you quickly find that after a few frames you have a pattern of lines on the screen that should be evenly spaced. Instead of guessing, or remembering how far your puppet has moved each frame, you can clearly see it on the screen. In our studios, a video camera is mounted to look through the 35mm film camera viewfinder and give us exactly the same view that will appear on film. This video picture is then fed into a computer system (Leitch/DPS PVR or Reality hard disk recorder using the 'Animate' programme). In this way we can play through the sequence of images already taken, and then add the one we plan to take next. After checking it to see if it is OK, and adjusting the model if necessary, we record it on the computer, adding it to the end of the sequence, and then shoot the new image on the film camera. In fact, we are watching the animation develop frame by frame as we do it.

This street set for *Limoland* is built on a steel table at the right height for animators to get in and out. We also left gaps for them between the buildings (which cannot be seen from the camera's viewpoint). To make things even more complex, we had to deal with a lot of 'practical' lights in the form of street lights, lights from cars and others in the buildings, all of which took a long time to set up.

Digital Frame Store We used to use an amateur video mixing desk for this task but have recently designed our own simple system for storing just one image at a time. We use it to store the image we have just taken, so that we can compare it with the one we are preparing to shoot. The frame store usually has a slider control so that the animator can mix gently between the two images, checking that every detail is correct. It is also invaluable for checking that nothing in the picture has moved that the animator did not want to move - or, in the case of the animator's worst disaster, when the puppet falls over during shot, it is possible to replace it in exactly the right position.

Lamps can be suspended from an overhead grid, right, or mounted, as below, on floor-mounted lighting stands.

The outer lamps in this group are fitted with Fresnel lenses which allow the beam angle to be adjusted.

Second and third from left are profile spots. Profile lamps give a more controllable beam of light which can be focused to give a hard-edged light or softened for a more subtle effect. Internal shutters can help to control the spread of light. You can also insert a 'gobo' - literally, something which comes between the lamp and the set. We use these to project a defined shape such as a window or a slatted venetian-blind pattern.

The Power of Lighting

Today we use lighting in just the same way as a conventional film studio, except that we work on a much smaller scale with relatively tiny sets and characters. In order to achieve precise lighting control on such small sets, we use lanterns designed for use in theatres, called 'profile' lamps. These are designed a little like slide projectors and can project a very controlled beam from quite a distance. In this way lamps positioned some distance from the set can illuminate very small areas of it without 'spill light' falling on other areas.

The amount of light illuminating a set does not have to be huge, even when shooting on film, as we can use long shutter speeds, often between one quarter to a full second. With video cameras, exposure is much less of a problem and a set can be lit quite adequately with a couple of anglepoise lamps. All video cameras have automatic exposure control but you may want to overide it and use manual exposure to ensure you get the full effect of the lighting you have set up. Manual mode will also prevent the camera from changing the exposure setting as you step in front of it to alter the positions of your models. Remember to set the camera for tungsten lighting when using normal electric lights, or 'white balance' the camera using a white card held under the lamps you are going to use. This will avoid causing a colour cast to your images and will also allow any coloured lights you might use to have their full effect.

The key light gives the characters their shape, making distinctive and readable shadows. The lamp is often placed to one side of the camera and a little higher than the character to give a 'normal' look. One side of the face will be fully illuminated and the other will be in shadow, which will show the character's features well. If there is a window in the set, the key light will come from that direction to suggest that the light is coming through the window.

The fill light fills in the shadow side of the subject, keeping a reasonable difference between the two, typically one or two stops (half or one quarter the amount of light coming from the key light) to prevent the shadows going

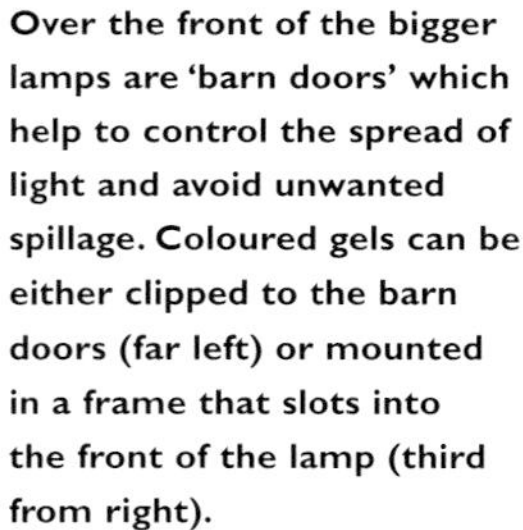

Over the front of the bigger lamps are 'barn doors' which help to control the spread of light and avoid unwanted spillage. Coloured gels can be either clipped to the barn doors (far left) or mounted in a frame that slots into the front of the lamp (third from right).

How lighting enhances the action. Clockwise from top left: Warm light from the fire is contrasted with the cold blue moonlight flooding in through the window; from *Wat's Pig*. Film noir suspense with deep shadows and a shaft of bright light in *The Wrong Trousers*. Car lights flash across the wall of the interview room in *Going Equipped*. Back lighting rims the worm/phallus shape of the character in *Ident* and makes him stand out from his background.

totally black. To avoid multiple shadows, this light is often a 'soft' light, diffused by tracing paper or similar which is placed over the front of the lamp, or by 'bouncing' the light off a white card to produce a diffused source. Bounced light is very useful, but the light 'falls off' (diminishes in power) very rapidly if the bounce board is too far from the subject.

The back light is used to 'rim' the subject with light, producing a highlight along all the top edges and separating the subject from the background. This is often called giving the subject 'an edge'. This light is placed quite high to the rear of the set pointing towards the camera. Care has to be taken not to have the light shining directly into the camera lens, so the lens may need to be shielded with a lens hood.

A very pleasing effect can be made using a 'three-quarter rear key'. This combines the effect of the back light and key light in one lamp by placing a lamp behind the subject and quite high, at about the 10 o'clock or 2 o'clock position. This gives strong shadows on the ground running towards the camera, and provides the subject with an edge as well as key-light modelling. The shadow

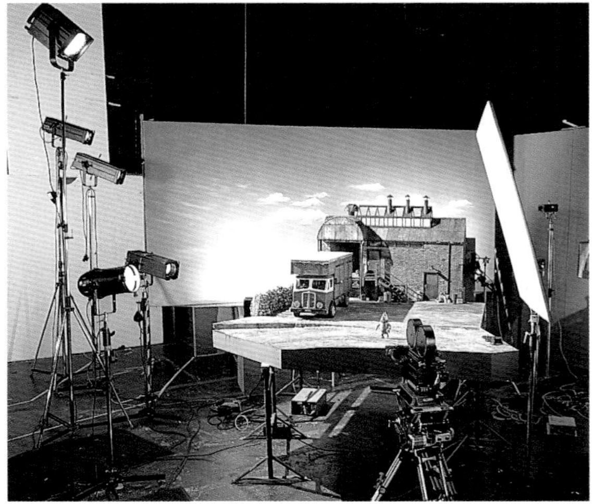

The lighting set-up for an outdoor shot in *A Close Shave*. For this shot the key light (1) assumes the sun position. The shadows are filled by 'bouncing' a narrow-beamed lamp (4) off the large white fill board (6). Three back lights (2,3,5) are used to give emphasis to certain parts of the set, such as the cabin of the truck and details on the rooftop. When positioning these, care is needed not to create secondary shadows from the camera's viewpoint (7).

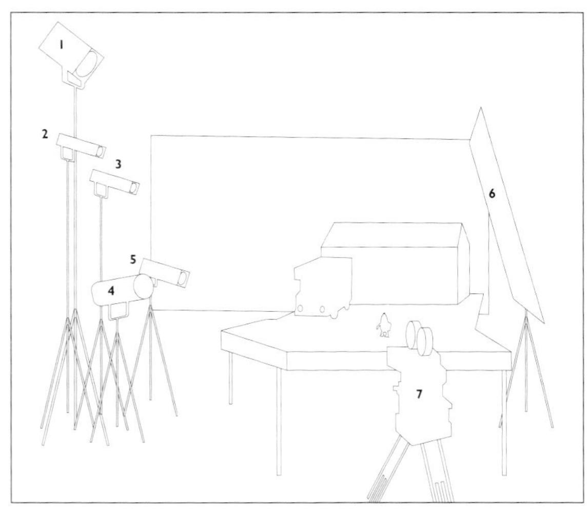

Preston at three times of day. For the daylight shot, left, the scene is keyed from the left as if the main source of light is from a high sun. The fill board to the right of the set bounces a soft light into the shadow areas.

side (facing the camera) is filled using soft light, and the exposure is made for the fill, with the result that the three-quarter key light looks bright and crisp.

Once your basic lights are in position, you can adjust the amount of light thrown on to the set by various means. First, think what kind of an overall effect you want. Do you want a bright, high-key look with little to no contrast - effectively shadowless - a style often used in comedies or to replicate an outdoor light without sun? Or do you want something more moody and low-key, with high contrast and plenty of shadows, the kind that goes best with thrillers?

Wiring up the headlight with a wire through the wheel arch. An important element in dressing and lighting night scenes is the use of 'practicals' such as these headlamps (actually torch or flashlight bulbs) which are connected to a low-voltage power supply.

The direction of the key light is very important - it is the key. In everyday life, people are usually seen illuminated from above - from the sky - or from lights in the ceilings of buildings, so we read human faces with shadows falling down the face or across it, as from a low sun or as the light comes through a window. A light placed below the face makes it look abnormal and even horrific, especially if the light is coloured! Side lighting brings out the character in the face, emphasising the contours, and side frontal lighting softens the contours and produces a flattering look, as used in shots for glossy magazines.

Soft back light can be produced by placing the lamp beside the camera and directing its beam over the top of the set to bounce off a white or foil-covered board above and behind the set. This gives good rim-lighting effects, but the lamp will need to be quite a bit stronger than the key light to read adequately.

Another good effect is to throw shadows on the wall of a set to look like sunlight pouring in through a window. Cut a window-frame shape out of card and place this close to the set and some distance away from a spotlight, positioning it so that it produces a slanting 'sun beam' across the wall. Putting a light orange filter on the light source will make it even more convincing.

Above left: It is dusk, and the scene is now keyed from the right using a lower light source and an added orange gel (filter) to give the impression of a setting sun. The advent of darkness is further emphasised by having very little frontal fill light and by using practicals such as the headlamps and lights in the building.

Above: The cold quality of night-time is achieved by using a blue gel on the fill light contrasted with a warmer tungsten light source skimming over the building as if emanating from practical light sources.

simple techniques

Simple Clay Animation

Working with modelling clay (Plasticine) is the perfect way to get started in animation. As a material it is cheap, flexible and instantly ready to use. Within minutes of opening the pack, you can be animating (not necessarily well, it is true, but certainly animating). So where to start? You have a camera, an empty table and a pack of clay. Take a piece of clay and roll it round in your hands to warm it up. Now practise some moves with it - let it stand up and flip over. Divide it into two lumps. Make them rotate around each other. Each time you move one forward, say 0.5in (1.2cm), press down on it a little. As it moves, it flattens itself. Let one piece grow taller. Before you move it, mark its position on the table with a loop of clay, lift it off the set, squeeze it out longer, then put it back on its mark. Look through the camera and check the new position.

Top: A simple bar of clay, straight from the pack - and never mind the finger-prints! Make it stand up, flip over and break into fragments.

Left: The raw material of clay animation. For filming we use English clay, firmer than the American type which is softer and has brighter colours. Clay is a simple tool, and you need no training to get started. There is nothing to stand between you - the creator - and your ideas.

Try to relax and not be too ambitious at first. Although you could go directly to making a clay figure, a little person or animal, that would be to risk becoming bogged down too soon in detail. Even at this first stage in animation, there are rules and techniques which are simple to follow and will enormously improve the finished result. Never forget that the frame you are animating is one of a sequence. It is not an end in itself. Never lose sight of how slow animation is. If you are working in double-frame, 12 separate moves will only make one second of animation. Time yourself going through a movement to get a sense of how fast your puppet can or should move. How much can you do, how far can you move in one second? If you have a stop-watch, use this to time movements. If not, try saying 'Tick-tock' at a normal rate of speaking; this takes about one second. If you need one second to move, say, 5 ft (1.5m), this means you can film your puppet travelling an equivalent distance - perhaps a complete walk cycle - in 12 frames. Divide up this space into 12 sections or frames to pinpoint each move.

Above: From a blob to a Morph in five moves. This is not so easy, and it would be wise to practise first with the simple sequences on this and the following pages. Have fun with what clay does so well. It is organic and flexible. Each sequence gives you 8-10 phases of movement, or nearly 1 second of film in double-frame (12fps). Put in 3-4 still frames at the beginning to announce your film, and 3-4 at the end to close it.

Top: Make an elongated ball and squash it down. Then squeeze it out longer into a horn shape and let it spring over in an arc and revert to its original form.

When this sequence is projected, it will appear that the ball has actually flown through the air.

Above (both pages): Make a smooth sausage shape and bend to make an undulating caterpillar. See how its back arches up to power its movement forward.

★ In between shots, clean your hands with baby wipes and rub over the table surface to remove any bits of clay that would show up on your film.

Top: Squeeze out two shapes that rise up, cross over and land in each other's places. Then they form columns, lean inward and intertwine.

Centre (both pages): Cartwheeling Morph. When a clay model is off-balance, support it with fine (invisible) fishing wire suspended out of shot from a rig.

★ Before you animate, use your own body to rehearse the movements and secure a smooth flow from one phase to the next. We call this 'acting through the puppet'.

Above: Frames from our Channel 4 Television logo sequence, made by animating the chest of drawers and the number 4, which squeezes in and out of various drawers. The beach location is an extra bit of surreal fun which makes the chest look more interesting than it would in a room setting.

Opposite: Room set ready for the opening shot. Objects such as the jug and glasses, and the base of the anglepoise, will remain in a fixed position throughout. Plan your own film with this in mind, allowing later arrivals enough space to perform their moves. At the beginning of your film, shoot 2-3 seconds of the same frame to establish the scene before everything starts moving, and to freeze it at the end when the action comes to a climactic halt.

Simple Object Animation

Most of this book is concerned with animating models in miniature sets. It is also perfectly possible to animate in the real world, using full-sized objects as props and employing the human body - your own or someone else's - as the puppet. When real people and locations are used, the process is called 'pixillation', the word suggesting the idea of figures jumping about as though bewitched. Because you do not have to build either sets or models, it is a wonderful medium for fast, improvised animation.

These techniques are not part of our mainstream work, but most of us at Aardman have experimented with pixillation early on in our careers, and most of us will jump at the opportunity to do it because it is great fun. While conventional animation requires the animator to work quietly and intensively on his or her own, pixillation is a process in which several people can animate, or be animated, at the same time.

There are masses of things you could animate in a room. They include: an anglepoise lamp; a clothes airer; a glass that fills and empties with liquid; a chest of drawers opening and shutting; curtains and blinds which open and close; a cupboard which opens and the contents jump out; books which change places; toys; things with wheels; counterweighted light fittings, and anything made in several sizes of the same design - weights from scales, saucepans, plates, Russian dolls.

When you lay out your set for object animation, think first of the end point and how to work towards it. Not everything has to be in the opening sequence. Bring some objects in later to create a surprise. Examples from our shots overleaf are: the abacus next to the guitar, the clothes airer, and the dominoes and Lego pieces which jump out of the box. Try to create relationships between the pieces: the clothes airer does not just yaw up and down, it also moves sideways towards the chest, the drawers of which open to allow towels and a scarf to slither out and on to the airer's rails. You need only a minimum of aids to make a room scene work: use tacky putty to hold the rug in position, and suspend the towels and scarf with cotton. As ever, when you move something to animate it, like the jug or glasses, be sure to mark its position with a loop of clay or tacky putty *before* you lift it. When selecting your camera position, choose a viewpoint where everything can be seen clearly and without distortion; in our example the lens is approximately at the eye-level of someone standing.

Now the action starts.
On the left, the baseball cap creeps up the wall unit, the cupboard door opens, a poster starts to unravel and the first tennis racquet comes into view. The clothes airer jumps across the room, in the corner there is now an abacus next to the guitar, and more and more cushions arrive on the sofa. In the foreground, the lamp comes on and focuses with rising astonishment on the box and its contents. The dominoes dance off in one direction and the Lego pieces turn themselves into tower blocks. Meanwhile, the glasses fill with orange juice and the jug empties. In the background, the curtains part, the blind slides up and flowers multiply like rabbits.

See how many other animated objects you can find in the pictures. If you make your own film, think about the story behind it all. Perhaps this is what happens every day, when the humans are out of the house and the things come out to play. Run the film backwards, and everything goes back to normal.

Dancing spoons, arranged in a serpentine layout, as made for the Golden Syrup commercial. A metal spoon, being inflexible, is typical of the objects we animate by substitution, shooting a separate model, or group of models, for each frame of film.

Other Animation Techniques

There is a very particular technique of puppet animation called 'substitution' that I always associate with the Dutch animator George Pal. Although I am sure he did not invent the technique, he raised it to a fine art. Substitution is utterly different from other forms of puppet animation, and actually has more in common with drawn animation. Instead of having one puppet which is repositioned, you use a separate model for each frame of film. Shooting in double-frame, you would need 12 separate models for 1 second of film. We have used the technique only a few times, for TV commercials, and although it is absurdly labour-intensive in the modelmaking department, and expensive, the results can be very satisfying.

Marching figures animated by substitution, also for the Golden Syrup commercial. The bread is from a giant loaf baked specially for us. The baker cut it in slices and we put these in plywood formers to go stale, so the slices would stay in the required shape during filming.

Substitution has three main advantages. Firstly, it offers a way of articulating materials that are otherwise very difficult to animate because for some reason they will not bend. For example, a character made out of shiny metal or glass is impossible to animate conventionally (the normal solution today would be to create a computer-generated character). However, you can make a series of models with a chrome finish and shoot them individually.

Secondly, the technique allows the sort of graphic exaggeration that is common in 2-D animation. George Pal used this to great effect in his films. A puppet's walk cycle can include extravagant stretching of the limbs, as demonstrated by the marching figures in the illustrations. With this kind of animation a puppet can change its mass from one frame to the next. Finally, if an action is repeated, it can be quite efficient to build an animation cycle. This is what we did for the Golden Syrup commercial, where all the puppets were required to do was to walk in a repeating cycle.

Substitution need not be the complicated and expensive process that I have outlined. You can make simple and very effective substitution cycles out of clay. This could be as simple as a bouncing-ball sequence, where the clay model shows all the squash and stretch usually associated with 2-D animation. To be a little more complicated, you could make a series of walking figures to show the legs reaching out in an exaggerated way. When you work with this technique, you can emphasise the importance of bodyweight in motion, letting the character almost sag into the ground and spring upward with each step, like a human bouncing ball.

models and modelmaking

Basic Principles

You have got your storyboard, at least in outline, and perhaps a few sketches of the character you want to make. Now is the time to think in some detail about the nature of the model and what you want it to do. Think about its size, shape, weight, and the kind of movements you need it to perform.

How big should you build it? If it is too small, there will not be room to accommodate the mechanical skeleton, known as an armature, which allows the model to be posed and to hold its position. The advantage of a larger model is that you can give it plenty of detail. On the other hand, the larger the model the larger the set has to be, and that can present its own problems. For many of our films we make the human-shaped characters about 8-10in (20-25cm) tall, and construct everything else to fit round this scale.

Morph has always been hand-made. To check that we always used the same amount of clay, we weighed him on these old scales.

Armatures for Wallace and Gromit. These mechanical skeletons are precisely designed and built from detailed drawings of the character (see page 99). You can make them yourself, though most amateur animators get theirs from specialist suppliers.

Weight, too, can be a problem. Say you have a character with a big head. Even if you use a hollow head, it will still need special support. How much support? Will a simple wire skeleton be enough, or will it need a tougher rod-and-joint armature? As ever, it is a balancing act between the artistic requirements of how big the head must be, and the practical question of how you can make that shape work.

Outwardly, Morph and Adam may look very similar. Both are human-shaped figures made of clay. In construction, though, they are quite different. While Morph is fairly earthbound, moving about over a horizontal surface, Adam has to be far more athletic, able to stand on one leg and bring off other balancing feats that Morph normally never has to. Morph can thus be made of solid clay, but Adam has to have ball-and-socket joints in the legs so he can keep his balance.

In his quiet way, Morph also has his moments, as demonstrated in the flick-through sequence at bottom right on pages 7-61. When a clay model has to be tilted off-balance, there are lots of cunning ways to stop him falling over - with a pin through the foot, magnets, a carefully disguised blob of stickyback (wax), a rod in the back which the camera cannot see, or very fine fishing wire suspended from a rig above the model. For further tips, look at the sequences on pages 78-81, and see also page 98.

One of the early traps is to think, 'I am a beginner, so I should use basic, clay-only models.' That may be fine for the very early days, but most people will then want to broaden out, and rightly so. You need to test the other options. Quite soon you will also

Building a wire-based figure - one of the troupe of chihuahuas featured in *Stage Fright*. Wire figures are easier to animate than clay models, and cheaper to make than armatured characters, but tend to snap if too much is demanded of them.

discover that unsupported clay is not all that easy to animate. It smudges and gets dirty, and you have to clean it and resculpt every two or three shots. Because of its weight, it is also relatively inflexible.

You might do better to go for a wire-based figure which has its rigid parts, such as the head, made of balsa wood or fibreglass to cut down on weight, and its skeleton covered with foam or cloth. A figure made like this will last longer and let you do more with it. It will also, by keeping its shape, retain the essentials of the character. This is important. With clay, you can shave off so many bits between shots, or unintentionally pull it so far out of shape, that you end up with a different-looking character. This will not endear you to audiences, who need to identify with a character that remains consistent and recognisable.

Don't be afraid to experiment. The more you do, the more you will build up an armoury of different solutions which you can apply in different contexts. At Aardman, in the course of designing and building a single character, we will look at dozens of different materials. In modelmaking there is no neat set of perfect answers. Every character calls for a different way of working.

Sometimes you do not need to build a whole character for a particular sequence. For a head-and-shoulders shot, it can be enough to build the top half of the body and put it on a central pole. As long as the character is held stable for the shot, it does not need to have legs as well.

Think also about the character's focus of interest. If a character has expressive hands, these will probably need a special armature. In *Loves Me ... Loves Me Not,* the character has to have long-fingered, extra-flexible hands so he can perform the delicate task of plucking individual petals off a flower. Hands break easily, by the way, so with a character like that you will need to make several replacement hands which can then be pegged on to the arm as required. To do this, you need to allow for a hole at the end of the arm when you design the basic figure.

As you can see, there is a lot of planning involved. It is a bit like cooking, really. You have to put in all the ingredients to get the right result. And in modelmaking, of course, you have to write the recipe as well.

The compulsive petal-plucking hero of *Loves Me ... Loves Me Not*. Because of the delicacy of his hand movements, and the amount of times he repeats the action, special armatures were made for his hands.

Wallace makes vain shooing noises at the horde of sheep happily camped out in his living room. Even though these sheep may seem to be mere extras, the detailing on them is precise. Necks and heads move about, and also give the modelmaker clues about how the model should be constructed.

Making a Sheep

In modelmaking terms, there are three types of sheep in *A Close Shave*, which we broadly categorised as Normal Sheep, Stunt Sheep and Thin Sheep. Thin Sheep were required for the scene in the wool shop when they run between Wallace and Wendolene, and we needed to show a mass of different woolly shapes going past while Wallace and Wendolene are still holding hands over their heads. They, obviously, had much narrower bodies than the normal type. Stunt Sheep were used for the shot where they plunge through the small trapdoor in Wallace's house, and when Shaun emerges shivering from the Knit-O-Matic. They had to be different again, with a lighter and more squashy build, and had skeletons made of mesh and coiled wire. Normal sheep were really quite complex, and had a variety of options built into their basic armature. This was made of K&S square-section metal tubing, and had two sets of holes in

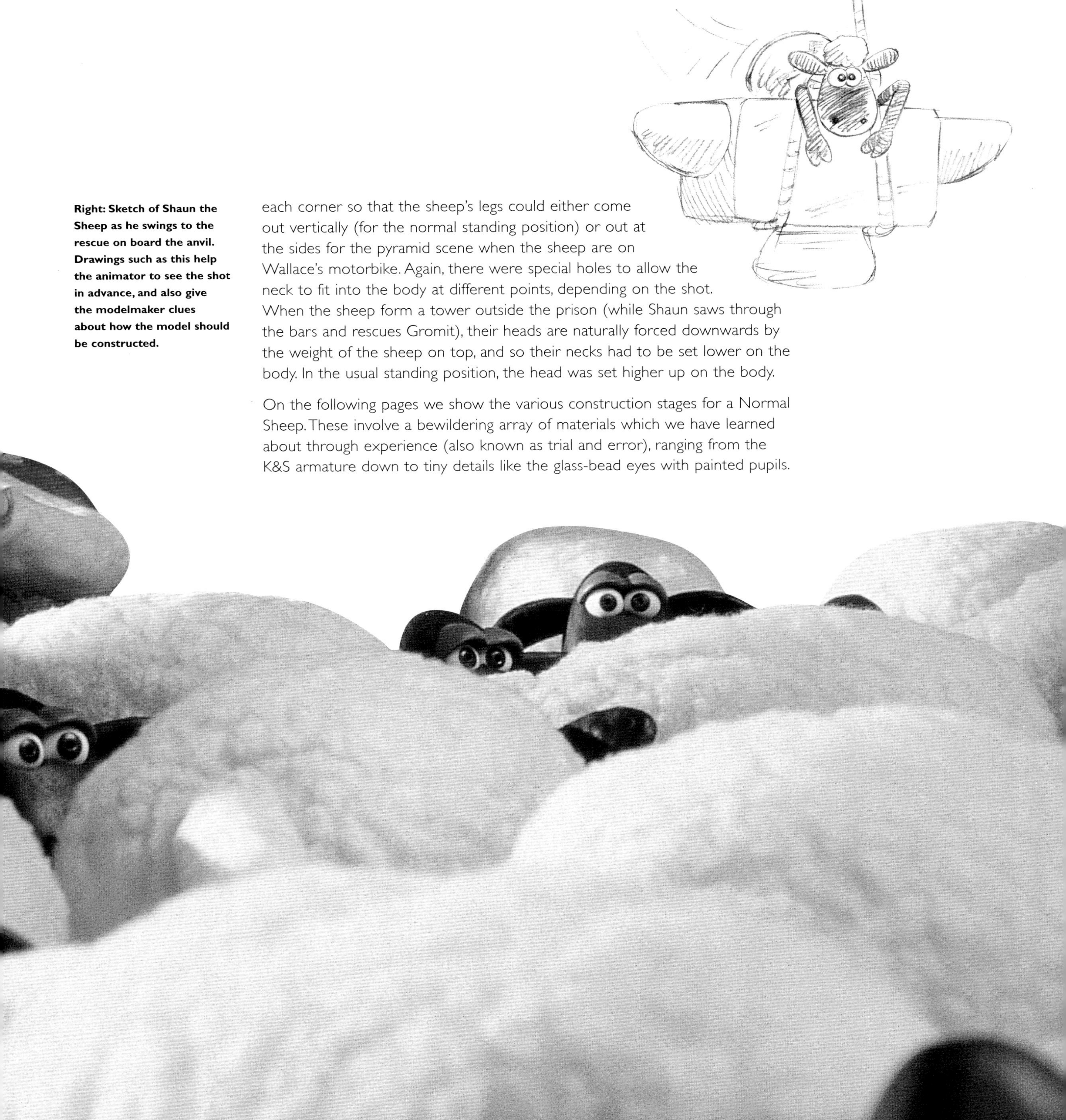

Right: Sketch of Shaun the Sheep as he swings to the rescue on board the anvil. Drawings such as this help the animator to see the shot in advance, and also give the modelmaker clues about how the model should be constructed.

each corner so that the sheep's legs could either come out vertically (for the normal standing position) or out at the sides for the pyramid scene when the sheep are on Wallace's motorbike. Again, there were special holes to allow the neck to fit into the body at different points, depending on the shot. When the sheep form a tower outside the prison (while Shaun saws through the bars and rescues Gromit), their heads are naturally forced downwards by the weight of the sheep on top, and so their necks had to be set lower on the body. In the usual standing position, the head was set higher up on the body.

On the following pages we show the various construction stages for a Normal Sheep. These involve a bewildering array of materials which we have learned about through experience (also known as trial and error), ranging from the K&S armature down to tiny details like the glass-bead eyes with painted pupils.

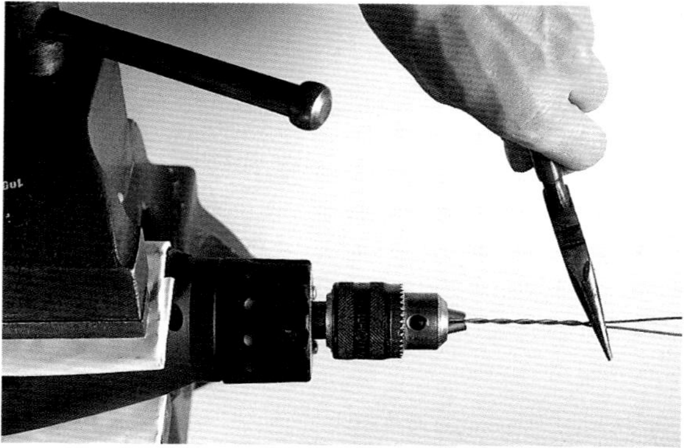

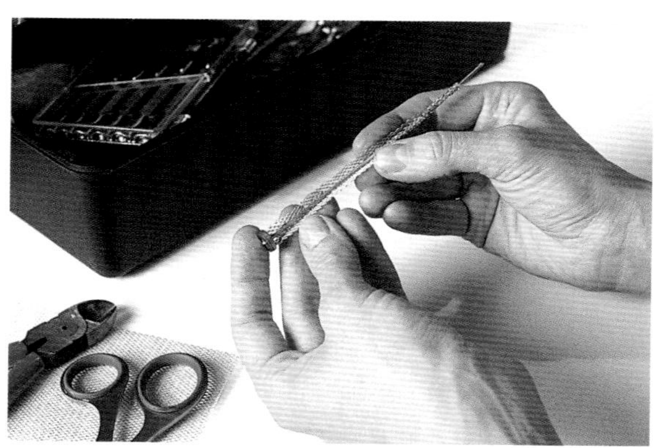

Left-hand column: Legs are made from lengths of twisted aluminium wire.

The feet are steel discs with holes for the leg and for a pin in case the leg needs extra support.

The leg is covered in mesh which is cut to size and squeezed round the aluminium wire.

The head is made of fast-cast resin. Once out of the mould, the holes and slots for eyes and ears are drilled to shape with an electric drill.

Right-hand column: The first stage completed, with pieces of K&S square-section tubing added last to join the legs to the body.

The eyes are white glass beads with pupils painted on using a paint brush and enamel paint. First, the glass bead is placed on a cocktail stick, then put in a drill and clamped with a vice. The drill is turned on to run slowly while the pupil is painted.

A covering of Plastazote - a hard, foam-like material - is put over the metal armature and trimmed with a scalpel, leaving the various holes clear for fitting the legs, neck and tail.

The ears are made of aluminium wire which is twisted to leave a loop at one end. Over the loop goes a piece of mesh, and over this goes the outer covering of maxi-plast rubber, which is sculpted and baked in an oven to retain its shape.

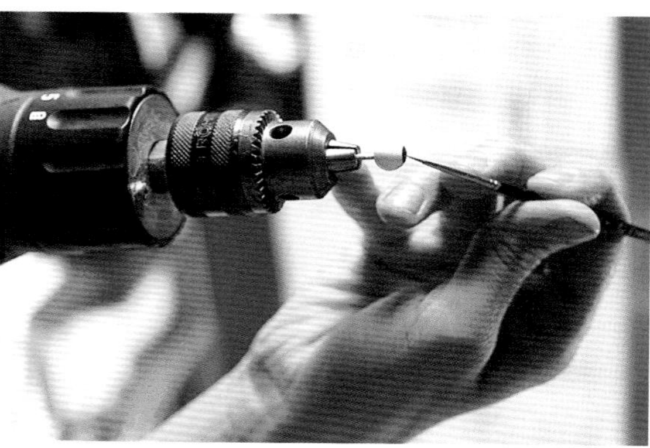

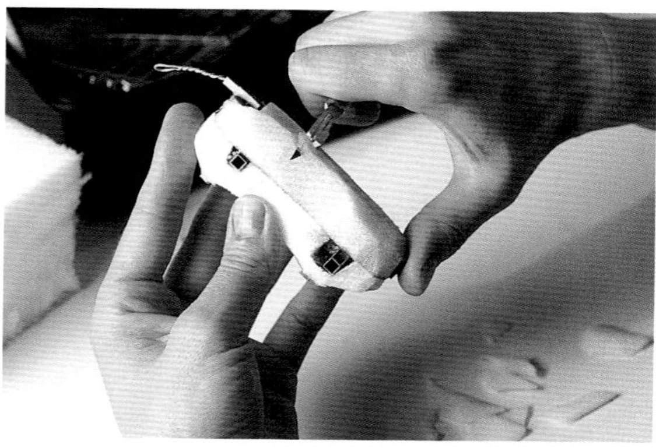

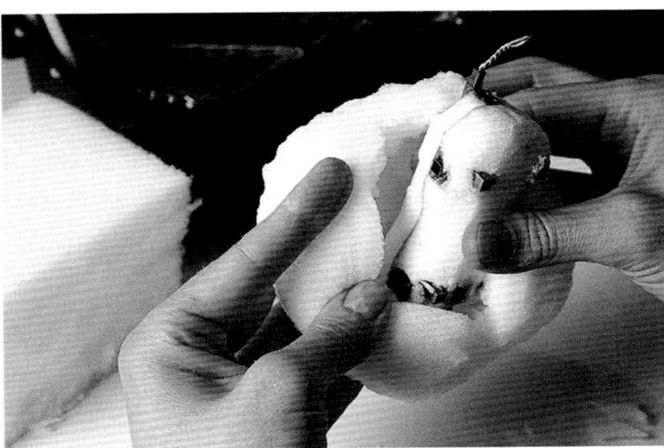

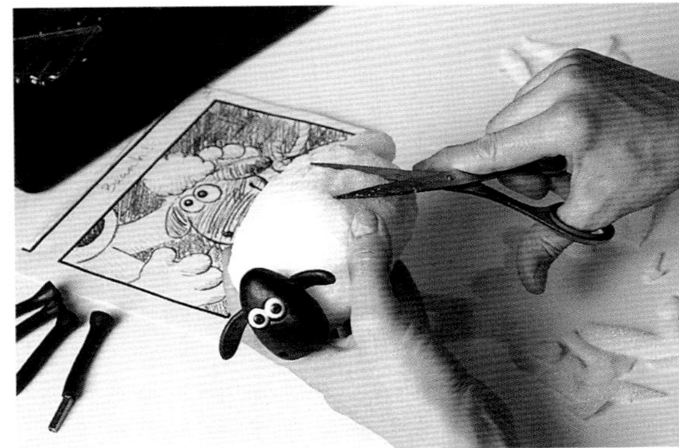

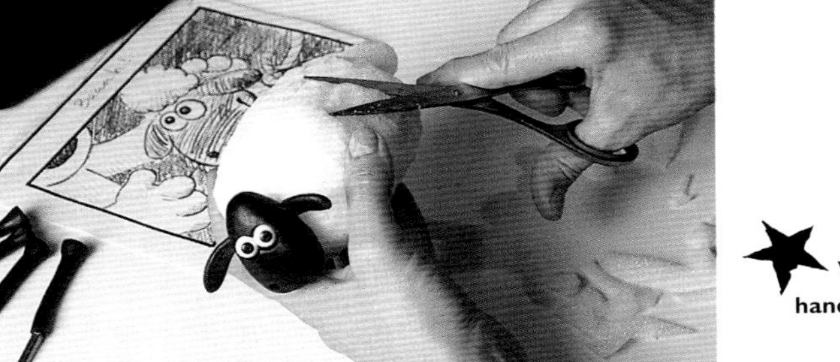

Left-hand column: The second stage completed, with Plastazote body and legs made of maxi-plast rubber which has been sculpted and baked.

Next, the body and tail are covered with a square of foam, which is trimmed to shape with scissors.

Right-hand column: Fur fabric, the final covering, is starched to make it lie down properly and avoid flickering on film. It is then trimmed from its backing, top, and glued over the foam layer, as shown in the next picture.

Eyelids are cast in coloured resin and then trimmed to shape. When the head is finally assembled, the ears and neck are glued into the head with epoxy-resin glue. The eyes, however, are bedded into a type of sticky wax which holds them in place but allows movement.

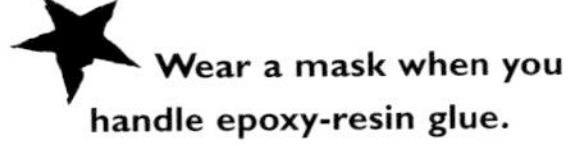

Wear a mask when you handle epoxy-resin glue.

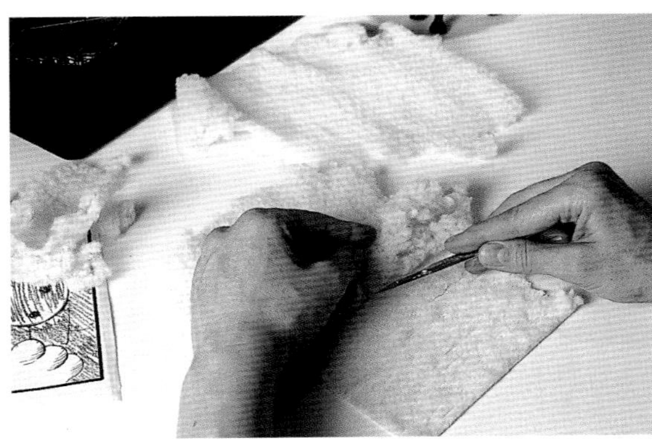

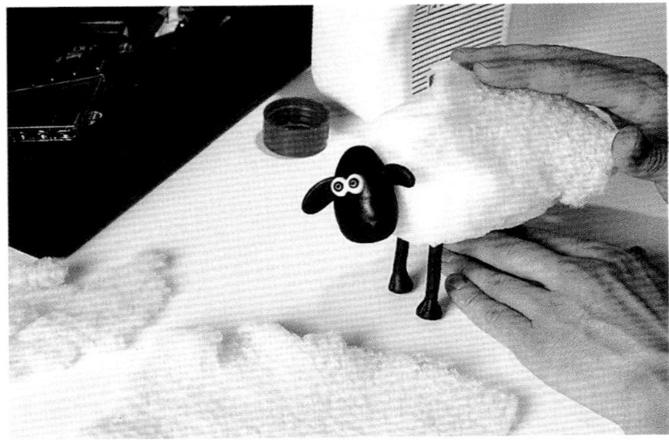

Gromit Construction

Gromit brings in the papers, ears raised on the alert.

In their progress from *A Grand Day Out* to *A Close Shave*, the Wallace and Gromit puppets have undergone a considerable evolution and are now much more rounded and three-dimensional than they used to be. Wallace had a much flatter face when he was building the rocket in the cellar in *A Grand Day Out*. At first he did not speak much, but when he did he suddenly developed cheeks and his brow got bigger. Now he is much fuller in the face with quite rounded cheeks, and his mouth expands quite enormously in a sideways direction when he speaks 'ee' sounds, especially in words like 'cheese', mention of which tends to make him grin as well. In the same way, Gromit's brow was much smaller in the beginning, and is now quite big. His nose or muzzle has meanwhile become shorter, and is less pear-shaped and more stubby. At first he was to have been a talking dog, with a mouth, but this idea was dropped when it became clear how expressive he could be just through small movements of the eyes, ears and brow.

Not all Gromit figures are the same. The one shown here is a standard Gromit standing on four legs. In other scenes where he is required to sit down, say in an armchair or at the controls of the rocket, he has to have a very different kind of ball-and-socket armature. This other type is much more human-looking, simply because our joints are not in the same places as those of dogs.

This Gromit consists basically of a ball-and-socket armature and a body made of fast-cast resin. Plastazote could also be used for the core of the body, which needs to be hard enough to be drilled for fixing the puppet's limbs to it. The body is then built up with modelling clay. In general it is a good idea to begin by adding clay to the armatured parts, since these tend to give off black metallic flakes and oil which makes the clay dirty. We block out the whole figure first, and then sculpt it to its final form, working the surfaces until they get smoother and smoother. Water is used to skim off clay, or lighter fluid, though this eats away at surfaces and is best reserved for tiny detailed parts.

Character sketches to work out the angles of head to body, the position of the eyes for looking up, down or sideways, and how the paws change from being conventional paw or hoof-like things, for walking on, to human-style hands with four stubby fingers.

Starting with the armature and fast-cast resin parts for the head and body, the Gromit shape is blocked out in clay and gradually smoothed down with a modelling tool. Then the final details can be added - the eyes, nose, ears and tail.

The eyes, like those of the sheep (see previous pages) are glass beads with painted-on pupils. The noses were mass-produced for something else, but when we saw they were just right for Gromit, we bought a bagful. The ears and tail are made from a wire twist. This can be coated with cotton, string or pipe-cleaners to help key on the clay, which is then added and smoothed into shape.

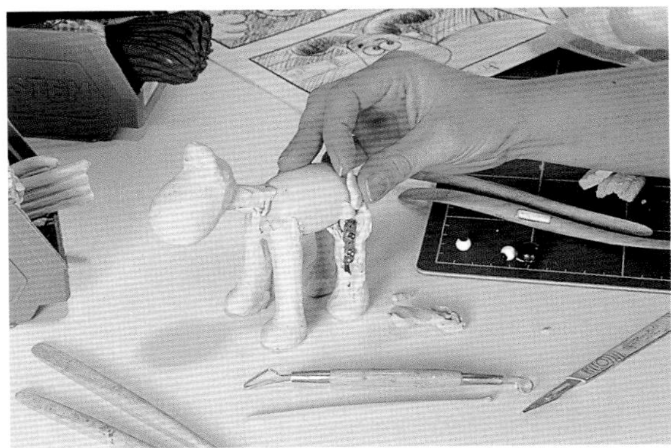

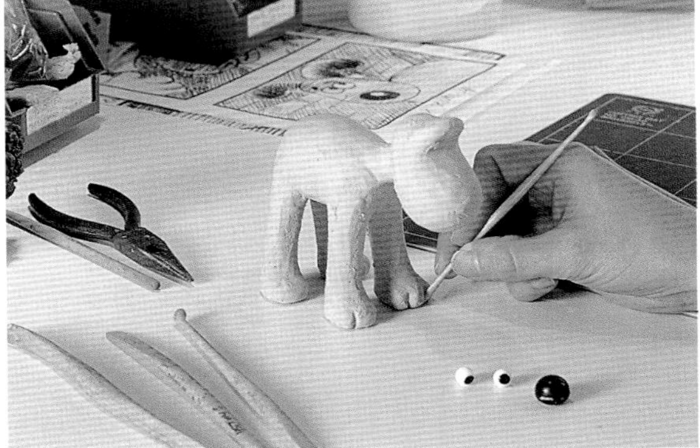

Wat and his brother, shown in split screen, essentially two characters cast from the same mould.

Wat Construction

Wat and his brother, in *Wat's Pig,* are good examples of the human-type everyman figure. When planning the model, we knew that he would have to move fluidly and often, and make a lot of emphatic gestures. The solution was to keep his build fairly spindly, as the drawing opposite shows. Basically, the head consists of a solid core covered with clay and sculpted, and the hands are also made of clay. The rest of the body is made of foam applied sparingly over a metal armature.

Construction falls into several main stages. It begins with the storyboard, where the film-maker can give real purpose to any previous sketches he may have made of the character. Once the story is working properly, the character's design can be finalised and drawn up. The figure is then sculpted in clay and a design drawing made for the armature. This shows in detail how the armature will be built and how it fits inside the character. When the armature is made, it is wrapped in plumber's tape to make a better bond with the latex covering. The clay sculpture is broken down into its component parts, such as the torso, and these are cast in plaster. This produces a plaster mould in which the armature is placed and coated with foam latex. The mould is baked and the finished torso (or whatever) is removed ready for colouring and assembly with the head, legs and hands.

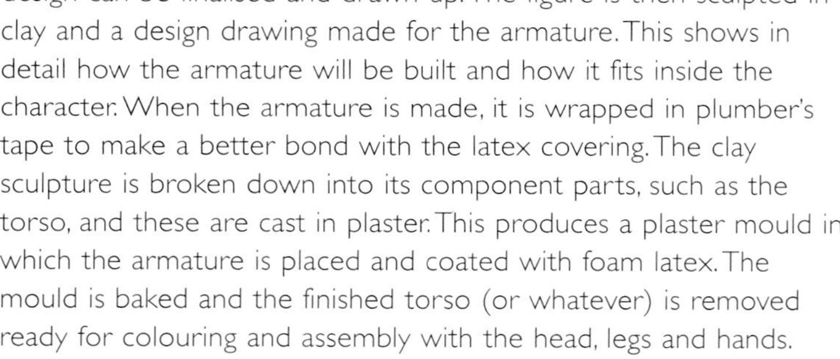

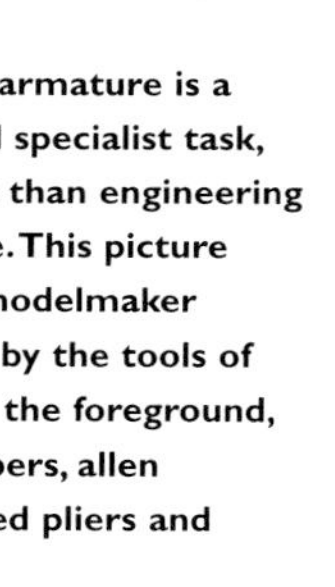

Making the armature is a delicate and specialist task, nothing less than engineering in miniature. This picture shows the modelmaker surrounded by the tools of his trade: in the foreground, vernier calipers, allen keys, assorted pliers and a hacksaw.

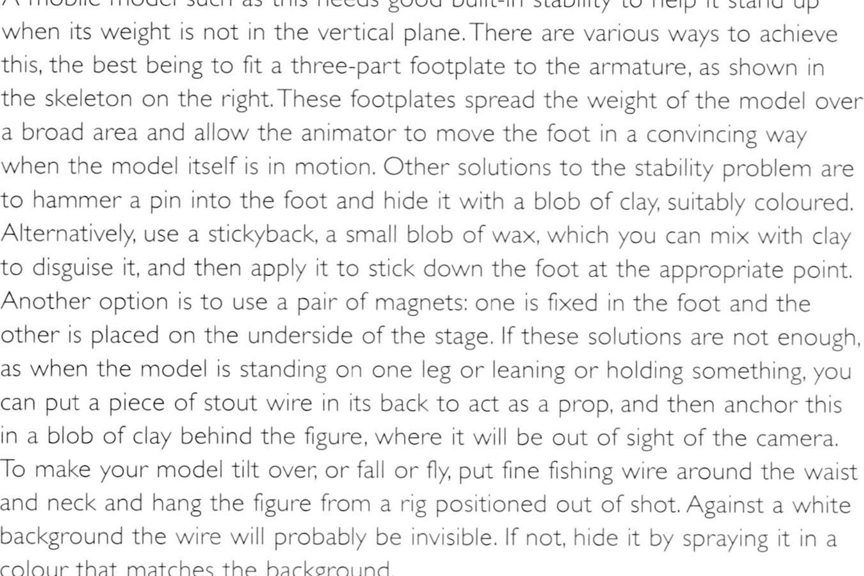

A mobile model such as this needs good built-in stability to help it stand up when its weight is not in the vertical plane. There are various ways to achieve this, the best being to fit a three-part footplate to the armature, as shown in the skeleton on the right. These footplates spread the weight of the model over a broad area and allow the animator to move the foot in a convincing way when the model itself is in motion. Other solutions to the stability problem are to hammer a pin into the foot and hide it with a blob of clay, suitably coloured. Alternatively, use a stickyback, a small blob of wax, which you can mix with clay to disguise it, and then apply it to stick down the foot at the appropriate point. Another option is to use a pair of magnets: one is fixed in the foot and the other is placed on the underside of the stage. If these solutions are not enough, as when the model is standing on one leg or leaning or holding something, you can put a piece of stout wire in its back to act as a prop, and then anchor this in a blob of clay behind the figure, where it will be out of sight of the camera. To make your model tilt over, or fall or fly, put fine fishing wire around the waist and neck and hang the figure from a rig positioned out of shot. Against a white background the wire will probably be invisible. If not, hide it by spraying it in a colour that matches the background.

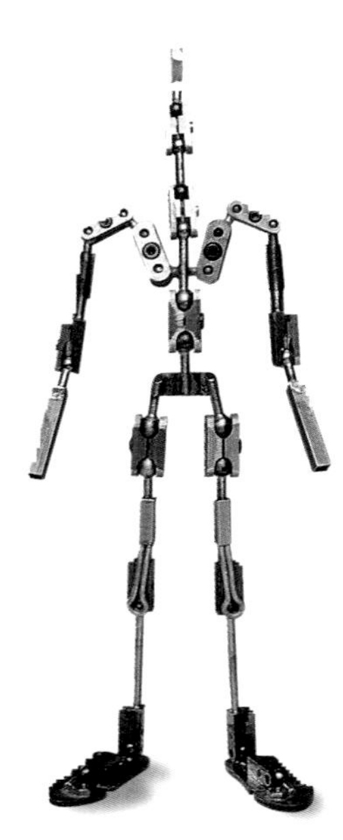

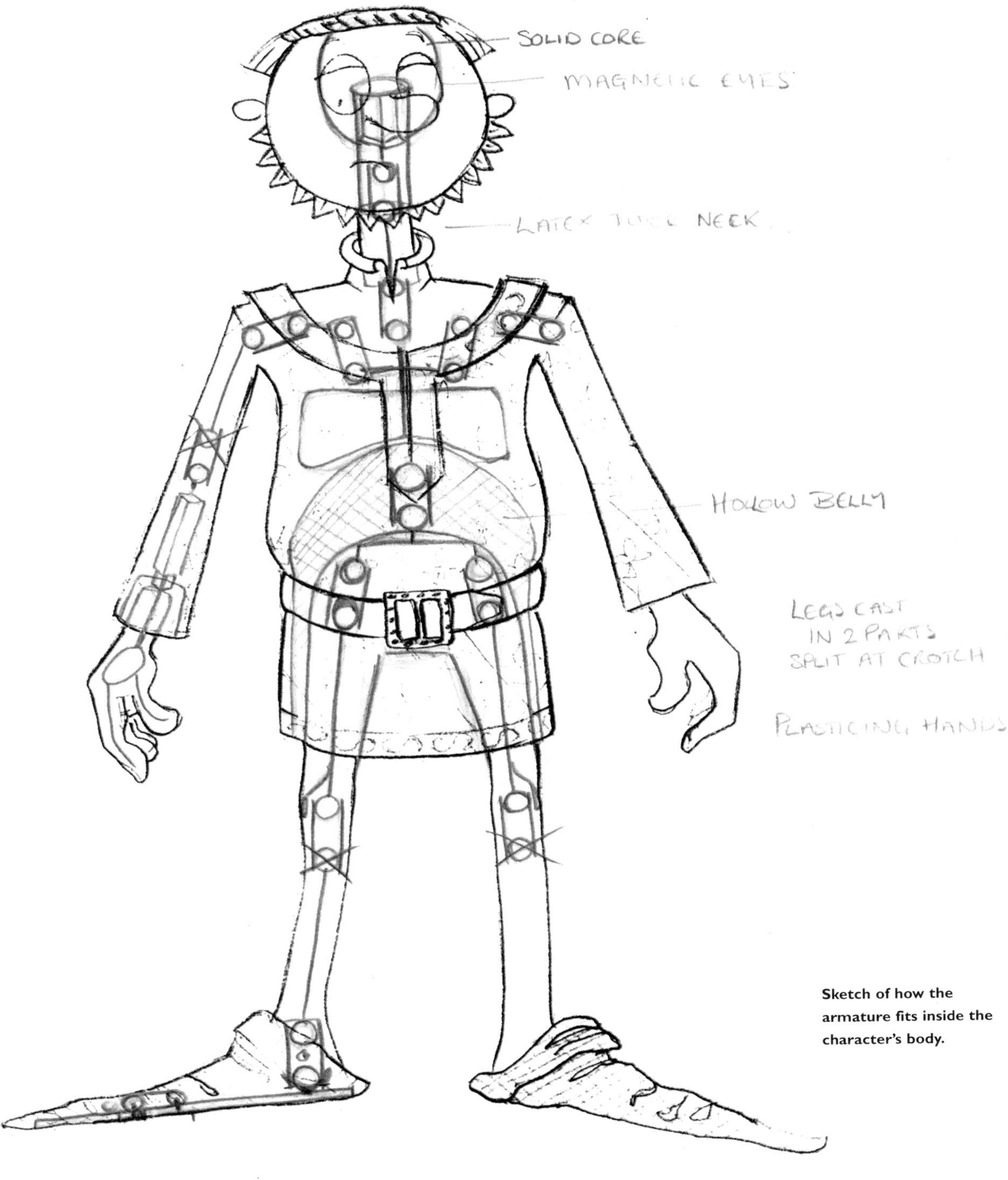

Sketch of how the armature fits inside the character's body.

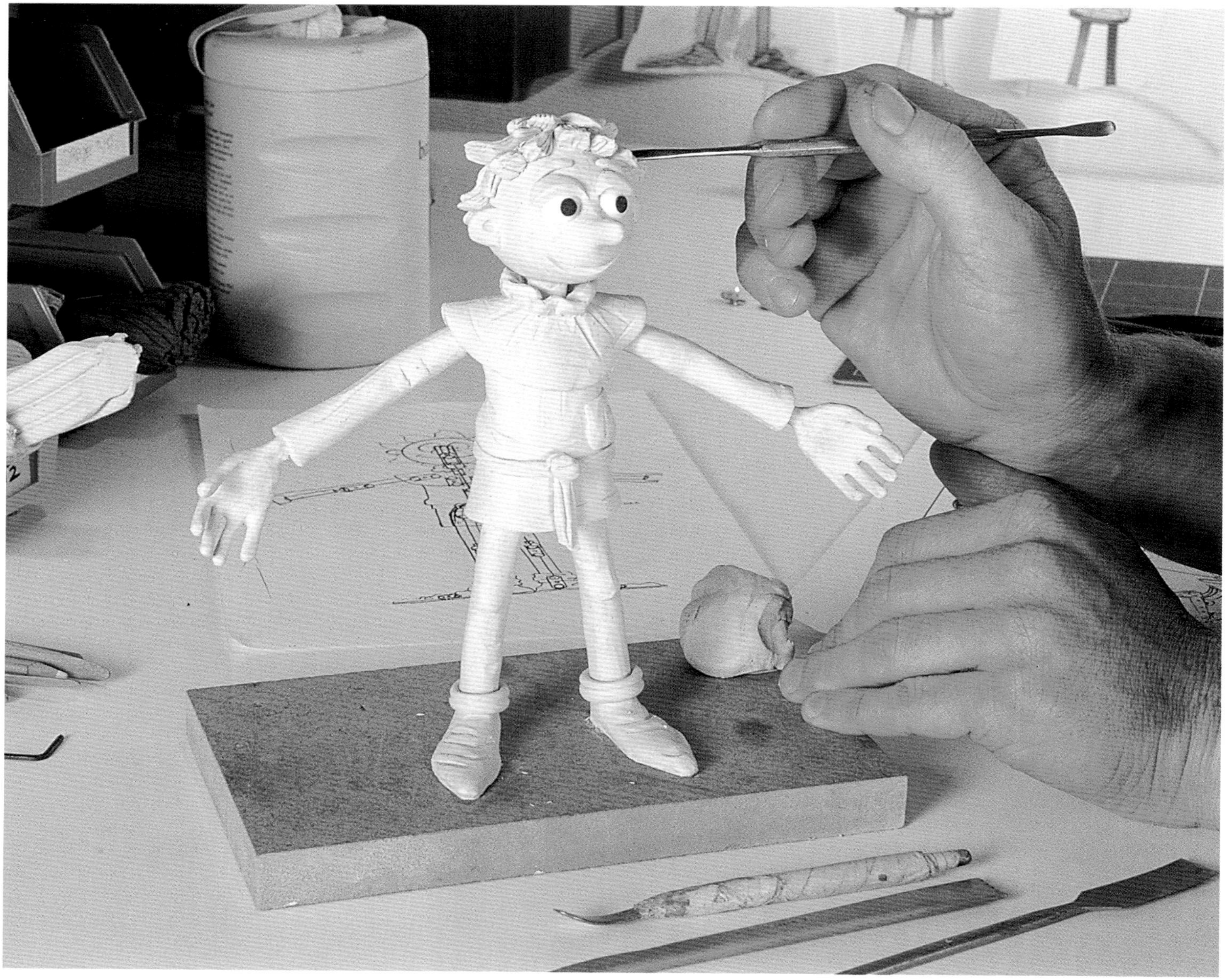

The original Wat figure is sculpted in Plasticine (modelling clay) on a simple wire armature. This has brass square-section fittings so that all the component parts can easily be taken apart.

The clay torso is laid up, ready to be cast in plaster.

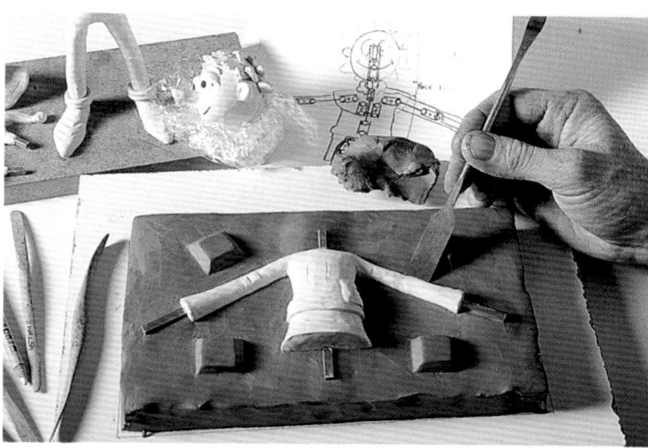

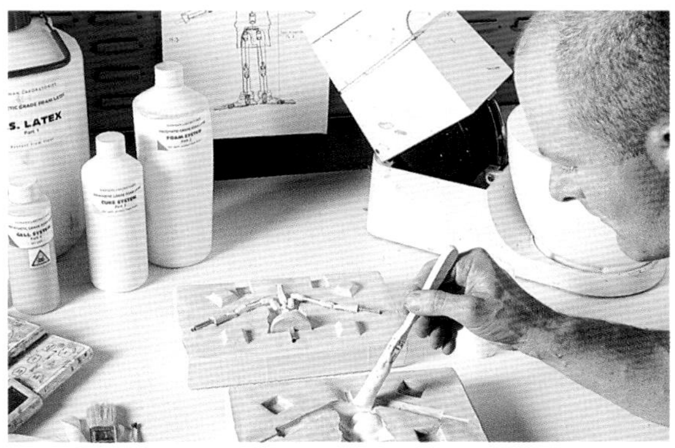

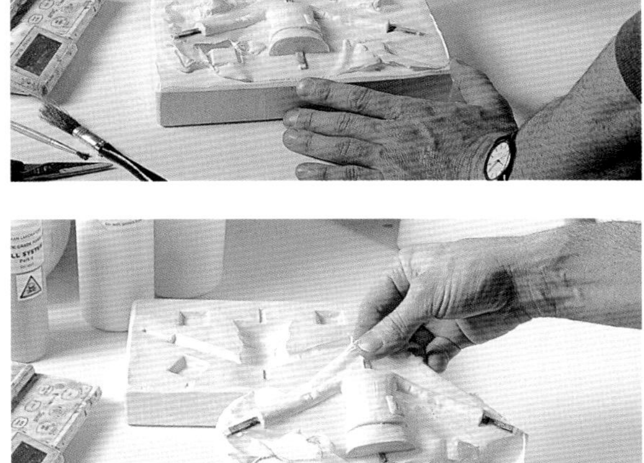

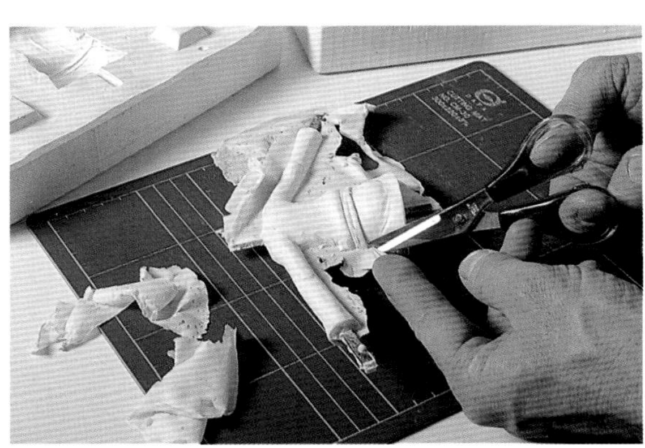

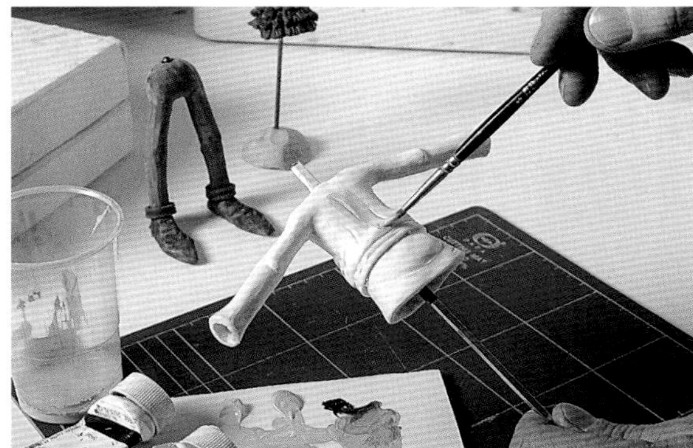

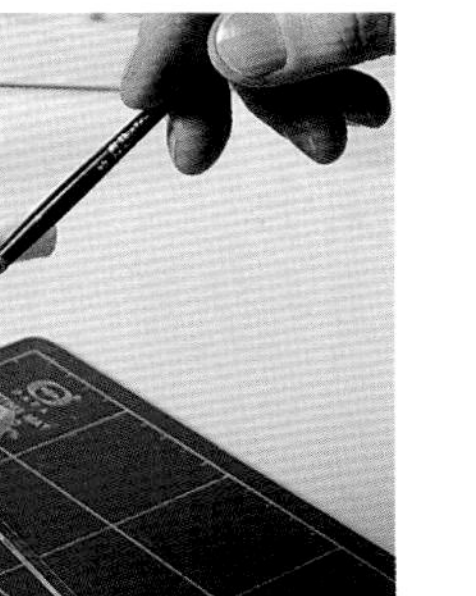

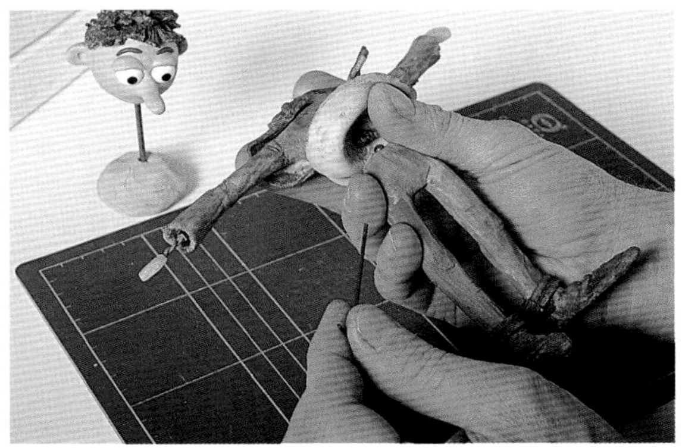

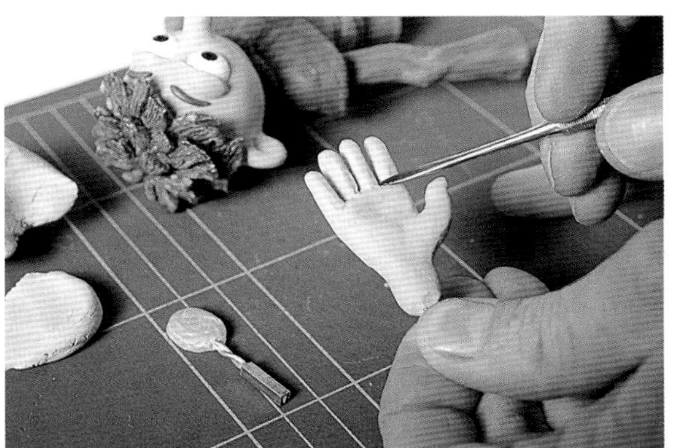

Left-hand column: Foam latex is brushed into the plaster mould, with the ball-and-socket armature wrapped in tape. The mould is separated after baking, the foam latex torso is removed and any excess foam is trimmed off.

Right-hand column: Colouring the torso with a diluted latex mixture. To colour figures, you can either spray the whole torso with the main colour and then hand-paint details such as the belt, or you can mask out the parts you do not want covered and spray the rest.

Assembling the puppet after painting.

Sculpting the hands in clay. A character such as Wat will use a lot of hand gestures in the course of a film, which means the hands will need replacing from time to time with new ones.

Rex Construction

Rex the Runt and the main characters in his series of adventures are flattish, not unlike gingerbread men. Their shape, and the way they are made, comes from the special way the series is filmed. This is the so-called 2-D technique of shooting the characters on an angled sheet of glass, often with a painted or photographic background positioned behind the glass so that the two elements can be combined in a single shot. Rex and the others - Wendy, Bad Bob and Vince - are not completely two-dimensional (even a gingerbread man has a certain minimal depth) but the way they can be used is very different from a fully rounded, three-dimensional character.

There are three main advantages to shooting on glass. Firstly, you do not need the complex armatures which have to be built for most of our conventional 3-D characters, such as Wallace and Gromit. Secondly, the characters are not bound by gravity and can be animated to jump or fly around the scene, more like they do in cel animation. Thirdly, the animator can sit in reasonable comfort at the sheet of glass, which is fixed at the angle of a drawing-board, with the camera shooting over the animator's shoulder.

Rex and Vince, ready for the camera. Once the basic figure is sprung from the press mould, the eyes, noses and clothing are added. The eyes consist of simple white beads with small holes in the pupil so the eye can be moved around expressively. Noses are made of solid resin, and Rex's mouth is a loop of clay.

Animating on glass. The characters are set up on the angled glass, often with a suitable background placed behind it, then filmed from a position over the animator's shoulder.

In the course of making a series, we get through several hundred main characters. Obviously, it is important that each one should look the same as its predecessors. At the same time, they have to be as simple as possible to make. The solution for us is to use press-moulds. The process begins, as ever, with a model drawing, which is then sculpted in clay. We then cast the character in rubber.

When the clay is removed, it leaves an impression that gives us the press mould. This is then surrounded by a plaster jacket to stop the mould distorting. The mould can be reused throughout the production to turn out new characters when they are needed.

Once the mould is ready for use, the first step is to dust it with talcum powder to prevent the clay from sticking to it. Then a thin layer of clay is rolled out and pressed into the mould. This is followed by more clay, pushed in carefully to make sure it works its way into all the detailing of the figure. The top surface is finally flattened out with a rolling pin. To extract the completed character from the mould, the trick is to bend it slowly and at just the right angle for it to pop out. The character is then ready for the usual finishing work - adding the eyes, nose, mouth and any other special features, such as Bad Bob's eye patch.

Above: A complete impression of the figure lies in the rubber mould after casting, while the modelmaker rolls out a thin layer of clay.

Centre left: Layers of clay are pressed into the mould and pushed into all the details of the figure.

Centre right: When the mould is full, it is flattened with a rolling pin.

Below: The rubber mould is separated from its plaster jacket and then gently bent to release the new figure.

Preston

Preston is the evil dog in *A Close Shave* who first appears as the thuggish sheep-rustler who rules the roost in Wendolene's blighted household. At the film's climax, he is transformed into a metallic monster, receives his just desserts and ends up as a crippled robotic wreck. He is thus seen in three completely different versions - the brutal but recognisably doggy dog, the gleaming robo-dog and the trembling has-been.

John Wright, who specialises in 'engineered' models, made the original armature for the basic Preston, which was then modelled in clay and dressed with the character's special spiked collar and wrist bands. The other, mechanical versions are much more elaborate and were made in John Wright's workshop in Bristol. He recalls, 'What was interesting about the robot Preston was that his armature was on the outside and became part of his villainous character.'

The three ages of Preston, in which the villainous bully dog is transformed into a metal robot clad in spikes, pipes and rivets, and later, after meeting a machine which is even bigger than he is, emerges a beaten-up, bandaged wreck gliding about on pram wheels.

The arms and legs are in fact part of a basic armature, with the visible parts dressed with extra screws and piping to make them look more mechanical and threatening. The body was machined in a chemical-wood material called Modelling Board and painted with a steel-finish paint. This was then dirtied up around the rivets to make it look as if it had been knocked about. On the chest (see main picture, right) is a miniature tape recorder, also specially made. The other main feature of this model is a hinge at the back of the head which allows the top of the head to lift back and reveal a mouth horrifically full of cogs, gears and piping.

Finally, after his disastrous experience in the Mutton-O-Matic, the crippled Preston is a mere shadow of his former brute self. The body is essentially the same, though tipped over into the horizontal, but in place of his fierce armature-legs he now stands on four much more spindly supports, made to look like wall units for a shelving system and mounted on pram wheels. For added pathos he sports a bandage wrapped round his forehead.

EVEN MORE

the Pits
Twist A-PEEL
PULP PALACE

set design and making

The Jaguar mourns the lack of space in his simple brick enclosure; from *Creature Comforts*.

Planning a Set

For about the first ten years of our career, Dave and I never had a set with more than three walls in it. That really is all you need at first, just something that neatly contains the miniature world you are filming.

Every set has to have a firm base which does not move. Even though your basic stage or tabletop may be solid and flat, it is a good idea to build each set with its own floor. It will then be completely transportable and can be stored out of the way when you do not need it, and brought back for use in another film. Also, your basic stage will soon get mucky and stop being very flat if it has to be host to a succession of different sets. Use a sheet of hardboard or plywood as the platform and colour it with emulsion paint.

As you design your set, think about where you will want to bring in the camera. In relative scale, the camera is about as big as a double-decker bus, so you have to make plenty of allowance for it. Think, too, about how you will light your set and leave enough space to get in and animate your characters, whether from the front, the side or by moving in over the top. Try to avoid situations where you risk brushing against, and moving, any part of the set. This is easier said than done, but if you move something and do not put it back exactly where it was, the shift will show up on your film.

Try to keep your first sets indoors, and confine everything within a space of about 4ft x 4ft (1.2m x 1.2m). For a simple room set, build two side walls and a back wall from foamboard or thick card. Cut out a window in a side or rear wall to give yourself extra lighting and shadow options. Hold the walls upright with supports glued on to the back, and fix the walls to the floor with blobs of tacky putty. If you need to take out a wall to shoot from a different angle, be sure to mark its position before you lift it.

Wallace in his sitting room, basically a simple three-walled set with a window on one side, through which different lighting effects could be used to suggest changes in the weather or time of day.

The furniture and other props need not be elaborate. Add simple chairs and a table if this fits the plot of your story. Look around local toy and model shops for ready-made pieces, or make everything yourself from simple materials such as balsa wood. Glue the parts together and colour them. Later you can move on to scenic artist's paints, but for now any water-based paint will do. If you want a tree to be visible outside the window, make the trunk and branches from a frame of twisted aluminium wire, cover it with masking tape and paint it. Cut leaves from coloured paper and glue them on to small frames of fine mesh, of the kind used to patch holes in the bodywork of cars.

Bear in mind that props should be more or less in scale with your characters, and that most human-shaped puppets are 8-10in (20-25cm) tall. Remember, too, that nothing has to be spot-on realistic. You are operating in a world populated by small clay creatures, and the important thing is that their chairs, their TV sets, cars and other worldly goods should look appropriate to them.

A Straightforward Set

From an entry-level set with just three walls, it is not such a big jump to Wallace and Gromit's sitting-room. The basic structure is the same, even though it is made with greater expertise and has more elaborate furniture and décor.

Our conventional room sets are free-standing table units. The whole structure has to be strong and solid enough not to move under temperature and atmospheric changes. The floors are usually made of perforated steel, which is strong enough not to bend and thin enough for magnets positioned underneath to hold and draw the puppets as they move around the set. The actual room finish - in the form of floorboards, carpet and so on - is fixed over the floor. The room walls are usually made of plywood and fixed in position by means of dowels - like pack-flat furniture - so they can be lifted out easily when shots need to be taken through the space they are occupying.

You can apply the same techniques to other more complicated sets such as a staircase and landing. Here, it is important to leave sufficient space under the stairs for the animators to get in and reposition the magnets - and to do so many times during the course of a sequence.

Outdoor and Landscape Sets

Outdoor sets are generally bigger and more difficult because you have different layers from front to back, and this all takes up a lot more space than a room set. In *Wat's Pig*, for

Set drawing for *Wat's Pig*, with Wat outside his hovel and the ground sloping up and away towards the castle. Opposite, a frame from the film shows the same scene.

example, we had a landscape set with three layers, and a track running through it. First was the foreground which sloped upwards from a flat plain that the characters could stand on. This was about 8ft (2.4m) deep. Then the land appeared to fall away - in fact it was a gap with nothing at all there - and behind that we had the next layer of hills, which was about 2ft (60cm) from front to back. However, the track appeared much narrower so the audience would understand that it was much farther away. Behind this was the third layer of hills with the castle perched on top.

Below is the same landscape seen from side-on. From the platform on the far right, where the characters stand, the ground rolls away in layers towards the horizon and painted sky.

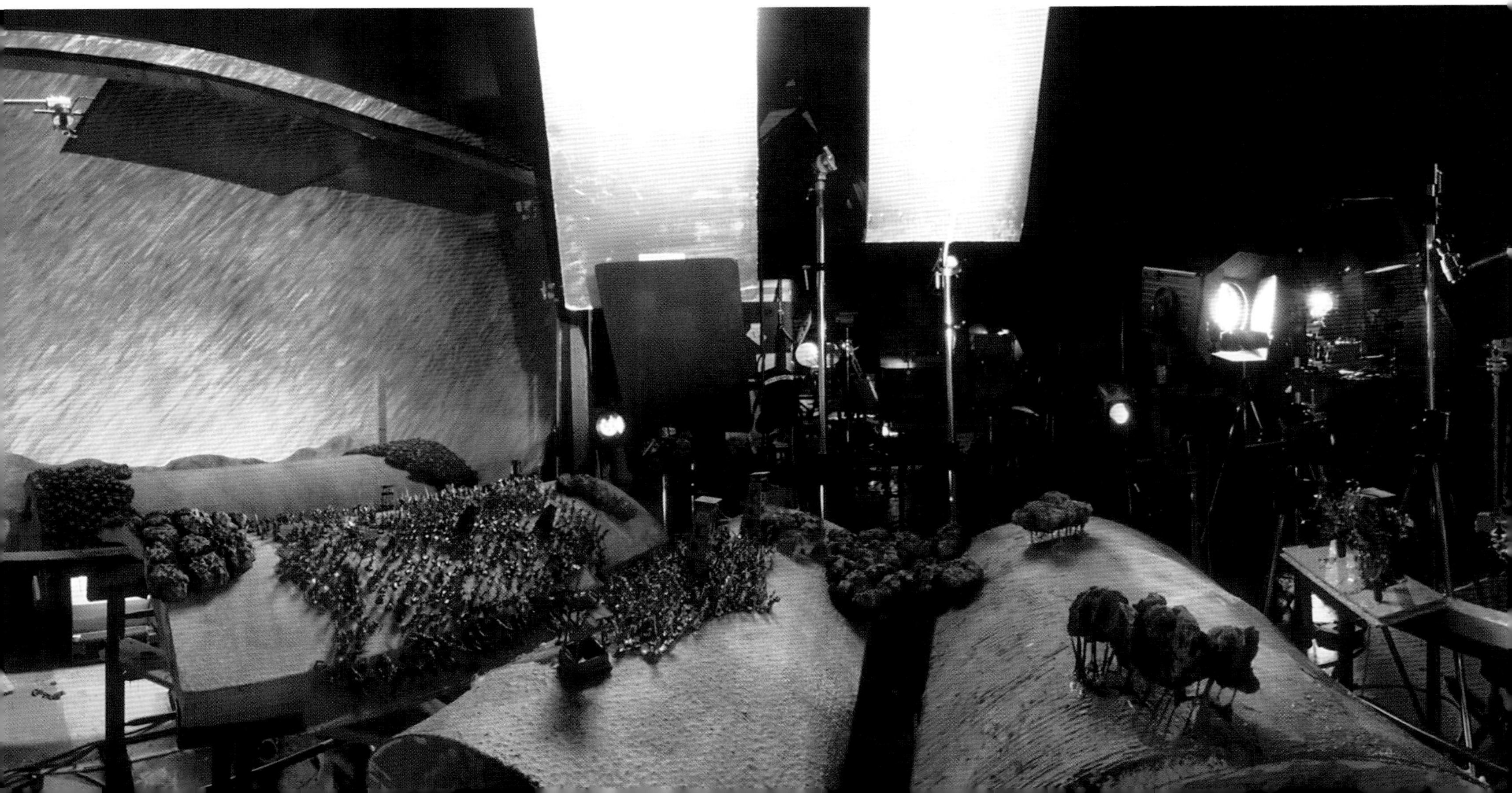

These hills were painted in paler colours to make them recede, and in the far background was a painted sky. It was all very graphic rather than realistic, but it suited the context of a fabled medieval world inhabited by peasants, warriors, a power-mad baron and a kindly smiling pig.

Matching Sets to Products

When the function of a set is to help advertise a product, it will tend to look more highly finished than usual. This is particularly true of scenes where the product itself is presented in some form. Clients want their product to look good, and sometimes the tone of a commercial is worked out from that point.

This by no means applies to all commercials, many of which take place in a complete fantasy land which is geared to promoting some idea about the product or special quality that the advertising agency has chosen to emphasise - its great taste, for example, or the fact that it is made of real fruit. However, when the product appears in the story, it will probably be handled straight, pretty much as you would see it in real life or in a brochure. In our commercials for Burger King, we peopled the set with a colourful mob of clay puppets, but the burgers, buns, chips, etc were handled in a realistic manner.

To make such items is specialist work, and here the boundaries become blurred between modelmaking and set-building. Whoever does the work, the important thing is to get the right blend between the animated models and the backgrounds against which they move. This can be seen in the Polo commercials, where the sturdy shape of the mints, with their chunky embossed lettering, seems to express a sympathetic bond with the shiny metal machines in the Factory of the Future (courtesy of 1930s Hollywood) which is obviously dedicated to production of the ultimate mint, and where every surface is studded with Polo-like rivets.

High-finish factory sets for the Polo commercials, crammed with glass and metal surfaces held together by Polo-shaped rivets.

In our Chevron commercials, we were dealing with a product which is virtually impossible to show - petrol. To resolve this, we created a range of vehicles which run on Chevron (and others that do not) and made them into central figures. They are strong characters with expressive features: the headlights are eyes, which swivel this way and that, their radiator grilles are mouths and their wipers act as highly mobile eyebrows. The sets were then matched to the cars, right down to the last

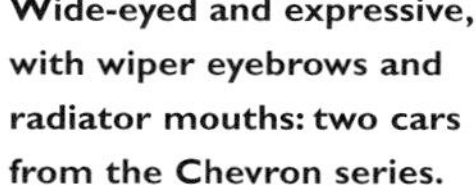

Wide-eyed and expressive, with wiper eyebrows and radiator mouths: two cars from the Chevron series.

Drawing for a Polo factory set, which by featuring an impressive length of conveyor belt, moving in a bold diagonal across the set and surrounded by machines, goes far beyond the conventional three-walled space of most 3-D animation sets.

petrol pump and telegraph pole, so that everything had the same graphic 'cartoon' quality. In other words, we built a believable world for those characters to inhabit.

Many advertisements finish by cutting to a pack shot of the product. You may see the company name and logo as well as the product, or just the product by itself. For this we often make a special larger version, it being much easier to make something look good if you make it bigger than life-size and build up its inherent textures. These packs may even be more perfect than the ones on sale in the supermarket. We can do this by taking off the bar code, for example, or some tiny detail such as a copyright line.

Then the pack has to sit perfectly in its setting, on a velvet cushion or surrounded by petals, each of which has to be exquisite and just right. All this adds a sense of high quality, hence desirability, which the client naturally wants people to associate with this particular product.

A Complex Set

The film *Stage Fright* started off as the story of an entertainer who passed through all the showbiz eras of this century. Beginning as a dog-juggler in music hall, he went into silent movies, then he tried talkies, and so on, and each time he failed in some dreadful way to make a go of it. As the planning went on, we could see it would be possible to make almost the entire film in a single music-hall setting, and this encouraged us to invest heavily in building one big set.

The theatre is based on the Bristol Old Vic, and we show it in two periods. One belongs to the cheerful past, when it was a proper music hall, and the other to the present after it has become a virtual ruin. To do this we built the theatre in its prime, decorated with shimmering gilt ornament and gas lamps, and filmed all the sequences relating to that period. Then we wrecked it, smashed the plasterwork and ripped up the seats until we had the right air of ultimate mournful decay.

Right, top: the auditorium in its distressed state, after we had trashed it to show the old music hall in its time of decay.

Right, below left: The theatre during construction, from which you can get an idea of its relatively huge scale for an animation film. Below right is the second proscenium arch where we filmed on-stage scenes to save time while the main auditorium was in use.

Set drawing for *Stage Fright*, the stalls and galleries filled with 80-90 characters. In some shots every one of them had to be animated, especially when they were applauding or jeering.

On the right is a plan view of the auditorium, showing the boxes near the stage which swung open like doors so that between shots the animators could move in and animate the characters.

It was a big set, measuring about 10ft (3m) from front to back, 6ft (1.8m) high and 6ft (1.8m) wide, and consisted of about thirty separate pieces. Fitting it all together was like doing a 3-D jigsaw puzzle. Along the side walls of the auditorium we had little boxes for members of the audience. We built these side parts as big doors which could be opened out on hinges. The animators could then go in, animate the figures in the audience, including those in the boxes, then close the door ready for the next shot. The hinges were disguised under architectural columns which looked like part of the theatre's design. We also built a second proscenium arch and front-stage area so we could film on-stage shots at the same time as the more complicated sequences were being photographed in the main theatre.

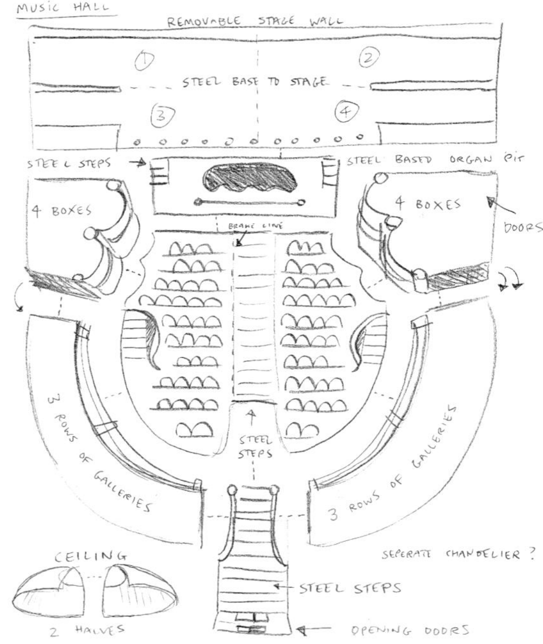

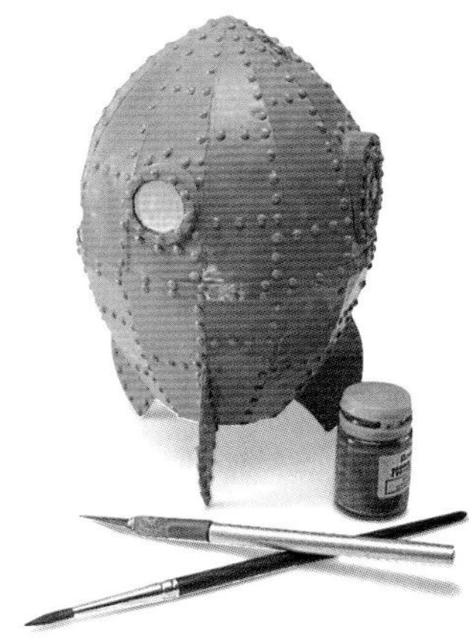

Below: The hand next to this display of Wallace's tool-kit gives an idea of how minute such props have to be. To compare the real-life scale of the saw in this group with the saw as it actually appears in the film frame, look at the picture on page 76.

Ingenuity and Props

Because we work in miniature, all our props are small. Some, however, are very small. Many of these are hand-held items - a toaster, a tea set, a hair-drier, a plate of burger and chips. All these things have to be made in the same scale as the hands that will hold or carry them, although that is not necessarily the same as the scale of the set. Hands are often made disproportionately large to cope with all the work they have to do, so if the same prop was held up to the character's head it would look ridiculous. To get over this, you probably have to make a smaller version of the prop. Close-ups, on the other hand, look better with a larger version. These are just some of the complications that our prop-makers have to bear in mind as they search for ingenious ways to convey the essence of an object. Over the years they acquire an extraordinary mental directory of solutions to cover anything from a tiny submarine to an electric fire that actually glows.

A Moon rocket no taller than a paint-brush, from *A Grand Day Out*, and a flying toaster made for an episode of Morph.

As ever, there are no fixed rules about materials or methods of construction. For fine or detailed work, prop-makers sometimes use rather finer materials than basic modelling clay. Products such as Fimo, Milliput and Sculpy are easier to model than standard Plasticine; the sculpted object can then be baked in an oven and hand-painted. Items of clothing are often sculpted in Plasticine, then a plaster mould is made and filled with latex which has lengths of wire inside it. If you want, for example, an apron or a coat that will flap in the wind, the wire helps it to hold its position. When several versions of the same prop are needed, such as shoes or hats, it may be best to use fast-cast resin and a silicone mould.

Graphic items such as newspapers or Wallace's travel and cheese magazines can usually be produced on the computer and reduced down. The same goes for posters, wall-signs and notices on shop-fronts. If a character needs to hold a newspaper while reading it, you can back the paper with heavy-duty foil to hold it firm while in shot. Household decorations, such as the pictures on the wall, the wallpaper and carpets in Wallace's living room are all hand-painted. You could make these by photocopying, but usually directors prefer things to have a home-made feel. We have also included a number of glass objects in our films. These are made for us by a professional glassblower.

Right: Gromit flies round on the end of a miniature power drill; from *A Grand Day Out*.

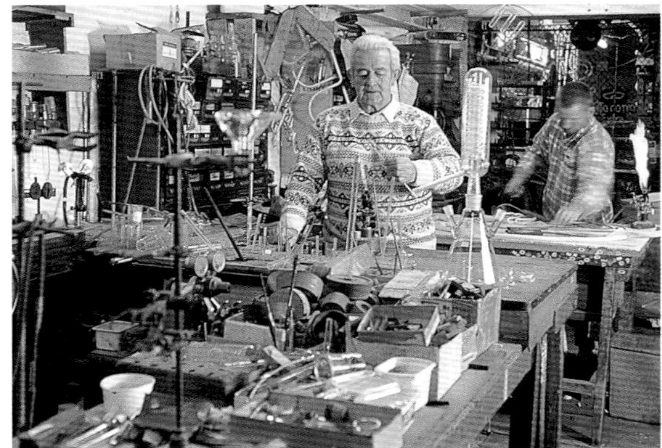

Prop-making for small worlds.

This page, from top: Making Wallace's favourite crackers, and the packets too.

Mocking up newspapers and other paper items. These may be needed for a character to hold and read, or for display in a newsagent's window, as shown. Newspaper props are backed with heavy-duty foil so they hold their position during shooting.

In the glassblower's workshop, where all manner of glass objects are made, including the milk bottles which feature at the end of the chase sequence in *The Wrong Trousers*.

Wallace's hair-drier with an action frame from *The Wrong Trousers*.

Opposite: A parade of objects to demonstrate the invention and artistry of the prop-makers. They include the submarine that journeyed through Vince's brain in the 'Rex the Runt' series, and the basket used by Tiny, the dog-juggler in *Stage Fright*.

BAKED BEANS
21p
BAKED BEANS
21p
Dog Juggler
Aards

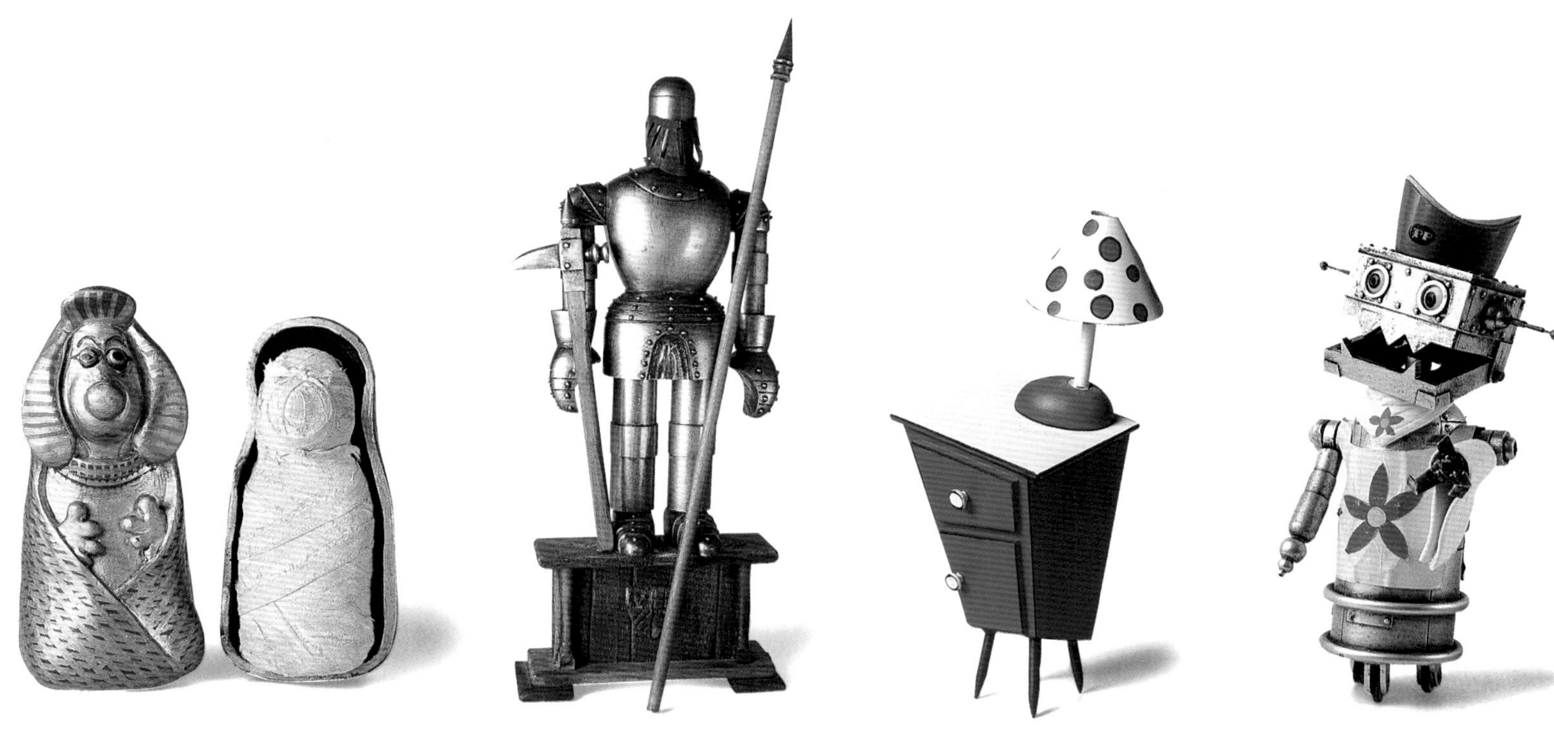

Left to right: Ancient exhibits from the museum in *The Wrong Trousers;* Contemporary table and lamp from *Not Without My Handbag;* fantastic creatures from the *Rex the Runt* series, an animated dustbin featured in *Morph,* and tiny instruments for Rex's band. Though beautifully crafted, some of these props were only seen for a fleeting second in the final film.

Miniature engineering from John Wright's workshop. Wallace's motor-bike is engineered like a real motor-bike, with welded parts and steel frames. Even the wheel spokes are individually stitched with wire and drilled into the wheel frame. The tyres are rubber, like real ones. Working parts such as the exhaust and engine are made of steel and chrome and heated to make them look scorched.

Big machines, like the Mutton-O-Matic, are made using foundry-cast brass parts. With such pieces, it is good to put everything on them, as for an all-round view, with all the rivets showing. When you are making the model, you never know which camera angle will finally be chosen.

He's leaving home. For this rain scene in *The Wrong Trousers*, we superimposed live-action rain. The water running down Gromit's cape was actually tiny blobs of glycerine which were animated frame by frame.

Special Effects

Some special effects are made principally with the camera. Others rely on physical factors such as the use of glass to lend invisible support, or artfully chosen props and materials which can be made to pass off as something else. Usually, though, a successful effect is a blend of both. How you light your scene is also important.

Right: Ghost effect in *Stage Fright*, basically achieved by double exposure.

Double exposure For double exposures, or superimpositions, which can be applied to produce ghost effects, you need a camera with a windback facility. First, expose your main scene, then wind back the film by the number of frames in which you want your ghost to appear. If you then expose this figure against a black background, it will show through on

Top: The secret of pouring tea is to use rolls of squashed-up brown Cellophane. This catches the light and makes it look as if it is moving; from *Palmy Days*.

Centre: Beads of sweat fly off the anxious Penguin's brow in *The Wrong Trousers*. The sweat was made by animating tiny perspex drops across the window in front of the character.

Bottom: Washing windows with a foam of white hair wax dotted with different-sized glass beads; from *A Close Shave*. As with all new solutions, once you have made the wonderful discovery that foam = white hair wax + added glass beads, you can apply the formula to other situations to make, say, shaving foam or bubble-bath.

the first exposure and be transparent, like a ghost. Black velvet is best for the background, because it reflects less light than black paper. You can extend this trick to other kinds of apparition, as the Victorian photographers did with their scenes of 'The soldier's dream of his loved-ones' and 'The fairies' dell', etc.

Mattes The simplest form is the split screen. Here you mask off one side of the picture and shoot the action that fits into the unmasked half. You rewind the film, swap the mask over and shoot the action for the other side. This process can be further developed by using a sheet of glass in front of the camera, on which an area of the image is masked off with black paint - for example, the action to be seen inside the windows of a miniature space-ship. The ship is shot with the window areas painted out on the glass. Then the film is rewound, the clear area painted black and the previously painted area scraped clear, and finally the action for the window is set up in front of the camera and shot.

Water and rain effects Water and other liquids are difficult to simulate, and animators have tried out various ways to convey the illusion. A classic method for flat water, say a lake or river, is to cut a perspex sheet to size and spray it with the colours you want, adding ripple effects and so on.

For the rain effect in *The Wrong Trousers,* we put little blobs of glycerine on glass and animated them by blowing them, frame by frame, down the glass. Then, every so often, we put in a random splash effect, a tiny winged object that looked like a very small butterfly and was made out of cel. We stuck this on Gromit's raincoat and on the ground, just for one frame, then took it off. In another scene in *The Wrong Trousers,* the Penguin is outside the museum window during the robbery, and beads of sweat fly off him. Again, we animated small perspex drops across the glass away from him. For the foam in the window-washing sequence in *A Close Shave,* we came up with a combination of white hair wax dotted with glass beads to represent the bubbles. To suggest bubbles bursting and new ones forming, we took beads out and put in new ones.

Advanced Special Effects

There are some special effects you cannot easily achieve with model animation. For example, it is difficult to convey the illusion of high-speed motion. If you animate objects moving fast across the screen, you often get jerky, 'strobing' movement because the distance between the positions of the models from one frame to another is too great for the brain to smooth out. The problem is exacerbated by the sharp images created by photographing static objects.

When shot as live-action film, fast-moving objects create a blurred image on each frame of the film because they are moving during the relatively long exposure made by the live-action camera. These blurred, indistinct images are more easily smoothed over by the brain than the hard-edged, sharp images

Left: The train chase scene in *The Wrong Trousers*. By moving the train and the camera together during a two-second exposure, it and the characters on board come out sharply defined, whereas the wallpaper background is blurred.

created by stop-frame animation. To avoid the jerky effects of fast-moving objects in animation, you have to create blurred images. In the train chase in *The Wrong Trousers* and the lorry chase in *A Close Shave,* we blurred the background by using long exposures (one or two seconds) and by physically moving the camera during the exposure.

To take the train example, the train on its track was attached to the camera, which was mounted on a dolly. For each frame, we pushed the dolly about 3-4in (8-10cm) and this carried the train along with it. At the same time we pressed the button to expose the film. The characters on the train come out sharply defined because they are moving with the camera, but in the course of the two-second exposure the camera moves fractionally past the wallpaper in the background, and this comes out blurred.

Blue-screen This process is used a great deal in films today. It is a way of putting difficult foreground action against a realistic background - for example, to show people falling out of a building. We use the technique frequently when we want to put animated characters into a live-action background. First, the foreground action (the people falling) is shot against a blue background. The blue is then electronically replaced by the chosen background (the building) using a sophisticated computer graphics system (it used to be done in the film laboratories, but this is rare nowadays). This has the effect of merging the two elements of the scene. Naturally, you have to be careful to match the lighting, perspective and camera angles, otherwise it can look like cut-out images stuck on another picture!

Douglas the Lurpak Butter man, filmed by the blue-screen process. First he is shot against a blue background, then the blue is electronically replaced by the table-top scene. We use blue as the background colour because human faces do not usually have much blue in them. Any strong colour will do, such as lime green, but it is important to ensure that the colour does not appear in the surrounding scene because it will also be removed in the process.

animation and performance

Movement

Like actors, animators communicate through the language of movement. We create characters, convey emotions and make people laugh through the movements, gestures and facial expressions of our puppets.

People often say that our work is naturalistic, which I think is meant as a compliment because the best model animation is regularly praised for its smooth and 'natural' movement. But in fact our work is not realistic at all. It is - and it should be - exaggerated. All the animated movements that we do, however understated or natural they may appear, are bigger, bolder and simpler than 'real life'. Real movement, the sort of thing you would see if you analysed film of a live actor, always looks weak and bland when it is closely imitated in an animated version. Some animators use previously shot live-action footage as reference material, or even copy it slavishly frame by frame to create their own animated performance. At Aardman we rarely do this. We prefer to act out the animation ourselves, so that we really understand it, then add our own degree of caricature and stylisation. The important thing is that the audience should be able to understand what the puppet character is doing and thinking, no matter how broad or subtle the style of animation. What we love doing is producing *performances* with our puppets that feel 'natural' because in some way they feel true. By simplifying and exaggerating gestures, we try to distil the essence of a particular movement or sequence of movements. This is far more important than copying from real life. When we get this right, it gives the audience a great sense of recognition. They think, 'Yes, that's exactly how people react or behave,' and they believe that what they have seen is uncannily natural.

Nick Park, stopwatch in hand, uses his own body to work through the jerky, exaggerated movements of the Wrong Trousers (seen right in action). Once he knows exactly how long it takes to get from A to B in a particular phase, he can plan how to animate the model within this timespan.

Posing the Character Obviously, animation is about movement. But few really expressive sequences are carried out through *continuous* movement. One of the classic symptoms of our earliest work is that the characters shift about constantly and restlesslessly, never daring to be still. Later we realised that the time between movements, when the puppet is still, often conveys far more character than the same number of seconds of elaborate animation.

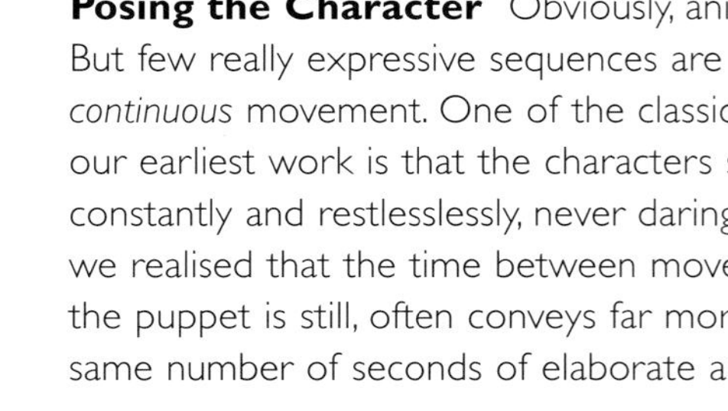

We talk of 'poses' and 'holds'. A pose is pretty obvious - a still position that conveys a lot of information about

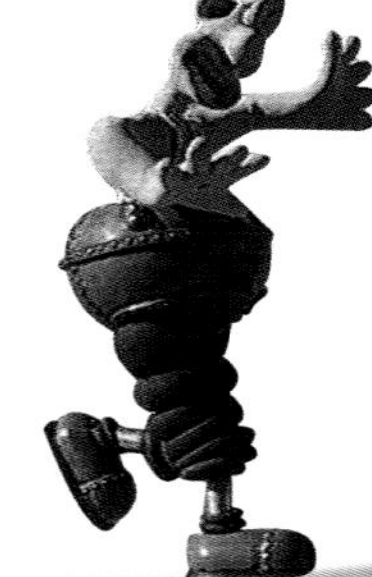

mood and emotion. A hold is the moment when the action stops - though it seldom freezes completely - and it can last for anything from a quarter of a second to half a minute. During these holds, the audience can see and understand far more than when the character is continually moving. The point to remember is that your puppet is never *just* sitting or standing or leaning - it should always be expressive in face and body. You should always know what your character is thinking and feeling - if you don't, who does? - and in the poses, you make it clear to the audience.

To be sure, I certainly do not mean that the pose has to be like some magnificent melodramatic gesture from a Victorian painting. Audiences are very sophisticated, and the pose can be as subtle, or as corny, as you can make it. If your puppet is frightened, he does not have to be cringing and quaking in extravagant terror. The fear can be communicated in the angle of the head, the tension in the shoulders and arms and the smallest obsessive gesture with one hand.

Remember that these holds should not be totally static. Watch television with the sound off, or watch people in the street. You often see people sit or stand for several minutes at a time, doing virtually nothing. However, they are moving in slight ways, and they *are* alive. If your puppet goes into a hold, keep it alive, don't let it freeze, and look on this as an opportunity to let the audience see what he or she is thinking and feeling.

Changing the Pace Of course, different actions happen at different speeds. Building a house of cards is a slow and careful business, whereas trying to extract a lighted cigarette from inside your clothing is going to be pretty frenetic. But whatever the speed of the sequence, try to vary the pace of individual parts of your animation. Try to avoid falling into a too-regular rhythm of move-hold-move-hold. Remember too that different parts of the body can move at different speeds. A thief may creep carefully through an empty house, but his head and eyes can move quickly and sharply.

In the animated sequences on the following pages, we show key frames to illustrate the essence of a movement. In a full sequence, there would be other, intervening frames.

When a hand or a foot - or a bottom or a nose - comes into contact with the ground, make it look as if it is firmly set. Make it lie flat and contact the ground at all points, so that no line of light is visible underneath. This makes the puppet feel larger and heavier.

Remember that your puppet has a centre of gravity, and needs to stay well balanced. Standing with his weight equally on both feet, you want him to step forward on to his right foot. To do this, he must first shift his body weight over his supporting foot, the left. The best demonstration is to try it yourself. Start with your feet very close together, and step forward on to your right foot. As you start, you move very slightly to the left. Starting with your feet a metre apart, you are forced to move a long way to the left before you can go forward. Now try moving off without shifting left and see how unnatural it feels.

Right: Everything about this puppet is downcast. His feet barely leave the ground, his head bounces slowly as if he has not got the strength to hold it up, and his arms swing heavily in small arcs.

Every step we take starts at the hip joint. Your puppet should do the same. When he prepares to move off, the supporting hip drops down as the body's weight is transferred on to it. The pelvis swivels and the stepping foot is released.

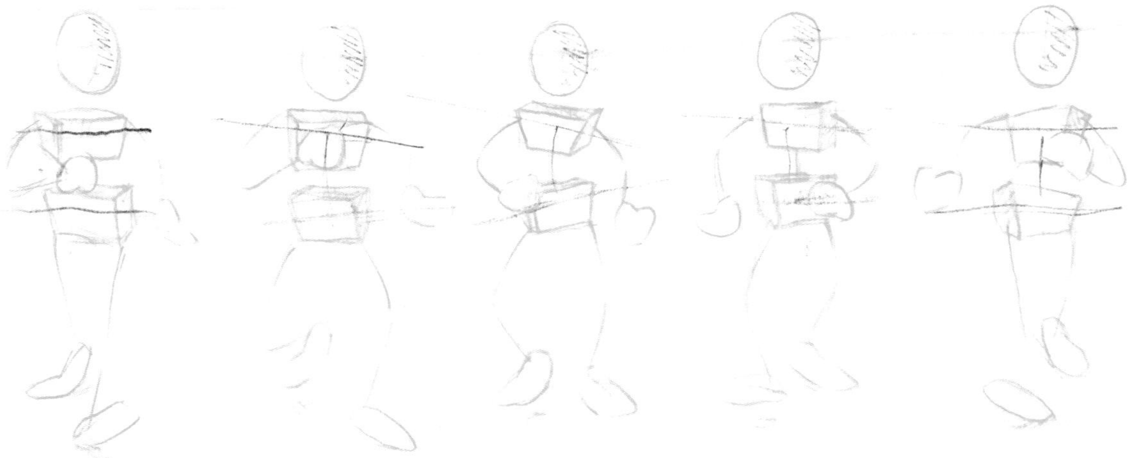

Walk Cycles in Action

Adam
Adam is so dejected, his whole body hangs heavily. As he plods slowly uphill, his arms barely swing.

Wallace
The Wrong Trousers take Wallace for a walk. The trousers move with an extreme mechanical step, which causes Wallace's hands and head to wave about in panic.

Loves Me ... Loves Me Not
As the puppet tangoes across the floor, his legs smooth out the action like shock absorbers.

Wat
In most 'real' walks, the head is kept quite still. In this scene Wat moves with exaggerated effort and his head bobs up and down wearily.

Substitution
The substitution technique allows us to create lovely smooth lines in the legs and feet, and gives extra stretch as the front foot reaches forward.

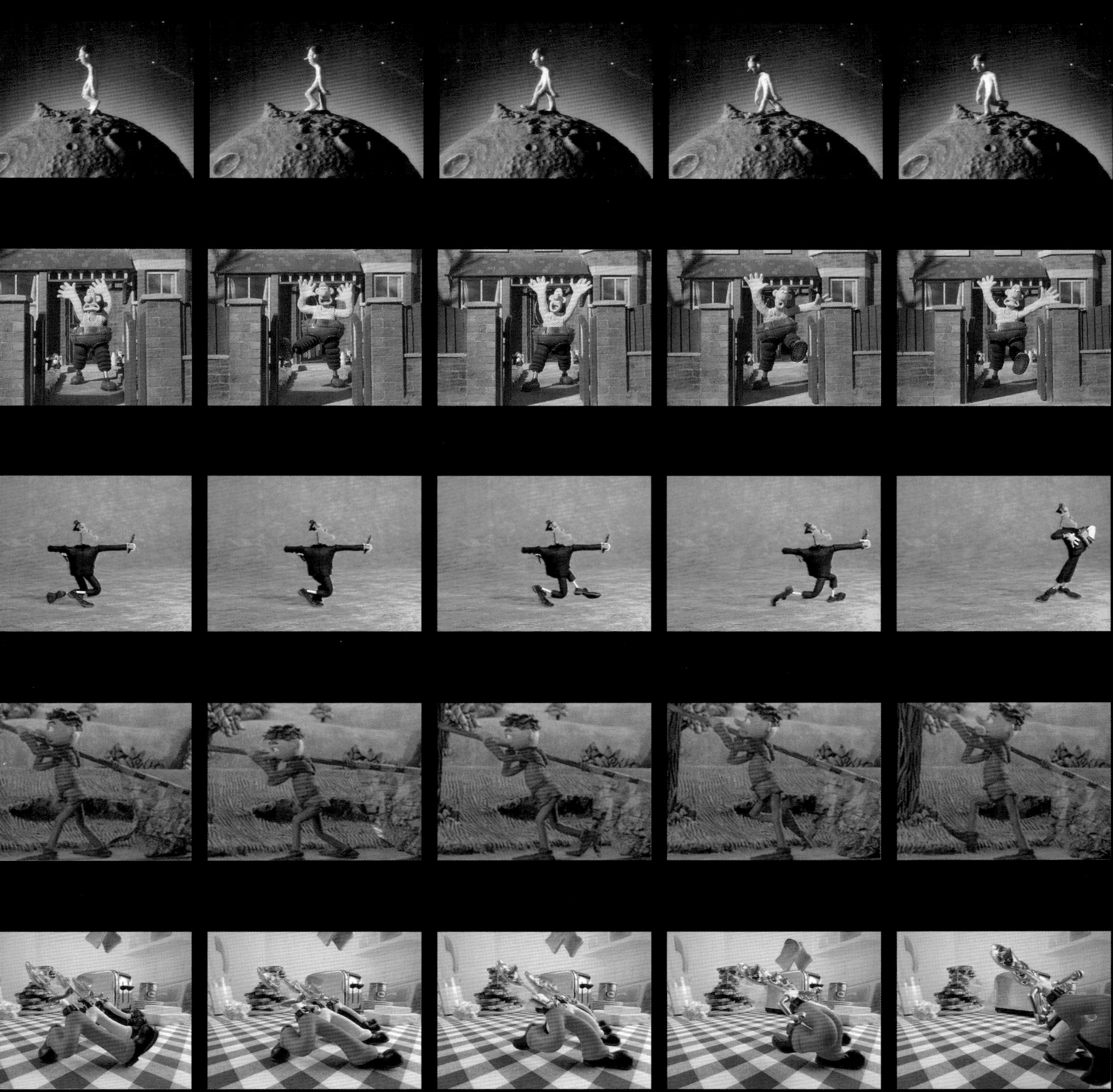

Most of the principles that make up good animation have something to do with the transference of weight and the animator's ability to make it believable.

Characters in animation are not bound by the Laws of Gravity. If you want to, you can make an elephant flit around as weightlessly as a butterfly. However, in nearly all our animation, we work hard to create the illusion that our puppets are earthbound. I often think that Plasticine lends itself best to creating solid, heavy-looking characters.

Making Movement Believable

Anticipation Before an animated figure starts moving in one direction, we usually anticipate the action by moving it the opposite way. This is not so strange when you think about it. If you want to jump up in the air, you first crouch down; if you want to throw a ball forward, the first thing your arm does is go back. Anticipation is 'realistic', and it also works well in film because the moment of anticipation prepares the audience for the action which is going to follow. This is why, in cartoon films, the anticipation is often stronger than the action itself.

Weight We make our characters more believable by making them look heavy. The weightlifter, above, nicely demonstrates this as he struggles to lift a barbell which only weighs a couple of ounces. The animator plans and rehearses the movement, miming it to understand how it works. Then he tries to make the puppet do the hard work. In stage 3 for example, he has just started to lift by pushing his legs and back straight, and stretching his arms. At stage 4, he has hauled the barbell as high as he can, it hangs in the air for a moment before it

Above: Think about the weightlifter's speed through the lift. Most of the action is quite slow, but at stage 4 he suddenly snatches up the weight, and at 5 he quickly gets his hands and arms below the barbell.

Top: Wallace walks across the museum ceiling in *The Wrong Trousers,* his leg movements controlled by Feathers McGraw from outside the window. The way he moves reflects both the character and his plight. The Penguin, mindful of the risks he is taking, moves the Trousers with exaggerated care. The knees come up high and the feet are planted with great caution, to make sure they stick. Inside the Trousers, Wallace moves to a linked but different pattern.

falls, and in that time he quickly gets his hands and body underneath it. When he finally holds the weight aloft in triumph, see how his arms and legs are locked straight. If they were not, the audience would not believe he could support a heavy weight.

Momentum Remember that, like the barbell, your head, body and limbs are also heavy. Because of this, they should not stop moving too quickly once they start. Try sprinting as fast as you can, then stopping. When your feet finally stop, thanks to friction, your head and body will want to carry on, tipping you forward. In animation, we often exaggerate this natural effect.

Acceleration and Deceleration Except in extreme cases, objects and people do not suddenly start or stop moving at full speed. They normally accelerate and decelerate. This is pretty obvious in the case of a sprinter running from the starting blocks, but it applies equally to small actions such as lifting your hand to scratch your ear. Remember that your hand and arm have weight, and have to be brought up to speed.

See how his arms swing like a pendulum, but always behind the movement of the feet. When a foot is forward, the arms swing helplessly back, then swing forward again as the next stride begins.

Very little human movement happens in straight lines. It can usually be broken down into a series of arcs. If you trace the path of the batter's foot, hand or hip, you should see a pattern of overlapping curves.

Putting it all together

The sequences here show a mix of all the animation principles mentioned in the previous pages. Swinging a baseball bat is a good example because the whole process is about storing up and using energy.

Stage 1 shows the batter poised to receive the ball. In 2 and 3 he moves back, anticipating the main action which will be forward. His shoulders rotate, storing energy, and his weight is entirely on the back foot, allowing him to raise the left foot. He steps forward on to his front foot, and by 5 has started to unwind his shoulders. As he accelerates, the bat moves a greater distance in each frame.

The bat has weight and is swinging in a big arc, so in 6 and 7 it is moving farther than anything else. All his weight is pushing on to the front foot, and his whole body is unwinding so that maximum force and speed are brought to bear on the ball at stage 7. At 8, the power which started in the hips and shoulders has now been transferred to the bat which is almost pulling him round in his follow-through. In a more 'cartoony' version, his bat would carry on and get wrapped round behind his head.

All the sequences on these pages demonstrate how movement flows through a gesture. I think of it as a wave that runs through the body from the first thing that moves to the last. Swinging the bat starts when the foot steps forward, followed by the knee, hip, chest, shoulder, elbow, hand and finally the bat.

Right: The force of the flying ball catches the man's hand and pulls him along in a sequence that runs from his hand down to his feet.

Running is notoriously difficult in model animation. Because the movement is fast, the gaps between frames are large. This means that although the effect is energetic, it is seldom smooth.

Left: The tumbling character demonstrates the effect of momentum. When he trips, his feet stop moving but his head keeps going forward (4). In turn, his tumbling body pulls his feet after him (6). When his head contacts the ground, the feet - still full of energy - carry on past (7) until they finally settle on the ground (8). If he was running faster, he would carry on tumbling longer.

Action and Reaction

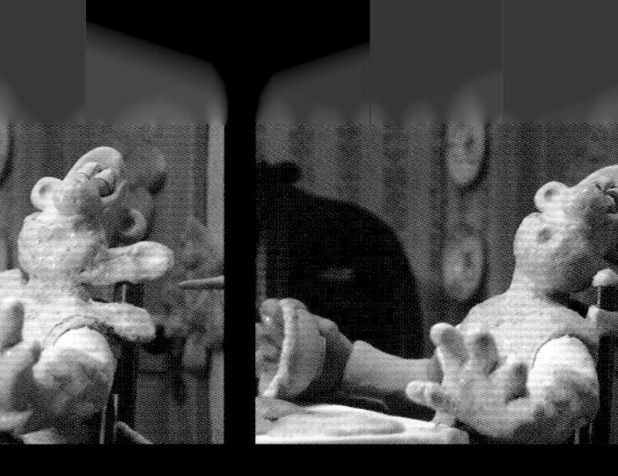

Porridge Power
The impact of the flying blob of porridge knocks Wallace back in his chair. Just as he recovers to an upright position, the action is repeated.

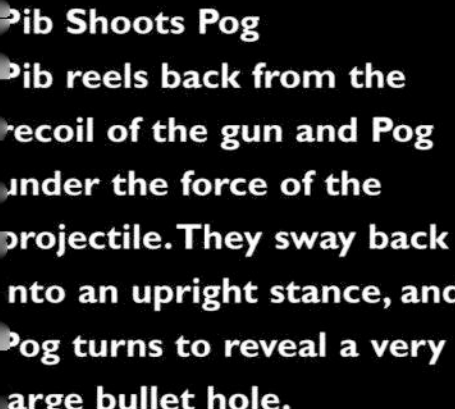

Pib Shoots Pog
Pib reels back from the recoil of the gun and Pog under the force of the projectile. They sway back into an upright stance, and Pog turns to reveal a very large bullet hole.

Carpet Trick
The boy's whirling legs ruck the carpet into extravagantly huge ridges. In classic cartoon style, when his legs touch the ground, they zoom off first, followed a moment later by the body and head.

Bungee Effect
Gromit's legs, helmet and bucket tell the story. In frame 3, when his body has stopped falling, his legs are the last things to stop. When he finds himself pulled up again (6), his legs are the last thing to start moving.

Adam Takes Strike
A study in anticipation as Adam coils himself up to strike. See how in frame 7 he has started to unwind into the stroke from his foot to the shoulder, but the pack is still in a state of anticipation – it has not yet moved.

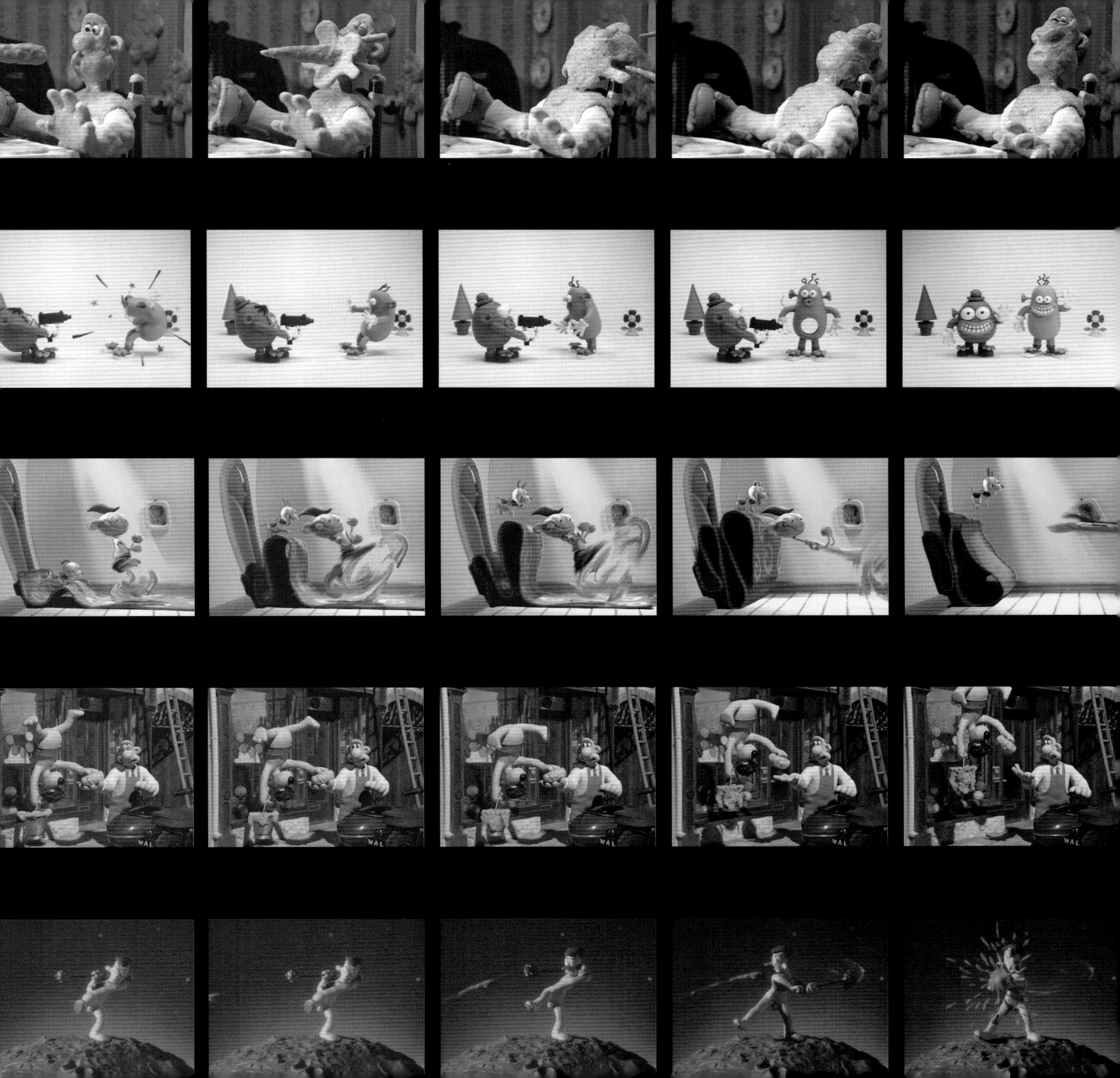
WAL

Special Movement Effects

We are often asked how the Penguin got into the bottle in *The Wrong Trousers*. In fact this was a relatively straightforward thing to do, relying on a quick substitution of both character and bottle. The sequence, illustrated below, begins with the empty milk bottle wobbling and vibrating after Gromit has crashed into the cupboard. Then it falls off the unit and Gromit catches it. Up till then we used an ordinary model bottle. For the next frames we had a thin replacement Penguin who is first seen entering the bottle before he becomes inescapably jammed up to the neck inside it. This was a different bottle, vacuum-formed and supplied in two halves. We pushed the thin clay Penguin against the side of one half and then sealed him in, hiding the join when we positioned the bottle to camera.

Another difficult part of this sequence was animating the Penguin after he has been shot up in the air and then falls to earth against a background of sky and clouds. Rather than try to show the Penguin in motion against a fixed background, we photographed him on glass with a parallel sky positioned behind him. In the following frames the Penguin is largely still, though from time to time we altered the position of his feet and the sack across his shoulder. The illusion of falling comes mainly from the sky itself, which we moved from side to side during a series of long exposures. This was a variant on the blurred-wallpaper effect which occurs earlier in the train chase (described on page 131).

Again, while shooting *Adam,* we had to go to great lengths of ingenuity to show him running round the circumference of the world. For most of the film, Adam stands on top of his globe, which was supported on the end of a scaffolding pole. This was fixed through the far side of the globe and so always remained out of shot. The pole also ran through a hole in the night-sky picture which was our backdrop. For the running sequence, it would have been incredibly painful to animate Adam by holding him on strings and changing their position after each shot, so we came up with another solution.

First we turned the globe-pole-sky unit on its side, through 90 degrees. Then we measured the circumference of the globe and cut a circular hole in a large

The Penguin falls to earth in *The Wrong Trousers*. The illusion of falling was mainly achieved by pulling the painted background from side to side during a series of long exposures.

How the Penguin got into the bottle. This was a two-bottle and two-Penguin trick. When the Penguin began entering the bottle, his body was exchanged for a special thin Penguin. The receiving bottle was also different - it came in two halves and was clamped round the Penguin between shots.

When Adam ran round the circumference of the globe, we shot him on glass. With one hip and one shoulder resting against the glass, he was far easier to animate than if we had tried somehow to suspend him on wires.

sheet of glass which fitted exactly round the globe on a north-south axis. So now, because everything was turned, we had the camera up in the roof shooting downward. After that, it was relatively easy to film Adam running round the world because he was lying with one shoulder and one hip flat on the glass.

If you should try something like that yourself, there are two snags: extra colour from the glass, and reflections. A sheet of glass may have some colour in it, and this is likely to show up when you move from the previous scene, which has no glass in it, into your with-glass scene, and similarly when you move out of it into the next scene. To avoid this, shoot a whole group of scenes with a sheet of glass in them, whether they need it or not, and the transition will not show up. To avoid picking up reflections thrown by the puppet lying on its side, shoot directly at 90 degrees to the glass. There may still be some reflection, but this should be minimal.

Arnold, the bully figure from *Stage Fright*, and some of the replacement mouths that helped to keep fame and fortune at a distance in his career as an entertainer.

His short pointy teeth, allied to fierce eyes and alarming carroty hair, give him a powerful expressive range. Think of this when deciding on the kind of facial effects you want your character to produce.

Expressions and Gestures

Although we spend a lot of time on mouths, working with dope sheets to synchronise speech and mouth movements, and yet more time making this work by constantly sculpting and resculpting mouths, or fitting replacement mouths, this part of the face is by no means the most expressive. The mouth is of course crucial to speech, but perhaps supplies only 5-10 per cent of a character's performance.

Those moments that really make you believe that this clay person is talking are all done with the eyes, eyebrows and gestures involving the face - nods, nose-scratching, stroking the cheek while thinking something over, and so on. Bear in mind, too, that a character can be highly expressive without speaking a single word. Gromit is a good example of this: almost all his expressiveness comes from the way his eyes are positioned. Many of our models' eyes are made of glass beads with a painted-on pupil, which has a hole at its centre. To move the eyes around, and make them look up, down or sideways, the animator inserts a cocktail stick into the hole in the pupil and swivels the eye to the desired position. Eyebrows are used to enhance certain facial expressions - surprise, for example - and eyelids, often made of fast-cast resin, are added if the character is required to blink, fall asleep or wake up.

Hand and arm gestures are also important in their own right, whether they involve touching the face or not. The amount they can be used will naturally depend on the build of the character. As Nick Park found while making *Creature Comforts,* not all animals are designed with the kind of front paws that can be waved about expressively: 'It was fine for the Jaguar and the Polar Bears, because they had these front legs and paws, but some animals did not have anything I could work with. The young Hippopotamus just had two cloven front hooves, which he needed to support himself while sitting up, and the Armadillo was even more limited. With the Bush Baby, it was enough to have her clinging on to the branch to bring out her insecurity. I also made her lift her glasses off, so people could see those two little timid eyes beneath.'

Clay faces and hands get dirty very quickly. The best way to clean them is very gently to scrape off the top layer. The important thing is to keep a constant balance between the tones of a model's face and any separate pieces, such as mouths and eyelids, that you may fix to it.

The more you scrape away, the more you have to add new bits of clay, and here too you can get differences in tone. Eventually, you reach a stage where you cannot get the dirt out of the face, and then you have to make a new one.

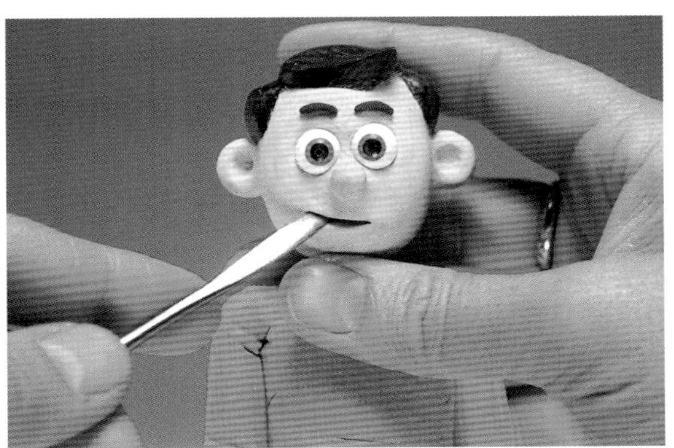

Eyes, brows, eyelids and mouth are the main elements that we can move to change a character's expression. Left-hand column: First the animator works on the mouth with a modelling tool, widening it and adding the characteristic dent in the cheek.

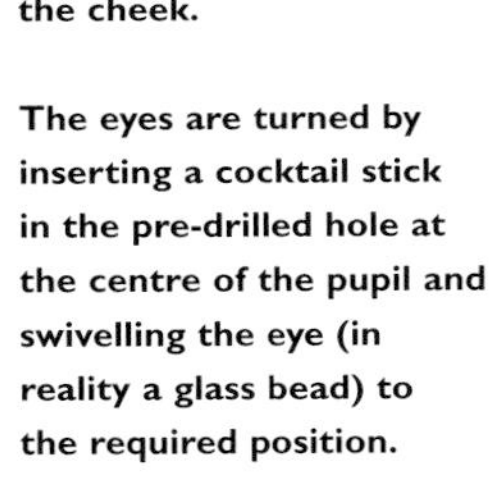

The eyes are turned by inserting a cocktail stick in the pre-drilled hole at the centre of the pupil and swivelling the eye (in reality a glass bead) to the required position.

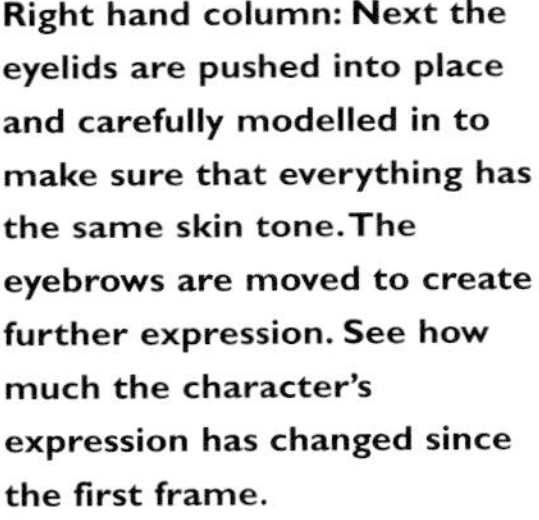

Right hand column: Next the eyelids are pushed into place and carefully modelled in to make sure that everything has the same skin tone. The eyebrows are moved to create further expression. See how much the character's expression has changed since the first frame.

Faces and Expressions

In Going Equipped, the characterisation is exaggerated but basically realistic.

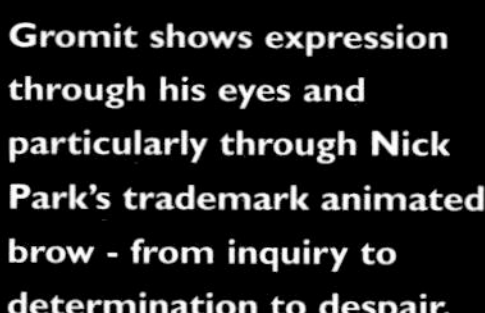

Gromit shows expression through his eyes and particularly through Nick Park's trademark animated brow - from inquiry to determination to despair.

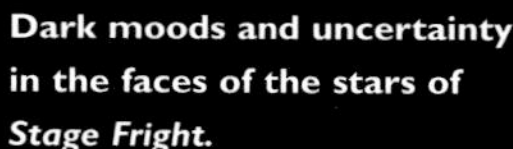

Dark moods and uncertainty in the faces of the stars of *Stage Fright.*

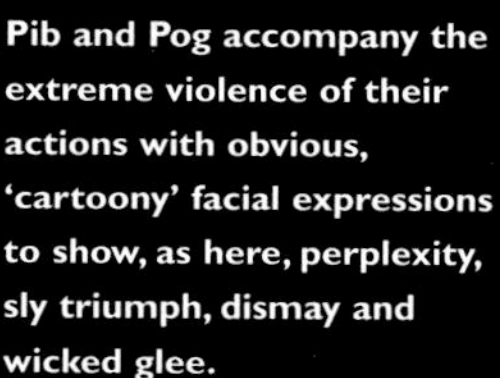

Pib and Pog accompany the extreme violence of their actions with obvious, 'cartoony' facial expressions to show, as here, perplexity, sly triumph, dismay and wicked glee.

Right and opposite: Sprawled across his tree perch, the Jaguar is free to gesture massively at the unreasonable fate which has befallen him.

Nick Park and Steve Box prepare Wendolene for her next scene in *A Close Shave,* matching gesture to storyboard.

Below is a chart of Wendolene sounds, each one pinpointing the position of the mouth.

Opposite, below, is a sample dope sheet, which provides the animator with an accurate map of the sounds a character will make, and how many frames each one will occupy. This is matched, top, with the face the audience sees while hearing the sounds on the soundtrack.

Lip Sync

We match voices to lip movements by a somewhat ancient method which has become traditional in the company. First, an editor marks all the syllables on the magnetic tape of the dialogue recording. Then he or she transfers all this to a bar chart, in which each bar covers a second of film (or 1ft of 35mm), so the animator can see exactly where each syllable starts and finishes. With the word 'Me', for example, the chart will show the 'M'-sound lasting for two frames, or whatever, and the longer 'eeeee' sound lasting for nine frames. If there is pre-recorded music, as there might be for a film which is set round a tune or song, this will also be sketched in, to show where the beats fall, or a particular run of notes which are important for the animator's timing.

The chart goes to the animator, who then copies the information on to a traditional animation dope sheet. There are 96 lines to a page, one line for each frame, covering 4 seconds, and the lines run vertically down the sheet. On the dope sheet you have more space to put other information, and that is the essential difference. Instead of having just a tiny gap per frame, as on the bar chart, here the animator has a whole line.

Now you have your own personal map of the sounds, and the gaps between them, and can begin to devise a performance for your character. From listening to the sound, you know when the voice goes up higher - which might indicate a questioning expression, with raised eyebrows. In *War Story,* the old man says

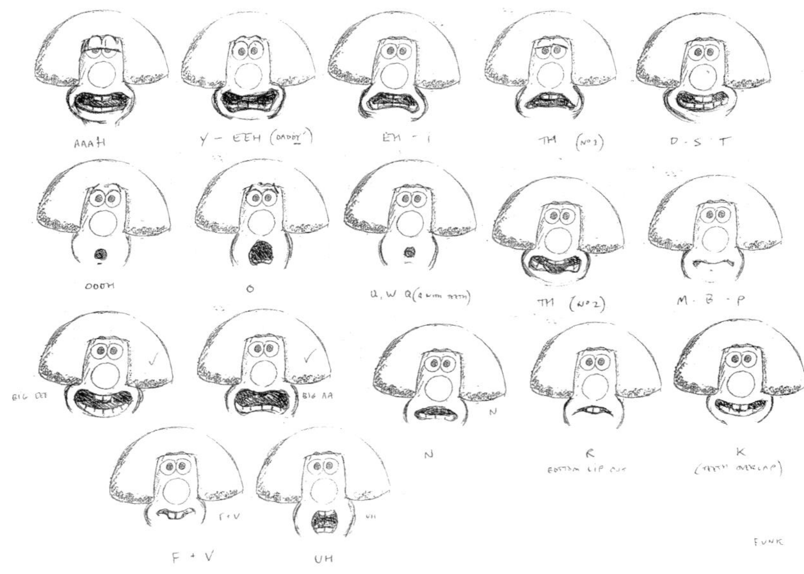

to his interviewer, 'I was out at the BAC, see, Pete?' You listen to that, and try to work out when he should raise his eyebrows, or tilt his head. Typically you listen over and over again, repeating it to yourself, copying the accent and intonation, trying to sense the right moment for the character to react. You can hear that he pauses after 'BAC', so you choose that as the moment. The dope sheet, meanwhile, tells you the exact space between 'C' and 'see' is 18 frames. This is the essential information you need both to plan ahead, and to animate.

How much an animator actually notes down on the dope sheet is a matter of personal choice. You could write down every detail, but with experience you tend to write less. Alongside our sample piece of speech, you might mark in certain movements, e.g. 'blink ... blink ... starts to raise hand to face - 18 frames (during that time, starts to tilt head to left) . . . tilts head to left - 12 frames'. And so on. Sometimes it can be deadening to analyse a movement too closely, fragment by fragment. Today I tend to write down just the key moments, where the timing is essential, and leave the rest to inspiration when we shoot. On the other hand, some gestures are so specific that it can be helpful to note down all the separate movements, of hands, eyebrows, angle of head, etc., to make sure you include them all and that they blend together.

One important tip is to look ahead at all times. It is too easy to develop a kind of tunnel vision with the frame you are working on, and then you can forget to start another movement in time, or you find that your character is out of position and cannot make the expressive move you want him to.

As for marrying the sounds to lip movements, a character can either have its own set of replacement mouths, each corresponding to a particular sound or group of sounds, or you can decide to resculpt the face itself each frame - what we call 'animating through'. Even with replacement mouths, you still have to do a certain amount of remodelling to clean up the face and sculpt in the new mouth so it fits perfectly.

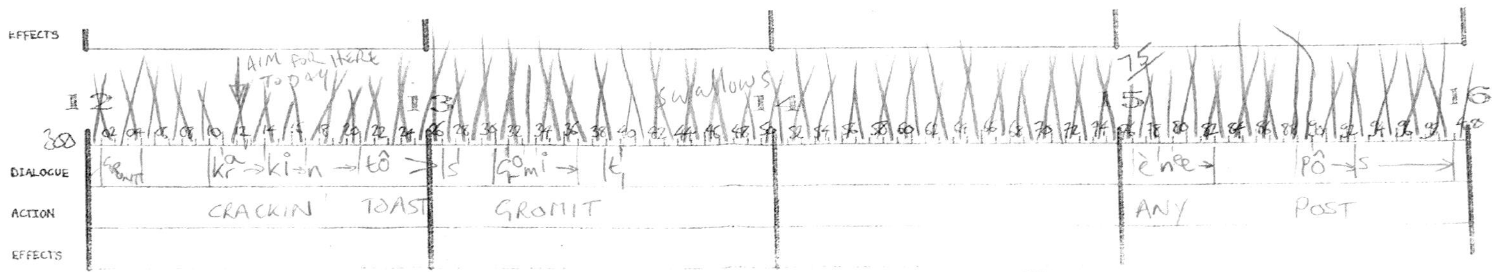

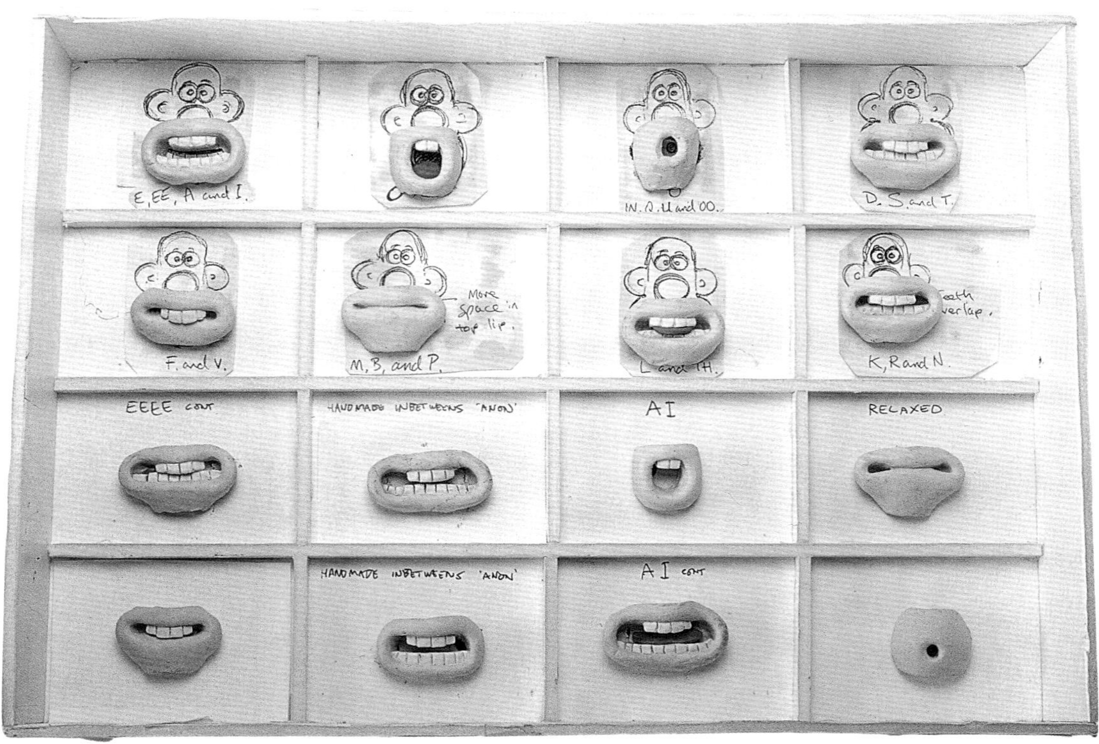

A box of Wallace's mouths, showing some of the sounds and expressions he can make with them, including the all-important 'relaxed' when he does not say anything at all or goes into listening mode.

Talking Heads

The idea of making up a set of replacement mouths for a character was conceived as a way of saving time. Because everything in animation takes so long, any time-saving device is to be welcomed. In theory, it should be quicker for the animator just to exchange one mouth for another, model it in to make sure the joins do not show, and shoot the next frame. Also, a replacement mouth has the advantage that it can be used a number of times, whereas if you reanimate a fixed mouth you lose that advantage. For all that, some animators still prefer the old-fashioned way, finding it more satisfactory to work with a head that remains a unified entity, and probably has less variation in skin tone, than with something that always consists of two halves that have to be constantly reunited.

Whichever way you choose, you have to be prepared to do a lot of cleaning and remodelling. If you have a mouth which you will only need for two or three frames, then this is not so important. But if it is a mouth you are going to use when the face comes to rest, and will be needed for a long sequence of frames, then you have to be sure that it is clean and that it tones in with the face.

The best cleaning liquid for clay is water. You can try lighter fluid, but this tends to strip away the whole surface of the face, leaving it sticky and more difficult to handle. For the best results, use water and gently scrape away at those parts you want to clean or remove.

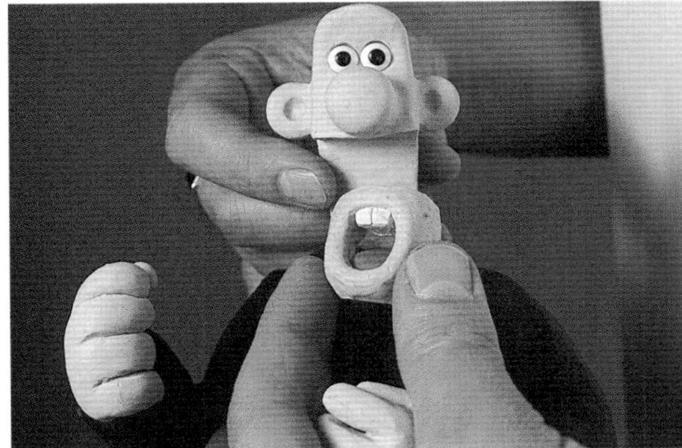

In this sequence, Wallace's 'ee' mouth is taken off and the new mouth which says 'o' is slid into place. The animator uses a modelling tool to mask the join and smooth down the new face.

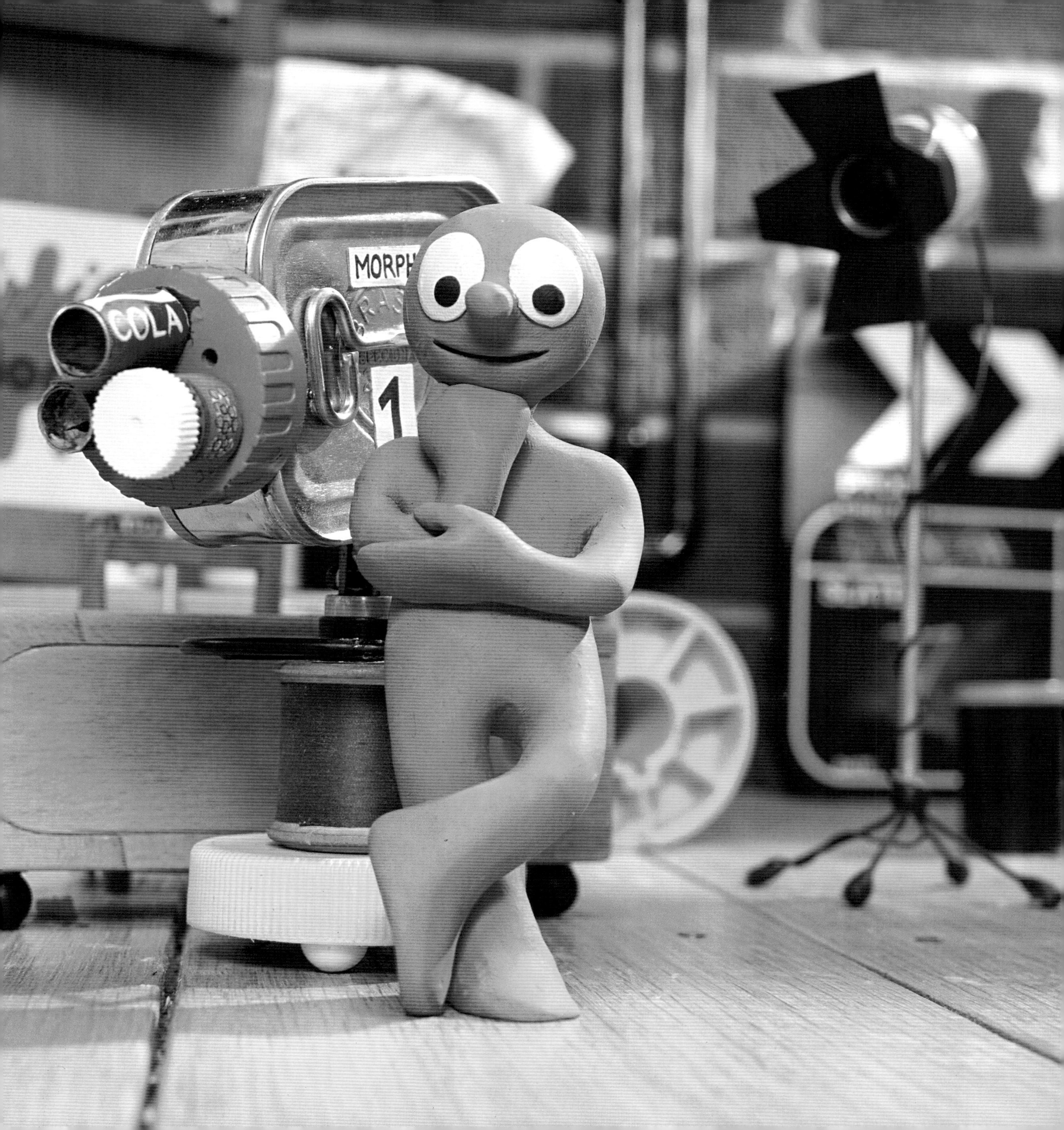
COLA
MORPH

making a film

Thinking about a Script

Whole stories do not fall ready-made from the sky. The best ones usually evolve slowly and take a huge amount of effort. Dave and I learned our trade in storytelling when we made films for 'Vision On' and 'Take Hart'. Those early films were very short - no more than sketches, really - but many of the same basic rules that we discovered then, apply equally to much longer and more complicated stories.

A story is usually about something, meaning that there is more to the story than simply what happens. Morph stories are usually about sibling rivalry, jealousy, pomposity pricked - things like that. But the seed from which the story grows may be very simple. It may be enough to think of a single gag, an absurd situation, an animation idea that you would love to try.

Morph, Chas and a computer keyboard - all the ingredients you need for a short sharp conflict. When we began making Morph films for the 'Vision On' series, our goal was to tell a story in under a minute - not a bad target for anyone setting out in animation.

When we were writing sketches for Morph, we had the freedom to choose any subject. For example, we might decide it would be fun to animate him as if he were on ice. That is not a story, but it is the seed from which the story grows. It is a situation that will be fun to do and will challenge the character. Now we need to work out how to simulate ice on Morph's table-top. He could invent an ice-making machine, or receive one through the post, like Wile E Coyote, or we could send him to the North Pole. Or we might decide that all this is much too complicated. Instead, Morph's alter ego Chas has polished the floor so hard that it becomes as slippery as ice. But Chas, being incredibly lazy, would never have polished the floor voluntarily. So he needs a reason that is funny and in character. The simplest reason is good old malice. Chas has booby-trapped the floor, and now lies in wait to watch the fun. Starting with an animation idea, a story is already forming.

All this is the set-up for the main part of the story, in which Morph tries to achieve something, and is constantly thwarted by the slippery floor. I am shy of giving rules, but we often found that you had to try three variations on a predicament to make it effective. In this case, discovering the slippery floor and falling over a few times is not enough. You have to invent *variations* on him falling over. Why does he do it, how does he avoid it, what are the consequences? And while he is falling over, while he is in conflict with Chas, we must not forget to have visual fun with Morph skating around. Finally, we need a punchline, an ending, a resolution. Knowing Morph, he eventually discovers that Chas is responsible and takes some terrible kind of revenge which leaves the audience with a feeling that justice has been done.

Nick Park and Peter Lord think chickens - devising the shape, look and individual characteristics of the stars of Chicken Run.

On a much bigger scale, the idea for *Wat's Pig* came during a holiday in France. I was in the Dordogne, where you can see these huge medieval castles standing in full view of one another. I thought, how difficult to have been a peasant in the middle of this lot, caught up in the intrigues of warring barons who held the key to everything you did in life. That was the starting-point. As we developed our plot, we settled on one particular castle rather than have two facing each other. Later came the idea of the twins who were separated by a thief who stole one of them. After that began the real job of knocking it all into a complete story, which took months of work.

Story-writing is like solving a great puzzle made up of dozens of elements. Think of Rubik's Cube. You twist the sides around to see if a given combination will work, then you twist it again, and again, until it comes out right. Along the way, you probably have to discard a few things as well, and that can be the hardest part.

Peter Lord, seen on the right animating his character Adam, planned the film by drawing up the main sequences in a series of rough sketches like those shown below. By shuffling these around, he was able to organise the film's structure, and also check whether he had captured the spirit of each individual sequence.

Creating a Storyboard for *Adam*

With only one location, two characters and no dialogue, *Adam* is a very simple film. Even so, storyboarding it was not easy. At the ideas stage, I had come up with a dozen or more situations that Adam would face - the effect of gravity, loneliness, a temper tantrum, etc. The job was then to put the sequences in the best order. so that the story unfolded in the right way to an audience. I drew up each short sequence very swiftly and roughly - to capture the ideas in my head. Then, with hundreds of scratchy little drawings on separate sheets of paper, it was easy to shuffle them around to try out different ways of structuring the film. The storyboard drawings did not need to convey anything to anybody else about the look of the film. What they did convey to me was the spirit of each sequence, and also whether or not a gag was working.

So, along with body posture and facial expression, the most important thing the storyboard told me was the size and shape of the shot. Is loneliness conveyed better in a soulful close-up, or in a wide shot which shows that there is nobody and nothing else around? Or both? And in which order? It seems to me that such questions - half artistic and half practical - are the main business of storyboarding.

Nick Park and Steve Box plan the scene where Gromit hides in a cardboard box to spy on the Penguin, and carves out a viewing slot like a pair of binoculars. On the wall, the storyboard shows the view from inside the box and from the Penguin's vantage point.
Right: Character sketches by Nick Park.

Creating a Storyboard for *The Wrong Trousers*

The storyboard can be a very exciting stage, the place where a film starts to come to fruition after all the preliminary work. Usually, one drawn storyboard picture represents one event in a shot. Some shots may contain two or three events, and if so we represent them all. We prepare the storyboard piece by piece, or scene by scene, then pin the sections on the wall to see how they fit together. The act of drawing the frames really helps you to grasp the story and get it into your head.

PASTE
PAINT

Sc 65. Shot 3. INT. DINING ROOM. NIGHT.
GROMIT CROSSES PENGUINS TRACK,
PENGUIN ABOUT TO COLLIDE WITH TRAIN.

Sc 65. Shot 3 continued.
WALLACE TRIES TO GRAB PENGUIN...

Sc 65. Shot 3 continued.
...BUT PENGUIN TRUNDLES ON ENGINELESS.

Sc 65. Shot 4. INT. DINING ROOM. NIGHT.
WALLACE HAS GRABBED THE ENGINE
TRACKING SHOT.

Sc 65. Shot 5. INT. DINING ROOM. NIGHT.
GROMITS TRAIN CURVES AROUND TO COME UP PARALLEL TO PENGUINS TRACK.
GROMIT RUNS OUT OF TRACK AND DISCARDS THE BOX. TRACK WITH PENGUIN.

Sc 65. Shot 6. INT. DINING ROOM. NIGHT.
PENGUINS P.O.V. TROUSERS STEP ON HIS TRACK. (WE'RE HEADING FOR KITCHEN)
TRACKING SHOT.

Sc 65. Shot 7. INT. DINING ROOM. NIGHT.
PANICKED PENGUIN TRIES TO BRAKE AND WALLACE AND GROMIT OVERTAKE.
TRACKING SHOT.

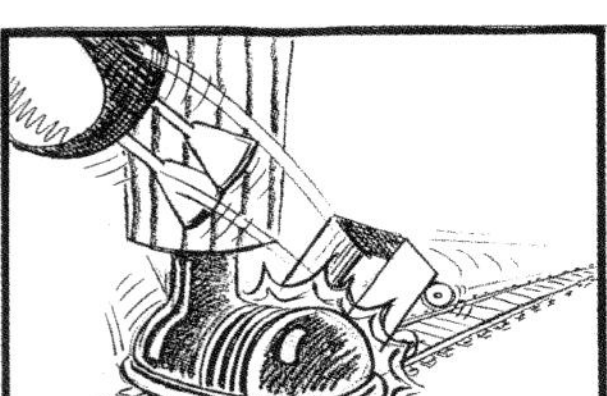
Sc 65. Shot 7. CONTINUED.
TROUSER FOOT COMES DOWN ON THE TRACK.
PENGUIN GOES FLYING.

Sc 66. Shot 1. INT. KITCHEN. NIGHT.
WALLACE REACHES UP TO GRAB PENGUIN.
TRACKING SHOT

Sc 66. Shot 2. INT. KITCHEN. NIGHT.
GROMIT ANTICIPATES A CATCH.
TRACKING SHOT.

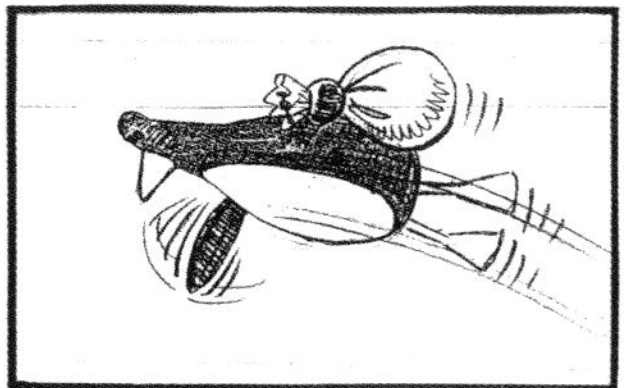
PENGUIN SAILS THROUGH THE AIR.
TRACKING SHOT.

Sc 66. Shot 4. INT. KITCHEN. NIGHT.
GROMIT SMASHES INTO KITCHEN UNIT CUPBOARDS.
TRACK THEN STOP.

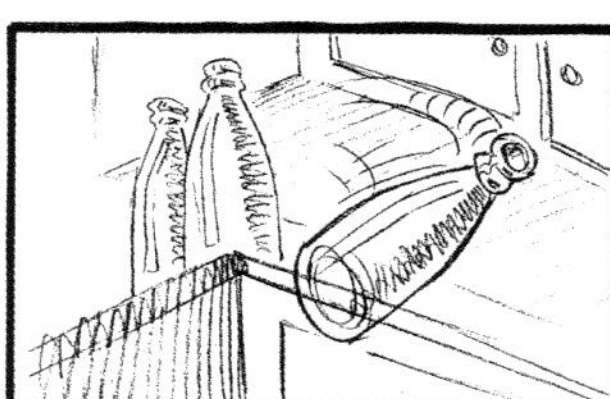
Sc 66. Shot 5. INT. KITCHEN. NIGHT.
THE CRASH CAUSES A BOTTLE TO TOPPLE OFF THE COUNTER.

Sc 66. Shot 6. INT. KITCHE. ... HT.
PENGUIN DESCENDS TRY TO FL... ? ONE WING.

Sc 66. Shot 7. INT. KITCHEN. NIGHT.
BOTTLE LANDS IN GROMIT LAP...

Sc 66. Shot 7 continued.
..PERFECTLY POSITIONED TO CATCH THE PENGUIN AND THE DIAMOND.
"ATTABOY GROMIT LAD!"

Sc 66. Shot 8. INT. KITCHEN. NIGHT.
WALLACE SLIDES INTO FRAME:
"WELL DONE! WE DID IT!"

Nick Park: 'This sequence in *The Wrong Trousers* was the first one we storyboarded. Even before we started writing the script, I storyboarded this whole sequence - and we stuck with it. Sometimes scenes change a lot, either when we shoot or in the cutting room, or they may be dropped entirely, but we managed to keep this one. It was edited down quite a lot, but the essence of the storyboard is still there.'

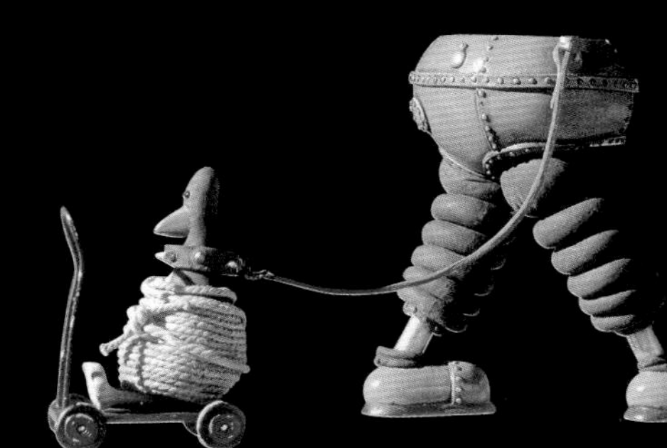

Creating a Storyboard for *A Close Shave*

Nick Park: 'We had less time to storyboard this film, so we tended to skip events and represent the shot in just one frame. I roughed out what we wanted and then Michael Salter, who was working with me, drew up the frames more elaborately. With most films we do the storyboard after the script has been written, so we already have a clear view of what we are going to do. The storyboard helps us to refine that view and put the words into a coherent visual form.'

The storyboard frames show Gromit flying in to attack Preston. In the completed version, right, he then opens fire with the porridge gun before Preston manages to get his paws on the propeller.

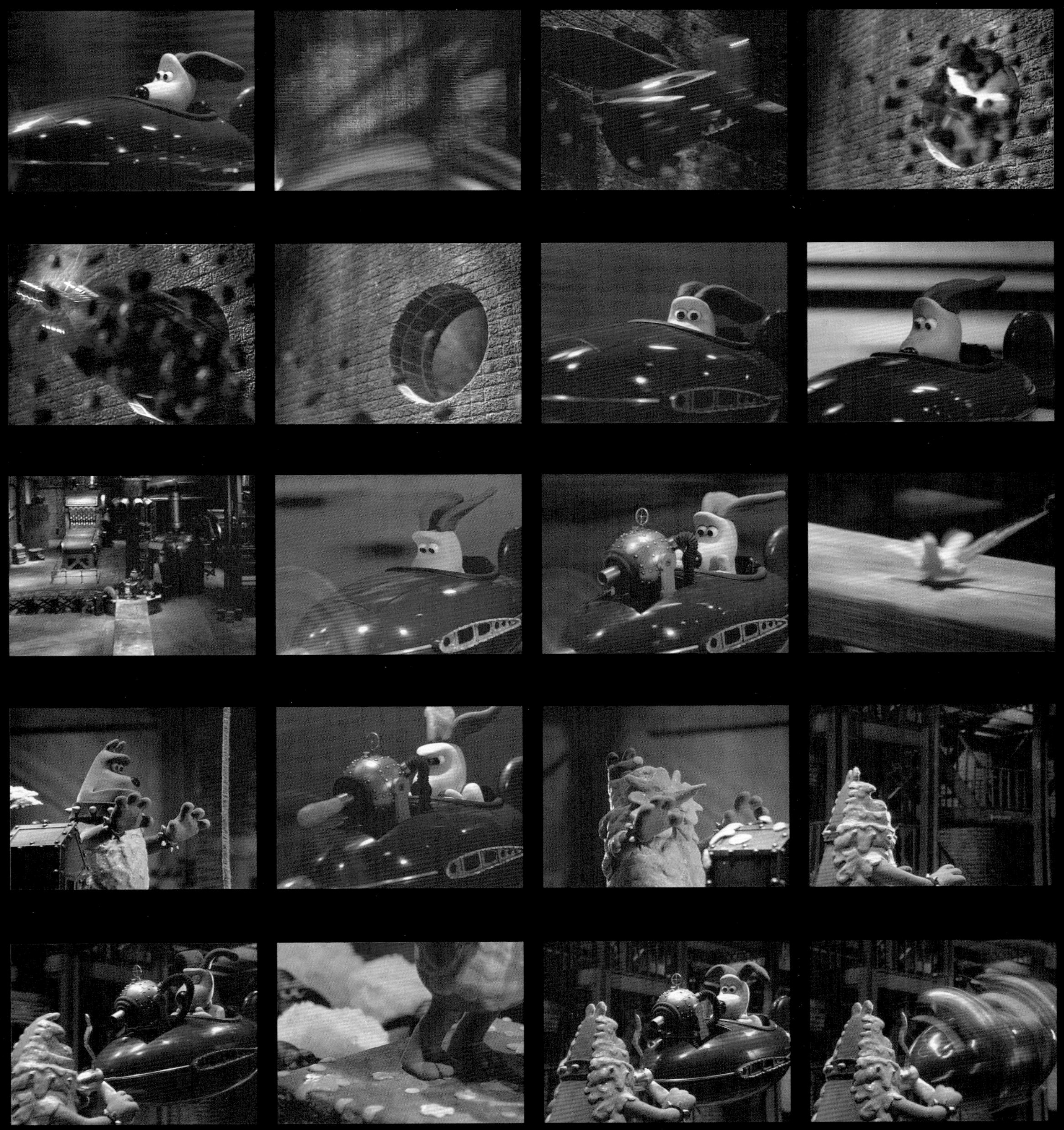

Opposite: Ginger in the escape tunnel, pulled along on a roller skate and clutching her digging equipment - a kitchen spoon.

Right: Rocky in 'flight'.

Below: Co-directors Nick Park and Peter Lord burst into fresh air from the tunnel, demonstrating the massive scale of the set, where the chicken huts were each as big as Wallace's entire house.

***Chicken Run* – the Challenge** Peter Lord

When faced with the prospect of making our first full-length feature film, we looked back at our past productions to calculate how long it would take, and what kind of crew we would need. The maths looked deceptively simple: a feature film is three times as long as our last thirty-minute short film, so we'd just multiply the time, the crew and the cost by three. Oh, and double it for safety. How far wrong could we be? Well the answer is: very. In longer-form films, every part of the process seems to grow exponentially, and provides you with huge problems of scale.

A Close Shave is thirty minutes long, and the total crew consisted of about thirty people, six of whom were animators. On *Chicken Run*, which is eighty minutes long, the number of animators grew to 34 and the crew to about two hundred. On that kind of scale, you can't just operate by common sense and instinct; you can't expect everyone on the crew to understand the bigger picture. You have to set up structures and systems to communicate your wishes to the whole team.

Nick and I both come from a background where basically you do everything yourself. When you start out in stop-frame, you're liable to be writer, director, animator, model-maker and caterer as well. As you gain experience, and take on bigger projects, you learn to delegate more of the processes, but instinctively you still feel the same way you always did. You still believe you can do everything yourself. The trick is to find a system that gives you all the control you need, without burying you under a mountain of work and drudgery.

We started with a terrific germ of an idea: we'd do a prisoner-of-war escape film - with chickens. We were happy to create the story by ourselves, but knew we would need a writer to dramatise it and write the screenplay. Nick and I spent a whole year kicking the idea around, shaping and re-shaping the story. I found it was helpful to map the plot out by pinning cards to a wall. It allows you to play with ideas and the ordering of events, and it keeps the whole story graphically in front of you. Otherwise you can easily end up with a muddled soup of ideas in your head.

It's surprising how few POW escape movies have been made, and we must have watched them all in our search for inspiration. In addition I'd been a big fan, as a schoolboy, of thrilling escape yarns like *The Colditz Story* and *The Wooden Horse*, so we quickly worked out what ingredients we wanted in our film. We decided we must have a tunnel escape at some stage; the good guard and the bad guard; a strong prisoner and a weak one, and a grumpy one; watchtowers, searchlights and dogs, of course. We were also influenced by *Stalag 17*, an American film with William Holden, in which there's a traitor in the camp. We loved that idea, and for ages we tried to incorporate into our story a crooked chicken who was selling the others out to the farmer – a sort of stool-pigeon chicken. We tried dozens of different ways of twisting and turning the plot to fit this in, until eventually, regretfully, we threw the whole idea out.

In our early attempts, the film used to open with the chickens not in captivity, but living happily on an idyllic, free-range farm. Following a comic catastrophe, they all got arrested and sent to Tweedy's Farm for punishment. We also had a huge, elaborate escape at the end involving farm equipment and a cannon, which we reluctantly abandoned. Between them, these ideas would have doubled the length of the film.

Of all the ideas that you take very seriously at the story stage, only about five per cent ever end up in the finished film. Not just jokes but whole setpieces and crucial characters are tried and then rejected. Even your central characters change and evolve. Rocky, in particular, went through all kinds of metamorphoses until he reached his final version. As a way of working, I don't actually mind this, but it is very greedy of ideas.

Early on, we were writing down versions of the film that, conservatively, were three hours long – great rambling storylines which make what finally appeared on the screen seem almost minimalist. We were probably still at the three-hour stage when we called in our screenwriter, Karey Kirkpatrick, whose job it then was to tell us gently that we could not possibly film our present story in the time allotted, and to encourage us to cut things down and simplify.

Once Karey had delivered a first draft of the script we started storyboarding -

Assorted chickens with domestic implements and a chicken feeder - more miniature marvels from the Modelmaking department. On the right, Mr Tweedy upends Ginger, here destined for the pie machine. For this scene, the scale problem was solved by pairing a standard 12 in (30 cm) Mr Tweedy with a miniature Ginger.

which is really another form of writing, only this time the ideas are visual. When you create the storyboard, you begin to direct the film. The choices you make – where and when and why to cut, when to use a close-up and when to go wide, why to move the camera – are all directorial decisions. It's also quite cheap to make those choices at this stage, working with just a pencil and paper, whereas it's very expensive to make them later. Nick and I storyboarded as much of the film as we could, then we had to take on other people to help us.

One thing that completely took me by surprise on *Chicken Run*, was how often the storyboarding was rethought and redone over the life of the movie. When you make a short film, and you do the storyboarding yourself, it's relatively easy to hold the whole film in your head. There's a good chance that a lot of your first storyboard will stay in the film. It's much more difficult to hold all of an eighty minute movie in your head. Of necessity, you divide the film up into shorter, manageable sequences. But there's a big danger lurking here, which we call Sequencitis. You refine and polish a short section of the film – perhaps three minutes long - but later you find you haven't paid due attention to how it fits in with the rest of the film. Because of Sequencitis, and because the story is continually evolving, you end up storyboarding the whole film many times over.

After storyboarding, we then make a story-reel, which at its simplest level is a filmed and assembled version of all the storyboard drawings. The idea is to make a 'sketch' of the whole film, partly to explain the film to other people and partly so that you understand it yourself! To make it readable you have to put in many more drawings than there are in the storyboard. If, for example, the point of the shot is to show someone opening a door, you need to draw the door first closed and then open. It's not animation, but it should give a clear impression of what is happening in each shot, and how long the shot is going to be. As well as the visuals, we add the dialogue using temporary voices. Various

Key animator Sergio Delfino animates Ginger and Rocky on one of the studio's thirty autonomous shooting units.

members of the studio staff stand in for the real actors - and some of them are surprisingly good. It brings out the inner thespian in all sorts of surprising people. We also put in a few key sound effects, and a temporary music-score.

Ultimately, you do all this so that when you start the shooting process you are as certain as you can be that you are filming exactly what you need. In the happy world of live action, it's a simple matter to film several big wide covering shots of each scene, and go in and shoot all the close-ups as well. Then, when you go into the editing room, you have a huge range of choices, maybe twenty minutes of film which you edit down to one minute. In animated films, however, we will have maybe one and a quarter minutes of film to edit down to one minute. Our filming process is very time-consuming, and this drives us not to waste anything, which is why we try to make all the story decisions before we shoot. To me this is one of the most difficult parts of animation, but without this system or discipline we would not be able to function properly.

Once the story-reel is complete, or as complete as we can make it, the actors record their parts and we finally get to the shoot. On *Chicken Run*, the challenges were endless. Our kind of animation is quite like a live performance in that you only get one go at it. You can shoot second and third takes of a shot, of course, but that may take a day, or days, and we don't have that kind of leeway in our schedules.

It's interesting to compare our way of animating with the CG process. Take the example of a single shot that lasts five seconds. In the CG world, an animator can block out the whole shot very roughly. First he creates key frames – the important poses he wants to hit within the shot. Then he can animate the whole shot roughly, and see how it's working out; perhaps the timing was wrong, perhaps the key-frame positions weren't exactly right. So the animator makes changes to any part of the shot – front, middle or end – and then animates again. And again. In this way the animator is constantly reviewing, refining and improving. In contrast, the stop-motion animator blocks a shot out roughly, by way of rehearsal – and may indeed shoot the whole shot quickly as a rehearsal, but for the final shot, the animator only has one go. He starts with the first frame of the shot and ploughs on to the end. And though you may have the clearest possible idea of what the end is going to be you simply can't be certain until you get there. It's real, it's spontaneous – each step is an

Above: Mrs Tweedy at her most menacing. For this shot, the puppet was placed on elevated rigging to make her loom over the assembled chickens she is leering at.

Above right: The ostrich stratagem. Chickens leg it for freedom under the dubious cover of a drinking trough.

experiment, and you can only check if it's right by going onwards. You can't go back. CG animation is all about refining and revising, whereas stop-frame animation is all about getting it perfect at the first attempt.

When *Chicken Run* was going full-pelt, we had thirty different 'units' in the studio at the same time, each working on a different shot of the film. On a typical day, ten units would be in preparation - the cameras were being set up, the models being adjusted and so on. But the other twenty units were shooting. Each set was a small self-contained studio with an animator, a camera, set, puppets and a full lighting rig. Nick and I divided the film up, and each of us was responsible for directing on fifteen units every day. We had to check the lighting, the camera move, the timing and above all the performance; and to make sure that when the film was finally completed people would not be aware that it was shot on so many different units by thirty different animators. Compare that with a live-action film where there's basically only one unit shooting at any one time. There may be a second unit filming landscapes or pick-ups somewhere else, but no more than that.

To make it even more difficult, on any given day there might be fifteen different animators all animating Ginger, the one character, and trying to make it look like one performance. Imagine a feature film with fifteen look-alike actors all playing the same role. Meanwhile, Nick and I were running round the studio like lunatics (highly disciplined lunatics) and on each set we had perhaps fifteen minutes to say our piece and then rush on to the next one. It was a mammoth operation, and extremely tiring as well. This is what I meant originally about the challenges being exponential. The bigger the film, the more there is to charge round and control. That is why it was so essential for each unit to have similar, interchangeable equipment such as the light-tight cameras which Tom Barnes describes in the next section.

Our largest set was a wide view of the whole farmyard with the Yorkshire Dales beyond. One particular scene shows Mrs. Tweedy inspecting the chickens

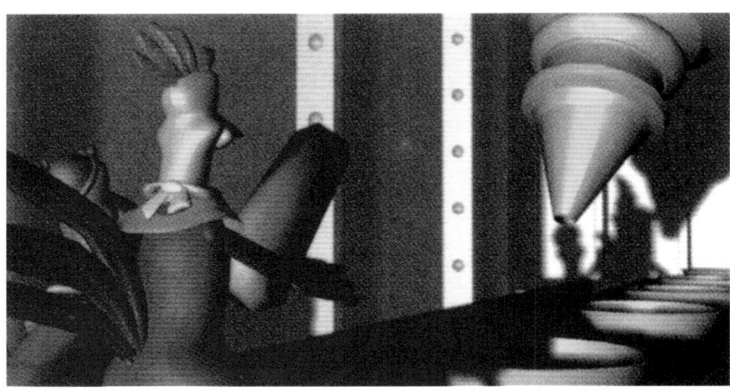

in the early morning. A huge light, representing the rising sun, was placed as far away from the set as we could get it, the idea being ideally to light the whole set with one enormous light-source. The sky itself was a gigantic painting some forty feet (12 m) wide and twenty feet (6 m) high. All the chickens were lined up standing at attention (though incidentally it's very rare in real poultry-farming to hold a roll-call for chickens). In the animation, Mrs Tweedy marches along, then turns to say something to the chickens. On her turn we cut to a close-up of her. That close-up might be shot three months later on a very small

Storyboard version and corresponding CGI visualisation frames of Ginger and Rocky trapped on the conveyor leading to the maw of the pie machine.

Ginger and Rocky on the belt of Doom. The pie machine, a descendant of the Mutton-O-Matic in *A Close Shave*, was based on the sleek, shiny industrial designs of the post-war period.

set, with a different sky, and a different light representing the sun. So everything is different, and it's the job of the DoP to make sure the audience don't think the two shots were filmed three months apart. And it's the job of the animator to pick up the exact speed of Mrs Tweedy's turn – the turn of the head and the shoulders – so that it all looks seamless.

Where you've filmed the wide shot first, that becomes a 'master shot' that sets the look for the entire scene. Sometimes, annoyingly, you are forced to shoot the close-up detail before the wide shot. Then you find yourself in the ridiculous position of establishing the look for a whole scene through a quick close-up shot. It's much more difficult to match a wide shot to the detail than the other way around.

Despite our best-laid plans we didn't finish the storyboard, or the story-reel, before we started on the shoot. In the mornings we'd direct the scenes that were being shot on the studio floor, and in the afternoons we'd have to work on the story-reel, which was constantly evolving as we shot. In an ideal world, you'd complete the storyboard and the story-reel, and only then would you start shooting the film. But in reality, these processes were always overlapping.

Right: Key animator Suzy Fagan working on a scene in which only Mr Tweedy's legs and boots appear. This is the large 3 ft (90 cm) version of Tweedy, awful to animate but OK for more static shots.

Far right: Working with the standard 12 in (30 cm) Mr Tweedy.

We were still working on storyboards and the story-reel when the film had only three months left to run.

We were still recording the actors voices as well, much to their amazement. An actor might imagine that once the big up-front recording session is over, their work is done. They'd be amazed to be asked back eighteen months later to re-record a scene which didn't seem to have changed substantially. They'd say 'But didn't we do this a year ago?' and we'd say, 'Yes, we did, and we're going to do it again'. Over months the scene gradually evolves and requires slightly different dialogue to make it perfect.

Another thing we learnt about shooting a feature film is that the number of puppets you need is massive. A star like Ginger will appear on pretty well every set, so you need thirty separate versions of her and maybe twenty versions of Rocky. That's something you can plan for, but there was also a huge cast of background chickens. A prison camp, or a chicken coop for that matter, is a crowded place. There would naturally be a lot of 'extras' in many scenes. Somehow, you always needed ten chickens in the background. That was OK; Nick and I liked having lots of chickens around. Sometimes, however, I'd get to the set and say, 'So where's my crowd of chickens?' And be told 'There's no chickens left. Nick's got them all.' So then, lacking whole chickens, you'd end up with heads on sticks, in the foreground or bobbing about in the extreme distance of a crowd shot. There were never enough chickens to go round

Then there was the scale problem. Ginger's puppet is very much the same classic size as Wallace, about ten inches (25 cm) high, which is comfortable to handle and animate. However, Wallace is meant to be a human being, so he is about one-sixth scale, but Ginger is a chicken so she's one-half scale. This means that the whole world around her has to be in half-scale too. The huts, for instance, had to be much bigger (and heavier) than our usual models; they were about five feet long (1.5 m) and two feet (60 cm) high – great hefty things the size of Wallace's whole house. Then we had to have human puppets interacting with the chickens. To be in scale, the human puppets would have to be about three feet (90 cm) tall, which is the animator's nightmare. We did make a Mr Tweedy that size, but it was awful trying to animate him and we soon gave up trying. We had to find another way, and in the end we decided to

Ginger's fears are echoed and magnified by a chorus of supporting chickens, part of a huge cast of 'extras' which ran into the hundreds.

operate on two different scales. The main Ginger puppet was 10 inches (25 cm) tall and Mr Tweedy was 12 inches (30 cm) tall, which on the face of it is ridiculous – you can't have chickens the same size as humans. So we had to build miniature chickens to go with the humans. These matched terribly well with the others, so well that I almost can't spot it myself.

There were also two classes of chickens, the ones that moved and the 'crowd chickens' that did not. For a big roll-call scene, where all the chickens were lined up, we had about three hundred miniature chickens, most of which couldn't move. This didn't matter much because it was a roll call and they were meant to be standing to attention. To make it realistic, we animated every tenth chicken, so they moved their heads round while the others stood stock-still. For special scenes we made big Tweedy hands to grab Ginger round the neck and big Tweedy boots to kick her into the gate. But those big models were terrible to use.

We got there in the end. After months and years of intensive work, by hundreds of highly talented people we finally got to the last shot, and the film was done, complete. One particular worry that remained was how our characters would look when magnified on cinema screens. After all, Ginger's head is only two and a half inches (6 cm) high, and if you take that and blow it up on a big screen in a big close-up, would it still look good? But I'm happy to say the puppets held up beautifully. If anything, we felt they looked rather too smooth and perfect so we plan to move back towards the handcrafted look in our current project, the new Wallace and Gromit movie.

Shooting *Chicken Run* – the Technical Side

Tom Barnes was the Technical Director on the film. Here he explains how Aardman geared themselves up to shoot their first-ever feature film.

'*Chicken Run* was the most ambitious project the company had taken on in terms of size, complexity and running time. None of us had ever done anything like it before, and although we had a good knowledge of animated film-making generally, we did not know what problems a feature film on that scale might bring. We just though it would be like *A Close Shave*, but harder.

'Towards the end of *A Close Shave* we were shooting simultaneously with about thirteen 35mm cameras. These were a mixed bag of old movie cameras from the 1930s onwards which had been converted and updated a little bit in America. Quite a lot of them had been used for studio-based TV shows. We also had a large assortment of lenses, no two of which were entirely similar. So, moving up to *Chicken Run,* we decided to make all the cameras completely consistent and interchangeable. We also wanted each camera to have through-the-lens video assist of the best quality we could afford in order to help the animators to shoot as efficiently as possible.

'The camera we chose was the old Mitchell BNC camera. These were were more light-tight than others we used, and we had them fitted with a reflex conversion designed and manufactured by Doug Fries in Los Angeles, giving us one single type of camera that would fulfil all the animation needs of the film. For each camera we built a geared head, which gave us motion-control pan and tilt moves of great accuracy and repeatability. By the time we got towards the end of filming, we were shooting on around thirty-four of these cameras.

'Because we were making a feature film, we had to set up our own projection and viewing room for looking at the day's rushes, and our own editorial department. We edited the film in the conventional way on AVIDs (digital editing machines). We had three AVIDs networked together so that several people could work on the film simultaneously. At times we increased that number, for instance when we had visiting film and music editors coming over from Dreamworks.

'For viewing rushes, we also cut the film conventionally on Steinbecks, which are flat-bed editing machines for reviewing and cutting film. This allowed us to run the previous day's picture with a 35mm sound track in sync. Both directors, Peter

A Fries converted 35mm Mitchell camera with pan and tilt head on a linear track. This allows camera moves similar to a live-action film in miniature.

Tom Barnes and Dave Alex Riddett (Director of Photography) with some of the cameras built for *Chicken Run*.

Lord and Nick Park, needed to see their rushes and review them with the animators as early as possible each morning so they could establish what progress had been made the day before, and plan for the day to come.

'We had two film prints back from the laboratory each morning. Logistically, this meant we had a cut-off time each night, when shooting had to finish. Our courier took the film rushes up to the Technicolor laboratories near Heathrow airport. The film had to arrive at Technicolor by 11 o'clock so that we could collect the rush prints at 6 o'clock the following morning and get them down to Bristol for about 8 o'clock. The film editors then took the two prints, made one of them up into a projection roll to project for technical approval of the shots, and broke the other one down into the shots that each of the directors had directed. They could then review these on film on an editing machine with the soundtracks running in sync with the shots. They checked the lip sync of the shots and the action simultaneously, and went through everything with the animators involved.

'This happened every single morning of the film. The day's plan was very much driven by the previous day's rushes. At that time we also reviewed all test results. We looked at lighting tests for motion-control moves, and at the basic block of character positions that the animator had carried out the previous day so the directors could approve the rough character positions through each shot.

'Looking back, I think I felt more pressure before the film started than once it was under way. Like other people doing preparatory work in different departments, I felt an enormous responsibility not to be the one person whose department was holding up the progress of the film. Once filming began, it became more a matter of troubleshooting, getting in more equipment, and dealing with whatever had to be mended.'

moustache
balanced on
on the
worked late.
newspaper
held
so many
scarcely

The Bookworms were created for the BBC's 'Big Read' series. They are CGI characters composited onto a live-action background.

Below: One of the award-winning Blobs created for BBC3 idents.

CGI Computer Generated Imagery

In the mid-1990s, Aardman began experimenting on a small scale with animated films made entirely using computers. This was at a time when computer-based work was becoming more commonplace within the special-effects industry and entirely digital films such as Disney/Pixar's innovative *Toy Story* (1995) were breaking the mould of how animated films were being made. The process of making a computer generated film is quite different from clay or stop-motion animation, but the animation skills needed are very much the same.

Today, Aardman has a thriving CGI Department producing a prolific range of commercials, short films, broadcast films, trailers and experimental work. Two of its members, Scott Pleydell-Pearce (Animation Lead) and Bobby Proctor (Lighting, Modeling and Rendering Lead), explain what CGI is and the process involved in making films on computer.

'CGI stands for Computer Generated Imagery. We use 3-D software which allows us to do every process of animation, from modeling, rigging skeletons, animating, texturing, lighting, rendering and post production.

'Some of these terms are common to conventional clay animation techniques, but for us they may describe very different procedures arising from the way we work. Take the models, for example. With CGI there are no solid models or props to help us. We have to build everything you see on screen, from scratch, in the computer. Computer generated models are made up of surfaces - where the computer creates geometry between a series of curved lines, or polygons - where the model is constructed from a series of intricately placed triangular shapes. The approach taken when modeling characters or props depends on the complexity of the design and the function of the model. Often we create the geometry starting with simple forms, such as spheres or cubes, which are then manipulated using 3D tools to create the desired shape. This process is often like digitally sculpting clay.

Once the models are built, they go through a process where texture is added. This involves adding material properties to the models to make them appear realistic, or at least believable. For example, a character's head may be given a material to give it a skin-like appearance, and clothing may be textured to look like it is made of cloth. Essentially, everything that is modeled digitally has to be taken through the texturing process to convince the audience they are looking at a genuine object, and not a computer-generated one.

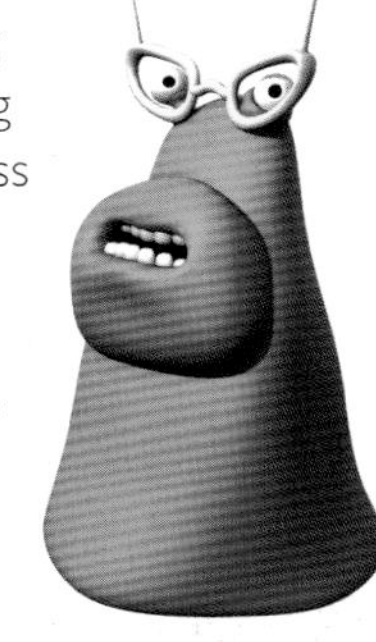

'With computer animation, you don't have to shoot the whole image in one go, as you do on camera, you can separate it into elements or layers. You may have a background or environment pass for example, and shoot the character or characters as a separate element. We can even separate characters from their shadows and have these elements in layers to give us finer image control during the post-production stage.

'One of the most important things about CGI is that it's like working in space. It's a void. There's no floor, no sky, no walls, no air. Every single thing that we want to be seen has to be created. If you want sunlight to filter through a room and show dust particles in the air, you have to create those yourself. If you want to bend a character's arm, you have to make that work in the computer using points in space. There are no givens, like with a clay model or a real-world lighting setup.

'In a way, it's like dealing with stupid maths. It's a highly complex process but it's also stupid because of what the computer doesn't know. It doesn't know that if you put an object on a table, for instance, in reality it would stay there. In the computer's view, the object could move through the table. What we have to do is input our own knowledge of the way the physical world works to make these things correct in the digital world; the computer has no common sense.

'There have been a lot of technical advances in recent years. In lighting for example, we have software which allows objects to reflect light as they would in the real world. Things like this make it easier for us to produce better, more realistic lighting effects.

'We spend much of our time balancing the really clever technical aspects of trying to copy real-world physics with our traditional craft-based skills. Nearly everyone working in CGI at Aardman has a traditional artistic background. They have skills in 2-D drawing, sculpting, painting, graphic design and so on. We then use the computer as a tool, like a pencil or a paint brush, to express ourselves. There is a popular misconception that once we have somehow set up our computers, they and the software will make the film for us. While there are some things that the computer will do automatically, this is definitely not the way we work. If we don't control everything very carefully, the results will look artificial and awful. It takes a great deal of work and creative input to make something look really good. To do the job well, we need not just our CGI skills but also all the knowledge we have of traditional animation, and how to cope with all the problems of motion, weight and dynamics.

'The software we use is sufficiently complex to produce the full Hollywood range of amazing special effects. But at Aardman we are more interested in character animation and storytelling, whether it's done with clay or CGI. We use whatever tools and mediums are required to allow us to create charming, believable characters and humorous, enjoyable films for a wide audience.

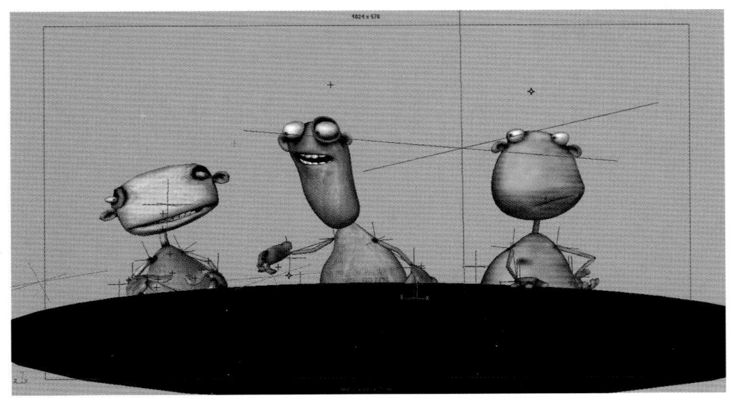

Images from 'The Deadline' episode of *The Presentators*. The first picture shows how the characters look while they are being animated, the second shows the final image once the characters have been lit and rendered. These characters have appeared on the Nickelodeon channel.

The Process

'For commercials, we are supplied with a script by the advertising agency. These can vary between the very prescriptive, which we have to follow closely, and the pretty vague, which allow us plenty of scope for adding our own input. We look at it and decide if the job is feasible and we have time to do it. If we want to go ahead, we may have to produce a Test, which shows how our treatment will work. This can be just a still or a small animation piece.

'Once we have got the job, we go on to produce a storyboard and draw up character designs. A director is appointed, who writes a treatment, which is his view of how the commercial should look. If it's a very experimental kind of job, we may have an R&D (Research and Development) phase to test out the approach and see how we can make it work.

'Next comes the build stage. Models are sculpted, and rigs and skeletons are placed inside the characters so they can be animated. To do this, we sculpt a character out of our 3-D mesh, and put the bones inside the skeleton, and then we attach the surface to the bones so that when, for example, the character bends an arm the surface moves with it. These skeletons are in fact the computer version of the armatures used inside clay models, the main difference being that we work in reverse, sculpting the hollow model first and then putting its bones inside it.

'Now we start animating the characters. In parallel with that, the characters are coloured and given their final appearance. Because ours is not a linear process, but more one of creating different layers, someone can be doing the animation while someone else, working on a separate machine, is texturing the character.

'Similarly, we do not have to do "straight-ahead" animation, like you do with stop-motion where you start with Frame 1, then you do Frame 2, then 3, and so on through the film. With 2-D drawn animation, you make key drawings every *x* number of frames, then you go back and make the in-between ones. With computer-generated animation, you can do a mixture of these processes, and also break the movement down into components of animation. For instance, if we are doing lip-sync, this can be done separately, whereas with stop-motion everything has to be done at the same time – when the lips

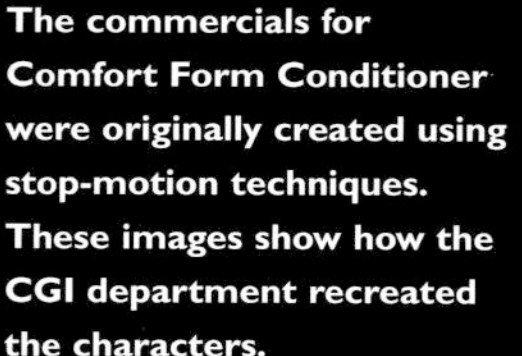

The commercials for Comfort Form Conditioner were originally created using stop-motion techniques. These images show how the CGI department recreated the characters.

1. Low resolution character

2. Wire frames showing construction

3. Animation approval grey model

4. Add bones and joints

5. The character posed to test bones and joints

6. Textures and lighting are added to give the finished look

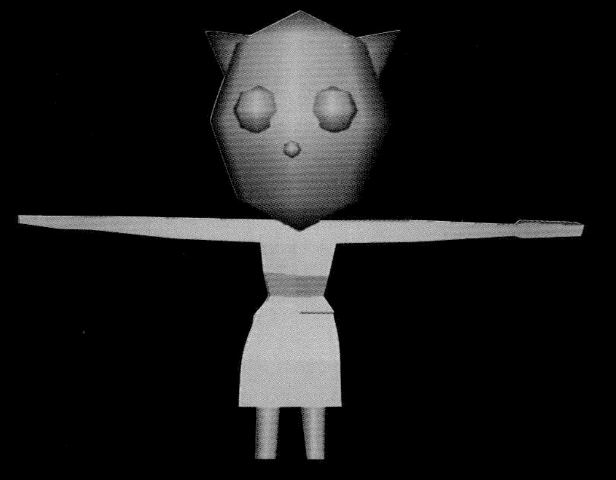

1

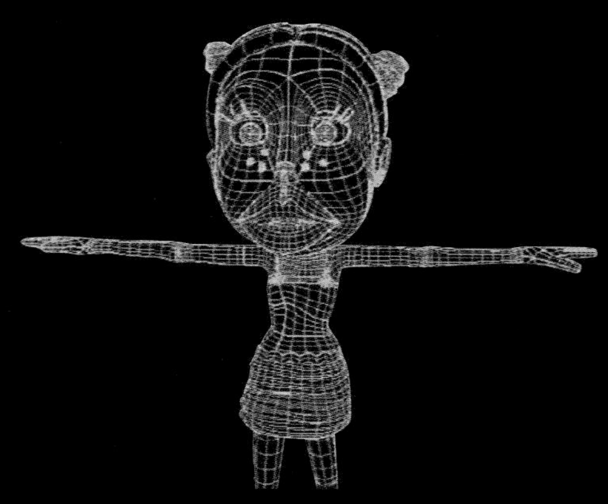

2

3

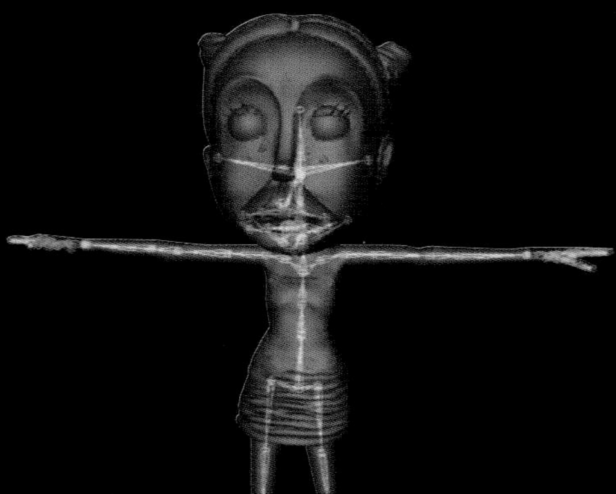

4

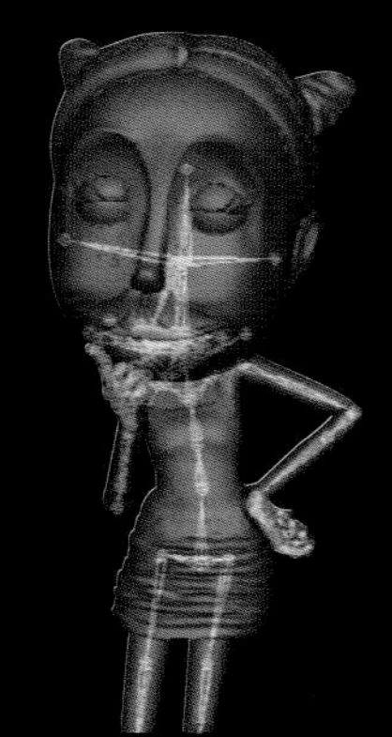

5

6

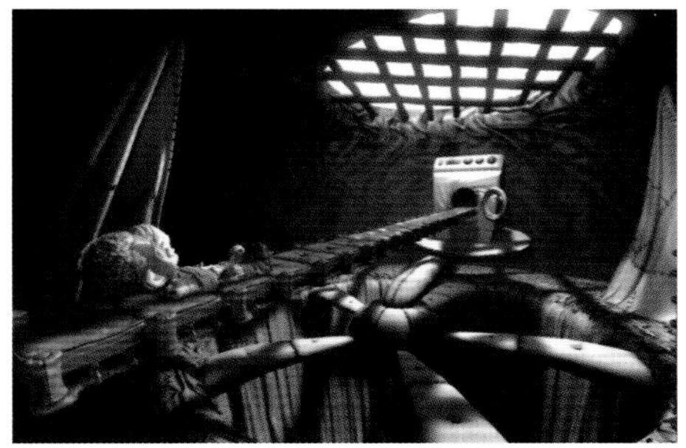

Storyboard and frame showing the finished character in action, about to be saved from 'getting all stretched and out of shape' in the commercial for Comfort Form Conditioner.

move, the eyes, hair, hands and whatever else have to move at the same time. Although we don't have to break the process down, it can sometimes be liberating, giving us more scope to experiment with the way we animate the characters. As ever, we are still bound to create our films in complete frames, which are screened at the standard rate of 25 frames per second, so every frame has to end up working perfectly by itself and in smooth conjunction with those around it.

'We usually leave the lighting stage until the animation is complete. This is because lighting works very differently in CGI. If, for example, using conventional animation, you shine a light at this table, it will reflect off the table because the surface is shiny. But, again, the computer doesn't know that, so you have to create the effect yourself, as you do all the shadows and other effects, giving the lights different temperatures and colours, and so on.

'People often ask if CGI is quicker than stop-motion. Sometimes we are ahead, and sometimes we are behind, but usually it takes the same amount of time. In our case, what really counts is the amount of experience we can build up, so that we know in advance how a certain texture will react to light, for example, and don't need to experiment to find a good solution. This is also true of stop-motion, of course, but a CGI animator will probably save more time as he becomes more experienced because the whole process is so complex. What we never say, however, is that CGI is better than stop-motion, or vice-versa. They are simply different ways of achieving the same end.

Top: The squash hits the water and swirls downwards, before it morphs into the dancers

Below: On-screen montage of visual concepts for the Robinson's commercial and (right) character design sheet for the dancers.

Robinson's Commercial

'One of the commercials we are developing at the moment is for Robinson's Squash. This is technically very challenging and we were very glad we could have some R&D time to work out how to do it. To explain the problem: as the commercial begins, you are looking inside a big jug of water. Then someone pours squash into it. This volume of squash then swirls and bubbles about and turns into a character, which turns into other characters as the squash spreads through the jug. Everything had to look like realistic squash in water, and move accordingly while being choreographed to music.

'The scenario presented us with all kinds of unknowns, not least of which was how to create and animate a character that looked as if was made of 100% fluid, and was in fluid at the same time, which meant that, with everything blending into everything else, there were none of the usual contacts or surfaces. It was very strange, creating this combination of something apparently amorphous which would then morph into recognisable shapes. Someone said it was like trying to sculpt smoke with fans.

'To our knowledge, this had not been done before, so we had no earlier models to study and learn from. Another problem was the lighting. At first we thought the squash and the characters would look shiny because when you look at liquids in a glass or a jug they reflect light. We did some tests in the studio, putting powder paint and all sorts of coloured media into water. We then found that these liquids were actually very flat. There were tones in there, but no shininess at all because things underwater do not reflect light. So, it was

Detailed storyboard showing how the dance evolves.

22. they both lean out, arms connected and stretched

23. they both snap back together....

24. ....with a splat !!!

25. The splat comes apart,

26. .....and forms into two seperate dancers,

27. As they dance to the music, the figure on the right stretches up and over the other guy who in turn

28.

29. the dancers return to a more equal size

30.. the two dancers lunge at each other....

31. ...and going into a whirlwind.

32. the camera pulls out to reveal that the spin was inside the fat guys belly.

33. he settles, does a few moves...

34. ...and then lunges backwards....

35. ...making his way into the distance..

36. like a fast, liquid slinky.

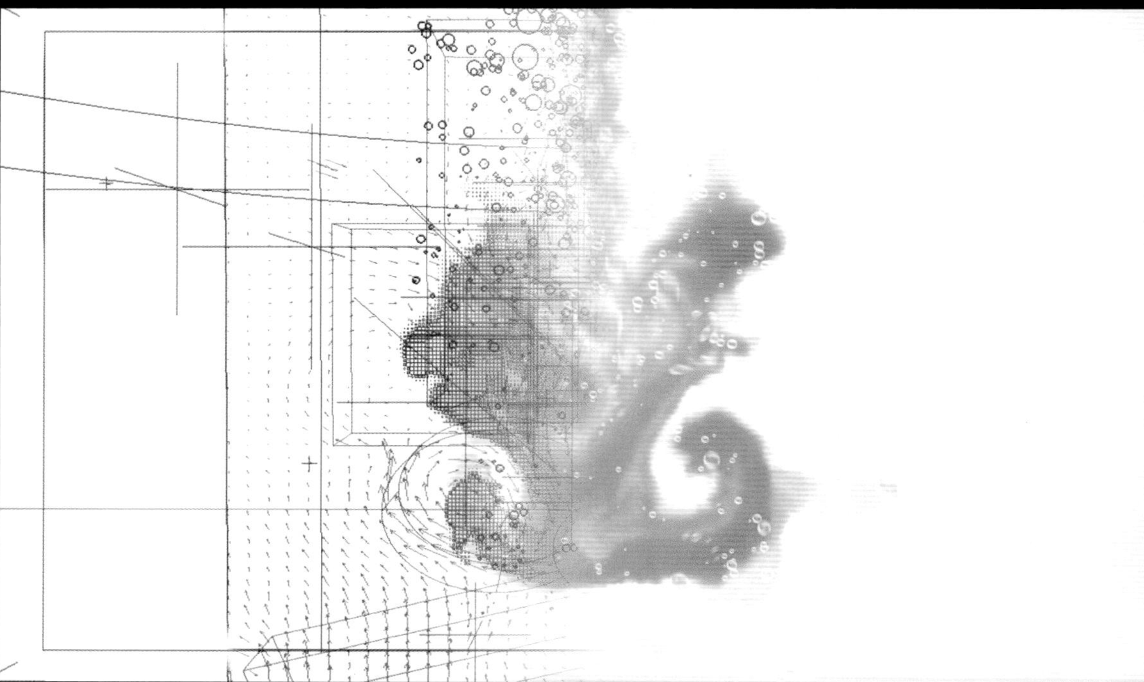

The Robinson's crew tested and filmed real fluid movement, which helped to inform the design process and final look of the commercial. These stills show the complex procedures behind creating the 'squash' look.

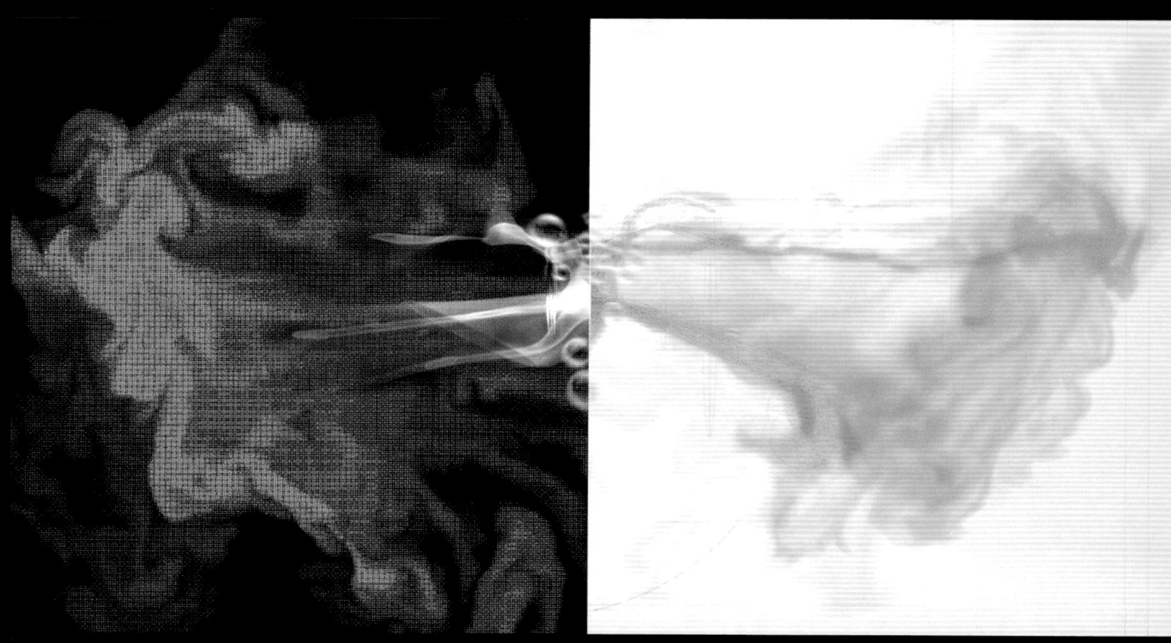

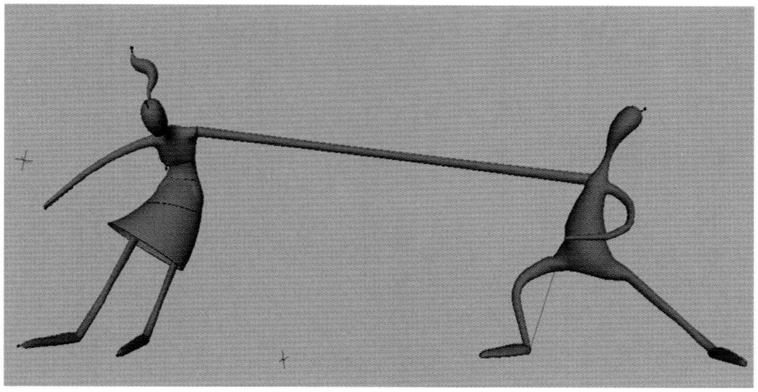

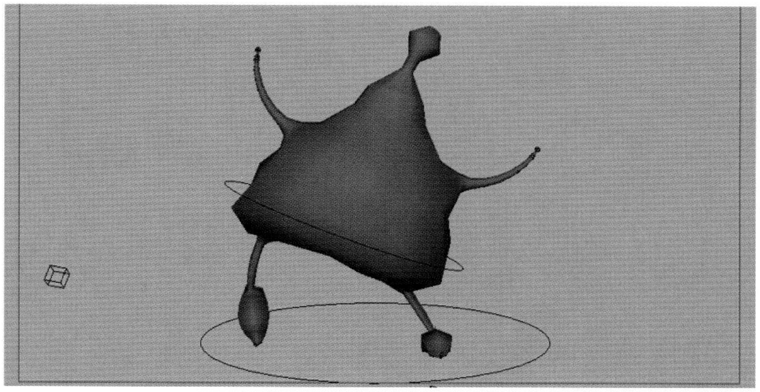

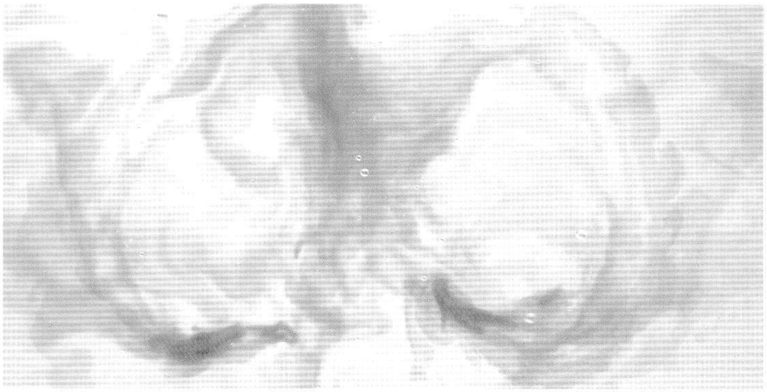

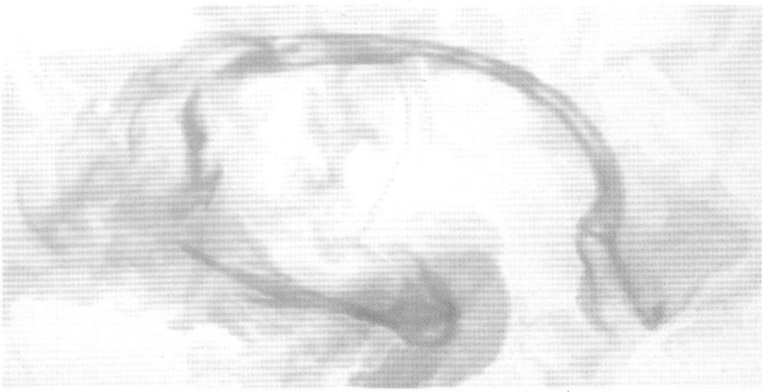

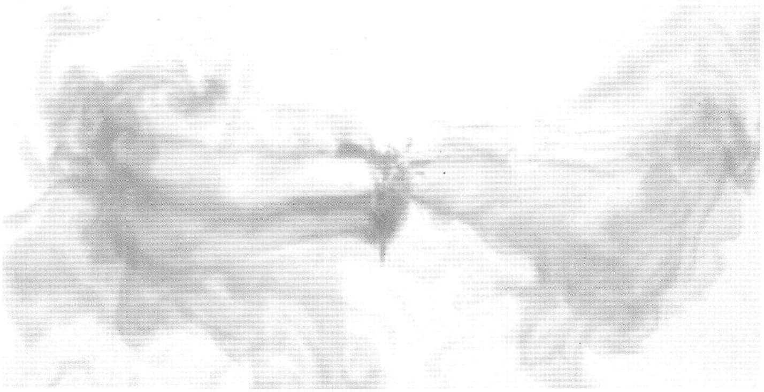

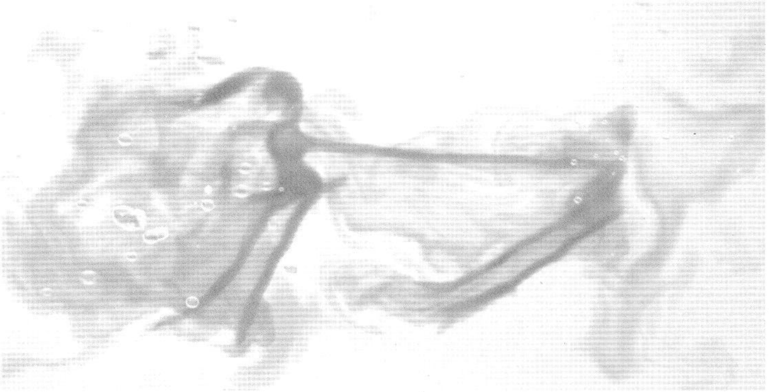

The character animation was created from a combination of multiple layers of diffuse squash, derived from density maps, and dynamic forces.

all much flatter than we thought, and we had to go through a huge experimental process to establish a look for the product and the film.

'For us, this commercial is a nice mix of a very technical job which also has a lot of charm and humour to it. It also has that essential Wow factor, which the advertising agency always wanted us to go for. They wanted people to watch it and wonder, "How on earth did they do that?"'

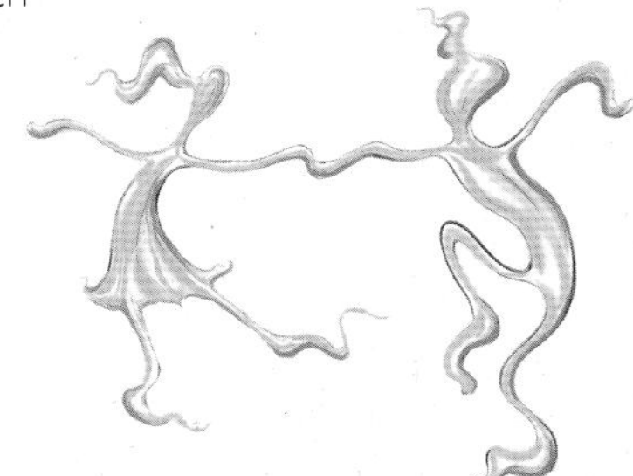

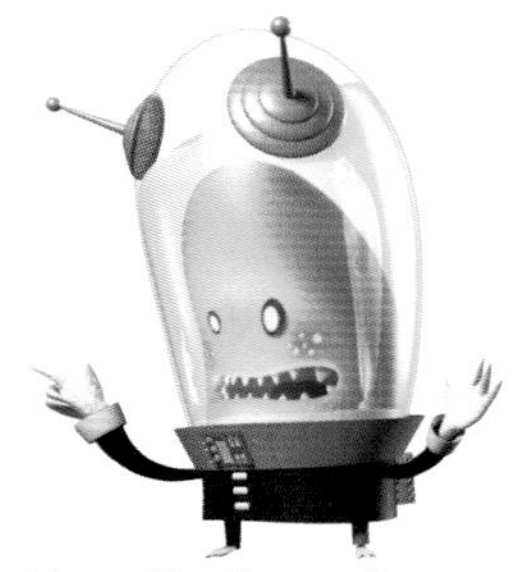

Chop Socky Chooks characters. Clockwise from top: Dr Wasabi, Bubba, Chuckie Chan, and a Ninja Chimp.

Chop Socky Chooks

'Chop Socky Chooks' or 'Kick-ass Chickens in Kung Fu Capers', as a current sub-title proclaims, is a new comedy/action series based on the old-style all-action Kung Fu movies. Aimed at boys around eight to ten years old, it was created by Sergio Delfino, who moved to the CGI department after working as a stop-frame animator on *A Close Shave* and *Chicken Run*. Here he explains how the series began:

'The show is designed around three superhero Kung Fu chickens: the spiritual Chuckie Chan, the streetwise KO Joe and the enigmatic *femme fatale* Chick P. They are a force for good and use their martial arts to fight the evil Dr Wasabi, a psychotic mutated piranha, with maniacal plans for world domination

'The idea came out of me whingeing to another animator about how laborious the lip-sync sculpting was on *Chicken Run*. I joked it would have been easier if we'd done it as a badly dubbed film, like one of those old Kung-Fu movies. "Yeah, it should've been *Kung Fu Chickens* ... or ... *Chop Socky Chooks*!" After two years on the feature I never wanted to animate another "chook" in my life, but the idea stuck, so like it or not I'm still working with chickens!

'The conception of the series coincided with my move to Aardman's CGI department. As I began to learn Maya – a computer animation programme – I realised how flexible and versatile CG animation could be, enabling you to move the camera around freely and have characters leap around without any complicated rigging.

' "Chop Socky Chooks" was largely inspired by the Kung Fu movies I used to watch as a kid. But I'm also a big fan of today's action films that utilise CGI to achieve complex camera work, spectacular fight

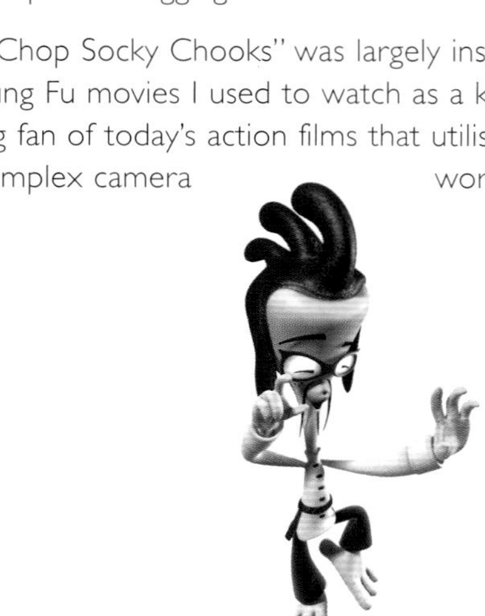

Inspired by Kung Fu movies, the style of Chop Socky Chooks draws on the latest CG technology and hi-tech designs. Below: KO Joe and Chick P.

sequences and stunning special effects. It's this kind of dynamic action that I had in mind for the series, and I realised that CGI was the way to do it.

'Before it moved into CGI, the initial design work was done in 2-D. Designer Danny Capozzi worked in Illustrator to develop the look of the characters and establish the visual style of the whole show. At the same time we were developing scripts. Initially, we recruited a British writer who established a lot of the ideas and worked up the comedy side of the characters. Later an American writer came on board, and he concentrated on the action element; between the two of them I think we found a great balance between action and comedy.

'It was difficult at first handing over your ideas to another person: inevitably a writer has his own take on it and things start to change. I had to learn not to be too precious, and appreciate that the collaboration was improving the show all the time.

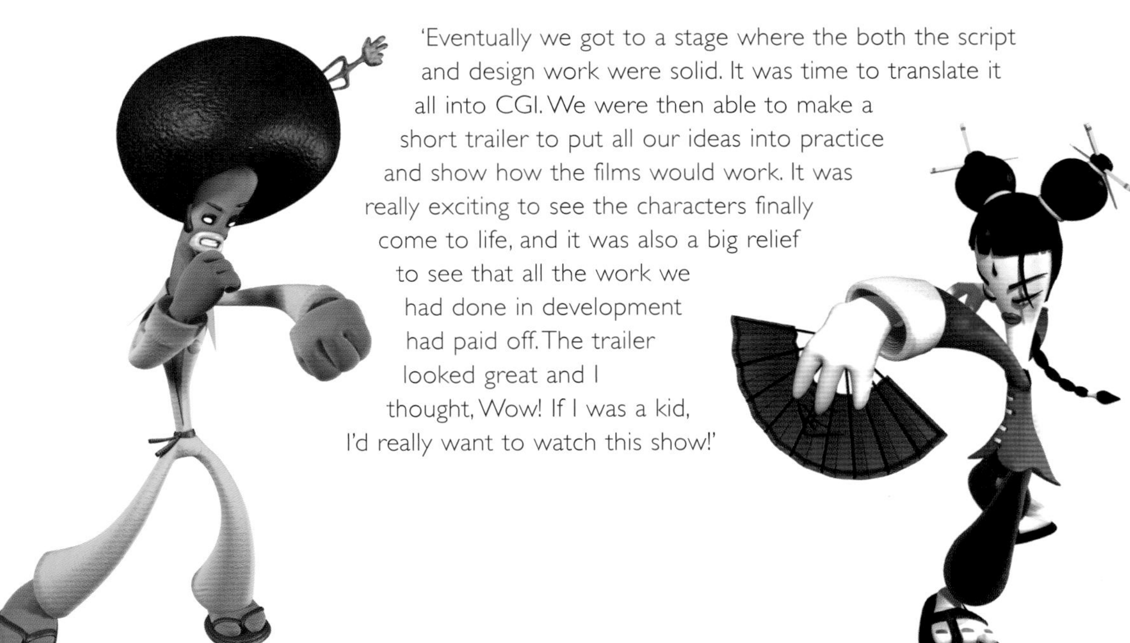

'Eventually we got to a stage where the both the script and design work were solid. It was time to translate it all into CGI. We were then able to make a short trailer to put all our ideas into practice and show how the films would work. It was really exciting to see the characters finally come to life, and it was also a big relief to see that all the work we had done in development had paid off. The trailer looked great and I thought, Wow! If I was a kid, I'd really want to watch this show!'

Tom Parkinson's Big Jeff character, created by Flash Animation, surrounded by his mates. Big Jeff's adventures were first released in 2004.

Using Flash Animation - Big Jeff

'Big Jeff is an Australian nudist. He's a beer-swilling, environmental freedom fighter, and a surrealist. In his world, anything is possible. Things can get pretty rude but Jeff's realm is very colourful and, I hope, funny as well.' This is Tom Parkinson's description of his genial Australian character, a 2-D animation hero with his own increasingly popular website, www.bigjeff.tv.

'It all started with a sketch of a nude guy on rollerskates leaping over a gang of midgets! I made him an Aussie because I wanted his world to be flawed but full of sunshine and optimism, just like an Australian soap opera. It also meant he could get away with swearing a lot and drinking massive quantities of beer.

'I use Flash Animation to do the "Big Jeff" stories. Flash is a 2-D animation tool

Images from 'Didgeridoo' and 'Nepal 1987'.

originally designed for the web. It is Vector-based, which means that the file size of the web-movie can be kept relatively low. I love the immediacy of Flash; I can draw straight into the computer using a Wacom tablet, a pen-and-tablet combination which is connected to the computer, and produce maybe ten seconds of animation in an hour, which is very fast compared to other methods. You can record voices straight in, add music to your film and edit it yourself. It is very hands-on, so you can direct your own work without anyone else needing to be involved.

The style is basic, but it has an urgency that I like, a sense that it could fall apart but somehow doesn't. Working at that speed, you can't produce highly crafted animation, but I think it makes up for that with a sense of organic vitality.

'If you push the software, you can get some really nice effects as well. I try to make the animation look as close to traditional 2-D cel animation as possible without generating massive file sizes. To do this, I use a mixture of drawing each frame separately (at 12 frames per second of animation) and a technique called 'tweening' which allows you to change an object's position, shape or colour automatically. I like my work to be as "non-slick" as possible, so I don't mind when the line quality fluctuates, giving it a "boil" or "rhubarb and custard" effect! This gives it more vibrancy and liveliness.

'Flash is an ideal method for someone starting out. It's cheap, all you need is a computer, and you can do it in your bedroom, as I did. I put together my first Showreel working at home in the evenings, animating with a Wacom pen in one hand and a microphone in the other. I did have a fine-art training, but no previous background in animation. I taught myself how to do that, or at least to animate in this particular style. I'm not really big on the technical merits of animation; if you've got an aesthetically exciting style and a good narrative, you can make great films. The slapped-together look is an important part of the "Big Jeff" series.'

Creating Angry Kid

The antics of the alarming boy anarchist won a cult following on the Internet before he moved to BBC3. Darren Walsh, his creator, describes how he developed the character and the unusual process they use to make the films:

Below: Line-up of masks worn by the actor who plays Angry Kid.

'Angry Kid started off as a joke voice I used to do about ten years ago to make my friends laugh. The voice is based on my brother, when he was a kid. He is three years older than me, and the character's look is based on him too, with his Seventies parka, chopper bike and so on. He didn't have red hair, but I thought I'd stick that on for good measure. He was horrible to me in those days, so it's all a revenge thing really.

'When we began, I was still learning to do lip-sync, so we did a test. We recorded the voice, made some masks for the actor to wear, and filmed this as a screen test. The idea was, you put a kid in front of a camera and for the first half minute or more he's having a good look at the camera – "What you lookin' at? You lookin' at me?" – but the real question was what he would do after that, when he had run out of things to say. In this case he attacks the camera and kicks it over. A simple enough storyline, but we thought we had captured something lively and interesting. Really, it was no more than an experiment, but it seemed to go down well when we showed it around, and gradually it built up a following at festivals.

'Then we thought, if we are going to make more "Angry Kid" films, we need to master the stupid little things he does – the sniffs, the snot, the awkward pauses, little bits of business like that. We don't know how old he is, somewhere betweeen eight and 13. It's difficult to decide, because sometimes he plays with toys and other times he really wants to be a grown-up. He's full of that angry innocence.

'When Atom Films came along and put "Angry Kid" on the Internet, the word must have spread quickly enough because by the end of the first year it had scored around ten million hits. Then BBC3 picked it up. They don't schedule it, they just put one on when they have a spare minute between programmes. This way, it's like he's infiltrating the airwaves – which is nice because they're not masterpieces, they're little snippets of "stuff".'

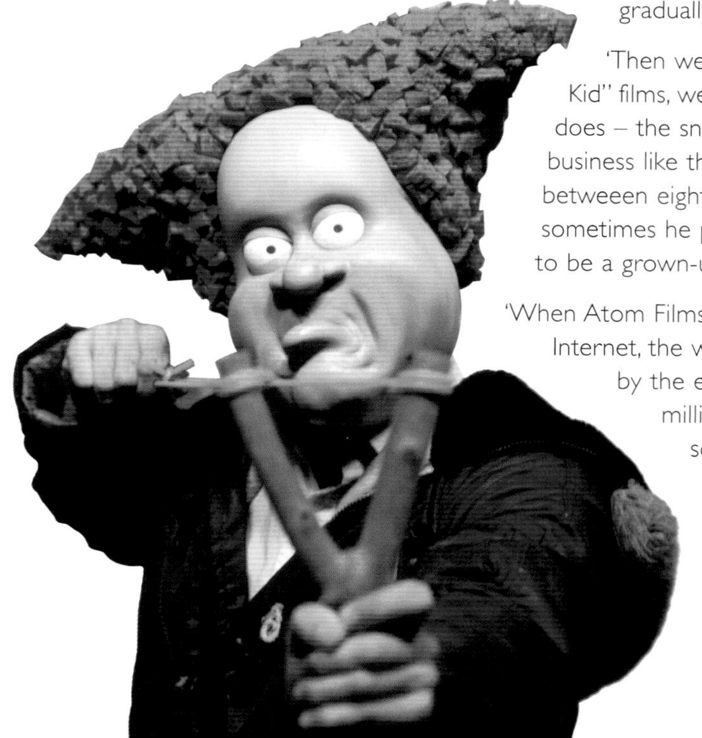

The 'Angry Kid' films are made by a combination of pixillation – animating a live actor – and replacement animation. The actor (Clayton Saunders) wears one of a series of masks to show the character's changing expressions (all the blinks, sniffs, twitches, smiles, etc, and all the vowel and consonant positions too). Each phase of a movement is shot (two frames), then he moves to the next position, maybe with a change of mask, and that is shot (two frames). It's a great strain on the actor because he can't see out through the mask and, along with the sensory deprivation, it gets very hot in there.

Above: Angry Kid, the boy who could ruin anyone's breakfast.

Right: Actor Clayton Saunders shaves his hands to make them look younger. Director Darren Walsh supplies the tea.

Far right: On the back seat of Dad's car, cut away to the basic elements the audience needs to see.

Characterisation - *Morph*

When Dave and I brought Morph into the BBC series 'Take Hart', he was not much more than a human-shaped blob. The challenge for us was to develop him into a fully-fledged character.

Back in 'Vision On' days, we had created a group of little clay characters, called the Gleebies, who ran round the tabletop and created havoc, knocking over paint pots and stuff like that. The producer liked them, and when he was preparing the 'Take Hart' series he asked us to create a new character who could interact with the artist Tony Hart, and who would apparently live in his studio. He also liked the fact that our plasticine characters could change shape. So we made a very simple terracotta-coloured figure who could instantly change back into a lump of plasticine. Because he could metamorphose, we called him Morph. The problem then was to find things for him to do.

Morph was a troublemaker from day one, and from that came his personality. He was disrespectful of authority, viz Tony Hart, and gradually, story by story, he acquired more and more characteristics. In each episode we set him a problem to solve, and the way he reacted to it gave him another dimension. We also decided to cut down on the amount he changed shape, because that did not interest us as much as his character.

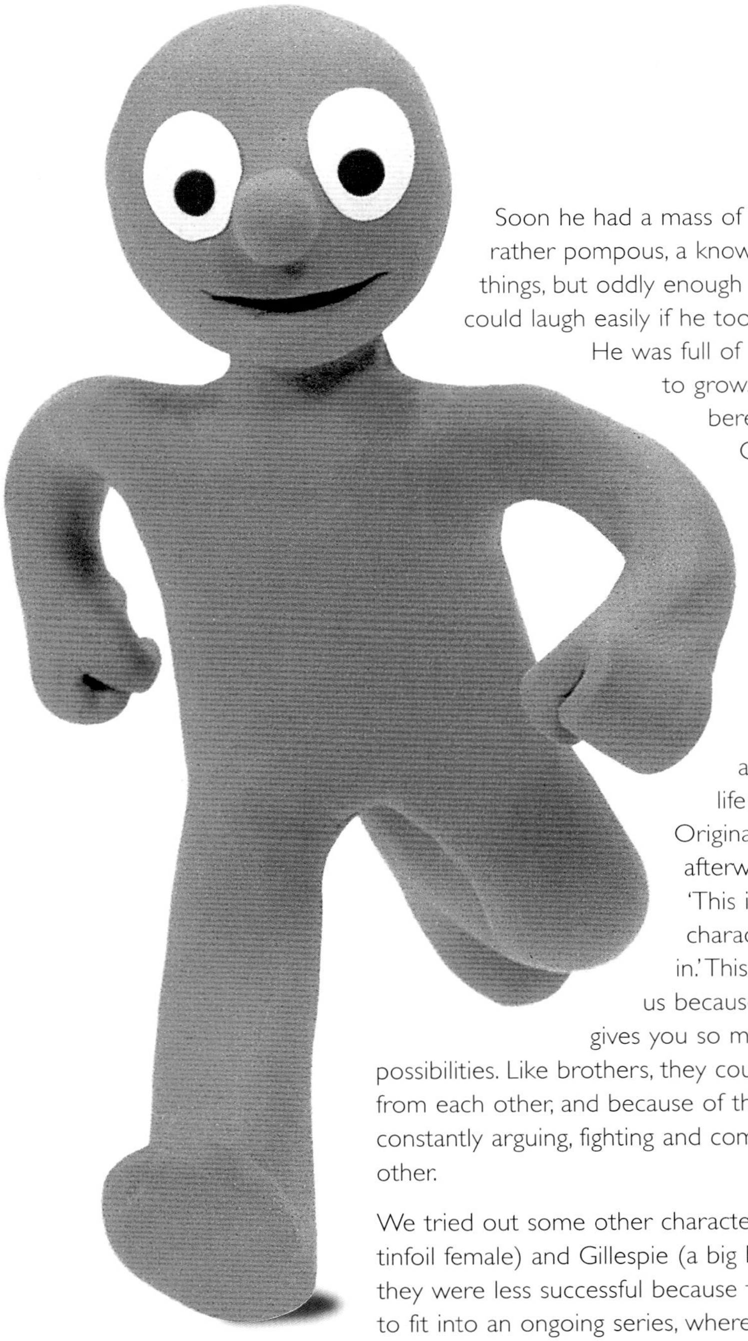

Soon he had a mass of distinctive traits: he was short-tempered, rather pompous, a know-all and a show-off - all rather negative things, but oddly enough they made him seem attractive. People could laugh easily if he took a prat-fall, but he was clearly not all bad. He was full of genuine enthusiasms, and these helped him to grow. For example, one day he appears wearing a beret and holding a palette and paint brush. Obviously he fancies himself as a great artist. He flings himself into his new role with huge energy. His paintings are pretty awful, but he strikes grand poses as if he is Van Gogh, and is insufferably pleased with his work.

Then Chas arrived, Morph's alter-ego. One day Morph is carving a statue of himself from some pale-coloured material. He chips away at the figure, which suddenly comes to life and immediately starts a fight with him. Originally this was just a story about a statue, then afterwards we thought, 'This is a good character, let's keep him in.' This was excellent for us because a double-act gives you so many more story possibilities. Like brothers, they could not get away from each other, and because of this they were constantly arguing, fighting and competing with each other.

We tried out some other characters too, like Folly (a tinfoil female) and Gillespie (a big blue figure), but they were less successful because they were *invented* to fit into an ongoing series, whereas Morph and Chas had the luxury to evolve through a much longer creative process. I'm sure it's made them much stronger as characters.

On these pages Morph displays some of his many characteristics. On the plus side, he is friendly and full of genuine enthusiasms. Less positively, he is pompous and definitely likes to get his own way, especially with Chas, the brother-figure he cannot stop arguing and fighting with.

Characterisation - *Creature Comforts*

The action takes place in a zoo where the animal characters - a Jaguar, a Gorilla, a Terrapin, three Polar Bears and others - talk about their lives and how they are treated. The film won director Nick Park his first Oscar. Here he discusses the characters and how he developed them.

The title frame of *Creature Comforts* shows a professional tape recorder. A voice says, 'Sound running. When you're ready'. This sets up the film as a series of interviews, and conveys to the viewer that the voices in the film are 'real'.

'The idea came from what Pete and Dave were doing on 'Conversation Pieces', using the voices of ordinary people on a pre-recorded soundtrack. Rather than get other people to do all the sound recording, I did half of it myself. Also, instead of eavesdropping on the subjects, we interviewed them. In my mind I had the zoo theme planned out, so in the interviews I tried to ask questions that would produce the kind of answers that animals might make. I found a Brazilian student living in Bristol, so I asked him not only what he thought about zoos but also about the weather, the food and student accommodation. He said a surprising amount of things which fitted perfectly. Asked about the food in his hall of residence, he said, " ... and food that look more like dog food than food proper for wild animals. All right?"

'He was so good that later I was able to let the soundtrack dictate to me what we should do when we filmed him as an animal. For some reason he kept mentioning double-glazing: "Here you have everything sorted out - double-glazing, your heating and everything, but you don't have *space*!" So I put a big glass window next to him to convey both the glazing and the fact that it helped to shut him in.

'Once we had recorded a voice, I tried to match it to a particular animal. People now say how well-suited the voices are to the animals, but in fact I changed things round a lot. At one point I thought the Brazilian could be a penguin rather than the Jaguar he became. My theory is that you can make anything fit anything. What is most important is how you do it.

'I found working with pre-recorded voices very refreshing. Although the format might seem rigid, and the filming process very straightforward, in fact it frees you up. Unlike a commercial, where you have to tell a complete story in thirty seconds, here you have time to let the voice give you ideas about how to animate and play with the character, all within the discipline of a static, held frame. To me this was liberating and very enjoyable to do.'

Each of the captive animals has a different view of what it is like to live in a zoo. Clockwise, from top left: The anxious but not unhappy Bush Baby - 'I know, whatever happens, they'll look after me'; Andrew the young Polar Bear, who takes a precociously global view of things; the Terrapins, reasonably comfortable but 'I can't actually get out and about'; the Armadillos, contented in a downtrodden sort of way; the young Hippopotamus who thinks that most of the cages are a bit small, and the philosophical Gorilla. Below: The spokesperson for the Birds, who reasons that animals in the zoo are better off than animals in the circus because 'they can do their own thing'.

DO NOT
CLIMB ON
THE WALL

A series of images showing 'Creature Comforts' characters at different stages of development, from first build to final shot.

New Creature Comforts

For some years after the success of the original *Creature Comforts*, Nick Park had wanted to go back and make more films with animals talking about their lives. When the opportunity came to go ahead, Nick was still heavily committed to feature film work and Richard Goleszowski took over as director of the new series. He describes how they developed the scenario further into a series of longer films, each taking a set theme such as 'The Circus', 'The Sea', 'Feeding Time' and so on.

'When we kicked off, we were not sure whether the talking animals would hold up well enough in a longer format. The original film was only five minutes long and now we were going to make a series of ten-minute films. But once we started to try it out, we realised that this need not be a problem. At first we were not thinking in terms of fully worked-out films. We had plenty of ideas, so we recorded lots of material very quickly on a range of different subjects and then decided which of these to use in the 13 episodes of the series.

'We used the established method of interviewing the kind of people who would talk and answer questions in a way that could be matched to a set of animal characters. For "The Circus", for example, we spoke to amateur actors, jugglers, street performers and so on. Although it very rarely happens, we found that the most successful characters start from a voice which sounds like a particular animal. The Posh Horse, for example, immediately came to mind once we had captured the voice on tape, giving us such wonderful lines as: "I think the standard of British food is first class ... somehow clean."

'This time we also introduced a computer-generated character: the Plankton. We wanted to get that look of a microscopic creature that you might see on Open University biology programmes. Because of the way these creatures are built, with tiny tentacles that wave about all the time as it bobs up and down in the water, it was much easier to achieve this effect on CGI than with Plasticine. We were very pleased with this character, and now we want to do an episode called "Micro World" which will feature a cast of germs, cells, plankton and other microscopic bodies.'

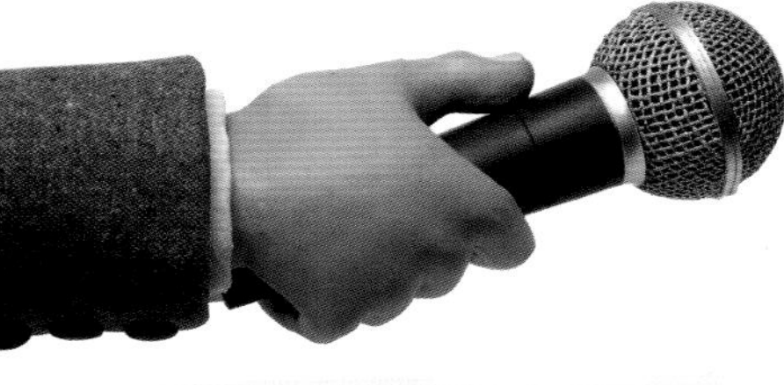

The public certainly enjoyed what they saw. When the new 'Creature Comforts' series went out on ITV, it was claiming audiences of up to 8 million. Naturally, a new series is on the way.

WAL I

Characterisation - Wallace and Gromit

Nick Park has won two Oscars and one nomination for his films featuring Wallace the inventor and Gromit, his dog. In chronological order they are *A Grand Day Out, The Wrong Trousers* and *A Close Shave*. Here, he describes how Wallace and Gromit came into being and how they have changed during the making of the three films.

'I sketched out my ideas for the characters way back in art school in Sheffield. I resurrected them at film school, and then I had this other idea about somebody - I did not know who - building a rocket in his basement and going to the Moon. I went back to the earlier characters to see if they could build the rocket. Gromit was then a cat, and I changed him into a dog. A dog would be chunkier and larger, and easier to work with in clay. I wrote a script, but this also changed a great deal once we started shooting. Some of the restrictions of working with clay started to dictate their characters.

'For example, Gromit originally had a voice, which we actually recorded. He was also going to leap about a lot and do tricks. At first I did not realise how difficult that would be to animate, but when we came to shoot the first scene I began to rethink the whole character. In this scene Wallace is sawing a door and Gromit is standing underneath acting as a trestle (see page 80). Because he was stuck under there, all I could move was his head, ears and eyebrows. So I did that, and then I saw I could get such a lot of character from just those little movements. This showed me that he did not need a stuck-on mouth as well, so we dropped the whole idea of Gromit speaking. It made a better contrast too, with Gromit now the quieter, more introverted character and Wallace the louder, more outgoing one.

Early sketches by Nick Park of Wallace and (a very different) Gromit.

'I find you can always make economy work for you, even if this is not at first apparent. For instance, it can be harder not to move something than it is to move it. Suppose you are shooting a character with a tail, and now it is eight hours since you last moved it. In film-time this may be only two seconds, but you can still get very impatient because you have not moved it. You have to watch this, otherwise your tail will be wiggling about the whole time and distracting the audience from the main character.

Wallace and Gromit - an unlikely but unbeatable combination. Wallace the loud one, the man in command, the eccentric inventor whose machines are never totally under control. Gromit, quiet, dependable, with much more sense than his master.

'As for the relationship between the two characters, this is still evolving. I am not one of those people who feels he has to know everything about his characters before shooting. People ask me questions like "What would Wallace buy Gromit for Christmas?" This is something I have never thought about, so I do not know the answer. I have not got there yet. I almost feel that they have their own life, so really I would have to ask them about it.'

Characterisation - War Story

An old man recounts his memories of the Second World War - under the bombs in Bristol, when the cupboard under the stairs doubled as a coalhouse and an air-raid shelter - 'I sits on the coal, then in comes 'er mother and sits on my lap, and my missus sits on 'er mother's lap. My missus was expecting a child at the moment, so I reckon I had about three of them on me. Humour and nostalgia were key notes in our treatment of the main character.

After 'Conversation Pieces', Channel 4 commissioned a similar series which we called 'Lip Synch'. We took the opportunity to try out new directors and new styles. In *War Story*, we abandoned the formula of recording conversations, and went instead for a recorded interview. We talked to Peter Lawrence of Radio Bristol, and he recommended this guy, Bill Perry, then probably in his seventies. Bill was a great raconteur, and Peter had interviewed him several times for radio. As usual, we decided not to meet him because we preferred to work in a state of innocence, so we asked Peter to do the interview, and he came back with two and a half hours of tape.

At the time I was quite tempted to do a serious piece, concentrating on the darker side of Bill's war memories. He had worked at the BAC aircraft factory

Images from the Home Front in the 1940s - a propeller aircraft at the BAC aircraft factory, Bristol, and the coalman emptying his sacks into the cupboard under the stairs.

on the outskirts of Bristol when it was bombed, and I thought I could make a faintly mournful, regretful film based on this side of his story. But, at about that time, I'd finished another film in the series, called *Going Equipped*. This was a serious piece about a petty criminal and the awful barren life he falls into. I liked the film, and still do, but simply because it did not have any laughs in it, people had been unsure how to react. This made me decide to go for a more light-hearted take on the material we had for *War Story*.

There was plenty of material to choose from, so we selected the bits we liked and tried to arrange them in a coherent order. One of the attractions was being able to mix scenes of the old man telling his stories in the present with others showing him acting them out as a younger man. The most difficult part was the ending. Bill had a lot of stories, but he never got to a really white-hot punchline with any of them. Fortunately, while describing the after-effects of sitting on a heap of coal with the other members of his family piled on top of him, he says, 'It was agony, Ivy, I was tattooed all over," which I believe is an old radio catch-phrase. Then I had him clamp his pipe firmly between his teeth with a loud "click", rather like Eric Morecambe used to do, waggle his eyebrows - and that was it. That was our ending. Not the world's best, perhaps, but it is quite a good example of how to bring your film to a pleasing end when the action or dialogue does not provide you with an obvious choice.

A happy ending - simply achieved with a click of National Health teeth on pipe, a grin and a quick waggle of the eyebrows.

Characterisation - Pib and Pog

This film is a highly knockabout version of a children's TV show. It features two bulbous characters, Pib and Pog, who do increasingly violent and nasty things to each other, and the slightly nannyish voice of the female presenter, who mostly pretends that everything is all right really. She is never seen. At the end, Pib and Pog are revealed as two old luvvie actors who probably perform these hooligan roles on a regular basis. The film was written and directed by Peter Peake, who describes his approach.

'I saw Pib and Pog as a couple of animated characters playing a part and giving the cameras what they want to see, which is a very stylised kind of Tom and Jerry violence. As characters they are equals, each as bad as the other. Neither is prepared to back down, which is reason enough for the violence to escalate all the time, starting with childish squabbling and finishing with a cannon which they point at each other in mounting panic before it blows up and blasts the pair of them off the stage.

'In a way, Pib and Pog inflict violence on each other like Laurel and Hardy used to do. One of them just stands there and waits while the other one plots a new trick, then comes up and smacks him. There is a dreadful inevitability about what is going to happen next. It is certainly going to be violent; the only question in the audience's mind is what form it will take. One of my problems, in portraying this kind of inevitable violence, was to keep the interest going. I tried to do this not only by making each assault nastier than the one before, but also by devising unexpected bits as well, like the bed of nails which Pog rapidly produces while Pib is still gleefully bouncing up in the air after his latest triumph. Next moment, he is impaled and helpless, and the initiative has passed back to Pog.

'Against this grim war of attrition you have the voice of the patronising presenter who is continually telling the imaginary child audience what fun Pib and Pog are having. I think both these aspects are still true of children's television programmes, where you can see acts of quite horrific violence on film, the after-effects of which are quickly soothed away by a presenter who almost seems to have no idea about what the kids at home have really been watching.

Welcome to the cosy teatime world of Pib and Pog. 'Hello Pib, hello Pog,' cries the off-screen presenter. 'What have you been up to?'

Now let the mayhem begin. Oh look, Pog's head is jammed in a bucket. A moment later he emerges with his face missing. 'Why,' coos the presenter, 'it's concentrated sulphuric acid!'

Now Pib saws Pog in half. Pog responds by trapping Pib on a bed of nails. What fun they're having!

After the show, the actors say goodbye. 'What a dreadful ham,' says the Pog luvvie, after electrocuting his partner.

'There is a further jab at the cosy world of the TV studio when Pib and Pog fall back to earth again after the cannon blast and sing their cutesy little signature tune. As a final punchline, perhaps a reminder that violence is always around us, or at least an affirmation that the two actors are just as bad as the roles they play, the luvvies amble off-stage mouthing compliments to each other, then one electrocutes the other with his parting handshake.'

New Directions for Animators David Sproxton

Chicken Run, Aardman's first feature film, was released in 2000. During the making of that film and in the period since, new and developing technologies have greatly extended the boundaries of how animation film-makers approach their work, and the potential media on which it might be shown

In a technical sense, for instance, the new 'Creature Comforts' has evolved into an interesting hybrid. We are now about to make our second series of new films for ITV. These are still made by stop-frame but are shot on video directly. This is a very interesting production approach, blending our traditional skills in modelmaking, sets and lighting with a shoot that is entirely digital, using some twenty video cameras instead of film cameras. The images are taken straight into hard drives on the animators' work stations, then go into an edit suite and are finally produced on tape. This method helps to speed up the production while at the same time keeping the production values at a high level. The new technology can actually enhance the creative process as well as making us more efficient.

Another new and developing direction for us has been the web. Some time ago, we thought it would be interesting to launch 'Angry Kid' on the web. In its first year it got an extraordinary number of hits as the word went round, and that made us sit up. Clearly, here was a new way of getting cartoon characters out to the public. Then we discovered 'Big Jeff', whose creator, Tom Parkinson, is making a series of 90-second episodes made in Flash Animation, which we will launch on the web following the pattern of 'Angry Kid'.

Screen shot from the 'Angry Kid' website.

In future we may also try projects out by putting them on mobile phones. Flash material is very good for this, because it is highly compressible. Putting images on mobile phones is a phenomenal business in Japan, and a great way of testing out new characters as well as showing established favourites. Japan is a very icon-led culture, which means they love looking at pictures, and because the country is a relatively compact landmass they can get very good mobile-phone coverage. Vast numbers of people there have a mobile phone and they love the idea of downloading images onto them. In this respect, the Japanese are way ahead of us. Unfortunately, the cellphone system in the United States is not nearly as good, and they have a lot of catching up to do. However, it is obviously an area with great future potential.

We are currently looking at the possibilities of providing images from 'Angry Kid' and 'Big Jeff', and also excerpts from 'Creature Comforts' and other films.

A further area that all animators can explore is the computer game. For instance, we have made a game called *Project Zoo* which was devised for us by Frontier Development. This came out at the end of 2003. It was a long, two-year project: Frontier cooperated closely in the early days with Nick Park to get the right look for the characters. The film revives the diabolical Penguin from *The Wrong Trousers*, but here he has captured and imprisoned all the baby animals from a zoo and the player, with Wallace and Gromit as his tools and assistants, has to liberate them and confound the villain.

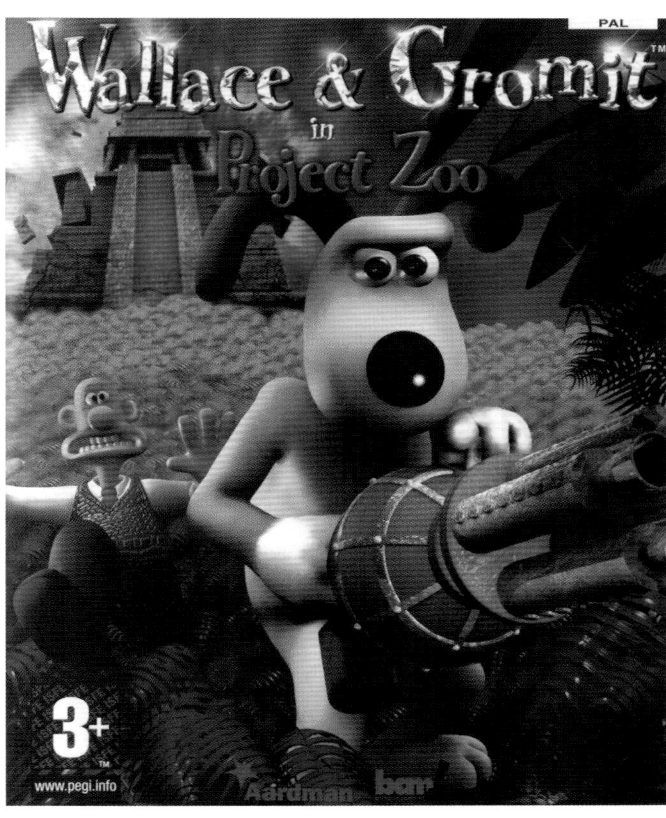

Cover of the Playstation 2 game *Project Zoo*, devised for Aardman by Frontier Development.

There has also been a big uptake of computer technology in schools, and we have been working with Nesta Futurelab, created by the National Endowment for Science Technology and the Arts. They are looking at ways you can provide education with play in all sorts of areas. Our project is a way to teach children about biology and the environment. Basically, it is a complex computer game in which you construct a creature out of body parts that are preset with characteristic needs and wants. Then the creature is set down in an environment which may or may not be suitable for it, and the player has test this out and introduce character changes until his creature and the environment are compatible.

It has been interesting for us to become involved in this project because it opens up new ways of thinking about what we produce, what we design and how we think. We have a lot of highly creative people at Aardman, and their creativity can be applied in new areas beyond our core businesses of making commercials and entertainment films. We have evolved a great deal in the last five years, and I hope we shall still be evolving and adapting to new needs and technologies five years from now.

Editing

Helen Garrard has edited many films for Aardman. Here she explains how the process begins.

'My first task on a film is to supervise the soundtrack. I am given a storyboard, and a script if there is dialogue in the film, and then I go to the dialogue recording. At Aardman, which is famous for its closely synchronised dialogue, we record the dialogue before any filming takes place. We come back with all the dialogue, choose the best takes and edit them down to a final version. It can be spaced out later, if necessary, but the essence of it is there. We then break down the dialogue phonetically and mark this on a series of charts. The animators work very closely to these when they match the movements of the characters to what they say. From the charts they can see the position of the mouth on each frame.'

Although much of Aardman's work is still shot on film, they now edit on computer using systems such as Avid or Final Cut Pro. The film material is transferred to tape on a regular basis during the shooting period (which lasts many months on a full-length feature film), and this is then loaded into the computer editing system, where the editor assembles the shots and does a 'rough cut', which at this stage is quite loose. The editor then works on tightening this edit, and often adds basic sound effects and music which can be done much more easily on a computer system than with the old method of cutting the actual film. This helps the director to see how a sequence is playing emotionally, even though all the sound components may

Capturing the right mood for title-sequence lettering: a theatrical type for *Stage Fright*, and a rough-edged thriller style for *The Wrong Trousers*.

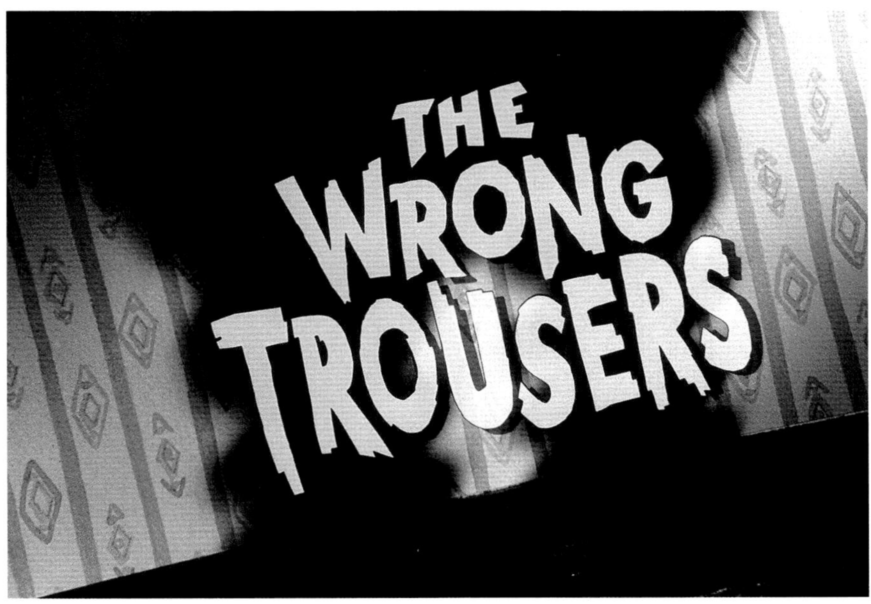

be replaced with specially created effects and music at a later date.

Computer editing also allows the editor to try a number of different versions of an edit and to keep them for comparison. This is simply not possible with traditional film editing. The systems also allow more than one editor to work on the material at the same time, which for a feature-length film is a huge advantage.

As the film takes shape, the composer is brought in to start work. Initially they compose themes and ideas; only when the picture has been finally edited can they begin putting music to the film in earnest, accurately matching cuts and pace to the music.

Similarly, 'track laying' also starts, although many aspects of the 'sound design' (for example how a certain contraption might sound, or the atmosphere a certain scene might need) will have been started much earlier. Again, computer systems are now used extensively for this process, and an almost infinite number of tracks can be laid. The sound editor can do 'mini-mixes' to assess how all the components will go together before the final mix happens many weeks later.

In the meantime, the film material itself will have been digitised to a very high quality and work started on any visual effects that need to be applied. Eventually, these film files are assembled to match the cutting copy in the computer editing system, and are printed back to film for cinema release. Although the laboratories will still need to be involved in the colour grading of the final release prints, the detailed grading that needs to be done for each sequence is now carried out beforehand on computer, allowing the director of photography to make much finer corrections than can be done in the film laboratory.

Sound

Adrian Rhodes is a specialist sound editor, or sound mixer. He has been responsible for the sound on a large number of live-action films as well as Aardman productions. Here he discusses his role.

'My job is to create sounds rather than to record them. I am not usually involved in the dialogue recording, but come in after about half the film has been shot and edited into a rough cut. At this stage I go through the material with the editor and the director, and then I can start to build up the sound effects that will be needed.

'Take the lorry in *A Close Shave*. In the beginning, I want to get the concept right, so I work on assembling appropriate lorry sounds that can be stretched or edited down later when filming is completed. I supply all the sounds needed in the film, not just the big ones like lorries or aircraft but also every footstep, rustle, or the noise that someone makes when they put their glasses down on a table. These little sounds are called foley or footstep sounds, and making them is specialised and highly skilled work. I work with a foley artist, who comes into the studio and acts out or makes up the sounds - walking along to the action pictures, for example, to provide the sound of footsteps. On the studio floor there is a panel of different surfaces - paving stone, floorboard, tarmac surface, etc. - which he can walk or run on to get the right sound.

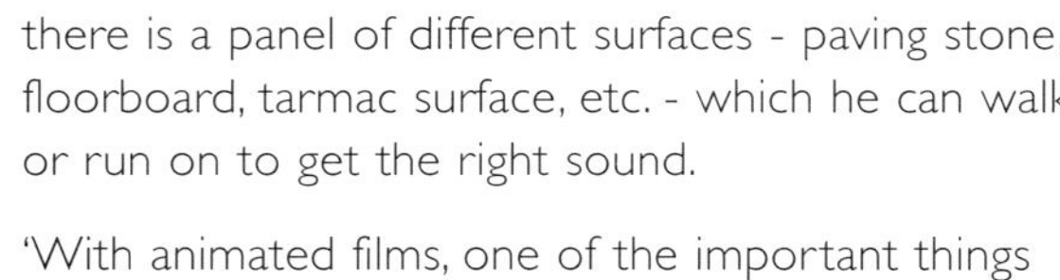

At the mixing desk for the final mix, when all the sound components are brought together and balanced out.

'With animated films, one of the important things to remember is that real sounds, ie those directly imitated from life, can often seem out of place or unsuitable. If you want an exterior sound of tweeting birds, for example, it is probably not a good idea to record real birds in a garden. This is because the characters in the film are not real but clay creatures living in their own fantasy world, and so the sound of real tweeting birds may not sit well on the film. For the Penguin's feet in *The Wrong Trousers*, it would have been a mistake to record a real penguin flapping about. Instead, we got the foley artist to do it, and his solution was very simple: he just slapped his hands on his thighs to the rhythm of the walk.

'One of our most complex scenes, from the sound point of view, was in the cellar in *A Close Shave*,

after Preston the dog had turned into a robot. The Preston sounds alone took up more than twenty different tracks, with different sound combinations for his head movements, feet, the roar, and so on. Also in that sequence there were several other elements - the conveyor belt, the machine that chews up the robot, the sheep, etc. What you can then do is focus on one particular element, building up the robot, for example, until you have got him working, and then you can mix all his separate tracks down to something more manageable, put them on one side and then focus on the sheep, and do the same for that character. This is what we call the premixing stage, where all the sounds are assembled and then mixed together so that, when we come to the final mix, all the sound components of the film have been reduced to the three strands of sound, dialogue and music. For the final mix we go into a big studio and all sit there together - the director, editor, sound editor and composer - and work through everything until we get the balance that we think is right.

'I would encourage anyone starting out to make films to try and get in as much sound as possible. Sound brings a film to life, and even the tiniest details can play a part in this, helping to make your film better and more believable.'

Music

Julian Nott composes music for film and television productions. He has written the music for several Aardman films, and here describes how he works.

'The composer can come in at various times, depending on the kind of film and the preferences of the director. In animated films, the music may be needed first if the film is dependent on a song which has to be written before anything else can be done. In more story-led films, I prefer to come in at the end when the editing is finished and I can write music to the pictures.

'This means you probably do not have much time, perhaps three or four weeks for a 30-minute Wallace and Gromit film, but at least I can be as certain as possible that the film will not be changed. If someone decides to change the cut, the composer often has to start work all over again. There is always the temptation to try desperately hard to change what you have already written to fit the new cut, but this never really works and so it means starting afresh.

'On most occasions I see rushes on a big screen, and when the film is finished I get a videotape to work from. At this time I have a meeting with the director, and he or she tells me what in general they are hoping to do with the music, and then we go through the film in more detail to decide where the cues should start and end.

'I take away the video, which has a time-code on it. This is a computer code which is on one of the audio channels of the tape. I can then lock all my computers and machines and instruments on to this time-code and write the music very specifically to each second of the film.

'When I have written a certain amount, I demo it to the director. Nowadays we have a lot of technology to help us, and even at this stage we can demo an orchestral score, using synthesisers which can make an accurate representation of the real instrument. Once the composer gets the final OK, he really has to work fast. With an orchestral score there is not time for him to do the orchestration and the parts copying for all the members of the orchestra. On *A Close Shave*, for instance, we had some 65 musicians in the orchestra and about 25 cues. That means providing the musicians with 1625 sheets, all of which have to be written out for a particular instrument. To cope with this, I sketch out the music and bring in an orchestrator, and he does the detailed orchestration for me. When the parts come back, someone books a studio and arranges for the musicians to come in.

Julian Nott's sketch for the beginning of the motorbike chase in *A Close Shave*. Sketches such as this go to the orchestrator who works out the orchestration in detail and prepares the parts for the musicians.

'Many film directors and producers feel quite overwhelmed when they hear the music being played for the first time against their pictures by a full orchestra. It is such a powerful sound. Once we are recording, it is very difficult for the director to make changes. In animated films, people do not have the kind of budget where you can waste time and keep 65 musicians hanging around while you change the music. When all the music is recorded, we mix it and then it goes off to be track-laid against the pictures. The composer may or may not be involved with this, but he will probably go to the final mix, where all the sounds and music are balanced and the film is then ready to go to the final print.'

A high-point from the motorbike chase in *A Close Shave*, which is accompanied by suitably heroic martial music.

A Career in Animation

With the development of animation in all its forms, and especially with the advancement of CGI, the animated film business is becoming an increasingly popular career choice. Although this makes the field highly competitive, it also provides the opportunity for those with real passion and enthusiasm to shine. Dedication is essential as jobs are limited, and anyone wanting to succeed will need to do plenty of research. Watch television, see films, go to events such as festivals and exhibitions, try to make personal contacts within the industry, and keep up to date with the relevant trade and technical press.

Although it is not essential to have completed a course at art school or film school, it is immensely helpful and is often desirable to employers. Very often people find their individual style during those years. For instance, most of Aardman's really successful directors – including Nick Park – laid down the foundations of their career in their student days. There are a number of courses available covering most aspects of animation: more information can be found online. Seek advice about the most appropriate course for what you're interested in.

Whether you have a traditional animation background or not, the most important asset for an aspiring animator is their showreel. When compiling a showreel, be creative and original, put your best work first and make sure your reel stands out. Remember that film companies will be looking for examples of your animation skills as well, so include a segment that demonstrates walk cycles or stretch and squash moments. Further guidelines can be found on the Aardman website. Remember too that all animation companies will have their own submission policy.

It is important to define what kind of work you are best suited to, developing your own style and individuality and considering which areas interest you most. There are a huge variety of jobs available and a career in animation does not necessarily mean directing films or being an animator. Aardman depends not only on well-established film craft skills - storyboard artist, scenic artist, cameraman, producer, modelmaker, set designer, technician, editor, and many more – but also skilled computer technicians who operate motion-control systems or support CGI software, engineers who design and manufacture specialist camera equipment as well as many of the traditional support roles you find in companies – accountants, chefs, site managers, and so on.

Whatever your age or experience, you can find all Aardman's most up-to-date guidelines, information and opportunities at: www.aardman.com.

DO NOT
CLIMB ON
THE WALL

Filmography

KEY
Series titles in quotes
Film titles in italics
D/A = Direction/Animation
D = Direction
A = Animation

Feature Films
2000
Chicken Run
D Peter Lord & Nick Park
81 min

Short Films
1978
'Animated Conversations'
Confessions of a Foyer Girl
Down and Out
D/A Peter Lord & David Sproxton, 5 min each

1981–83
'The Amazing Adventures of Morph' – 26 episodes
D/A Peter Lord & David Sproxton, 5 min each

'Conversation Pieces'
On Probation
Sales Pitch
Palmy Days
Early Bird
Late Edition
D/A Peter Lord & David Sproxton, 5 min each

1986
Babylon
D/A Peter Lord & David Sproxton
14 min 30 sec

1989
'Lip Synch'
Next
D/A Barry Purves
Ident
D/A Richard Goleszowski
Going Equipped
D/A Peter Lord
Creature Comforts
D/A Nick Park
War Story
D/A Peter Lord
5 min each

*A Grand Day Out**
D/A Nick Park, 23 min
*Produced by the National Film & Television School and finished with the help of Aardman Animations

Lifting the Blues
D David Sproxton
52 min

1990–91
Rex the Runt – How Dinosaurs Became Extinct
D/A Richard Goleszowski
2 min

1991
Rex the Runt – Dreams
D/A Richard Goleszowski
2 min

Adam
D/A Peter Lord, 6 min

1992
Never Say Pink Furry Die
D/A Louise Spraggon, 12 min

Loves Me ... Loves Me Not
D/A Jeff Newitt, 8 min

1993
The Wrong Trousers
D Nick Park
A Nick Park, Steve Box
29 min

Not Without My Handbag
D/A Boris Kossmehl, 12 min

1994
Pib & Pog
D/A Peter Peake, 6 min

1995
A Close Shave
D Nick Park
A Nick Park, Steve Box, Peter Peake, Lloyd Price, Gary Cureton, Ian Whitlock, Sergio Delfino, 29 min

1996
Pop
D/A Sam Fell, 5 min

Wat's Pig
D Peter Lord
A Peter Lord, Sam Fell, Mike Booth, 11 min

'Rex the Runt' Pilot, *North by North Pole*
D Richard Goleszowski
A Richard Goleszowski, Chris Sadler, Dave Osmond, Sergio Delfino, Grant White
6 min

1997
Stage Fright
D Steve Box
A Steve Box, Jason Spencer-Galsworthy, Gary Cureton, Lloyd Price, Dave Osmand
11 min

Owzat
D/A Mark Brierley, 5 min

'Rex the Runt' series – 13 episodes
D Richard Goleszowski
A Various
10 min each

1998
Hum Drum
D/A Peter Peake, 6 min

Al Dente
D/A Mark Brierley, 2 min

Angry Kid X3
D/A Darren Walsh
11 min each

1999
Minotaur and Little Nerkin
D/A Nick Mackie, 2 min

'Angry Kid' Series 1 (13 episodes)
D/A Darren Walsh
1 min each
'Rabbits' Pilot
D Sam Fell
A Will Byles, Gary Cureton, Chris Sadler, 4 min 20 sec

2000
'Aztec Shorts'
Chunga Chui
D/A Stefano Cassini
Comfy
D/A Seth Watkins
Ernest
D/A Darren Robbie
Hot Shot
D/A Michael Cash
IQ 552
D/A Ian Whitlock
Non-Domestic Appliance
D/A Sergio Delfino
The Drifter
D/A Andy Symanowski
1 min each

2001
The Deadline
D Stefan Marjoram
A Stefan Marjoram, Dan Lane, Wee Brian
2 min 32 sec

'Rex the Runt' Series 2 (13 episodes)
Created by Richard Goleszowski
D Sam Fell (3 episodes), Peter Peake (3), Chris Sadler (3), Dan Capozzi (4), approx 10 min each

2002
'Angry Kid' Series 2 (13 episodes)
D/A Darren Walsh
1 min each

Chump
D/A Sam Fell, 4 min

'Wallace and Gromit's Cracking Contraptions' (10 episodes)
D Christopher Sadler & Loyd Price
Originated and produced by Nick Park, approx 2 min each
Vacation
D Scott Pleydell-Pierce
2 min 15 sec

Hobbies
D Nick Mackie
1 min 30 sec

Lens Lens
D Rich Webber
2 min 45 sec

White Trash
D Dave Osmand, 1 min

2003
The Tales
D Dan Lane
A Dan Lane, Wee Brian
50 sec

'Creature Comforts' Series 1 (13 episodes)
D Richard Goleszowski
approx 9 min each

The Adventures of Big Jeff
D Tom Parkinson
Prod Helen Brunsdon
1 min 10 sec

Commercials
1982-2004
Films completed for the following clients/products: Access, Ace Bars, American Express Travel, Ameritrade Proctor, Ariston, Asthma Awareness, BBC Christmas Stings, Big Read, Bitza Pizza, BBC3 Idents, Bowyers Sausages, Britannia Building Society, BT, Burger King, Cadbury's Coronation Street, Central Office of Information, Chevron, Chewits, Coca Cola, Colgate, Comfort, Comfort Blue, Cook Electric, Crunchie, Cuprinol, Daewoo, Daily Telegraph, Dairylea, Dairylea Dunkers, Dishwash Electric, Domestos, Dr Pepper, Duracell, Electricity Board, Enterprise Computers, Frisps, Glico Putchin

Pudding, Grolsch, Guardian, Guinness, Hamburger Helper, Hamlet, Henkel, Hershey Big Kat, Homepride, Jacobs, Jordans Crunchy Bars, Kangoo, Kellogg's, KP, Lego, Lifesavers, Lipton, Little Caesars, Lurpak, Lyles Golden Syrup, May Co., Maynards, McVities, Naturesweet, Nestle, Nike Footlocker, Perrier, PG Tips, Polo, Prevacid, Pringles, Quavers, Quickbrew, Ready-Brek, Rice Krispies, Ritz Bits, Ruffles, Savlon, Scotch Videotape, Scottish Health Education Group, Serta Mattresses, Shower Electric, Smarties, St Ivel, Starburst, Tennent's, Terence Higgins Trust, Total Heating, Twistables, Wagon Wheels, Walkers French fries, Weetabix, Weetos, WWF.

Bibliography

Archer, Steve, *Willis O'Brien: Special Effects Genius* (McFarland & Co Inc, Jefferson, North Carolina) 1993

Bendazzi, Giannalberto, *Cartoons: One hundred years of cinema animation* (John Libbey, London) 1994

Bocek, Jaroslav, *Jiri Trnka: Historie dila a jeho tvurce Statni nakladatelstvi krasne literatury a umeni v Praze*, 1963

Canemaker, John, *Winsor McCay: His Life and Art* (Abbeville Press (New York, NY) 1987

Crafton, Donald, *Emile Cohl, Caricature and Film* (Princeton University Press, Princeton, NJ) 1990

ibid, *Before Mickey: The Animated Film, 1898-1928* (MIT Press, Cambridge, Mass) 1982

Edera, Bruno & (ed) Halas, John, *Full Length Animated Feature Films* (Focal Press, London) 1977

Frierson, Michael, *Clay Animation: American Highlights 1908 to the Present* (Twayne Publishers / Simon & Schuster Macmillan, New York, NY) 1994

Halas, John, *Masters of Animation* (BBC Books, London) 1987

Halas, John & Manvell, Roger, *The Technique of Film Animation* (Focal Press, London) 1968

Harryhausen, Ray, *Film Fantasy Scrapbook* (Titan Books London) 1989

Hickman, Gail Morgan, *The Films of George Pal* (AS Barnes and Co Inc, South Brunswick, NJ) 1977

Holliss, Richard & Sibley, Brian *The Disney Studio Story* (Octopus, London / Crown, New York, NY) 1988

Holman, L Bruce, *Puppet Animation in the Cinema* (AS Barnes and Co Inc, South Brunswick, NJ) 1975

Home, Anna, *Into the Box of Delights: A History of Children's Television* (BBC Books, London) 1993

Horne, Maurice (ed), *The World Encyclopedia of Cartoons* (Chelsea House Publishers, New York, NY) 1980

Martin, Leona Beatrice & Martin, François, *Ladislas Starewitch* (JICA Diffusion, Bibliography 2 Annecy) 1991

Pilling, Jayne (ed), *Starewich 1882-1965* (Film House, Edinburgh) 1983

Robinson, David, *George Méliès: Father of Film Fantasy* (Museum of the Moving Image, London) 1993

Sibley, Brian (ed), *Wallace & Gromit Storyboard Collection: A Close Shave* (BBC Worldwide Publishing Ltd, London) 1997

Thomas, Bob, *Walt Disney the Art of Animation* (Golden Press, New York, NY) 1958

Thompson, Frank, *Tim Burton's Nightmare Before Christmas: The Film, The Art, The Vision* (Hyperion, New York, NY) 1993

Picture Acknowledgments

Our grateful thanks to the following for permission to reproduce illustrations:

AB Productions: 38 (courtesy of the BBC)
Bare Boards Productions: 55
BBC Photo Library (Blobs and Bookworms)
BFI: 20 © DACS 1998, 21, 24, 25,
26t, 26b Condor-Hessisches/SGR/Film Four, 28t C4, 28b, 39b, 46
Columbia: 47 (courtesy of Kobal)
CM Dixon: 16
Mary Evans Picture Library: 17t & b, 18t & b, 19t
Janie Fitzgerald/Axisimages: 111b
Fremantle Media Ltd (Wind in the Willows)
Krátny Film Prague (tel. 420.2.32.67091.154): 27 (courtesy of Kobal), 32
Pearson International: 38t
Philips, Eindhoven: 29t
Photofest: 22, 29b, 30, 31t & b, 36, 37, 40, 48, 50t
RKO/Warner/Time: 44 & 45 (courtesy of Kobal)
SC4/BBC/Christmas Films Russia: 34, 35
Touchstone/Burton/Di Novi: 41 & 43 (courtesy of Kobal)
Viacom: 50b (courtesy of Kobal)

Thanks to the following for permission to reproduce images from advertising commercials:

APL/Hasbro (Burger King)
Mr Potato Head® is a trademark of Hasbro, Inc. ©Hasbro, Inc. All rights reserved. Used with permission.
BMP/DDB Needham Ltd (Lurpak, 'Love Story')
Dilly Gent/Parlophone Records (Limoland, 'In Your Wildest Dreams')
Electricity Association (Heat Electric commercials)
Greys/Starburst Fruits (Starburst)
Robinsons Soft Drinks Ltd (Robinsons Squash)
Lyle's (Golden Syrup)
J. Walter Thompson/Nestlé Rowntree (Polo)
Unilever/Ogilvy & Mather (Comfort)
Virgin/Sledgehammer (Sledgehammer)
Young & Rubican/Chevron (Chevron)

Index

Page numbers in *italics* refer to picture captions.

Aardman Animations 9–15, 17, 53–65
Aardman Cartoon (Lord and Sproxton) *10*, 11–12
Academy nominations and Awards 9, 17, 56, 58, 59, 62, 200, 205
Achilles (Purves) *57*, 58
acting out parts *85*, 134, *134*
Adam (Lord) 9, 17, 62, 94, *138*, *146*, 148–9, *149*, 162, *162*
Adventures of Mark Twain, The (Vinton) 51–2, *52*
'Adventures of Twizzle, The' (Anderson) 39
advertising see commercials
'Aesop's Fables' (Terry) 25
Alice (Svankmajer) *28*, 29
Alice in Wonderland (Bunin) 41, *41*
Anderson, Gerry 39
Andy Pandy 37
'Angry Kid' (Walsh) 64, *64*, 196, *196*, *197*, 210, *210*, 211
Animals and the Brigands, The (Trnka) 34
'Animated Conversations' (Aardman) 54, 55
'Animated Grouch Chasers, The' (Barre) 24–5
Animated Matches, The (Cohl) 26–7
Antz 64
armatures 17, 94, *94*, 95, 98, 100, *101*, 102, *102*, *103*, *104*, 108
Armstrong, Todd 48, *49*
AVID (editing system) 180, 212

Babylon (Aardman) 60
back light 77, *78*, 79
backgrounds 25, 129, 131
Barbera, Hanna 9
Barnes, Tom 180–1, *181*
Barre, Raoul 24–5
Bass, Jules 42
BBC3 Blobs idents *183*
Beautiful Leukanida, The (Starewich) 27
Beda, Galina 37, *37*
Beetlejuice (Burton) 43
Bergen, Edgar 37
'Big Jeff' (Aardman) 194–5, *194*, *195*, 210, 211
'Big Read' Bookworm ident *14*, *183*
Bill and Ben, The Flowerpot Men 37–8
Blackton, J Stuart 24, 25
blue-screen process 131, *131*
blurred images 130–1, *131*
'Bobby Bump' (Hurd) 25
Box, Steve *17*, 61–2, *154*, *164*, 174–5
box-projectors 21–2
Brambley Hedge (Cosgrove Hall) 42
Bray, J R 25
Brough, Peter 37
Bug's Life, A 64
Bunin, Lou *41*, 42
Burger King commercials *62*, 116
Burton, Tim 42–3, *42*, *45*

Cabinet of Jan Svankmajer, The: Prague's Alchemist of Film (Brothers Quay) 30
'Camberwick Green' (Murray) 40
camera obscura 19
Cameraman's Revenge, The (Starewich) 27
cameras 68–70, 180
motion control 70, 74
tripods see tripods
video 68, 70
video assist 74–5
Capozzi, Danny 193
Caprino, Ivo 37
cel animation *10*, 11–12, 17, 34–3, 49, 64
chalk animation 9–10, 11, 24, *24*
Channel 4 logo sequence *86*
Chaplin, Charlie 26, *27*
characterisation 198–209
Chevron commercial 59, 116–17, *116*
Chicken Run (Lord and Park) 13–14, 62–3, *161*, 171–81, *171–81*, 210
Chimney Sweep, The (Trnka) 34–5
Chiodo, Stephen 43
'Chop Socky Chooks' (Aardman) 64, 192–3, *192*, *193*
Christmas Films 37, *37*
Christmas Gift, A (Vinton) 51
Cinderella (Cooper) 26
cine film 68–9, 70
Cinématographe 22–3
'Clangers, The' (Smallfilms) 40
Clash of the Titans, The (Harryhausen) 48
clay animation 11, 17, 25, 44–63
2-D figures 106, *106*, *107*, 176
cleaning 84, 150, 156
hands 95, *95*, 102, *105*, 120, 150
heads 102
joints 94, *94*
modelmaking 94–5
simple techniques 82–5
see *also* armatures; figures; modelmaking
Claymation 51
Claymation Christmas Celebration, A (Vinton and Gatz) 51
Clokey, Art 49–51, *50*
Close Shave, A (Park) 56, 57, 61, *78*, *79*, 96–9, *96–9*, 100, 108, *108*, *126*, 129, *129*, 131, *154*, 168, *168*, 169, 180, 205, *205*, 214–15, *216*
Closed Mondays (Vinton and Gardiner) 51
Clutterbuck, Graham 40
Cohl, Emile 24, 26–7
coloured lighting 76, 79, *79*
colouring models *105*, 120
Comet Quest (Vinton) 51–2, *52*
Comfort Form Conditioner commercials *186*, *187*
commercials 26, 29, 52, *52*, 56, 59–60, *59*, *60*, 91, *91*, 116–17, 185
computer generated imagery (CGI) 14, 18, 25, 63–4, 69, 70, 174–5, 183–93, 210–13, 216
computerised editing 212–13
Confessions of a Foyer Girl (Aardman) 54
'Conversation Pieces' (Aardman) 54, *54*, 55–6, *55*, 200
Cook, Luis 62
Cooper, Arthur Melbourne 25–6
Cooper, Merian C 47, *47*
Cosgrove, Brian 40–2
Cosgrove Hall 40–2, 56
Crandall, Roland 48
'Crapston Villas' (Kennedy) 61
Creation (Vinton and Gatz) 51
Creature Comforts (Park) 59, 65, *65*, *112*, 150, *152*, 200, *200*, 202, *202*, 210, 211
cut-outs 10, 17, 29

Danot, Serge 40, *40*, 53
Delfino, Sergio *174*, 192–3
Delgardo, Marcel 47
Demon (Kawamoto) 36
Destination Moon (Pal) 33
Devil on Springs, The (Trnka) 34–5
digital frame store 75
Dimensions of Dialogue (Svankmajer) 30
Dinky Doodle 25
Dinosaur (Vinton) 51
Dinosaurs (Goleszowski) 61
Disney Studio 42–3, 49, 53, 54–5
Disney, Walt 9, 25, 61
Dojoji (Kawamoto) 36
dope sheets *154*
double exposures (impositions) 126–7
double-frame animation (doubles; twos) 68, 69, 83, *83*
Dowling, Patrick 11
drawn animation 17, 21, 24–5, *24*, *25*
model animation compared 18–19
Dreams (Goleszowski) 61
Dreams of Toyland (Cooper) 26, *26*
Dreamworks 64

Edison, Thomas 21, 23
editing 212–13
Edward Scissorhands (Burton) 43
Emperor's Nightingale, The (Trnka) 35, 36
Evans, Mortimer 21
Execution of Mary Queen of Scots, The 23
eyes *98*, 150, *151*

facial expression 150, *150–5*, 156, *156*, *157*, *162*
Fagan, Suzy *178*
Fall of the House of Usher, The (Svankmajer) 29–30
Fantasmagorie (Cohl) 24
Faust (Svankmajer) *29*, 30
Felix the Cat 25
Fell, Sam 62, 64
fibreglass 95
figures
2-D 106, *106*, *107*, 176
evolution, character 100
focus of interest 95, *95*
size, consistency of *94*, 95, 178–9
wire-based *94*, 95
see *also* armatures; clay animation; modelmaking
fill light 76–7, *78*, 79, *79*
Filmfare 40
Fimo 120
Finding Nemo 64, 70
'Fireball XL5' (Anderson) 39
Firman, Peter 40
Fisherman and the Little Fish, The (Ptushko) 30–1
Fleischer, Dave 25
Fleischer, Max 48
Flushed Away (Aardman and Dreamworks) 64
foam see latex foam
'Four Feather Falls' (Anderson) 39
Fox Talbot, William Henry 19
Frankenweenie (Burton) 43
Fresnel lenses 76
Fries, Doug 180
Friese-Williams, William 21

Gabriel, Peter, *Sledgehammer* video 60, *61*
Gardiner, Bob 51
Garrard, Helen 212–13
Gatz, Joan 51
Geesink, Joop 33
Gertie the Trained Dinosaur (McCay) 25, *25*
gestures 150–5
Gibson, EB 47
Gilliam, Terry 53
Gingerbread Cottage, The (Pojar) 35
glass, angled, shooting on 106, *106*, 176–7
glue, epoxy-resin 99
gobos 76, *76*
Godzilla 10
Gogs (Morris and Mort) 61
Going Equipped (Lord) 59, *77*, *152*, 207
Golden Syrup commercial 91, *91*
Goleszowski, Richard 56–7, *58*, 61, *63*, 65, *65*, 176–7, 200
Good Soldier Schweik, The (Trnka) 35
Grand Day Out, A (Park) 56, *56*, 100, *120*, 205
Grandpa Planted a Beet (Trnka) 34
Great Cognito, The (Vinton) 51
Gromit *100*, *120*, *128*, *146*, 150, *152*, *164*, *168*
construction 100–1, *101*
see *also* Wallace and Gromit
Gross, Yoram 37
Gumby series (Clokey) 49–51, *50*

Halas and Manvell, *The Technique of Film Animation* 54
Hall, Mark 40–2
Hand, The (Trnka) *34*, 35
hands 95, *95*, *102*, *105*, 120, 150
Hansel and Gretel (Myerberg) *33*
Harryhausen, Ray 33, 47–8, *48*, *49*, 53, 59, 60
Hart, Tony 53, 198
Harvey, Laurence *33*
Haunted Hotel, The (Blackton and Smith) 25
headlamps *75*, *79*
Heat Electric commercials 59
Henson, Jim 37
Homer, William George 20
House of Fire (Kawamoto) 36
'Howdy Doody' (Smith) 37, *39*
Hulk, The 63
Humorous Phases of Funny Faces (Blackton) 24, *24*
Humpty Dumpty Circus, The (Blackton and Smith) 25
Hunchback of Notre Dame, The (Disney) 55
Hurd, Earl 25

Ident (Goleszowski) 57, *58*, 61, *77*
impositions see double exposures

Jabberwocky (Svankmajer) 29–30
Jackson, Peter 63
James and the Giant Peach (Selick) 44
Jason and the Argonauts (Harryhausen) 48, *49*, 53, 59
Jasper series (Pal) 33
John Henry and the Inky Poo (Pal) 33
Johnson, Steve 60, *61*
Joseph the Dreamer (Gross) 37
Jurassic Park 63

Kawamoto, Kihachiro 36, 55
Keaton, Buster 44, 47
Kennedy, Sarah Ann 61
key light 76, 79
Kinetoscope 23
King Kong (Cooper) 47, *47*
Kirkpatrick, Karey 172
Knobs in Space (Riddett and Cook) 62

Lantz, Walter 25
Last Trick, The (Svankmajer) 29
latex foam 17, 99, 102
casting 102, *104*, *105*, 120
Lawrence, Peter 206
lighting 76–5
Limoland (Aardman) 74, *74*, *75*
line animation see drawn animation
Lion and the Song, The (Pojar) 35
lip sync technique 70, 154–5, *154*, *212*
Lip Synch (Aardman) 57–9, *58*, 60,

206
Little Golden Key, The (Ptushko) 29
Little Nemo in Slumberland (McCay) 24
Little Prince, The (Vinton) 51
Little Red Riding Hood (Harryhausen) 33
live-action
and animation compared 18
used with animation 47–6, 47, 49, 52, 55, *128*
Lord, Peter 9–15, 9, *13*, 17, 18–19, 20, 48, 53–65, *53*, 62–3, 64, 65, *161*, *162*, 171–81, *171*
Lord of the Rings, The trilogy 63–4
Love in Black and White (Starewich) 26, *27*
Loves Me ... Loves Me Not (Aardman) *12*, 95, *95*, *138*
Lucanus Cervus (Starewich) 26–7
Luce, Ralph 49
Lumière, Auguste and Louis 22–3
Lurpack Butterman 59–60, *60*, *131*

McCay, Winsor 24, *25*
Magic Clock, The (Starewich) 26–7
Magic Lamp, The (Pal) 31
'Magic Roundabout, The' (Danot) 40, *40*, 53
Martin the Cobbler (Vinton) 51
Mary, Etienne-Jules 21
Mascot, The (Starewich) 28–9
Matches: An Appeal (Cooper) 26
Matrix, The 63
mattes 129
May, Virginia 47
Méliès, Georges 22–3, *22*, 28
Mesmer, Otto 25
Midsummer Night's Dream, A (Trnka) 35
Milliput 120
Milo 70
Mix, Tom 26
model animation 17
drawn animation compared 18–19
video assist 74–5
Modelling Board 108
modelmaking
2-D figures 106, *106*, *107*
basic principles 94–5
joints 94, *94*
size, consistency of 94, *94*
see *also* clay animation; figures
Mona Lisa Descending a Staircase (Gatz) 51
Monsters of the Past (May) 47
montage *188*
'Monty Python's Flying Circus' 53
Morph (Aardman) *72*, *73*, *83*, *85*, 94, *120*, *124*, 160, *160*, 198–9, *199*
'Morph' series (Aardman) 53, *53*
Morris, Deiniol 61
Mort, Michael 61
Mother Goose Stories (Harryhausen) 33
motion control 70, 74
moulds
for latex foam 102, *104*, *105*
plaster 102, *104*, *105*, 120
press 106, *107*
rubber 106, *107*
silicone 120
mouths 150–5, 212
movement 134–49
acceleration and deceleration 141
anticipation 140
high-speed 130–1, *131*
model mobility 102
special effects 148–9
Muat, Maria 37
Muffin the Mule 37
'Muppet Show, The' 37
Murray, Gordon 40
music 214–16
Muybridge, Eadweard 19–20, *19*

New Gulliver, The (Ptushko) 30, *30*
Newitt, Jeff *12*
Next (Purves) 57–8, *57*
Nightmare Before Christmas (Burton) 43–4, *43*, *45*
No Credit (Tregillus and Luce) 49
Noah's Ark (Cooper) 26
Noah's Ark (Disney) 42
Nocturna artificialia (Brothers Quay) 30
Noddy (Cosgrove Hall) 41
Not Without My Handbag (Aardman) *124*
Nott, Julian 215–16

Oakie Doke (Cosgrove Hall) 41–2
object animation 17, 29, 59, 86–9, *91*
substitution 91, *91*
O'Brien, Willis 44, 47, *47*, 48
Old Czech Legends (Trnka) 35
On Probation (Aardman) 54, *54*
One Too Many (Pojar) 35
'Operavox' series 37
optical toys 20–1, *20*
Oscars see Academy nominations and Awards
'Out of the Inkwell' (Fleischer) 25, 48
outdoor and landscape sets 114–15, *114*, *115*

Pal, George 31–4, *31*, *32*, *33*, 42, 91
Palmy Days (Aardman) 55–6, *129*
pans 70
Pantomimes Lumineuses 21
Paris, Dr John Ayrton 20
Park, Nick 9, 13, 56–7, *56*, 59, 62–3, 65, *134*, *154*, *161*, *164*, 166, *166*, 171–81, *171*, 200, 202, 205, 211
Parkinson, Tom 194–5, 210
Pastrone, Giovanni 26
Peake, Peter 61, 208–9
Perry, Bill 206–7
persistence of vision 17, 68
Phenakistiscope 20, *20*
photography 19–20
Pib and Pog (Peake) 61, *146*, *152*, 208–9, *208*
Pickford, Mary 26
Pinchcliffe Grand Prix, The (Caprino) 37
Pit and the Pendulum, The (Svankmajer) 30
Pixar Animation Studio 64
pixillation 11, 30, 64, 86, 196
Plasticine 11, 14, 44, 53, 82–5, *104*, 120
see *also* clay animation
Plateau, Joseph 20, *20*
Pleydell-Pearce, Scott 183
Pocahontas (Disney) 55
Poet's Life, A (Kawamoto) 36
'Pogles' Wood' 40
Pojar, Bretislav 35
Polo commercials 60, 116, *116*, *117*
Pop (Fell) 62
poses 134–5
Postgate, Oliver 40
'Postman Pat' 40
Praxinoscope *20*, *21*
Presentaters, The (Aardman) *185*
Preston *78*, *79*, 108, *108*, *168*
Proctor, Bobby 183
Proem (Tregillus and Luce) 49
profile lamps 76
Project Zoo (Frontier Development) 211, *211*
props 113, 120, *120–2*
Ptushko, Alexander 30, *30*
Punch and Judy 37
puppet animation 17, 24, 25, 28–42, 61, 65
'Puppetoons' 31–3, *32*
Purves, Barry 56–8, *57*

Quay, Stephen and Timothy 30, *30*, 60

rain *128*, 129
replacement animation 196
resin, cast *98–9*, 100, *101*, 120
Return to Oz (Disney) 52
Rex the Runt (Goleszowski) 61, *63*, 106, *106*, *107*, *122*, *124*, 176–7, *176*, *177*
Reynaud, Emile 21, *21*, 22
Rhodes, Adrian 214–15
Riddett, Dave Alex 62, *181*
Rigoletto (Purves) *57*, 58
Rip Van Winkle (Vinton) 51
Robinson's commercial 188–9, *188–9*

Sales Pitch (Aardman) 55, *55*
Sallis, Peter 56
Salter, Michael 168
Screen Play (Purves) 57, *58*
scripts and stories 160–1, 212
Sculpy 120
Selick, Henry 43–4
'Sesame Street' 37
set design and construction 112–19, 120
7th Voyage of Sinbad, The (Harryhausen) 48
shadows 76–7, *77*, *78*, *79*
'Shakespeare, The Animated Tales' *36*, 37
sheep, construction 96–9, *98–9*
Ship of the Ether, The (Pal) 31, *31*
Shrek 64, 70
Sinbad the Sailor (Pal) 31
single-frame animation (singles; ones) 69, 70
Smallfilms 40
Smith, Albert E 25
Smith, Bob *39*
Sokolov, Stanislav *36*, 37
Song of the Prairie (Trnka) 35
sound 174, 214–16
editing 212–13
lip sync 154–5, *154*, 212
synchronised 49
temporary voices 173–4
special effects 128–31
movement effects 148–9
Spider-man 63
split screen 129
Sproxton, Dave 9–15, 17, 48, 53–65, *53*, 160, 210–11
Stage Fright (Box) 61–2, *95*, 118, *118*, *122*, *150*, *152*, 174–5, *174*, *212*
Star Wars 63
Starewich, Ladislaw (Ladislas Starevitch) 26–9, *27*, *28*, 37, 40
Steamboat Willie (Disney) 49
Stereoscope 20
still frames *83*
'Stingray' (Anderson) 39
stop motion (stop action) 23–4, 25–6, 34, 40, 43, 70, 174
Story of King Midas, The (Harryhausen) 33
Story of Rapunzel, The (Harryhausen) 33
story-reels 173–4, 177–8
storyboards 102, *154*, 162–9, *162–9*, 172–3, 177–8, *189*, 212
Street of Crocodiles (Brothers Quay) 30, *30*
studios and studio equipment 72–5
substitution method *32*, 91, *91*, *138*
Sullivan, Pat 25
'Supercar' (Anderson) 39
Svankmajer, Jan 29, *29*
Symposium on Popular Songs, A (Disney) 42

'Take Hart' (Aardman) 160, 198
Tale of the Fox, The (Starewich) 28
Terry, Paul 25
'Testament' series 37, *37*
Thaumatrope 20
Théâtre Optique 21, *21*, 22
Three Ages, The (Keaton) 44, 47
3-D animation see model animation
'Thunderbirds' (Anderson) 39
Time Machine, The (Pal) 33
timing movements and frames 83
Tippett, Phil 63
Trnka, Jan 34–7, *34*
Tom Thumb (Pal) 34
'Torchy the Battery Boy' (Anderson) 39
Town Rat, Country Rat (Starewich) 28, *28*
Toy Story (Disney) 64, 70
Toymaker's Dream, The (Cooper) 26
Trash 10
Tregillus, Leonard 49
tripods 68, 69, 72, 73
Truckers (Cosgrove Hall) 42
'Trumpton' (Murray) 40
Tubby the Tuba (Pal) 31–2, *31*
Tulips Shall Grow (Pal) 32
2-D animation
angled glass, shooting on 106, *106*, 176–7
see *also* drawn animation

video assist 74–5
video cameras 66, 69
Vincent (Burton) 42–3, *42*
Vinton, Will 51–2, *52*
'Vision On' (Aardman) 11–12, 17, 53, *53*, 72, 160, 198
Voyage to the Moon (Méliès) 22–3, *22*

Wallace and Gromit 56, *56*, *94*, 100–1, 113–14, *113*, *120*, *138*, *141*, *146*, *156–7*, *164–9*, *171*, 205
'Wallace and Gromit's Cracking Contraptions' 65
Walsh, Darren 64, *64*, 196, *197*
War and the Dream of Momi (Pastrone) 26
War Story (Lord) 59, 154–5, 206–7, *206*, *207*
War of the Worlds (Pal) 33
water, special effects *128*, 129, *129*
Wat's Pig (Lord) *13*, 14–15, 62, 77, 102–5, *114*, *115*, *138*, 161
When Worlds Collide (Pal) 33
Wind in the Willows, The (Cosgrove Hall) 40–1, *41*, 56
wire-based figures 95, *95*, *98*
'Wombles, The' 40, 53
Wonderful World of the Brothers Grimm, The 33, 34
Woodentops 37
Woody Woodpecker 25
Wright, John 108, *126*
Wrong Trousers, The (Park) *17*, 56, 61, 77, *122*, *124*, *128*, 129, *129*, 131, *131*, *134*, *138*, *141*, 148, *148*, 164, *164–7*, 205, *213*

Zoetrope 20, *21*

ACKNOWLEDGMENTS

Many thanks also to everyone at or connected with Aardman who in some way helped to make this book happen, especially:

Photography	Tristan Oliver, Dave Alex Riddett
Text Contributions	Tom Barnes, Steve Box, Helen Brunsdon, Mark Brierley, Trisha Budd, Sergio Delfino, Helen Garrard, Richard Goleszowski, Angie Last, Phil Lewis, Julian Nott, Nick Park, Tom Parkinson, Peter Peake, Scott Pleydell-Pearce, Bobby Proctor, Adrian Rhodes, Dave Alex Riddett, Jan Sanger, Debbie Smith, David Sproxton, Darren Walsh, John Wright
Special Photography:	
Photographer	Richard Laing
Art Director	Darren Walsh
Producer	Zoe Goleszowski
Animation	Peter Lord, Seamus Malone, Loyd Price, Darren Walsh
Modelmaking	Zennor Box, Jeff Cliff, Will La Trobe-Bateman, Debbie Smith, John Wright, Kevin Wright, Mr Jones the Glassmaker
Modelmaking Coordination	Chris Entwhistle, Kerry Evans, Jan Sanger
Set Design	Phil Lewis
Director of Photography	Dave Alex Riddett
Sparks	John Truckle
Rigger	Nick Upton
Additional Artwork	Darren Walsh
Archive Stills/Footage/Artwork	Kieran Argo, Janie Conley, Maggie O'Connor, Andrea Redfern, Sharron Traer
Special Thanks	Jo Allen, Amy Anderson, Rachael Carpenter, Alison Cook, Kirstie Cooksley, Mike Cooper, Liz Keynes, Julie Lockhart, Helen Neno, Paula Newport, Amy Robinson, Alina Roberts, Michael Rose, Arthur Sheriff, Kate Strudwick, Jacqueline White

A Sears Pocknell book

Editorial Direction	Roger Sears
Art Direction	David Pocknell
Editor	Michael Leitch
Designers	Jonathan Allan and Bob Slater

Library of Congress Cataloging-in-Publication Data

Lord, Peter.
Creating 3-D animation : the Aardman book of filmmaking / Peter Lord and
Brian Sibley ; foreword by Nick Park. — Rev. ed.
p. cm.
Includes bibliographical references and index.
ISBN 0-8109-4971-7 (hardcover)
1. Animation (Cinematography) 2. Three-dimensional display systems. 3. Aardman Animations (Firm) I. Title: Creating three-D animation. II. Sibley, Brian. III. Aardman Animations (Firm) IV. Title.

TR897.5.L67 2004
778.5'347—dc22 2004010921

This is a revised and expanded edition of Creating 3-D Animation, The Aardman Book of Filmmaking, published in 1998 by Harry N. Abrams, Inc.

Published in 2004 by Harry N. Abrams, Incorporated, New York

Published in Great Britain under the title *Cracking Animation: The Aardman Book of 3-D Animation*
Printed and bound in Singapore by Imago

10 9 8 7 6 5 4 3 2 1

Harry N. Abrams, Inc.
100 Fifth Avenue
New York, N.Y. 10011
www.abramsbooks.com

Abrams is a subsidiary of

GOOD HOUSEKEEPING

COOKING for EVERYONE

GOOD HOUSEKEEPING INSTITUTE

EBURY PRESS
LONDON

Published by Ebury Press
National Magazine House
72 Broadwick Street
London W1V 2BP

First impression 1984

ISBN 0 85223 304 3

Designed by Bob Hall   Edited by Maria Mosby

Jacket photographed by James Jackson shows Sage and Bacon Stuffed Pork (page 81), Broccoli Amandine (page 171) and Strawberry Vacherin (page 229)

Filmset by Advanced Filmsetters (Glasgow) Ltd
Printed and bound in Italy by New Interlitho S.p.a. Milan

CONTENTS

Starters 7
Soups 21
Main Courses: Fish 34
Main Courses: Meat & Poultry 53
Eggs & Cheese 147
Pasta & Rice 179
Salads 195
Sauces & Stuffings 209
Desserts 217
Baking 239
Jams & Jellies 267
Drinks 273
Index 281

STARTERS

Lemony Bean Appetiser

100 g (4 oz) FLAGEOLETS, SOAKED OVERNIGHT AND DRAINED
FINELY GRATED RIND AND JUICE OF 1 LEMON
90 ml (6 tbsp) OLIVE OIL
1 CLOVE GARLIC, SKINNED AND CRUSHED
15 ml (1 tbsp) SNIPPED CHIVES
SALT AND FRESHLY GROUND PEPPER
225 g (8 oz) FIRM TOMATOES, SKINNED AND SLICED THINLY
FRENCH BREAD, TO SERVE

Serves 4

1. Bring a saucepan of water to the boil and cook the flageolets until tender, about 1 hour. Drain.
2. In a screw-top jar, shake together the lemon rind, juice, oil, garlic, chives and seasoning.
3. Pour the dressing over the warm beans and leave to cool. Cover and chill.
4. Arrange the tomato slices on four individual plates. Pile the beans, together with all the dressing, on the tomatoes. Serve with French bread.

Melon Seafood Salad

175 g (6 oz) SKATE
1 SMALL CARROT, PEELED AND SLICED
1 SMALL ONION, SKINNED AND SLICED
1 BAY LEAF
6 WHOLE BLACK PEPPERCORNS
5 ml (1 tsp) WINE VINEGAR
SALT AND FRESHLY GROUND PEPPER
125 g (4 oz) WHITE CRABMEAT
15 ml (1 tbsp) LEMON JUICE
45 ml (3 tbsp) DOUBLE CREAM, LIGHTLY WHIPPED
A FEW LETTUCE LEAVES
1 SMALL MELON—OGEN, GALIA OR CHARANTAIS—ABOUT 800 g (1¾ lb), SEEDED, SKINNED AND SLICED INTO 4 RINGS
4 LEMON SLICES, TO GARNISH

Serves 4

1. Just cover the skate with fresh cold water, add the carrot and onion slices, bay leaf and peppercorns with the vinegar and a good pinch of salt. Poach gently until the fish is just tender; drain well then flake the flesh, discarding skin and bones.
2. Flake the crabmeat and mix with the skate and lemon juice. Season and fold in the cream.
3. Line four individual dishes with lettuce and place a melon ring on each. Pour in the fish mixture and garnish with lemon twists.

Photographed opposite

Salami Antipasta

50 g (2 oz) PASTA SHAPES
100 g (4 oz) SALAMI, CUT INTO STRIPS
½ RED PEPPER, SEEDED AND FINELY SLICED
½ GREEN PEPPER, SEEDED AND FINELY SLICED
18 BLACK OLIVES, HALVED AND STONED
15 ml (1 tbsp) OIL
5 ml (1 tsp) VINEGAR

Serves 2

1. Bring a pan of salted water to the boil and cook the pasta shapes for 9–10 minutes until tender. Drain and leave to cool.
2. Put the cooled pasta, salami, peppers and olives into a bowl. Mix the oil and vinegar in a jug, pour over the pasta mixture and toss. Serve on individual plates.

Smoked Mackerel Mousse

300 ml (½ pint) MILK
1 ONION, SKINNED AND SLICED
1 CARROT, PEELED AND SLICED
1 BAY LEAF
10 ml (2 tsp) GELATINE
30 ml (2 tbsp) WATER
25 g (1 oz) BUTTER
30 ml (2 tbsp) PLAIN FLOUR
275 g (10 oz) SMOKED MACKEREL FILLETS
1 SMALL ONION, SKINNED AND ROUGHLY CHOPPED
15 ml (1 tbsp) CREAMED HORSERADISH
142 g (5 oz) CARTON NATURAL YOGURT
15 ml (1 tbsp) LEMON JUICE
SALT AND FRESHLY GROUND PEPPER
2 EGG WHITES
WATERCRESS SPRIGS OR LEMON SLICES, TO GARNISH
WARM FRENCH BREAD, TO SERVE

Serves 6

1. Put the milk into a saucepan with the onion, carrot and bay leaf and bring slowly to the boil. Remove from the heat, cover the pan and leave to infuse for 30 minutes.
2. Meanwhile, sprinkle the gelatine over the water in a small bowl and leave to soak for at least 10 minutes.
3. Melt the butter in a small pan, stir in the flour and cook gently for 1 minute, stirring. Remove from the heat. Strain the infused milk and gradually add it to the butter, stirring until smooth. Return to the heat and bring to the boil slowly. Continue to cook, stirring, until the sauce thickens.
4. Remove from the heat and stir in the soaked gelatine. Stir until dissolved. Pour into a bowl and cool.
5. Flake the mackerel, discarding the skin. Put the cooled sauce, fish, onion and horseradish into a blender and liquidise until smooth. Pour into a bowl and stir in the yogurt, lemon juice and seasoning to taste.
6. Whisk the egg whites until standing in soft peaks, then fold them gently through the fish mixture.
7. Spoon into six ramekin dishes and refrigerate until set. Garnish with watercress sprigs or a twist of lemon; serve chilled with warm French bread.

Melon Seafood Salad

Cheese Palmiers

Cheese Palmiers

227 g (8 oz) PACKET PUFF PASTRY, THAWED
1 EGG, BEATEN
75 g (3 oz) CHEDDAR CHEESE, GRATED
SALT AND FRESHLY GROUND PEPPER
PAPRIKA

Makes 10

1. On a lightly floured board, roll out the dough to an oblong 30 × 25 cm (12 × 10 inches). Brush with the egg.
2. Scatter over the grated cheese and sprinkle with salt, pepper and paprika.
3. Roll the dough up tightly lengthways, rolling from each side until the rolls meet in the centre. Cut across into ten pieces.
4. Dampen a baking sheet and place the dough pieces, cut side down, on it. Flatten with a round-bladed knife.
5. Bake in the oven at 200°C (400°F) mark 6 for 15–18 minutes or until brown and crisp. Ease off the baking sheet and cool on a wire rack.

Photographed left

Spiced Onions

25 g (1 oz) BUTTER
15 ml (1 tbsp) GROUND CUMIN
700 g ($1\frac{1}{2}$ lb) BUTTON ONIONS, SKINNED
1 LARGE GREEN PEPPER, SEEDED AND DICED
226 g (8 oz) CAN TOMATOES
15 ml (1 tbsp) CIDER VINEGAR
12 BLACK OLIVES, HALVED AND STONED
SALT AND FRESHLY GROUND PEPPER
WATERCRESS SPRIGS, TO GARNISH
MELBA TOAST, TO SERVE

Serves 6

1. Melt the butter in a medium-sized saucepan and gently fry the cumin for 1–2 minutes.
2. Add the onions and pepper and cook, stirring, for a few minutes before adding the tomatoes, vinegar and olives. Simmer very gently until the onions and pepper are cooked—at least 10 minutes. Season, pour into a bowl and leave to cool. Cover and chill well.
3. Transfer to individual dishes. Garnish with watercress and serve with Melba toast.

Onion and Tomato Salad

4 TOMATOES, SKINNED AND VERY THINLY SLICED
2 ONIONS, SKINNED AND VERY THINLY SLICED
45 ml (3 tbsp) OIL
15 ml (1 tbsp) VINEGAR
10 ml (2 tsp) SNIPPED CHIVES

Serves 4

1. Arrange the tomato and onion slices alternately in a shallow dish.
2. Mix the oil and vinegar in a jug and add the chives. Pour over the salad then cover and chill well.

Tuna Rice Bakes

25 g (1 oz) LONG-GRAIN RICE
98 g ($3\frac{1}{2}$ oz) CAN TUNA FISH IN OIL, REFRIGERATED OVERNIGHT, DRAINED AND FLAKED
1 EGG
MILK
5 ml (1 tsp) LEMON JUICE
15 ml (1 tbsp) CHOPPED PARSLEY
SALT AND FRESHLY GROUND PEPPER

Serves 2

1. Bring a pan of salted water to the boil and cook the rice until tender, about 15 minutes. Drain and add to the tuna.

2. Beat the egg in a measuring jug and make up to 150 ml ($\frac{1}{4}$ pint) with milk. Add the egg mixture to the fish and rice; add lemon juice and parsley and season. Divide the mixture between two 11.5 cm ($4\frac{1}{2}$ inch) foil patty-type dishes.

3. Stand the dishes in a roasting tin with 2.5 cm (1 inch) of cold water. Bake in the oven at 180°C (350°F) mark 4 for 30 minutes. Serve at once.

Prawn Cocktail

60 ml (4 tbsp) MAYONNAISE (see page 210)
60 ml (4 tbsp) SINGLE CREAM
10 ml (2 tsp) TOMATO PUREE
10 ml (2 tsp) LEMON JUICE
A DASH OF WORCESTERSHIRE SAUCE
A DASH OF DRY SHERRY
SALT AND FRESHLY GROUND PEPPER
225 g (8 oz) PEELED PRAWNS
A FEW LETTUCE LEAVES, SHREDDED
4 LEMON SLICES, TO GARNISH
THINLY SLICED BREAD AND BUTTER, TO SERVE

Serves 4

1. In a small bowl, mix together the mayonnaise, cream, tomato purée, lemon juice, Worcestershire sauce and sherry. Season then add the prawns and stir to coat.

2. Put the shredded lettuce into four glasses and top with the prawn mixture. Garnish each glass with a lemon slice. Serve with thinly sliced bread and butter.

Grilled Grapefruit

3 GRAPEFRUIT, HALVED
90 ml (6 tbsp) MEDIUM SHERRY
ABOUT 90 ml (6 tbsp) DEMERARA SUGAR

Serves 6

1. Run a serrated or grapefruit knife around each half, keeping the blade between the flesh and pith. Take care not to puncture the skin.

2. Cut around each segment to loosen from the pith, then ease out the pith and membrane.

3. Just before serving, spoon 15 ml (1 tbsp) sherry over each grapefruit half and sprinkle with sugar. Flash under a hot grill until golden. Serve at once.

Blue Cheese Dip

142 ml (5 fl oz) CARTON SOURED CREAM
1 GARLIC CLOVE, SKINNED AND CRUSHED
175 g (6 oz) BLUE STILTON CHEESE, CRUMBLED
JUICE OF 1 LEMON
SALT AND FRESHLY GROUND PEPPER
SNIPPED CHIVES, TO GARNISH
SAVOURY COCKTAIL BISCUITS, PRETZELS, CRISPS AND STUFFED OLIVES

Serves 6–8

1. Combine all the ingredients, except the chives, in a bowl and beat together well. Do not add too much salt as Stilton can be salty. Put into a small dish and chill.

2. Garnish with snipped chives. Serve with savoury cocktail biscuits, pretzels, crisps and stuffed olives.

Photographed opposite

VARIATION: CORN DIP

Omit the Stilton and garlic, adding instead 100 g (4 oz) cottage cheese and a 227 g (8 oz) drained can of corn niblets.

Avocado Appetiser

2 CRISP GREEN EATING APPLES, CORED AND THINLY SLICED
1 AVOCADO, SKINNED AND SLICED
JUICE OF $\frac{1}{2}$ LEMON
A FEW LETTUCE LEAVES OR WATERCRESS SPRIGS
45 ml (3 tbsp) OIL
15 ml (1 tbsp) VINEGAR
CHOPPED PARSLEY, TO GARNISH

Serves 4

1. Toss the apple and avocado slices in the lemon juice.

2. Arrange the lettuce leaves on four individual serving plates and spoon the avocado mixture on top.

3. Mix the oil and vinegar in a jug and pour a little dressing over each serving. Garnish with parsley and serve at once.

Herby Cheese Dip

15 ml (1 tbsp) CHOPPED FRESH MINT
15 ml (1 tbsp) CHOPPED FRESH PARSLEY
225 g (8 oz) CHEDDAR CHEESE, GRATED
125 g (4 oz) COTTAGE CHEESE
1 GARLIC CLOVE, SKINNED AND CRUSHED
6 COCKTAIL GHERKINS, CHOPPED
SALT AND FRESHLY GROUND PEPPER
WHOLE RADISHES, CUCUMBER SLICES AND CELERY STICKS, TO SERVE

Serves 6

1. Put the herbs and cheeses into a bowl and beat well until smooth. Add the garlic, gherkins and seasoning.

2. Chill and serve with radishes, cucumber and celery.

Blue Cheese Dip

Stuffed Mushrooms

Sweet Pickled Mushrooms

700 g ($1\frac{1}{2}$ lb) SMALL BUTTON MUSHROOMS, WIPED AND STALKS TRIMMED
1 SMALL ONION, SKINNED AND FINELY CHOPPED
50 g (2 oz) PICKLED GHERKINS, ROUGHLY CHOPPED
60 ml (4 tbsp) MANGO CHUTNEY, ROUGHLY CHOPPED
15 ml (1 tbsp) CHILLI SEASONING
150 ml ($\frac{1}{4}$ pint) WATER
45 ml (3 tbsp) WHITE WINE VINEGAR
SALT AND FRESHLY GROUND PEPPER
1 SMALL LETTUCE, WASHED
WARM ROLLS, TO SERVE

Serves 6

1. Put the mushrooms into a large saucepan with a tight-fitting lid together with the onion. Stir in the gherkins and mango chutney with the chilli seasoning.

2. Pour in the water and wine vinegar and bring to the boil. Cover and simmer for 5–10 minutes—do not overcook or the mushrooms will shrink. Season to taste and leave to cool in the cooking liquid, then chill well.

3. Line six individual dishes with lettuce, add the mushrooms and a little of the cooking liquid and serve accompanied by warm rolls.

Stuffed Mushrooms

75 g (3 oz) BUTTER
12 LARGE MUSHROOMS, ABOUT 350 g (12 oz) TOTAL WEIGHT, WIPED AND STALKS FINELY CHOPPED
4 STICKS CELERY, TRIMMED AND FINELY CHOPPED
1 SMALL ONION, SKINNED AND FINELY CHOPPED
50 g (2 oz) SHELLED WALNUTS, FINELY CHOPPED
75 g (3 oz) FRESH BREADCRUMBS
60 ml (4 tbsp) CHOPPED PARSLEY
30 ml (2 tbsp) LEMON JUICE
SALT AND FRESHLY GROUND PEPPER
1 EGG, BEATEN
50 g (2 oz) CHEDDAR CHEESE, GRATED
90 ml (6 tbsp) CHICKEN STOCK

Makes 12

1. Heat the butter in a medium-sized frying pan and lightly brown the rounded sides of the mushrooms, a few at a time.

2. Remove from the pan and drain on absorbent kitchen paper. Add the chopped mushroom stalks to the pan with the celery, onion and walnuts. Fry quickly for 2–3 minutes, stirring occasionally.

3. Remove from the heat and stir in the breadcrumbs, parsley, lemon juice and seasoning. Bind with the beaten egg.

4. Spoon the mixture into the mushroom caps and place side-by-side in a shallow ovenproof dish to just fit. Sprinkle a little cheese over each mushroom and pour the stock around the edges of the dish. Bake in the oven at 180°C (350°F) mark 4 for 20–25 minutes. Serve hot.

Photographed opposite

Jumbo Stuffed Tomatoes

8 LARGE TOMATOES, ABOUT 900 g (2 lb)
1 EATING APPLE, CORED AND CHOPPED
450 ml ($\frac{3}{4}$ pint) WATER
125 g (4 oz) LONG-GRAIN RICE
5 ml (1 tsp) TURMERIC
1 GREEN PEPPER, SEEDED AND FINELY CHOPPED
50 g (2 oz) SULTANAS
SALT AND FRESHLY GROUND PEPPER
142 ml (5 fl oz) CARTON SOURED CREAM

Serves 8

1. Cut the tops off the tomatoes and, using a teaspoon, scoop out the insides of the tomatoes to form shells. Turn these upside down on a flat plate and leave them to drain thoroughly.

2. Chop the tomato tops and add to the tomato flesh with the apple.

3. Salt the water, add the rice and the turmeric and bring to the boil. Add the green pepper and sultanas and season with salt and pepper. Continue cooking for 8 minutes then drain the mixture thoroughly.

4. Mix the apple mixture into the rice and pile into the tomato shells. Put them into an ovenproof dish and bake at 190°C (375°F) mark 5 for 15–20 minutes until the tomatoes are soft. Serve at once with a little soured cream.

Savoury Eggs with Stilton

50 g (2 oz) BUTTER, SOFTENED
125 g (4 oz) STILTON CHEESE, CRUMBLED
45 ml (3 tbsp) SINGLE CREAM
6 HARD-BOILED EGGS, SHELLED AND HALVED LENGTHWAYS
50 g (2 oz) WALNUT PIECES
2 STICKS CELERY, TRIMMED AND VERY FINELY CHOPPED
SALT AND FRESHLY GROUND PEPPER
WATERCRESS SPRIGS, TO GARNISH
FRENCH BREAD, TO SERVE

Serves 6

1. Beat the butter in a bowl until quite smooth and gradually work in the cheese and the cream. Scoop out the egg yolks and press them through a sieve into the cheese mixture.

2. Finely chop half the walnuts and beat them into the cheese mixture with the celery. Season to taste and spoon the mixture into a piping bag fitted with a 1 cm ($\frac{1}{2}$ inch) plain nozzle. Pipe the cheese filling into the centre of each of the egg whites.

3. Arrange the eggs side-by-side around the edge of a shallow-rimmed serving dish and sprinkle with the remaining walnut pieces. Cover and chill until 30 minutes before serving.

4. Fill the centre of the dish with watercress sprigs and serve with French bread.

Sardine Savouries

124 g ($4\frac{3}{8}$ oz) CAN SARDINES IN OIL
1 STICK CELERY, TRIMMED AND CHOPPED
SALT AND FRESHLY GROUND PEPPER
20 ml (4 tsp) LEMON JUICE
5 ml (1 tsp) CHOPPED PARSLEY
225 g (8 oz) STREAKY BACON RASHERS, RINDED AND HALVED
HOT TOAST, TO SERVE

Serves 4–6

1. Halve the sardines, remove the backbones and mash the flesh with the oil.
2. Add the celery to the sardines with the seasoning, lemon juice and parsley.
3. Stretch the halved bacon rashers with a knife. Put a small spoonful of sardine mixture on to each rasher and roll them up. Cover and chill for 30 minutes.
4. Grill the rolls, turning them frequently and serve with hot toast.

Seafood Scallops

175 g (6 oz) HADDOCK
150 ml ($\frac{1}{4}$ pint) DRY WHITE WINE
1 BUTTON ONION, SKINNED
1 PARSLEY SPRIG
1 BAY LEAF
350 g (12 oz) POTATOES, PEELED
50 g (2 oz) BUTTER
50 g (2 oz) BUTTON MUSHROOMS, WIPED AND SLICED
45 ml (3 tbsp) PLAIN FLOUR
200 ml (7 fl oz) MILK
50 g (2 oz) CHEDDAR CHEESE, GRATED
50 g (2 oz) POTTED SHRIMPS
SALT AND FRESHLY GROUND PEPPER

Serves 4

1. Put the haddock into a saucepan with the wine, onion, parsley and bay leaf. Bring to the boil and simmer for about 15 minutes.
2. Drain, reserving the liquid. Add enough water to make up to 150 ml ($\frac{1}{4}$ pint). Skin and flake the fish. Bring the potatoes to the boil in a saucepan of salted water and cook for about 20 minutes until tender. Drain, mash and set aside.
3. Melt half the butter in a saucepan, fry the mushrooms and set aside. In another pan, melt the remaining butter, stir in the flour and cook gently for 1 minute, stirring. Remove the pan from the heat and gradually stir in the strained fish liquid and the milk. Bring to the boil slowly and continue to cook, stirring, until the sauce thickens.
4. Add the flaked fish, mushrooms, cheese and potted shrimps to the sauce. Adjust the seasoning.
5. Put the mashed potato into a piping bag fitted with a star nozzle and pipe around the edge of four scallop shells or individual dishes. Spoon the fish mixture into the centre and brown under a hot grill.

Photographed right

Seafood Scallops

Tzaziki

Halibut Cocktail

225 g (8 oz) HALIBUT
5 ml (1 tsp) LEMON JUICE
½ BAY LEAF
SALT AND FRESHLY GROUND PEPPER
142 g (5 oz) CARTON NATURAL YOGURT
30 ml (2 tbsp) SEAFOOD SAUCE
½ SMALL RED PEPPER, SEEDED AND CHOPPED
A FEW WATERCRESS SPRIGS, CHOPPED
A FEW LETTUCE LEAVES, SHREDDED
PAPRIKA, TO GARNISH

Serves 4

1. Put the halibut, lemon juice and bay leaf into a small pan. Season, barely cover with water and poach gently until the fish begins to flake—about 10 minutes. Cool in the water.

2. Drain and flake the fish, discarding the bones and skin.

3. Combine the yogurt and seafood sauce and add the red pepper and watercress, then gently fold in the flaked fish.

4. Put a little shredded lettuce into four individual glass dishes, top with the fish cocktail mixture and garnish with paprika.

Anchovy Egg Appetiser

56 g (2 oz) CAN ANCHOVY FILLETS, DRAINED
60 ml (4 tbsp) MILK
100 g (4 oz) BUTTER, SOFTENED
FRESHLY GROUND BLACK PEPPER
6 HARD-BOILED EGGS, SHELLED AND HALVED LENGTHWAYS
30 ml (2 tbsp) LEMON JUICE
1 SMALL LETTUCE, WASHED
WHOLEMEAL BREAD, TO SERVE

Serves 6

1. Soak the anchovies in the milk for 20 minutes, to remove excess salt.

2. Strain the anchovies and pound them in a bowl with the butter and plenty of black pepper until smooth.

3. Sieve the egg yolks and combine them with the butter mixture and lemon juice. Adjust the seasoning and stuff the mixture into the egg whites, reshaping into whole eggs. Cover and chill well.

4. Line six individual plates with lettuce, place an egg in each and serve accompanied by wholemeal bread.

Minted Pear Vinaigrette

125 g (4 oz) STREAKY BACON, RINDED
90 ml (6 tbsp) OIL
30 ml (2 tbsp) VINEGAR
30 ml (2 tbsp) CHOPPED MINT
3 LARGE RIPE DESSERT PEARS
1 SMALL LETTUCE, WASHED

Serves 6

1. Grill the bacon until crisp, cool and scissor-snip into tiny pieces. Mix the oil and the vinegar in either a bowl or screw-topped jar with the mint and whisk or shake well together.

2. Peel and halve one of the pears and scoop out the core with a teaspoon. Brush both sides of each half immediately with a little of the dressing to prevent discoloration. Repeat with the other pears.

3. Arrange lettuce leaves on six individual serving plates. Place a pear half, cut-side up, on each plate and spoon over the remaining dressing. Sprinkle with the bacon and serve at once.

Chicken Liver Toasties

125 g (4 oz) THIN CUT STREAKY BACON RASHERS, RINDED AND CUT INTO SMALL PIECES
25 g (1 oz) BUTTER
225 g (8 oz) CHICKEN LIVERS, FINELY CHOPPED
45 ml (3 tbsp) CHOPPED PARSLEY
2 HARD-BOILED EGGS, SHELLED AND FINELY CHOPPED
SALT AND FRESHLY GROUND PEPPER
30 ml (2 tbsp) MAYONNAISE
12 SLICES THIN-CUT WHITE BREAD

Makes 24

1. Fry the bacon until crisp then drain off all the bacon fat.

2. Add the butter and chicken livers and fry quickly until the livers change colour then lower the heat and cook for 5 minutes.

3. Stir in the parsley and chopped egg. Season and bind with the mayonnaise.

4. Spread the mixture over half the bread slices, cover with the remaining slices and press down well. Remove the crusts, cut into triangles and grill until golden.

Tzaziki

½ CUCUMBER, ROUGHLY DICED
SALT AND FRESHLY GROUND PEPPER
142 g (5 oz) NATURAL YOGURT (A FIRM SET ONE IF POSSIBLE)
1 GARLIC CLOVE, SKINNED AND CRUSHED
15 ml (1 tbsp) CHOPPED MINT

Serves 4

1. Put the cucumber into a colander, sprinkle with salt and leave to stand for 30 minutes to draw out the juices. Rinse, drain well and dry with absorbent kitchen paper.

2. Transfer the cucumber to a serving bowl. Pour over the yogurt, add the garlic, mint, seasoning and mix well. Cover and chill in the refrigerator before serving.

Photographed opposite

Chicken Liver Pâté

Chicken Liver Pâté

450 g (1 lb) CHICKEN LIVERS
50 g (2 oz) BUTTER
1 ONION, SKINNED AND CHOPPED
1 GARLIC CLOVE, SKINNED AND CRUSHED
75 ml (5 tbsp) DOUBLE CREAM
15 ml (1 tbsp) TOMATO PUREE
15 ml (1 tbsp) BRANDY
SALT AND FRESHLY GROUND PEPPER
50 g (2 oz) MELTED BUTTER
PARSLEY SPRIGS, TO GARNISH
MELBA TOAST OR FRENCH BREAD, TO SERVE

Serves 8

1. Pat the chicken livers dry with absorbent kitchen paper.

2. Heat the butter in a saucepan, add the onion and garlic and cook for about 5 minutes until the onion is soft. Add the chicken livers and cook for a further 5 minutes.

3. Cool and add the fresh cream, tomato purée and brandy; season well.

4. Purée the mixture in a blender and put into a serving dish. Pour the melted butter over the top to prevent it drying out. Chill in the refrigerator.

5. Garnish with parsley sprigs and serve with Melba toast or French bread.

Photographed above

SOUPS

Red Cabbage and Sausage Soup

15 ml (1 tbsp) OIL
75 g (3 oz) ONIONS, SKINNED AND THINLY SLICED
225 g (8 oz) RED CABBAGE, FINELY SHREDDED
1 GARLIC CLOVE, SKINNED AND CRUSHED
1.1 litres (2 pints) LIGHT STOCK
397 g (14 oz) CAN TOMATOES
15 ml (1 tbsp) RED WINE VINEGAR
1.25 ml (¼ tsp) DRIED THYME
SALT AND FRESHLY GROUND PEPPER
213 g (7½ oz) CAN RED KIDNEY BEANS, DRAINED
240 g (8½ oz) PACKET SMOKED PORK SAUSAGE, CUT INTO 2 cm (¾ inch) DIAGONAL SLICES
142 ml (5 fl oz) CARTON SOURED CREAM

Serves 6

1. Heat the oil in a saucepan and fry the onion and cabbage for a few minutes.
2. Add garlic, stock, tomatoes and their juice, vinegar, thyme and seasoning. Bring to the boil, lower the heat, cover and simmer for about 25 minutes.
3. Add the beans and sausages to the soup and cook for a further 15 minutes. Adjust the seasoning and serve with a swirl of soured cream.

Mulligatawny Soup

50 g (2 oz) BUTTER
1 ONION, SKINNED AND FINELY CHOPPED
125 g (4 oz) CARROTS, PEELED AND FINELY CHOPPED
125 g (4 oz) SWEDES, PEELED AND FINELY CHOPPED
1 SMALL EATING APPLE, PEELED, CORED AND FINELY CHOPPED
50 g (2 oz) STREAKY BACON, FINELY CHOPPED
25 g (1 oz) PLAIN FLOUR
15 ml (1 tbsp) MILD CURRY PASTE
15 ml (1 tbsp) TOMATO PUREE
30 ml (2 tbsp) MANGO CHUTNEY
1.4 litres (2½ pints) BEEF STOCK
5 ml (1 tsp) DRIED MIXED HERBS
PINCH OF GROUND MACE
PINCH OF GROUND CLOVES
SALT AND FRESHLY GROUND PEPPER
50 g (2 oz) LONG-GRAIN RICE
150 ml (5 fl oz) DOUBLE CREAM

Serves 6

1. Melt the butter in a large saucepan and fry the onion, carrot, swede, apple and bacon until lightly browned.
2. Stir in the flour, curry paste, tomato purée and chutney. Cook for 1–2 minutes before adding the stock, herbs and seasonings.
3. Bring to the boil, skim and simmer, covered, for 30–40 minutes. Sieve the soup or purée in a blender.
4. Return the soup to the pan, bring to the boil, add the rice and boil gently for about 12 minutes, until the rice is tender.
5. Adjust the seasoning. Stir in the cream, reserving a little. Do not boil. Pour into a tureen or bowls and swirl with the remainder of the cream.

Photographed opposite

Cream of Parsley Soup

100 g (4 oz) BUTTER OR MARGARINE
450 g (1 lb) PARSLEY, TRIMMED AND ROUGHLY CHOPPED
450 g (1 lb) ONIONS, SKINNED AND SLICED
225 g (8 oz) CELERY, TRIMMED AND SLICED
90 ml (6 tbsp) PLAIN FLOUR
4 litres (7 pints) CHICKEN STOCK, PREFERABLY JELLIED
SALT AND FRESHLY GROUND PEPPER
300 ml (10 fl oz) SINGLE CREAM

Serves 16

1. Melt the butter in a large saucepan and add the parsley, onions and celery. Cover the pan and cook gently until the vegetables are quite soft, shaking the pan from time to time.
2. Stir in the flour and cook for 1 minute, stirring. Stir in the stock, season and bring to the boil.
3. Cover the pan and simmer for 25–30 minutes. Cool a little then purée in a blender. Return to the rinsed-out pan, adjust the seasoning and stir in cream just before serving the soup.

White Bean Soup

125 g (4 oz) ONIONS, SKINNED AND FINELY CHOPPED
1 SMALL GARLIC CLOVE, SKINNED AND CRUSHED
175 g (6 oz) HARICOT BEANS, SOAKED OVERNIGHT AND DRAINED
1.4 litres (2½ pints) LIGHT STOCK
2.5 ml (½ tsp) DRIED ROSEMARY
125 g (4 oz) RED LEICESTER CHEESE, GRATED
SALT AND FRESHLY GROUND PEPPER

Serves 6

1. Put the onion into a large saucepan with the garlic, beans and stock. Add the dried rosemary and bring to the boil. Simmer gently, covered, for about 50 minutes or until beans are tender.
2. Pour off half the stock and purée in an electric blender with half the beans.
3. Return the purée to the pan, add the cheese and adjust the seasoning. Reheat and serve at once.

Mulligatawny Soup

Curried Parsnip Soup

Golden Vegetable Soup

25 g (1 oz) BUTTER OR MARGARINE
75 g (3 oz) ONIONS, SKINNED AND FINELY SLICED
125 g (4 oz) CARROTS, PEELED AND SLICED INTO STRIPS 4 cm ($1\frac{1}{2}$ inches) LONG
125 g (4 oz) CELERY, TRIMMED AND SLICED INTO STRIPS 4 cm ($1\frac{1}{2}$ inches) LONG
125 g (4 oz) SWEDES, PEELED AND SLICED INTO STRIPS 4 cm ($1\frac{1}{2}$ inches) LONG
225 g (8 oz) CAULIFLOWER, BROKEN INTO SMALL FLORETS
2.5 ml ($\frac{1}{2}$ tsp) GROUND TURMERIC
1.1 litres (2 pints) LIGHT STOCK
SALT AND FRESHLY GROUND PEPPER
SNIPPED CHIVES, TO GARNISH

Serves 6

1. Melt the butter in a pan and add the vegetables. Cover the pan and cook gently for a few minutes, shaking the pan from time to time.
2. Add the turmeric and cook for a further few minutes. Add the stock and adjust the seasoning. Bring to the boil and simmer gently for about 15 minutes, or until the vegetables are tender. Serve garnished with snipped chives sprinkled on the top.

Spinach and Orange Soup

RIND AND JUICE OF 2 ORANGES
100 g (4 oz) MARGARINE
1 kg ($2\frac{1}{4}$ lb) FRESH LEAF SPINACH, COARSELY CHOPPED
225 g (8 oz) ONIONS, SKINNED AND FINELY CHOPPED
60 ml (4 tbsp) PLAIN FLOUR
900 ml ($1\frac{1}{2}$ pints) MILK
900 ml ($1\frac{1}{2}$ pints) CHICKEN STOCK
SALT AND FRESHLY GROUND PEPPER

Serves 6–8

1. Grate the rind of both the oranges, reserving a few strips for garnish. Bring a small pan of water to the boil and blanch the orange strips for a few minutes. Drain and set aside.
2. Melt the margarine in a large heavy-based pan, add the vegetables and grated rind. Cover with a piece of dampened greaseproof paper and the lid and sweat for about 25 minutes or until soft.
3. Stir in the flour and cook, stirring, for 1 minute. Remove from the heat and gradually add the milk and stock. Return to the heat, bring to the boil, season, and simmer for 15 minutes.
4. Purée the mixture in a blender, then return to the rinsed-out saucepan and reheat. Add the orange juice at the last minute and garnish with the orange rind.

Curried Parsnip Soup

40 g ($1\frac{1}{2}$ oz) BUTTER
1 ONION, SKINNED AND SLICED
700 g ($1\frac{1}{2}$ lb) PARSNIPS, PEELED AND FINELY DICED
5 ml (1 tsp) CURRY POWDER
2.5 ml ($\frac{1}{2}$ tsp) GROUND CUMIN
1.4 litres ($2\frac{1}{2}$ pints) CHICKEN STOCK
SALT AND FRESHLY GROUND PEPPER
142 ml (5 fl oz) CARTON SINGLE CREAM
PAPRIKA, TO GARNISH

Serves 6

1. Heat the butter in a large pan and fry the onion and parsnips together for about 3 minutes.
2. Stir in the curry powder and cumin and fry for a further 2 minutes.
3. Add the stock, bring to the boil, lower the heat and simmer covered for about 45 minutes, until the vegetables are tender.
4. Cool slightly, then, using a slotted spoon, transfer the vegetables to a blender, add a little stock and purée until smooth.
5. Return to the pan. Adjust the seasoning, add the cream and reheat to serving temperature but do not boil. Serve sprinkled with paprika.

Photographed opposite

Cannellini and Chicken Soup

225 g (8 oz) CANNELLINI BEANS, SOAKED OVERNIGHT AND DRAINED
175 g (6 oz) ONIONS, SKINNED AND CHOPPED
125 g (4 oz) CARROTS, PEELED AND COARSELY SLICED
1 STICK CELERY, TRIMMED AND COARSELY SLICED
1 LARGE CHICKEN LEG PORTION
1 BAY LEAF
1.1 litres (2 pints) WATER
SALT AND FRESHLY GROUND PEPPER
CHOPPED PARSLEY, TO GARNISH

Serves 4

1. Put the beans into a pan, cover with cold water, bring to the boil and boil for 1 hour. Drain.
2. Put the onions, carrots and celery into a large pan with the chicken portion, beans, bay leaf and water. Bring to the boil, season well, cover and simmer for 45 minutes.
3. Remove the chicken portion, discard the skin and bone. Discard the bay leaf.
4. Roughly purée the beans and vegetables, the chicken meat and a little cooking liquid in a blender.
5. Return the purée to the rinsed-out saucepan and stir in the rest of the cooking liquid. Adjust the seasoning and reheat to serving temperature. Garnish with chopped parsley.

Watercress and Carrot Soup

50 g (2 oz) BUTTER
450 g (1 lb) CARROTS, PEELED AND SLICED
225 g (8 oz) ONIONS, SKINNED AND SLICED
1.1 litres (2 pints) LIGHT STOCK
SALT AND FRESHLY GROUND PEPPER
1 LARGE BUNCH WATERCRESS, TRIMMED AND FINELY CHOPPED
60 ml (4 tbsp) SINGLE CREAM
2.5 ml ($\frac{1}{2}$ tsp) FRESHLY GROUND NUTMEG

Serves 6

1. Melt the butter in a pan and fry the carrots and onions until they begin to soften.
2. Add the stock and seasoning and bring to the boil. Lower the heat and simmer, covered for about 40 minutes until the vegetables are tender.
3. Purée in a blender and return to the rinsed-out pan with the watercress. Simmer gently for 10 minutes. Stir in the cream and nutmeg and bring to serving temperature—do not boil.

Leek and Split Pea Soup

75 g (3 oz) STREAKY BACON RASHERS, RINDED AND SNIPPED
75 g (3 oz) SPLIT PEAS, SOAKED OVERNIGHT AND DRAINED
1.1 litres (2 pints) LIGHT STOCK
SALT AND FRESHLY GROUND PEPPER
700 g ($1\frac{1}{2}$ lb) LEEKS, TRIMMED AND THINLY SLICED

Serves 6

1. Put the bacon into a large pan and heat until the fat runs. Add the split peas, stock and seasoning. Bring to the boil and simmer gently for about 45 minutes.
2. Add the leeks to the pan and continue cooking for a further 30 minutes, or until the leeks are tender. Adjust the seasoning and serve.

Celery and Stilton Soup

40 g ($1\frac{1}{2}$ oz) BUTTER OR MARGARINE
175 g (6 oz) CELERY, TRIMMED AND FINELY CHOPPED
45 ml (3 tbsp) PLAIN FLOUR
300 ml ($\frac{1}{2}$ pint) MILK
600 ml (1 pint) LIGHT STOCK, PREFERABLY UNSEASONED
225 g (8 oz) STILTON CHEESE, GRATED
SALT AND FRESHLY GROUND PEPPER

Serves 6

1. Melt the butter in a pan and gently fry the celery for 5 minutes—do not allow it to colour.
2. Stir in the flour and cook for 1 minute, stirring. Remove from the heat and gradually add the milk and stock. Bring to the boil then cover and simmer for 15 minutes, or until the celery is tender.
3. Gradually add the Stilton and stir in until melted. Add seasoning and reheat gently to serving temperature.

Bortsch

Bortsch

6 SMALL RAW BEETROOT, ABOUT 1 kg ($2\frac{1}{4}$ lb), PEELED AND COARSELY GRATED
2 ONIONS, SKINNED AND CHOPPED
1.1 litres (2 pints) BEEF STOCK
SALT AND FRESHLY GROUND PEPPER
30 ml (2 tbsp) LEMON JUICE
90 ml (6 tbsp) DRY SHERRY
142 ml (5 fl oz) CARTON SOURED CREAM
SNIPPED FRESH CHIVES, TO GARNISH

Serves 4

1. Put the beetroot into a pan with the onion, stock and seasoning. Bring to the boil and simmer, covered, for 45 minutes.

2. Strain, discard the vegetables and add the lemon juice and sherry to the liquid. Adjust the seasoning. Cool and chill well.

3. Serve swirled with soured cream and sprinkled with snipped chives.

Photographed above

Hot and Sour Soup

225 g (8 oz) BUTTON MUSHROOMS, THINLY SLICED
100 ml (4 fl oz) MEDIUM SHERRY
75 ml (5 tbsp) SOY SAUCE
30 ml (2 tbsp) CHOPPED FRESH CORIANDER
1.1 litres (2 pints) WATER
225 g (8 oz) COOKED TURKEY MEAT, THINLY SHREDDED
125 g (4 oz) SPRING ONIONS, THINLY SHREDDED
125 g (4.4 oz) JAR WHOLE BABY SWEETCORN, DRAINED AND THINLY SLICED
75 ml (5 tbsp) WHITE WINE VINEGAR
SALT AND FRESHLY GROUND PEPPER

Serves 4

1. Put the mushrooms into a large saucepan with the sherry, soy sauce, coriander and water. Bring to the boil and simmer uncovered for 15 minutes.

2. Stir the turkey, spring onions and sweetcorn into the mushroom mixture, with the wine vinegar and seasoning. Simmer for a further 5 minutes before serving.

Photographed opposite

Hot and Sour Soup

Curried Pasta Soup

50 g (2 oz) LEEKS, TRIMMED AND CUT INTO STRIPS 4 cm ($1\frac{1}{2}$ inches) LONG
30 ml (2 tbsp) OIL
100 g (4 oz) CARROTS, PEELED AND SLICED INTO STRIPS 4 cm ($1\frac{1}{2}$ inches) LONG
100 g (4 oz) CELERY, TRIMMED AND SLICED INTO STRIPS 4 cm ($1\frac{1}{2}$ inches) LONG
50 g (2 oz) ONIONS, SKINNED AND SLICED INTO STRIPS 4 cm ($1\frac{1}{2}$ inches) LONG
5 ml (1 tsp) MILD CHILLI POWDER
10 ml (2 tsp) HOT CURRY POWDER
2.3 litres (4 pints) BEEF STOCK
100 g (4 oz) EACH SWEDES AND PARSNIPS, PEELED AND CUT INTO STRIPS 4 cm ($1\frac{1}{2}$ inches) LONG
100 g (4 oz) PASTA SHELLS
SALT AND FRESHLY GROUND PEPPER

Serves 8–10

1. Bring a pan of salted water to the boil and cook the leeks for 1 minute. Set aside.
2. Heat the oil in a large pan, add the carrots, celery and onions and cook, covered, for 5 minutes. Add the spices and cook for a further 2 minutes.
3. Stir in the stock with the swedes and parsnips, bring to the boil and add the pasta and seasoning. Simmer gently for 12–15 minutes.
4. Spoon into individual serving bowls and garnish with the leeks.

Photographed opposite

Brussels Sprouts and Potato Purée

25 g (1 oz) BUTTER OR MARGARINE
225 g (8 oz) BRUSSELS SPROUTS, TRIMMED AND COARSELY CHOPPED
225 g (8 oz) POTATOES, PEELED AND SLICED
900 ml ($1\frac{1}{2}$ pints) LIGHT STOCK
SALT AND FRESHLY GROUND PEPPER
150 ml ($\frac{1}{4}$ pint) MILK
30 ml (2 tbsp) DOUBLE CREAM
CHOPPED WALNUTS, TO GARNISH

Serves 6

1. Heat the butter, add the sprouts and fry for a few minutes. Add the potatoes, stock and seasoning and bring to the boil. Simmer, covered, for 25 minutes or until the potatoes are tender.
2. Cool slightly, then purée the vegetables and stock in a blender.
3. Return to the rinsed-out pan then add the milk and heat thoroughly. Add the cream, adjust the seasoning and reheat, without boiling. Serve in individual bowls and scatter a few walnuts over the surface of each.

Cheese and Celery Potage

50 g (2 oz) BUTTER
400 g (14 oz) CELERY, TRIMMED AND THINLY SLICED
50 g (2 oz) LONG-GRAIN BROWN RICE
75 g (3 oz) SMOKED STREAKY BACON, RINDED AND COARSELY CHOPPED
30 ml (2 tbsp) PLAIN FLOUR
600 ml (1 pint) MILK
600 ml (1 pint) WATER
125 g (4 oz) MATURE CHEDDAR CHEESE, COARSELY GRATED
SALT AND FRESHLY GROUND PEPPER

Serves 4

1. Melt the butter in a pan, add the celery, rice and bacon and fry until golden, about 3–4 minutes.
2. Stir in the flour and cook, stirring, for 1 minute. Remove from the heat and gradually add the milk and water. Bring to the boil. Cover and simmer for 1 hour, or until the rice is tender.
3. Remove from the heat and stir in half the cheese. Season and transfer to a flameproof dish or individual flameproof bowls. Sprinkle the remaining cheese on top and brown under a hot grill for 2–3 minutes before serving. This soup may have a curdled appearance.

Cauliflower Buttermilk Soup

50 g (2 oz) BUTTER OR MARGARINE
175 g (6 oz) ONIONS, SKINNED AND COARSELY CHOPPED
1 GARLIC CLOVE, SKINNED AND CRUSHED
15 ml (1 tbsp) PLAIN FLOUR
900 ml ($1\frac{1}{2}$ pints) MILK
900 g (2 lb) CAULIFLOWER, BROKEN INTO SMALL FLORETS
2 EGGS, BEATEN
300 ml ($\frac{1}{2}$ pint) BUTTERMILK
PINCH OF FRESHLY GRATED NUTMEG
SALT AND FRESHLY GROUND PEPPER
25 g (1 oz) FLAKED ALMONDS
15 ml (1 tbsp) CHOPPED PARSLEY

Serves 6

1. Melt half the butter in a pan and gently fry the onion and garlic for 3–4 minutes until golden. Stir in the flour and cook, stirring, for 1 minute. Remove from the heat and gradually add the milk. Stir in the cauliflower and return to the heat. Bring to the boil, cover and simmer for 25–30 minutes until the cauliflower is very soft. Purée the mixture in a blender.
2. Return the purée to the rinsed-out saucepan. Beat in the eggs, buttermilk, nutmeg and seasoning. Reheat very gently—do not boil.
3. Melt the remaining fat and gently fry the almonds and parsley together until the nuts are golden. Scatter over the soup before serving.

Curried Pasta Soup

Mussel Bisque

40 g ($1\frac{1}{2}$ oz) BUTTER
45 ml (3 tbsp) PLAIN FLOUR
900 ml ($1\frac{1}{2}$ pints) MILK
150 ml ($\frac{1}{4}$ pint) WHITE WINE
SALT AND FRESHLY GROUND PEPPER
FOUR 113 g (4 oz) CANS MUSSELS, DRAINED
2 EGG YOLKS
45 ml (3 tbsp) DOUBLE CREAM
15 ml (1 tbsp) CHOPPED PARSLEY, TO GARNISH

Serves 6

1. Melt the butter in a pan, stir in the flour and cook gently for 1 minute, stirring. Remove from the heat and gradually add the milk, stirring until smooth. Add the white wine and season well. Return to the heat and bring to the boil slowly. Continue to cook slowly until the sauce thickens.

2. Add the mussels and, stirring all the time, cook over low heat for 10 minutes to heat the fish thoroughly.

3. Mix the egg yolks with the double cream in a small bowl. Add a little of the fish liquid to the cream and pour into the soup. Reheat without boiling.

4. Spoon into bowls and sprinkle with parsley.

Swede and Lentil Purée

50 g (2 oz) MARGARINE
700 g (1½ lb) SWEDES, PEELED AND THINLY SLICED
125 g (4 oz) ONIONS. SKINNED AND SLICED
ABOUT 2.3 litres (4 pints) BONE STOCK OR BEEF STOCK
225 g (8 oz) LENTILS, SOAKED IN BOILING WATER FOR 2 HOURS, DRAINED
SALT AND FRESHLY GROUND BLACK PEPPER
142 ml (5 fl oz) CARTON SOURED CREAM, WELL STIRRED
CHOPPED PARSLEY, TO GARNISH

Serves 8–10

1. Melt the margarine in a large, heavy-based pan and gently fry the swedes and onions for 10 minutes.
2. Add the stock, drained lentils and seasoning. Bring to the boil, cover and simmer for about 45 minutes or until the vegetables are really soft.
3. Purée the soup in a blender and return to the rinsed-out pan to reheat. Adjust the seasoning, adding more stock if necessary. Serve with soured cream and garnished with parsley.

Mushroom and Rice Broth

50 g (2 oz) ONIONS, SKINNED AND FINELY CHOPPED
50 g (2 oz) BROWN RICE
1.4 litres (2½ pints) LIGHT STOCK
SALT AND FRESHLY GROUND PEPPER
25 g (1 oz) BUTTER OR MARGARINE
225 g (8 oz) MUSHROOMS, WIPED AND SLICED
30 ml (2 tbsp) PLAIN FLOUR
SNIPPED CHIVES, TO GARNISH

Serves 6

1. Put the onion into a large pan with the brown rice, stock and seasoning. Bring to the boil and simmer, covered, for about 40 minutes, or until the rice is tender.
2. Melt the butter in a large saucepan and gently fry the mushrooms for about 3 minutes. Stir in the flour, mixing well to coat the mushrooms and cook over low heat for 5 minutes.
3. Slowly stir in the stock and rice mixture and bring to the boil. Simmer gently for 5 minutes, stirring. Serve sprinkled with snipped chives.

Carrot and Cardamom Soup

50 g (2 oz) BUTTER
200 g (7 oz) CARROTS, PEELED AND COARSELY GRATED
125 g (4 oz) ONIONS, SKINNED AND THINLY SLICED
10 WHOLE GREEN CARDAMOMS, SEEDS REMOVED AND CRUSHED
50 g (2 oz) LENTILS
1.1 litres (2 pints) CHICKEN STOCK
SALT AND FRESHLY GROUND PEPPER

Serves 4

1. Melt the butter in a pan and gently fry the carrot and onion for 4–5 minutes. Stir in the cardamom seeds with the lentils. Cook, stirring for a further 1–2 minutes.
2. Add the chicken stock and bring to the boil. Cover and simmer gently for about 20 minutes, or until the lentils are just tender. Season before serving.

Chicken and Macaroni Broth

2 GOOD-SIZED CHICKEN PORTIONS
1.6 litres (2¾ pints) WATER
125 g (4 oz) ONIONS, SKINNED AND CHOPPED
175 g (6 oz) SWEDES, PEELED AND DICED
125 g (4 oz) PARSNIPS, PEELED AND DICED
SALT AND FRESHLY GROUND PEPPER
50 g (2 oz) SHORT-CUT MACARONI
125 g (4 oz) CARROTS, PEELED AND GRATED
60 ml (4 tbsp) CHOPPED PARSLEY

Serves 6

1. Put the chicken portions into a large pan with the water. Add the onion, swede, parsnip and plenty of seasoning. Bring to the boil, lower the heat and simmer, covered, for about 1 hour.
2. Remove the chicken portions. Stir in the macaroni and carrot and continue cooking for a further 15 minutes.
3. Meanwhile, discard the skin and bones from the chicken and shred the flesh into bite-sized pieces.
4. Return the chicken meat to the soup and stir in the parsley. Cook for a further 5 minutes. Adjust the seasoning.

Cream of Onion Soup

25 g (1 oz) BUTTER
450 g (1 lb) ONIONS, SKINNED AND THINLY SLICED
568 ml (1 pint) MILK
300 ml (½ pint) WATER; AND 45 ml (3 tbsp)
SALT AND FRESHLY GROUND PEPPER
20 ml (4 tsp) CORNFLOUR
45 ml (3 tbsp) SINGLE CREAM
PARSLEY SPRIGS, TO GARNISH

Serves 4

1. Heat the butter in a saucepan, add the onions, cover and cook gently until softened, shaking the pan occasionally to prevent browning.
2. Add the milk, 300 ml (½ pint) water and seasoning and bring to the boil, stirring. Lower the heat and simmer covered for about 25 minutes, until the onion is tender.
3. Blend the cornflour with 45 ml (3 tbsp) water, stir into the soup and bring to the boil. Cook gently for a few minutes until slightly thickened, stirring.
4. Add the cream, adjust the seasoning and reheat without boiling. Garnish with parsley sprigs and serve at once.

Photographed opposite

Cream of Onion Soup

Shropshire Pea Soup

Shropshire Pea Soup

50 g (2 oz) BUTTER
1 SMALL ONION, SKINNED AND FINELY CHOPPED
900 g (2 lb) FRESH PEAS, SHELLED
1.1 litres (2 pints) CHICKEN STOCK
2.5 ml ($\frac{1}{2}$ tsp) CASTER SUGAR
2 LARGE MINT SPRIGS
SALT AND FRESHLY GROUND PEPPER
2 EGG YOLKS, SIZE 2
142 ml (5 fl oz) CARTON DOUBLE CREAM
1 MINT SPRIG, TO GARNISH (optional)

Serves 4

1. Melt the butter in a large saucepan, add the onion and cook for 5 minutes until soft. Add the peas, stock, sugar and mint sprigs. Bring to the boil and cook for about 30 minutes.

2. Put the soup through a fine sieve or purée in a blender. Return to the pan and add the seasoning.

3. In a bowl, beat together the yolks and cream and add to the soup. Heat gently, stirring, but do not boil otherwise it will curdle.

4. Transfer to a soup tureen and garnish with a mint sprig, if wished.

Photographed above

Speedy Tomato and Pepper Soup

TWO 400 g (14 oz) CANS TOMATOES
200 g (7 oz) CAN PIMIENTOS, DRAINED
30 ml (2 tbsp) OIL
1 LARGE GARLIC CLOVE, SKINNED AND CRUSHED
50 g (2 oz) ONIONS, SKINNED AND FINELY CHOPPED
30 ml (2 tbsp) PLAIN FLOUR
600 ml (1 pint) CHICKEN STOCK
SALT AND FRESHLY GROUND PEPPER
SNIPPED CHIVES, TO GARNISH

Serves 6–8

1. Purée the tomatoes and pimientos in a blender, then sieve to remove the seeds.

2. Heat the oil in pan and add the garlic and onion. Cover the pan and cook until the onion is soft, about 10 minutes.

3. Stir in the flour and gradually stir in the stock. Add the puréed ingredients and bring to the boil. Simmer gently for about 15 minutes.

4. Adjust the seasoning and garnish with snipped chives before serving.

MAIN COURSES
·FISH·

Omelette Arnold Bennett

100 g (4 oz) SMOKED HADDOCK
50 g (2 oz) BUTTER
150 ml ($\frac{1}{4}$ pint) DOUBLE CREAM
3 EGGS, SEPARATED
SALT AND FRESHLY GROUND PEPPER
50 g (2 oz) CHEDDAR CHEESE, GRATED

Serves 2

1. Put the fish into a saucepan and cover with water. Bring to the boil and simmer gently for 10 minutes. Drain and flake the fish, discarding skin and bones.

2. Put the fish into a pan with half the butter and 30 ml (2 tbsp) double cream. Toss over a high heat until the butter melts. Leave to cool.

3. Beat the egg yolks in a bowl with 15 ml (1 tbsp) double cream and seasoning. Stir in the fish mixture. Stiffly whisk the egg whites and fold in.

4. Heat the remaining butter in an omelette pan. Fry the egg mixture, but make sure it remains fairly fluid. Do not fold over. Slide it on to a flameproof serving dish.

5. Blend the cheese and remaining double cream and spread on top of the omelette, then quickly bubble under a high grill. Slide on to a heatproof serving plate.

Photographed right

Fresh Sardines with Herbs

60 ml (4 tbsp) CHOPPED MINT
60 ml (4 tbsp) CHOPPED PARSLEY
60 ml (4 tbsp) CHOPPED SAGE
GRATED RIND OF 2 LEMONS
120 ml (8 tbsp) LEMON JUICE
300 ml ($\frac{1}{2}$ pint) OIL
225 g (8 oz) ONIONS, SKINNED AND FINELY SLICED
SALT AND FRESHLY GROUND PEPPER
900 g (2 lb) FRESH SARDINES (AT LEAST 12), CLEANED
LEMON WEDGES, TO GARNISH

Serves 12 buffet portions

1. Reserve 5 ml (1 tsp) each of the herbs. Mix the remainder with the lemon rind, juice, oil, onions and seasoning.

2. Grill the sardines for 5–7 minutes each side, basting with the herb dressing. Leave in the dressing to cool completely. Sprinkle with the reserved herbs before serving. Garnish with lemon wedges.

Omelette Arnold Bennett

Fish Croquettes

Fish Croquettes

350 g (12 oz) FRESH HADDOCK OR COD FILLET
300 ml (½ pint) MILK
1 SMALL ONION, SKINNED AND SLICED
1 SMALL CARROT, PEELED AND SLICED
1 BAY LEAF
SALT AND FRESHLY GROUND PEPPER
50 g (2 oz) MARGARINE
PLAIN FLOUR
30 ml (2 tbsp) FINELY CHOPPED PARSLEY
30 ml (2 tbsp) CAPERS, ROUGHLY CHOPPED
5 ml (1 tsp) LEMON JUICE
CAYENNE PEPPER
1 EGG, BEATEN
50 g (2 oz) DRIED WHITE BREADCRUMBS
OIL, FOR DEEP-FRYING
TARTARE SAUCE, TO SERVE (see page 210)

Makes 12 croquettes

1. Put the fish into a medium-sized frying pan. Pour over the milk and add the onion, carrot and bay leaf with a good pinch of salt. Bring slowly to the boil, cover the pan and simmer gently for about 10 minutes, or until the fish is cooked—it flakes when tested with a fork.

2. Lift the fish out of the milk with a fish slice, and place on a plate. Flake the fish with two forks, discarding the skin and bones. Strain and reserve the milk.

3. Melt the margarine in a saucepan. Stir in 50 g (2 oz) flour and cook over a moderate heat for 1 minute, stirring occasionally. Remove from the heat and pour on the reserved milk, all at once, then stir until evenly blended. Return to the heat, bring to the boil, stirring all the time and cook for 2 minutes. It will be very thick.

4. Remove from the heat and stir in the fish, beating until smooth. Stir in the parsley with the capers and lemon juice, mixing well. Season to taste with salt and ground pepper and add a sprinkling of cayenne pepper.

5. Turn the fish mixture into a 15 cm (6 inch) square shallow dish—not a metallic one and leave until cold. Cover tightly with cling film and chill for several hours until firm.

6. When firm, divide the fish mixture in half and mark each portion into six fingers. With lightly floured hands, roll each portion into a sausage shape, about 7.5 cm (3 inches) long.

7. Brush a few croquettes at a time with beaten egg. Lift out of the egg with a slotted spoon and coat in the crumbs. Using a palette knife press the crumbs over the croquettes. Chill for 30 minutes.

8. Half fill a medium-sized saucepan with oil and heat gently to 180°C (350°F). Place a few croquettes at a time into a frying basket and lower gently into the oil. Fry for 2–3 minutes, or until golden brown. Drain on absorbent kitchen paper; keep warm, uncovered, in a low oven while frying the remaining croquettes. Serve with Tartare Sauce.

Photographed opposite

Smoked Cod Patties

450 g (1 lb) SMOKED COD FILLET
1 BAY LEAF
150 ml (¼ pint) MILK
25 g (1 oz) MARGARINE
125 g (4 oz) CARROTS, PEELED AND COARSELY GRATED
75 ml (5 tbsp) PLAIN FLOUR
GRATED RIND OF 1 LEMON
SALT AND FRESHLY GROUND PEPPER
1 EGG, BEATEN
50 g (2 oz) FRESH WHITE BREADCRUMBS
OIL, FOR FRYING

Makes 8

1. Put the cod, bay leaf and milk into a small saucepan and poach gently for 12–15 minutes. Drain well, reserving liquid. Discard the bay leaf.

2. Melt the margarine in a saucepan. Stir in the carrot and 60 ml (4 tbsp) flour. Cook, stirring for 1 minute, before adding the reserved liquid. Bring to the boil, stirring briskly, then simmer for 2 minutes until thickened.

3. Skin and flake the fish. Stir into the sauce with the lemon rind and seasoning. Turn on to a plate and leave to cool.

4. With wet hands shape the mixture into eight patties, about 1 cm (½ inch) in depth. Season the remaining flour and coat the patties in it, then in the egg and breadcrumbs. Chill for at least 20 minutes before frying.

5. Heat sufficient oil in a large frying pan to come halfway up the sides of the patties. Fry the patties for 3–4 minutes on each side.

Deep-fried Fish Fillets

125 g (4 oz) PLAIN FLOUR
PINCH OF SALT
1 EGG
150 ml (¼ pint) MILK OR MILK AND WATER
OIL OR FAT, FOR DEEP-FRYING
700 g (1½ lb) WHITE FISH FILLETS
SEASONED FLOUR

Serves 4

1. Mix together the flour and salt, make a well in the centre and break in the egg. Add the liquid gradually beating until smooth.

2. Heat the oil or fat to 177–188°C (350–370°F). Test with a thermometer or by dropping in a bread cube, which should brown in 1 minute.

3. When the oil is hot, coat each piece of fish with seasoned flour and then with batter.

4. Lower the fish gently into the fat, cooking two at a time to avoid lowering the temperature. Cook 5–10 minutes, until golden.

5. Remove the fish pieces and drain thoroughly on absorbent kitchen paper. Keep hot while cooking the remaining pieces.

Stir-fried Prawns

75 ml (5 tbsp) WATER
30 ml (2 tbsp) CORNFLOUR
20 ml (4 tsp) SOY SAUCE
5 ml (1 tsp) SUGAR
60 ml (4 tbsp) OIL
25–50 g (1–2 oz) BLANCHED ALMONDS
350 g (12 oz) CHINESE CABBAGE, TRIMMED AND CUT INTO 5 cm (2 inch) PIECES
6 SPRING ONIONS, TRIMMED AND CUT INTO 2.5 cm (1 inch) PIECES
50 g (2 oz) SHELLED PEAS
15 ml (1 tbsp) SALT
450 (1 lb) SHELLED PRAWNS, THAWED AND DRAINED, IF FROZEN
2.5 ml ($\frac{1}{2}$ tsp) GROUND GINGER
2.5–5 ml ($\frac{1}{2}$–1 tsp) PAPRIKA
120 g ($4\frac{1}{4}$ oz) CAN WHOLE MUSHROOMS, DRAINED
30 ml (2 tbsp) DRY SHERRY

Serves 4

1. Mix the water, cornflour, soy sauce and sugar in a bowl and set aside. Heat 30 ml (2 tbsp) oil in a large frying pan and fry the almonds until lightly browned, stirring frequently. Remove and drain well.
2. Stir-fry the cabbage, spring onions and peas with 5 ml (1 tsp) salt in the oil remaining in the pan for 2 minutes, or until the vegetables are tender but still slightly crisp.
3. Stir 15 ml (1 tbsp) of the cornflour mixture into the vegetables. Cook until it thickens and coats the vegetables, then remove to a serving dish and keep hot.
4. Put the remaining oil in the pan and add the prawns, ginger, paprika and remaining salt. Stir-fry for 3–4 minutes until the prawns are heated through, then add the mushrooms, sherry and remaining cornflour mixture. Stir-fry for a further 3–4 minutes until the mixture thickens and coats the prawns.
5. Spoon the prawn mixture over the vegetables and sprinkle with the almonds.

Haddock Kedgeree

175 g (6 oz) BROWN RICE
350 g (12 oz) SMOKED HADDOCK
2 HARD-BOILED EGGS, SHELLED
75 g (3 oz) BUTTER OR MARGARINE
SALT AND FRESHLY GROUND PEPPER
CHOPPED PARSLEY, TO GARNISH

Serves 4

1. Cook the rice the night before: bring a large saucepan of lightly salted water to the boil. Stir in the rice, cover and simmer for 40–45 minutes or until the rice is just tender. Drain, rinse in cold water to stop the cooking process and drain again. Leave to cool completely, then cover and chill overnight.
2. The next day, put the haddock in a large bowl or jug and cover with boiling water. Leave for 10–15 minutes or until the haddock is tender, then drain, skin and flake the fish.
3. Chop one egg and slice the other into rings. Melt the butter in a pan, add the rice, fish, chopped egg, seasoning and stir over a moderate heat for about 5 minutes or until hot.
4. Pile on to a warmed serving dish and garnish with parsley and the sliced egg.

Prawn Curry

25 g (1 oz) BUTTER
2 ONIONS, SKINNED AND CHOPPED
1 COOKING APPLE, PEELED AND CHOPPED
15 ml (1 tbsp) CURRY POWDER
5 ml (1 tsp) CURRY PASTE
15 ml (1 tbsp) PLAIN FLOUR
300 ml ($\frac{1}{2}$ pint) CHICKEN STOCK
15 ml (1 tbsp) SWEET CHUTNEY
15 ml (1 tbsp) TOMATO PUREE
PINCH CAYENNE PEPPER
LEMON JUICE
350 g (12 oz) SHELLED PRAWNS, THAWED AND DRAINED, IF FROZEN
SALT
30–45 ml (2–3 tbsp) SINGLE CREAM (optional)

Serves 3–4

1. Melt the butter in a large saucepan, add the onions and apple. Fry gently for 5–8 minutes without browning. Add the curry powder and paste and cook for 5 minutes, stirring occasionally.
2. Stir in the flour and cook for 1 minute. Gradually add the stock and bring to the boil, continuing to stir. Add the chutney, tomato purée, cayenne pepper and a squeeze of lemon juice. Cover and simmer for about 45 minutes.
3. Add the prawns to the sauce and heat through. Adjust the seasoning and stir in a little cream if a slightly milder flavour is preferred.

Trout in Cream

4 TROUT, CLEANED WITH HEADS LEFT ON, IF WISHED
JUICE OF 1 LEMON
15 ml (1 tbsp) CHOPPED CHIVES
15 ml (1 tbsp) CHOPPED PARSLEY
15 ml (1 tbsp) WATER
142 ml (5 fl oz) CARTON SINGLE CREAM
30 ml (2 tbsp) FRESH BREADCRUMBS
A LITTLE BUTTER, MELTED

Serves 4

1. Butter a shallow flameproof dish and lay the fish in it.
2. Sprinkle over the lemon juice, herbs and about 15 ml (1 tbsp) water. Cover with foil.
3. Cook in the oven at 180°C (350°F) mark 4 for 10–15 minutes, until tender.
4. Heat the cream gently and pour over the fish. Sprinkle with breadcrumbs and melted butter and brown under a hot grill. Serve immediately.

Photographed opposite

Trout in Cream

Cod with Coriander in Cream

Cod with Coriander in Cream

30 ml (2 tbsp) PLAIN FLOUR
10 ml (2 tsp) GROUND CORIANDER
SALT AND FRESHLY GROUND PEPPER
450 g (1 lb) THICK CUT COD FILLET, SKINNED AND DIVIDED INTO 4
50 g (2 oz) BUTTER
15–30 ml (1–2 tbsp) LEMON JUICE
15 ml (1 tbsp) CAPERS
1 EGG YOLK
90 ml (6 tbsp) SINGLE CREAM

Serves 4

1. Mix the flour, ground coriander and seasoning together and coat the fish pieces with this mixture.

2. Heat the butter in a medium-sized frying pan and cook the fish gently until golden on both sides, turning only once.

3. Add 15 ml (1 tbsp) lemon juice to the pan with the capers, cover tightly and continue cooking for a further 4–5 minutes, until the fish is tender. Place the fish on a warm serving dish.

4. Mix the egg yolk and cream together, stir into the pan juices and heat gently until the sauce thickens—do not boil. Adjust the seasoning, adding extra lemon juice, if wished, and spoon the sauce over the fish.

Photographed left

Baked Fillets with Lemon Sauce

700 g ($1\frac{1}{2}$ lb) SOLE OR PLAICE FILLETS, SKINNED
SALT AND FRESHLY GROUND PEPPER
40 g ($1\frac{1}{2}$ oz) BUTTER
15 ml (1 tbsp) PLAIN FLOUR
150 ml ($\frac{1}{4}$ pint) CHICKEN STOCK
15 ml (1 tbsp) LEMON JUICE
1 EGG YOLK
5 ml (1 tsp) WATER
4 STUFFED OLIVES, SLICED, TO GARNISH

Serves 4

1. Grease a large ovenproof dish and arrange the fillets in it. Sprinkle them with salt and pepper and dot with 25 g (1 oz) butter.

2. Bake the fish at 180°C (350°F) mark 4 for 10 minutes or until tender. Spoon off any cooking liquid and discard it.

3. Make the sauce. Melt the remaining butter in a small saucepan and stir in the flour. Cook gently for 2–3 minutes. Gradually add the chicken stock and lemon juice and cook until the sauce thickens slightly, stirring all the time.

4. Beat the egg yolk with the water and add a little of the hot sauce, stirring rapidly. Pour the mixture slowly back into the sauce and cook without boiling until it has thickened, stirring all the time. Adjust the seasoning to taste.

5. Pour the sauce over the baked fish and garnish with the sliced olives.

Barley-stuffed Mackerel

100 g (4 oz) TOASTED BARLEY FLAKES
100 g (4 oz) BUTTER OR MARGARINE
1 SMALL ONION, SKINNED AND FINELY CHOPPED
GRATED RIND AND JUICE OF 1 LEMON
SALT AND FRESHLY GROUND PEPPER
4 MACKEREL, CLEANED AND HEADS REMOVED
LEMON SLICES AND WATERCRESS, TO GARNISH

Serves 4

1. Beat together the barley flakes and the butter. Add the onion with the lemon rind and juice and the seasoning.

2. Lightly grease a shallow ovenproof dish. Divide the stuffing into four and use to fill the fish. Place the fish in the prepared dish. Cover and bake in the oven at 180°C (350°F) mark 4 for 30 minutes, until tender. Garnish with lemon slices and watercress.

Smothered Mackerel

4 MACKEREL, CLEANED AND HEADS REMOVED
1 LARGE ONION, SKINNED AND SLICED
2 TOMATOES, SKINNED AND SLICED
GRATED RIND AND JUICE OF 1 LEMON
SALT AND FRESHLY GROUND PEPPER
1 BAY LEAF
15 ml (1 tbsp) CHOPPED PARSLEY
2.5 ml (½ tsp) GROUND MACE

Serves 4

1. Put the fish into an ovenproof dish and cover with the onion and tomatoes. Add the remaining ingredients and cover the dish.

2. Bake in the oven at 190°C (375°F) mark 5 for 30 minutes. Uncover and cook for a further 10 minutes until the fish are tender.

Curried Haddock Crêpes

175 g (6 oz) PLAIN FLOUR; PLUS 45 ml (3 tbsp)
50 g (2 oz) SALTED PEANUTS, FINELY CHOPPED
2 EGGS
15 ml (1 tbsp) VEGETABLE OIL
450 ml (¾ pint) MILK OR WATER MIXED
BUTTER, FOR FRYING
700 g (1½ lb) SMOKED HADDOCK, COD, OR WHITING FILLETS
568 ml (1 pint) MILK
125 g (4 oz) CELERY, CHOPPED
10 ml (2 tsp) MILD CURRY POWDER
SALT AND FRESHLY GROUND PEPPER
75 ml (5 tbsp) SINGLE CREAM
50 g (2 oz) CHEDDAR CHEESE, GRATED
CHOPPED PARSLEY, TO GARNISH

Serves 6

1. To make the batter: whisk the 175 g (6 oz) flour, peanuts, eggs, oil and half the milk and water mixture until quite smooth. Whisk in the remaining liquid.

2. Melt a knob of butter in a 19 cm (7½ inch) frying pan, tilting the pan so that the melted butter coats the base. Pour in enough batter to cover the base of the pan and cook for about 3 minutes until golden underneath. Turn and cook the other side. Repeat with the remaining batter to make twelve pancakes. Keep them covered.

3. Put the fish into a deep frying pan with the milk, cover and poach gently until the fish is quite tender and begins to flake—about 12 minutes. Strain off and reserve the fish stock.

4. Flake the fish, discarding the skin and bones.

5. Melt 50 g (2 oz) butter in a heavy-based pan, fry the celery and curry powder together for 1 minute, stirring. Remove from the heat, stir in the remaining flour, reserved fish stock and seasoning—be cautious with salt as the fish may be salty enough. Bring to the boil, stirring. Boil for 1 minute then remove from the heat and fold in the cream and flaked fish.

6. Grease a shallow ovenproof dish. Divide the filling between the pancakes, roll up and place side-by-side in a single layer in the dish. Sprinkle the grated cheese over the top and cover loosely with foil. Bake at 180°C (350°F) mark 4 for about 40 minutes. Serve really hot sprinkled with parsley.

Haddock and Mushroom Puffs

397 g (14 oz) PACKET FROZEN PUFF PASTRY, THAWED
450 g (1 lb) HADDOCK FILLET, SKINNED AND CUT INTO 4 PIECES
213 g (7½ oz) CAN CREAMED MUSHROOMS
5 ml (1 tsp) LEMON JUICE
20 ml (4 tsp) CAPERS, CHOPPED
15 ml (1 tbsp) CHOPPED FRESH CHIVES OR 5 ml (1 tsp) DRIED
SALT AND FRESHLY GROUND PEPPER
1 EGG, BEATEN, FOR GLAZING

Serves 4

1. On a lightly floured surface, roll the pastry into a 40 cm (16 inch) square. Using a sharp knife, cut into four squares, trim the edges and reserve the trimmings. Place the squares on dampened baking sheets.

2. Place a piece of fish diagonally across each of the pastry squares.

3. Combine the creamed mushrooms, lemon juice, capers, chives, and seasoning. Mix well, then spoon over the fish.

4. Brush the edges of each square lightly with water. Bring the four points of each square together and seal the edges to form an envelope. Decorate with the pastry trimmings and make a small hole in the centre of each parcel.

5. Glaze the pastry with beaten egg and bake in the oven at 220°C (425°F) mark 7 for about 20 minutes, or until the pastry is golden brown and well risen.

Photographed opposite

Haddock and Mushroom Puffs

Butter Bean and Fish Pie

Butter Bean and Fish Pie

175 g (6 oz) DRIED BUTTER BEANS, SOAKED OVERNIGHT AND DRAINED
700 g ($1\frac{1}{2}$ lb) POTATOES, PEELED
350 g (12 oz) COD FILLET, SKINNED
ABOUT 600 ml (1 pint) MILK
SALT AND FRESHLY GROUND PEPPER
40 g ($1\frac{1}{2}$ oz) BUTTER OR MARGARINE
45 ml (3 tbsp) PLAIN FLOUR
45 ml (3 tbsp) CHOPPED PARSLEY
15 ml (1 tbsp) LEMON JUICE
1 EGG, BEATEN, TO GLAZE

Serves 4

1. Put the beans into a pan, cover with water and bring to the boil. Lower the heat and simmer for about 50 minutes. Drain well. Boil the potatoes and drain.

2. Meanwhile, poach the fish in 450 ml ($\frac{3}{4}$ pint) seasoned milk. Drain, reserving the cooking liquid. Flake the fish, discarding any bones.

3. Melt the butter in a pan, stir in the flour and cook gently for 1 minute, stirring. Remove from the heat and gradually add the reserved liquid, stirring until smooth. Add the parsley, lemon juice and seasoning.

4. Spoon the fish and half the beans into a pie dish. Pour over the sauce.

5. Purée the rest of the beans with half the remaining milk in a blender.

6. Mash the potatoes and combine with the beans adding enough milk to give a spreading consistency. Season well and use to top the fish mixture.

7. Brush with beaten egg and bake at 200°C (400°F) mark 6 for about 30 minutes or until golden.

Photographed above

Fish en Papillote

50 g (2 oz) BROWN RICE
SALT AND FRESHLY GROUND PEPPER
25 g (1 oz) MARGARINE OR BUTTER
50 g (2 oz) SPRING ONIONS, TRIMMED AND FINELY CHOPPED
½ SMALL BUNCH WATERCRESS, TRIMMED AND FINELY CHOPPED
50 g (2 oz) DRIED APRICOTS, SOAKED OVERNIGHT, DRAINED AND SNIPPED INTO SMALL PIECES
15 ml (1 tbsp) LEMON JUICE
2 MACKEREL, ABOUT 275–350 g (10–12 oz) EACH CLEANED, FILLETED AND HEADS AND TAILS REMOVED
OIL OR LARD, FOR FRYING
LEMON WEDGES, TO GARNISH

Serves 2

1. Bring a pan of salted water to the boil and cook the rice for about 40 minutes until tender. Drain well.

2. Melt the margarine in a pan and gently fry the onion until golden. Remove from the heat and stir in the cooked brown rice together with the chopped watercress, apricots and lemon juice. Season well and turn on to a plate to cool.

3. Pat the two fish dry with absorbent kitchen paper and divide the stuffing between them. Fill a large saucepan of about 25 cm (10 inches) diameter, with oil or lard to a depth of about 6.5 cm (2½ inches). Heat gently to 320°C (170°F), testing with a fat thermometer.

4. Cut two 30 cm (12 inch) squares of greaseproof paper, grease well and place one fish in the centre of each. Season the fish and wrap the paper over to form a loose parcel, making several folds along the join to ensure a good seal. Twist the ends firmly and secure with paper (not plastic) twist ties.

5. Carefully lower the parcels into the oil. Adjust the heat to maintain a steady temperature of 170°C (320°F) and fry the fish for 7 minutes. Lift out the parcels with a slotted spoon and drain briefly on absorbent kitchen paper. Serve at once with lemon wedges.

Photographed below

Fish en Papillote

Fisherman's Hot Pot

Skate Portuguese

25 g (1 oz) BUTTER
100 g (4 oz) TOMATOES, SKINNED AND THINLY SLICED
6 STUFFED GREEN OLIVES, THINLY SLICED
SALT AND FRESHLY GROUND WHITE PEPPER
5 ml (1 tsp) TOMATO PUREE
350 g (12 oz) SKATE, IN TWO PIECES, TRIMMED
CHOPPED PARSLEY, TO GARNISH

Serves 2

1. Melt the butter in a shallow pan, add the tomatoes and cook gently to a pulp. Add the olives, seasoning and tomato purée.

2. Grease two large squares of foil and place a piece of fish on each. Spoon the tomato mixture over the skate and wrap in the foil, sealing well.

3. Put into a steamer and cook for about 25 minutes, or until the fish flakes easily. Open up the foil, sprinkle with chopped parsley and serve from the parcels. Alternatively cook without foil between two greased plates over a saucepan of boiling water.

Fisherman's Hot Pot

450 g (1 lb) COD FILLET, SKINNED AND CUT IN 2 cm ($\frac{3}{4}$ inch) SQUARES
40 g ($1\frac{1}{2}$ oz) PLAIN FLOUR
700 g ($1\frac{1}{2}$ lb) POTATOES, PEELED
15–30 ml (1–2 tbsp) LEMON JUICE
SALT AND FRESHLY GROUND PEPPER
1 ONION, SKINNED AND THINLY SLICED
225 g (8 oz) MUSHROOMS, WIPED AND SLICED
15 g ($\frac{1}{2}$ oz) BUTTER
150 ml ($\frac{1}{4}$ pint) MILK
100 g (4 oz) CHEDDAR CHEESE, GRATED

Serves 4

1. Toss the fish squares in 25 g (1 oz) flour.

2. Butter an ovenproof casserole. Boil the potatoes until tender, but not soft, then slice them thinly. Arrange one-third on the bottom of the casserole. Cover with half the cod, sprinkle with lemon juice and season well.

3. Combine the onion and mushrooms and arrange half the mixture over the fish. Cover with the remaining cod, lemon juice, one-third of the potatoes and the remaining onions and mushrooms.

4. Melt the butter in a pan, stir in the remaining 15 g ($\frac{1}{2}$ oz) flour and cook gently for 1 minute, stirring. Remove the pan from the heat and gradually stir in the milk. Return to the heat and bring to the boil. Continue to cook, stirring, until the sauce thickens, then add half the cheese and seasoning to taste.

5. Pour the sauce over the ingredients in the casserole, put the remaining potato slices on top and sprinkle with the remaining cheese.

6. Bake in the oven, uncovered, at 200°C (400°F) mark 6 for about 40 minutes, until golden.

Photographed opposite

Cod Roe Patties with Corn Sauce

75 g (3 oz) INSTANT MASHED POTATO (DRY WEIGHT)
200 g (7 oz) CAN PRESSED COD ROE
25 g (1 oz) GRATED ONIONS
30 ml (2 tbsp) CHOPPED PARSLEY
SALT AND FRESHLY GROUND PEPPER
1 EGG, BEATEN
50 g (2 oz) FRESH BREADCRUMBS
25 g (1 oz) MARGARINE
20 ml (4 tsp) PLAIN FLOUR
300 ml ($\frac{1}{2}$ pint) MILK
326 g ($11\frac{1}{2}$ oz) CAN CORN NIBLETS, DRAINED
OIL, FOR FRYING

Serves 4

1. Add just enough hot water to the potato to make a fairly stiff mixture. Mash the cod roe, onion and parsley and blend with the potato. Season.

2. With lightly floured hands, mould into 8–10 flat patties. Chill for about 20 minutes then coat in the beaten egg and breadcrumbs.

3. Melt the margarine in a saucepan and stir in the flour. Cook for 2 minutes, stirring. Add the milk, stir until thickened then add the corn with seasoning. Keep hot.

4. Heat a little oil in a frying pan and shallow-fry the patties for about 10 minutes, turning once. Drain on absorbent kitchen paper and serve at once with the sauce poured over.

Cod and Cucumber Mornay

4 LARGE COD CUTLETS
SALT AND FRESHLY GROUND PEPPER
10 ml (2 tsp) CHOPPED PARSLEY
150 ml ($\frac{1}{4}$ pint) DRY CIDER
$\frac{1}{2}$ CUCUMBER, PEELED AND DICED
150 ml ($\frac{1}{4}$ pint) MILK
100 g (4 oz) CHEDDAR CHEESE, GRATED

Serves 4

1. Put the fish into an ovenproof dish, season, add the parsley and pour over the cider. Cover and bake in the oven at 180°C (350°F) mark 4 for about 20 minutes, or until the fish is cooked and slightly flaky.

2. Meanwhile, put the cucumber into a pan with the milk, season to taste and simmer gently for 10 minutes. When the fish is cooked, pour over the cucumber mixture and sprinkle with the grated cheese. Put under a hot grill for a few minutes until the cheese melts and turns golden brown.

Stuffed Mackerel Fillets

25 g (1 oz) BUTTER
175 g (6 oz) COOKING APPLES. PEELED, CORED AND CHOPPED
75 g (3 oz) CELERY, TRIMMED AND CHOPPED
4 GHERKINS, CHOPPED
2.5 ml ($\frac{1}{2}$ tsp) DRIED THYME
5 ml (1 tsp) VINEGAR
45 ml (3 tbsp) FRESH WHITE BREADCRUMBS
SALT AND FRESHLY GROUND PEPPER
4 LARGE MACKEREL FILLETS
5 ml (1 tsp) ARROWROOT
5–10 ml (1–2 tsp) SUGAR
150 ml ($\frac{1}{4}$ pint) APPLE JUICE
SLICED GHERKINS, TO GARNISH

Serves 4

1. Make the stuffing: melt the butter in a pan and cook the apple and celery until the apple is pulpy. Add the gherkins, thyme, vinegar, breadcrumbs and seasoning and mix well.
2. Spread the stuffing over the fillets and fold each one in half. Arrange them in an ovenproof dish and bake uncovered at 180°C (350°F) mark 4 for 25–30 minutes or until tender.
3. Blend the arrowroot and sugar with a little apple juice. Warm the remaining apple juice and stir in the arrowroot mixture. Bring to the boil and cook, stirring, until thickened.
4. Garnish the mackerel fillets with sliced gherkins and glaze them with some of the sauce. Serve the remaining sauce separately.

Quenelles

75 g (6 oz) BUTTER
100 ml (4 fl oz) WATER; PLUS 900 ml ($1\frac{1}{2}$ pints)
135 ml (9 tbsp) PLAIN FLOUR, SIFTED
2 EGGS
450 g (1 lb) PIKE, WHITING OR BRILL FILLET, SKINNED, FINELY MINCED TWICE AND CHILLED
1 EGG WHITE
SALT AND FRESHLY GROUND PEPPER
142 ml (5 fl oz) CARTON DOUBLE CREAM
18 FRESH UNSHELLED PRAWNS
150 ml ($\frac{1}{4}$ pint) DRY WHITE WINE
227 g (8 oz) PACKET OF FROZEN PUFF PASTRY, THAWED
1 EGG, BEATEN, TO GLAZE

Serves 4

1. Make a choux paste: cut up 50 g (2 oz) butter and put into a pan with 100 ml (4 fl oz) water. Heat gently until the butter melts, then bring to a fast boil. Remove from the heat and immediately beat in 105 ml (7 tbsp) flour until the mixture is just smooth. Cool slightly and gradually beat in the eggs, keeping the mixture stiff. Cool and then chill.
2. Put the minced fish into a large bowl placed in a pan of iced water. Break up the egg white with a fork and beat into the fish, a little at a time, using a wooden spoon and keeping the mixture stiff. Steady the bowl with one hand to prevent any iced water splashing into it.
3. Gradually add the chilled choux paste to the fish mixture, beating well between each addition. Add 2.5 ml ($\frac{1}{2}$ tsp) salt and plenty of ground pepper and beat into the fish with 60 ml (4 tbsp) cream, a little at a time until the consistency of a creamed cake mixture. Cover and chill the quenelle mixture for at least 1 hour.
4. Twist the heads off the prawns and discard them. Carefully ease the body shell and any roe away from the prawn flesh. Soften 50 g (2 oz) butter and pound the shells and roe with it until well mixed. Sieve to remove the shells. Cover and chill with the prawns.
5. Pour 900 ml ($1\frac{1}{2}$ pints) water into a large frying pan and add the wine with 1.25 ml ($\frac{1}{4}$ tsp) salt. Bring to the boil. Using two damp dessertspoons, shape the quenelle mixture into ovals and push them gently out of the spoons into the simmering liquid. Add sufficient shapes to half fill the pan—they swell on cooking.
6. Cover the pan and simmer very gently for 10–12 minutes. The liquid should just tremble. When the quenelles are well puffed up and firm to the touch, lift them out of the pan using slotted spoons. Drain on absorbent kitchen paper, then keep warm, covered, in a low oven. Shape and poach the remaining quenelles in the same way.
7. On a lightly floured surface, roll out the pastry to 5 mm ($\frac{1}{4}$ inch). Using a fluted pastry cutter, stamp out crescent shapes and place them well apart on baking sheets. Glaze with beaten egg. Bake at 220°C (425°F) mark 7 for about 12 minutes, or until well risen and golden.
8. Boil the cooking liquid and reduce to 250 ml (8 fl oz). Melt the remaining butter, stir in the remaining flour, followed by the reduced stock. Season, bring to the boil, stirring, and cook for 1–2 minutes. Remove from the heat, stir in the remaining cream and whisk in the prawn butter. Reheat gently without boiling. Adjust the seasoning and spoon over the quenelles. Garnish with the prawns and serve with the pastry crescents.

Photographed opposite

Grilled Herrings

4 HERRINGS, CLEANED AND HEADS REMOVED
SALT AND FRESHLY GROUND PEPPER
VEGETABLE OIL OR MELTED BUTTER
MUSTARD SAUCE, TO SERVE (see page 211)

Serves 4

1. Make two or three diagonal cuts in the flesh on both sides of the fish. Sprinkle with salt and pepper and brush with oil or melted butter. Grease the grill rack and put the fish on it.
2. Grill the herrings under a moderate heat, turning them once, for 10–15 minutes or until thoroughly cooked; test with a fork. Serve with mustard sauce.

Quenelles

Golden Glazed Coley

450 g (1 lb) COLEY FILLET, SKINNED AND CUT INTO SERVING PIECES
300 ml (½ pint) MILK
SALT AND FRESHLY GROUND PEPPER
25 g (1 oz) MARGARINE
225 g (8 oz) LEEKS, TRIMMED AND SLICED
30 ml (2 tbsp) PLAIN FLOUR
5 ml (1 tsp) CURRY PASTE
2 HARD-BOILED EGGS, SHELLED
50 g (2 oz) CHEDDAR CHEESE, GRATED

Serves 4

1. Put the fish into a wide, shallow pan and pour over the milk. Season, cover and simmer until just flaking apart. Drain, reserving the milk. Keep the fish warm on a serving dish.
2. Melt the margarine and gently fry the leeks until tender. Stir in the flour and curry paste and cook for about 2 minutes. Remove from the heat and gradually add the milk. Return to the pan and cook, stirring, until thickened.
3. Roughly chop the egg white and add to the sauce with the cheese. Season to taste.
4. Glaze the fish with the sauce and garnish with the sieved egg yolk.

Crispy Fish Dumplings

450 g (1 lb) FILLET OF HADDOCK
1 BAY LEAF
568 ml (1 pint) MILK
25 g (1 oz) BUTTER OR MARGARINE
225 g (8 oz) PLAIN FLOUR
75 g (3 oz) GHERKINS, FINELY CHOPPED
50 g (2 oz) CAPERS, FINELY CHOPPED
FINELY GRATED RIND OF 1 LEMON
SALT AND FRESHLY GROUND PEPPER
1 EGG
OIL, FOR DEEP FRYING

Serves 4

1. Put the fish into a pan with the bay leaf and 300 ml (½ pint) milk and poach for about 10 minutes. Strain, reserving the liquid.
2. Melt the butter in a saucepan, stir in 50 g (2 oz) flour and cook, stirring for 1–2 minutes. Remove from the heat and gradually add the reserved liquid and 150 ml (¼ pint) milk. Return to the heat and simmer until thickened, then stir in the flaked fish, gherkins, capers, lemon rind and seasonings. Leave until cool.
3. Divide the mixture into twelve and shape into balls with well floured hands. Season 50 g (2 oz) flour and coat the fish in it.
4. Make the batter: sift the remaining flour with a pinch of salt. Make a well in the centre and beat in the egg and remaining milk.
5. Heat the oil to 180°C (350°F). Dip the fish in the batter and fry for about 3 minutes until puffed and golden in colour.

Haddock au Gratin

175 g (6 oz) FRESH HADDOCK FILLET
175 g (6 oz) SMOKED HADDOCK FILLET
300 ml (½ pint) WATER
60 ml (4 tbsp) DRY WHITE WINE
6 WHOLE BLACK PEPPERCORNS
1 BAY LEAF
1 SMALL ONION, SKINNED AND SLICED
50 g (2 oz) BUTTER
125 g (4 oz) BUTTON MUSHROOMS, WIPED AND SLICED
30 ml (2 tbsp) PLAIN FLOUR
50 g (2 oz) RED LEICESTER CHEESE, GRATED
FRESHLY GROUND BLACK PEPPER
25 g (1 oz) FRESH BREADCRUMBS

Serves 6

1. Put the fresh and smoked fish into a saucepan with the water and wine. Add the peppercorns, bay leaf and onion and bring to the boil. Cover and poach gently for about 15 minutes.
2. Strain off the liquid and reserve. Flake the fish, discarding the skin and bones. Also discard the flavouring ingredients.
3. Melt the butter in a frying pan and gently cook the mushrooms for 2 minutes, stir in the flour and cook gently for 1 minute, stirring. Remove the pan from the heat and gradually stir in the strained cooking liquid. Return to the heat and bring to the boil. Continue to cook, stirring, until the sauce thickens, then add the fish, half the grated cheese and seasoning to taste.
4. Spoon the mixture into six individual soufflé dishes. Top with the remaining cheese and the crumbs.
5. Bake in the oven at 220°C (425°F) mark 7 for about 15 minutes, until golden brown. Serve hot.

Photographed opposite

Smoked Haddock Chowder

175 g (6 oz) ONIONS, SKINNED AND GRATED
225 g (8 oz) POTATOES, PEELED AND GRATED
125 g (4 oz) CELERY, TRIMMED AND FINELY CHOPPED
600 ml (1 pint) WATER
450 g (1 lb) SMOKED HADDOCK FILLET, SKINNED
568 ml (1 pint) MILK
SALT AND FRESHLY GROUND PEPPER
15 ml (1 tbsp) LEMON JUICE
PAPRIKA, TO GARNISH

Serves 4

1. Put the onions, potatoes and celery into a saucepan. Cover with the water, bring to the boil, lower the heat, cover and cook for 10 minutes, then drain.
2. Rinse the fish under cold running water and put into a pan with the vegetables.
3. Add the milk and seasoning to the pan and bring to the boil. Lower the heat, cover and simmer until the fish is tender, about 15 minutes.
4. Lift the fish from the cooking liquid using a slotted spoon and flake, discarding the bones.
5. Return the fish to pan. Add the lemon juice, adjust the seasoning and sprinkle with paprika.

Haddock au Gratin

Savoury Haddock Crumble

450 g (1 lb) HADDOCK
300 ml ($\frac{1}{2}$ pint) MILK
SALT AND FRESHLY GROUND PEPPER
2 HARD-BOILED EGGS, SHELLED AND CHOPPED
1 ONION, SKINNED AND CHOPPED
40 g ($1\frac{1}{2}$ oz) MARGARINE
90 g ($3\frac{1}{2}$ oz) PLAIN WHEATMEAL FLOUR
25 g (1 oz) ROLLED OATS
CHOPPED PARSLEY, TO GARNISH

Serves 4

1. Put the haddock, milk and seasoning into a saucepan and simmer gently for 10–15 minutes until the haddock is tender. Drain, reserving the milk, and skin and flake the fish. Put the haddock, eggs and onion into a shallow ovenproof dish.
2. Melt 15 g ($\frac{1}{2}$ oz) margarine in a saucepan, stir in 15 g ($\frac{1}{2}$ oz) flour and cook for 1–2 minutes. Remove from the heat. Make the reserved milk up to 300 ml ($\frac{1}{2}$ pint) with a little more milk, if necessary, and gradually stir into the flour mixture. Return to the heat and bring to the boil, stirring. Cook for a further 1–2 minutes until thick. Season, then stir into the fish mixture.
3. To make the crumble topping, rub the remaining margarine into the remaining flour until the mixture resembles breadcrumbs, then stir in the oats. Sprinkle the topping over the fish mixture and bake in the oven at 190°C (375°F) mark 5 for 20 minutes until golden brown. Garnish with chopped parsley.

Cod Steak with Mushrooms and Spinach

100 g (4 oz) BUTTER
700 g ($1\frac{1}{2}$ lb) COD, HALIBUT OR HAKE STEAK
2.5 ml ($\frac{1}{2}$ tsp) SALT
225 g (8 oz) MUSHROOMS, WIPED AND SLICED
30 ml (2 tbsp) LEMON JUICE
275 g (10 oz) SPINACH, TRIMMED
LEMON WEDGES, TO GARNISH

Serves 4

1. Melt the butter in a large frying pan, add the fish and sprinkle it with salt. Cook gently for 5 minutes, then turn the fish and cook for a further 4–5 minutes or until the thickest flesh flakes easily when tested with a fork.
2. With a fish slice, transfer the fish to a large serving dish and keep warm.
3. Add the mushrooms and lemon juice to the pan and cook for about 5 minutes until the mushrooms are tender. Remove them from the pan with a slotted spoon and reserve.
4. Add the spinach to the juices in the pan and cook for 2–3 minutes or until tender, stirring occasionally. Stir in the mushrooms and cook for a further few minutes to heat them through.
5. Spoon the vegetables round the fish and pour the juices remaining in the pan over it. Garnish with the lemon wedges before serving.

Summer Fish Hot Pot

450 g (1 lb) NEW POTATOES, SCRAPED
700 g ($1\frac{1}{2}$ lb) FIRM WHITE FISH FILLETS (COD OR HADDOCK), SKINNED
275 g (10 oz) FLORENCE FENNEL, TRIMMED AND THINLY SLICED
25 g (1 oz) BUTTER
40 g ($1\frac{1}{2}$ oz) PLAIN FLOUR
415 g (15 oz) CAN CREAM OF CELERY SOUP
SALT AND FRESHLY GROUND PEPPER
60 ml (4 tbsp) CHOPPED PARSLEY
10 ml (2 tsp) LEMON JUICE
PARSLEY, TO GARNISH

Serves 4

1. Put the potatoes into a large pan of salted water and boil until tender. Drain.
2. Put the fish into a pan of shallow water. Bring to the boil, remove from the heat and drain. Cut into fork-size pieces.
3. Blanch the fennel: put into a pan of salted water for 2 minutes. Drain well.
4. Melt the butter in a flameproof casserole and add the flour. Cook for 2 minutes then gradually add the soup. Bring to the boil, and cook for 2 minutes. Season.
5. Add the fennel, parsley and lemon juice to the sauce and mix well. Stir in the fish, taking care not to break up the flesh. Cool.
6. Slice the potatoes, stir the ends into the casserole. Arrange the slices of potato on top and cover the dish with buttered foil.
7. Bake, covered, in the oven at 180°C (350°F) mark 4 for about 50 minutes or until the fish is cooked. Garnish with parsley.

Marinated Halibut Steaks

2 HALIBUT STEAKS, EACH WEIGHING ABOUT 350 g (12 oz)
75 ml (5 tbsp) VEGETABLE OIL
75 ml (5 tbsp) TARRAGON VINEGAR
2 BAY LEAVES
30 ml (2 tbsp) CHOPPED PARSLEY
1.25 ml ($\frac{1}{4}$ tsp) TARRAGON
5 ml (1 tsp) WORCESTERSHIRE SAUCE
SALT AND FRESHLY GROUND PEPPER

Serves 4

1. Put the halibut steaks into a shallow dish large enough to take the fish steaks in a single layer.
2. Mix the oil and vinegar, add the herbs, Worcestershire sauce and seasoning and stir well. Pour over the fish, turning them to coat well on both sides.
3. Cover the dish with foil and refrigerate for at least 3 hours, turning the fish occasionally.
4. Place the fish steaks on the grill rack and grill for 15 minutes or until the fish is tender, basting occasionally with the juices. The flesh should flake easily when tested with a fork.

MAIN COURSES
MEAT & POULTRY

Steak and Kidney Pudding

600 g ($1\frac{1}{4}$ lb) STEWING STEAK, CUT INTO 1 cm ($\frac{1}{2}$ inch) CUBES
225 g (8 oz) OX KIDNEY, CORED AND DICED
125 g (4 oz) ONIONS, SKINNED AND FINELY CHOPPED
30 ml (2 tbsp) CHOPPED PARSLEY
45 ml (3 tbsp) PLAIN FLOUR
SALT AND FRESHLY GROUND PEPPER
FINELY GRATED RIND OF $\frac{1}{2}$ LEMON
275 g (10 oz) SELF-RAISING FLOUR
150 g (5 oz) SHREDDED SUET
ABOUT 200 ml (7 fl oz) WATER; PLUS 120 ml (8 tbsp)
BUTTER OR MARGARINE
PARSLEY SPRIG, TO GARNISH

Serves 4

1. Put the meat cubes and kidneys into a bowl with the onion and parsley. Sprinkle with the plain flour and season well. Add the lemon rind and stir well.

2. Mix the self-raising flour in a bowl with the suet and a good pinch of salt. Cut and stir in just enough water to form a soft, but manageable, dough. Knead lightly and roll out, on a lightly floured surface, to a round about 35.5 cm (14 inches) in diameter. Cut out one-quarter of the dough in a fan shape to within 2.5 cm (1 inch) of the centre.

3. Lightly grease a 1.7 litre (3 pint) pudding basin. Dust the top surface of the pastry with flour and fold the dough in half, then in half again. Lift the dough into the basin, unfold, press into the base and up the sides, taking care to seal the join well. The pastry should overlap the basin top by about 2.5 cm (1 inch).

4. Spoon the meat mixture into the lined pudding basin, taking care not to puncture the pastry lining. Spread the meat out evenly. Add about 120 ml (8 tbsp) water. This should come about two-thirds of the way up the meat mixture. Add more water if necessary.

5. Roll out the remaining dough on a lightly floured surface to a round 2.5 cm (1 inch) larger than the top of the basin. Damp the exposed edge of dough lining the basin. Lift the round of dough on top of the filling and push the pastry edges together to seal. Trim around the top of the basin to neaten. Roll the sealed edges inwards around the top of the basin.

6. Cut a piece of greaseproof paper and a piece of foil large enough to cover the basin. Place them together and make a pleat across the middle. Lightly butter the greaseproof side and put them over the pudding, greaseproof side down. Tie securely on to the basin and make a string handle across the basin top.

7. Bring a large pan of water to the boil. Fit a steamer over the pan and steam the pudding, covered, for about 5 hours. Top up with boiling water as necessary.

8. To serve, uncover and place the basin on a serving plate. Garnish with a sprig of parsley.

Photographed right

Steak and Kidney Pudding

Boeuf Bourguignonne

50 g (2 oz) BUTTER
30 ml (2 tbsp) VEGETABLE OIL
100 g (4 oz) BACON, IN ONE PIECE, DICED
900 g (2 lb) BRAISING STEAK OR TOPSIDE, CUBED
1 GARLIC CLOVE, SKINNED AND CRUSHED
45 ml (3 tbsp) PLAIN FLOUR
SALT AND FRESHLY GROUND PEPPER
1 BOUQUET GARNI
150 ml ($\frac{1}{4}$ pint) BEEF STOCK
300 ml ($\frac{1}{2}$ pint) RED WINE
12 SMALL ONIONS, SKINNED
6 oz (175 g) BUTTON MUSHROOMS, WIPED
CHOPPED PARSLEY, TO GARNISH

Serves 4

1. Melt half the butter and oil in a large flameproof casserole and quickly brown the bacon. Drain and set aside. Brown the meat, in small amounts, then return the bacon to the casserole with the garlic. Sprinkle the flour over and stir in well. Add seasoning, the bouquet garni, stock and wine. Bring to the boil, stirring all the time. Cover and cook in the oven at 170°C (325°F) mark 3 for about $1\frac{1}{2}$ hours.

2. Meanwhile, heat the remaining butter and oil together and gently fry the whole onions until they are glazed and golden brown. Remove from the pan and fry the mushrooms. Remove the mushrooms and add them with the onions to the casserole and cook for a further 30 minutes.

3. Remove the bouquet garni from the casserole, skim off the surface fat and serve the casserole garnished with chopped parsley.

Cottage Pie

900 g (2 lb) POTATOES
15 g ($\frac{1}{2}$ oz) BUTTER
450 g (1 lb) MINCED BEEF
1 PACKET ONION SAUCE MIX
150 ml ($\frac{1}{4}$ pint) WATER
2 CANNED PIMIENTO, DRAINED AND CHOPPED
225 g (8 oz) TOMATOES, SKINNED AND CHOPPED
ABOUT 90 ml (6 tbsp) MILK
SALT AND FRESHLY GROUND PEPPER

Serves 4

1. Boil the potatoes in salted water for about 20 minutes, or until tender. Drain.

2. Melt the butter in a saucepan and add the mince. Cook, stirring, for about 10 minutes. Sprinkle over the onion sauce mix and add the water, pimiento, and tomatoes. Stir well and cook for a further 10 minutes.

3. Mash the potatoes with the milk. Mix until smooth.

4. Adjust the seasoning of the mince mixture and turn into an ovenproof dish. Top with the creamed potatoes and fork over the surface. Place the dish on a baking sheet and cook in the oven at 220°C (425°F) mark 7 for about 30 minutes or until the potato topping is a deep golden brown.

Beef and Potato Braise

Beef and Potato Braise

30 ml (2 tbsp) OIL
450 g (1 lb) BRAISING STEAK, CUT INTO LARGE CHUNKS
2 LEEKS, TRIMMED AND THINLY SLICED
700 g ($1\frac{1}{2}$ lb) POTATOES, PEELED AND CUT INTO 5 mm ($\frac{1}{4}$ inch) SLICES
SALT AND FRESHLY GROUND PEPPER
300 ml ($\frac{1}{2}$ pint) BEEF STOCK
225 g (8 oz) TOMATOES, SKINNED AND QUARTERED

Serves 4

1. Heat the oil in a shallow frying pan and fry the meat for about 5 minutes until evenly brown. Remove from the heat.

2. Put the meat into a 2 litre ($3\frac{1}{2}$ pint) shallow ovenproof casserole. Top with the leeks and potatoes and season well.

3. Pour over the beef stock and cook covered in the oven at 170°C (325°F) mark 3 for $1\frac{1}{2}$ hours, then raise to 190°C (375°F) mark 5 and continue to cook uncovered for 30 minutes. Any potato surface protruding from the surface lightly brush with oil.

4. A quarter of an hour before the end of the cooking, tuck the tomatoes in among the other vegetables.

Photographed above

Brewers' Braise

100 g (4 oz) STONED PRUNES
30 ml (2 tbsp) VEGETABLE OIL
700 g ($1\frac{1}{2}$ lb) STEWING BEEF, CUT INTO FORK-SIZED PIECES
2 LARGE ONIONS, SKINNED AND SLICED
15 ml (1 tbsp) PLAIN FLOUR
275 ml (9.68 fl oz) CAN OF BEER
298 ml ($10\frac{1}{2}$ oz) CAN CONDENSED CREAM OF TOMATO SOUP
225 g (8 oz) CARROTS, PEELED AND SLICED
SALT AND FRESHLY GROUND PEPPER

Serves 4

1. Cover the prunes with boiling water and leave to stand for 30 minutes. Drain.

2. Heat the oil in a flameproof casserole and brown the meat well. Remove with a slotted spoon and set aside. Add the onions to the oil remaining in the pan and brown lightly. Stir in the flour and cook for 1 minute. Stir in the beer, the undiluted soup, prunes and carrots. Bring to the boil and season well.

3. Return the meat to the pan, cover and cook in the oven at 170°C (325°F) mark 3 for $1\frac{1}{2}$–2 hours until tender when tested with a fork.

Cannelloni au Gratin

12 CANNELLONI
15 ml (1 tbsp) OIL
100 g (4 oz) STREAKY BACON, RINDED AND FINELY CHOPPED
450 g (1 lb) MINCED STEAK
100 g (4 oz) ONIONS, SKINNED AND FINELY SLICED
60 g ($2\frac{1}{4}$ oz) CAN TOMATO PUREE
2.5 ml ($\frac{1}{2}$ tsp) DRIED MIXED HERBS
40 g ($1\frac{1}{2}$ oz) BUTTER
25 g (1 oz) PLAIN FLOUR
450 ml ($\frac{3}{4}$ pint) MILK
100 g (4 oz) MATURE CHEDDAR CHEESE, GRATED
SALT AND FRESHLY GROUND PEPPER
PINCH OF FRESHLY GRATED NUTMEG
PINCH OF CAYENNE

Serves 4

1. Cook the cannelloni as directed on the packet, cool under running water and drain carefully.
2. Heat the oil in a frying-pan and fry the bacon until crisp. Add the minced steak and onion and fry until the meat is fully cooked.
3. Drain off any surplus fat then stir in the tomato purée and the herbs.
4. Using a teaspoon and standing the cooked cannelloni up on end, carefully fill. Grease an ovenproof dish and lay the cannelloni flat in the dish.
5. Melt the butter in a saucepan and stir in the flour. Cook for 1–2 minutes. Remove from the heat and gradually stir in the milk. Return to the heat and bring to the boil. Cook for 2–3 minutes until thickened. Stir in the cheese and season with salt and pepper.
6. Pour the sauce over the cannelloni. Lightly sprinkle with the spices and bake in the oven at 200°C (400°F) mark 6 for about 30 minutes until bubbling and golden.

Calcutta Curry

25 g (1 oz) LARD
600 g ($1\frac{1}{4}$ lb) SHIN OF BEEF, CUT INTO 3 cm ($1\frac{1}{4}$ inch) CUBES
300 ml ($\frac{1}{2}$ pint) WATER
2 ONIONS, SKINNED AND SLICED
1 GARLIC CLOVE, SKINNED AND CRUSHED
15 ml (1 tbsp) HOT CURRY POWDER
2.5 ml ($\frac{1}{2}$ tsp) TURMERIC
2.5 ml ($\frac{1}{2}$ tsp) GROUND CUMIN
150 ml ($\frac{1}{4}$ pint) MILK
SALT

Serves 4

1. Melt half the lard in a heavy saucepan or flameproof casserole and fry the meat cubes quickly to seal. Stir in the water, cover and simmer very gently for about $1\frac{1}{2}$ hours until the beef is tender.
2. Melt the remaining lard in another pan and fry the onions for 5 minutes until golden brown. Stir in the garlic and spices and fry gently, stirring, for a further 4–5 minutes. Blend in the milk, then add to the cooked meat with salt, to taste. Simmer, uncovered, for about 10 minutes or until the juices are reduced slightly.

Aduki Bean and Beef Bake

50 g (2 oz) BUTTER
175 g (6 oz) ONIONS, SKINNED AND CHOPPED
450 g (1 lb) LEAN MINCED BEEF
60 ml (4 tbsp) PLAIN FLOUR
200 ml (7 fl oz) BEEF STOCK
396 g (14 oz) CAN TOMATOES
15 ml (1 tbsp) TOMATO PUREE
175 g (6 oz) ADUKI BEANS, SOAKED OVERNIGHT AND DRAINED
SALT AND FRESHLY GROUND PEPPER
450 ml ($\frac{3}{4}$ pint) MILK
1 EGG, BEATEN
100 g (4 oz) CHEDDAR CHEESE, GRATED

Serves 6

1. Melt half the butter in a frying pan and cook the onions until soft. Stir in the mince and cook until just coloured.
2. Stir in 15 ml (1 tbsp) flour, cook for 2 minutes, stirring then add the stock, tomatoes with their juice, tomato purée and beans and seasoning. Cover and simmer for about 30 minutes. Turn into a 1.7 litre (3 pint) ovenproof dish.
3. To make the sauce: melt the remaining butter, and stir in the remaining flour and cook for 2 minutes. Remove from the heat and add the milk gradually. Return to the heat and cook until thickened. Beat in the egg and cheese. Season.
4. Cover the mince mixture with the sauce and bake at 200°C (400°F) mark 6 for about 20 minutes.

Carbonade of Beef

SALT AND FRESHLY GROUND PEPPER
900 g (2 lb) STEWING STEAK, CUT INTO 1 cm ($\frac{1}{2}$ inch) CUBES
50 g (2 oz) BEEF DRIPPING OR BUTTER
75 g (3 oz) LEAN BACON, RINDED AND CHOPPED
60 ml (4 tbsp) PLAIN FLOUR
300 ml ($\frac{1}{2}$ pint) BEER
300 ml ($\frac{1}{2}$ pint) BEEF STOCK OR WATER
30–45 ml (2–3 tbsp) VINEGAR
450 g (1 lb) ONIONS, SKINNED AND CHOPPED
1 GARLIC CLOVE, SKINNED AND CHOPPED
1 BOUQUET GARNI

Serves 4

1. Season the meat. Heat the fat in a large pan and fry the meat for about 5 minutes until brown. Add the bacon and continue cooking for a few minutes. Remove the meat and bacon from the pan and set aside.
2. Stir the flour into the pan and brown lightly. Gradually add the beer, stock and vinegar, stirring constantly until the mixture thickens.
3. Fill a casserole with layers of meat, bacon, onions and garlic. Pour the sauce over and add the bouquet garni. Cover and cook in the oven at 150°C (300°F) mark 2 for $3\frac{1}{2}$–4 hours. Add a little more beer while cooking, if necessary.
4. Just before serving, remove the bouquet garni.

Chilli Beef with Beans

90 ml (6 tbsp) ORANGE JUICE
15 ml (1 tbsp) LEMON JUICE
10 ml (2 tsp) BEEF EXTRACT
30 ml (2 tbsp) CHILLI SEASONING
5 ml (1 tsp) CORNFLOUR
SALT AND FRESHLY GROUND PEPPER
275 g (10 oz) RUMP STEAK, TRIMMED AND CUT INTO 1 cm ($\frac{1}{2}$ inch) CUBES
ABOUT 45 ml (3 tbsp) PEANUT OIL
175 g (6 oz) RED PEPPER, SEEDED AND DICED
125 g (4 oz) ONION, SKINNED AND DICED
425 g (15 oz) CAN BLACK EYE BEANS, DRAINED

Serves 4

1. Whisk together the orange and lemon juice, beef extract, chilli seasoning, cornflour and seasoning and pour over the beef. Leave to marinate for 1 hour.

2. Heat 45 ml (3 tbsp) oil in a wok or large frying pan until smoky hot. Drain the beef, reserving the marinade and brown a few pieces at a time. Remove with a slotted spoon.

3. Add the pepper and onion to the pan. Fry, stirring all the time, for 2–3 minutes, adding more oil if necessary. Return the beef with the beans and marinade mixture. Cook, stirring, for a further 2–3 minutes, until the sauce thickens and glazes the ingredients. Adjust the seasoning.

Goulash

700 g ($1\frac{1}{2}$ lb) STEWING STEAK, CUT INTO 1 cm ($\frac{1}{2}$ inch) CUBES
45 ml (3 tbsp) SEASONED FLOUR
30 ml (2 tbsp) VEGETABLE OIL
2 ONIONS, SKINNED AND CHOPPED
1 GREEN PEPPER, SEEDED AND CHOPPED
10 ml (2 tsp) PAPRIKA
45 ml (3 tbsp) TOMATO PUREE
A LITTLE FRESHLY GRATED NUTMEG
SALT AND FRESHLY GROUND PEPPER
50 g (2 oz) PLAIN FLOUR
300 ml ($\frac{1}{2}$ pint) BEEF STOCK
2 LARGE TOMATOES, SKINNED AND QUARTERED
1 BOUQUET GARNI
150 ml ($\frac{1}{4}$ pint) BEER

Serves 4

1. Coat the meat with seasoned flour. Heat the oil in a pan and lightly fry the onions and pepper for 3–4 minutes. Add the meat and fry lightly on all sides until golden brown, about 5 minutes.

2. Add the paprika to the pan and fry for a further minute. Stir in the tomato purée, nutmeg, seasoning and flour and cook for a further 2–3 minutes.

3. Add the stock, tomatoes and bouquet garni, transfer to a casserole and cook in the oven at 170°C (325°F) mark 3 for $1\frac{1}{2}$–2 hours. Add the beer, cook for a few minutes longer and remove the bouquet garni.

Beefburgers

450 g (1 lb) LEAN MINCED BEEF
50 g (2 oz) FRESH BREADCRUMBS
60 ml (4 tbsp) MILK
1 SMALL ONION, SKINNED AND FINELY GRATED
2.5 ml ($\frac{1}{2}$ tsp) PREPARED MUSTARD
5 ml (1 tsp) WORCESTERSHIRE SAUCE
SALT AND FRESHLY GROUND PEPPER
40 g ($1\frac{1}{2}$ oz) BUTTER
BUNS, LETTUCE AND SLICED TOMATO, TO SERVE

Serves 4

1. Combine all the ingredients, except the butter, and divide into four equal-sized pieces. Shape each into a 1 cm ($\frac{1}{2}$ inch) thick cake.

2. Heat the butter in a frying pan. Add the burgers and fry briskly for 1 minute on each side.

3. Lower the heat and cook more slowly for a further 6–8 minutes, turning twice. Serve in a bun with lettuce, sliced tomatoes and barbecue sauce (see page 210) if wished.

Photographed opposite

VARIATIONS

CHEESE BURGER

When the burger is cooked, place a slice of Cheddar cheese over the top and grill until the cheese bubbles.

GRATED CHEESE AND MAYONNAISE TOPPED BURGER

Mix together 50 g (2 oz) grated Cheddar cheese, and 30 ml (2 tbsp) mayonnaise; use to top the burger.

CHEESE TIERED SPECIAL BURGER

Use two burgers inside the bun, with a slice of Cheddar cheese between the two and crumbled Blue Stilton cheese on the top. Serve with relishes.

Beef in Wine

2 PIECES QUICKFRY STEAK, ABOUT 225 g (8 oz) EACH
100 g (4 oz) MUSHROOMS, WIPED AND FINELY CHOPPED
$\frac{1}{2}$ SMALL GREEN PEPPER, SEEDED AND SLICED
4 STUFFED OLIVES, SLICED
30 ml (2 tbsp) TOMATO PUREE
15 ml (1 tbsp) LEMON JUICE
SALT AND FRESHLY GROUND PEPPER
60 ml (4 tbsp) RED WINE

Serves 4

1. Beat the steaks until fairly thin and halve each.

2. Mix together the mushrooms, pepper, olives, tomato purée and lemon juice in a small bowl and divide the mixture between the four steaks. Sprinkle lightly with salt and pepper and roll each one up.

3. Place each steak on a piece of foil. Pour 15 ml (1 tbsp) red wine over each and make a parcel with the foil.

4. Place in a baking tin and cook in the oven at 180°C (350°F) mark 4 for about 30 minutes. Remove from the foil, place on a serving plate and spoon over the juices.

Beefburgers

Steak with Cream Sauce

Steak with Cream Sauce

4 FILLET STEAKS, 175 g (6 oz) EACH
2 GARLIC CLOVES, SKINNED AND CRUSHED
SALT AND FRESHLY GROUND PEPPER
50 g (2 oz) BUTTER
125 g (4 oz) BUTTON MUSHROOMS, WIPED AND VERY THINLY SLICED
25 g (1 oz) ONIONS, SKINNED AND VERY FINELY CHOPPED
15 ml (1 tbsp) LEMON JUICE
30 ml (2 tbsp) WORCESTERSHIRE SAUCE
15–30 ml (1–2 tbsp) BRANDY
142 ml (5 fl oz) CARTON SINGLE CREAM
15 ml (1 tbsp) FINELY CHOPPED PARSLEY
4 PARSLEY SPRIGS, TO GARNISH

Serves 4

1. Rub the steaks with the garlic and season well.
2. Heat half the butter in a frying pan and fry the steaks over a high heat for about 2 minutes on each side to brown. Cook for longer, if the steaks are preferred well done. Put into a warm serving dish to keep hot.
3. Heat the remaining butter and quickly fry the mushrooms and onion in the pan until tender. Add the lemon juice, Worcestershire sauce and brandy and bring to the boil.
4. Stir in the fresh cream and parsley, bring almost to the boil, adjust the seasoning, then quickly pour over the steaks and serve garnished with a sprig of parsley.

Photographed above

Oriental Meatballs

50 g (2 oz) BUTTER OR MARGARINE
1 ONION, SKINNED AND FINELY CHOPPED
450 g (1 lb) MINCED BEEF
50 g (2 oz) FRESH BROWN BREADCRUMBS
5 ml (1 tsp) WORCESTERSHIRE SAUCE
1 EGG
SALT AND FRESHLY GROUND PEPPER
45 ml (3 tbsp) VEGETABLE OIL
1 GREEN PEPPER, SEEDED AND ROUGHLY CHOPPED
1 RED PEPPER, SEEDED AND ROUGHLY CHOPPED
30 ml (2 tbsp) SOFT BROWN SUGAR
10 ml (2 tsp) SOY SAUCE
30 ml (2 tbsp) VINEGAR
150 ml ($\frac{1}{4}$ pint) ORANGE JUICE
150 ml ($\frac{1}{4}$ pint) BEEF STOCK
15 ml (1 level tbsp) CORNFLOUR

Serves 4

1. Heat the butter in a pan, add the onion and cook for about 5 minutes until softened. Stir in the mince, breadcrumbs, Worcestershire sauce and egg and season well. Cool.
2. Use damp hands to shape the mixture into twelve balls and chill for 20 minutes. Heat the oil in a large frying pan and brown the meatballs well. Remove with a slotted spoon and set aside.
3. Add the peppers to the pan and fry gently for 2 minutes. Stir in the sugar, soy sauce, vinegar, orange juice, stock and seasoning. Bring to the boil and return the meatballs to the pan.
4. Cover and cook in the oven at 180°C (350°F) mark 4 for about 45 minutes. Skim if necessary. Drain the cooking liquid from the meatballs and keep them warm in a serving dish.
5. Mix the cornflour to a smooth paste with a little water. Stir into the pan juices and bring to the boil. Cook stirring for 2–3 minutes and pour over the meatballs.

Peasant-style Roulades

4 SLICES TOPSIDE OF BEEF, 100 g (4 oz) EACH
SALT AND FRESHLY GROUND PEPPER
2 SLICES COOKED HAM, FINELY CHOPPED
75 g (3 oz) POTATO, PEELED, FINELY CHOPPED
25 g (1 oz) BUTTER
100 g (4 oz) ONIONS, PEELED AND CHOPPED
2 SMALL CARROTS, PEELED AND THINLY SLICED
½ TURNIP, PEELED AND THINLY SLICED
1 STICK CELERY, TRIMMED AND THINLY SLICED
1 SMALL LEEK, TRIMMED AND SLICED
5 WHOLE BLACK PEPPERCORNS
½ BAY LEAF
5 WHOLE ALLSPICE
30 ml (2 tbsp) SOURED CREAM

Serves 4

1. Beat out the slices of beef until fairly thin. Season the ham and potato and divide between the slices of beef. Roll up and secure with cotton.
2. Melt the butter and fry the onions lightly, add the remaining vegetables, season and turn together. Place as a bed in a casserole which is just large enough to take the rolls in a single layer.
3. If necessary add a little more butter to the pan and well brown the roulades on all sides. Arrange over the vegetables. Tie the peppercorns, bay leaf and allspice in muslin and tuck the bag into the vegetables. Cover and cook in the oven at 170°C (325°F) mark 3 for 1½ hours or until the beef is fork tender.
4. To serve, remove the cotton and discard with the spices. Arrange the roulades in a hot dish and keep warm. Quickly pass the vegetables and juices through a sieve or purée in a blender. Heat through with soured cream, adjust the seasoning and pour over the meat.

Braised Beef with Lentils

SALT AND FRESHLY GROUND PEPPER
450 g (1 lb) LEAN MINCED BEEF
15 ml (1 tbsp) VEGETABLE OIL
2 ONIONS, SKINNED AND SLICED
1.25 ml (¼ tsp) CHILLI POWDER
175 g (6 oz) RED LENTILS
45 ml (3 tbsp) SOY SAUCE
5 ml (1 tsp) WORCESTERSHIRE SAUCE
15 ml (1 tbsp) YEAST EXTRACT
226 g (8 oz) CAN TOMATOES
600 ml (1 pint) WATER
CHOPPED SPRING ONION, TO GARNISH

Serves 4

1. Season the minced beef and shape into eight patties. Heat the oil in a flameproof casserole and brown the patties well on both sides. Remove and set aside.
2. Brown the onions in the pan, then stir in the chilli powder. Cook for 2 minutes before stirring in all the remaining ingredients, except the garnish. Bring to the boil, cover and simmer for 30 minutes. Place the beef patties on the lentil mixture, cover and finish cooking in the oven at 180°C (350°F) mark 4 for 30 minutes. If necessary skim off the fat. Serve sprinkled with chopped spring onion.

Mince and Bacon Pie

225 g (8 oz) PLAIN FLOUR; AND 30 ml (2 tbsp)
PINCH OF SALT
50 g (2 oz) LARD, CUT INTO SMALL PIECES
50 g (2 oz) MARGARINE, CUT INTO SMALL PIECES
45–60 ml (3–4 tbsp) WATER; AND 300 ml (½ pint)
100 g (4 oz) STREAKY BACON RASHERS, RINDED, AND SNIPPED
450 g (1 lb) MINCED BEEF
1 BEEF STOCK CUBE
15 ml (1 tbsp) DRIED ONION FLAKES
15 ml (1 tbsp) DRIED CELERY FLAKES
GRAVY BROWNING
MILK, TO GLAZE

Serves 4

1. Make the shortcrust pastry: sift the 225 g (8 oz) flour and the salt into a bowl. Rub in the fat until the mixture resembles fine breadcrumbs. Mix to a firm dough with about 45 ml (3 tbsp) water.
2. Cook the bacon slowly in a frying pan until the fat begins to run. Add the mince and continue to cook slowly until it is lightly browned.
3. Crumble in the stock cube with the onion, celery and the remaining flour, stir and slowly add the 300 ml (½ pint) water. Bring to the boil, lower the heat and simmer for 20 minutes. Add the browning and cool.
4. On a lightly floured surface, roll out about half the pastry to line a 20 cm (8 inch) pie plate. Add the cooled filling. Roll out the remaining pastry and cover the dish. Brush with milk and make a hole in the centre.
5. Bake in the oven at 200°C (400°F) mark 6 for about 45 minutes.

Beef Olives

25 g (1 oz) BUTTER
50 g (2 oz) BACON, RINDED AND CHOPPED
50 g (2 oz) MUSHROOMS, WIPED AND CHOPPED
50 g (2 oz) SHREDDED SUET
50 g (2 oz) FRESH WHITE BREADCRUMBS
15 ml (1 tbsp) CHOPPED PARSLEY
1 EGG, BEATEN
SALT AND FRESHLY GROUND PEPPER
45 ml (3 tbsp) PLAIN FLOUR
8 THIN SLICES TOPSIDE OF BEEF, 100 g (4 oz) EACH
30 ml (2 tbsp) VEGETABLE OIL
2 ONIONS, SKINNED AND SLICED
600 ml (1 pint) BEEF STOCK
15 ml (1 tbsp) TOMATO PUREE

Serves 4

1. To make the stuffing: melt the butter in a pan and fry the bacon and mushrooms for 8–10 minutes until golden brown. Stir in the suet, breadcrumbs and parsley and add just enough egg to bind.
2. Add the seasoning to the flour. Spread the stuffing on to the meat slices and roll up. Secure with string and toss in the seasoned flour.
3. Heat the oil in a frying pan and fry the beef rolls for 5 minutes until lightly browned on all sides. Remove from the pan and put into an ovenproof casserole.
4. Add the onion slices to the pan, cook for 5 minutes and put into the casserole with the beef olives.
5. Add the remaining flour to the pan and cook for 1 minute. Stir in the stock and tomato purée and bring to the boil. Pour over the beef olives. Cover and cook in the oven at 180°C (350°F) mark 4 for 1½ hours. Remove the string before serving.

Pepperbag Steak

15 g (½ oz) BUTTER
1 SHALLOT, SKINNED AND CHOPPED
50 g (2 oz) MUSHROOMS, WIPED AND CHOPPED
50 g (2 oz) RED PEPPERS, SEEDED AND CHOPPED
50 g (2 oz) GREEN PEPPERS, SEEDED AND CHOPPED
15 ml (1 tbsp) FRESH WHITE BREADCRUMBS
SALT AND FRESHLY GROUND PEPPER
450 g (1 lb) RUMP STEAK, 2.5 cm (1 inch) THICK
15 ml (1 tbsp) OIL

Serves 2–3

1. Melt the butter in a small pan and soften the shallot. Add the mushrooms and peppers and cook for 2 minutes. Remove from the heat and stir in breadcrumbs. Season well.
2. Slit the steak along one side to make a pocket. Spread the filling in the centre of the steak. Replace the top flap and secure with 2–3 wooden cocktail sticks.
3. Brush the steak with oil and grill under a hot grill for 5–7 minutes each side.
4. Before serving, remove the cocktail sticks and make several slits in the top of the steak to reveal the filling.

Roast Beef

SIRLOIN, RIB, RUMP, TOPSIDE, AITCH-BONE
50 g (2 oz) BEEF DRIPPING (optional)
FRESHLY GROUND BLACK PEPPER (optional)
5 ml (1 tsp) DRY ENGLISH MUSTARD (optional)

Serves 100–150 g (4–6 oz) off the bone per person; 150–300 g (6–12 oz) on the bone per person

1. Weigh the meat and calculate the cooking time. For rare meat, allow 20 minutes per 450 g (1 lb) plus 20 minutes; 25 minutes per 450 g (1 lb) plus 25 minutes for medium meat and 30 minutes per 450 g (1 lb) plus 30 minutes for well-done meat. *Use these times regardless of whether the meat is on the bone, boned or rolled.*
2. Put the meat into a shallow roasting tin, preferably on a grid, with the thickest layer of fat uppermost and the cut sides exposed to the heat. Add the dripping if the meat is lean. Season with pepper and mustard, if wished.
3. Roast the joint at 170°C (325°F) mark 3 and cook for the calculated time, basting occasionally with the juices from the tin.
4. If Yorkshire Pudding is to be cooked at the same time, raise the temperature to 220°C (425°F) mark 7 for the duration of the cooking time of the pudding, and move the meat to the coolest part of the oven.

Individual Yorkshire Puddings

50 g (2 oz) PLAIN FLOUR
PINCH OF SALT
1 EGG
150 ml (¼ pint) MILK
15 g (½ oz) LARD OR DRIPPING

Makes 10–12

1. Sift the flour and salt into a bowl, make a well in the centre and break in the egg. Add half the liquid, gradually work in the flour using a wooden spoon and beat the mixture until it is smooth.
2. Add the remaining liquid gradually and beat until well mixed and the surface is covered with tiny bubbles. The batter may be used at once or left to stand in a cool place. If it is left to stand it may be necessary to add a little more milk before using.
3. Divide the dripping or lard and put in a 4-cup Yorkshire pudding pan or 10–12 patty tins. Place the pan or tin towards the top of the oven at 220°C (425°F) mark 7. When the fat in the tin shows a haze and is really hot, pour in the batter and return to the oven to cook for 15–20 minutes.

Photographed opposite

VARIATION

For a large Yorkshire pudding, use 125 g (4 oz) plain flour, a pinch of salt, 1 egg, 300 ml (½ pint) milk (or two-thirds milk and one-third water), and 25 g (1 oz) lard or dripping, and cook for 40–45 minutes. This quantity will fill a tin measuring about 18 cm (7 inch) square.

Roast Beef with Yorkshire Puddings

Pot-au-feu

1 kg ($2\frac{1}{4}$ lb) LEAN BEEF (BRISKET, FLANK OR TOPSIDE), TIED SECURELY
3 litres ($5\frac{1}{4}$ pints) WATER
SALT AND FRESHLY GROUND PEPPER
1 CARROT, PEELED AND QUARTERED
1 TURNIP, PEELED AND QUARTERED
1 ONION, SKINNED AND QUARTERED
1 PARSNIP, PEELED AND QUARTERED
2 SMALL LEEKS, TRIMMED AND QUARTERED
2 CELERY STICKS, TRIMMED AND QUARTERED
1 SMALL CABBAGE, TRIMMED AND HALVED
1 BOUQUET GARNI
30 ml (2 tbsp) SEED PEARL TAPIOCA

Serves 4

1. Put the meat into a large saucepan, add the water and 10 ml (2 tsp) salt. Cover and simmer for 2 hours.
2. Add the vegetables to the pan (except the cabbage) and the bouquet garni and cook for a further 2 hours.
3. Add the cabbage to the pan and continue cooking for a final 30 minutes, or until it is soft. Strain off most of the liquid, put into a pan, bring to the boil, sprinkle in the tapioca and simmer for about 15 minutes, or until the tapioca clears. If wished, this can be served as a starter, or, serve with the sliced meat and vegetables. Adjust the seasoning and remove the bouquet garni before serving.

Brown Stew with Doughboys

15 g ($\frac{1}{2}$ oz) DRIPPING
450 g (1 lb) STEWING STEAK, TRIMMED AND CUBED
225 g (8 oz) ONIONS, SKINNED AND SLICED
225 g (8 oz) CARROTS, PEELED AND SLICED
15 g (1 oz) PLAIN FLOUR
750 ml ($1\frac{1}{4}$ pints) STOCK
SALT AND FRESHLY GROUND PEPPER
1 BOUQUET GARNI
75 g (3 oz) SELF-RAISING FLOUR
40 g ($1\frac{1}{2}$ oz) SHREDDED SUET
2.5 ml ($\frac{1}{2}$ tsp) DRIED MIXED HERBS
5 ml (1 tsp) CHOPPED PARSLEY

Serves 4

1. Melt the dripping in a frying pan and quickly seal the meat. Put the meat into a large casserole. Reheat the pan fat, adding more if necessary and brown the onions and carrots. Put them with the meat in the casserole.
2. Add the flour to the pan, stir well and gradually add the stock. Bring to the boil, season well, pour over the meat and vegetables and add the bouquet garni. Cover and cook in the oven at 170°C (325°F) mark 3 for about $1\frac{1}{2}$ hours.
3. Make the doughboys: in a bowl combine the self-raising flour, suet, herbs, parsley and seasoning. Add just enough cold water to make an elastic dough. Turn on to a lightly floured board and shape into eight balls.
4. Remove the bouquet garni from the casserole, adjust the seasoning and add the dumplings. Cover and continue to cook for a further 20 minutes.

Spicy Meatballs

450 g (1 lb) LEAN MINCED BEEF
100 g (4 oz) FRESH BREADCRUMBS
1 EGG, BEATEN
70 ml ($2\frac{1}{2}$ fl oz) MILK
SALT AND FRESHLY GROUND PEPPER
2.5 ml ($\frac{1}{2}$ tsp) DRIED THYME
15 ml (1 tbsp) OIL
1 ONION, SKINNED AND CHOPPED
1 GARLIC CLOVE, SKINNED AND CRUSHED
15 ml (1 tbsp) PLAIN FLOUR
396 g (14 oz) CAN TOMATOES
150 ml ($\frac{1}{4}$ pint) BEEF STOCK
5 ml (1 tsp) TOMATO PUREE
CHOPPED PARSLEY, TO GARNISH

Serves 6

1. In a bowl, mix together the meat, breadcrumbs, egg, milk, and seasonings and herbs. Form the mixture into 2 cm ($\frac{3}{4}$ inch) balls.
2. Heat the oil in a frying pan and cook the meatballs until brown. Remove from the pan and place in a casserole dish.
3. Fry the onion and garlic until soft and add the flour, mix well and stir in the tomatoes, stock and purée. Cook until thick and adjust the seasoning.
4. Pour the sauce over the meatballs and cover the casserole. Cook in the oven at 180°C (350°F) mark 4 for 45 minutes.
5. Serve hot, garnished with chopped parsley.

Photographed opposite

Chunky Beef with Celery

50 g (2 oz) RED KIDNEY BEANS, SOAKED OVERNIGHT AND DRAINED
25 g (1 oz) LARD OR DRIPPING
4 CHUNKY PIECES OF TOP RIB BEEF, 125 g (4 oz) EACH
225 g (8 oz) CELERY, TRIMMED AND CUT INTO 5 cm (2 inch) LENGTHS
1 ONION, SKINNED AND SLICED
450 ml ($\frac{3}{4}$ pint) BEEF STOCK
30 ml (2 tbsp) SHERRY
SALT AND FRESHLY GROUND PEPPER
30 ml (2 tbsp) CORNFLOUR

Serves 4

1. Put the beans into a saucepan of water. Bring to the boil and boil rapidly for 10 minutes, then drain again.
2. Melt the fat in a flameproof casserole and brown the meat quickly. Remove with a slotted spoon and set aside.
3. Add the celery and onion to the casserole and brown lightly. Mix in the beans and sit the meat on top of the vegetables. Pour the stock and sherry over and season well. Bring to the boil then cover and bake in the oven at 170°C (325°F) mark 4 for about 2 hours.
4. Strain off the juices and transfer the meat and vegetables to a shallow dish. Mix the cornflour to a paste with a little water. Stir into the juices, bring slowly to the boil and cook for 2–3 minutes to thicken. Pour a little over the meat and serve the rest separately.

Spicy Meatballs

Beefy Macaroni Bake

100 g (4 oz) SHORT-CUT MACARONI
50 g (2 oz) MARGARINE
100 g (4 oz) ONIONS, SKINNED AND SLICED
450 g (1 lb) MINCED BEEF
5 ml (1 tsp) DRIED SAGE
45 ml (3 tbsp) PLAIN FLOUR
SALT AND FRESHLY GROUND PEPPER
225 g (8 oz) CAN TOMATOES
300 ml ($\frac{1}{2}$ pint) MILK
2.5 ml ($\frac{1}{2}$ tsp) FRESHLY GRATED NUTMEG
1 EGG, BEATEN

Serves 4

1. Bring a pan of salted water to the boil and cook the macaroni until tender. Drain.
2. Melt half the margarine and gently fry the onion until soft. Stir in the minced beef and cook quickly to seal. Add the sage, 15 ml (1 tbsp) flour and seasoning.
3. Layer the macaroni and mince mixture in a 1.7 litre (3 pint) ovenproof dish. Add the tomatoes and their juice.
4. Melt the remaining margarine in a pan and stir in the flour. Cook, stirring, for 2 minutes. Remove from the heat and gradually add the milk. Beat in the nutmeg, egg and seasonings, to taste. Return to the heat and stir until thickened.
5. Pour the sauce over the mince mixture and bake at 200°C (400°F) mark 6 for 30 minutes.

Braised Beef in Aspic

15 g ($\frac{1}{2}$ oz) LARD
225 g (8 oz) CARROTS, PEELED AND DICED
125 g (4 oz) ONIONS, SKINNED AND DICED
125 g (4 oz) BACK BACON, RINDED AND DICED
15 ml (1 tbsp) TOMATO PUREE
1.25 ml ($\frac{1}{4}$ tsp) GROUND ALLSPICE
900 g (2 lb) SILVERSIDE
150 ml ($\frac{1}{4}$ pint) RED WINE
SALT AND FRESHLY GROUND PEPPER
TWO 28.3 g (1 oz) PACKETS ASPIC POWDER
SMALL GHERKINS, TO GARNISH

Serves 8 buffet portions

1. Melt the lard in a deep flameproof casserole and gently fry the vegetables and bacon for 5–7 minutes. Stir in the tomato purée and allspice. Place the beef on top, pour over the wine. Season and bring to the boil. Cover tightly and cook at 170°C (325°F) mark 3 for about 2$\frac{3}{4}$ hours, basting once.

2. Remove the beef from the casserole and cool completely. Strain off the liquid and reserve. Cool the vegetables and bacon.

3. Make the reserved juices up to 1.1 litre (2 pints) with water. Chill and skim off the fat. Bring the juices to the boil and dissolve the aspic powder in the hot liquid.

4. Meanwhile, thinly slice the beef. Layer with the vegetables and bacon in a 2 litre (3$\frac{1}{2}$ pint) serving dish. Pour over 900 ml (1$\frac{1}{2}$ pint) aspic and chill to set. Garnish with small gherkins and spoon over the remaining aspic.

Four-in-one Beef Casserole

SALT AND FRESHLY GROUND PEPPER
15 ml (1 tbsp) PLAIN FLOUR
30 ml (2 tbsp) CORN OIL
450 g (1 lb) SHIN OF BEEF, TRIMMED AND CUBED
75 g (3 oz) CELERY, TRIMMED AND SLICED
75 g (3 oz) CARROTS, PEELED AND SLICED
125 g (4 oz) ONIONS, SKINNED AND SLICED
1 GARLIC CLOVE, SKINNED AND CRUSHED
175 g (6 oz) TOMATOES, SKINNED, SEEDED AND ROUGHLY CHOPPED
6 BLACK OLIVES, HALVED AND STONED
1.25 ml ($\frac{1}{4}$ tsp) DRIED OREGANO
75 ml (5 tbsp) RED WINE, DRY CIDER OR LIGHT BEER
200 ml (7 fl oz) STOCK

Serves 4

1. Season the flour and toss the meat in it. Heat the oil in a flameproof casserole and brown the meat on all sides. Remove from the casserole using a slotted spoon.

2. Add the celery, carrots and onion to the fat remaining in the pan and fry until lightly coloured. Add the garlic.

3. Return the meat to the casserole with the tomatoes, olives and oregano. Pour over the wine, cider or beer and the stock. Add seasoning to taste. Cover and cook in the oven at 170°C (325°F) mark 3 for about 2 hours or until the meat is fork tender.

Barbecued Beef and Beans

SALT AND FRESHLY GROUND PEPPER
450 g (1 lb) BRAISING STEAK, TRIMMED AND CUT INTO LARGE CUBES
15 g ($\frac{1}{2}$ oz) LARD
15 ml (1 tbsp) PLAIN FLOUR
2 LARGE ORANGES, RIND GRATED AND JUICE SQUEEZED FROM ONE ORANGE; THE OTHER PEELED AND SLICED
15 ml (1b tbsp) TOMATO KETCHUP
30 ml (2 tbsp) MALT VINEGAR
15 ml (1 tbsp) CLEAR HONEY
15 ml (1 tbsp) WORCESTERSHIRE SAUCE
1.5 ml ($\frac{1}{4}$ tsp) CHILLI SAUCE
425g (15 oz) CAN RED KIDNEY BEANS, DRAINED

Serves 4

1. Rub the seasoning into the meat. Melt the lard in a frying pan and brown the meat on all sides. Remove and set aside. Lightly skim the surface of the pan to remove any excess fat. Blend in the flour. Gradually add the orange juice, ketchup, vinegar, honey, Worcestershire sauce and chilli sauce until smoothly combined. Heat, stirring, until thickened. Remove from the heat.

2. Put the meat into an ovenproof casserole. Sprinkle the orange rind over and cover with the sauce. Bake, covered at 150°C (300°F) mark 2 for about 2$\frac{1}{2}$ hours until meat is fork tender. After 2 hours add the beans. Remove the cover, fork through the juices before serving with a garnish of orange slices.

Steak and Kidney Pie

700 g (1$\frac{1}{2}$ lb) STEWING STEAK, CUT INTO CUBES
225 g (8 oz) OX KIDNEY, CUT INTO CUBES
25 g (1 oz) SEASONED FLOUR
25 g (1 oz) LARD
1 ONION, SKINNED AND SLICED
225 g (8 oz) BUTTON MUSHROOMS
150 ml ($\frac{1}{4}$ pint) BEEF STOCK
30 ml (2 tbsp) TOMATO KETCHUP
45 ml (3 tbsp) CHOPPED PARSLEY
SALT AND FRESHLY GROUND PEPPER
368 g (13 oz) PACKET FROZEN PUFF PASTRY, THAWED
1 EGG, BEATEN

Serves 6

1. Toss the steak and kidney in the seasoned flour. Melt the lard in a pan and fry the onion, meats and mushrooms quickly.

2. Add the stock, ketchup and parsley to the pan, bring to the boil and season.

3. Place a pie funnel in the centre of a 1.1 litre (2 pint) pie dish. Fill the dish with the meat mixture and allow it to cool.

4. Roll out the pastry on a lightly floured surface and cover the pie, decorating it with pastry trimmings. Glaze with the beaten egg. Bake in the oven at 230°C (450°F) mark 8 for 20 minutes. Cover loosely with foil and lower the heat to 180°C (350°F) mark 4. Bake for a further 2 hours.

Braised Brisket with Red Wine

SALT AND FRESHLY GROUND PEPPER
15 ml (1 tbsp) PLAIN FLOUR
1.1 kg ($2\frac{1}{2}$ lb) PIECE LEAN ROLLED BRISKET
15 ml (1 tbsp) VEGETABLE OIL
225 g (8 oz) CARROTS, PEELED AND DICED
225 g (8 oz) PARSNIPS, PEELED AND DICED
2 ONIONS, SKINNED AND DICED
150 ml ($\frac{1}{4}$ pint) BEEF STOCK
15 ml (1 tbsp) TOMATO PUREE
60 ml (4 tbsp) RED WINE
2.5 ml ($\frac{1}{2}$ tsp) DRIED THYME
1 BAY LEAF
10 ml (2 tsp) CORNFLOUR

Serves 6

1. Season the flour and roll the brisket joint in it until well coated.
2. Heat the oil in a 2.3 litre (4 pint) flameproof casserole and brown the joint well. Remove the meat and set aside. Stir the vegetables into the fat remaining in the pan and fry for 2 minutes. Add the stock, tomato purée, wine, thyme, bay leaf and seasoning. Bring to the boil. Return the meat to the pan, pushing it well down into the vegetables.
3. Cover tightly and cook in the oven at 170°C (325°F) mark 3 for about $2\frac{1}{4}$ hours or until the meat is tender when pierced with a fine skewer. Remove the meat and carve into slices. Arrange on a serving dish with the vegetables, cover and keep warm. Mix the cornflour to a paste with a little water. Stir into the juices, bring slowly to the boil and cook for 2–3 minutes to thicken. Adjust the seasoning and serve separately.

Chilli con Carne

225 g (8 oz) DRIED RED KIDNEY BEANS, SOAKED OVERNIGHT AND DRAINED
15 ml (1 tbsp) VEGETABLE OIL
2 ONIONS, SKINNED AND CHOPPED
700 g ($1\frac{1}{2}$ lb) LEAN MINCED BEEF
1 LARGE GARLIC CLOVE, SKINNED AND CRUSHED
15 ml (1 tbsp) SALT
FRESHLY GROUND PEPPER
2.5 ml ($\frac{1}{2}$ tsp) CHILLI POWDER
15 ml (1 tbsp) PLAIN FLOUR
30 ml (2 tbsp) TOMATO PUREE
793 g (28 oz) CAN TOMATOES

Serves 6

1. Put the beans into a pan and cover with water. Bring to the boil and boil rapidly for 10 minutes then boil gently for about 45 minutes until tender. Drain.
2. In a large saucepan, heat the oil and fry the onions, add the mince and cook until brown and crumbly. Add the garlic, salt, pepper and chilli seasoning to the mince. Sprinkle on the flour and stir it in. Add the tomato purée and the tomatoes with their juice. Bring to the boil and add the beans.
3. Lower the heat, cover and simmer for 30 minutes, stirring occasionally.

Mince in a Crust

25 g (1 oz) MARGARINE
100 g (4 oz) ONIONS, SKINNED AND CHOPPED
450 g (1 lb) LEAN MINCE
100 g (4 oz) FRESH WHITE BREADCRUMBS
5 ml (1 tsp) LEMON JUICE
SALT AND FRESHLY GROUND PEPPER
350 g (12 oz) SELF-RAISING FLOUR
10 ml (2 tsp) CURRY POWDER
60 ml (4 tbsp) OIL
20 ml (4 tsp) MADE MUSTARD
75 g (3 oz) CHEDDAR CHEESE, GRATED
MILK, TO GLAZE
SESAME SEEDS

Serves 4

1. Melt the margarine in a large pan and cook the onion until soft. Add mince and brown evenly, then add the breadcrumbs and lemon juice. Adjust the seasoning.
2. Sift the flour and curry powder into a bowl. Stir in the oil and enough cold water to bind to a firm but manageable dough.
3. Roll out the dough on a lightly floured surface to a rectangle 25 × 33 cm (10 × 13 inches). Trim the edges. Spread with mustard to within 2.5 cm (1 inch) of the edge and sprinkle with the cheese.
4. Spoon the savoury mixture down the centre. Dampen the edges and bring each edge over the filling. Seal.
5. Place seam-side down on a baking sheet. Roll out the trimmings and cut strips to garnish. Brush pastry with milk, arrange the decorative strips, reglaze and sprinkle with sesame seeds. Cut a slit on top and bake at 190°C (375°F) mark 5 for about 30 minutes.

Braised Beef with Soured Cream

45 ml (3 tbsp) VEGETABLE OIL
550 g ($1\frac{1}{4}$ lb) BONED TOP RIB BEEF, CUT INTO STRIPS 5 × 1 cm (2 × $\frac{1}{2}$ inch)
1 ONION, SKINNED AND SLICED
30 ml (2 tbsp) PLAIN FLOUR
300 ml ($\frac{1}{2}$ pint) BEEF STOCK
SALT AND FRESHLY GROUND PEPPER
1 SMALL GREEN PEPPER, HALVED, SEEDED AND SLICED
175 g (6 oz) BUTTON MUSHROOMS, WIPED AND SLICED
142 ml (5 fl oz) CARTON SOURED CREAM, STIRRED
CHOPPED PARSLEY, TO GARNISH

Serves 4

1. Heat the oil in a small flameproof casserole and brown the meat then remove with a slotted spoon and set aside. Add the onion and brown lightly. Stir in the flour and cook for 1 minute. Stir in the stock and seasoning and bring to the boil, stirring.
2. Return the meat to the pan, cover tightly and cook in the oven at 170°C (325°F) mark 3 for about $1\frac{3}{4}$ hours.
3. Stir the pepper and mushrooms into the casserole, cover and return to the oven for 15 minutes. Stir in the soured cream. Adjust the seasoning and sprinkle with chopped parsley.

Fillet of Lamb with Black Beans

396 g (14 oz) CAN TOMATOES
2.5 ml (½ tsp) DRIED OREGANO
1 GARLIC CLOVE, SKINNED AND CRUSHED
225 g (8 oz) ONIONS, SKINNED AND FINELY CHOPPED
1.1 kg (2½ lb) LEG FILLET OF LAMB
225 g (8 oz) BLACK BEANS
300 ml (½ pint) STOCK
30 ml (2 tbsp) CORNFLOUR
SALT AND FRESHLY GROUND PEPPER

Serves 6

1. Purée together the tomatoes, oregano and garlic and stir in the onion.
2. Put the lamb in a polythene bag in a bowl. Pour over puréed tomato, seal the bag with twist tie and leave to marinate overnight. Soak the beans overnight in water.
3. Put the lamb, marinade and stock into a flameproof casserole with a tight-fitting lid. Drain the beans and scatter into the liquid surrounding the joint.
4. Bring to the boil, cover and cook in the oven at 180°C (350°F) mark 4 for about 2 hours.
5. Remove the lamb to a serving dish and keep warm. Mix the cornflour to a smooth paste with a little water and stir into the casserole juices. Bring to the boil, simmer until thickened. Season and serve separately.

Marinaded Lamb Cutlets with Rosemary

TWO 1.1 kg (2½ lb) BEST END NECKS OF LAMB, TRIMMED OF EXCESS FAT AND CHINE BONE REMOVED
450 ml (¾ pint) MEDIUM WHITE WINE
120 ml (8 tbsp) VEGETABLE OIL
20 ml (4 tsp) DRIED ROSEMARY
SALT AND FRESHLY GROUND PEPPER
1 LARGE GARLIC CLOVE, SKINNED AND CRUSHED

Serves 12 buffet portions

1. Score the fat of the chops lightly. Put the meat into a shallow glass dish or other container but not a metal one, as the flavour will be affected.
2. Mix the wine, oil, rosemary, seasoning and garlic together and pour over the meat. Cover with cling film and marinate in a cool place for 12 hours, turning once.
3. Remove the meat from the marinade, reserving the marinade, and place on a rack standing over a roasting tin.
4. Cook in the oven at 180°C (350°F) mark 4 for about 1½ hours or until the meat is tender, basting occasionally.
5. While still warm divide the meat into cutlets and spoon over the marinade. Baste and turn occasionally until cold.

Lamb with Orange Sauce

75 g (3 oz) FRESH WHITE BREADCRUMBS
2 ORANGES, RINDS GRATED, 1 ORANGE SQUEEZED, THE OTHER PEELED AND SEGMENTED
2.5 ml (½ tsp) DRIED MINT
1 EGG, BEATEN
SALT AND FRESHLY GROUND PEPPER
2 LARGE BREASTS OF LEAN LAMB, BONED AND TRIMMED OF EXCESS FAT
4 ONIONS, SKINNED AND HALVED CROSSWAYS
300 ml (½ pint) STOCK
10 ml (2 tsp) CORNFLOUR
5 ml (1 tsp) DEMERARA SUGAR
5 ml (1 tsp) WORCESTERSHIRE SAUCE

Serves 4

1. Combine the breadcrumbs, half the grated orange rind, mint, egg and seasoning. Spread over the meat, roll up and tie with fine string.
2. Put the lamb into an ovenproof casserole with the onions, cut-side up. Season and add 60 ml (4 tbsp) stock.
3. Cover the casserole and cook at 180°C (350°F) mark 4 for about 50 minutes, uncover for the last 20 minutes to brown.
4. Meanwhile, in a small pan, blend a little of the remaining stock with the cornflour, add the rest with the sugar, Worcestershire sauce and the remaining grated rind and the orange juice. Bring to the boil, stirring. Cook 1–2 minutes and season.
5. Serve the lamb in thick slices with the orange sauce and the reserved orange segments.

Blanquette d'Agneau

700 g (1½ lb) LEAN SHOULDER OF LAMB, DICED
100 g (4 oz) CARROTS, PEELED AND SLICED
1 ONION, SKINNED AND SLICED
2 STICKS CELERY, TRIMMED AND SLICED
1 SMALL BAY LEAF
5 ml (1 tsp) DRIED THYME
SALT AND FRESHLY GROUND PEPPER
300 ml (½ pint) STOCK OR WATER
25 g (1 oz) BUTTER, SOFTENED
45 ml (3 tbsp) PLAIN FLOUR
1 EGG YOLK
142 ml (5 fl oz) CARTON SINGLE CREAM
CHOPPED PARSLEY, TO GARNISH

Serves 4

1. Put the meat, carrots, onion, celery, flavourings and seasonings in a large pan. Cover with stock or water, cover and simmer for 1½ hours. Remove the bay leaf.
2. Blend together the softened butter and flour, and when mixed add to the stew in small knobs and stir until thickened. Simmer for 10 minutes, adding more liquid if necessary.
3. Blend together the egg yolk and cream, add to the stew and reheat without boiling. Garnish with parsley before serving.

Photographed opposite

Blanquette d'Agneau

Savoury Lamb and Mushrooms

2 ONIONS, SKINNED AND SLICED
3 TOMATOES, SKINNED AND SLICED
100 g (4 oz) MUSHROOMS, WIPED AND SLICED
4 LAMB CHOPS, TRIMMED OF FAT
BUTTER OR MARGARINE
SALT AND FRESHLY GROUND PEPPER

Serves 4

1. Put the onions, tomatoes and mushrooms into an ovenproof dish. Arrange the chops on top of the vegetables, place a knob of butter on each and season with salt and pepper.

2. Cook in the oven at 200°C (400°F) mark 6 for 45 minutes or until the chops are tender.

Irish Stew

900 g (2 lb) POTATOES, PEELED AND SLICED
2 LARGE ONIONS, SKINNED AND SLICED
8 MIDDLE NECK LAMB CHOPS, TRIMMED OF EXCESS FAT
SALT AND FRESHLY GROUND PEPPER
CHOPPED PARSLEY, TO GARNISH

Serves 4

1. Place alternate layers of the vegetables and meat in a saucepan, seasoning with salt and pepper and finishing with a layer of potatoes. Add sufficient water to half cover.

2. Cover with a lid and either simmer very slowly for 3 hours or cook the stew in a casserole in the oven at 190°C (375°F) mark 5 for $2\frac{1}{2}$–3 hours. Serve sprinkled with chopped parsley.

Cheshire Lamb Crumble

350 g (12 oz) COOKED ROAST LAMB
1 ONION, SKINNED
115 g ($4\frac{1}{2}$ oz) PLAIN FLOUR
15 ml (1 tbsp) TOMATO PUREE
300 ml ($\frac{1}{2}$ pint) BEEF STOCK
SALT AND FRESHLY GROUND PEPPER
50 g (2 oz) BUTTER
50 g (2 oz) CHESHIRE CHEESE, GRATED
2.5 ml ($\frac{1}{2}$ tsp) DRIED MIXED HERBS

Serves 4

1. Mince together the meat and onion. Mix in 15 g ($\frac{1}{2}$ oz) flour, the tomato purée, stock and seasoning and turn into a shallow ovenproof dish.

2. In a bowl, rub the butter into the remaining flour until it resembles fine breadcrumbs, then stir in the grated cheese, herbs and seasoning. Spoon the crumble over the meat.

3. Bake in the oven at 190°C (375°F) mark 5 for 45 minutes–1 hour. Serve immediately.

Photographed right

Sweet and Sour Lamb with Pasta

4 LARGE BREASTS OF LAMB, BONED, SKINNED AND CUT INTO 5 cm (2 inch) STRIPS
30 ml (2 tbsp) VEGETABLE OIL
225 g (8 oz) ONIONS, SKINNED AND SLICED
10 ml (2 tsp) GROUND GINGER
45 ml (3 tbsp) PLAIN FLOUR
300 ml ($\frac{1}{2}$ pint) CHICKEN STOCK
300 ml ($\frac{1}{2}$ pint) DRY CIDER
30 ml (2 tbsp) SOY SAUCE
15 ml (1 tbsp) WORCESTERSHIRE SAUCE
45 ml (3 tbsp) CLEAR HONEY
45 ml (3 tbsp) WINE VINEGAR
340 g (12 oz) CAN PINEAPPLE CUBES, DRAINED WITH JUICE RESERVED
SALT AND FRESHLY GROUND PEPPER
125 g (4 oz) SMALL PASTA SHELLS
PARSLEY SPRIGS, TO GARNISH

Serves 8

1. Put the meat into a pan, cover with cold water, bring to the boil and bubble for 5 minutes. Drain and cool.

2. Heat the oil in a large flameproof casserole and brown the meat well, a little at a time. Remove and set aside.

3. Add the onions, ground ginger and flour to the oil remaining in the pan and fry gently for 3 minutes. Stir in the next six ingredients with the pineapple juice, seasoning and meat.

4. Bring to the boil, cover and cook in the oven at 150°C (300°F) mark 2 for 1 hour. Add the pineapple chunks and the pasta. Re-cover and cook for a further 40 minutes, adjust the seasoning. Garnish with parsley before serving.

Cheshire Lamb Crumble

Shoulder of Lamb Stuffed with Apricots

50 g (2 oz) FRESH WHOLEMEAL BREADCRUMBS
60 ml (4 tbsp) NATURAL YOGURT
1 GARLIC CLOVE, SKINNED AND CRUSHED
SALT AND FRESHLY GROUND PEPPER
A LITTLE FRESHLY GRATED NUTMEG
4 APRICOTS, STONED AND CHOPPED
30 ml (2 tbsp) CHOPPED MINT
15 ml (1 tbsp) CHOPPED THYME
½ SHOULDER OF LAMB, BONED AND TRIMMED OF FAT
300 ml (½ pint) CHICKEN STOCK

Serves 4

1. To make the stuffing, mix the breadcrumbs, half the yogurt, the garlic, seasoning and nutmeg and leave for 15 minutes.

2. Mix half the apricots into the breadcrumb mixture with half the chopped mint and the thyme. Spread the cut surface of the meat with the mixture. Re-shape the meat and tie with fine string. Set the meat on a rack in a roasting tin and roast at 180°C (350°F) mark 4 for 1½ hours, until tender.

3. Remove the lamb from the tin and place on a warm carving dish. Pour away any fat from the pan juices and put the pan on top of the cooker. Pour in the stock and bring to the boil, stirring in any residue from the bottom of the pan. Mix the remaining apricots into the stock with the remaining mint. Leave to simmer gently while carving the lamb. Remove the pan from the heat and mix the remaining yogurt into the sauce.

4. To serve, arrange the stuffed lamb slices on a warm serving dish and pour the apricot sauce over the top.

Lamb and Apricot Kebabs

60 ml (4 tbsp) OLIVE OIL
JUICE OF 1 LEMON
1 GARLIC CLOVE, SKINNED AND CRUSHED
PINCH OF SALT
5 ml (1 tsp) GROUND CUMIN
5 ml (1 tsp) GROUND CORIANDER
PINCH OF CAYENNE PEPPER
700 g (1½ lb) BONED LEAN SHOULDER OF LAMB, CUT INTO 2.5 cm (1 inch) CUBES
12 APRICOTS, HALVED AND STONED
2 LARGE ONIONS, SKINNED AND QUARTERED

Serves 4

1. In a large bowl, whisk together the oil, lemon juice, garlic, salt and spices until well blended. Stir in the cubes of lamb and leave to marinate at room temperature for at least 4 hours.

2. Drain the lamb and put alternate pieces of lamb, apricot and onion on to eight kebab skewers. Grill the kebabs under a high heat, turning them frequently, for about 12 minutes or until the cubes of lamb are browned on all sides.

Casseroled Lamb with Aubergine

700 g ($1\frac{1}{2}$ lb) AUBERGINES
SALT AND FRESHLY GROUND PEPPER
50 g (2 oz) LARD
1.8–2 kg (4–$4\frac{1}{2}$ lb) LEG OF LAMB, BONED AND SLICED INTO THIN STRIPS
60 ml (4 tbsp) PLAIN FLOUR
450 ml ($\frac{3}{4}$ pint) CHICKEN STOCK
90 ml (6 tbsp) MEDIUM SHERRY
5 ml (1 tsp) DRIED MARJORAM
700 g ($1\frac{1}{2}$ lb) TOMATOES, SKINNED AND SLICED
45 ml (3 tbsp) VEGETABLE OIL
CHOPPED PARSLEY, TO GARNISH

Serves 8

1. Cut the aubergines into 5 mm ($\frac{1}{4}$ inch) slices, sprinkle with salt and leave for 30 minutes to draw out the bitter juices. Rinse under cold water and dry with absorbent kitchen paper.

2. Heat the lard in a pan and brown the meat, a few strips at a time. Remove from the pan and place in a shallow ovenproof dish. Stir the flour into the pan juices, add the stock, sherry and marjoram. Season, bring to the boil and pour over the lamb.

3. Top with the tomatoes and finally the sliced aubergines. Brush with oil. Cover and bake in the oven at 180°C (350°F) mark 4 for $1\frac{1}{2}$ hours. Uncover, brush the aubergines with the cooking juices and bake at 230°C (450°F) mark 8 for a further 20 minutes or, until golden. Sprinkle with parsley.

Lamb and Maître d'Hôtel Butter

4 LARGE LOIN LAMB CHOPS, TRIMMED
175 g (6 oz) BUTTER
50 g (2 oz) BUTTON MUSHROOMS, WIPED AND FINELY CHOPPED
50 g (2 oz) HAM, FINELY CHOPPED
GRATED RIND OF 1 SMALL LEMON AND 5 ml (1 tsp) JUICE
SALT AND FRESHLY GROUND PEPPER
25 g (1 oz) FRESH BREADCRUMBS
1 BEATEN EGG
15 ml (1 tbsp) OIL
30 ml (2 tbsp) FINELY CHOPPED PARSLEY

Serves 4

1. Using a sharp knife, slit the lean eye of the chop horizontally through the fat edge.

2. Melt 25 g (1 oz) butter in a frying pan and lightly fry the mushrooms until soft. Add the ham, lemon rind, seasoning and breadcrumbs and bind with a little beaten egg. Allow to cool then stuff the mixture into the incisions in the chops. Secure each chop with string.

3. Heat the oil and 25 g (1 oz) butter in a large frying pan and over a high heat, fry the chops well on both sides. Lower the heat and cook for 20 minutes.

4. Whisk the remaining butter until soft but not oily. Add salt and pepper to taste, then the lemon juice and parsley. Cover and chill.

5. Remove the string from the chops. Cut the chilled maître d'hôtel butter into 1 cm ($\frac{1}{2}$ inch) slices and put one on each of the chops.

Photographed below

Lamb and Maître d'Hôtel Butter

Eastern Casserole of Lamb

- 450 g (1 lb) TOMATOES, SKINNED AND QUARTERED
- 45 ml (3 tbsp) VEGETABLE OIL
- 1.4 kg (3 lb) LEAN BONED LAMB OR MUTTON, CUT INTO LARGE CUBES
- 350 g (12 oz) ONIONS, SKINNED AND SLICED
- 30 ml (2 tbsp) GROUND CORIANDER
- 10 ml (2 tsp) GROUND CUMIN
- 5 ml (1 tsp) GROUND GINGER
- 1.25 ml (¼ tsp) TURMERIC
- 1.25 ml (¼ tsp) CAYENNE PEPPER
- 30 ml (2 tbsp) PLAIN FLOUR
- 15 ml (1 tbsp) TOMATO PUREE
- 450 ml (¾ pint) CHICKEN STOCK
- 75 g (3 oz) SULTANAS
- SALT AND FRESHLY GROUND PEPPER

Serves 8

1. Sieve the tomatoes to remove the seeds.
2. Heat the oil in a large flameproof casserole and brown the meat well, a few pieces at a time. Remove from the casserole and set aside.
3. Brown the onions in the fat remaining in the pan. Add the coriander, cumin, ginger, turmeric and cayenne and cook for 2 minutes, then add the flour and cook for a further 2 minutes. Add the remaining ingredients and season well. Return the meat to the pan, cover the casserole and cook in the oven at 170°C (325°F) mark 3 for about 1¾ hours for lamb, 2½ hours for mutton.

Minted Lamb Casserole

- 4 LAMB CHUMP CHOPS, BONED AND TRIMMED OF EXCESS FAT
- FRESHLY GROUND PEPPER
- 25 g (1 oz) LARD
- 1 ONION, SKINNED AND CHOPPED
- 396 g (14 oz) CAN TOMATOES
- PINCH OF GARLIC SALT
- 2.5 ml (½ tsp) SALT
- 5 ml (1 tsp) SUGAR
- 5 ml (1 tsp) DRIED MINT OR 15 ml (1 tbsp) CHOPPED MINT
- 1 BAY LEAF
- 50 g (2 oz) CHEDDAR CHEESE, GRATED
- 50 g (2 oz) FRESH BREADCRUMBS

Serves 4

1. Sprinkle both sides of the meat with pepper. Heat the lard in a pan and brown the chops on both sides. Drain on absorbent kitchen paper to remove most of the fat.
2. Fry the onion in the fat remaining in the pan for about 3 minutes. Remove using a slotted spoon and place in an ovenproof casserole with the chops.
3. Mix the tomatoes with their juices, seasonings, sugar and herbs. Pour over the meat.
4. Cover and cook in the oven at 170°C (325°F) mark 3 for 1 hour. Remove the bay leaf. Combine the cheese and breadcrumbs and sprinkle over the dish. Bake, uncovered, for a further 30 minutes until golden.

Lamb with Fennel

- 8 LAMB CUTLETS, ABOUT 150 g (5 oz) EACH, TRIMMED AND BONED
- 450 g (1 lb) FLORENCE FENNEL, TRIMMED AND SLICED
- 10 ml (2 tsp) LEMON JUICE
- ABOUT 30 ml (2 tbsp) PEANUT OIL
- 1 GARLIC CLOVE, SKINNED AND CRUSHED
- 15 ml (1 tbsp) TOMATO PUREE
- PINCH OF SUGAR
- 90 ml (6 tbsp) RED WINE
- 45 ml (3 tbsp) GRATED PARMESAN
- 12 BLACK OLIVES, HALVED AND STONED
- SALT AND FRESHLY GROUND PEPPER

Serves 4

1. Shape the lamb cutlets into rounds and secure with wooden cocktail sticks. Toss the fennel in the lemon juice.
2. Heat 30 ml (2 tbsp) oil with the garlic in a wok or large frying pan until smoky hot. Add the lamb and fry for about 4 minutes, until brown on all sides.
3. Stir in the fennel, adding more oil if necessary. Cook over a high heat for a further 4–5 minutes, stirring all the time, until the fennel begins to soften.
4. Add the tomato purée, sugar and red wine. Lower the heat, stir for 2–3 minutes, until well blended. Stir in the Parmesan and olives. Season and serve immediately.

Lamb and Cider Hotpot

- 1.8 kg (4 lb) LAMB SHOULDER, BONED, CUT INTO 5 cm (2 inch) PIECES
- 50 g (2 oz) PLAIN FLOUR
- 90 ml (6 tbsp) VEGETABLE OIL
- 90 g (3½ oz) BUTTER
- 225 g (8 oz) ONIONS, SKINNED AND SLICED
- 350 g (12 oz) CELERY, TRIMMED AND CHOPPED
- 450 g (1 lb) COOKING APPLES, PEELED, CORED AND SLICED
- 600 ml (1 pint) CHICKEN STOCK
- 327 ml (11½ fl oz) CAN CIDER
- SALT AND FRESHLY GROUND PEPPER
- 450 g (1 lb) POTATOES, THINLY SLICED
- PARSLEY SPRIGS, TO GARNISH

Serves 8

1. Toss the meat in the flour. Heat the oil and 50 g (2 oz) butter in a frying pan and quickly brown the meat. Drain and put into a 2.8 litre (5 pint) pie or ovenproof dish, sprinkling in any excess flour.
2. Add the onions, celery and apples to the frying pan and brown lightly. Spoon on top of the meat. Pour the stock and cider with plenty of seasoning over the meat and vegetables. Top with a layer of potatoes and dot with remaining butter.
3. Stand the dish on a baking sheet and bake in the oven at 180°C (350°F) mark 4 about 1½ hours, or until the meat is tender and the potatoes crisp. Serve garnished with parsley.

Lamb Pot Roast with Bean Stuffing

225 g (8 oz) ROSE COCOA BEANS, SOAKED OVERNIGHT AND DRAINED
30 ml (2 tbsp) CHOPPED MINT OR 10 ml (2 tsp) DRIED
60 ml (4 tbsp) FRESH BREADCRUMBS
1 EGG, BEATEN
SALT AND FRESHLY GROUND PEPPER
2–2.3 kg (4½–5 lb) LEG OF LAMB, BONED
300 ml (½ pint) CHICKEN STOCK
20 ml (4 tsp) CORNFLOUR

Serves 8–10

1. Divide the beans into two equal portions. Put one portion of beans into a pan, cover with water and bring to the boil. Lower the heat and simmer for about 1 hour, or until tender. Drain.
2. Mash the cooked beans lightly with back of a wooden spoon to break them down a little. Mix with half the mint, the breadcrumbs, egg and seasoning.
3. Use to stuff the cavity of the meat and tie securely. Cook any extra stuffing separately.
4. Place the meat in a large deep casserole and put the rest of the beans round. Pour over the stock with the remaining mint added. Season, cover and cook in the oven at 150°C (300°F) mark 2 for 3–3½ hours until the meat and beans are tender.
5. Pour off the juices and keep the meat and beans warm. Skim the fat from the juices. Blend the cornflour with cold water and stir into the juices. Bring to the boil, stirring and season.
6. Serve the lamb with the whole beans and hand the gravy separately.

Lamb and Aubergine Moussaka

900 g (2 lb) AUBERGINES, THINLY SLICED
SALT AND FRESHLY GROUND PEPPER
VEGETABLE OIL
350 g (12 oz) LEAN LAMB, MINCED
2 ONIONS, SKINNED AND CHOPPED
45 ml (3 tbsp) TOMATO PUREE
150 ml (¼ pint) DRY WHITE WINE
226 g (8 oz) CAN TOMATOES
2.5 ml (½ tsp) DRIED OREGANO
2.5 ml (½ tsp) DRIED BASIL
30 ml (2 tbsp) PLAIN FLOUR
75 g (3 oz) FRESH BREADCRUMBS
15 g (½ oz) BUTTER
300 ml (½ pint) MILK
75 g (3 oz) CHEDDAR CHEESE, GRATED
1 EGG YOLK

Serves 4

1. Sprinkle the aubergines generously with salt and leave in a colander to drain for 30 minutes.
2. Heat 15 ml (1 tbsp) oil in a saucepan and brown the lamb well. Stir in the onion, tomato purée, wine, tomatoes with juices, herbs and 15 ml (1 tbsp) flour. Bring to the boil, cover and simmer for 30 minutes. Season to taste.
3. Rinse the aubergines, squeeze and pat dry with absorbent kitchen paper. In a frying pan, fry them a few at a time in hot oil, until brown. Drain well.
4. Layer the aubergines in a 1.4 litre (2½ pint) shallow ovenproof dish, with the lamb and 50 g (2 oz) breadcrumbs.
5. To make the sauce, melt the butter in a pan, stir in the remaining flour and cook gently for 1 minute, stirring. Remove the pan from the heat and gradually stir in the milk. Return to the heat and bring to the boil. Continue to cook, stirring, until the sauce thickens. Remove from the heat, then stir in 50 g (2 oz) cheese and the egg yolk.
6. Spoon the sauce over the moussaka, sprinkle with the remaining cheese and breadcrumbs. Bake in the oven at 180°C (350°F) mark 4 for 45 minutes, until golden. Serve immediately.

Photographed opposite

Lamb and Spinach au Gratin

900 g (2 lb) SPINACH
75 g (3 oz) BUTTER
1.4 kg (3 lb) FILLET END LEG OF LAMB, BONED AND MINCED
1 GARLIC CLOVE, SKINNED AND CRUSHED
700 g (1½ lb) TOMATOES, SKINNED AND CHOPPED
75 g (3 oz) PLAIN FLOUR
10 ml (2 tsp) OREGANO
10 ml (2 tsp) ROSEMARY
300 ml (½ pint) DRY WHITE WINE
SALT AND FRESHLY GROUND PEPPER
16 SHEETS COOKED LASAGNE, 12.5 × 9 cm (5 × 3½ inches) ABOUT 275 g (10 oz)
900 ml (1½ pints) MILK
125 g (4 oz) LANCASHIRE CHEESE, GRATED
125 g (4 oz) MOZZARELLA CHEESE, GRATED

Serves 10

1. In a pan, gently cook the spinach (do not add liquid) for 3–4 minutes. Drain well and chop.
2. Melt 25 g (1 oz) butter in a frying pan and brown the lamb well. Drain off all the fat and stir in the garlic, spinach, tomatoes, 45 ml (3 tbsp) flour and the herbs. Cook for 1–2 minutes before adding the wine and seasoning. Bring to the boil, simmer for about 30 minutes, uncovered and cool.
3. Spread the mixture over the sheets of lasagne and roll up each sheet of lasagne from the short side. Cut the rolls into three, stand upright and pack tightly together in a large or two small 5 cm (2 inch) deep, straight-sided ovenproof dishes.
4. Melt the remaining butter in a pan and stir in the remaining flour. Remove from the heat and gradually stir in the milk. Return to the pan, season and stir until the sauce thickens. Pour over the pasta and cover.
5. Bake at 200°C (400°F) mark 6 for about 40 minutes, uncover, sprinkle with the cheese and grill until golden.

Lamb and Aubergine Moussaka

Lamb Tikka Kebab

142 g (5 oz) CARTON NATURAL YOGURT
5 ml (1 tsp) GARAM MARSALA
5 ml (1 tsp) GROUND CUMIN SEED
1.25 ml (¼ tsp) GROUND CORIANDER
1.25 ml (¼ tsp) GROUND TURMERIC
1.25 ml (¼ tsp) FRESHLY GROUND NUTMEG
2.5 ml (½ tsp) GARLIC POWDER
2.5 ml (½ tsp) CHILLI SEASONING
JUICE AND FINELY GRATED RIND OF 1 LEMON
450 g (1 lb) LEAN LAMB FILLET, CUBED
8–12 BUTTON ONIONS, SKINNED
1 SMALL GREEN PEPPER, SEEDED AND CUT INTO 2.5 cm (1 inch) SQUARES
175 g (6 oz) BUTTON MUSHROOMS, WIPED
LEMON WEDGES, TO GARNISH

Serves 4

1. To make the marinade: combine the first nine ingredients in a large bowl. Add the lamb and turn to coat evenly. Leave to marinate in the refrigerator for 2 days giving it an occasional stir.

2. Put the onions into a pan of water. Bring to the boil and simmer for 10 minutes. Put the green pepper into a small pan of water. Bring to the boil and simmer for 1–2 minutes. Drain the onions and peppers.

3. Remove the lamb from the marinade. Thread the lamb, mushrooms, onions and pepper squares alternately on to flat skewers and place on a baking sheet. Place under a moderate grill for 15–20 minutes or until the meat is cooked. Garnish with lemon wedges.

Piquant Lamb with Rosemary

900 g (2 lb) PIECE LEG OF LAMB, ABOUT 700 g (1½ lb) BONED, CUT INTO 2.5 cm (1 inch) CUBES
GRATED RIND OF 1 LEMON
90 ml (6 tbsp) LEMON JUICE
30 ml (2 tbsp) FRESH ROSEMARY OR 15 ml (1 tbsp) DRIED
1 LARGE GARLIC CLOVE, SKINNED AND CRUSHED
45 ml (3 tbsp) OIL
900 g (2 lb) SMALL NEW POTATOES
10 ml (2 tsp) CORNFLOUR
SALT AND FRESHLY GROUND PEPPER
ROSEMARY SPRIGS, TO GARNISH

Serves 4

1. Put the lamb cubes into a bowl with the lemon rind, lemon juice, rosemary and garlic. Cover and marinate for at least 1 hour.

2. Drain the lamb and reserve the marinade. Heat the oil in a large flameproof casserole. Brown the lamb well, a few pieces at a time. Remove with a slotted spoon.

3. In the same pan, gently fry the potatoes for 1–2 minutes. Return the lamb to the pan with the marinade and bring to the boil.

4. Cover tightly and bake at 180°C (350°F) mark 4 for 1–1½ hours or until the lamb and potatoes are tender.

5. Drain the juices from the casserole into a measuring jug. Make up to 150 ml (¼ pint) with water. Whisk in the cornflour and bring to the boil, stirring. Simmer until thickened and clear. Season and spoon over the lamb. Garnish with rosemary.

Photographed opposite

Apple and Lemon Lamb

15 ml (1 tbsp) OIL
450 g (1 lb) LEAN FILLET OF LAMB, CUT INTO 5 cm (2 inch) STRIPS
1 LEMON, THINLY SLICED
5 ml (1 tsp) DRIED THYME
SALT AND FRESHLY GROUND PEPPER
150 ml (¼ pint) STOCK
1 EATING APPLE, CORED AND SLICED
CHOPPED PARSLEY, TO GARNISH

Serves 4

1. Heat the oil in a shallow flameproof casserole and brown the meat. Cover with the lemon slices.

2. Stir the thyme, salt and pepper into the stock and pour over the lamb. Bring to the boil and simmer for 20 minutes.

3. Arrange the apple slices over the lemon. Cook for a further 10 minutes, or until the lamb, apple and lemon are tender. Serve garnished with parsley.

Peppered Lamb Stew

25 g (1 oz) DRIPPING
700 g (1½ lb) MIDDLE NECK OF LAMB
175 g (6 oz) ONIONS, SKINNED AND SLICED
225 g (8 oz) CARROTS, PEELED AND SLICED
225 g (8 oz) TURNIPS, PEELED AND SLICED
30 ml (2 tbsp) PLAIN FLOUR
600 ml (1 pint) WATER OR STOCK
30 ml (2 tbsp) WORCESTERSHIRE SAUCE
SALT AND FRESHLY GROUND PEPPER

Serves 4

1. Heat the dripping in a flameproof casserole and fry the meat to brown on all sides. Drain the meat and set aside.

2. Add the vegetables to the casserole and cook gently for 5 minutes. Add the flour and cook, stirring, until pale golden. Add the liquid and bring to the boil, stirring.

3. Return the meat to the pan with the Worcestershire sauce and seasoning. Cover and simmer for 1½ hours, or until the meat is fork tender.

Piquant Lamb with Rosemary

Lamb in Tomato Sauce

700 g ($1\frac{1}{2}$ lb) TOMATOES, SKINNED AND QUARTERED
CHICKEN STOCK
30 ml (2 tbsp) VEGETABLE OIL
1.4 kg (3 lb) SHOULDER OF LAMB, BONED, CUT INTO LARGE CUBES
1 ONION, SKINNED AND SLICED
20 ml (4 tsp) PLAIN FLOUR
30 ml (2 tbsp) TOMATO PUREE
2.5 ml ($\frac{1}{2}$ tsp) DRIED ROSEMARY
60 ml (4 tbsp) RED WINE
SALT AND FRESHLY GROUND PEPPER
50 g (2 oz) BUTTER, SOFTENED
15 ml (1 tbsp) CHOPPED PARSLEY
8 SLICES FRENCH BREAD

Serves 4

1. Sieve the tomatoes to remove the seeds. Make up the tomato juice to 300 ml ($\frac{1}{2}$ pint) with stock.

2. Heat the oil in a flameproof casserole and brown the lamb pieces. Remove from the casserole and set aside. Fry the onion in the fat remaining in the pan. Stir in the flour and gradually add the measured stock, tomatoes, tomato purée, rosemary and wine. Bring to the boil stirring. Return the meat to the pan and season.

3. Cover the casserole and cook in the oven at 170°C (325°F) mark 3 for about $1\frac{1}{4}$ hours.

4. Put the butter into a bowl, add the parsley and mix together thoroughly. Spread on the bread.

5. Uncover the casserole, place the bread butter side up on top. Cook for a further 1 hour.

Spiced Pork with Dumplings

45 ml (3 tbsp) OIL
450 g (1 lb) LEAN BELLY PORK, SKINNED, BONED AND CUT INTO STRIPS
175 g (6 oz) ONIONS, SKINNED AND QUARTERED
175 g (6 oz) CARROTS, PEELED AND QUARTERED
45 ml (3 tbsp) PLAIN FLOUR
20 ml (4 tsp) GROUND CORIANDER
2.5 ml (½ tsp) GROUND CUMIN
700 ml (1¼ pints) STOCK
100 g (4 oz) ADUKI BEANS, SOAKED OVERNIGHT AND DRAINED
SALT AND FRESHLY GROUND PEPPER
100 g (4 oz) SELF-RAISING FLOUR
50 g (2 oz) SHREDDED SUET
30 ml (2 tbsp) CHOPPED PARSLEY

Serves 4

1. Heat the oil in a flameproof casserole and brown the meat. Add the vegetables and fry gently.
2. Stir in the flour and spices, cook for 2 minutes, then stir in the stock and beans. Season, bring to the boil, cover and simmer for 1 hour, stirring occasionally.
3. Sift the self-raising flour with a pinch of salt and pepper, add suet and parsley. Add enough cold water to bind, and form into eight even-sized balls. Add the dumplings to the stew. Cover and cook for 15–20 minutes.

Cassoulet

25 g (1 oz) LARD
450 g (1 lb) ONIONS, SKINNED AND SLICED
225 g (8 oz) STREAKY SALT PORK, RINDED AND CUT INTO STRIPS
225 g (8 oz) LEAN SHOULDER LAMB, CUT INTO STRIPS
600 ml (1 pint) BONE STOCK
225 g (8 oz) DRIED HARICOT BEANS, SOAKED OVERNIGHT AND DRAINED
1 BAY LEAF
1 GARLIC CLOVE, SKINNED AND CRUSHED
100 g (4 oz) GARLIC SAUSAGE, SLICED
15 ml (1 tbsp) FRESH CHOPPED WINTER SAVORY
SALT AND FRESHLY GROUND PEPPER

Serves 6

1. Melt the fat in a 2.8 litre (5 pint) flameproof casserole and gently fry the onions until soft. Add the meats and cook to seal.
2. Add the stock, beans, bay leaf, garlic, garlic sausage, savory and seasoning. Bring to the boil, cover and simmer gently for 1½–2 hours or until the beans and meat are tender.

Pork and Apricot Parcels

50 g (2 oz) DRIED APRICOTS, THINLY SLICED
25 g (1 oz) BLANCHED ALMONDS, SHREDDED
45 ml (3 tbsp) BRANDY
30 ml (2 tbsp) OIL
4 PORK LOIN CHOPS, BONED AND TRIMMED OF EXCESS FAT
SALT AND FRESHLY GROUND BLACK PEPPER
CHOPPED PARSLEY, TO GARNISH

Serves 4

1. Put the apricots and almonds into a bowl, pour over the brandy and marinate overnight.
2. Heat the oil in a frying pan and quickly brown the chops to seal, turning once.
3. Place each chop on a square of foil. Spoon a little of the apricot mixture over each and season well. Fold the foil over each chop, loosely, sealing the edges well.
4. Put into a steamer over boiling water, cover and steam for 50–60 minutes. Serve from the parcels, garnished with parsley.

Celery-stuffed Pork Shoulder

900 g (2 lb) SHOULDER NECK END OF PORK, BONE REMOVED AND RESERVED
OIL, FOR BRUSHING
50 g (2 oz) MARGARINE
125 g (4 oz) CELERY, TRIMMED AND FINELY CHOPPED
50 g (2 oz) DATES, STONED AND CHOPPED
10 ml (2 tsp) LEMON JUICE
45 ml (3 tbsp) FRENCH MUSTARD
225 g (8 oz) WHITE BREADCRUMBS
50 g (2 oz) SHREDDED SUET
SALT AND FRESHLY GROUND PEPPER
50 g (2 oz) BUTTER
25 g (1 oz) DEMERARA SUGAR
3 RED SKINNED APPLES, CORED AND QUARTERED

Serves 6

1. With a sharp knife, remove the rind from the pork joint in one piece. Score it and brush with oil.
2. Melt the margarine in a pan and gently fry the celery for 5 minutes until softened. Stir in the chopped dates, lemon juice, 30 ml (2 tbsp) mustard, breadcrumbs and suet. Season well.
3. Make three deep slashes down the joint to within 1 cm (½ inch) of the base.
4. Press the stuffing down the slashes in the meat. Secure with skewers and spread with the remaining mustard.
5. Place the joint in a roasting tin with the reserved bones, and the pork rind beside it. Roast at 170°C (325°F) mark 3 for about 2¼ hours, covering loosely with foil after the first hour.
6. In a second tin, melt the butter, stir in the sugar and apple quarters and turn to coat them. Place alongside the meat for the last 10 minutes of cooking time. Serve the pork with the apple quarters and gravy made from the pan juices. If wished, serve the dish with sautéed lentils and celery.
Photographed opposite

Celery-stuffed Pork Shoulder

Parcelled Pork

25 g (1 oz) BUTTER
4 PORK CHOPS, 175 g (6 oz) EACH, TRIMMED OF RINDS AND EXCESS FAT
1 ONION, SKINNED AND FINELY CHOPPED
225 g (8 oz) MUSHROOMS, WIPED AND SLICED
90 ml (6 tbsp) DRY CIDER
30 ml (2 tbsp) LEMON JUICE
142 ml (5 fl oz) CARTON SOURED CREAM
SALT AND FRESHLY GROUND PEPPER

Serves 4

1. Melt the butter in a large frying pan and brown the chops well. Remove the chops from the pan and place on pieces of foil about 20 cm (8 inches) square.

2. Add the onion and mushrooms to the butter remaining in the pan and cook for 5 minutes.

3. Stir in the cider and lemon juice and bring to the boil. Reduce the liquid over a high heat until reduced by half, then remove from the heat and stir in the soured cream. Season well.

4. Place a quarter of the mushroom mixture on top of each chop, then shape the foil into neat parcels and seal well.

5. Place the parcels in a small ovenproof dish and bake in the oven at 180°C (350°F) mark 4 for about 50 minutes, until the chops are tender.

6. To serve, place each parcel on a plate and open carefully so that no juices escape. Serve with small new potatoes, boiled in their jackets, and green beans.

Photographed opposite

Peppered Pork with Fruit

12 STONED PRUNES
50 g (2 oz) BUTTER OR MARGARINE
566 g (20 oz) CAN SMALL SLICES PINEAPPLE, DRAINED, WITH JUICE RESERVED
6 LARGE PORK CHOPS, TRIMMED OF EXCESS FAT
30 ml (2 tbsp) PLAIN FLOUR
90 ml (6 tbsp) SHERRY
30 ml (2 tbsp) WHOLE BLACK PEPPERCORNS, CRUSHED
SALT

Serves 6

1. Put the prunes into a pan, cover with boiling water and leave to stand for 30 minutes. Drain.

2. Heat the fat in a large frying pan and brown the chops well. Place side-by-side in a shallow ovenproof casserole.

3. Brown the pineapple slices, a few at a time, in the fat remaining in the pan. Spoon over the chops.

4. Stir the flour into the pan with the sherry, pineapple juice, crushed peppercorns and salt and bring to the boil. Stir in the prunes and spoon the mixture over the chops.

5. Cover the dish tightly and cook in the oven at 180°C (350°F) mark 4 for about 50 minutes. Serve on a shallow dish with the juices spooned over.

Pork and Apple Loaf

100 g (4 oz) ONIONS, SKINNED AND FINELY CHOPPED
225 g (8 oz) COOKING APPLE, PEELED, CORED AND FINELY CHOPPED
450 g (1 lb) MINCED LEAN BELLY PORK
100 g (4 oz) FRESH WHITE BREADCRUMBS
2 EGGS, BEATEN
2.5 ml ($\frac{1}{2}$ tsp) DRIED SAGE
SALT AND FRESHLY GROUND BLACK PEPPER
BUTTER OR MARGARINE
CHOPPED PARSLEY OR SNIPPED CHIVES

Serves 4–6

1. Combine the onion and apple with the pork, breadcrumbs, eggs, sage and seasonings, mixing well.

2. Thoroughly grease a 1.1 litre (2 pint) loaf tin or a round soufflé dish. Base-line with greaseproof paper and grease the paper. Turn the pork mixture into it.

3. Cover with greased foil and put into a steamer over boiling water. Cover and steam for about $1\frac{1}{2}$ hours. Turn out, slice and serve with the juices spooned over. Garnish with parsley or chives.

Baked Stuffed Pork Chops

50 g (2 oz) LONG-GRAIN BROWN RICE
30 ml (2 tbsp) VEGETABLE OIL
4 SPARE RIB PORK CHOPS, TRIMMED AND BONED
1 SMALL ONION, SKINNED AND FINELY CHOPPED
50 g (2 oz) SEEDLESS RAISINS
226 g (8 oz) CAN PINEAPPLE, DRAINED AND CHOPPED, JUICE RESERVED
45 ml (3 tbsp) CHOPPED PARSLEY
SALT AND FRESHLY GROUND PEPPER

Serves 4

1. Bring a pan of salted water to the boil and cook the rice for about 30 minutes until almost tender. Drain well.

2. Heat the oil in a large pan and brown the chops well. Cool them, then slit three-quarters of the way through each chop to form a large pocket.

3. Brown the onion in the oil remaining in the pan. Stir in the raisins with the pineapple, cooked rice, parsley and seasoning.

4. Place the chops in a shallow ovenproof dish. Use the rice mixture to stuff them. Spoon round 60 ml (4 tbsp) pineapple juice. Season, cover the dish tightly and cook in the oven at 180°C (350°F) mark 4 for 1–$1\frac{1}{4}$ hours. Baste once with the juice during cooking.

Parcelled Pork

Sage and Bacon Stuffed Pork

1 kg ($2\frac{1}{4}$ lb) BONED LOIN OF PORK, WELL SCORED
225 g (8 oz) BACK BACON RASHERS, RINDED
12 FRESH OR DRIED SAGE LEAVES AND A SPRIG OF FRESH SAGE, TO GARNISH
COOKING OIL
SALT

Serves 6

1. Ask the butcher to bone the pork and score the rind deeply and evenly. Place the joint on a flat surface, fat side down, and cut the flesh at intervals to open it out a little.

2. Lay the rashers over the flesh and place the sage leaves at intervals. Roll up carefully and secure firmly with string, parcel fashion. Put in a roasting tin. Rub the rind well with oil and salt. Roast in the oven at 190°C (375°F) mark 5 for about 2 hours. Remove the strings and place the meat on a serving dish garnished with a sprig of fresh sage.

Photographed on the cover

Pork with Tomato and Barley

4 SPARE RIB PORK CHOPS, TRIMMED AND BONED
30 ml (2 tbsp) VEGETABLE OIL
225 g (8 oz) ONIONS, SKINNED AND SLICED INTO ROUNDS
396 g (14 oz) CAN TOMATOES
300 ml ($\frac{1}{2}$ pint) CHICKEN STOCK
50 g (2 oz) PEARL BARLEY
1 LARGE GARLIC CLOVE, SKINNED AND CRUSHED
5 ml (1 tsp) DRIED OREGANO
SALT AND FRESHLY GROUND PEPPER

Serves 4

1. Divide each chop into three pieces. Heat the oil in a flameproof casserole and brown the chops well. Remove and set aside.

2. Lightly brown the onions in the fat remaining in the pan. Add the tomatoes and their juice with the stock, barley, garlic, oregano and seasoning. Bring to the boil.

3. Return the pork to the casserole, cover tightly and cook in the oven at 170°C (325°F) mark 3 for about $1\frac{1}{2}$ hours.

Crumbed Pork with Leeks

125 g (4 oz) MARGARINE
50 g (2 oz) DRIED BREADCRUMBS
15 g ($\frac{1}{2}$ oz) GRATED PARMESAN
2 PIECES BELLY PORK, TOTAL WEIGHT 900 g (2 lb), RIND REMOVED AND CUT INTO STRIPS
175 g (6 oz) PEARL BARLEY
600 ml (1 pint) LIGHT STOCK
450 g (1 lb) LEEKS, TRIMMED AND SLICED
30 ml (2 tbsp) PLAIN FLOUR
600 ml (1 pint) MILK
SALT AND FRESHLY GROUND PEPPER

Serves 6

1. Rub 75 g (3 oz) margarine into the breadcrumbs and Parmesan to form a paste.
2. Score the surface fat of the pork and press the cheese mixture well on to the fat.
3. Put the pearl barley and stock into a roasting tin. Put the pork joints on a rack over the tin. Cook in the oven at 180°C (350°F) mark 4 for $2\frac{1}{2}$ hours. Cover after the first hour. In a separate tin put the crackling strips into the oven, and raise the temperature to 200°C (400°F) mark 6.
4. Transfer the pork to a serving dish and keep warm.
5. Melt the remaining margarine in a saucepan and lightly fry the leeks. Stir in the flour and cook for 1 minute before adding the barley and juices from the roasting tin. Remove from the heat and gradually add the milk. Bring to the boil, simmer for 2 minutes and season. Serve with the carved pork.

Pork with Mushrooms

900 g (2 lb) PORK FILLET, CUBED
75 g (3 oz) PLAIN FLOUR
5 ml (1 tsp) SALT
FRESHLY GROUND PEPPER
75 g (3 oz) BUTTER
350 g (12 oz) ONIONS, SKINNED AND SLICED
450 g (1 lb) BUTTON MUSHROOMS, WIPED AND SLICED
900 ml ($1\frac{1}{2}$ pints) CHICKEN STOCK
100 ml (4 fl oz) DRY SHERRY

Serves 6

1. Toss the meat in the flour and seasonings to coat evenly.
2. Melt the butter in a frying pan and cook the onions and meat until lightly browned. Add the mushrooms, stir in any remaining flour and fry gently for 1 minute. Gradually stir in the stock and sherry.
3. Bring to the boil, cover and simmer for 30–40 minutes, until the meat is tender.

Photographed right

Pork with Mushrooms

Rolled Pork Tenderloins

2 FILLETS OF PORK, 350 g (12 oz) EACH
25 g (1 oz) BUTTER
125 g (4 oz) CELERY, TRIMMED AND CHOPPED
225 g (8 oz) LEEKS, TRIMMED AND CHOPPED
125 g (4 oz) EATING APPLES, PEELED, CORED AND ROUGHLY CHOPPED
50 g (2 oz) WALNUT PIECES, ROUGHLY CHOPPED
125 g (4 oz) EDAM CHEESE, COARSELY GRATED
SALT AND FRESHLY GROUND PEPPER
60 ml (4 tbsp) OIL

Serves 6

1. Make a cut in each fillet almost through to the base. Open out and lay, cut side down, on a flat surface. Cover with greaseproof paper and beat out with a rolling pin until completely flat and very thin.

2. Melt the butter in a large frying pan and gently fry the celery, leek, apple and walnuts for 3–4 minutes, until the celery has softened. Remove from the pan and cool.

3. Stir 75 g (3 oz) of the cheese into the cooled mixture and season.

4. Lay the pork fillets on a flat surface, overlapping the longest edges by about 2.5 cm (1 inch). Spoon the stuffing mixture evenly along the pork fillets and fold up the sides to enclose the stuffing. Tie securely at intervals with fine string.

5. Heat the oil in the frying pan and brown the pork well. Transfer pork and oil to a roasting tin, and cook at 200°C (400°F) mark 6 for 40 minutes.

6. Sprinkle the remaining cheese over the pork. Return to the oven for a further 10 minutes.

Photographed below

Orange-glazed Spare Ribs

30 ml (2 tbsp) SOY SAUCE
45 ml (3 tbsp) ORANGE MARMALADE
25 g (1 oz) SOFT BROWN SUGAR
GRATED RIND AND 60 ml (4 tbsp) JUICE OF 1 ORANGE
1.4 kg (3 lb) AMERICAN CUT PORK SPARE RIBS
15 ml (1 tbsp) OIL
125 g (4 oz) CARROTS, PEELED AND ROUGHLY CHOPPED
225 g (8 oz) ONIONS, SKINNED AND ROUGHLY CHOPPED

Serves 4

1. Combine the soy sauce, marmalade and sugar. Add the orange rind and juice. Spoon over the spare ribs and leave to marinate for 1–2 hours, turning occasionally.

2. Heat the oil in a frying pan and gently fry the vegetables lightly for 2 minutes. Spoon into an oven-proof dish and place the spare ribs and marinade on top.

3. Cook in the oven, uncovered at 190°C (375°F) mark 5 for about $1\frac{1}{4}$ hours, turning the ribs occasionally.

Rolled Pork Tenderloins

Cider Pork Sauté

Cider Pork Sauté

450 g (1 lb) GREEN EATING APPLES
450 g (1 lb) FLOURY POTATOES, PEELED AND CUT INTO SMALL CHUNKS
SALT AND FRESHLY GROUND PEPPER
50 g (2 oz) BUTTER
15 ml (1 tbsp) OIL
450 g (1 lb) PORK ESCALOPE, CUT INTO FINE STRIPS
50 g (2 oz) ONIONS, SKINNED AND FINELY CHOPPED
15 ml (1 tbsp) PLAIN FLOUR
300 ml ($\frac{1}{2}$ pint) DRY CIDER
30 ml (2 tbsp) CAPERS
1 EGG, BEATEN, FOR GLAZING

Serves 4

1. Quarter, peel and core half the apples and thickly slice. Cook together with the potatoes in boiling, salted water for 20 minutes, or until the potatoes are tender. Drain well. Press the potatoes and apples through a sieve and beat in half the butter. Season and spoon the mixture down both ends of a 1.5 litre ($2\frac{1}{2}$ pint) shallow ovenproof dish.
2. Quarter, core and thickly slice the remaining apples. Keep covered in cold water.
3. Heat the remaining butter with the oil in a large frying pan. Brown the pork strips a few at a time and remove with a slotted spoon.
4. Add the onion to the pan, fry gently for 2–3 minutes. Return all the pork strips to the pan and stir in the flour. Cook, stirring, for 1–2 minutes before adding the cider. Bring to the boil, stir in the drained apple slices, simmer gently for 4–5 minutes, or until the pork is tender but the apple still holds its shape. Stir in the capers and season.
5. Spoon into the centre of the dish. Brush the potato with beaten egg and bake at 200°C (400°F) mark 6 for 25–30 minutes.

Photographed above

Bean and Pork Patties

- 125 g (4 oz) DRIED ADUKI BEANS, SOAKED OVERNIGHT AND DRAINED
- 225 g (8 oz) MINCED PORK
- 2 GARLIC CLOVES, SKINNED AND CRUSHED
- 25 g (1 oz) FRESH WHITE BREADCRUMBS
- 175 g (6 oz) ONIONS, SKINNED AND FINELY CHOPPED
- 1 EGG, BEATEN
- 7.5 ml (1½ tsp) DRIED ROSEMARY, CRUSHED
- SALT AND FRESHLY GROUND PEPPER
- 30 ml (2 tbsp) PLAIN FLOUR
- OIL
- 450 g (1 lb) TOMATOES, SKINNED, SEEDED AND CHOPPED
- 5 ml (1 tsp) SUGAR
- 10 ml (2 tsp) WORCESTERSHIRE SAUCE
- 10 ml (2 tsp) SOY SAUCE
- 20 ml (4 tsp) MANGO CHUTNEY
- 5 ml (1 tsp) CIDER VINEGAR
- 450 ml (¾ pint) LIGHT STOCK
- 15 ml (1 tbsp) CORNFLOUR

Serves 4

1. Put the beans into a pan, cover with water and bring to the boil. Lower the heat and simmer for about 30 minutes until tender. Drain.

2. Mash the beans and mix with the pork, 1 garlic clove, breadcrumbs, half the onion, the egg, rosemary and seasonings. Shape into 16 balls, roll in the flour and flatten.

3. Heat a little oil in a pan and fry the patties for about 15 minutes until well browned. Drain and place in an ovenproof dish.

4. Fry the remaining onion and the tomatoes with the remaining garlic clove and the other remaining ingredients except the cornflour. Season well and simmer for about 10 minutes. Mix the cornflour to a paste with a little water. Add a spoonful of the pan juices and stir the mixture back into the pan. Pour over the meatballs.

5. Cover and cook in the oven at 180°C (350°F) mark 4 for about 30 minutes.

Photographed opposite

Pork and Corn Pan Supper

- 30 ml (2 tbsp) VEGETABLE OIL
- 25 g (1 oz) BUTTER
- 4 SPARE RIB PORK CHOPS, BONED AND SLICED INTO FORK-SIZED PIECES
- 225 g (8 oz) ONIONS, SKINNED AND SLICED
- 45 ml (3 tbsp) PLAIN FLOUR
- 5 ml (1 tsp) PAPRIKA
- 450 ml (¾ pint) CHICKEN STOCK
- SALT AND FRESHLY GROUND PEPPER
- 198 g (7 oz) CAN CORN NIBLETS
- 60 ml (4 tbsp) NATURAL YOGURT, STIRRED
- CHOPPED PARSLEY, TO GARNISH

Serves 4

1. Heat the oil and butter in a frying pan and brown the meat well. Remove the meat from the pan and set aside.

2. Add the onions and brown well, then stir in the flour and paprika and fry gently for 1 minute. Stir in the stock and bring to the boil, stirring. Season and add the drained corn niblets. Return the pork to the pan.

3. Cover the pan tightly and simmer gently for about 45 minutes, stirring occasionally. Blend the stirred yogurt into the juices and scatter with parsley.

Spring Pork Casserole

- 15 ml (1 tbsp) VEGETABLE OIL
- 4 SPARE RIB PORK CHOPS, TRIMMED
- 1 ONION, SKINNED AND SLICED
- 450 g (1 lb) SMALL NEW CARROTS, SCRAPED AND LEFT WHOLE
- 450 g (1 lb) POTATOES, PEELED AND DICED
- 2.5 ml (½ tsp) DRIED MIXED HERBS
- 300 ml (½ pint) CHICKEN STOCK
- SALT AND FRESHLY GROUND PEPPER
- CHOPPED PARSLEY, TO GARNISH

Serves 4

1. Heat the oil in a pan and quickly fry the chops on both sides until brown. Remove from the pan and set aside. Add the onion to the pan and fry until golden.

2. Combine the carrots with the potatoes and place in a shallow casserole. Add the herbs and pour the stock over the vegetables. Lay the chops on the vegetables with the onion and season with salt and pepper.

3. Cover and cook in the oven at 180°C (350°F) mark 4 for about 1 hour until the chops are tender. Serve garnished with parsley.

Stir-fried Pork and Vegetables

- 60 ml (4 tbsp) SOY SAUCE
- 15 ml (1 tbsp) DRY SHERRY
- 12.5 ml (2½ tsp) CORNFLOUR
- 6.25 ml (1¼ tsp) SUGAR
- 2.5 ml (½ tsp) FINELY CHOPPED FRESH GINGER OR 1.25 ml (¼ tsp) GROUND GINGER
- 2 PORK FILLETS, 350 g (12 oz) EACH, THINLY SLICED
- 150 ml (¼ pint) VEGETABLE OIL
- 450 g (1 lb) VEGETABLES SUCH AS CAULIFLOWER FLORETS, BEANSPROUTS, CARROTS, SLICED AND BROCCOLI FLORETS
- 225 g (8 oz) MUSHROOMS, SLICED
- 1.25 ml (¼ tsp) SALT
- 30 ml (2 tbsp) WATER

Serves 6

1. Mix the soy sauce, sherry, cornflour, sugar and ginger in a bowl; add the pork and toss well.

2. Heat 60 ml (4 tbsp) of the oil in a flameproof casserole and add the vegetables, mushrooms and salt. Fry quickly, stirring, until the vegetables are coated with oil. Add the water and continue to stir-fry until the vegetables are tender but still crisp. Place the vegetables and liquid on a heated serving dish and keep hot.

3. Heat the remaining oil in the casserole until very hot. Add the meat mixture and stir-fry for about 2 minutes until the meat is browned. Return the vegetables to the casserole and heat through.

Photographed on page 191

Bean and Pork Patties

Bacon in Cider

1.1 kg (2½ lb) SMOKED COLLAR OF BACON
4 CLOVES
300 ml (½ pint) DRY CIDER
1 BAY LEAF
125 g (4 oz) FRESH WHITE BREADCRUMBS
175 g (6 oz) SELF-RAISING FLOUR
5 ml (1 tsp) SAGE
50 g (2 oz) SHREDDED SUET
25 g (1 oz) MARGARINE
175 g (6 oz) ONIONS, SKINNED AND COARSELY GRATED
SALT AND FRESHLY GROUND PEPPER

Serves 6

1. Put the bacon into a saucepan of cold water and bring slowly to the boil. Drain off the water. Slice off the rind if it is not cooked enough to peel away. Stud the fat with cloves.

2. Put the bacon into a shallow casserole with the cider and bay leaf. Cover tightly and cook in the oven at 180°C (350°F) mark 4 for about 2¼ hours.

3. Meanwhile, combine the breadcrumbs, flour, sage and suet. Rub in the margarine, add the onion and bind to a soft dough with water. Season lightly and shape into twelve dumplings.

4. About 45 minutes before the end of cooking time add the dumplings to the juices surrounding the bacon. Cover again and finish cooking.

Peanut-glazed Bacon Hock

1.1 kg (2½ lb) BACON HOCK
1 SMALL CARROT, PEELED
1 SMALL ONION, SKINNED
1 BAY LEAF
30 ml (2 tbsp) LEMON MARMALADE
30 ml (2 tbsp) DEMERARA SUGAR
10 ml (2 tsp) LEMON JUICE
DASH OF WORCESTERSHIRE SAUCE
25 g (1 oz) SALTED PEANUTS, CHOPPED

Serves 6

1. Put the bacon into an ovenproof casserole with the carrot, onion, bay leaf and enough water to come halfway up the joint. Cover and cook at 180°C (350°F) mark 4 for about 2¼ hours.

2. Remove the bacon, carefully cut off the rind and score the fat.

3. Combine the marmalade, sugar, lemon juice and Worcestershire sauce. Spread over the surface of the joint and sprinkle on the chopped peanuts.

4. Put the joint into a roasting tin. Raise the oven temperature to 220°C (425°F) mark 7 and return the joint to the oven for a further 15 minutes to glaze.

Caramelled Gammon

2 GAMMON RASHERS, 1 cm (½ inch) THICK, RINDED
40 g (1½ oz) BUTTER
226 g (8 oz) CAN PINEAPPLE RINGS, DRAINED AND JUICE RESERVED
60 ml (4 tbsp) DEMERARA SUGAR
WATERCRESS SPRIGS, TO GARNISH

Serves 4

1. Snip the rasher fat at intervals and cut each rasher in half. Poach the rashers in a little water for 1–2 minutes. Drain.

2. Melt the butter in a pan and fry the rashers until golden brown on both sides—about 2 minutes. Remove the rashers and cool the butter remaining in the pan. Add the pineapple juice and sugar, dissolve over a low heat and bring to the boil. Return the rashers to the pan, lower the heat, cover and simmer for about 20 minutes, or until tender.

3. Arrange the rashers on a serving dish. Reduce the liquid in the pan by boiling rapidly. Add the pineapple rings and heat through. Arrange them on top of the rashers and pour the glaze over them. Garnish with watercress and serve with rice.

Photographed opposite

Roast Gammon

1.8 kg (4 lb) PIECE BONELESS GAMMON, SOAKED IN WATER 2–3 HOURS
50 g (2 oz) DEMERARA SUGAR
150 g (5 oz) MARMALADE
10 ml (2 tsp) MADE MUSTARD
2 ORANGES, THINLY SLICED
CLOVES

Serves 10

1. Drain the gammon well and put into a large pan, skin side down. Cover with fresh cold water and add the sugar. Bring slowly to the boil, skimming off the scum as it rises. Lower the heat, cover and simmer for 50 minutes–1 hour. Top up with extra boiling water when necessary.

2. Drain the joint. Carefully cut off the rind and score the fat into squares. Wrap the joint in foil, place in a roasting tin and roast at 180°C (350°F) mark 4 for 40 minutes.

3. Put the marmalade and mustard together in a small saucepan and stir over gentle heat until the marmalade is melted. Remove the gammon from the oven, remove the foil and brush the gammon with glaze.

4. Raise the temperature to 220°C (425°F) mark 7 and cook uncovered for a further 20 minutes.

5. Halve the orange slices and arrange them in rows, overlapping slightly, over the gammon. Fasten them in place with cloves. Brush the remaining warm marmalade glaze gently over the orange slices.

6. Return the gammon to the oven for 10 minutes or until the orange slices are heated through.

Caramelled Gammon

Curried Bacon Flan

175 g (6 oz) PLAIN FLOUR
PINCH OF SALT
40 g ($1\frac{1}{2}$ oz) BUTTER, CUT INTO SMALL PIECES
40 g ($1\frac{1}{2}$ oz) LARD, CUT INTO SMALL PIECES
ABOUT 45 ml (3 tbsp) WATER
25 g (1 oz) BUTTER
125 g (4 oz) CELERY HEART, TRIMMED AND SLICED
125 g (4 oz) STREAKY BACON, RINDED AND DICED
5 ml (1 tsp) CURRY POWDER
3 EGGS, BEATEN
142 g (5 oz) CARTON NATURAL YOGURT
SALT AND FRESHLY GROUND PEPPER
225 g (8 oz) TOMATOES, SKINNED AND THINLY SLICED

Serves 4–6
1. Make the pastry: sift the flour and salt into a bowl and rub in the fat until the mixture resembles fine breadcrumbs, and add just enough water to make a firm dough.
2. Roll out the pastry on a lightly floured surface, and use to line a 22 cm ($8\frac{1}{2}$ inch), loose-bottomed French fluted flan tin. Bake blind with foil and beans in the oven at 200°C (400°F) mark 6 for 10–15 minutes until set.
3. Melt the butter in a small frying pan and gently cook the celery and bacon until golden brown. Stir in the curry powder and cook for 2 minutes.
4. In a bowl, blend the egg with the yogurt. Add the pan ingredients and seasoning. Remove the foil and beans from the flan and turn the mixture into it. Top with tomato slices.
5. Bake in the oven at 190°C (375°F) mark 5 for about 25 minutes until golden brown and set. Serve hot or cold.
Photographed opposite

Midweek Bacon Stew

700 g ($1\frac{1}{2}$ lb) BACON SLIPPER JOINT, RINDED AND CUT INTO 2.5 cm (1 inch) CUBES
25 g (1 oz) LARD
225 g (8 oz) TURNIPS, PEELED AND COARSELY DICED
225 g (8 oz) PARSNIPS, PEELED AND COARSELY DICED
30 ml (2 tbsp) PLAIN FLOUR
7.5 ml ($1\frac{1}{2}$ tsp) DRY MUSTARD
600 ml (1 pint) UNSEASONED CHICKEN STOCK
100 g (4 oz) DRIED BUTTER BEANS, SOAKED OVERNIGHT AND DRAINED
FRESHLY GROUND PEPPER
CHOPPED PARSLEY, TO GARNISH

Serves 6
1. Put the meat cubes into a pan of cold water, bring to the boil and simmer for 5 minutes. Drain well.
2. Melt the fat in a flameproof casserole and gently fry the vegetables for 5 minutes. Stir in the flour and mustard, cook for 1 minute then gradually stir in the stock. Stir until boiling.
3. Add the beans, meat and pepper. Cover and simmer for about $1\frac{1}{2}$ hours. Serve garnished with parsley.

Asparagus and Bacon Quiche

700 g ($1\frac{1}{2}$ lb) ASPARAGUS SPEARS, ABOUT 24
225 g (8 oz) PLAIN FLOUR
125 g (4 oz) BUTTER OR MARGARINE
ABOUT 60 ml (4 tbsp) WATER
125 g (4 oz) THIN SLICED STREAKY BACON RASHERS, RINDED
3 EGG YOLKS
200 ml (7 fl oz) SINGLE CREAM
100 g (4 oz) SAMSOE CHEESE, GRATED
SALT AND FRESHLY GROUND PEPPER

Serves 8 buffet portions
1. Trim the heads off the asparagus to the length of about 4 cm ($1\frac{1}{2}$ inches). Blanch the heads: put into a pan of boiling salted water for 5 minutes. Drain well.
2. Sift the flour into a bowl and rub in the fat until the mixture resembles fine breadcrumbs. Mix in enough water to make a firm dough. Roll out on a lightly floured surface, and use to line a 25 cm (10 inch) loose-bottomed fluted flan tin. Bake blind with foil and beans until set but not browned.
3. Stretch the bacon with a palette knife and wrap a small piece around each asparagus head.
4. Mix the egg yolks, cream, cheese and seasoning together and spoon into the flan case.
5. Arrange the bacon rolls in the custard. Bake at 180°C (350°F) mark 4 for 30–35 minutes, or until set and golden brown. Serve warm.

Bacon Blintzes

125 g (4 oz) PLAIN FLOUR
1 EGG, BEATEN
300 ml ($\frac{1}{2}$ pint) MILK AND WATER, HALF AND HALF
LARD, FOR FRYING
225 g (8 oz) LEAN STREAKY BACON, RINDED AND FINELY SNIPPED
225 g (8 oz) MUSHROOMS, WIPED AND CHOPPED
75 g (3 oz) SPRING ONIONS, TRIMMED AND FINELY CHOPPED
FRESHLY GROUND PEPPER
OIL, FOR DEEP FRYING

Serves 4
1. Make the batter: sift the flour into a bowl and beat in the egg and milk and water until smooth. Heat a knob of lard in a small frying pan tilting the pan so that the melted lard coats the base. Pour in enough batter to cover the base of the pan and cook for about 3 minutes until golden underneath. Turn and cook the other side. Repeat with remaining batter to make eight pancakes.
2. Add the bacon to the pan and fry in its own fat for a few minutes.
3. Add the mushrooms and onions to the pan. Cook gently, stirring until the vegetables are soft and there is no free liquid. Season well.
4. Fill the pancakes with the bacon mixture and roll up like a parcel with the ends tucked in to enclose the filling. Secure with cocktail sticks.
5. Heat the oil and deep-fry the pancakes quickly for about 2 minutes, or until crisp. Drain and serve the blintzes at once.

Curried Bacon Flan

Cottage Cheese and Ham Cocottes

40 g ($1\frac{1}{2}$ oz) BUTTER
1 SMALL ONION, SKINNED AND FINELY CHOPPED
225 g (8 oz) COTTAGE CHEESE, SIEVED
2 EGGS
1 SLICE OF HAM, TRIMMED OF FAT AND CHOPPED
100 g (4 oz) BUTTON MUSHROOMS, WIPED AND SLICED
SALT AND FRESHLY GROUND PEPPER
30 ml (2 tbsp) CHOPPED PARSLEY
50 g (2 oz) CHEDDAR CHEESE, GRATED

Serves 4

1. Melt 15 g ($\frac{1}{2}$ oz) butter in a pan and fry the onion for 5 minutes, until soft, then drain.

2. Melt the remaining butter in another pan and use to brush four individual ovenproof dishes. Place them on a baking sheet.

3. Beat the cottage cheese and eggs together. Stir in the ham, mushrooms and onion, then season to taste and mix in half the herbs. Divide the mixture between the four dishes and sprinkle with grated cheese.

4. Bake in the oven at 200°C (400°F) mark 6 for 10–15 minutes until golden. Garnish with the remaining herbs and serve immediately.

VEAL

Fricassée of Veal

900 g (2 lb) STEWING VEAL, CUT INTO 4 cm ($1\frac{1}{2}$ inch) SQUARES
450 g (1 lb) CARROTS, PEELED AND CUT INTO THICK STRIPS
1 ONION, SKINNED AND SLICED
15 ml (1 tbsp) CHOPPED FRESH THYME, OR 2.5 ml ($\frac{1}{2}$ tsp) DRIED THYME
150 ml ($\frac{1}{4}$ pint) DRY WHITE WINE
900 ml ($1\frac{1}{2}$ pints) WATER
SALT AND FRESHLY GROUND PEPPER
A LITTLE STOCK (optional)
50 g (2 oz) BUTTER
50 g (2 oz) PLAIN FLOUR
2 EGG YOLKS
142 ml (5 fl oz) CARTON SINGLE CREAM
CHOPPED PARSLEY, TO GARNISH

Serves 6

1. Cover the meat with cold water, bring to the boil and bubble for 1 minute. Strain through a colander and rinse under a cold tap to remove all scum. Rinse out the pan thoroughly and replace the meat.

2. Add the carrots to the pan with the onion, herbs, wine, water and plenty of seasoning. Bring slowly to the boil, cover and simmer gently for about $1\frac{1}{4}$ hours until the veal is quite tender.

3. Strain off the cooking liquid, make up to 700 ml ($1\frac{1}{4}$ pints) with stock if necessary and reserve; keep the veal and vegetables warm in a covered serving dish.

4. Melt the butter in a pan, stir in the flour and cook gently for 1 minute, stirring. Remove from the heat and gradually stir in the strained cooking liquid and season well. Return to the heat and bring to the boil, stirring all the time. Simmer the sauce for 5 minutes.

5. Mix the egg yolks with the fresh cream; remove the sauce from the heat and stir in the cream mixture. Return to the heat and warm gently—without boiling—until the sauce becomes slightly thicker; adjust the seasoning.

6. Pour the sauce over the meat and serve garnished with parsley.

Photographed right

Fricassée of Veal

Veal with Okra and Apple

Veal with Okra and Apple

125 g (4 oz) GREEN EATING APPLE, CORED AND THICKLY SLICED
15 ml (1 tbsp) CIDER VINEGAR
2 VEAL ESCALOPES, ABOUT 175 g (6 oz) EACH
SEASONED FLOUR
85 g (3 oz) PACKET FULL FAT SOFT CHEESE
1 EGG, BEATEN
50 g (2 oz) DRIED WHITE BREADCRUMBS
90–105 ml (6–7 tbsp) PEANUT OIL
350 g (12 oz) OKRA, TRIMMED
200 ml (7.04 fl oz) CARTON APPLE JUICE
SALT AND FRESHLY GROUND PEPPER

Serves 4

1. Put the apple slices into a bowl with the cider vinegar and toss well to coat.

2. Place the veal escalopes between sheets of cling film. Beat with a rolling pin until very thin then coat with seasoned flour.

3. Spread one side of one escalope with the cream cheese. Place the other escalope on top and press down well. Slice the veal into 1 cm ($\frac{1}{2}$ inch) wide strips.

4. Coat again in seasoned flour, dip into the egg and coat in breadcrumbs. Chill well for about 30 minutes.

5. Heat 90 ml (6 tbsp) oil in a wok or large frying pan. Fry the veal slices over a medium heat for 4–5 minutes, until golden brown. Remove with a slotted spoon and keep warm.

6. Add the okra to the pan, adding extra oil if necessary. Fry, stirring, over a medium heat for 3–4 minutes then add the apple juice. Bring to the boil and simmer, covered, for about 10 minutes. Stir in the apple slices and vinegar and season.

7. Return the veal strips to the pan. Shake over a high heat for a further 2–3 minutes to heat through. Serve immediately.

Photographed above

Hungarian Veal

1.4 kg (3 lb) SPINACH
75 g (3 oz) BUTTER
45 ml (3 tbsp) VEGETABLE OIL
700 g (1½ lb) TOMATOES, SKINNED AND SLICED
1 LARGE GARLIC CLOVE, SKINNED AND CRUSHED
700 g (1½ lb) FILLET OF VEAL SLICED INTO 7.5 cm (3 inch) LONG STRIPS
60 ml (4 tbsp) PLAIN FLOUR
7.5 ml (1½ tsp) PAPRIKA
200 ml (7 fl oz) CHICKEN STOCK
200 ml (7 fl oz) WHITE WINE
SALT AND FRESHLY GROUND PEPPER
45 ml (3 tbsp) SOURED CREAM

Serves 6

1. In a pan, gently cook the spinach (do not add liquid) for 3–4 minutes. Drain well.
2. Heat the butter and oil in a pan and fry the tomatoes and garlic for 1–2 minutes. Transfer to a shallow ovenproof dish.
3. Briskly fry the veal a few strips at a time in the oil remaining in the pan, for 3 minutes each side. Spoon on top of the spinach. Stir the flour and paprika into the pan juices, cook for 1 minute, stir in the stock and wine and simmer for 2 minutes. Season, cool slightly and whisk in the soured cream.
4. Spoon the sauce over the veal and cover. Cook in the oven at 200°C (400°F) mark 6, for about 40 minutes.

Veal Kiev

4 VEAL ESCALOPES, 450 g (1 lb) TOTAL WEIGHT, HALVED
100 g (4 oz) BUTTER
FINELY GRATED RIND OF ½ LEMON
15 ml (1 tbsp) LEMON JUICE
30 ml (2 tbsp) CHOPPED PARSLEY
SALT AND FRESHLY GROUND BLACK PEPPER
30 ml (2 tbsp) PLAIN FLOUR
1 EGG, BEATEN
50 g (2 oz) DRIED WHITE BREADCRUMBS
OIL, FOR DEEP-FAT FRYING
LEMON WEDGES, TO GARNISH

Serves 4

1. Beat out each escalope thinly between sheets of greaseproof paper.
2. Cream the butter, mix in the lemon rind, juice, parsley and seasoning.
3. Divide the parsley butter between the eight escalopes, roll up each one to enclose the butter completely. Tie with fine string and chill well.
4. Season the flour and coat the escalopes in it and then in the egg and breadcrumbs. Chill again while heating the oil.
5. Deep-fry the escalopes at 185°C (365°F) for 6–8 minutes until golden brown. Drain on absorbent kitchen paper, remove the string and serve immediately garnished with lemon wedges.

Veal and Kidney Deep Dish Pie

50 g (2 oz) DRIPPING OR LARD
450 g (1 lb) STEWING VEAL, CUT INTO FORK-SIZED PIECES
450 g (1 lb) CALVES' KIDNEY, CUT INTO FORK-SIZED PIECES
225 g (8 oz) ONIONS, SKINNED AND SLICED
60 ml (4 tbsp) PLAIN FLOUR
600 ml (1 pint) STOCK
700 g (1½ lb) CARROTS, PEELED AND SLICED
15 ml (1 tbsp) ROSEMARY
10 ml (2 tsp) WORCESTERSHIRE SAUCE
SALT AND FRESHLY GROUND PEPPER
175 g (6 oz) SHREDDED SUET
325 g (12 oz) SELF-RAISING FLOUR
ABOUT 90 ml (6 tbsp) COLD WATER

Serves 8

1. Melt the dripping in a heavy-based pan and fry the meat to seal on all sides. Add the onion and cook for 3–4 minutes.
2. Stir in the flour, then gradually add the stock, stirring until thickened and boiling.
3. Add the carrots to the pan with the rosemary, Worcestershire sauce and seasoning. Cover and simmer for 30 minutes. Turn into a 1.7 litre (3 pint) pie dish and cool.
4. In a bowl, stir the suet into the flour with enough cold water to mix to a light manageable dough. Roll out on a lightly floured surface and use to cover the pie dish.
5. Bake at 200°C (400°F) mark 6 for 35 minutes, or until the crust is crisp and golden.

Ragout of Veal

900 g (2 lb) PIE VEAL, CUBED
45 ml (3 tbsp) SEASONED FLOUR
75 ml (5 tbsp) VEGETABLE OIL
175 g (6 oz) LEAN BACON RASHERS, RINDED AND ROUGHLY CHOPPED
16 BUTTON ONIONS, SKINNED
396 g (14 oz) CAN TOMATOES, DRAINED AND HALVED
150 ml (¼ pint) DRY WHITE WINE
2.5 ml (½ tsp) PAPRIKA
SALT AND FRESHLY GROUND PEPPER
113 g (4 oz) PACKET FROZEN PEAS
45 ml (3 tbsp) SOURED CREAM, BEATEN UNTIL RUNNY
CHOPPED PARSLEY, TO GARNISH

Serves 8

1. Toss the veal in the seasoned flour. Heat the oil and fry the veal quickly. Transfer to a large casserole.
2. Add the bacon to the pan and fry with the onions for 3 minutes. Transfer to the casserole. Add the tomatoes to the casserole with the wine. Season with paprika, and plenty of salt and pepper.
3. Cover and cook in the oven at 150°C (300°F) mark 2 for about 2½ hours. Twenty minutes before the cooking is finished, stir in the peas and return to oven.
4. Swirl the soured cream over the casserole and sprinkle with chopped parsley.

Casserole of Rolled Stuffed Veal

75 g (3 oz) FRESH BREADCRUMBS
125 g (4 oz) HAM, VERY FINELY CHOPPED
30 ml (2 tbsp) SNIPPED CHIVES
60 ml (4 tbsp) SOURED CREAM
15 ml (1 tbsp) WHOLE GRAIN MUSTARD
25 g (1 oz) WALNUT PIECES, CHOPPED
SALT AND FRESHLY GROUND PEPPER
2 kg ($4\frac{1}{2}$ lb) BREAST OF VEAL, WEIGHT WITH BONE, BONED AND TRIMMED
450 g (1 lb) MUSHROOMS, WIPED AND SLICED
150 ml ($\frac{1}{4}$ pint) WHITE STOCK, PREFERABLY VEAL BONE
30 ml (2 tbsp) WHITE WINE
CHOPPED PARSLEY, TO GARNISH

Serves 8

1. Mix together the breadcrumbs, ham, chives, 30 ml (2 tbsp) soured cream, mustard, walnuts and seasoning.
2. Spread the mixture over the inside of the meat. Roll up the meat as tightly as possible and sew together with fine string.
3. Place the mushrooms in the bottom of a flameproof casserole. Pour over the stock and wine and bring to the boil. Place the veal on top of the casserole, cover tightly, and cook in the oven at 150°C (300°F) mark 2 for about 3 hours.
4. Remove the meat from the casserole to slice for serving. Stir the remaining soured cream into the mushrooms and juices and boil to reduce for about 5 minutes. Pour over the veal. Garnish with parsley.

Veal Goulash with Caraway Dumplings

75 g (3 oz) BUTTER
1.4 kg (3 lb) STEWING VEAL, CUT INTO 4 cm ($1\frac{1}{2}$ inch) PIECES
700 g ($1\frac{1}{2}$ lb) ONIONS, SKINNED AND THINLY SLICED
450 g (1 lb) CARROTS, PEELED AND THINLY SLICED
60 ml (4 tbsp) PAPRIKA
30 ml (2 tbsp) PLAIN FLOUR
900 ml ($1\frac{1}{2}$ pints) CHICKEN STOCK
60 ml (4 tbsp) DRY WHITE WINE
SALT AND FRESHLY GROUND PEPPER
225 g (8 oz) SELF-RAISING FLOUR
125 g (4 oz) SHREDDED SUET
10 ml (2 tsp) CARAWAY SEEDS
142 ml (5 fl oz) CARTON SOURED CREAM
75 ml (5 tbsp) WATER

Serves 8

1. Heat the butter in a frying pan and brown the veal, a little at a time. Drain and put into a shallow ovenproof dish.
2. Fry the onions and carrots in the butter remaining in the pan until lightly browned. Add the paprika and plain flour and fry for 2 minutes. Gradually stir in the stock, wine and seasoning, bring to boil and pour over the veal.
3. Cover tightly, cook in the oven at 150°C (300°F) mark 2 for 2 hours.
4. Mix the next four ingredients together with the water, seasoning well. Divide into 16 dumplings, place on top of the goulash and sprinkle with extra caraway seeds (if wished). Return to the oven, covered, for a further 45 minutes.

Photographed opposite

Osso Buco

65 g ($2\frac{1}{2}$ oz) BUTTER
15 ml (1 tbsp) VEGETABLE OIL
1 ONION, SKINNED AND VERY FINELY CHOPPED
8 SLICES SHIN OF VEAL, WEIGHING ABOUT 1.75 kg ($3\frac{1}{2}$ lb), WITH BONE SAWED INTO PIECES 6.5 cm ($2\frac{1}{2}$ inches) THICK, SECURELY TIED
45 ml (3 tbsp) PLAIN FLOUR
SALT AND FRESHLY GROUND PEPPER
150 ml ($\frac{1}{4}$ pint) DRY WHITE WINE
300 ml ($\frac{1}{2}$ pint) BEEF STOCK
396 g (14 oz) CAN TOMATOES
5 ml (1 tsp) GRATED LEMON RIND
$\frac{1}{2}$ GARLIC CLOVE, SKINNED AND VERY FINELY CHOPPED
15 ml (1 tbsp) CHOPPED PARSLEY

Serves 4

1. Heat the butter and oil in a flameproof dish, large enough to contain all the meat in a single layer and with a tightly fitting lid. Gently fry the onion for about 5 minutes, until soft.
2. Meanwhile, coat the pieces of veal with the flour, shaking off any excess. Add the meat to the onion in the pan and brown well on both sides. Season with salt and pepper. Pour over the wine and boil rapidly for 5 minutes, turning the veal over several times.
3. Add the beef stock and tomatoes with their juice, cover the pan and cook over very low heat for about 2 hours. Carefully turn and baste the veal bones every 15 minutes. If necessary add more stock during the cooking. If, by the time the meat is cooked, the sauce is too thin, remove the veal from the pan and reduce the liquid by boiling rapidly.
4. Mix together the lemon rind, garlic and parsley. Remove the string from the bones and serve piping hot with the sauce poured over the meat and the lemon rind mixture sprinkled on top. Serve with a green salad.

Photographed on page 194

Veal Goulash with Caraway Dumplings

Scalloped Chicken with Potatoes

700 g ($1\frac{1}{2}$ lb) POTATOES, PEELED AND THINLY SLICED
4 CHICKEN THIGH AND DRUMSTICK PORTIONS, SKINNED
30 ml (2 tbsp) PLAIN FLOUR
198 g (7 oz) CAN CORN NIBLETS, DRAINED
1 SMALL GREEN PEPPER, SEEDED AND DICED
SALT AND FRESHLY GROUND BLACK PEPPER
568 ml (1 pint) MILK
50 g (2 oz) GRUYERE CHEESE, GRATED
CHOPPED PARSLEY, TO GARNISH

Serves 4

1. Lightly grease a 1.7 litre (3 pint) shallow ovenproof dish and put half the potatoes into it.
2. Divide each chicken portion into two. Coat lightly with flour and lay on top of the potatoes.
3. Surround the chicken with the corn and green pepper and season well.
4. Arrange the remaining potatoes neatly on top. Pour over the milk and sprinkle the cheese on top.
5. Stand the dish on a baking sheet and cook at 170°C (325°F) mark 3 for about $1\frac{3}{4}$ hours, covering if necessary towards the end. Sprinkle with chopped parsley before serving.

Chicken Chinese

4 CHICKEN JOINTS, SKINNED, ABOUT 225 g (8 oz) EACH
30 ml (2 tbsp) OIL
45 ml (3 tbsp) SOY SAUCE
30 ml (2 tbsp) TOMATO PUREE
1 ONION, SKINNED AND SLICED
2 CARROTS, PEELED AND CUT INTO MATCHSTICKS
$\frac{1}{2}$ GREEN PEPPER, SEEDED AND FINELY SLICED
100 g (4 oz) MUSHROOMS, WIPED, STEMS REMOVED, SLICED
270 g ($9\frac{1}{2}$ oz) CAN BEANSPROUTS, DRAINED
283 g (10 oz) CAN BAMBOO SHOOTS, DRAINED AND FINELY CUT INTO MATCHSTICKS
15 ml (1 tbsp) DRY SHERRY (optional)
SMALL PINCH OF MONOSODIUM GLUTAMATE

Serves 4

1. Cut the flesh from the chicken joints and slice into strips.
2. Heat the oil, add the chicken and quickly fry, stirring all the time. Stir in the soy sauce and tomato purée. Add the onion, carrots and green pepper and fry for 5 minutes, stirring frequently.
3. Add the mushrooms, beansprouts and bamboo shoots to the pan, then add the sherry (if used) and the monosodium glutamate. Heat through, stirring well.

Baked Drumsticks with Peanuts

8 CHICKEN DRUMSTICKS, SKINNED AND BONED
15 ml (1 tbsp) PEANUT BUTTER
50 g (2 oz) SALTED PEANUTS, CHOPPED
FINELY GRATED RIND OF 1 LEMON
15 ml (1 tbsp) LEMON JUICE
75 g (3 oz) ONIONS, SKINNED AND COARSELY GRATED
1 EGG, BEATEN
30 ml (2 tbsp) CHOPPED PARSLEY
SALT AND FRESHLY GROUND PEPPER
50 g (2 oz) PLAIN FLOUR

Serves 4

1. Skin the drumsticks, slit along the flesh of each and ease out the bone.
2. Mix together the peanut butter, 25 g (1 oz) peanuts, the lemon rind, lemon juice and the onion.
3. Open out the boned drumsticks and spread a little of the mixture on to each. Fold together again.
4. Mix together the beaten egg, parsley, remaining peanuts and seasonings. Season the flour and roll each drumstick in it, and then coat in the egg mixture and thread on to skewers.
5. Oil a piece of foil, put the kebabs on it and place on a baking sheet. Cover loosely with foil and bake at 190°C (375°F) mark 5 for 45–50 minutes. Uncover for the last 10–15 minutes of cooking time.

Curried Chicken Pilaff

1.5 kg ($3\frac{1}{4}$ lb) OVEN-READY CHICKEN
25 g (1 oz) BUTTER, MELTED
SALT AND FRESHLY GROUND PEPPER
4 STREAKY BACON RASHERS, RINDED
30 ml (2 tbsp) CHICKEN FAT
175 g (6 oz) ONIONS, SKINNED AND SLICED
175 g (6 oz) LEEKS, TRIMMED AND SLICED
15 ml (1 tbsp) MADRAS CURRY POWDER
225 g (8 oz) LONG-GRAIN RICE
600 ml (1 pint) CHICKEN STOCK
25 g (1 oz) SULTANAS
CHOPPED PARSLEY, TO GARNISH

Serves 4

1. Put the chicken into a deep roasting tin, brush with melted butter and sprinkle with salt and pepper. Lay the bacon rashers over the breast. Roast in the oven at 200°C (400°F) mark 6 for about $1\frac{1}{2}$ hours, or until the chicken is tender. Baste occasionally.
2. Cool the chicken, discard the skin and bone and roughly chop the flesh.
3. Melt the fat in a flameproof casserole and gently fry the onion and leek with the curry powder for 1 minute.
4. Add the rice and cook gently for 2 minutes, stirring. Gradually add the stock, with the sultanas and seasoning.
5. Bring to the boil, cover and simmer for 10 minutes. Add the chicken and simmer a further 5 minutes until the rice is cooked and the liquid is absorbed. Adjust the seasoning and serve sprinkled with parsley.

Coronation Chicken

Coronation Chicken

2.3 kg (5 lb) OVEN-READY CHICKEN
50 g (2 oz) BUTTER, SOFTENED
4 RASHERS STREAKY BACON, RINDED (optional)
1 SMALL ONION, SKINNED AND FINELY CHOPPED
15 ml (1 tbsp) CURRY PASTE
15 ml (1 tbsp) TOMATO PUREE
100 ml (4 fl oz) RED WINE
1 BAY LEAF
JUICE OF $\frac{1}{2}$ LEMON
4 CANNED APRICOTS, FINELY CHOPPED
300 ml ($\frac{1}{2}$ pint) MAYONNAISE (see page 210)
150 ml (5 fl oz) WHIPPING CREAM
SALT AND FRESHLY GROUND PEPPER
CUCUMBER SLICES, TO GARNISH

Serves 8

1. Put the chicken into a deep roasting tin, brush with half the butter and lay the bacon rashers (if using) over the breast. Roast in the oven at 200°C (400°F) mark 6 for 2 hours or until tender. Cool, then discard the skin and bones and dice the flesh.
2. In a small pan, heat the remaining butter, add the onion and cook for 3 minutes, until softened. Add the curry paste, tomato purée, wine, bay leaf and lemon juice.
3. Simmer, uncovered, for about 10 minutes, until well reduced. Strain and cool.
4. Sieve the apricots to produce a purée. Beat the cooled sauce into the mayonnaise with the apricot purée.
5. Whip the fresh cream until standing in soft peaks and fold into the mixture. Season, adding a little lemon juice if necessary.
6. Toss the chicken pieces into the sauce and garnish with sliced cucumber.

Photographed above

Honey Barbecued Chicken

Curried Chicken Envelopes

25 g (1 oz) MARGARINE
100 g (4 oz) ONIONS, SKINNED AND CHOPPED
10 ml (2 tsp) MADRAS CURRY POWDER
175 g (6 oz) BUTTON MUSHROOMS, WIPED AND SLICED
30 ml (2 tbsp) PLAIN FLOUR
1 CHICKEN STOCK CUBE
300 ml (½ pint) BOILING WATER
275 g (10 oz) COOKED CHICKEN MEAT, DICED
212 g (7½ oz) PACKET FROZEN PUFF PASTRY, THAWED
1 BEATEN EGG, TO GLAZE

Serves 4

1. Melt the margarine in a pan and gently fry the onions with the curry powder until soft. Add the mushrooms and cook gently for a few minutes. Stir in the flour and cook, stirring, for 2 minutes.
2. Dissolve the stock cube in the water and add to the pan, stirring. Bring to the boil and cook for 2 minutes. Add the chicken to the sauce. Allow to cool.
3. Roll out the pastry thinly on a lightly floured surface, to a large square. Cut into four squares.
4. Divide the filling between each square and fold the corners up to form envelopes. Seal with beaten egg.
5. Place on a dampened baking sheet, brush with beaten egg and bake at 220°C (425°F) mark 7 for about 20 minutes. Eat while hot.

Poached Chicken with Horseradish Cream Sauce

SMALL BOILING CHICKEN, ABOUT 2 kg (4½ lb)
1 ONION, SKINNED
1 CARROT, PEELED
1 BAY LEAF
6 WHOLE BLACK PEPPERCORNS
50 g (2 oz) MARGARINE
50 g (2 oz) PLAIN FLOUR
60 ml (4 tbsp) GRATED BOTTLED HORSERADISH
SALT AND FRESHLY GROUND BLACK PEPPER
30 ml (2 tbsp) CHOPPED PARSLEY
113 ml (4 fl oz) CARTON DOUBLE CREAM

Serves 6

1. Put the chicken into a large pan with the onion, carrot, bay leaf and peppercorns. Add sufficient salted water to just cover and bring to the boil. Lower the heat, cover and simmer for 2–2½ hours, or until the chicken is tender.
2. Remove the chicken from the pan, strain off the stock and reserve. Skin and joint the chicken and keep warm in a covered dish.
3. Prepare the sauce: melt the margarine in a heavy-based pan, stir in the flour and add 600 ml (1 pint) of the reserved stock with the horseradish and seasoning.
4. Bring to the boil, stirring and simmer gently for 5 minutes. Add the parsley and cream. Adjust the seasoning and spoon the sauce over chicken before serving.

Honey Barbecued Chicken

50 g (2 oz) BUTTER
100 g (4 oz) ONIONS, SKINNED AND FINELY CHOPPED
1 GARLIC CLOVE, SKINNED AND FINELY CHOPPED (optional)
396 g (14 oz) CAN TOMATOES
30 ml (2 tbsp) WORCESTERSHIRE SAUCE
15 ml (1 tbsp) HONEY
SALT AND FRESHLY GROUND PEPPER
100 g (4 oz) LONG-GRAIN RICE
4 CHICKEN DRUMSTICKS
MUSHROOMS, TOMATOES AND PARSLEY, TO GARNISH

Serves 4

1. To make the barbecue sauce, combine the butter, onions, garlic (if used), tomatoes and their juice, Worcestershire sauce, honey and plenty of salt and freshly ground pepper in a saucepan. Gently cook for 30 minutes.
2. Meanwhile, cook the rice in a saucepan of fast boiling salted water until tender, but not soft. Set aside and keep hot.
3. Place the chicken drumsticks in the grill pan and brush liberally with the barbecue sauce. Grill for 10 minutes on each side, brushing frequently with more sauce.
4. Serve on a bed of rice garnished with grilled mushrooms and tomatoes and sprigs of parsley. Serve any remaining sauce separately.

Photographed opposite

Bird in a Pot

1.8 kg (4 lb) BOILING CHICKEN, HALVED LENGTHWAYS, TRIMMED OF EXCESS FAT
450 g (1 lb) CARROTS, PEELED AND ROUGHLY CHOPPED
450 g (1 lb) ONIONS, SKINNED AND ROUGHLY CHOPPED
225 g (8 oz) PARSNIPS, PEELED AND ROUGHLY CHOPPED
SALT AND FRESHLY GROUND PEPPER
1 BOUQUET GARNI
10 ml (2 tsp) CORNFLOUR
15 ml (1 tbsp) CHOPPED PARSLEY
LEMON JUICE

Serves 4–6

1. Place the bird, cut-side down, in a flameproof casserole, then nestle the vegetables round and pour in just enough water to cover.
2. Add the seasoning and bouquet garni, Cover tightly and cook in the oven at 150°C (300°F) mark 2 for about 3 hours until tender.
3. Remove the meat from the bones in largish pieces. Strain the juices from the casserole and remove the bouquet garni. Return the chicken meat to the vegetables and keep hot.
4. Skim off as much fat as possible from the juices. Blend the cornflour with a little water to a paste, add the juices and return to a pan, bring to the boil. Add the parsley and cook for 1–2 minutes. Adjust the seasoning with lemon juice, salt and pepper. Pour over the chicken and serve.

Chicken with Tarragon Sauce

6 CHICKEN BREASTS
75 g (3 oz) BUTTER
25 g (1 oz) PLAIN FLOUR
450 ml ($\frac{3}{4}$ pint) CHICKEN STOCK
30 ml (2 tbsp) TARRAGON VINEGAR
10 ml (2 tsp) FRENCH MUSTARD
5 ml (1 tsp) FRESH TARRAGON, CHOPPED, OR
2.5 ml ($\frac{1}{2}$ tsp) DRIED TARRAGON
50 g (2 oz) CHEDDAR CHEESE, GRATED
SALT AND FRESHLY GROUND PEPPER
142 ml (5 fl oz) CARTON SINGLE CREAM

Serves 6

1. In a covered pan, slowly cook the chicken breasts in 50 g (2 oz) butter, for about 20 minutes, until tender, turning once.
2. Meanwhile, melt the remaining butter in a pan, stir in the flour and gradually stir in the stock and vinegar.
3. Stir in the mustard, tarragon and cheese; bring to the boil, stirring. Season, simmer for 3 minutes. Remove from the heat and add the fresh cream.
4. Return to the heat and heat gently without boiling. Place drained chicken on a serving dish and spoon over the sauce.

Photographed right

Chicken and Leek Pudding

4 CHICKEN BREASTS, TOTAL WEIGHT 450 g (1 lb), SHREDDED
225 g (8 oz) LEEKS, TRIMMED AND SLICED
100 g (4 oz) CARROTS, PEELED AND COARSELY GRATED
45 ml (3 tbsp) PLAIN FLOUR
FINELY GRATED RIND OF $\frac{1}{2}$ LEMON
SALT AND FRESHLY GROUND BLACK PEPPER
225 g (8 oz) SELF-RAISING FLOUR
100 g (4 oz) SHREDDED SUET
150 ml ($\frac{1}{4}$ pint) CHICKEN STOCK

Serves 4

1. Combine the chicken, leeks, carrots, plain flour, lemon rind and seasoning.
2. Sift the self-raising flour with a pinch of salt and stir in the suet, with enough cold water to make a light manageable dough.
3. Grease a 1.4 litre ($2\frac{1}{2}$ pint) pudding basin. Roll the dough out on a lightly floured surface and use two-thirds to line the basin.
4. Turn the filling into the lined basin and spoon over the stock. Roll out the remaining pastry as a lid. Cover the basin and seal the edges well.
5. Cut a piece of greaseproof paper and a piece of foil large enough to cover the basin. Place them together and make a pleat across the middle. Lightly grease the greaseproof side and put them over the pudding, greaseproof side down. Tie securely on to the basin, and make a string handle across the basin top.
6. Bring a large pan of water to the boil. Fit a steamer over the pan and steam the pudding, covered, for 3–$3\frac{1}{2}$ hours. Top up with boiling water as necessary.

Chicken with Tarragon Sauce

Chicken with Lemon and Almonds

1.4 kg (3 lb) CHICKEN
50 g (2 oz) BLANCHED ALMONDS
1 LEMON, THINLY SLICED
1 GARLIC CLOVE, SKINNED
25 g (1 oz) BUTTER, SOFTENED
SALT AND FRESHLY GROUND PEPPER
450 ml ($\frac{3}{4}$ pint) STOCK MADE FROM THE GIBLETS
125 g (4 oz) BUTTON MUSHROOMS, WIPED AND SLICED
15 ml (1 tbsp) CORNFLOUR
60 ml (4 tbsp) SINGLE CREAM
WATERCRESS, TO GARNISH

Serves 4

1. Loosen the chicken skin all over the breast with the fingertips. Slip the almonds under the skin.

2. Stuff the lemon into the chicken cavity with the garlic. Truss or tie the bird securely.

3. Place the chicken in a roasting tin and spread butter all over its surface. Season well. Pour the stock around the chicken and roast in the oven at 200°C (400°F) mark 6 for 1 hour, basting frequently.

4. Add the mushrooms to the roasting tin. Lay a piece of foil over the bird and continue cooking for a further 20 minutes, until the bird is tender.

5. Drain the bird, discard the lemon and garlic. Joint the chicken.

6. Blend the cornflour with a little water until smooth, pour into the pan juices and heat, stirring, until thickened. Add the fresh cream without re-boiling the sauce. Adjust the seasoning and spoon over the bird for serving. Garnish with watercress.

Photographed below

Chicken with Lemon and Almonds

Chicken and Barley Broth

Chicken and Barley Broth

2 CHICKEN QUARTERS, ABOUT 700 g (1½ lb) TOTAL WEIGHT
SALT AND FRESHLY GROUND PEPPER
1 SMALL CARROT, PEELED AND SLICED
1 SMALL ONION, PEELED AND SLICED
6 WHOLE BLACK PEPPERCORNS
1 BAY LEAF
1.1 litres (2 pints) WATER; AND 60 ml (4 tbsp)
75 g (3 oz) PEARL BARLEY
30 ml (2 tbsp) CHOPPED PARSLEY
2.5 ml (½ tsp) DRIED TARRAGON
30 ml (2 tbsp) CORNFLOUR
PINCH OF GROUND TURMERIC
142 ml (5 fl oz) CARTON SINGLE CREAM

Serves 4

1. Put the chicken, a good pinch of salt, the carrot and onion slices, peppercorns and bay leaf into a large saucepan with the 1.1 litres (2 pints) water. Bring to the boil, cover and simmer for 45–50 minutes, or until the chicken is tender. Remove the chicken and cool; strain and reserve the stock.

2. Bring a pan of water to the boil and cook the barley until tender, about 1 hour. Drain well.

3. Skin the chicken pieces. Remove the flesh and cut into bite-sized pieces. Skim the reserved stock and measure out 900 ml (1½ pints). Put into a saucepan with the chicken, barley, parsley and tarragon.

4. Mix the cornflour and turmeric to a smooth paste with 60 ml (4 tbsp) water. Stir into the chicken mixture and bring to the boil, stirring, then simmer for 10–15 minutes. Stir in the single cream. Season and reheat gently without boiling.

Photographed above

Roast Chicken

Chicken Hotpot

1.4 kg (3 lb) OVEN-READY CHICKEN, SKINNED AND BONED
700 g ($1\frac{1}{2}$ lb) FLOURY POTATOES, PEELED AND SLICED INTO THICK MATCHSTICKS
225 g (8 oz) LEEKS, TRIMMED AND SLICED
439 g ($15\frac{1}{2}$ oz) CAN BUTTER BEANS, DRAINED
SALT AND FRESHLY GROUND PEPPER
450 ml ($\frac{3}{4}$ pint) CHICKEN STOCK
10 ml (2 tsp) DIJON MUSTARD
15 ml (1 tbsp) TOMATO PUREE
25 g (1 oz) BUTTER
CHOPPED PARSLEY, TO GARNISH

Serves 4

1. Dice the chicken flesh into 2.5 cm (1 inch) pieces, including any scraps.

2. Put one-third of the potatoes into the centre of a 2.4 litre ($4\frac{1}{2}$ pint) ovenproof casserole. Layer the chicken, leeks and beans round them. Season each layer well.

3. Mix the stock with the mustard and tomato purée and pour into the dish. Top with remaining potatoes and dot with butter. Cover and bake in the oven at 180°C (350°F) mark 4 for about 1 hour until the potatoes are tender.

4. Uncover and return to the oven at 220°C (425°F) mark 7 for about 30 minutes, until the top is golden and crisp. Sprinkle with parsley for serving.

Chicken and Sweetcorn Potato Cakes

200 ml (7 fl oz) MILK
2 EGGS
125 g (4 oz) PLAIN FLOUR
SALT AND FRESHLY GROUND PEPPER
450 g (1 lb) POTATOES, PEELED AND COARSELY GRATED
225 g (8 oz) ONIONS, SKINNED AND THINLY SLICED
225 g (8 oz) COOKED CHICKEN, FINELY CHOPPED
198 g (7 oz) CAN SWEETCORN KERNELS, DRAINED
OIL, FOR SHALLOW FRYING

Makes 12

1. Make the batter: put the milk and eggs into a blender, add the flour and a pinch of salt. Switch on for about 1 minute, then refrigerate.
2. Blanch the potato and onion: put them together in boiling salted water for 2–3 minutes. Drain well and press out as much liquid as possible.
3. Stir the chicken into the batter with the sweetcorn, potato and onion. Season.
4. Heat 5 mm (¼ inch) oil in a frying pan. Spoon heaped tablespoons of mixture into the pan and fry for about 4 minutes on each side. Drain well and keep warm, uncovered, in a low oven.
5. Repeat with the remaining mixture until it has all been used. Serve the potato cakes immediately.

Pot Roast Chicken with Onion Sauce

25 g (1 oz) MARGARINE
450 g (1 lb) ONIONS, SKINNED AND FINELY CHOPPED
LIVER FROM THE CHICKEN, FINELY CHOPPED
25 g (1 oz) WALNUT PIECES, FINELY CHOPPED
225 g (8 oz) FRESH WHITE BREADCRUMBS
30 ml (2 tbsp) LEMON JUICE
30 ml (2 tbsp) CHOPPED PARSLEY
25 g (1 oz) COARSE OATMEAL
25 g (1 oz) SHREDDED SUET
SALT AND FRESHLY GROUND PEPPER
1.5 kg (3 lb) OVEN-READY CHICKEN
OIL, FOR FRYING
300 ml (½ pint) MILK
1 BAY LEAF
15 ml (1 tbsp) CORNFLOUR

Serves 6

1. Melt the margarine and gently fry 225 g (8 oz) onions, the liver and walnuts for 3–4 minutes. Mix together with the breadcrumbs, lemon juice, chopped parsley, oatmeal and shredded suet. Season well with salt and ground pepper.
2. Spoon all but 60 ml (4 tbsp) stuffing into the chicken. Gently ease the chicken skin away from either side of the breastbone to form two pockets. Press in the reserved stuffing.
3. Heat enough oil to cover the base of a flameproof casserole—there should not be too much space around the chicken. Brown the chicken and remove it from the casserole.
4. Put the remaining onion, the milk and bay leaf into the casserole. Return the chicken to the casserole and cook covered at 180°C (350°F) mark 4 for about 1¾ hours, until tender.
5. Remove the chicken to a serving dish and keep warm.
6. Make the onion sauce: mix the cornflour to a paste with a little water. Stir into the pan juices to thicken them, then taste and adjust the seasoning.
7. Carve the chicken and pour over the onion sauce, or if preferred pour the sauce into a sauceboat and serve it separately.

Roast Chicken

1.8–2.3 kg (4–5 lb) OVEN-READY CHICKEN
HERB STUFFING (see page 214)
1 ONION, SKINNED
1 LEMON WEDGE (optional)
BUTTER, FOR ROASTING
SALT AND FRESHLY GROUND PEPPER
STREAKY BACON RASHERS (optional)

Serves 4–6

1. If the chicken is frozen, allow it to thaw out completely, discarding the bag of giblets. A 1.8 kg (4 lb) bird will take 8–10 hours at room temperature.
2. Wash the bird and dry thoroughly and stuff with the herb stuffing at the neck end before folding the neck skin over. For added flavour put the onion, lemon wedge (if using) together with a knob of butter into the body of the bird.
3. Weigh the chicken and place it in a deep roasting tin, brush with melted butter and sprinkle with salt and freshly ground pepper.
4. A few strips of streaky bacon may be laid over the chicken breast to prevent it from becoming dry. Roast in the oven at 200°C (400°F) mark 6, basting from time to time, and allowing 20 minutes per 450 g (1 lb) plus 20 minutes.
5. Put a piece of greaseproof paper over the breast if it shows signs of overbrowning. Alternatively, wrap the chicken in foil before roasting. Allow the same cooking time, but open the foil for the final 15–20 minutes to allow the bird to brown.
6. Bacon rolls, chipolata sausages, bread sauce (see page 210) and gravy are the usual accompaniments. Serve with a green vegetable such as broccoli.

Photographed opposite

Turkey in Spiced Yogurt

ABOUT 1.1 kg ($2\frac{1}{2}$ lb) TURKEY LEG MEAT ON THE BONE
7.5 ml ($1\frac{1}{2}$ tsp) GROUND CUMIN
7.5 ml ($1\frac{1}{2}$ tsp) GROUND CORIANDER
2.5 ml ($\frac{1}{2}$ tsp) GROUND TURMERIC
2.5 ml ($\frac{1}{2}$ tsp) GROUND GINGER
SALT AND FRESHLY GROUND PEPPER
300 g (10 fl oz) NATURAL YOGURT
30 ml (2 tbsp) LEMON JUICE
45 ml (3 tbsp) VEGETABLE OIL
225 g (8 oz) ONIONS, SKINNED AND SLICED
45 ml (3 tbsp) DESICCATED COCONUT
30 ml (2 tbsp) PLAIN FLOUR
150 ml ($\frac{1}{4}$ pint) CHICKEN STOCK OR WATER
CHOPPED PARSLEY, TO GARNISH

Serves 6

1. Cut the turkey meat off the bone into large fork-sized pieces, discarding the skin; there should be about 900 g (2 lb) meat.

2. In a large bowl, mix the spices with the seasoning, yogurt and lemon juice. Stir well until evenly blended.

3. Fold through the turkey meat until coated with the yogurt mixture. Cover tightly with cling film and refrigerate for several hours.

4. Heat the oil in a medium flameproof casserole and lightly brown the onion. Add the coconut and flour and fry gently, stirring, for about 1 minute.

5. Remove from the heat and stir in the turkey with its marinade and the stock. Return to the heat and bring slowly to the boil, stirring all the time. Cover tightly and cook in the oven at 170°C (325°F) mark 3 for 1–$1\frac{1}{4}$ hours, or until the turkey is tender.

6. Adjust the seasoning and serve garnished with parsley.

Photographed right

Turkey in Spiced Yogurt

Turkey Escalopes with Hazelnut Cream Sauce

450 g (1 lb) TURKEY FILLET, THINLY SLICED
50 g (2 oz) BUTTER
60 ml (4 tbsp) SWEET SHERRY
60 ml (4 tbsp) DOUBLE CREAM
25 g (1 oz) HAZELNUTS, FINELY CHOPPED
SALT AND FRESHLY GROUND PEPPER
PAPRIKA, TO GARNISH

Serves 4

1. Beat out the slices of turkey, between two sheets of damp greaseproof paper, into small escalopes.
2. Melt the butter in a frying pan and cook the escalopes quickly for 4–5 minutes, turning once. Remove from the pan and keep warm.
3. Lower the heat and stir in the sherry, fresh cream and hazelnuts. Season and cook, stirring, for 1 minute. Pour over the escalopes and serve immediately with a light dusting of paprika.

Photographed below

Turkey Escalopes with Hazelnut Cream Sauce

Turkey Kebabs

Turkey Kebabs

1 EGG
150 ml (¼ pint) MILK
125 g (4 oz) PLAIN FLOUR
SALT
5 ml (1 tsp) DRIED TARRAGON
225 g (8 oz) TURKEY FILLET, CUT INTO 1 cm (½ inch) PIECES
175 g (6 oz) GOUDA CHEESE, CUT INTO 1 cm (½ inch) PIECES
75 ml (5 tbsp) SAGE AND ONION STUFFING MIX
75 ml (5 tbsp) DRIED WHITE BREADCRUMBS
OIL, FOR FRYING

Serves 4

1. Put the egg and milk into a blender, add the flour and a pinch of salt. Switch on for about 1 minute, stir in the tarragon and turn into a wide, shallow dish.

2. Thread the turkey and cheese pieces alternately on to four 15 cm (6 inch) small metal skewers.

3. Combine the stuffing mix and breadcrumbs on a plate.

4. Roll each skewer in the batter, coating evenly, shake off any excess, then roll in the stuffing mixture.

5. Heat 2.5 cm (1 inch) oil in a large frying pan and fry the kebabs for 4–5 minutes, turning once. Serve immediately.

Photographed above

Turkey 'Sirloin'

125 g (4 oz) CHICK PEAS, SOAKED OVERNIGHT AND DRAINED
30 ml (2 tbsp) VEGETABLE OIL
50 g (2 oz) ONIONS, SKINNED AND CHOPPED
50 g (2 oz) STREAKY BACON PIECES, FINELY SNIPPED
50 g (2 oz) FRESH WHITE BREADCRUMBS
10 ml (2 tsp) DRIED TARRAGON
1 LARGE EGG
15 ml (1 tbsp) LEMON JUICE
SALT AND FRESHLY GROUND PEPPER
600 g ($1\frac{1}{4}$ lb) TURKEY BREAST ROAST
600 ml (1 pint) CHICKEN OR TURKEY STOCK
10 ml (2 tsp) ARROWROOT
DASH OF GRAVY BROWNING

Serves 6

1. Put the chick peas into a pan, cover with water and bring to the boil. Lower the heat and simmer until tender, at least 2 hours. Drain and mash.
2. Heat the oil and fry the onion and bacon until the onion is golden. Remove from the heat, and mix in the next four ingredients with the chick peas and seasoning.
3. Put the turkey roast into a small roasting tin. Press the chick-pea mixture round the joint to form a collar then wrap a strip of greased foil around the outside.
4. Pour 150 ml ($\frac{1}{4}$ pint) stock into the tin and roast at 180°C (350°F) mark 4 for about $1\frac{1}{2}$ hours. Lift the joint on to a serving plate and remove the foil.
5. Add the remaining stock to the pan juices and bring to the boil. Mix the arrowroot to a paste with a little water and stir into the pan juices. Adjust the seasoning and add a dash of gravy browning.
6. Slice off the chick-pea crust before carving. Serve, if wished, with sauté potatoes and mushrooms with peas.

Photographed below

Turkey 'Sirloin'

Turkey Ragout with Savoury Scones

Turkey Ragout with Savoury Scones

30 ml (2 tbsp) OIL
700 g ($1\frac{1}{2}$ lb) BONELESS DARK TURKEY MEAT, SKINNED AND CUT INTO BITE-SIZED PIECES
125 g (4 oz) ONIONS, SKINNED AND SLICED
225 g (8 oz) COOKING APPLE, PEELED AND SLICED
350 g (12 oz) CARROTS, PEELED AND SLICED
SALT AND FRESHLY GROUND PEPPER
10 ml (2 tsp) GROUND PAPRIKA
10 ml (2 tsp) GROUND CORIANDER
2.5 ml ($\frac{1}{2}$ tsp) GROUND TURMERIC
30 ml (2 tbsp) PLAIN FLOUR
450 ml ($\frac{3}{4}$ pint) STOCK
225 g (8 oz) SELF-RAISING FLOUR
5 ml (1 tsp) BAKING POWDER
40 g ($1\frac{1}{2}$ oz) BLOCK MARGARINE
30 ml (2 tbsp) CHOPPED PARSLEY
ABOUT 150 ml ($\frac{1}{4}$ pint) MILK

Serves 4

1. Heat the oil in a large pan and brown the turkey all over. Remove from the pan and add the onion, apple and carrot to the pan with the seasoning, spices and plain flour and fry for 2–3 minutes, stirring.

2. Blend in the stock and bring to the boil, return the turkey meat to the pan. Cover and simmer for about 1 hour.

3. For the scones, sift together the self-raising flour, baking powder, 1.25 ml ($\frac{1}{4}$ tsp) salt and a little pepper. Rub in the margarine. Add the chopped parsley and add just enough milk to bind. Turn out on a lightly floured surface and shape into a 15 cm (6 inch) round, transfer to a baking sheet. Mark into eight wedges and brush with more milk. Bake at 220°C (425°F) mark 7 for about 15 minutes.

4. Adjust the seasoning of the turkey and serve with the warm scones. Place some on top of the dish or serve them separately.

Photographed above

Poacher's Pie

225 g (8 oz) PLAIN FLOUR
PINCH OF SALT
50 g (2 oz) BUTTER, CUT INTO SMALL PIECES
50 g (2 oz) LARD, CUT INTO SMALL PIECES
45–60 ml (3–4 tbsp) WATER
4 RABBIT JOINTS, CHOPPED
3–4 RASHER BACON, RINDED AND CHOPPED
2 POTATOES, PEELED AND SLICED
1 LEEK, TRIMMED AND SLICED
SALT AND FRESHLY GROUND PEPPER
15 ml (1 tbsp) CHOPPED PARSLEY
1.25 ml ($\frac{1}{4}$ tsp) DRIED MIXED HERBS
STOCK OR WATER
BEATEN EGG, TO GLAZE

Serves 4

1. Make the pastry: sift the flour and salt into a bowl. Rub in the fat until the mixture resembles fine breadcrumbs and add just enough water to mix to a firm dough. Cover and chill for 10 minutes.

2. Fill a pie dish with alternate layers of rabbit, bacon and vegetables, sprinkling each layer with seasoning and herbs. Half fill the dish with stock or water.

3. Roll the dough out on a lightly floured surface and cover the pie dish. Make a hole in the centre. Decorate with pastry trimmings, if wished, and brush with egg.

4. Bake in the oven at 220°C (425°F) mark 7 until the pastry is set, then lower the temperature to 170°C (325°F) mark 3 and cook for about $1\frac{1}{4}$ hours, until the meat is tender. Cover with foil if the pie starts to overbrown.

Cider Baked Rabbit with Cabbage

60 ml (4 tbsp) VEGETABLE OIL
225 g (8 oz) STREAKY BACON RASHERS, RINDED AND SNIPPED INTO SMALL PIECES
2 ONIONS, SKINNED AND SLICED
350 g (12 oz) COOKING APPLES, PEELED AND SLICED
1.4 kg (3 lb) FIRM WHITE CABBAGE, COARSELY SHREDDED
SALT AND FRESHLY GROUND PEPPER
8 RABBIT JOINTS, ABOUT 1.4 kg (3 lb) TOTAL WEIGHT
60 ml (4 tbsp) PLAIN FLOUR
15 ml (1 tbsp) FRENCH MUSTARD
300 ml ($\frac{1}{2}$ pint) DRY CIDER
450 ml ($\frac{3}{4}$ pint) CHICKEN STOCK
CHOPPED PARSLEY, TO GARNISH

Serves 8

1. Heat the oil in a large frying pan and lightly brown the bacon, onions and apples. Remove with a slotted spoon, mix with the cabbage and plenty of seasoning and put into a large ovenproof casserole.

2. Brown the rabbit joints well in the oil remaining in the pan and place on top of the cabbage.

3. Stir the flour and mustard into the pan. Gradually add the cider and stock, stirring. Season and bring to the boil.

4. Pour over the rabbit; cover tightly and cook in the oven at 170°C (325°F) mark 3 for $1\frac{1}{2}$–$1\frac{3}{4}$ hours, or until the rabbit is tender. Adjust the seasoning and garnish with plenty of parsley.

Rabbit and Forcemeat Pie

175 g (6 oz) PLAIN FLOUR; AND 30 ml (2 tbsp)
40 g ($1\frac{1}{2}$ oz) BUTTER, CUT INTO SMALL PIECES
40 g ($1\frac{1}{2}$ oz) LARD, CUT INTO SMALL PIECES
ABOUT 45 ml (3 tbsp) WATER
4 RABBIT PORTIONS 600 g ($1\frac{1}{4}$ lb) TOTAL WEIGHT
30 ml (2 tbsp) OIL
225 g (8 oz) BUTTON MUSHROOMS, WIPED
225 g (8 oz) SMALL ONIONS, SKINNED AND QUARTERED
1 GARLIC CLOVE, SKINNED AND CRUSHED
100 ml (4 fl oz) PORT
300 ml ($\frac{1}{2}$ pint) STOCK
12 JUNIPER BERRIES, CRUSHED
350 g (12 oz) SAUSAGEMEAT
45 ml (3 tbsp) CHOPPED PARSLEY
30 ml (2 tbsp) MADE ENGLISH MUSTARD
SALT AND FRESHLY GROUND PEPPER

Serves 4

1. Make the pastry: sift the 175 g (6 oz) flour and a pinch of salt into a bowl and rub in the fat until the mixture resembles fine breadcrumbs and add just enough water to mix to a firm dough. Cover and chill for about 20 minutes.

2. Toss the rabbit portions in the remaining flour.

3. Heat the oil in a pan and gently fry the mushrooms, onions and garlic until beginning to brown. Remove with a slotted spoon to a 1.7 litre (3 pint) pie dish.

4. In the same pan, brown the rabbit portions. Stir in the port, stock and juniper berries. Bring to the boil, scraping any sediment from the bottom and add to the pie dish.

5. Mix together the sausagemeat, parsley, mustard and seasoning. Shape into eight balls and add to the pie dish.

6. On a lightly floured surface, roll out the dough and cover the pie dish. Make a hole in the centre. Bake at 190°C (375°F) mark 5 for 30 minutes. Cover loosely with foil and lower the temperature to 180°C (350°F) mark 4 for a further 1 hour.

Photographed opposite

Pigeon with Prunes

4 YOUNG PIGEONS
FLOUR, FOR DUSTING
50 g (2 oz) LARD OR DRIPPING
1 RASHER FAT BACON
1 ONION, SKINNED AND CHOPPED
2 CARROTS, PEELED AND CHOPPED
225 g (8 oz) TOMATOES, CHOPPED
50 g (2 oz) MUSHROOMS, WIPED
600 ml (1 pint) BEEF STOCK
1 BAY LEAF
1 BOUQUET GARNI
PINCH OF SUGAR
225 ml (8 fl oz) RED WINE
12 PRUNES
SWEET CHUTNEY
12 ALMONDS, BLANCHED

Serves 4

1. Dust the pigeons in flour. Melt the lard in a pan and brown the birds then remove and place in a deep casserole. Add the bacon and chopped vegetables and mushrooms to the fat remaining in the pan and brown them.
2. Add the stock, herbs and sugar and simmer for 10 minutes. Push through a sieve, adjust the seasoning and add 100 ml (4 fl oz) wine. Pour the liquid over the birds and simmer in a closed casserole for 1½–2 hours.
3. Meanwhile, simmer the prunes in the rest of the wine until tender. Remove their stones, fill with chutney and one almond.
4. Remove the birds to an open dish and pour over the sauce. Garnish with the stuffed prunes.

Wood Pigeons in Beer

4 SMALL WOOD PIGEONS
30 ml (2 tbsp) VEGETABLE OIL
25 g (1 oz) BUTTER
450 g (1 lb) ONIONS, SKINNED AND SLICED
45 ml (3 tbsp) PLAIN FLOUR
20 ml (4 tsp) FRENCH MUSTARD
600 ml (1 pint) LIGHT ALE
20 ml (4 tsp) SOFT BROWN SUGAR
30 ml (2 tbsp) VINEGAR
142 ml (5 fl oz) CARTON SOURED CREAM
200 g (7 oz) CAN OF PIMIENTOS, DRAINED AND THINLY SLICED

Serves 4

1. Cut the backbone from each pigeon, leaving the rest of the bird whole. Heat the oil in a large flameproof casserole. Add the butter and when frothing brown the birds lightly on all sides. Remove the birds.
2. Fry the onions until golden. Stir in the flour, mustard, ale, sugar, vinegar, salt and pepper. Bring to the boil, stirring.
3. Return the birds to the casserole. Cover tightly and cook in the oven at 170°C (325°F) mark 3 for about 2½ hours, or until tender. Serve the pigeon on a heated dish. Reheat the juices with the soured cream and pimientos. Spoon over the pigeons.

Partridge with Grapes

2 YOUNG PARTRIDGES, HALVED
30 ml (2 tbsp) VEGETABLE OIL
175 ml (6 fl oz) CHICKEN STOCK
90 ml (6 tbsp) DRY WHITE WINE
15 ml (1 tbsp) CORNFLOUR
1 EGG YOLK
30 ml (2 tbsp) DOUBLE CREAM
125 g (4 oz) WHITE GRAPES, SKINNED, HALVED AND PIPPED
CHOPPED PARSLEY, TO GARNISH

Serves 2

1. Remove the backbones from the partridges and carefully pull off the skin. Heat the oil in a large flameproof casserole and lightly brown the birds.
2. Pour over the stock and wine, season and bring to the boil. Cover tightly and cook gently on top of the stove for about 25 minutes or until the meat is tender.
3. Drain the partridges and keep warm on a serving dish.
4. Blend together the cornflour, egg yolk and cream. Add to the pan juices with the grapes and cook gently without boiling, until the sauce thickens. Adjust the seasoning. Spoon the sauce over the partridges and garnish with parsley.

Pheasant with Cranberries

175 g (6 oz) CRANBERRIES
30 ml (2 tbsp) CASTER SUGAR
75 g (3 oz) ONIONS, SKINNED AND FINELY CHOPPED
75 g (3 oz) CELERY, TRIMMED
75 g (3 oz) STREAKY BACON, RINDED AND FINELY CHOPPED
75 g (3 oz) BUTTER OR MARGARINE
125 g (4 oz) FRESH BROWN BREADCRUMBS
SALT AND FRESHLY GROUND PEPPER
1 LARGE OVEN-READY PHEASANT
15 ml (1 tbsp) VEGETABLE OIL
15 ml (1 tbsp) PLAIN FLOUR
150 ml (¼ pint) RED WINE
150 ml (¼ pint) CHICKEN STOCK

Serves 4

1. Put the cranberries, caster sugar and 10 ml (2 tsp) water in a pan over a low heat. Heat, covered, until the cranberries burst. Uncover, raise the heat for 2–3 minutes until moisture has evaporated, cool.
2. Melt 25 g (1 oz) butter in a pan and gently fry the onion, celery and bacon for 3–4 minutes then stir in the breadcrumbs and cranberries. Season then cool.
3. With poultry shears or strong scissors cut along the backbone and breastbone of the pheasant to split the bird in two. Pack the stuffing into the halves.
4. Place the oil and remaining butter in a small roasting tin. Add the pheasant halves skin side down and roast in the oven at 230°C (450°F) mark 8 for 10 minutes then at 200°C (400°F) mark 6 for a further 25–30 minutes.
5. To serve, split each piece of pheasant in half, keep warm. Make a gravy from the pan juices and remaining ingredients. Spoon a little over the pheasant and serve the rest separately.

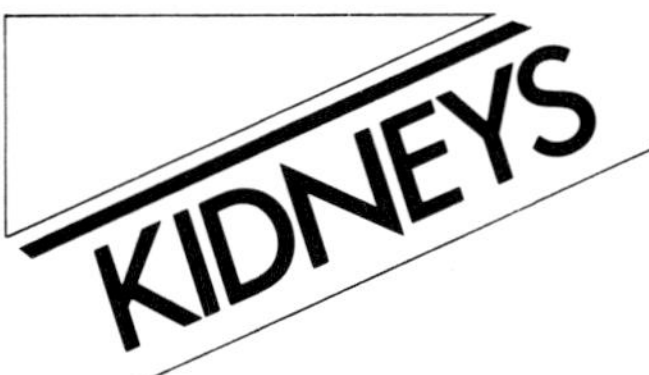

Sautéed Kidneys

40 g (1½ oz) MARGARINE
100 g (4 oz) MUSHROOMS, WIPED AND SLICED
2 SPRING ONIONS, TRIMMED AND SLICED
2 CALF OR LAMB KIDNEYS WEIGHING ABOUT 450 g (1 lb), CORED AND CUT INTO 2.5 cm (1 inch) CUBES
100 ml (4 fl oz) CHICKEN STOCK
30 ml (2 tbsp) MADEIRA
1.25 ml (¼ tsp) SALT
4 SLICES BREAD, CRUSTS REMOVED
CHOPPED PARSLEY, TO GARNISH

Serves 4

1. Melt the margarine in a frying pan and cook the mushrooms and spring onions for about 5 minutes until tender. Remove from the pan and set aside.
2. Cook the kidneys in the margarine remaining in the pan for about 3 minutes until lightly browned, stirring occasionally.
3. Add the mushroom mixture to the pan, with the stock, Madeira and salt and bring to the boil. Cover and simmer for 30 minutes or until the kidneys are tender.
4. Toast the bread and cut each slice in half to form eight triangles. Serve the kidneys on the toast garnished with parsley.

Kidneys à la Crème

225 g (8 oz) LONG-GRAIN RICE
25 g (1 oz) BUTTER
8 LAMBS' KIDNEYS, CORED AND HALVED
1 SMALL ONION, SKINNED AND CHOPPED
1 GARLIC CLOVE, SKINNED AND CRUSHED
30 ml (2 tbsp) PLAIN FLOUR
150 ml (¼ pint) BEEF STOCK
142 ml (5 fl oz) CARTON DOUBLE CREAM
SALT AND FRESHLY GROUND PEPPER
CHOPPED PARSLEY, TO GARNISH (optional)

Serves 4

1. Bring a large pan of salted water to the boil and cook the rice for about 15 minutes until tender.
2. Melt the butter in a pan, add the kidneys, onion and garlic and cook for 3–4 minutes, until the kidneys are evenly browned.
3. Push the kidneys to one side of the pan, stir in the flour and cook for 2 minutes, gradually adding the stock and fresh cream. Stir gently and reheat without boiling.
4. Drain the rice and transfer to a serving dish. Season the kidney mixture and spoon on to the rice. Season well and serve garnished with parsley, if wished.

Photographed opposite

Kidney and Mushroom Pie with Lemon

225 g (8 oz) LEEKS, TRIMMED AND SLICED
30 ml (2 tbsp) OIL
50 g (2 oz) BUTTER
450 g (1 lb) CALVES OR LAMBS' KIDNEYS, CORED AND CUT INTO FORK-SIZED PIECES
100 g (4 oz) MUSHROOMS, WIPED AND QUARTERED
60 g (4 tbsp) PLAIN FLOUR
450 ml (¾ pint) STOCK
15 ml (1 tbsp) DIJON MUSTARD
GRATED RIND OF ½ LEMON
15 ml (1 tbsp) LEMON JUICE
SALT AND FRESHLY GROUND BLACK PEPPER
175 g (6 oz) SELF-RAISING FLOUR
75 g (3 oz) SHREDDED SUET
ABOUT 100 ml (4 fl oz) WATER
BEATEN EGG OR MILK, TO GLAZE

Serves 4

1. Blanch the leeks: put into a pan of boiling water for 2 minutes. Drain well.
2. Heat the oil and butter in a pan and brown the kidneys. Remove and set aside. Add the mushrooms to seal quickly and remove.
3. Stir the flour into the pan and cook slowly to a straw colour, adding more fat if necessary. Blend in the stock, mustard, lemon rind, juice and seasoning. Simmer for 2–3 minutes.
4. Put the kidneys, mushrooms, leeks and sauce into a 1.1 litre (2 pint) pie dish. Cool.
5. Sift the flour with 2.5 ml (½ tsp) salt. Add the suet and mix. Stir in cold water to form an elastic dough. On a lightly floured surface, knead the dough and roll out. Cover the dish and glaze the dough with beaten egg. Make a hole in the centre and bake at 190°C (375°F) mark 5 for about 45 minutes.

Kidney and Celery Broth

45 ml (3 tbsp) OIL
450 g (1 lb) OX KIDNEYS, CORED AND CUT INTO SMALL PIECES
225 g (8 oz) CELERY, TRIMMED AND THINLY SLICED
100 g (4 oz) ONIONS, SKINNED AND FINELY SLICED
1.7 litre (3 pints) BEEF STOCK
SALT AND FRESHLY GROUND BLACK PEPPER
50 g (2 oz) LONG-GRAIN RICE

Serves 6–8

1. Heat the oil in a large heavy-based saucepan and brown the kidneys. Remove and set aside. Add the vegetables and soften for 10 minutes, then stir in the stock and seasoning. Bring to the boil, replace the kidneys and simmer gently, covered, for 15 minutes.
2. Add the rice to the pan, continue simmering for about 15 minutes, or until the rice is tender. Adjust the seasoning.

Kidneys à la Crème

Kidney and Bacon Roly Poly

25 g (1 oz) BUTTER OR MARGARINE
4 LAMBS' KIDNEYS, CORED AND FINELY CHOPPED
100 g (4 oz) STREAKY BACON, RINDED AND CUT INTO THIN STRIPS
50 g (2 oz) ONIONS, SKINNED AND FINELY CHOPPED
30 ml (2 tbsp) TOMATO PUREE
SALT AND FRESHLY GROUND PEPPER
200 g (7 oz) SELF-RAISING FLOUR
100 g ($3\frac{1}{2}$ oz) SHREDDED SUET
ABOUT 90 ml (6 tbsp) WATER
PARSLEY SPRIGS, TO GARNISH

Serves 4

1. Heat the butter in a heavy-based pan and gently fry the kidney, bacon and onion until the kidney is lightly coloured and the onion transparent. Add the tomato purée and seasonings. Cool.

2. Sift the flour with a pinch of salt and add the suet. Stir in just enough cold water to bind.

3. Roll out the dough on a lightly floured surface to a rectangle 30 × 20 cm (12 × 8 inches). Spread the filling to within 1 cm ($\frac{1}{2}$ inch) of the edges. Dampen the edges and roll up from the narrow end, sealing the ends.

4. Grease a piece of foil and place the kidney roll on it, fold the foil over loosely and seal. Put into a steamer over boiling water, cover and steam for about $1\frac{1}{2}$ hours. Serve garnished with parsley.

Kidneys in Batter

225 g (8 oz) PLAIN FLOUR
PINCH OF SALT
2 EGGS
568 ml (1 pint) MILK
75 g (3 oz) BUTTER
8 LAMBS' KIDNEYS, CORED AND CHOPPED
1 LARGE ONION, SKINNED AND VERY FINELY CHOPPED
350 g (12 oz) MUSHROOMS, WIPED AND FINELY CHOPPED
1 GARLIC CLOVE, SKINNED AND CRUSHED
2 GLASSES DRY SHERRY
142 ml (5 fl oz) CARTON DOUBLE CREAM
SALT AND FRESHLY GROUND PEPPER

Serves 4

1. Make the batter: sift the flour and salt into a bowl. Beat in the eggs and milk gradually and whisk until smooth.

2. Melt 50 g (2 oz) butter in a frying pan and gently cook the kidneys and onion until the onion is transparent; add the mushrooms, garlic and sherry. Cook gently for a few minutes and add the fresh cream.

3. Simmer gently until the sauce is reduced and thick, then season.

4. Heat the remaining butter in a flan dish, add the batter and pour the kidney mixture in the centre. Bake in the oven at 200°C (400°F) mark 6 for 35 minutes, until the pastry is crisp, golden and well risen. Serve at once.

Photographed below

Kidneys in Batter

Kidney and Pasta Soup

Kidney and Pasta Soup

25 g (1 oz) BUTTER
15 ml (1 tbsp) OIL
225 g (8 oz) LAMB'S KIDNEYS, CORED AND ROUGHLY CHOPPED
1 GARLIC CLOVE, SKINNED AND CRUSHED
5 ml (1 tsp) TOMATO PUREE
15 ml (1 tbsp) PLAIN FLOUR
1.1 litres (2 pints) BEEF STOCK
GRATED RIND AND JUICE OF 1 ORANGE
225 g (8 oz) DRIED TORTELLINI
450 g (1 lb) FIRM TOMATOES, SKINNED, HALVED, SEEDED AND ROUGHLY CHOPPED
30 ml (2 tbsp) CHOPPED PARSLEY
SALT AND FRESHLY GROUND PEPPER

Serves 4

1. Heat the butter and oil in a large saucepan and brown the kidney a few pieces at a time.

2. Return all the kidney to the saucepan with the garlic and tomato purée. Cook, stirring, for 1–2 minutes. Add the flour and cook for a further minute. Stir in the stock, orange rind, juice and tortellini.

3. Bring to the boil, cover and simmer for 12–15 minutes or until the tortellini are tender.

4. Stir the tomatoes into the soup with the parsley. Heat gently, season and serve.

Photographed above

Kidneys in Sherry Sauce

Kidneys in Sherry Sauce

225–275 g (8–10 oz) LONG-GRAIN BROWN RICE
SALT AND FRESHLY GROUND PEPPER
45 ml (3 tbsp) OIL
75 g (3 oz) CARROTS, PEELED AND CUT INTO 5 mm (¼ inch) CUBES
50 g (2 oz) ONIONS, SKINNED AND CUT INTO 5 mm (¼ inch) CUBES
20 ml (4 tsp) PLAIN FLOUR
ABOUT 600 ml (1 pint) BEEF STOCK, PREFERABLY HOMEMADE
15 ml (1 tbsp) TOMATO PUREE
1 SMALL GARLIC CLOVE, SKINNED AND CRUSHED
1 BAY LEAF
90 g (3½ oz) BUTTER
12 LAMBS' KIDNEYS, ABOUT 700 g (1½ lb), CORED AND SLICED
30 ml (2 tbsp) MEDIUM SHERRY
50 g (2 oz) SEEDLESS RAISINS
225 g (8 oz) ONIONS, SKINNED AND SLICED
45 ml (3 tbsp) CHOPPED PARSLEY
WATERCRESS, TO GARNISH

Serves 4–6

1. Bring a large pan of salted water to the boil and cook the rice for 35–40 minutes or until just tender.

2. Meanwhile, heat the oil in a saucepan. Add the vegetables, cover the pan and cook gently until they begin to look shrivelled but are barely coloured. Stir in the flour and cook gently, stirring occasionally, until the flour and vegetables are a light brown—about 5 minutes.

3. Stir in 450 ml (¾ pint) of the stock with the tomato purée, crushed garlic and seasoning. Bring slowly to the boil, stirring all the time. Add the bay leaf, lower the heat, half cover the pan and simmer very gently for 25–30 minutes stirring occasionally.

4. Melt 40 g (1½ oz) butter in a large frying pan. When it is frothing, add the kidneys, cut side down. Fry briskly over a high heat until the kidneys 'seize up' and turn brown. Turn once only, frying on each side for 2 minutes.

5. Uncover the sauce, add half the remaining stock and bring to the boil. Remove from the heat and tilt the pan slightly, then, using a metal spoon, skim off any fat or scum that has risen to the surface. Repeat to ensure the fat is removed.

6. Add the sherry to the browned kidneys and bring to the boil. Strain in the sauce. Press the vegetables lightly to extract all the juice, without pushing them through the sieve, and add to the kidneys in the pan. Cover and reheat, without boiling, for about 5 minutes. The kidneys should be slightly pink near the centre. Skim and adjust the seasoning.

7. About 5 minutes before the end of cooking time for the rice, stir in the raisins. Drain thoroughly.

8. Melt the remaining butter in a large saucepan and fry the sliced onions until golden. Add the rice, raisins, parsley and seasoning. Stir over a high heat for a few minutes, then spoon on to plates and serve with the kidneys and sauce. Garnish with watercress.

Photographed left

Potted Liver Pop-ins

50 g (2 oz) MARGARINE
50 g (2 oz) ONIONS, PEELED AND FINELY CHOPPED
225 g (8 oz) CHICKEN LIVERS
15 ml (1 tbsp) DIJON MUSTARD
SALT AND FRESHLY GROUND BLACK PEPPER
6 ROUND CRUSTY ROLLS, SLICED OPEN
BUTTER OR MARGARINE
3 TOMATOES, THINLY SLICED
1 ONION, SKINNED AND SLICED INTO RINGS
WATERCRESS, TO GARNISH

Serves 6

1. In a small pan melt the margarine and soften the chopped onion. Add the livers and cook over a high heat until firm. Turn into bowl and cool.
2. Chop the liver mixture finely and combine with the mustard and seasoning.
3. Spread the rolls with butter or margarine. Fill with potted liver, sliced tomatoes and onion rings. Garnish with watercress.

Liver and Sausage Casserole

30 ml (2 tbsp) VEGETABLE OIL
225 g (8 oz) PORK CHIPOLATA SAUSAGES
225 g (8 oz) LAMBS' LIVER, SLICED
225 g (8 oz) SMALL ONIONS, SKINNED AND QUARTERED
30 ml (2 tbsp) PLAIN FLOUR
450 ml ($\frac{3}{4}$ pint) CHICKEN STOCK
15 ml (1 tbsp) FRENCH MUSTARD
SALT AND FRESHLY GROUND PEPPER
30 ml (2 tbsp) SHERRY (optional)
PARSLEY SPRIGS, TO GARNISH

Serves 4

1. Heat the oil in a large shallow flameproof casserole and brown the sausages, add the liver and brown quickly. Drain and set aside. Halve the sausages.
2. Add the onions to the pan and brown lightly. Stir in the flour and fry gently for 1–2 minutes. Mix in the stock, mustard and seasoning and bring to the boil. Return the liver and the sausages to the pan. Cover the pan tightly and simmer gently for about 15 minutes, or until the meat and vegetables are just tender.
3. Adjust the seasoning and stir in the sherry (if used) for serving. Garnish with parsley.

Photographed opposite

Chicken Livers Aloha

50 g (2 oz) BUTTER
100 g (4 oz) CELERY, TRIMMED AND CHOPPED
50 g (2 oz) ONIONS, SKINNED AND CHOPPED
1 GREEN PEPPER, SEEDED AND SLICED
700 g ($1\frac{1}{2}$ lb) CHICKEN LIVERS
439 g ($15\frac{1}{2}$ oz) CAN PINEAPPLE CHUNKS, DRAINED
30 ml (2 tbsp) SOFT BROWN SUGAR
15 ml (1 tbsp) CORNFLOUR
7.5 ml ($1\frac{1}{2}$ tsp) SALT
175 ml (6 fl oz) WATER
30 ml (2 tbsp) CIDER VINEGAR

Serves 4

1. Melt the butter in a large frying pan. Add the celery, onion and green pepper and cook gently for about 5 minutes, or until the vegetables are tender but still slightly crisp.
2. Add the chicken livers and cook for a further 10 minutes, stirring frequently. Add the pineapple chunks and stir them in.
3. Mix the brown sugar, cornflour and salt in a bowl and stir in the water and vinegar. Gradually add to the chicken livers and cook, stirring, until the mixture thickens. Serve at once.

Baked Liver with Dumplings

45 ml (3 tbsp) VEGETABLE OIL
350 g (12 oz) LAMBS' LIVER, SLICED AND CUT INTO FORK-SIZED PIECES
1 ONION, SKINNED AND SLICED
75 g (3 oz) CELERY, TRIMMED AND SLICED
225 g (8 oz) COOKING APPLES, PEELED AND SLICED
30 ml (2 tbsp) PLAIN FLOUR
300 ml (10 fl oz) CHICKEN STOCK
200 ml (7 fl oz) CIDER
SALT AND FRESHLY GROUND PEPPER
125 g (4 oz) SELF-RAISING FLOUR
50 g (2 oz) SHREDDED SUET
PAPRIKA, TO GARNISH

Serves 4

1. Heat the oil in a pan and brown the liver. Transfer to a shallow 1.7 litre (3 pint) ovenproof dish.
2. Brown the onion, celery and apples lightly in the oil remaining in the pan. Stir in the plain flour, stock, cider and seasonings, bring to the boil, cover and simmer for 20 minutes.
3. Mix the self-raising flour and suet and season with salt and pepper. Bind to a soft dough with water and shape into eight dumplings.
4. Pour the hot sauce over the liver and place the dumplings on top.
5. Cover the dish and bake in the oven at 190°C (375°F) mark 5 for about 40 minutes. Sprinkle the top with paprika before serving.

Liver and Sausage Casserole

Liver with Rice in Tomato Sauce

600 ml (1 pint) WATER; AND 150 ml ($\frac{1}{4}$ pint)
SALT AND FRESHLY GROUND PEPPER
275 g (10 oz) PUDDING RICE
1 ONION, SKINNED AND FINELY CHOPPED
50 g (2 oz) STREAKY BACON, RINDED AND SNIPPED INTO SMALL PIECES
225 g (8 oz) LAMBS' LIVER, CUT INTO VERY SMALL PIECES
15 ml (1 tbsp) TOMATO PUREE
5 ml (1 tsp) LEMON JUICE
30 ml (2 tbsp) PLAIN FLOUR
OIL, FOR FRYING
376 g (13$\frac{1}{4}$ oz) CAN TOMATO AND ONION COOK-IN-SAUCE

Serves 4

1. Bring 600 ml (1 pint) salted water to the boil. Add the rice and the onion. Cover and simmer gently for about 13 minutes until the liquid has been absorbed and the rice is tender. Allow to cool slightly.
2. Lightly fry the bacon until the fat runs. Stir in the liver and fry briskly for 1–2 minutes until just coloured. Remove from the heat and stir in the tomato purée and lemon juice.
3. Stir the liver mixture into the rice. Season. Using wet hands, shape into 12 balls, pressing the mixture together well. Season the flour and coat the balls in it.
4. Fry the balls briskly in a little oil for 1–2 minutes to seal. Transfer to an ovenproof dish. Stir 150 ml ($\frac{1}{4}$ pint) water into the Cook-in-Sauce and pour into the dish. Cover and cook in the oven at 180°C (350°F) mark 4 for 35–40 minutes.

Potato Topped Liver with Leeks

25 g (1 oz) DRIPPING
350 g (12 oz) LAMBS' LIVER, SLICED AND CUT INTO THIN STRIPS
350 g (12 oz) LEEKS, TRIMMED AND SLICED
100 g (4 oz) ONIONS, SKINNED AND SLICED
30 ml (2 tbsp) PLAIN FLOUR
300 ml ($\frac{1}{2}$ pint) MEAT OR VEGETABLE STOCK
SALT AND FRESHLY GROUND PEPPER
700 g (1$\frac{1}{2}$ lb) POTATOES, PEELED AND CHOPPED
30 ml (2 tbsp) MILK
30 ml (2 tbsp) FINELY CHOPPED PARSLEY
225 g (8 oz) TOMATOES, SKINNED AND SLICED

Serves 4

1. Heat the dripping in a heavy pan and fry the liver quickly to seal. Add the leeks and onion and cook until lightly browned.
2. Stir in the flour, followed by the stock and stir well over a moderate heat until thickened. Season well, cover and simmer for about 15 minutes.
3. Cook the potatoes in boiling salted water. Mash with the milk, adjust the seasoning and add parsley.
4. Put the liver mixture into a 1.7 litre (3 pint) ovenproof dish and arrange a layer of sliced tomatoes over it. Fork the potato mixture over the top.
5. Either place the dish under a hot grill to brown, or bake at 200°C (400°F) mark 6 for 15–20 minutes.

Mexican Liver

SALT AND FRESHLY GROUND PEPPER
30 ml (2 tbsp) PLAIN FLOUR
450 g (1 lb) LAMBS' LIVER, SLICED
25 g (1 oz) BUTTER OR MARGARINE
90 ml (6 tbsp) VEGETABLE OIL
2 ONIONS, SKINNED AND SLICED
225 g (8 oz) TOMATOES, SKINNED AND SLICED
1 RED PEPPER, SEEDED AND SLICED
300 ml ($\frac{1}{2}$ pint) CHICKEN STOCK
100 g (4 oz) LONG-GRAIN RICE

Serves 4

1. Season 30 ml (2 tbsp) flour and toss the liver in it. Heat the butter and oil in a frying pan and fry it lightly for 5 minutes, then put it into a casserole.
2. Fry the onions, tomatoes and red pepper (reserving a few slices of pepper) for 5 minutes and add to the liver.
3. Stir the remaining flour into the fat left in the pan and gradually add the stock. Bring to the boil, stirring all the time, season well and pour over the liver. Cover and cook in the oven at 180°C (350°F) mark 4 for about 45 minutes.
4. Meanwhile, bring a pan of salted water to the boil and cook the rice. Drain. Serve the liver on the rice and garnish with the reserved sliced pepper.

Goujons of Liver

450 g (1 lb) PIGS' LIVER, CUT INTO THIN STRIPS
A LITTLE MILK (optional)
99 g (3$\frac{1}{2}$ oz) PACKET SAGE AND ONION STUFFING MIX
25 g (1 oz) MARGARINE
225 g (8 oz) ONIONS, SKINNED AND CHOPPED
30 ml (2 tbsp) PLAIN FLOUR
5 ml (1 tsp) DRY MUSTARD
300 ml ($\frac{1}{2}$ pint) BEEF STOCK
SALT AND FRESHLY GROUND PEPPER
50 g (2 oz) DRIPPING OR LARD

Serves 4

1. If wished, to lessen the strong flavour of pigs' liver, it can be soaked in a little milk for a few hours. Drain before using.
2. Toss the strips of liver in the stuffing mix to coat evenly.
3. Melt the margarine in a large pan and fry the onion very gently until soft. Add the flour and mustard and cook gently for 2 minutes, stirring. Gradually add the stock, then stir over a moderate heat until thickened. Season with salt and pepper. Keep hot while preparing the liver.
4. Melt the dripping in a wide, shallow pan and fry the liver strips until evenly browned. Serve immediately, with the onion sauce poured over.

Liver Jardinière

450 g (1 lb) OX LIVER, SLICED
30 ml (2 tbsp) PLAIN FLOUR
100 g (4 oz) STREAKY BACON, RINDED
2 ONIONS, SKINNED AND SLICED
2 LARGE GREEN PEPPERS, SEEDED AND THINLY SLICED
226 g (8 oz) CAN TOMATOES, DRAINED WITH JUICE RESERVED
SALT AND FRESHLY GROUND PEPPER

Serves 4

1. Lightly coat the liver slices with flour.
2. Fry the bacon in its own fat until crisp. Drain, crumble and set aside. Pour off all but 45 ml (3 tbsp) fat from the pan and reserve it.
3. Reheat the fat in the pan and fry the liver a few pieces at a time until lightly browned on both sides, removing the pieces as they brown.
4. Add 30 ml (2 tbsp) reserved bacon fat to the pan and lightly brown the onions and green peppers. Add the tomato juice and season.
5. Place the liver on top of the vegetables, cover and cook gently for 25 minutes or until the liver is tender when tested with a knife.
6. Towards the end of cooking time, add the tomatoes to heat through. Serve garnished with the crumbled bacon sprinkled on top.

Eastern Spiced Liver

25 g (1 oz) DESICCATED COCONUT
150 ml (¼ pint) BOILING WATER
45 ml (3 tbsp) VEGETABLE OIL
25 g (1 oz) BUTTER OR MARGARINE
350 g (12 oz) LAMBS' LIVER, SLICED INTO LARGE FORK-SIZED PIECES
2 ONIONS, SKINNED AND SLICED
15 ml (1 tbsp) CHILLI SEASONING
15 ml (1 tbsp) GROUND CORIANDER
5 ml (1 tsp) PAPRIKA
2.5 ml (½ tsp) TURMERIC
30 ml (2 tbsp) PLAIN FLOUR
450 ml (¾ pint) CHICKEN STOCK
30 ml (2 tbsp) MANGO CHUTNEY
SALT AND FRESHLY GROUND PEPPER
LEMON TWISTS AND POPADUMS, TO SERVE

Serves 4

1. Soak the coconut in the boiling water for 15 minutes, strain, reserving the juices.
2. Heat the oil and butter in a pan and brown the liver slices thoroughly. Remove from the pan.
3. Add the sliced onions to the pan and fry until golden; stir in the spices and flour and cook for 1 minute, stirring.
4. Add the stock with the coconut 'milk', chutney and seasoning and bring to the boil.
5. Replace the liver, cover and simmer for 15–20 minutes. Garnish with lemon twists and serve with popadums.

Liver Goujons with Orange Sauce

350 g (12 oz) LAMBS' LIVER, SLICED AND CUT INTO NARROW FINGER-SIZE PIECES
SALT AND FRESHLY GROUND PEPPER
75 ml (5 tsp) PLAIN FLOUR
1 EGG, BEATEN
100 g (4 oz) MEDIUM OATMEAL
1 ONION, SKINNED AND SLICED
50 g (2 oz) BUTTER
300 ml (½ pint) CHICKEN STOCK
GRATED RIND AND JUICE OF 1 ORANGE
5 ml (1 tsp) RUBBED SAGE
DASH OF GRAVY BROWNING
60 ml (4 tbsp) VEGETABLE OIL
CABBAGE AND PASTA SHAPES, TO SERVE

Serves 4

1. Season 45 ml (3 tbsp) of the flour thoroughly. Coat the liver pieces in the flour, the egg and oatmeal. Refrigerate while preparing the sauce.
2. Melt 25 g (1 oz) butter in a pan and fry the onion until golden. Add the remaining flour and cook gently for 2 minutes, stirring.
3. Add the stock, orange rind and juice with the sage and seasoning. Bring to the boil and simmer for 10–15 minutes. Add the gravy browning and adjust seasoning.
4. Heat the remaining butter and the oil in a pan and fry the goujons until tender.
5. Serve with freshly boiled cabbage and pasta shapes, accompanied by the sauce.

Liver-stuffed Cannelloni

25 g (1 oz) MARGARINE
100 g (4 oz) ONIONS, SKINNED AND FINELY CHOPPED
225 g (8 oz) PIGS' LIVER, FINELY CHOPPED
226 g (8 oz) PACKET FROZEN CHOPPED SPINACH, THAWED AND WELL DRAINED
40 g (1½ oz) FRESH WHITE BREADCRUMBS
SALT AND FRESHLY GROUND PEPPER
FRESHLY GRATED NUTMEG
12 CANNELLONI
396 g (14 oz) CAN TOMATOES, ROUGHLY CHOPPED
300 ml (½ pint) CHICKEN STOCK
50 g (2 oz) CHEDDAR CHEESE, GRATED

Serves 4

1. Melt the margarine and gently fry the onion and liver for 8–10 minutes, stirring frequently.
2. Stir in the spinach, breadcrumbs, seasoning and a pinch of nutmeg.
3. Use the spinach mixture to stuff the uncooked cannelloni. Grease a shallow ovenproof dish and pack the stuffed cannelloni in tightly in a single layer. Spoon over the tomatoes with the juice and the stock.
4. Cover with foil and bake at 190°C (375°F) mark 5 for 30 minutes. Uncover, sprinkle with cheese and return to the oven until melted.

Fried Liver and Bacon

8 RASHERS STREAKY BACON, RINDED
450 g (1 lb) LAMBS' LIVER, SLICED ABOUT 5 mm (¼ inch) THICK
30 ml (2 tbsp) PLAIN FLOUR
1.25 ml (¼ tsp) SALT
LEMON JUICE
CHOPPED PARSLEY, TO GARNISH
4 LEMON WEDGES, TO GARNISH (optional)

Serves 4

1. Fry the bacon in a frying pan in its own fat until crisp, drain on absorbent kitchen paper and keep hot. Pour off all but 30 ml (2 tbsp) fat.
2. Coat the slices of liver in flour.
3. Reheat the bacon fat in the pan and fry the liver for 4 minutes, turning once; do not overcook it—it should be crisp and browned on the outside and still pink on the inside.
4. Add the salt and a squeeze of lemon juice to the pan and stir in. Arrange the liver and bacon on a heated dish and sprinkle the chopped parsley over them. Garnish with lemon wedges, if wished.

Liver and Bacon Chops

4 LOIN OF LAMB CHOPS, ABOUT 75 g (3 oz) EACH, TRIMMED
50 g (2 oz) MARGARINE
1 ONION, SKINNED AND FINELY CHOPPED
175 g (6 oz) LAMBS' LIVER, FINELY CHOPPED
25 g (1 oz) FRESH BREADCRUMBS
30 ml (2 tbsp) DIJON MUSTARD
30 ml (2 tbsp) CHOPPED FRESH PARSLEY
SALT AND FRESHLY GROUND PEPPER
4 THIN RASHERS STREAKY BACON, RINDED

Serves 4

1. Grease a baking sheet and place the lamb chops on it. Fold the ends of the chops in to form a circle.
2. Melt the margarine in a pan and fry the onion for 3–4 minutes until softened. Off the heat stir in the liver and the breadcrumbs. Add 15 ml (1 tbsp) mustard, the parsley and seasoning.
3. Divide the stuffing mixture between the chops, spooning it into the centre of each one. Spread the remaining mustard on the outside of the chops.
4. Stretch the bacon rashers with the back of a knife. Wrap around each chop to enclose the stuffing. Secure with wooden cocktail sticks or skewers.
5. Bake in the oven at 190°C (375°F) mark 5 for 45–50 minutes. Cover with foil after 25 minutes.

Quick-fried Liver with Red Beans

100 g (4 oz) DRIED RED KIDNEY BEANS, SOAKED OVERNIGHT
30 ml (2 tbsp) VEGETABLE OIL
4 RASHERS STREAKY BACON, CUT INTO NARROW STRIPS
2 ONIONS, SKINNED AND SLICED
½ RED PEPPER, SEEDED AND THINLY SLICED
225 g (8 oz) LAMBS' LIVER, SLICED INTO 4 cm × 5 mm (1½ × ¼ inch) PIECES
120 g (4 oz) BUTTON MUSHROOMS, WIPED AND SLICED THINLY
300 ml (½ pint) CHICKEN STOCK
30 ml (2 tbsp) MEDIUM SHERRY
SALT AND FRESHLY GROUND PEPPER
45 ml (3 tbsp) CHOPPED FRESH PARSLEY, TO GARNISH

Serves 4

1. Drain the beans and place in a saucepan of water. Bring to the boil and boil rapidly for 10 minutes then boil gently for about 45 minutes until tender. Drain well.
2. Heat the oil and fry the bacon, onion and pepper until brown. Remove from the pan.
3. Over a high heat, add the liver and mushrooms; brown. Return the bacon, onion and pepper to the pan, add the beans and cook for a further 2 minutes, stirring frequently.
4. Add the stock and sherry and season well. Cook for 5–7 minutes, uncovered, until some of the liquid has evaporated and the liver is cooked. Serve garnished with parsley.

Liver in Stroganoff Sauce

450 g (1 lb) LAMBS' LIVER, THINLY SLICED INTO STRIPS
30 ml (2 tbsp) PLAIN FLOUR
SALT AND FRESHLY GROUND PEPPER
225 g (8 oz) ONIONS, SKINNED AND THINLY SLICED
75 g (3 oz) BUTTER
450 g (1 lb) TOMATOES, SKINNED AND QUARTERED, OR 396 g (14 oz) CAN TOMATOES, DRAINED
10 ml (2 tsp) DRIED SAGE
142 ml (5 fl oz) CARTON SOURED CREAM, STIRRED

Serves 4

1. Season the flour and toss the liver strips in it.
2. In a frying pan, melt the butter and lightly brown the onions. Add the tomatoes, push to the side of the pan, then add the liver and cook over a high heat for about 5 minutes.
3. Sprinkle over the sage. Lower the heat and spoon in the stirred soured cream.
4. Combine the pan ingredients, adjust seasoning and heat, but do not boil. Serve hot.

Liver and Sausage Ragout

30 ml (2 tbsp) VEGETABLE OIL
225 g (8 oz) PORK CHIPOLATA SAUSAGES
225 g (8 oz) LAMBS' LIVER, SLICED
225 g (8 oz) SMALL ONIONS, SKINNED AND QUARTERED
30 ml (2 tbsp) PLAIN FLOUR
450 ml ($\frac{3}{4}$ pint) CHICKEN STOCK
15 ml (1 tbsp) FRENCH MUSTARD
SALT AND FRESHLY GROUND PEPPER
30 ml (2 tbsp) SHERRY (optional)

Serves 4

1. Heat the oil in a large frying pan or shallow saucepan and brown the sausages, add the liver and quickly brown. Remove the sausages and liver from the pan, drain them and halve the sausages.
2. Brown the onions lightly in the oil left in the pan; stir in the flour and fry gently for 1–2 minutes.
3. Mix in the stock, mustard and seasoning and bring to the boil. Replace the liver and the halved sausages.
4. Cover the pan tightly and simmer gently for about 15 minutes, or until the meat and vegetables are just tender.
5. Adjust the seasoning and stir in the sherry if used.

Chicken Liver Sauté

50 g (2 oz) BUTTER
700 g ($1\frac{1}{2}$ lb) CHICKEN LIVERS
1 ONION, SKINNED AND ROUGHLY CHOPPED
25 g (1 oz) PLAIN FLOUR
450 ml ($\frac{3}{4}$ pint) CHICKEN STOCK
50 ml (2 fl oz) MEDIUM SHERRY
7.5 ml ($1\frac{1}{2}$ tsp) SALT
CHOPPED PARSLEY, TO GARNISH
SLICES OF TOAST, TO SERVE (optional)

Serves 4

1. Melt the butter in a pan and gently fry the chicken livers and the onion for about 10 minutes, stirring all the time.
2. Remove the chicken liver and the onion, draining them well so that the cooking juices are left in the pan.
3. Add the flour to the pan, stir well into the cooking juices and cook for a few minutes.
4. Gradually add the stock and cook, stirring, until the sauce thickens.
5. Stir in the sherry, salt and livers and onion. Heat through then serve, garnished with the chopped parsley. Serve with toast, if wished.

Rumaki

9 RASHERS STREAKY BACON, RINDED AND HALVED
225 g (8 oz) CHICKEN LIVERS, CUT INTO CHUNKS
227 g (8 oz) CAN WATER CHESTNUTS, DRAINED
100 ml (4 fl oz) SOY SAUCE
2.5 ml ($\frac{1}{2}$ tsp) CURRY POWDER
1.25 ml ($\frac{1}{4}$ tsp) GROUND GINGER

Makes 18

1. Wrap each piece of bacon around a piece of liver and a water chestnut. Fasten the rolls with wooden cocktail sticks.
2. In a bowl, stir together the soy sauce, curry powder and ginger, add the liver rolls and toss them carefully. Cover with cling film and chill for at least 1 hour, turning occasionally.
3. Just before serving, drain the rumaki and place them in a single layer on a rack in the grill pan.
4. Grill the rumaki under a high heat, turning them frequently, for about 10 minutes or until the liver is cooked. Serve hot.

Orange and Chicken Liver Skewers

200 ml (7 fl oz) UNSWEETENED ORANGE JUICE
2 SMALL ORANGES, RIND OF ONE GRATED; BOTH SEGMENTED
5 ml (1 tsp) CHOPPED FRESH TARRAGON OR 2.5 ml ($\frac{1}{2}$ tsp) DRIED
450 g (1 lb) CHICKEN LIVERS, CUT IN HALF
25 g (1 oz) FRESH WHITE BREADCRUMBS
1 GREEN PEPPER, ABOUT 175 g (6 oz), SEEDED AND ROUGHLY CHOPPED
1 ONION, SKINNED AND ROUGHLY CHOPPED
275 g (10 oz) BEANSPROUTS
SMALL BUNCH OF CHIVES, TRIMMED AND SNIPPED
SALT AND FRESHLY GROUND PEPPER

Serves 4

1. Simmer the orange juice with the grated rind and the tarragon for 2–3 minutes to reduce by half.
2. Toss the chicken livers lightly in breadcrumbs. Place in a lightly greased grill pan and grill for 2 minutes each side or until just firm.
3. Thread the green pepper and the onion on to four skewers alternately with the livers.
4. Place the skewers in the grill pan and spoon over a little of the reduced orange juice. Grill for 2–3 minutes on each side, basting occasionally.
5. Meanwhile, steam the beansprouts for 2–3 minutes. Warm the orange segments with the remaining juice.
6. Mix the beansprouts with the snipped chives and seasoning and arrange on a serving dish. Top with the skewers and spoon over the orange segments and juices.

Ragout of Ox Heart with Lemon

25 g (1 oz) LARD
1 ONION, SKINNED AND SLICED
450 g (1 lb) OX HEART, TRIMMED, CORED AND CUT INTO 1 cm (½ inch) WIDE STRIPS
15 ml (1 tbsp) PLAIN FLOUR
100 ml (4 fl oz) BEEF STOCK
FINELY GRATED RIND OF 1 SMALL LEMON
5 ml (1 tsp) LEMON JUICE
2.5 ml (½ tsp) DRIED MIXED HERBS
SALT AND FRESHLY GROUND PEPPER
142 ml (5 fl oz) CARTON SOURED CREAM
15 ml (1 tbsp) CHOPPED PARSLEY, TO GARNISH

Serves 4

1. Melt the lard in a flameproof casserole and gently fry the onion until golden. Fry the strips of heart quickly in the fat, to seal them on all sides.
2. Stir the flour into the pan and cook for 1 minute, then gradually blend in the stock with the lemon rind, juice and herbs. Bring to the boil and add salt and pepper to taste. Cover and cook in the oven at 150°C (300°F) mark 2 for about 2 hours.
3. Adjust the seasoning, stir in the soured cream and sprinkle with freshly chopped parsley.

Boiled Ox Tongue

1 SALTED OX TONGUE, WEIGHING ABOUT 1.6 kg (3½ lb)
1 ONION, SKINNED AND HALVED
1 CARROT, PEELED AND SLICED
1 TURNIP, PEELED AND SLICED
6 PEPPERCORNS
1 BOUQUET GARNI

Serves 8–10

1. Soak the tongue in water for several hours then drain and put it into a pan with fresh cold water to cover. Bring to the boil then drain again.
2. Add the remaining ingredients, cover with fresh cold water and bring to the boil again. Cover and simmer for 2½–3 hours, skimming off the scum from the surface.
3. Plunge the tongue into cold water, then skin it and remove the bones and gristle from the base.
4. Serve hot, or fit into a cake tin and fill with stock. Weight down and leave to cool and set. Turn out and cut into slices to serve.

Oxtail Paprika

75 ml (5 tbsp) VEGETABLE OIL
2 OXTAILS, ABOUT 1.6 kg (3½ lb) TOTAL WEIGHT, TRIMMED AND CUT UP
225 g (8 oz) ONIONS, SKINNED AND SLICED
30 ml (2 tbsp) PAPRIKA
60 ml (4 tbsp) PLAIN FLOUR
396 g (14 oz) CAN TOMATOES
2 PIECES CANNED PIMIENTO, DRAINED AND SLICED
600 ml (1 pint) BEEF STOCK
SALT AND FRESHLY GROUND PEPPER
142 ml (5 fl oz) CARTON SOURED CREAM
CHOPPED PARSLEY, TO GARNISH

Serves 6

1. Heat the oil in a large flameproof casserole and brown the oxtail well, a few pieces at a time. Remove from the pan.
2. Brown the onion in the oil remaining in the pan. Stir in the paprika and flour and cook gently for 1 minute. Stir in the tomatoes with their juice, sliced pimientos, stock and plenty of seasoning. Bring to the boil and return the meat to the casserole.
3. Cover the casserole tightly and cook in the oven at 170°C (325°F) mark 3 for about 3 hours or until the meat is really tender.
4. Shortly before serving, skim all fat from the surface of the casserole. Bring the casserole slowly to the boil, simmer gently for 10 minutes, covered. Remove from the heat and stir in the soured cream, then warm gently. Garnish with parsley.

Sweetbreads Meunière

450 g (1 lb) VEAL SWEETBREADS
SALT
LEMON JUICE
1.25 ml (¼ tsp) GROUND GINGER (optional)
100 g (4 oz) MARGARINE
25 g (1 oz) DRIED BREADCRUMBS
CHOPPED PARSLEY, TO GARNISH

Serves 3–4

1. Put the sweetbreads into a pan with hot water to cover. For every 900 ml (1½ pints) water, add 5 ml (1 tsp) salt and 15 ml (1 tbsp) lemon juice. Add the ginger, if wished.
2. Bring the pan to the boil, lower the heat, cover tightly and simmer for 20 minutes.
3. Drain the sweetbreads and place in cold water to cool, then remove the membrane, veins and thick connective tissue. Slice in half lengthways.
4. Melt the margarine in a small saucepan. Dip the sweetbreads into the margarine, then in the breadcrumbs. Reserve the remaining margarine.
5. Grease the rack in the grill pan and put the sweetbreads on it. Grill for 8–10 minutes until lightly browned, turning once. Remove to a heated serving dish.
6. Reheat the margarine, stir in 30 ml (2 tbsp) lemon juice and pour over the sweetbreads. Garnish with parsley.

Lambs' Tongues Portugaise

700 g (1½ lb) LAMBS' TONGUES
1 ONION, SKINNED
1 CARROT, PEELED
1 BAY LEAF
6 WHOLE BLACK PEPPERCORNS
45 ml (3 tbsp) OIL
100 g (4 oz) ONIONS, SKINNED AND DICED
100 g (4 oz) CARROTS, PEELED AND DICED
60 ml (4 tbsp) PLAIN FLOUR
226 g (8 oz) CAN TOMATOES
SALT AND FRESHLY GROUND PEPPER
CHOPPED PARSLEY, TO GARNISH

Serves 4

1. Blanch the lambs' tongues: put into a saucepan, cover with water and bring to the boil, drain and refresh in cold, preferably iced, water. Drain again.

2. Return the tongues to the rinsed-out pan with the onion, carrot, bay leaf and peppercorns. Cover with water, bring to the boil and simmer for about 2 hours or until tender.

3. Drain the tongues, discarding the vegetables and reserving the stock, then skin and slice the tongues removing any small bones.

4. Heat the oil in a pan and cook the diced vegetables until softened. Stir in the flour, cook to a straw colour, stirring frequently. Mix in 300 ml (½ pint) of the reserved tongue stock, together with the tomatoes with their juice and seasoning. Bring to the boil and simmer gently for 20 minutes.

5. Add the tongues to the sauce and heat over a low heat for 10 minutes. Adjust the seasoning and garnish with parsley.

Lancashire Tripe and Onions

450 g (1 lb) DRESSED TRIPE
225 g (8 oz) SHALLOTS, SKINNED
SALT AND FRESHLY GROUND PEPPER
568 ml (1 pint) MILK
PINCH OF FRESHLY GRATED NUTMEG
½ BAY LEAF (optional)
25 g (1 oz) BUTTER
45 ml (3 tbsp) PLAIN FLOUR
CHOPPED PARSLEY, TO GARNISH

Serves 4

1. Simmer the tripe, shallots, seasonings, milk, nutmeg and bay leaf (if used) in a covered pan for about 2 hours, or until tender. Alternatively, cook in a casserole in the oven at 150°C (300°F) mark 2 for 3 hours. Strain off the liquid and measure 600 ml (1 pint).

2. Melt the butter, stir in the flour and cook for 2–3 minutes. Remove the pan from the heat and gradually stir in the cooking liquid. Return to the heat and bring to the boil. Continue to stir until it thickens.

3. Add the tripe and shallots to the pan and reheat. Adjust the seasoning and sprinkle over with chopped parsley before serving.

Sweetbreads in Mushrooms and Cream

450 g (1 lb) LAMBS' SWEETBREADS
JUICE OF 1 LEMON
50 g (2 oz) BUTTER OR MARGARINE
225 g (8 oz) MUSHROOMS, WIPED AND SLICED
30 ml (3 tbsp) PLAIN FLOUR
150 ml (¼ pint) WHITE WINE
150 ml (¼ pint) CHICKEN STOCK
SALT AND FRESHLY GROUND WHITE PEPPER
1 BOUQUET GARNI
45 ml (3 tbsp) DOUBLE CREAM

Serves 4

1. Soak the sweetbreads in cold water and the lemon juice for 1 hour. Strain well. Remove any white tissue and pat dry with absorbent kitchen paper.

2. Heat the butter in a flameproof casserole and cook the sweetbreads until coloured lightly. Remove from the casserole and gently fry the mushrooms in the remaining fat for 2 minutes. Add the flour and cook for 2 minutes. Pour in the wine and stock and replace the sweetbreads. Season lightly and add the bouquet garni.

3. Cover and cook in the oven at 190°C (375°F) mark 5 for about 45 minutes until the sweetbreads are tender. Stir in the double cream before serving.

Lambs' Hearts in a Casserole

50 g (2 oz) BUTTER OR MARGARINE
1 ONION, SKINNED AND CHOPPED
125 g (4 oz) MUSHROOMS, WIPED AND CHOPPED
125 g (4 oz) STREAKY BACON, RINDED AND CHOPPED
2.5 ml (½ tsp) DRIED SAGE OR THYME
225 g (8 oz) FRESH BREADCRUMBS
FINELY GRATED RIND OF 1 LEMON
SALT AND FRESHLY GROUND PEPPER
1 EGG, BEATEN
8 LAMBS' HEARTS, ABOUT 175 g (6 oz) EACH, TRIMMED AND CORED
60 ml (4 tbsp) PLAIN FLOUR
30 ml (2 tbsp) VEGETABLE OIL
300 ml (½ pint) CHICKEN STOCK
45 ml (3 tbsp) SHERRY

Serves 8

1. Heat half the butter in a frying pan and lightly brown the onion, mushrooms and bacon. Remove from the heat and stir in the herbs, breadcrumbs, lemon rind and seasoning. Bind with the egg.

2. Fill the hearts with the stuffing and sew up neatly. Toss the hearts in the flour. Heat the remaining butter and oil in a flameproof casserole and brown the hearts well. Pour over the stock and sherry, season well and bring to the boil.

3. Cover the dish and cook in the oven at 150°C (300°F) mark 2 for about 2 hours, or until tender. Skim the juices and slice the hearts. Pour the juices over the hearts and serve.

Toad in the Hole

100 g (4 oz) PLAIN FLOUR
PINCH OF SALT
1 EGG
300 ml (½ pint) MILK
15 ml (1 tbsp) BUTTER, MELTED
450 g (1 lb) PORK SAUSAGES

Serves 4

1. Sift the flour and salt into a bowl. Beat to a smooth batter with the egg, half the milk and the melted butter. Stir in the remaining milk.
2. Arrange the sausages in a small shallow baking tin and bake in the oven at 220°C (425°F) mark 7 for 10 minutes.
3. Remove from the oven, pour the batter over the sausages and bake for a further 30 minutes.
4. Lower the temperature to 200°C (400°F) mark 6 and bake for a further 15–20 minutes. Serve immediately.

Photographed opposite

VARIATION: PICKLE POPOVERS
Using the same batter and omitting the sausages, cook in 12 buttered patty tins. When cooked, put a little pickle in the centre of each and serve immediately.

Frankfurter Ratatouille

25 g (1 oz) MARGARINE
100 g (4 oz) GREEN PEPPERS, SEEDED AND THINLY SLICED
100 g (4 oz) BUTTON MUSHROOMS, WIPED AND QUARTERED
225 g (8 oz) CAULIFLOWER, BROKEN INTO SMALL FLORETS
100 g (4 oz) PASTA SHELLS OR TWISTS
SALT AND FRESHLY GROUND BLACK PEPPER
396 g (14 oz) CAN TOMATOES
150 ml (¼ pint) STOCK
210 g (7 oz) PACKET FRANKFURTERS
75 g (3 oz) CHEDDAR CHEESE

Serves 4

1. Grease a 2 litre (3½ pint) pudding basin with the margarine and layer the vegetables, pasta, seasoning and tomatoes with their juice and the stock.
2. Grease a piece of foil, cover the basin and steam for 1 hour or until the vegetables and pasta are tender.
3. Heat the frankfurters as directed on the packet, slice and fold into the vegetables with the grated cheese.

Mini Heroes

454 g (1 lb) PACKET BROWN BREAD MIX
1 EGG, BEATEN
175 g (6 oz) BUTTER OR MARGARINE
45 ml (3 tbsp) HORSERADISH RELISH
THREE 113 g (4 oz) PACKETS SLICED DANISH SALAMI
298 g (10½ oz) CAN GREEN CUT ASPARAGUS SPEARS, DRAINED

Serves 8

1. Prepare and knead the dough according to the packet instructions. Wrap about one-sixth in greaseproof paper and keep in the refrigerator.
2. Lightly grease three baking sheets. Divide the remaining dough into 16 even pieces and shape into finger rolls. Place on the baking sheets loosely covered with oiled cling film. Leave to rise in a warm place until double in size.
3. Shape the refrigerated dough into 16 plaits the same length as the rolls. Make an indentation along each roll and place a plait in each. Glaze with egg and bake in the oven at 220°C (425°F) mark 7 for 15–20 minutes. Cool.
4. Cream the butter and horseradish together, split the rolls (which should be eaten fresh) and spread each half with the creamed mixture.
5. Spread out the salami slices and top each with an asparagus spear. Roll them up and put one inside each buttered roll.

Sausage Double-crust Pie

50 g (2 oz) MARGARINE
175 g (6 oz) CELERY, TRIMMED AND CHOPPED
50 g (2 oz) ONIONS, SKINNED AND CHOPPED
450 g (1 lb) SAUSAGEMEAT
15 ml (1 tbsp) TOMATO PUREE
2.5 ml (½ tsp) DRIED SAGE
SALT AND FRESHLY GROUND PEPPER
225 g (8 oz) PLAIN FLOUR
50 g (2 oz) BUTTER, CUT INTO SMALL PIECES
50 g (2 oz) LARD, CUT INTO SMALL PIECES
45–60 ml (3–4 tbsp) WATER
MILK, TO GLAZE

Serves 4

1. Melt the margarine and gently fry the celery and onion until soft.
2. Add the sausagemeat to the pan together with the tomato purée, sage and seasonings. Work the ingredients together until well blended.
3. Make the shortcrust pastry: sift the flour and a pinch of salt into a bowl. Rub in the fat and mix to a firm dough with the water. Roll out on a lightly floured surface and use half to line a deep 22 cm (8½ inch) pie plate.
4. Press in the sausage filling then cover the pie with the remaining pastry, sealing the edges well. Decorate with pastry trimmings and glaze with milk. Bake at 190°C (375°F) mark 5 for about 40 minutes.

Toad in the Hole

Beans with Sauerkraut and Frankfurters

Beans with Sauerkraut and Frankfurters

175 g (6 oz) DRIED BLACK EYE BEANS, SOAKED OVERNIGHT AND DRAINED
450 g (1b lb) JAR OR CAN SAUERKRAUT
30 ml (2 tbsp) OIL
350 g (12 oz) FRANKFURTER SAUSAGES, SCORED
1 ONION, SKINNED AND CHOPPED
425 g (15 oz) CAN READY-TO-SERVE CHICKEN SOUP
150 ml ($\frac{1}{4}$ pint) CIDER
1.25 ml ($\frac{1}{4}$ tsp) DILLWEED
2.5 ml ($\frac{1}{2}$ tsp) ENGLISH MUSTARD
SALT AND FRESHLY GROUND PEPPER
2 EATING APPLES

Serves 4

1. Put the beans into a pan, cover with water and bring to the boil. Lower the heat and simmer for about 40 minutes or until almost tender.
2. Turn the sauerkraut into a pan and boil rapidly for 5 minutes. Drain thoroughly.
3. Heat the oil and fry the sausages until golden. Remove from pan, add the onion and fry until brown.
4. Pour in the soup and cider. Bring to the boil, stir in the beans, sauerkraut, dillweed, mustard and seasonings.
5. Transfer the bean mixture to a wide casserole dish. Place the sausages on top (cut in half, if large), cover and cook at 180°C (350°F) mark 4 for about 45 minutes.
6. Peel and cut apples into chunks, stir into the casserole and continue to cook, covered, for a further 20 minutes.

Photographed above

Sausage Yorkshires with Onion Sauce

350 g (12 oz) PORK SAUSAGEMEAT
175 g (6 oz) COOKING APPLE, PEELED AND CORED
5 ml (1 tsp) CHOPPED PARSLEY
SALT AND FRESHLY GROUND PEPPER
125 g (4 oz) PLAIN FLOUR; PLUS 15 ml (1 tbsp)
2 EGGS
568 ml (1 pint) MILK
LARD
175 g (6 oz) ONIONS, SKINNED AND SLICED
15 g ($\frac{1}{2}$ oz) BUTTER

Serves 4

1. Put the sausagemeat into a bowl. Grate the apple into the bowl. Stir in the parsley and seasoning. Work the ingredients together and form into 16 small balls.

2. Sift the 125 g (4 oz) flour and a pinch of salt into a bowl. Beat in the eggs and 300 ml ($\frac{1}{2}$ pint) milk gradually. Whisk until smooth.

3. Heat a little lard in the bases of four 300 ml ($\frac{1}{2}$ pint) individual ramekin dishes until sizzling hot. Place four sausage balls in each and cook in a 220°C (425°F) mark 7 oven for 10 minutes.

4. Pour the batter over the sausage balls and return to the oven for 35–40 minutes until risen and golden.

5. Meanwhile, put the remaining milk into a pan and cook the onion until soft. To make the sauce, melt the butter in a pan, stir in the 15 ml (1 tbsp) flour and cook gently for 1 minute, stirring. Remove the pan from the heat and gradually stir in the onions and milk. Return to the heat and bring to the boil. Continue to cook, stirring, until the sauce thickens, then add seasoning to taste.

6. When the Yorkshires are baked, turn out and pour a little onion sauce into the centre of each.

Photographed below

Sausage Yorkshires with Onion Sauce

Pan Pizza

283 g (10 oz) PACKET WHITE BREAD MIX
VEGETABLE OIL
450 g (1 lb) TOMATOES, SKINNED AND SLICED
15 ml (1 tbsp) FRESH CHOPPED BASIL OR 5 ml (1 tsp) DRIED
SALT AND FRESHLY GROUND PEPPER
100 g (4 oz) CAN TUNA FISH, DRAINED AND FLAKED
50 g (2 oz) RINDED, SLICED SALAMI, CHOPPED
100 g (4 oz) STREAKY BACON, RINDED AND CHOPPED
100 g (4 oz) BUTTON MUSHROOMS, WIPED AND SLICED
175 g (6 oz) ANY HARD CHEESES, GRATED

Serves 4

1. Make up bread mix and knead according to packet directions. Roll out to two 25 cm (10 inch) rounds, press into pizza pans or place on baking sheets and brush with oil.
2. Cover the dough bases with sliced tomatoes and sprinkle over the herbs and seasoning. Top with tuna, salami, bacon and mushrooms arranging them in quarter sections on each dough base. Sprinkle the cheese over the top.
3. Bake at 230°C (450°F) mark 8 for about 20 minutes.

Spinach and Lentil Roulade

175 g (6 oz) RED LENTILS
1 SMALL ONION, SKINNED AND FINELY CHOPPED
30 ml (2 tbsp) TOMATO KETCHUP
15 ml (1 tbsp) CREAMED HORSERADISH
125 g (4 oz) BUTTER
SALT AND FRESHLY GROUND PEPPER
450 g (1 lb) SPINACH, TRIMMED
50 g (2 oz) PLAIN FLOUR
300 ml (½ pint) MILK
2 EGGS, SEPARATED
DRY BREADCRUMBS

Serves 4

1. Butter and line a 28 cm (11 inch) Swiss-roll tin.
2. Bring a large pan of salted water to the boil and cook the lentils with the onion until tender. Drain well, then return to the pan and heat to evaporate excess moisture. Add the tomato ketchup, horseradish and 50 g (2 oz) butter. Rub through a sieve or purée in a blender. Season and set aside.
3. In a pan, gently cook the spinach, sprinkled with salt (do not add any liquid), for 3–4 minutes. Turn into a colander, press with a potato masher, and chop finely.
4. To make the sauce, melt the remaining butter in a pan, stir in the flour and cook gently for 1 minute, stirring. Remove the pan from the heat and gradually stir in the milk. Return to the heat and bring to the boil. Continue to cook, stirring, until the sauce thickens. Remove from the heat. Stir in the spinach and egg yolks. Season.
5. Whisk the egg whites until stiff and gently fold into the spinach mixture. Spoon into the prepared tin. Level the surface and bake in the oven at 200°C (400°F) mark 6 for 20 minutes, or until well risen and golden.
6. Turn out on to greaseproof paper sprinkled with dried breadcrumbs. Peel off the greaseproof lining. Spread the lentil purée over the surface. Roll up Swiss-roll style and return to the oven for 5 minutes.

Photographed opposite

Vegetable Pot

175 g (6 oz) HARICOT BEANS, SOAKED OVERNIGHT AND DRAINED
40 g (1½ oz) MARGARINE
1 ONION, SKINNED AND SLICED
3 COURGETTES, TRIMMED AND SLICED
1 SMALL GREEN PEPPER, SEEDED AND SLICED
1 GARLIC CLOVE, SKINNED AND CRUSHED
2.5 ml (½ tsp) GROUND CORIANDER
2.5 ml (½ tsp) GROUND CUMIN
40 g (1½ oz) PLAIN WHOLEMEAL FLOUR
600 ml (1 pint) VEGETABLE STOCK
SALT AND FRESHLY GROUND PEPPER
4 TOMATOES, SKINNED AND ROUGHLY CHOPPED
30 ml (2 tbsp) TOMATO PUREE
15 ml (1 tbsp) WHEATGERM

Serves 4

1. Put the beans into a pan, cover with water and bring to the boil. Lower the heat and simmer for about 1–1½ hours or until the beans are tender. Drain.
2. Melt the margarine in a large saucepan and add the onion, courgettes, green pepper, garlic and spices. Fry gently for about 15 minutes or until the vegetables are soft.
3. Stir in the flour and cook for 2 minutes. Gradually stir in the stock and bring to the boil to thicken, then season well.
4. Stir the tomatoes into the pan with the beans and tomato purée. Cover and simmer gently for 35 minutes, until all the vegetables are tender. Spoon into a warm serving dish and sprinkle with the wheatgerm.

Spinach and Lentil Roulade

Quick Pizza

Quick Pizza

225 g (8 oz) SELF-RAISING FLOUR
2.5 ml ($\frac{1}{2}$ tsp) SALT
65 g ($2\frac{1}{2}$ oz) BUTTER
150 ml ($\frac{1}{4}$ pint) MILK
1 LARGE ONION, SKINNED AND SLICED
3 LARGE TOMATOES, SKINNED AND THINLY SLICED, OR 200 g (7 oz) CAN TOMATOES, DRAINED AND MASHED
SALT AND FRESHLY GROUND PEPPER
2.5 ml ($\frac{1}{2}$ tsp) DRIED MIXED HERBS
175 g (6 oz) CHEDDAR CHEESE, THINLY SLICED
2 RASHERS STREAKY BACON, CUT INTO NARROW STRIPS

Serves 4

1. Grease a baking sheet. Sift the flour and salt into a bowl, then rub in 50 g (2 oz) of butter until the mixture resembles fine breadcrumbs. Add the milk and mix to a soft dough.

2. Turn on to a floured work surface and knead until smooth. Roll out to one large or four individual circles, 1 cm ($\frac{1}{2}$ inch) thick. Put on to the prepared baking sheet.

3. Melt the remaining butter in a frying pan and fry the onion. Place on the pizza base and top with the tomato slices, seasoning, mixed herbs and cheese. Garnish with the bacon strips, arranged in a pattern.

4. Bake in the oven at 220°C (425°F) mark 7 for 20–25 minutes, until cooked and golden. Serve hot.

Photographed above

Bean and Vegetable Stew

175 g (6 oz) CANNELLINI BEANS, SOAKED OVERNIGHT AND DRAINED
700 ml ($1\frac{1}{4}$ pints) CHICKEN STOCK
25 g (1 oz) BUTTER
225 g (8 oz) COURGETTES, TRIMMED AND SLICED
225 g (8 oz) AUBERGINES, TRIMMED AND SLICED
100 g (4 oz) CELERY, TRIMMED AND SLICED
100 g (4 oz) ONIONS, SKINNED AND SLICED
100 g (4 oz) RED PEPPERS, SEEDED AND SLICED
150 ml ($\frac{1}{4}$ pint) DRY CIDER
2.5 ml ($\frac{1}{2}$ tsp) DRIED THYME
15 ml (1 tbsp) CORNFLOUR
SALT AND FRESHLY GROUND PEPPER

Serves 4–6

1. Put the beans into a pan with the stock and bring to the boil, cover and simmer for 45 minutes. The beans should be tender but still a little firm.

2. Melt the butter in a large deep frying pan and cook the vegetables a few at a time until golden.

3. Add the vegetables to the beans and stock. Add the cider and thyme, cover and simmer gently for 15 minutes, or until the beans and vegetables are tender.

4. Blend the cornflour to a paste with a little cold water and stir into the pan. Bring to the boil, stirring and cook until thickened. Adjust the seasoning before serving.

Tomato and Onion Flan

175 g (6 oz) PLAIN FLOUR
SALT
40 g ($1\frac{1}{2}$ oz) BUTTER, CUT INTO SMALL PIECES
40 g ($1\frac{1}{2}$ oz) LARD, CUT INTO SMALL PIECES
ABOUT 45 ml (3 tbsp) WATER
30 ml (2 tbsp) OIL
700 g ($1\frac{1}{2}$ lb) ONIONS, SKINNED AND THINLY SLICED
1 GARLIC CLOVE, SKINNED AND CRUSHED
350 g (12 oz) TOMATOES, SKINNED AND ROUGHLY CHOPPED
15 ml (1 tbsp) TOMATO PUREE
2.5 ml ($\frac{1}{2}$ tsp) DRIED OREGANO
50 g (2 oz) CAN ANCHOVY FILLETS, DRAINED AND HALVED LENGTHWAYS
45 ml (3 tbsp) MILK
ABOUT 10 BLACK OLIVES, HALVED AND STONED
SALT AND FRESHLY GROUND PEPPER

Serves 4–6

1. Sift the flour and a pinch of salt into a large bowl. Rub the fat in until the mixture resembles fine breadcrumbs. Sprinkle over enough water to make a firm dough. Wrap and chill for about 20 minutes.

2. Heat the oil in a large frying pan and add the onions and garlic. Press greaseproof paper down on top of the onions. Cover tightly and 'sweat' the onions over a gentle heat for about 40 minutes. They should be very soft and well browned. Don't uncover the pan during cooking.

3. On a lightly floured surface, gently knead the pastry into a neat round. Roll out to a circle about 28 cm (11 inches) in diameter.

4. Place a 20 cm (8 inch) diameter, 4 cm ($1\frac{1}{2}$ inch) deep flan ring on a baking sheet and carefully ease the pastry into it. Neaten the edges.

5. Prick the base of the pastry case then bake blind with foil and beans in a 200°C (400°F) mark 6 oven for about 10 minutes or until just set. Remove the beans and foil. Bake for a further 8 minutes, or until the pastry has dried out, but not browned.

6. Meanwhile, put the tomatoes into a small saucepan, stir in the tomato purée and oregano. Boil until the tomato flesh breaks down and the mixture reduces by half, stirring occasionally. Soak the anchovies in the milk for about 10 minutes.

7. Remove the pastry case from the oven and carefully ease off the metal ring. Stir the tomato mixture into the softened onions and season. Spoon the onion mixture into the pastry case.

8. Drain the anchovies and arrange over the onion filling to form a lattice. Garnish with olive halves and bake for a further 10 minutes or until really hot. Serve at once.

Photographed below

Tomato and Onion Flan

Onion Pizza Pie

283 g (10 oz) PACKET BROWN BREAD MIX
50 g (2 oz) BUTTER
125 g (4 oz) STREAKY BACON, RINDED AND SNIPPED INTO SMALL PIECES
600 g ($1\frac{1}{4}$ lb) ONIONS, SKINNED AND THINLY SLICED
2 EGGS (SIZE 2)
15 ml (1 tbsp) PLAIN FLOUR
284 ml ($\frac{1}{2}$ pint) CARTON SINGLE CREAM
SALT AND FRESHLY GROUND PEPPER
2.5 ml ($\frac{1}{2}$ tsp) CARAWAY SEEDS

Serves 4–6

1. Make up and knead the bread mix according to packet instructions. Place in an oiled bowl, cover with oiled cling film and leave to double in size—about 40 minutes.

2. Melt the butter in a large covered pan and cook the bacon and onions until the onions are translucent. Cool.

3. Whisk the eggs, flour, cream, seasonings and caraway seeds together and stir in the cooled onion mixture.

4. On a lightly floured surface, knock down the dough and roll out to fit a 33 × 23 × 2 cm (13 × 9 × $\frac{3}{4}$ inch) non-stick Swiss-roll type tin. Spoon the onion mixture on top.

5. Bake at 200°C (400°F) mark 6 for about 35 minutes, or until just set. Ease out of the tin and cut into wedges for serving.

Cheesy-stuffed Aubergines

2 AUBERGINES, STALKS REMOVED, HALVED LENGTHWAYS
50 g (2 oz) HAM, CHOPPED
15 ml (1 tbsp) CHOPPED PARSLEY
1 TOMATO, SKINNED AND CHOPPED
50 g (2 oz) FRESH BREADCRUMBS
$\frac{1}{2}$ ONION, SKINNED AND GRATED
SALT AND FRESHLY GROUND PEPPER
175 g (6 oz) CHEDDAR CHEESE, GRATED
CHOPPED PARSLEY, TO GARNISH

Serves 4

1. Scoop out the flesh of the aubergines to leave a 5 mm ($\frac{1}{4}$ inch) shell. Roughly chop the flesh.

2. Make the stuffing by combining the ham, parsley, tomato, breadcrumbs, onion, seasoning and 50 g (2 oz) cheese with the aubergine flesh.

3. Place the aubergine shells in a baking dish and fill with the mixture. Sprinkle with the remaining cheese and cover with foil.

4. Bake in the oven at 200°C (400°F) mark 6 for 20 minutes, then uncover and cook for a further 5–10 minutes until crisp and golden. Serve hot, garnished with chopped parsley.

Photographed right

Cheesy-stuffed Aubergines

Whole Stuffed Cabbage

Cheese and Tomato Fries

12 SLICES WHITE BREAD
BUTTER OR SOFT MARGARINE
DIJON MUSTARD
350 g (12 oz) EDAM CHEESE, THINLY SLICED
225 g (8 oz) TOMATOES, SKINNED AND THINLY SLICED
SALT AND FRESHLY GROUND BLACK PEPPER
OIL AND BUTTER, FOR SHALLOW-FRYING
GHERKINS, TO GARNISH

Serves 6

1. Spread the slices of bread with butter or margarine and mustard.

2. Sandwich the slices of bread together with the cheese and tomato slices, placing the tomatoes in the centre with plenty of seasoning. Press well together, cut off the crusts and divide the sandwiches into triangles.

3. Heat a little oil and butter and fry the triangles quickly until golden brown on both sides and the cheese starts to ooze.

4. Serve as soon as possible garnished with gherkins.

Whole Stuffed Cabbage

WINTER CABBAGE ABOUT 900 g (2 lb) IN WEIGHT, TRIMMED
75 g (3 oz) BUTTER OR MARGARINE
125 g (4 oz) ONIONS, SKINNED AND FINELY CHOPPED
50 g (2 oz) CELERY, TRIMMED AND FINELY CHOPPED
10 ml (2 tsp) GROUND CORIANDER
225 g (8 oz) SMOKED PORK SAUSAGE, FINELY CHOPPED
50 g (2 oz) FRESH BREADCRUMBS
30 ml (2 tbsp) CHOPPED PARSLEY
10 ml (2 tsp) LEMON JUICE
1 EGG, BEATEN
SALT AND FRESHLY GROUND PEPPER
A LITTLE SEASONED STOCK
SOY SAUCE

Serves 4

1. Using a potato peeler gouge out some of the stem from the cabbage. Cut a 2 cm ($\frac{3}{4}$ inch) slice off the top. Tie with string around the middle.

2. Bring a pan of salted water to the boil and blanch the cabbage for 8–10 minutes, then run under a cold tap to cool and drain well. Scoop out and reserve the centre of the cabbage leaving a 1 cm ($\frac{1}{2}$ inch) shell.

3. Melt 50 g (2 oz) butter in a pan and gently fry the onion and celery with the coriander for about 7 minutes until the vegetables are softened. Stir in the sausage with the breadcrumbs, parsley, lemon juice, egg and seasoning.

4. Pack the stuffing well into the cabbage shell. Place in a shallow ovenproof dish with 5 mm ($\frac{1}{4}$ inch) of stock and a dash of soy sauce. Cover loosely with buttered foil. Bake at 190°C (375°F) mark 5 for about $1\frac{1}{4}$ hours.

5. Lightly boil the reserved cabbage. Drain and toss in the remaining butter. Season well and serve with the stuffed cabbage and baking juices.

Photographed opposite

Onion and Cheese Pie

2 ONIONS, SKINNED AND CHOPPED
100 g (4 oz) CHEDDAR CHEESE, GRATED
30 ml (2 tbsp) NATURAL YOGURT
1 EGG, BEATEN
SALT AND FRESHLY GROUND PEPPER
175 g (6 oz) PLAIN WHOLEMEAL FLOUR
PINCH OF SALT
75 g (3 oz) BUTTER OR MARGARINE, CUT INTO SMALL PIECES
ABOUT 30 ml (2 tbsp) WATER

Serves 4

1. Bring a pan of salted water to the boil and cook the onions for 5 minutes until soft. Drain and mix with the cheese and yogurt. Add nearly all the beaten egg and season to taste.

2. Make the pastry; sift the flour and salt into a bowl. Rub in the butter until the mixture resembles fine breadcrumbs. Sprinkle in just enough water to make a firm dough.

3. Roll out half the pastry on a lightly floured surface and use to line an 18 cm (7 inch) pie plate. Pour the cheese mixture into the centre.

4. Roll out the remaining pastry to form a lid. Dampen the edges of the pastry on the plate with water and cover with the lid, pressing the edges well together. Flake and scallop the edge and brush with the remaining beaten egg. Make a hole in the centre and bake in the oven at 200°C (400°F) mark 6 for about 30 minutes, or until the pastry is golden brown.

Penny Pinchers' Pizza

225 g (8 oz) WHOLEMEAL FLOUR
15 ml (1 tbsp) BAKING POWDER
50 g (2 oz) BLOCK MARGARINE
MILK, TO BIND
198 g (7 oz) CAN CHOPPED HAM LOAF, CUT INTO THIN STRIPS
225 g (8 oz) TOMATOES, SLICED
SALT AND FRESHLY GROUND PEPPER
5 ml (1 tsp) DRIED MIXED HERBS
100 g (4 oz) EDAM CHEESE, SLICED

Serves 4

1. Sift together the dry ingredients with a pinch of salt and rub in the margarine evenly. Add enough milk to bind to a firm but light dough.

2. Lightly grease a baking sheet. On a lightly floured surface, roll out the dough to a 20 cm (8 inch) round and place on the baking sheet.

3. Layer the ham strips and tomatoes over the dough, sprinkling between the layers with seasoning and mixed herbs.

4. Top with slices of cheese and bake at 220°C (425°F) mark 7 for about 25 minutes. Serve hot, cut into wedges.

Spinach Potato Wedges

Spinach Potato Wedges

450 g (1 lb) POTATOES, PEELED
450 g (1 lb) FRESH SPINACH, TRIMMED
30 ml (2 tbsp) OIL
50 g (2 oz) ONIONS, SKINNED AND CHOPPED
50 g (2 oz) RICOTTA OR COTTAGE CHEESE
65 g (2½ oz) GRATED PARMESAN CHEESE
50 g (2 oz) SALAMI, SHREDDED
1 EGG YOLK, PLUS 1 EGG
PINCH FRESHLY GRATED NUTMEG
SALT AND FRESHLY GROUND PEPPER
3.75 ml (¾ tsp) BAKING POWDER
125 g (4 oz) PLAIN FLOUR
PARSLEY SPRIGS, TO GARNISH

Serves 4

1. Boil 350 g (12 oz) potatoes for 20 minutes, or until tender. In a small saucepan, gently cook the spinach (do not add any liquid) for 3–4 minutes. Drain well.

2. Coarsely grate the remaining potatoes and finely chop the spinach.

3. Heat the oil in a pan and fry the grated potato and onion for 2 minutes. Add the spinach and fry for a further 2 minutes. Off the heat add the Ricotta, 50 g (2 oz) Parmesan, salami, egg yolk, nutmeg and seasoning. Cool.

4. Grease a baking sheet. Drain and sieve the cooked potatoes. Beat in the egg, baking powder and flour and knead on a well floured surface. Roll out to a 23 cm (9 inch) square and place on the baking sheet. Pile the spinach mixture in the centre of the dough. Bring the corners of dough to the centre, pressing lightly together. Mark lines on the dough and sprinkle over the remaining Parmesan.

5. Bake at 200°C (400°F) mark 6 for about 40 minutes. Serve hot, cut into wedges and garnished with parsley.

Photographed above

Cauliflower and Celery Pie

450 g (1 lb) CAULIFLOWER, TRIMMED AND BROKEN INTO FLORETS
40 g ($1\frac{1}{2}$ oz) BUTTER OR MARGARINE
75 g (3 oz) CELERY, TRIMMED AND THINLY SLICED
4 RASHERS LEAN BACON, RINDED AND SNIPPED
45 ml (3 tbsp) PLAIN FLOUR
SALT AND FRESHLY GROUND PEPPER
300 ml ($\frac{1}{2}$ pint) MILK
30 ml (2 tbsp) CHOPPED PARSLEY
1 EGG, BEATEN
10 ml (2 tsp) BEEF EXTRACT
45 ml (3 tbsp) WATER
175 g (6 oz) SELF-RAISING FLOUR
75 g (3 oz) SHREDDED SUET

Serves 4

1. Bring a pan of salted water to the boil and lightly cook the florets. Drain.
2. Melt the butter in a frying pan and gently fry the celery for 3–4 minutes. Stir in the bacon, and fry for a further 2 minutes.
3. Stir in the plain flour, cook for 1 minute, bring to the boil, simmer for 2 minutes, season. Remove from the heat and gradually stir in the milk. Return to the heat and stir until thickened. Stir in the cauliflower, parsley and beaten egg. Leave to cool, then spoon into a 22 cm ($8\frac{1}{2}$ inch) shallow pie dish.
4. Mix the beef extract with the water and use to bind the self-raising flour and suet to a manageable dough. Add more water if needed.
5. On a lightly floured surface, roll out the pastry to fit the top of the dish. Cut a 7.5 cm (3 inch) circle from the centre. Cover the pie dish with the pastry. Replace the circle and glaze with milk.
6. Bake at 190°C (375°F) mark 5 for about 50 minutes. Cover, if necessary, towards end of the cooking time. To serve, lift out pastry circle and cut up separately.

Chilli Pizza Fingers

15 ml (1 tbsp) OIL
225 g (8 oz) MINCED BEEF
2.5 ml ($\frac{1}{2}$ tsp) CHILLI POWDER
1 GARLIC CLOVE, SKINNED AND CRUSHED
125 g (4 oz) ONIONS, SKINNED AND CHOPPED
125 g (4 oz) GREEN PEPPERS, SEEDED AND CHOPPED
125 g (4 oz) MUSHROOMS, WIPED AND SLICED
225 g (8 oz) TOMATOES, SKINNED AND CHOPPED
213 g (7.51 oz) CAN RED KIDNEY BEANS, DRAINED
150 ml ($\frac{1}{4}$ pint) BEEF STOCK
225 g (8 oz) PLAIN WHOLEMEAL FLOUR
50 g (2 oz) MEDIUM OATMEAL
15 ml (1 tbsp) BAKING POWDER
SALT
50 g (2 oz) BUTTER, CUT INTO SMALL PIECES
1 EGG, BEATEN
ABOUT 60 ml (4 tbsp) MILK
15 ml (1 tbsp) TOMATO PUREE
175 g (6 oz) MOZZARELLA CHEESE, THINLY SLICED

Serves 6

1. Heat the oil in a pan and fry the mince with the chilli powder and garlic for 3–4 minutes, stirring occasionally.
2. Add the onion, green pepper and mushrooms to the pan and fry for a further 1–2 minutes. Stir in the tomatoes with the kidney beans and stock. Bring to the boil and simmer for about 15 minutes, or until most of the liquid has evaporated.
3. Meanwhile, make the pizza base, combine the flour, oatmeal, baking powder and a pinch of salt. Rub in the butter until the mixture resembles fine breadcrumbs. Bind to a soft dough with the egg and milk. Knead lightly.
4. Turn on to a lightly floured surface and roll out to a 25 × 18 cm (10 × 7 inch) rectangle. Lift on to a baking sheet then spread carefully with the tomato purée. Pile the chilli mixture on top and cover with the Mozzarella cheese.
5. Bake at 200°C (400°F) mark 6 for about 30 minutes. Cut into fingers for serving.

Kidney Bean and Tomato Flan

125 g (4 oz) DRIED RED KIDNEY BEANS, SOAKED OVERNIGHT AND DRAINED
175 g (6 oz) PLAIN FLOUR
SALT
40 g ($1\frac{1}{2}$ oz) BUTTER, CUT INTO SMALL PIECES
40 g ($1\frac{1}{2}$ oz) LARD, CUT INTO SMALL PIECES
ABOUT 45 ml (3 tbsp) WATER
2 EGGS
90 ml (6 tbsp) SINGLE CREAM
90 ml (6 tbsp) MILK
45 ml (3 tbsp) GRATED PARMESAN CHEESE
FRESHLY GROUND PEPPER
25 g (1 oz) BUTTER
1 ONION, SKINNED AND FINELY CHOPPED
450 g (1 lb) RIPE TOMATOES, SKINNED AND CHOPPED
1.25 ml ($\frac{1}{4}$ tsp) DRIED OREGANO
2.5 ml ($\frac{1}{2}$ tsp) SUGAR

Serves 4

1. Put the beans into a pan, cover with water and bring to the boil, boil for 10 minutes, then lower the heat and simmer for about 45 minutes, until tender.
2. Meanwhile, make the pastry: sift the flour and a pinch of salt into a bowl and rub in the fat until the mixture resembles fine breadcrumbs and add just enough water to make a firm dough.
3. Roll out on a lightly floured surface and use to line a 20 cm (8 inch) deep flan dish. Chill for 10 minutes.
4. Prick the base of the pastry case and bake blind with foil and beans in a 200°C (400°F) mark 6 oven for about 10 minutes or until just set. Remove the foil and beans.
5. Beat the eggs, cream, milk and Parmesan together. Season and pour into the flan case. Bake at 180°C (350°F) mark 4 for about 25 minutes, until lightly set.
6. Meanwhile, melt the butter in a pan and slowly fry the onion. Stir in the tomatoes, oregano, sugar and seasoning to taste. Simmer in the open pan for about 15 minutes, until the liquid has evaporated.
7. Drain the beans and add to the hot tomato mixture. Reheat and spoon over the flan filling. Serve hot.

Baked Tuna-stuffed Potato

Baked Tuna-stuffed Potatoes

4 LARGE POTATOES, SCRUBBED AND PRICKED
198 g (7 oz) CAN TUNA, FLAKED
25 g (1 oz) BUTTER
142 ml (5 fl oz) CARTON SOURED CREAM
SALT AND FRESHLY GROUND PEPPER
125 g (4 oz) STREAKY BACON, CHOPPED

Serves 4

1. Bake the potatoes in the oven at 180°C (350°F) mark 4 for $1\frac{1}{2}$–2 hours, until just tender.
2. Slice the tops off the potatoes and scoop out the flesh, leaving a thin shell.
3. Mash the potato flesh, then stir in the tuna with its oil, the butter, soured cream and seasoning.
4. Spoon the tuna mixture back into the potato shells and mark the surface with a knife.
5. Sprinkle the bacon on top of the potatoes.
6. Place the potatoes in a shallow ovenproof dish and return to the oven at 220°C (425°F) mark 7 for 20–25 minutes. Serve with freshly cooked green beans or a mixed salad (see page 203).

Photographed above

Millet and Nut Burgers

175 g (6 oz) MILLET
125 g (4 oz) SHELLED MIXED NUTS, ROUGHLY CHOPPED
50 g (2 oz) FRESH WHOLEMEAL BREADCRUMBS
SALT AND FRESHLY GROUND PEPPER
1 EGG (SIZE 6), BEATEN
VEGETABLE OIL

Makes 8

1. Bring a pan of salted water to the boil and cook the millet until just tender, about 20 minutes. Drain well and put into a large bowl.
2. Add the nuts to the bowl and stir in the breadcrumbs and seasonings. Bind the mixture with the egg.
3. With floured hands, shape the mixture into eight 7.5 cm (3 inch) rounds. Place them on a flat tray, cover lightly and chill for at least 1 hour.
4. Brush the burgers lightly with vegetable oil, then grill them for about 4 minutes each side and leave to cool.

EGGS & CHEESE

Omelette in a Roll

2 EGGS
15 ml (1 tbsp) WATER
BUTTER
1 PIECE CANNED PIMIENTO, DRAINED AND CHOPPED
TWO 15 cm (6 inch) LONG CRUSTY POPPY SEED ROLLS, SLIT
MUSTARD

Serves 2

1. Lightly whisk the eggs with the water and season.
2. In a 15–18 cm (6–7 inch) pan melt enough butter to grease the base and swirl round.
3. Add the pimiento to the egg and pour half into the heated butter. Cook over moderate heat, lifting the edges up to let the liquid egg run through. Leave a few seconds to set then roll up in the pan and turn out. Keep warm. Immediately make a second omelette.
4. Lightly toast the inside of the rolls under the grill. Spread with butter and a little mustard. Place an omelette inside each roll and serve.

Eggs Fricassée

200 ml (7 fl oz) MILK
1 SMALL ONION, SKINNED AND THICKLY SLICED
1 SMALL CARROT, PEELED AND THICKLY SLICED
1 BAY LEAF
6 WHOLE BLACK PEPPERCORNS
212 g ($7\frac{1}{2}$ oz) PACKET FROZEN PUFF PASTRY, THAWED
25 g (1 oz) BUTTER
30 ml (2 tbsp) PLAIN FLOUR
142 ml (5 fl oz) CARTON SOURED CREAM
2.5 ml ($\frac{1}{2}$ tsp) DRIED TARRAGON
6 HARD-BOILED EGGS, SHELLED AND SLICED

Serves 4

1. In a saucepan, bring the milk to the boil with the onion, carrot, bay leaf and peppercorns and leave to infuse for at least 10 minutes. Strain.
2. Roll out the pastry on a lightly floured surface to a rectangle 25 × 10 cm (10 × 4 inches). Divide into two, lengthways, and cut each strip into 10 triangles. Dampen a baking sheet, put the triangles on it and bake in the oven at 220°C (425°F) mark 7 for 12–15 minutes until golden brown and well risen.
3. Meanwhile, melt the butter in a pan and stir in the flour. Remove from the heat and gradually stir in the milk, soured cream, tarragon and season. Return to the heat, bring to the boil, stirring all the time, until the sauce thickens. Simmer for about 5 minutes.
4. Reserving the yolk from one of the eggs, add the egg slices to the sauce and simmer to warm the eggs. Sieve the reserved egg yolk and use to garnish. Serve with pastry triangles.

Photographed right

Eggs Fricassée

Baked Eggs and Egg and Bacon Pilaff

Egg and Spinach Croûtes

2 LARGE SLICES BREAD, 2.5 cm (1 inch) THICK
125 g (4 oz) SPINACH, TRIMMED
2 EGGS
65 g ($2\frac{1}{2}$ oz) BUTTER
15 ml (1 tbsp) PLAIN FLOUR
150 ml ($\frac{1}{4}$ pint) MILK
SALT AND FRESHLY GROUND PEPPER
FRESHLY GRATED NUTMEG
1 GARLIC CLOVE, SKINNED AND CRUSHED

Serves 2

1. With a pastry cutter, stamp out as large rounds as possible from the slices of bread.

2. In a pan, gently cook the spinach (do not add liquid) for 3–4 minutes. Drain well and chop.

3. Bring a pan of water to the boil and put the eggs on to poach lightly.

4. Meanwhile, melt 15 g ($\frac{1}{2}$ oz) butter in a small saucepan and stir in the flour. Cook for 1 minute then remove from the heat and gradually add the milk. Bring to the boil, simmer for 1–2 minutes, stirring constantly. Stir in the spinach and season well with salt, pepper and nutmeg.

5. Toast the bread rounds on one side. Mix the rest of the butter with the garlic and spread on the untoasted side. Grill again until golden.

6. Drain the eggs. On a heated plate, top each toast croûte with an egg, spoon over the creamed spinach and serve at once.

Egg and Bacon Pilaff

30 ml (2 tbsp) VEGETABLE OIL
125 g (4 oz) ONIONS, SKINNED AND THINLY SLICED
125 g (4 oz) STREAKY BACON RASHERS, RINDED AND SNIPPED
175 g (6 oz) LONG-GRAIN RICE
2.5 ml ($\frac{1}{2}$ tsp) GROUND TURMERIC
300 ml ($\frac{1}{2}$ pint) LIGHT STOCK
SALT AND FRESHLY GROUND BLACK PEPPER
150 ml ($\frac{1}{4}$ pint) DRY CIDER
4 EGGS
CHOPPED PARSLEY, TO GARNISH (optional)

Serves 4

1. Heat the oil in a shallow, flameproof casserole or deep frying pan and fry the onion and bacon together to a golden brown. Stir in the rice and turmeric and cook 1 minute.

2. Add the stock and seasoning and bring to the boil, stirring. Cover and simmer gently for about 10 minutes.

3. Pour the cider into the casserole and adjust the seasoning. Make small 'wells' in the rice with the back of a spoon. Break the eggs, one by one, into a cup and tip carefully into the wells.

4. Cover the casserole or pan and continue to simmer gently for a further 7–8 minutes, or until the eggs are just set, adding a little more stock if necessary. Serve from the casserole, garnished with parsley, if wished.

Photographed opposite

Baked Eggs

50 g (2 oz) BUTTER, MELTED
4 EGGS
SALT AND FRESHLY GROUND PEPPER

Serves 4

1. Place four individual ovenproof dishes or cocottes on a baking sheet, and put one-quarter of the butter in each.

2. Break an egg into each dish and sprinkle with a little salt and pepper. Bake in the oven at 180°C (350°F) mark 4 for 5–8 minutes until the eggs are just set. Serve at once.

Photographed opposite

Baked Eggs with Mushrooms

50 g (2 oz) BUTTER
175 g (6 oz) BUTTON MUSHROOMS, WIPED AND FINELY CHOPPED
50 g (2 oz) ONIONS, SKINNED AND FINELY CHOPPED
5 ml (1 tsp) DRIED TARRAGON
SALT AND FRESHLY GROUND PEPPER
2 EGGS

Serves 2

1. Melt half the butter in a frying pan, add the vegetables and fry until golden and all excess moisture has evaporated. Add the herbs and season, cool.

2. Divide the mushroom mixture between two ramekin or cocotte dishes and make a well in the centre of each.

3. Carefully break an egg into each dish, dot with the reserved butter and stand the ramekins in a roasting tin. Pour water into the tin to come halfway up the sides of the ramekins.

4. Place the covered roasting tin in the oven and bake at 180°C (350°F) mark 4 for 12–15 minutes, or until the eggs are just set. Serve at once.

Chinese-style Egg Drop Soup

1.1 litres (2 pints) CHICKEN STOCK
5 ml (1 tsp) SOY SAUCE
PINCH OF GROUND GINGER
SALT AND FRESHLY GROUND BLACK PEPPER
25 g (1 oz) LONG-GRAIN RICE
50 g (2 oz) COOKED WHITE CHICKEN MEAT, FINELY SHREDDED
198 g (7 oz) CAN SWEETCORN, DRAINED
15 ml (1 tbsp) SHERRY
2 EGGS, BEATEN

Makes 1.4 litres ($2\frac{1}{2}$ pints)

1. Put the stock into a large saucepan. Add the soy sauce, ginger and seasoning, and bring to the boil.

2. Add the rice and simmer for 10 minutes. Add the chicken, sweetcorn and sherry and simmer for a further 5 minutes, or until the rice is cooked.

3. Trickle the eggs into the soup in a very thin stream, stirring well so that the egg sets in fine strings in the soup. Adjust the seasoning and serve very hot.

All-in-one Egg Supper

700 g ($1\frac{1}{2}$ lb) POTATOES, PEELED
450 g (1 lb) CABBAGE, TRIMMED AND ROUGHLY CHOPPED
75 g (3 oz) BUTTER OR MARGARINE
SALT AND FRESHLY GROUND BLACK PEPPER
450 ml ($\frac{3}{4}$ pint) MILK
1 SMALL CARROT, PEELED AND SLICED
1 SMALL ONION, SKINNED AND SLICED
1 BAY LEAF
6 WHOLE BLACK PEPPERCORNS
30 ml (2 tbsp) PLAIN FLOUR
2.5 ml ($\frac{1}{2}$ tsp) GROUND PAPRIKA
6–8 HARD-BOILED EGGS, SHELLED AND HALVED
25 g (1 oz) FRESH WHITE BREADCRUMBS

Serves 4

1. Boil the potatoes for about 20 minutes, or until tender. Drain and mash. Cook the cabbage in boiling salted water for 1 minute. Drain well. Combine the potatoes and cabbage and cook with 25 g (1 oz) butter over a high heat, stirring often, to remove any moisture. Season to taste.

2. Bring the milk just to the boil with the carrot, onion, bay leaf and peppercorns. Remove from the heat and leave to infuse for about 15 minutes.

3. Melt a further 25 g (1 oz) fat in a heavy-based pan. Add the flour and paprika and cook gently for 1 minute. Remove from the heat and stir in the strained milk. Return to the heat and bring to the boil, stirring. Season to taste, simmer 2 minutes, stirring occasionally.

4. Grease a shallow, ovenproof dish, and spoon the hot potato mixture into either end. Place the halved eggs in the centre.

5. Spoon over the sauce. Sprinkle with breadcrumbs and dot with shavings from the rest of the butter. Grill gently until golden brown.

Tarragon Buttered Eggs on Pasta

50 g (2 oz) BUTTER
75 g (3 oz) ONIONS, SKINNED AND THINLY SLICED
1 GARLIC CLOVE, SKINNED AND CRUSHED
GRATED RIND AND JUICE OF $\frac{1}{2}$ SMALL LEMON
2.5 ml ($\frac{1}{2}$ tsp) DRIED TARRAGON
SALT AND FRESHLY GROUND PEPPER
125 g (4 oz) TAGLIATELLE VERDI
4 EGGS

Serves 2

1. Melt the butter in a saucepan. Add the onion, garlic, lemon rind, juice and tarragon. Cook over a low heat for 4–5 minutes until the onion is soft. Season to taste.

2. Bring a pan of salted water to the boil and cook the pasta for 10–12 minutes until just tender. Drain well. Toss in half the butter mixture and spoon into a serving dish. Keep warm covered in a low oven.

3. Bring a pan of water to the boil and gently poach the eggs until just set. Drain and transfer to the pasta. Coat the eggs with the remaining butter mixture. Serve immediately.

Egg and Tomato Gratin

225 g (8 oz) LEEKS, TRIMMED AND SLICED
25 g (1 oz) MARGARINE
30 ml (2 tbsp) PLAIN FLOUR
300 ml ($\frac{1}{2}$ pint) MILK
SALT AND FRESHLY GROUND BLACK PEPPER
8 HARD-BOILED EGGS, SHELLED AND THICKLY SLICED
225 g (8 oz) TOMATOES, SKINNED AND SLICED
50 g (2 oz) CHEDDAR CHEESE

Serves 4

1. Blanch the leeks: put into a pan of boiling salted water for 5 minutes. Drain well.

2. Melt the margarine in a pan and stir in the flour. Remove from the heat and gradually stir in the milk. Return to the heat and bring to the boil, stirring all the time until it thickens. Season.

3. Layer the eggs with the leeks in four individual 300 ml ($\frac{1}{2}$ pint) gratin dishes. Spoon over the white sauce and cover with sliced tomatoes. Top with the grated cheese. Cook at 220°C (425°F) mark 7 for about 15 minutes until golden brown.

Bacon and Egg Croquettes

25 g (1 oz) MARGARINE
125 g (4 oz) GREEN STREAKY BACON RASHERS, RINDED AND ROUGHLY CHOPPED
200 ml (7 fl oz) MILK
1 SMALL CARROT, PEELED AND SLICED
1 SMALL ONION, SKINNED AND SLICED
1 BAY LEAF
6 WHOLE BLACK PEPPERCORNS
105 ml (7 tbsp) PLAIN FLOUR
1 EGG YOLK
30 ml (2 tbsp) SINGLE CREAM OR TOP OF MILK
4 HARD-BOILED EGGS, SHELLED AND CHOPPED
SALT AND FRESHLY GROUND BLACK PEPPER
1 WHOLE EGG, BEATEN
50 g (2 oz) DRY WHITE BREADCRUMBS
FRYING OIL, FOR DEEP-FRYING
PARSLEY SPRIGS, TO GARNISH

Serves 4

1. Melt the margarine in a heavy-based pan and gently fry the bacon. Meanwhile, bring the milk to the boil with the carrot, onion, bay leaf and peppercorns. Remove from the heat and leave about 15 minutes to infuse.

2. Stir 75 ml (5 tbsp) flour into the bacon. Remove from the heat then add the strained milk. Return to the heat and bring to the boil, stirring.

3. Beat the egg yolk into the cream and add to the milk mixture with the hard-boiled eggs and seasoning, to taste. Chill well.

4. Roll the egg mixture into sausage shapes on a floured board, brush with beaten egg and coat in the breadcrumbs—leave for 15 minutes for a crisper coat.

5. Heat the fat to 180°C (350°F) and deep-fry a few croquettes at a time until golden. Drain and serve at once garnished with parsley.

Curried Egg Deckers

3 EGGS
30 ml (2 tbsp) MILK
SALT AND FRESHLY GROUND PEPPER
25 g (1 oz) BUTTER OR MARGARINE
5 ml (1 tsp) MILD CURRY POWDER
6 LARGE SLICES BROWN BREAD
6 LARGE SLICES WHITE BREAD
BUTTER, FOR SPREADING
30 ml (2 tbsp) CHOPPED PARSLEY
10 ml (2 tsp) LEMON JUICE
PARSLEY SPRIGS, TO GARNISH

Serves 6

1. Whisk the eggs, milk and seasoning together.
2. Melt the butter or margarine in a saucepan, add the curry powder and cook gently for 1 minute. Stir in the egg mixture and cook over a low heat stirring all the time until the mixture becomes a soft scrambled consistency. Turn out on to a plate and cool.
3. Butter one side only of each slice of brown and white bread.
4. Spread the white slices with the egg mixture and sprinkle parsley and lemon juice over three of the brown slices.
5. Layer up four slices of brown and white bread topping with a plain brown slice, making three decker sandwiches in all.
6. Cut off the crusts then slice each sandwich into four triangles, place on a serving platter and garnish with parsley sprigs.

Soft-boiled Eggs on Brown Rice

125 g (4 oz) BROWN RICE
25 g (1 oz) BUTTER OR MARGARINE
125 g (4 oz) STREAKY BACON, RINDED AND SNIPPED
½ BUNCH WATERCRESS, TRIMMED AND CHOPPED
2.5 ml (½ tsp) DRIED OREGANO
15 ml (1 tbsp) DRY SHERRY
30 ml (2 tbsp) SINGLE CREAM
SALT AND FRESHLY GROUND PEPPER
15 ml (1 tbsp) OIL
125 g (4 oz) ONIONS, SKINNED AND THINLY SLICED
2 EGGS (size 2)

Serves 2

1. Bring a pan of salted water to the boil and cook the rice for 40–45 minutes, until tender. Drain well.
2. Melt the butter in a frying pan and stir in the bacon. Fry gently for 1–2 minutes. Add the rice, watercress and oregano. Heat gently for 3–4 minutes. Remove from the heat and stir in the sherry and cream. Season and spoon on to a serving dish. Cover and keep warm in a low oven.
3. Heat the oil and gently fry the onion until brown.
4. Soft-boil the eggs for 6 minutes. Shell while still hot and carefully place on the rice. Split the eggs and scatter with the onion just before serving.

Stuffed Egg Mayonnaise

4 HARD-BOILED EGGS, SHELLED AND HALVED LENGTHWAYS
75 g (3 oz) BLUE BRIE, RINDED
75 g (3 oz) FULL-FAT CREAM CHEESE
45–60 ml (3–4 tbsp) SINGLE CREAM
SALT AND FRESHLY GROUND PEPPER
225 g (8 oz) TOMATOES, SKINNED
150 ml (¼ pint) MAYONNAISE (see page 210)
PARSLEY SPRIGS, TO GARNISH

Serves 4

1. Sieve the egg yolks. Rinse and carefully dry the egg whites.
2. Beat the cheese until smooth. Work in the cream cheese with the sieved egg yolks, cream and seasoning, beating until smooth and pipeable in consistency.
3. Put the cream cheese mixture into a piping bag fitted with a 1 cm (½ inch) star vegetable nozzle and pipe into the egg whites.
4. Slice half the tomatoes and arrange in four individual serving dishes; place the stuffed eggs on top. Refrigerate for 30 minutes.
5. Halve, seed and roughly chop the remaining tomatoes and stir into the mayonnaise.
6. Spoon a little mayonnaise over each egg and garnish with parsley sprigs.

Curried Egg and Potato Slice

TWO 113 g (4 oz) PACKETS SLICED COOKED HAM SLICES HALVED
15 ml (1 tbsp) POWDERED GELATINE
45 ml (3 tbsp) WATER
6 EGGS
60 ml (4 tbsp) SINGLE CREAM
10 ml (2 tsp) MILD CURRY POWDER
SALT AND FRESHLY GROUND PEPPER
25 g (1 oz) BUTTER
60 ml (4 tbsp) MAYONNAISE
75 g (3 oz) RADISHES, TRIMMED AND ROUGHLY CHOPPED
3 STICKS CELERY, TRIMMED AND ROUGHLY CHOPPED
538 g (1 lb 3 oz) CAN NEW POTATOES, DRAINED AND ROUGHLY CHOPPED
45 ml (3 tbsp) CHOPPED PARSLEY

Serves 6

1. Line a 1.1 litre (2 pint) loaf tin with ham slices. Soak the gelatine in the water in a small bowl.
2. Whisk the eggs, cream, curry powder and seasoning together.
3. Melt the butter in a heavy-based pan, add the egg mixture and stir over a low heat until lightly set, turn out into a bowl.
4. Stir the soaked gelatine into the hot egg mixture until dissolved. Mix in the mayonnaise with the radishes, celery and potatoes.
5. Spoon the vegetable mixture into the loaf tin alternating with layers of chopped parsley and refrigerate to set.

Hot Savoury Soufflé

65 g ($2\frac{1}{2}$ oz) GRATED PARMESAN CHEESE
200 ml (7 fl oz) MILK
1 SMALL ONION, SKINNED AND SLICED
1 SMALL CARROT, PEELED AND SLICED
1 BAY LEAF
6 WHOLE BLACK PEPPERCORNS
75 g (3 oz) GRUYERE CHEESE, FINELY GRATED
25 g (1 oz) BUTTER OR MARGARINE
30 ml (2 tbsp) PLAIN FLOUR
10 ml (2 tsp) DIJON MUSTARD
SALT AND FRESHLY GROUND PEPPER
CAYENNE PEPPER
4 EGGS, SEPARATED, PLUS 1 EGG WHITE (SIZE 3)

Serves 2

1. Lightly grease a 1.3 litre ($2\frac{1}{4}$ pint) soufflé dish. Sprinkle 15 ml (1 tbsp) of the Parmesan into the dish. Tilt the dish, tapping the sides until they are evenly coated.
2. Put the milk into a medium-sized saucepan with the onion and carrot slices, bay leaf and peppercorns. Bring slowly to the boil then remove from the heat. Cover the pan and leave the ingredients to infuse for at least 15 minutes. Strain off and reserve the milk.
3. Mix the Gruyère with 50 g (2 oz) of the Parmesan cheese.
4. Melt the butter in a pan. Add the flour and mustard and stir for 1 minute. Remove from the heat and gradually add the milk. Return to the heat and bring slowly to the boil, stirring all the time. Season well and add a pinch of cayenne. Continue to boil for 2 minutes, stirring. Cool a little.
5. Beat the egg yolks into the cooled sauce one at a time. Sprinkle the mixed cheeses over the sauce reserving 15 ml (1 tbsp). Stir in the cheese until evenly blended.
6. Whisk the egg whites gently until the mixture stands in soft peaks.
7. Mix a large spoonful of egg white into the sauce. Gently pour the sauce over the remaining egg whites and cut and fold the ingredients together lightly, using a metal spoon, until the egg whites are just incorporated.
8. Pour the soufflé mixture carefully into the prepared dish—the mixture should come about three-quarters of the way up the side of the dish. Smooth the surface with a palette knife and sprinkle the reserved cheese over the top.
9. Put the soufflé on a baking sheet and cook in the oven at 180°C (350°F) mark 4 for about 30 minutes or until golden brown on the top, well risen and just firm to the touch. Serve at once.

Photographed opposite

Spanish-style Omelette

30 ml (2 tbsp) VEGETABLE OIL
125 g (4 oz) LEEKS, TRIMMED AND THINLY SLICED
125 g (4 oz) BUTTON MUSHROOMS, WIPED AND SLICED
2 PIECES CANNED PIMIENTO, DRAINED AND SHREDDED
6 EGGS
SALT AND FRESHLY GROUND BLACK PEPPER

Serves 4

1. Heat the oil in a 22 cm ($8\frac{1}{2}$ inch) non-stick frying pan and soften the leeks. Increase the heat and fry the leeks and mushrooms together until golden brown. Stir in the pimiento.
2. With a fork combine the eggs and seasoning until just blended and pour into the pan over the vegetables. Cook over a moderate heat, shaking the pan occasionally to prevent the omelette sticking, for about 4 minutes, or until the omelette is barely set.
3. Turn out on to a warm serving plate and cut into wedges for serving.

Omelette Niçoise

125 g (4 oz) FRENCH BEANS, TRIMMED AND CHOPPED
SALT AND FRESHLY GROUND PEPPER
3 EGGS (SIZE 2)
30 ml (2 tbsp) WATER
25 g (1 oz) BUTTER
125 g (4 oz) TOMATOES, SKINNED AND CHOPPED
6–10 BLACK OLIVES, HALVED AND STONED
99 g ($3\frac{1}{2}$ oz) CAN TUNA FISH, DRAINED AND FLAKED
ANCHOVY FILLETS AND CHOPPED PARSLEY, TO GARNISH

Serves 2

1. Bring the beans to the boil in a pan of salted water. Lower the heat and simmer 7–10 minutes until just tender.
2. Whisk the eggs with 30 ml (2 tbsp) water and season well.
3. Melt the butter in a 23 cm (9 in) omelette pan. When the foam subsides, pour in the egg mixture. Cook the omelette over a moderate heat, lifting it up round the edges with a spatula to allow the liquid egg to run underneath. When the omelette is almost set, but still runny on top, allow the underside to colour a little.
4. Spoon on the tomatoes, beans, olives and tuna fish. Season. Place the pan under a hot grill for 3 minutes to heat the filling. Fold the omelette in half, tilting the pan away from the handle and turn on to a dish. Garnish with fine strips of anchovy and chopped parsley. Serve immediately.

Breakfast in a Pan

50 g (2 oz) BUTTER
25 g (1 oz) STREAKY BACON, RINDED AND SNIPPED
50 g (2 oz) COARSE OATMEAL
25 g (1 oz) OAT FLAKES
25 g (1 oz) SHELLED HAZELNUTS, ROUGHLY CHOPPED
2 EGGS (size 2)
SALT AND FRESHLY GROUND PEPPER

Serves 2

1. Melt the butter in a frying pan and gently fry the bacon for 1–2 minutes until the fat runs. Add the oatmeal, oat flakes and nuts. Stir to coat in the butter.
2. Carefully break the two eggs on to the oatmeal mixture. Cover with a lid or foil and cook gently for 4–5 minutes until lightly set. Season before serving.

Hot Savoury Soufflé

Egg and Anchovy Crispy Fries

56 g (2 oz) CAN ANCHOVIES, DRAINED
30 ml (2 tbsp) MILK
6 HARD-BOILED EGGS, SHELLED AND HALVED LENGTHWAYS
50 g (2 oz) BUTTER, SOFTENED
15 ml (1 tbsp) TOMATO PUREE
15 ml (1 tbsp) LEMON JUICE
SALT AND FRESHLY GROUND BLACK PEPPER
ABOUT 30 ml (2 tbsp) PLAIN FLOUR
1 EGG, BEATEN
25 g (1 oz) DRIED WHITE BREADCRUMBS
DEEP FAT, FOR FRYING

Makes 6

1. Soak the anchovies in the milk for about 15 minutes. Drain and chop finely.

2. Carefully remove the egg yolks from the whites and sieve the yolks. Pound them with the butter, tomato purée, lemon juice, anchovies and seasoning.

3. Stuff the anchovy mixture into the egg whites, placing two halves together again. Coat the eggs in flour, beaten egg, and crumbs, and then again in egg and crumbs. Chill well.

4. Heat the oil to 180°C (350°F) and fry the eggs until golden brown. Drain well and serve hot.

Poached Eggs with Cucumber and Coriander Sauce

50 g (2 oz) BUTTER OR MARGARINE
225 g (8 oz) CUCUMBER, PEELED AND FINELY CHOPPED
30 ml (2 tbsp) PLAIN FLOUR
10 ml (2 tsp) GROUND CORIANDER
300 ml ($\frac{1}{2}$ pint) MILK
SALT AND FRESHLY GROUND PEPPER
900 g (2 lb) POTATOES, PEELED
4 EGGS

Serves 4

1. Melt 25 g (1 oz) of the butter in a pan and gently fry the cucumber until beginning to soften. Stir in the flour and coriander. Cook for 1 minute. Remove from the heat and gradually stir in the milk. Return to the heat and bring to the boil. Simmer for 3 minutes and season.

2. Grease a flameproof dish. Cook the potatoes in a pan of boiling salted water. Drain well and mash with the remaining butter. Season and spoon round the edge of the dish. Brown under the grill.

3. Meanwhile, bring a pan of water to the boil and softly poach the eggs. Drain and slip into the centre of the potato. Spoon over the cucumber sauce and serve at once.

Macaroni Cheese

175 g (6 oz) SHORT-CUT MACARONI
40 g ($1\frac{1}{2}$ oz) BUTTER
60 ml (4 tbsp) PLAIN FLOUR
568 ml (1 pint) MILK
SALT AND FRESHLY GROUND PEPPER
PINCH OF FRESHLY GRATED NUTMEG, OR 2.5 ml ($\frac{1}{2}$ tsp) PREPARED MUSTARD
175 g (6 oz) MATURE CHEDDAR CHEESE, GRATED
30 ml (2 tbsp) FRESH BREADCRUMBS

Serves 4

1. Bring a pan of salted water to the boil and cook the macaroni for 10 minutes. Drain well.
2. Melt the butter in a pan, stir in the flour and cook gently for 1 minute. Remove the pan from the heat and gradually stir in the milk. Return to the heat, bring to the boil and continue to cook, stirring, until the sauce thickens. Remove from the heat and add seasonings, 100 g (4 oz) cheese and the macaroni.
3. Pour into an ovenproof dish and sprinkle with the remaining cheese and the breadcrumbs.
4. Place on a baking sheet and bake in the oven at 200°C (400°F) mark 6 for about 20 minutes, until golden and bubbling, or brown under a very hot grill.

Photographed right

Hot Blue Cheese and Celery Mousse

225 g (8 oz) CELERY, TRIMMED AND FINELY SLICED
30 ml (2 tbsp) SINGLE CREAM OR TOP OF MILK
75 g (3 oz) DANISH BLUE CHEESE
3 EGG YOLKS
FRESHLY GROUND BLACK PEPPER
4 EGG WHITES
BUTTER
GRATED PARMESAN, TO GARNISH

Serves 4–6

1. Cook the celery in the minimum of water in a covered pan until really soft, about 30 minutes. Remove the lid and boil to evaporate the water completely.
2. Purée the celery with the cream and cheese until smooth. Cool slightly and beat in the egg yolks and black pepper. Whisk the egg whites until standing in stiff peaks and fold into the celery purée.
3. Lightly grease a 1.4 litre ($2\frac{1}{2}$ pint) soufflé dish and turn the mixture into it. Cover with greased foil.
4. Put into a steamer over boiling water, cover and steam for about 30 minutes. Serve at once dusted with Parmesan.

Macaroni Cheese

Blue Cheese Rarebits

125 g (4 oz) Danish blue cheese, grated
45 ml (3 tbsp) white wine
4 egg yolks, beaten
45 ml (3 tbsp) milk
salt and freshly ground black pepper
8 small slices rye bread, toasted

Serves 4

1. Put the cheese into a small heavy-based pan. Add the wine and stir over a low heat until the cheese has melted. Remove from the heat. Add the egg yolks to the milk and gradually stir into the cheese. Beat in the seasoning. Return to the heat and cook gently, stirring all the time until the mixture thickens.

2. Adjust the seasoning and spoon on to the slices of toast, pop under a hot grill to glaze golden brown. Serve as soon as possible.

Cheese and Corn Soufflé

142 g (5 oz) packet full-fat soft cheese with garlic and herbs
60–75 ml (4–5 tbsp) soured cream
198 g (7 oz) can sweetcorn niblets, drained
4 eggs, separated
salt and freshly ground pepper

Serves 4

1. Grease a 1.1 litre (2 pint) soufflé dish. Put the cheese into a large bowl and cream well with the soured cream. Stir in the sweetcorn niblets. Add the egg yolks. Season well and beat thoroughly.

2. Whisk the egg whites until standing in stiff peaks and gently fold into the cheese mixture. Turn into the prepared dish.

3. Bake at 180°C (350°F) mark 4 for about 40 minutes until well risen and golden on top. Serve immediately.

Grandma's Cheese Pudding

1.1 litres (2 pints) milk
125 g (4 oz) fresh breadcrumbs
450 g (1 lb) Cheddar cheese, grated
8 eggs
5 ml (1 tsp) French mustard
salt and freshly ground pepper

Serves 8

1. Bring the milk to the boil in a saucepan. Put the breadcrumbs into a bowl and pour the milk over. Stir in the cheese.

2. In a bowl, lightly beat the eggs with the mustard and with the milk and breadcrumbs. Season.

3. Butter a large, shallow 2.8 litre (5 pint) ovenproof dish well and pour in the cheese pudding mixture. Bake in the oven at 180°C (350°F) mark 4 for about 45 minutes, until lightly set and golden.

4. Serve with a mixed salad, see page 203.

Photographed on page 158

Grandma's Cheese Pudding

Courgettes au Gratin

6 COURGETTES, ABOUT 700 g ($1\frac{1}{2}$ lb), TRIMMED
50 g (2 oz) BUTTER
1 SMALL ONION, SKINNED AND CHOPPED
198 g (7 oz) CAN SWEETCORN, DRAINED
100 g (4 oz) PEELED PRAWNS
SALT AND FRESHLY GROUND PEPPER
30 ml (2 tbsp) PLAIN FLOUR
300 ml ($\frac{1}{2}$ pint) MILK
150 g (5 oz) CHEDDAR CHEESE, GRATED

Serves 6

1. Blanch the courgettes: put into a pan of boiling salted water for 8 minutes. Drain well. Cut a slice off the top of each and scoop out the flesh, leaving a 5 mm ($\frac{1}{4}$ inch) rim around the edge. Roughly chop the flesh, including the top slices. Turn the shells upside down and drain.

2. Melt half the butter in a pan and fry the onion until lightly browned. Stir in the chopped courgette flesh and cook over a high heat for a few minutes. Mix in the sweetcorn, the prawns and plenty of seasoning.

3. Place the courgette shells in a shallow ovenproof dish and fill with the prawn mixture.

4. Melt the remaining butter in a pan, stir in the flour and cook gently for 1 minute, stirring. Remove from the heat and gradually stir in the milk. Season, then return to the heat and bring to the boil. Continue to cook, stirring, until the sauce thickens. Remove from the heat and stir in 125 g (4 oz) cheese. Adjust the seasoning.

5. Spoon the cheese sauce over the courgettes and sprinkle with the remaining cheese. Cook in the oven at 200°C (400°F) mark 6 for 15–20 minutes, until golden.

Photographed opposite

Courgettes au Gratin

Leeks in Cheese Sauce

Leeks in Cheese Sauce

8 LEEKS, TRIMMED
50 g (2 oz) BUTTER
75 ml (5 tbsp) PLAIN FLOUR
568 ml (1 pint) MILK
100 g (4 oz) CHEDDAR CHEESE, GRATED
SALT AND FRESHLY GROUND PEPPER
8 THIN SLICES OF HAM OR BACON
30 ml (2 tbsp) FRESH BREADCRUMBS

Serves 4

1. Bring a pan of salted water to the boil and cook the whole leeks gently for 20 minutes, until soft. Drain and keep warm.

2. Meanwhile, melt about three-quarters of the butter in a pan, stir in the flour and cook gently for 1 minute, stirring. Remove the pan from the heat and gradually stir in the milk. Return to the heat and bring to the boil. Continue to cook, stirring, for about 5 minutes, then add 75 g (3 oz) cheese and seasoning to taste.

3. Wrap each leek in a slice of ham or bacon, place in an ovenproof dish and coat with the sauce. Top with breadcrumbs and the remaining cheese. Dot with the remaining butter and brown under the grill.

Photographed above

Cheese Fondue

1 GARLIC CLOVE, SKINNED AND CRUSHED
150 ml ($\frac{1}{4}$ pint) DRY CIDER OR DRY WHITE WINE
225 g (8 oz) MATURE CHEDDAR CHEESE, GRATED
10 ml (2 tsp) CORNFLOUR
FRESHLY GROUND PEPPER
PINCH OF FRESHLY GRATED NUTMEG
1 LIQUEUR GLASS BRANDY OR KIRSCH

Serves 4

1. Rub the inside of a fondue pot or flameproof dish with the garlic and pour in the cider or wine. Place the dish over a gentle heat and warm the liquid.

2. Add the cheese gradually and continue to heat gently, stirring, until all the cheese has melted.

3. Blend the cornflour and seasonings to a smooth paste with the brandy or kirsch and add to the cheese mixture. Continue cooking for a further 2–3 minutes. When the fondue reaches a very smooth consistency, it is ready to serve.

4. Fondue is traditionally served in the centre of the table, kept warm over a spirit lamp. Crusty cubes of bread are speared on long-handled forks and dipped into it.

Photographed opposite

Cheese Fondue

Savoury Cheesecake

Savoury Cheesecake

- 50 g (2 oz) BUTTER
- 75 g (3 oz) PLAIN POTATO CRISPS (PREFERABLY UNSALTED), CRUSHED
- 50 g (2 oz) WATER BISCUITS, CRUSHED
- 175 g (6 oz) FULL-FAT SOFT CREAM CHEESE
- 175 g (6 oz) ROQUEFORT CHEESE
- 3 EGGS
- 200 ml (7 fl oz) SINGLE CREAM
- 10 ml (2 tsp) GRATED ONIONS
- 2.5 ml ($\frac{1}{2}$ tsp) DRIED ROSEMARY
- FRESHLY GROUND PEPPER
- GHERKINS, TO GARNISH

Serves 4

1. Melt the butter in a pan and stir into the crisp and biscuit crumbs. Press over the base of a 23 cm (9 inch) flan dish. Cover and chill.

2. Beat the cheeses together until smooth, then beat in the eggs, cream, onion, rosemary and season with pepper.

3. Pour the cheese mixture into the flan case and cook at 180°C (350°F) mark 4 for about 40 minutes, or until well risen, just set and golden brown. Serve warm (not straight from the oven) garnished with gherkins.

Photographed above

VEGETABLES

Cauliflower Fritters

150 ml (¼ pint) MILK OR HALF MILK AND HALF WATER MIXED
15 ml (1 tbsp) CORN OIL
1 EGG, SEPARATED
125 g (4 oz) PLAIN FLOUR; PLUS 30 ml (2 tbsp)
SALT AND FRESHLY GROUND PEPPER
125 g (4 oz) CHEDDAR CHEESE, COARSELY GRATED
900 g (2 lb) CAULIFLOWER, TRIMMED AND BROKEN INTO LARGE FLORETS
OIL, FOR DEEP-FRYING
TOMATO SAUCE, TO SERVE (optional) (see page 210)

Serves 4

1. Put the milk, oil and egg yolk into a blender; add the 125 g (4 oz) flour and a pinch of salt. Switch on for 1 minute, then chill for 30 minutes.

2. Add the cheese to the chilled batter. Whisk the egg white in a bowl until standing in stiff peaks and lightly fold into the batter.

3. Bring a pan of salted water to the boil and cook the cauliflower until nearly tender, about 10 minutes. Drain well.

4. Season the remaining flour and dust the cauliflower in it. Lightly turn it in the batter, using a spoon and fork to coat it evenly. Heat the oil to 180°C (350°F) and fry the florets, a few at a time for 1–2 minutes, or until golden. Keep warm on a wire rack in a cool oven, uncovered, until they are all done. Serve at once with hot tomato sauce if wished.

Photographed opposite

Oven-fried Potato Balls

900 g (2 lb) OLD POTATOES, PEELED
2 EGGS, SEPARATED
SALT AND FRESHLY GROUND PEPPER
100 g (4 oz) FRESH WHITE BREADCRUMBS
90 ml (6 tbsp) CHOPPED PARSLEY
100 g (4 oz) MARGARINE

Serves 4

1. Cook the potatoes in boiling salted water until tender, about 20 minutes. Drain, return to the heat to dry and mash well. Beat in the egg yolks and season well. Cool and shape into 20 balls.

2. Mix the breadcrumbs and parsley. Whisk the egg whites lightly. Coat the potato balls first in the egg white and then in the breadcrumbs. Repeat.

3. Melt the margarine in a roasting tin, add the potato balls, shake the tin gently to coat with fat. Bake for 1½ hours in a 180°C (350°F) mark 4 oven.

Stir-fried Cabbage with Caraway

25 g (1 oz) BUTTER
45 ml (3 tbsp) OIL
450 g (1 lb) LAMBS' LIVER, THINLY SLICED AND CUT INTO 5 cm (2 inch) STRIPS
450 g (1 lb) GREEN CABBAGE, TRIMMED AND FINELY SHREDDED
225 g (8 oz) ONIONS, SKINNED AND CHOPPED
225 g (8 oz) EATING APPLES, CORED AND THINLY SLICED
15 ml (1 tbsp) CARAWAY SEEDS
30 ml (2 tbsp) CIDER VINEGAR
15 ml (1 tbsp) DEMERARA SUGAR

Serves 4

1. Heat together the butter and oil in a deep frying pan or wok. Brown the liver a few pieces at a time, stirring all the time—don't overcook them, the centres should be juicy. Remove with a slotted spoon.

2. Stir the cabbage and onion into the pan. Stir over a high heat for 4–5 minutes until the vegetables begin to soften.

3. Add the apples, caraway seeds, vinegar and sugar. Cook, stirring over a moderate heat for 1–2 minutes. Return the liver to the pan, season and reheat very quickly. Serve immediately.

Hot Corn-filled Tomatoes

8 LARGE TOMATOES, ABOUT 1.4 kg (3 lb) IN WEIGHT
50 g (2 oz) BUTTER
50 g (2 oz) PLAIN FLOUR
150 ml (¼ pint) MILK
198 g (7 oz) CAN SWEETCORN KERNELS, DRAINED
125 g (4 oz) FROZEN PRAWNS, THAWED
225 g (8 oz) GOUDA CHEESE, GRATED
5 ml (1 tsp) ANCHOVY ESSENCE
5 ml (1 tsp) LEMON JUICE
SALT AND FRESHLY GROUND PEPPER
PARSLEY SPRIGS, TO GARNISH

Serves 4

1. Cut a thin slice from the top of each tomato, scoop out and reserve the pulp leaving the tomato shell intact.

2. Melt the butter, stir in the flour. Cook for 2 minutes. Remove from the heat and gradually stir in the milk. Return to the heat and bring to the boil, stirring briskly. Continue to cook for another 3–4 minutes, stirring all the time as the consistency will be very thick. Remove from the heat, add the sweetcorn, prawns and 175 g (6 oz) of the cheese.

3. Sieve the tomato pulp into the sauce. Stir in the anchovy essence and lemon juice. Season.

4. Lightly season the inside of each tomato shell and divide the filling between them. Place in a baking tin.

5. Top with the remaining cheese. Bake uncovered at 200°C (400°F) mark 6 for 10–15 minutes. Garnish with parsley sprigs.

Cauliflower Fritters

Braised Celery

Braised Celery

50 g (2 oz) BUTTER
1 SMALL ONION, SKINNED AND FINELY CHOPPED
50 g (2 oz) CARROTS, PEELED AND FINELY CHOPPED
1 GARLIC CLOVE, SKINNED AND CRUSHED
4 SMALL CELERY HEARTS
150 ml ($\frac{1}{4}$ pint) CHICKEN STOCK
CHOPPED PARSLEY, TO GARNISH

Serves 4

1. Melt half the butter in a pan and gently fry the onion and carrot for 5 minutes. Add the garlic and transfer to an ovenproof casserole.

2. Evenly brown the celery hearts in the remaining butter and put on top of the vegetables. Spoon over the stock and season well.

3. Cover tightly and bake in the oven at 180°C (350°F) mark 4 for about $1\frac{1}{2}$ hours. Turn the celery hearts in the juices to glaze. Serve hot, scattered with chopped parsley.

Photographed left

Cabbage and Hazelnut Croquettes

450 g (1 lb) POTATOES, PEELED
900 g (2 lb) CABBAGE, TRIMMED AND ROUGHLY CHOPPED
45 ml (3 tbsp) MILK (optional)
50 g (2 oz) HAZELNUTS
50 g (2 oz) MARGARINE
50 g (2 oz) PLAIN FLOUR
SALT AND FRESHLY GROUND PEPPER
2 EGGS, BEATEN
225 g (8 oz) DRIED WHITE BREADCRUMBS
OIL, FOR DEEP-FRYING

Makes 16

1. Cook the potatoes in salted water for about 20 minutes, until tender. Drain and mash without adding any liquid.

2. Cook the cabbage in boiling salted water until just tender. Drain well. Purée in a blender, adding the milk if required—you should have 450 ml ($\frac{3}{4}$ pint) of purée.

3. Spread the hazelnuts out on a baking sheet and brown in the oven at 180°C (350°F) mark 4 for 15–20 minutes. Put into a soft tea-towel and rub off the skins. Chop.

4. Melt the margarine in a pan and stir in the flour. Cook for 1 minute and stir in the cabbage purée. Cook for 2 minutes, stirring then add the hazelnuts.

5. Stir the mashed potatoes into the sauce, season and mix well. Transfer to a bowl, cool, cover and chill well for at least $1\frac{1}{2}$ hours or until firm.

6. Grease a baking sheet. With dampened hands, shape the mixture into 16 croquettes, place on the baking sheet and chill again. Coat the croquettes in egg and breadcrumbs.

7. Heat the oil to 180°C (350°F) and fry the croquettes for about 4 minutes.

Mixed Glazed Vegetables

15–30 ml (1–2 tbsp) SESAME OIL
15–30 ml (1–2 tbsp) PEANUT OIL
175 g (6 oz) CARROTS, PEELED AND THINLY SLICED DIAGONALLY
175 g (6 oz) LEEKS, TRIMMED AND THINLY SLICED DIAGONALLY
175 g (6 oz) CELERY, TRIMMED AND THINLY SLICED DIAGONALLY
175 g (6 oz) CAULIFLOWER, TRIMMED AND BROKEN INTO SMALL FLORETS
225 g (8 oz) FROZEN GREEN BEANS OR 225 g (8 oz) BROCCOLI, TRIMMED AND BROKEN INTO SMALL HEADS
SMALL PIECE OF FRESH ROOT GINGER, PEELED AND SHREDDED, ABOUT 5 ml (1 tsp)
425 g (15 oz) CAN WHOLE BABY SWEETCORN, DRAINED
50 g (2 oz) DEMERARA SUGAR
45 ml (3 tbsp) LEMON JUICE
SALT AND FRESHLY GROUND PEPPER

Serves 4

1. Heat 15 ml (1 tbsp) each of the oils in a wok or large frying pan until smoky hot. Add all the vegetables and half the ginger. Cook over a high heat, stirring, for 2–3 minutes, adding more oil if necessary.

2. Stir in the sugar and lemon juice. Lower the heat, cook, stirring, for a further 3–4 minutes, until all the vegetables are just tender, yet still crunchy. Season and garnish with the remaining ginger. Serve immediately.

Photographed opposite

Potato and Courgette Savoury

900 g (2 lb) POTATOES, PEELED AND CUT INTO 3 mm ($\frac{1}{8}$ inch) SLICES
SALT AND FRESHLY GROUND PEPPER
75 g (3 oz) BUTTER OR MARGARINE
450 g (1 lb) COURGETTES, TRIMMED AND THINLY SLICED
225 g (8 oz) ONIONS, SKINNED AND THINLY SLICED
3 EGGS
450 ml ($\frac{3}{4}$ pint) MILK
15 ml (1 tbsp) DIJON MUSTARD
5 ml (1 tsp) DRIED BASIL

Serves 6

1. Blanch the potatoes: put into a pan of boiling salted water for 5–7 minutes, or until just tender. Drain well.

2. In a large frying pan, melt half the fat. Add the courgettes and onions and fry gently for 10–12 minutes, or until softened. Remove from the pan using slotted spoons.

3. In the same pan, melt the remaining fat. Gently fry the potato slices until pale golden.

4. Beat together the eggs, milk, mustard, basil and seasoning.

5. Layer the vegetables and milk mixture in a shallow 1.7 litre (3 pint) ovenproof dish, ending with a neat potato layer.

6. Place the dish in a roasting tin, half filled with water. Bake at 170°C (325°F) mark 3 for about 1$\frac{1}{4}$ hours until set and well browned.

Creamed Brussels

1 kg (2 lb) BRUSSELS SPROUTS, TRIMMED
SALT AND FRESHLY GROUND PEPPER
300 ml ($\frac{1}{2}$ pint) MILK
1 BABY CARROT, PEELED
1 BUTTON ONION, SKINNED
1 BAY LEAF
6 WHOLE BLACK PEPPERCORNS
50 g (2 oz) BUTTER
30 ml (2 tbsp) PLAIN FLOUR
LARGE PINCH OF FRESHLY GRATED NUTMEG
2 EGGS
25 g (1 oz) FRESH BREADCRUMBS

Serves 6

1. Cook the sprouts in boiling salted water for about 12 minutes, until tender. Drain and chop finely.

2. Bring the milk to the boil with the carrot, onion, bay leaf and peppercorns. Remove from the heat and leave to infuse for 10 minutes. Strain.

3. Melt 25 g (1 oz) butter in a saucepan, stir in the flour and cook gently for 1 minute, stirring. Remove from the heat and gradually stir in the strained milk. Season with salt and pepper.

4. Return to the heat and bring to the boil. Continue to cook, stirring, until the sauce thickens. Simmer for 2 minutes. Remove from the heat, stir in the chopped sprouts with a generous grating of nutmeg. Adjust the seasoning and beat in the eggs.

5. Lightly grease a 1.7 litre (3 pint) shallow soufflé dish. Spoon the mixture into it and sprinkle with the breadcrumbs. Dot with remaining butter and bake in the oven at 180°C (350°F) mark 4 for about 50 minutes, until set and golden.

Spicy Cauliflower Medley

30 ml (2 tbsp) SUNFLOWER OIL
2.5 ml ($\frac{1}{2}$ tsp) GROUND CUMIN
2.5 ml ($\frac{1}{2}$ tsp) GROUND CORIANDER
2.5 ml ($\frac{1}{2}$ tsp) MUSTARD POWDER
2.5 ml ($\frac{1}{2}$ tsp) GROUND TURMERIC
PINCH OF CAYENNE PEPPER
1 LARGE CAULIFLOWER, TRIMMED AND BROKEN INTO FLORETS
225 g (8 oz) CARROTS, PEELED AND SLICED
1 ONION, SKINNED AND CHOPPED
1 COOKING APPLE, PEELED, CORED AND CHOPPED
100 ml (4 fl oz) WATER
300 ml ($\frac{1}{2}$ pint) NATURAL YOGURT

Serves 4

1. Heat the oil in a large pan, add the spices and cook gently for 2 minutes, stirring. Add the cauliflower florets to the pan with the carrots, onion and apple. Cook for 5 minutes, stirring, until soft.

2. Add the water and yogurt, stir well, cover and simmer gently for about 10 minutes or until the vegetables are just tender.

Mixed Glazed Vegetables

Stir-fried Greens

30–45 ml (2–3 tbsp) OIL
450 g (1 lb) SPRING GREENS, TRIMMED AND FINELY SHREDDED
50 g (2 oz) STREAKY BACON, RINDED AND THINLY SLICED
125 g (4 oz) FROZEN PEAS
50 g (2 oz) ALFALFA SPROUTS
SALT AND FRESHLY GROUND PEPPER
142 g (5 oz) CARTON NATURAL YOGURT

Serves 4

1. Heat 30 ml (2 tbsp) oil in a wok or large frying pan until smoky hot. Stir in the greens, bacon and peas. Cook over a high heat for 3–4 minutes, until the peas are tender. Stir all the time, adding a little more oil if necessary. Stir in the alfalfa sprouts. Cook for 1 minute to heat through.

2. Season well and serve immediately drizzled with the yogurt.

Layered Potatoes and Swede

700 g (1½ lb) POTATOES, PEELED AND THINLY SLICED
700 g (1½ lb) SWEDES, PEELED AND CUT INTO THIN MATCHSTICKS
10 ml (2 tsp) CONCENTRATED BOUGHT MINT SAUCE
600 ml (1 pint) STOCK
SALT AND FRESHLY GROUND PEPPER
1.25 ml (¼ tsp) PAPRIKA
25 g (1 oz) MARGARINE OR BUTTER

Serves 4

1. Overlap half the potatoes around the edge of a shallow ovenproof dish and put half the swede in the centre.

2. Pour over the mint sauce and the stock. Season well and top with the remaining vegetables.

3. Sprinkle the paprika on to the margarine and beat it in then melt the mixture and spread on the vegetables. Bake uncovered at 180°C (350°F) mark 4 for 1½ hours.

Souffléed Parsnips

700 g (1½ lb) PARSNIPS, PEELED AND SLICED
2 EGGS, SEPARATED
300 ml (½ pint) MILK
75 g (3 oz) CHEDDAR CHEESE, GRATED
SALT AND FRESHLY GROUND PEPPER

Serves 4

1. Cook the parsnips in boiling salted water until tender, about 15 minutes. Drain well. Purée with the egg yolks and milk and mix with 50 g (2 oz) cheese and seasoning.

2. Whisk the egg whites and fold them into the purée.

3. Grease a deep 1.7 litre (3 pint) ovenproof dish. Turn the puréed mixture into it and top with the remaining cheese. Bake in the oven at 180°C (350°F) mark 4 for about 30 minutes.

Courgettes with Walnuts and Sage

4 LARGE COURGETTES, 700 g (1½ lb) TOTAL WEIGHT, TRIMMED
90 g (3½ oz) BUTTER
100 g (4 oz) ONIONS, SKINNED AND FINELY CHOPPED
50 g (2 oz) WALNUT PIECES, CHOPPED
50 g (2 oz) FRESH WHITE BREADCRUMBS
10 ml (2 tbsp) CHOPPED SAGE
15 ml (1 tsp) TOMATO PUREE
1 EGG, BEATEN
SALT AND FRESHLY GROUND PEPPER
30 ml (2 tbsp) PLAIN FLOUR
300 ml (½ pint) CHICKEN STOCK
30 ml (2 tbsp) CHOPPED PARSLEY
142 ml (5 fl oz) CARTON SINGLE CREAM

Serves 2

1. Score down the courgettes' skin at 1 cm (½ inch) intervals, halve lengthways and hollow out the centres using a teaspoon. Blanch: put into a pan of boiling water for 4 minutes. Drain well and cool. Butter an ovenproof dish.

2. Melt 25 g (1 oz) butter in a pan and fry the onion until golden. Remove from the heat and stir in the walnuts, breadcrumbs, half the sage, tomato purée, egg and plenty of seasoning.

3. Sandwich the courgettes with the stuffing. Put into the ovenproof dish and dot with 15 g (½ oz) butter.

4. Bake the courgettes covered at 190°C (375°F) mark 5 for about 35 minutes. Meanwhile, melt the remaining butter in a pan and stir in the flour. Cook for 1 minute then gradually add the stock, the remaining sage and the parsley. Stir until the sauce thickens and season.

5. When the courgettes are cooked, reheat the sauce, adding the cream at the last minute and pour over the courgettes.

Photographed opposite

Stir-fried Mushrooms and Beansprouts

15 g (½ oz) BUTTER
15 ml (1 tbsp) SUNFLOWER OIL
1 ONION, SKINNED AND FINELY SLICED
450 g (1 lb) MUSHROOMS, WIPED AND SLICED
225 g (8 oz) MUNG BEANSPROUTS
SALT AND FRESHLY GROUND PEPPER
GRATED RIND AND JUICE OF ½ AN ORANGE
25 g (1 oz) PEANUTS OR CASHEW NUTS

Serves 4

1. Heat the butter and oil in a large saucepan and fry the onion for 5 minutes until soft. Add the mushrooms and fry for a further 5 minutes until just tender.

2. Stir in the beansprouts, seasoning and orange rind and juice. Cook for a further 2–3 minutes, then spoon into a heated serving dish. Sprinkle with nuts and serve immediately.

Courgettes with Walnuts and Sage

Broccoli Amandine

1 kg (2 lb) BROCCOLI, TRIMMED
SALT AND FRESHLY GROUND PEPPER
50 g (2 oz) BUTTER
50 g (2 oz) FLAKED ALMONDS
30 ml (2 tbsp) LEMON JUICE

Serves 6

1. Cook the broccoli in boiling salted water for 10–15 minutes.

2. Meanwhile, melt the butter in another pan. Add the almonds and cook over a gentle heat for about 5 minutes until golden brown. Stir in the lemon juice and seasoning.

3. Drain the broccoli well and turn into a warmed serving dish. Spoon over the almond mixture.

Photographed on the cover

Creamed Butter Beans

350 g (12 oz) DRIED BUTTER BEANS, SOAKED OVERNIGHT AND DRAINED
50 g (2 oz) BUTTER
SALT AND FRESHLY GROUND PEPPER
CHOPPED PARSLEY, TO GARNISH

Serves 6

1. Put the beans into a pan, cover with water and bring to the boil. Lower the heat and simmer for $1\frac{1}{2}$–$1\frac{3}{4}$ hours, until the beans are quite tender.

2. Drain, then return to the pan and mash until smooth.

3. Push the purée to one side of the pan, melt the butter on the other side, then stir into the purée with seasoning. Stir over a low heat until thoroughly hot.

4. Spoon into a serving dish and scatter generously with parsley for serving.

Sauté Potatoes

- 1.4 kg (3 lb) POTATOES, SCRUBBED NOT PEELED
- SALT AND FRESHLY GROUND PEPPER
- 60 ml (4 tbsp) VEGETABLE OIL
- 50 g (2 oz) BUTTER
- 60 ml (4 tbsp) CHOPPED FRESH PARSLEY

Serves 8

1. Put the potatoes into a large pan of cold salted water, bring to the boil and cook steadily for 20 minutes, until almost tender.

2. Drain and keep warm. Peel and cut into large wedge-shaped pieces. Heat the oil in a large frying pan, add the butter and, when bubbling spoon in the potatoes.

3. Fry over a moderate heat, turning occasionally, until golden brown and flaky. Season well, add the parsley and serve.

Photographed right

Courgettes Provençale

- 25 g (1 oz) BUTTER
- 1 SHALLOT OR SMALL ONION, SKINNED AND CHOPPED
- 1 GARLIC CLOVE, SKINNED AND FINELY CHOPPED
- 6 COURGETTES, TRIMMED AND THICKLY SLICED
- 450 g (1 lb) TOMATOES, SKINNED AND SLICED
- 100 g (4 oz) CHEDDAR CHEESE, GRATED
- SALT AND FRESHLY GROUND PEPPER

Serves 4

1. Melt the butter and gently fry the shallot or onion and garlic for 2 minutes, until soft. Add the courgettes and fry for 10 minutes, turning frequently, until tender. Add the tomatoes and cook for a few minutes more, until the tomatoes are slightly pulpy.

2. Arrange the vegetables in layers with the grated cheese in an ovenproof dish, seasoning each vegetable layer with salt and pepper and finishing with a layer of cheese. Cook in the oven at 180°C (350°F) mark 4 for 30–40 minutes until the top is golden.

Mushrooms and Peas

- 50 g (2 oz) MARGARINE OR BUTTER
- 12 BIG FLAT MUSHROOMS, 350–450 g (12 oz–1 lb), STALKS REMOVED AND CHOPPED
- 75 g (3 oz) SPRING ONIONS, TRIMMED AND SNIPPED
- 225 g (8 oz) FROZEN PEAS
- SALT AND FRESHLY GROUND PEPPER

Serves 4

1. Melt the margarine in a pan and gently fry the mushroom stalks and spring onions. Stir in the frozen peas and season well.

2. Arrange the mushrooms in a single layer in a baking dish. Spoon the pea mixture on top. Cover and cook at 180°C (350°F) mark 4 for about 30 minutes.

Sauté Potatoes

Ratatouille

Onion and Carrot with Parsnip Sauce

225 g (8 oz) PARSNIPS, TRIMMED
300 ml ($\frac{1}{2}$ pint) MILK
50 g (2 oz) BUTTER
15 ml (1 tbsp) PLAIN FLOUR
1.25 ml ($\frac{1}{4}$ tsp) FRESHLY GRATED NUTMEG
SALT AND FRESHLY GROUND PEPPER
450 g (1 lb) CARROTS, PEELED AND CUT INTO 5 cm (2 inch) WEDGES
30 ml (2 tbsp) OIL
450 g (1 lb) ONIONS, SKINNED AND QUARTERED
30 ml (2 tbsp) CHOPPED PARSLEY

Serves 4

1. Bring a pan of salted water to the boil and cook the parsnips until tender. Drain and peel. Purée the parsnips and milk in a blender to give a smooth consistency.
2. Melt 25 g (1 oz) butter in a pan, stir in the flour and cook for 2 minutes before gradually stirring in the parsnip purée. Add the nutmeg and seasoning and bring to the boil, stirring, bubble gently for 3 minutes and keep warm.
3. Boil the carrots until tender, about 12 minutes and drain.
4. Heat the oil and the remaining butter in a frying pan and fry the onions until well browned and just tender. Arrange the onions and carrots in a serving dish. Keep warm loosely covered.
5. Before serving, stir the parsley into the sauce and pour over the vegetables.

Photographed opposite

Lentil Celery Ragout

50 g (2 oz) MARGARINE
350 g (12 oz) CELERY, TRIMMED AND CUT IN CHUNKS
175 g (6 oz) ONIONS, SKINNED AND CHOPPED
15 ml (1 tbsp) PAPRIKA
225 g (8 oz) RED LENTILS
600 ml (1 pint) STOCK
SALT AND FRESHLY GROUND PEPPER
45 ml (3 tbsp) NATURAL YOGURT

Serves 4

1. Melt the margarine in a pan and gently fry the celery and onions for 2 minutes. Stir in the paprika and cook 1 further minute, stirring.
2. Add the lentils and stock. Bring to the boil. Stir well and adjust the seasoning. Simmer uncovered for about 25 minutes, until all the liquid is absorbed, stirring occasionally. Stir in the yogurt before serving.

Ratatouille

5 ml (1 tsp) OLIVE OIL
225 g (8 oz) ONIONS, SKINNED AND SLICED
225 g (8 oz) GREEN AND YELLOW PEPPERS, SEEDED AND THINLY SLICED
225 g (8 oz) AUBERGINES, TRIMMED AND CUT INTO QUARTERS LENGTHWAYS
1 GARLIC CLOVE, SKINNED AND FINELY CHOPPED
SALT AND FRESHLY GROUND PEPPER
5 ml (1 tsp) DRIED OREGANO
4 TOMATOES, SKINNED AND CHOPPED
10 ml (2 tsp) WHITE WINE VINEGAR

Serves 6

1. Heat the oil in a wide heavy-based saucepan. Add the onions, cover the pan and cook for 5 minutes, until soft. Add the peppers, cover and continue cooking slowly for another 10 minutes until soft.

2. Cut the aubergines across into 5 mm ($\frac{1}{4}$ inch) slices. Stir the garlic into the softened onions and peppers. Mix in the aubergine and season with salt, pepper and the oregano. Cover and simmer for 10 minutes, turning once.

3. Add the tomatoes and vinegar, cover and cook gently for another 10 minutes until tender. Adjust the seasoning and serve hot or cold.

Photographed opposite

)nion and Carrot with Parsnip Sauce

Broad Beans in Parsley Sauce

1.8 kg (4 lb) BROAD BEANS, SHELLED
50 g (2 oz) BUTTER
75 ml (5 tbsp) PLAIN FLOUR
450 ml (¾ pint) CHICKEN STOCK
SALT AND FRESHLY GROUND PEPPER
2 EGG YOLKS
90 ml (6 tbsp) SINGLE CREAM
45 ml (3 tbsp) CHOPPED FRESH PARSLEY
30 ml (2 tbsp) LEMON JUICE

Serves 6

1. Cook the beans in a large pan of boiling water for about 15 minutes until tender. Drain and place in a vegetable dish. Keep warm, covered.

2. Prepare the sauce: melt the butter in a pan, stir in the flour and cook gently for 1 minute, stirring. Gradually stir in the stock, bring to the boil, and continue to cook, stirring, until the sauce thickens. Season and simmer for about 5 minutes.

3. Beat the egg yolks with the cream in a bowl, add 90 ml (6 tbsp) of the hot sauce and stir until blended.

4. Remove the pan from the heat, add the egg mixture and stir well. Return to the heat and cook over a low heat without boiling until the sauce thickens a little more. Stir in the parsley and lemon juice. Adjust the seasoning and pour over the broad beans.

Photographed opposite

Vichy Carrots

450 g (1 lb) NEW CARROTS, TRIMMED AND SCRUBBED
450 ml (¾ pint) COLD WATER
25 g (1 oz) BUTTER
SALT AND FRESHLY GROUND PEPPER
5 ml (1 tsp) DEMERARA SUGAR
CHOPPED PARSLEY, TO GARNISH

Serves 4

1. Put the carrots into a pan with the water, half the butter, a pinch of salt and the sugar. Bring to the boil and cook uncovered over a low heat, shaking occasionally towards the end, for about 45 minutes, until all the liquid has evaporated.

2. Add the remaining butter and ground pepper and toss the carrots until glazed. Sprinkle with parsley.

Fondant Potatoes

40 g (1½ oz) BUTTER
700 g (1½ lb) SMALL EVEN-SIZED NEW POTATOES, SCRUBBED
SALT

Serves 4

1. Melt the butter in a deep frying pan with a lid. Add the potatoes, cover and cook over a low heat. Shake the pan from time to time but do not lift the lid for the first 10 minutes as the steam inside helps the cooking and prevents sticking.

2. Test for tenderness, cook further if necessary. Serve sprinkled with salt.

Pease Pudding

350 g (12 oz) GREEN SPLIT PEAS, SOAKED OVERNIGHT AND DRAINED
1 SMALL CUBE OF HAM OR HALF A THIN BACON RASHER, CHOPPED
40 g (1½ oz) BUTTER
2 EGGS (optional)
SALT AND FRESHLY GROUND PEPPER

Serves 4

1. Tie the peas loosely in a cloth with the ham cube and place in a large pan of salted water. Boil gently about 2½ hours.

2. Remove the peas from the bag, discard the ham, beat in the butter and eggs (if using) and cook over a gentle heat to thicken slightly. Season with pepper.

Sweetcorn Fritters

125 g (4 oz) SELF-RAISING FLOUR
1.25 ml (¼ tsp) GROUND TURMERIC
PINCH OF SALT
1 EGG
JUST OVER 45 ml (3 tbsp) MILK
45 ml (3 tbsp) NATURAL YOGURT
198 g (7 oz) CAN SWEETCORN KERNELS, DRAINED
OIL, FOR SHALLOW-FRYING

Serves 4

1. In a bowl mix together the flour, turmeric, pinch of salt, egg, milk and yogurt. Stir in the sweetcorn.

2. Heat a little oil in a frying pan and drop in large spoonfuls of the sweetcorn batter. When browned on one side, about 2 minutes, turn the fritters over and brown the other side. Serve fresh from the pan.

Leek and Corn Slaw

700 g (1½ lb) LEEKS, TRIMMED AND THINLY SLICED
350 g (12 oz) WHITE CABBAGE, THINLY SLICED
335 g (11.8 oz) CAN SWEETCORN KERNELS, DRAINED
30 ml (2 tbsp) TOMATO KETCHUP
30 ml (2 tbsp) MAYONNAISE
SALT AND FRESHLY GROUND PEPPER

Serves 8

1. Blanch the leeks and cabbage together: put into a pan of boiling salted water for 2 minutes. Drain well. Rinse in cold water and drain.

2. Toss together the cabbage, leeks and sweetcorn. Add the tomato ketchup and mayonnaise and seasoning, stirring well to mix.

3. Spoon into a serving bowl, cover and refrigerate for several hours before serving. Take out of the refrigerator 30 minutes before eating, stir well.

Broad Beans in Parsley Sauce

Savoury Spring Cabbage

Spinach with Nutmeg

1.8 kg (4 lb) SPINACH, TRIMMED
SALT AND FRESHLY GROUND PEPPER
50 g (2 oz) BUTTER
LARGE PINCH OF FRESHLY GRATED NUTMEG

Serves 6

1. In a pan, gently cook the spinach (do not add liquid) for 3–4 minutes. Drain well and chop roughly.

2. Melt the butter in a saucepan, add the spinach with plenty of seasoning and cook over a moderate heat, stirring occasionally, until piping hot.

3. Add a generous grating of nutmeg and spoon into a serving dish.

Savoury Spring Cabbage

50 g (2 oz) BUTTER
700 g ($1\frac{1}{2}$ lb) YOUNG CABBAGE, FINELY SHREDDED
1 ONION, SKINNED AND GRATED
2 RASHERS STREAKY BACON, RINDED AND CHOPPED
PINCH OF FRESHLY GRATED NUTMEG

Serves 4

1. Heat the butter in a large saucepan. Add all the remaining ingredients. Cover the pan and cook very gently for 20–30 minutes, until the cabbage is just tender, shaking the pan frequently.

Photographed above

PASTA & RICE

Spaghetti Napoletana

30 ml (2 tbsp) OLIVE OIL
1.1 kg (2½ lb) TOMATOES, SKINNED AND QUARTERED
1 SMALL GARLIC CLOVE, SKINNED AND CRUSHED
2.5 ml (½ tsp) DRIED BASIL
5 ml (1 tsp) GROUND BAY LEAVES
10 ml (2 tsp) CASTER SUGAR
SALT AND FRESHLY GROUND PEPPER
275–350 g (10–12 oz) SPAGHETTI
25 g (1 oz) BUTTER, MELTED
50 g (2 oz) GRATED PARMESAN CHEESE

Serves 4

1. Heat the oil in a heavy-based pan. Add the tomatoes, garlic, herbs, sugar and seasoning. Bubble gently, uncovered until the tomatoes cook down to a thickish pulp, adjust the seasoning.
2. Meanwhile bring a large pan of salted water to the boil and cook the spaghetti for about 11 minutes. Drain, toss in the butter.
3. Spoon the tomato sauce over the spaghetti and top with grated Parmesan.

Pasta with Kidney Sauce

275–350 g (10–12 oz) PASTA BOWS
50 g (2 oz) BUTTER
75 g (3 oz) ONIONS, SKINNED AND THINLY SLICED
125 g (4 oz) BUTTON MUSHROOMS, WIPED AND THINLY SLICED
450 g (1 lb) LAMBS' KIDNEYS, CORED AND THINLY SLICED
60 ml (4 tbsp) PORT WINE
10 ml (2 tsp) CORNFLOUR
30 ml (2 tbsp) WATER
60 ml (4 tbsp) TOMATO CHUTNEY
SALT AND FRESHLY GROUND PEPPER
DASH OF VINEGAR

Serves 4

1. Bring a pan of salted water to the boil and cook the pasta for 10 minutes, stirring occasionally.
2. Melt the butter in a frying pan, add the onions and mushrooms and fry gently for 2 minutes, then add the kidneys and cook until they change colour. Add the port and bubble for 2 minutes.
3. Blend the cornflour to a cream with the water. Stir into the pan and use to thicken the sauce. Cook, stirring, for 3 minutes.
4. Add the tomato chutney and seasoning then add vinegar to taste.
5. Drain the pasta and put into a warmed serving dish. Pour over the kidney sauce.

Tortellini Bake

450 g (1 lb) AUBERGINES, TRIMMED AND CHOPPED
25 g (1 oz) BUTTER
450 g (1 lb) TOMATOES, SKINNED AND CHOPPED
1 GARLIC CLOVE, SKINNED AND CRUSHED
SALT AND FRESHLY GROUND PEPPER
225 g (8 oz) TORTELLINI
150 ml (¼ pint) MILK
227 g (8 oz) PACKET FULL-FAT CREAM CHEESE
15 ml (1 tbsp) GRATED PARMESAN CHEESE
30–45 ml (2–3 tbsp) DRIED BREADCRUMBS

Serves 4

1. Sprinkle the aubergines with salt and leave for 15–20 minutes. Rinse well, pat dry.
2. Melt the butter in a deep frying pan and slowly cook the aubergines, tomatoes and garlic until very soft. Season well.
3. Bring a pan of salted water to the boil and cook the tortellini for 15–18 minutes. Drain well.
4. Spoon the vegetable mixture into a shallow, ovenproof dish and layer the tortellini on top.
5. In a bowl, gradually beat the milk into the cream cheese whisking until smooth. Stir in 5 ml (1 tsp) Parmesan. Spoon evenly over the tortellini. Sprinkle the top with breadcrumbs and the remaining Parmesan.
6. Bake at 200°C (400°F) mark 6 for 25–30 minutes.

Pasta Bake

450 g (1 lb) MINCED BEEF
1 RED PEPPER, SEEDED AND SLICED
1 ONION, SKINNED AND CHOPPED
100 g (4 oz) BUTTON MUSHROOMS, WIPED AND SLICED
396 g (14 oz) CAN TOMATOES
5 ml (1 tsp) TABASCO SAUCE
SALT AND FRESHLY GROUND PEPPER
100 g (4 oz) WHOLEWHEAT SPAGHETTI RINGS
300 g (10 oz) NATURAL YOGURT
1 EGG, BEATEN
50 g (2 oz) PLAIN FLOUR
2 TOMATOES, SLICED
CHOPPED PARSLEY, TO GARNISH

Serves 4

1. In a saucepan, gently fry the mince in its own fat, until turning brown. Drain off any fat. Add the pepper, onion, mushrooms, the can of tomatoes and their juice, Tabasco sauce and seasoning; simmer gently for 10 minutes.
2. Meanwhile, bring a pan of salted water to the boil and cook the pasta for about 10 minutes, or until tender, but not soft. Drain. Place in a 1.4 litre (2½ pint) ovenproof dish and top with the mince mixture.
3. Beat together the yogurt, egg and flour until smooth and pour over the mince. Bake in the oven at 180°C (350°F) mark 4 for 40 minutes. Serve hot, garnished with tomatoes and chopped parsley.

Photographed opposite

Pasta Bake

Pasta with Peas and Ham in Cream Sauce

Pasta with Peas and Ham in Cream Sauce

275–350 g (10–12 oz) TAGLIATELLE OR SPAGHETTI
100 g (4 oz) FRESH OR FROZEN PEAS
100 g (4 oz) BUTTER
1 LARGE ONION, SKINNED AND SLICED
100 g (4 oz) HAM, CUT INTO THIN STRIPS
60 ml (4 tbsp) SINGLE CREAM
100 g (4 oz) CHEDDAR CHEESE, GRATED
SALT AND FRESHLY GROUND PEPPER

Serves 4

1. Bring a large pan of salted water to the boil and cook the pasta for about 10 minutes until tender, but not soft.
2. Meanwhile, bring a small pan of salted water to the boil and cook the peas.
3. Drain the pasta and the peas. Melt the butter in a pan, add the onion and cook for about 3 minutes until the onion is soft. Add the ham and peas and cook for a further 5 minutes.
4. Add the pasta, stir well and then add the cream and most of the cheese. Toss gently, add seasoning and serve at once, sprinkled with the remaining cheese.

Photographed opposite

Curried Seafood Pasta

225 g (8 oz) COD OR HADDOCK FILLETS
ABOUT 4 WHOLE BLACK PEPPERCORNS
150 ml (¼ pint) WATER
50 g (2 oz) BUTTER
50 g (2 oz) MUSHROOMS, WIPED AND SLICED
7.5 ml (1½ tsp) MILD CURRY POWDER
1 SMALL GARLIC CLOVE, SKINNED AND CRUSHED
30 ml (2 tbsp) PLAIN FLOUR
75 ml (5 tbsp) MILK
10 ml (2 tsp) LEMON JUICE
98 ml (3½ oz) CAN SHRIMPS
2.5 ml (½ tsp) WORCESTERSHIRE SAUCE
SALT AND FRESHLY GROUND PEPPER
150 g (5 oz) LARGE PASTA SHELLS
30 ml (2 tbsp) CHOPPED PARSLEY

Serves 2

1. Put the fish and the peppercorns in a saucepan with the water. Bring to boil, cover and poach gently for 10–15 minutes. Strain, reserving the stock.
2. Melt 25 g (1 oz) butter, add the mushrooms, curry powder, and garlic. Stir in the flour and cook for 1 minute. Remove from the heat and gradually add the milk. Return to the heat and stir in the lemon juice, fish stock, juices from the shrimps and Worcestershire sauce. Bring to boil, stirring briskly. Lower the heat and simmer for 5 minutes. Season.
3. Bring a pan of salted water to the boil and cook the pasta shells for about 12 minutes. Drain well.
4. In a deep frying pan melt the remaining butter, toss in the pasta, flaked fish, shrimps and parsley. Heat through. Season. Turn the pasta into a serving dish. Spoon over the hot curry and mushroom sauce.

Spinach and Ham Cannelloni

700 g (1½ lb) FRESH SPINACH
175 g (6 oz) BUTTER
50 g (2 oz) PLAIN FLOUR
300 ml (½ pint) MILK
125 g (4 oz) GOUDA CHEESE, GRATED
SALT AND FRESHLY GROUND PEPPER
6 SHEETS 18 × 7.5 cm (7 × 3 inch) LASAGNE
12 THIN SLICES OF COOKED SHOULDER HAM, PRE-PACKED
3 EGG YOLKS
10 ml (2 tsp) MADE MUSTARD
10 ml (2 tsp) LEMON JUICE
15 ml (1 tbsp) SNIPPED CHIVES

Serves 4

1. Well butter a round, shallow ovenproof dish. In a pan, gently cook the spinach (do not add liquid) for 3–4 minutes. Drain well and chop finely.
2. Melt 50 g (2 oz) butter in a pan and stir in the flour. Cook for 1 minute. Remove from the heat and gradually stir in the milk. Add the cheese and spinach. Return to the heat and bring to the boil. Cook, stirring, until it thickens, then season well.
3. Bring a large pan of salted water to the boil and cook the lasagne for about 15 minutes. Drain and halve each sheet crossways.
4. Place half the lasagne on a flat surface. Lay a slice of ham on top of each and top with a layer of spinach mixture. Roll up. Repeat, reversing spinach and ham.
5. Place the rolls in a single layer in the dish. Cover tightly with foil and bake at 200°C (400°F) mark 6 for 40–45 minutes.
6. Meanwhile, in a small bowl over simmering water, beat together the egg yolks, made mustard and lemon juice until the mixture thickens. Very gradually, beat in the remaining butter in small pieces to give a smooth thick sauce. Add the snipped chives. Pour into a jug and serve separately.

Tuna and Pasta in Soured Cream

225 g (8 oz) PASTA SPIRALS OR SHELLS
25 g (1 oz) BUTTER
142 ml (5 fl oz) CARTON SOURED CREAM
5 ml (1 tsp) ANCHOVY ESSENCE
30 ml (2 tbsp) MALT VINEGAR
198 g (7 oz) CAN TUNA, DRAINED AND FLAKED
4 HARD-BOILED EGGS, SHELLED AND CHOPPED
60 ml (4 tbsp) CHOPPED PARSLEY
SALT AND FRESHLY GROUND PEPPER

Serves 4

1. Bring a pan of salted water to the boil and cook the pasta for about 15 minutes. Drain well.
2. Melt the butter in a deep frying pan and toss in the pasta. Stir in the soured cream, anchovy essence and vinegar.
3. Add the tuna and eggs to the pan with the parsley. Season well and warm through over a low heat, stirring occasionally. Serve immediately.

Pasta with Broccoli

450 g (1 lb) BROCCOLI, TRIMMED AND BROKEN INTO FLORETS
90 ml (6 tbsp) OLIVE OIL
1 SMALL ONION, SKINNED AND SLICED INTO RINGS
4 ANCHOVY FILLETS
45 ml (3 tbsp) SULTANAS, SOAKED IN WARM WATER
25 g (1 oz) PINE NUTS
SALT AND FRESHLY GROUND BLACK PEPPER
400 g (14 oz) MACARONI OR LARGE-CUT TUBULAR PASTA
25 g (1 oz) BUTTER
50 g (2 oz) GRATED PARMESAN CHEESE

Serves 4 as a first course

1. Bring a large pan of salted water to the boil and cook the broccoli for 5–7 minutes, until tender. Drain well and set aside.
2. Heat 60 ml (4 tbsp) oil in a pan and gently fry the onion until soft and golden, but not brown. While the onion is cooking, heat the remaining oil in a small pan. Remove from the heat, add the anchovy fillets and mash with a fork.
3. Add the broccoli and anchovy paste to the onion and stir gently over low heat. Drain the sultanas and add to the broccoli sauce with the pine nuts. Season with pepper, taste and add salt if necessary.
4. Bring a pan of salted water to the boil and cook the pasta until it is firm to the bite. Drain it and turn into a warm serving dish. Toss with the butter and the cheese. Pour over the broccoli sauce and serve at once.

Chicken Apricot Pasta

175 g (6 oz) WHOLEWHEAT PASTA RINGS
25 g (1 oz) MARGARINE
1 ONION, SKINNED AND SLICED
1 SMALL RED PEPPER, SEEDED AND CHOPPED
25 g (1 oz) PLAIN FLOUR
600 ml (1 pint) CHICKEN STOCK
75 g (3 oz) DRIED APRICOTS, SOAKED OVERNIGHT AND DRAINED
350 g (12 oz) COLD COOKED CHICKEN
SALT AND FRESHLY GROUND PEPPER
10 ml (2 tsp) WORCESTERSHIRE SAUCE
CHOPPED PARSLEY, TO GARNISH

Serves 4

1. Bring a pan of salted water to the boil and cook the pasta for 15 minutes or until tender. Drain well and keep warm.
2. Melt the margarine in a saucepan and fry the onion and red pepper for 5 minutes until soft. Stir in the flour and cook for 2 minutes. Gradually stir in the stock and bring to the boil, stirring, to thicken.
3. Roughly chop the apricots and chicken, stir into the sauce, season well and add the Worcestershire sauce. Cover and simmer for 20 minutes.
4. Add the pasta to the mixture and mix well. Spoon into a heated serving dish and sprinkle with parsley.

Pasta and Frankfurter Scramble

4 EGGS
45 ml (3 tbsp) MILK
SALT AND FRESHLY GROUND PEPPER
175 g (6 oz) PASTA SHELLS
113 g (4 oz) PACKET FROZEN PEAS
25 g (1 oz) BUTTER OR MARGARINE
213 g (7½ oz) PACKET FRANKFURTERS, THINLY SLICED
SMALL BUNCH SPRING ONIONS, TRIMMED AND CHOPPED
5 ml (1 tsp) GROUND CUMIN

Serves 4

1. Whisk the eggs, milk and seasoning well together.
2. Bring a pan of salted water to the boil and cook the pasta until tender, adding the frozen peas for the last 5 minutes of cooking time.
3. Melt the fat in a large frying pan, add the frankfurters, onions and cumin and fry gently for about 5 minutes.
4. Drain the pasta and peas and add to the frankfurters with plenty of seasoning. Reheat, stirring, for 2–3 minutes.
5. Lower the heat and pour in the egg mixture stirring all the time until the eggs lightly scramble through the pasta. Serve at once.

Photographed opposite

Vegetable Lasagne

175 g (6 oz) GREEN LASAGNE
30 ml (2 tbsp) OIL
350 g (12 oz) COURGETTES, TRIMMED AND THINLY SLICED
225 g (8 oz) ONIONS, SKINNED AND THINLY SLICED
350 g (12 oz) TOMATOES, SKINNED AND THINLY SLICED
2.5 ml (½ tsp) DRIED BASIL
15 ml (1 tbsp) TOMATO PUREE
SALT AND FRESHLY GROUND PEPPER
25 g (1 oz) WALNUT PIECES, CHOPPED
454 g (16 oz) CARTON NATURAL YOGURT
2 EGGS
1.25 ml (¼ tsp) GROUND CUMIN
75 g (3 oz) CHEDDAR CHEESE, GRATED

Serves 4

1. Bring a pan of salted water to the boil and cook the lasagne for 15 minutes.
2. Heat half the oil in a pan. Reserve a few courgettes and fry the rest of the vegetables until the tomatoes begin to break down. Stir in the basil, tomato purée and season well.
3. Grease a 2 litre (3½ pint) deep-sided roasting tin. Drain the lasagne. Layer the lasagne, vegetables and nuts in the dish, ending with a layer of lasagne.
4. Season the yogurt, beat in the eggs and stir in the cumin and cheese. Pour over the lasagne.
5. Garnish with the reserved courgettes and brush with the remaining oil. Bake in the oven at 200°C (400°F) mark 6 for about 40 minutes until set.

Pasta and Frankfurter Scramble

Lasagne al Forno

Lasagne al Forno

OIL
125 g (4 oz) ONIONS, SKINNED AND ROUGHLY CHOPPED
50 g (2 oz) CARROTS, PEELED AND ROUGHLY CHOPPED
125 g (4 oz) BUTTON MUSHROOMS, WIPED AND THICKLY SLICED
50 g (2 oz) STREAKY BACON, RINDED AND SNIPPED
1 GARLIC CLOVE, SKINNED AND CRUSHED
450 g (1 lb) LEAN MINCED BEEF
227 g (8 oz) CAN TOMATOES, ROUGHLY CHOPPED
15 ml (1 tbsp) TOMATO PUREE
150 ml ($\frac{1}{4}$ pint) DRY WHITE WINE
300 ml ($\frac{1}{2}$ pint) BEEF STOCK
2 BAY LEAVES
SALT AND FRESHLY GROUND PEPPER
900 ml ($1\frac{1}{2}$ pints) MILK
1 SMALL ONION, SKINNED AND SLICED
1 SMALL CARROT, SKINNED AND SLICED
1 STICK CELERY, TRIMMED AND SLICED
6 WHOLE BLACK PEPPERCORNS
125 g (4 oz) BUTTER
75 g (3 oz) PLAIN FLOUR
225 g (8 oz) COOKED LASAGNE
75 g (3 oz) GRATED PARMESAN CHEESE

Serves 4

1. Heat 30 ml (2 tbsp) oil in a large frying pan, add the onion, carrot, mushrooms, bacon and garlic. Fry, stirring, for 1–2 minutes. Add the beef and cook over a high heat for a further 2 minutes. Stir in the tomatoes and juices, tomato purée, wine, stock and a bay leaf. Season. Bring to the boil, lower the heat to a simmer, cover and cook for about 35 minutes.

2. Meanwhile, pour the milk into a saucepan, add the sliced onion, carrot and celery, the peppercorns and remaining bay leaf. Bring slowly to the boil, remove from the heat, cover and leave to infuse for about 15 minutes.

3. Make the white sauce: strain the flavoured milk into a measuring jug. Melt the butter in a saucepan and stir in the flour until evenly blended. Remove from the heat and gradually add the milk, stirring all the time, until smooth. Return to the heat, bring to the boil, stirring. Cook for 1–2 minutes. Season.

4. Lightly grease the sides of a 2.8 litre (5 pint) shallow ovenproof dish. Spoon half the meat sauce over the base of the dish. Cover this with half the pasta, and spread over half of the white sauce. Repeat these layers once more topping with the white sauce to cover the pasta completely. Sprinkle the Parmesan over.

5. Stand the dish on a baking sheet. Cook in the oven at 180°C (350°F) mark 4 for about 1 hour, covering if necessary.

Photographed above

Spaghetti alla Carbonara

4 EGGS
142 ml (5 fl oz) CARTON SINGLE CREAM
25 g (1 oz) BUTTER
225 g (8 oz) STREAKY BACON, RINDED AND CHOPPED
350 g (12 oz) SPAGHETTI
175 g (6 oz) CHEDDAR CHEESE, GRATED
SALT AND FRESHLY GROUND PEPPER
30 ml (2 tbsp) CHOPPED FRESH PARSLEY

Serves 4

1. In a bowl, beat together the eggs and cream. Melt the butter in a frying pan and fry the bacon until crisp.

2. Meanwhile, bring a pan of salted water to the boil and cook the spaghetti for about 8 minutes until tender, but not soft. Drain and add it to the bacon.

3. Cook for 1 minute, stirring all the time. Remove from the heat and add the egg mixture. Mix well. (The heat of the spaghetti will be enough to cook the eggs.)

4. Stir in 125 g (4 oz) cheese and season with salt and pepper. Transfer to a serving dish and serve immediately, sprinkled with the parsley and remaining cheese.

Photographed below

Spaghetti alla Carbonara

Sausage Pasta Rolls

350 g (12 oz) WHOLEWHEAT LASAGNE
450 g (1 lb) FRESH BROCCOLI SPEARS
1.1 litre (2 pint) MILK
900 g (2 lb) PORK SAUSAGEMEAT
FINELY GRATED RIND AND JUICE OF 2 LEMONS
100 g (4 oz) FRESH WHITE BREADCRUMBS
SALT AND FRESHLY GROUND PEPPER
100 g (4 oz) BUTTER
100 g (4 oz) PLAIN FLOUR
100 g (4 oz) GRUYERE CHEESE, GRATED
225 g (8 oz) MATURE CHEDDAR CHEESE, GRATED

Serves 8

1. Bring a pan of salted water to the boil and cook the lasagne for 15–17 minutes.
2. In another pan, boil the broccoli for 15 minutes. Drain and chop roughly. Purée in a blender with 90 ml (6 tbsp) of the milk. Cool.
3. In a bowl, combine the sausagemeat, lemon rind and juice, breadcrumbs, cold broccoli purée and season well.
4. Grease two 1.7 litre (3 pint) shallow ovenproof dishes. Drain the lasagne. Halve each sheet crossways. Roll up with sausagemeat filling inside each piece. Place the rolls in a single layer in the dishes.
5. Melt the butter in a pan and stir in the flour. Cook for 1 minute. Remove from the heat and gradually stir in the remaining milk. Return to the heat and stir in the Gruyère cheese and seasoning. Continue to cook until thickened. Pour over the rolls and sprinkle Cheddar cheese on top.
6. Bake at 200°C (400°F) mark 6 for about 40 minutes, or until golden.

Red Pepper and Pasta Casserole

50 g (2 oz) LARD
900 g (2 lb) STEWING STEAK, CUBED
225 g (8 oz) ONIONS, SKINNED AND CHOPPED
10 ml (2 tsp) GROUND GINGER
10 ml (2 tsp) SOY SAUCE
1.1 litre (2 pint) BEEF STOCK
60 ml (4 tbsp) CHOPPED PARSLEY
SALT AND FRESHLY GROUND PEPPER
GRATED RIND OF 1 LARGE LEMON
350 g (12 oz) PASTA BOWS
400 g (14 oz) CAN PIMIENTO, DRAINED AND SLICED

Serves 8

1. Melt the lard in a large flameproof casserole and fry the meat a few pieces at a time.
2. Return all the meat to the pan with the onion, ginger, and soy sauce. Cook, stirring, for a few minutes.
3. Stir in the stock and parsley. Bring to the boil and season. Cover and simmer very gently for about 1½ hours until the meat is tender.
4. Add the lemon rind, pasta bows and pimiento. Cook gently for a further 15 minutes until the pasta is tender and much of the excess liquid has been absorbed. Adjust the seasoning.

Noodles in Walnut Sauce

75 g (3 oz) BUTTER, SOFTENED
30 ml (2 tbsp) PLAIN FLOUR
300 ml (½ pint) MILK
SALT AND FRESHLY GROUND PEPPER
100 g (4 oz) WALNUT PIECES
1 SMALL GARLIC CLOVE, SKINNED
275 g (10 oz) GREEN TAGLIATELLE
100 g (4 oz) LANCASHIRE CHEESE, GRATED

Serves 2 as a main course, 4 as a starter

1. In a blender, mix together 25 g (1 oz) butter, the flour and milk. Turn into a saucepan, bring slowly to the boil, stirring. Simmer gently for about 6 minutes, season well.
2. In the blender mix together the walnuts, remaining butter and the garlic.
3. Bring a pan of salted water to the boil and cook the tagliatelle for 6 minutes. Drain well. Return to the pan with the nut butter and heat through gently, stirring all the time.
4. Spoon into four large, individual gratin-type dishes. Coat with the sauce and scatter the grated cheese on top.
5. Grill for 5–10 minutes, until brown and bubbling. Serve immediately.

Photographed opposite

Spaghetti Bolognese

450 g (1 lb) MINCED BEEF
25 g (1 oz) BUTTER OR MARGARINE
100 g (4 oz) MUSHROOMS, SLICED (optional)
175 g (6 oz) ONIONS, SKINNED AND CHOPPED
2.5 ml (½ tsp) DRIED MARJORAM
1 BAY LEAF
15 ml (1 tbsp) PLAIN FLOUR
60 ml (4 tbsp) WATER
1 BEEF STOCK CUBE
396 g (14 oz) CAN TOMATOES
15 ml (1 tbsp) TOMATO PUREE
450 g (1 lb) SPAGHETTI
100 g (4 oz) GRATED PARMESAN CHEESE

Serves 4

1. In a saucepan, slowly fry the beef until beginning to brown. Turn out of the saucepan. Add 25 g (1 oz) butter to the pan and fry the sliced mushrooms (if using) for 5 minutes. Drain and set aside.
2. Reheat the fat in pan, add the onions and cook until beginning to brown. Stir in the marjoram, bay leaf, flour and mince. Slowly add the water, crumbled beef cube, tomatoes and purée. Bring to the boil, stir, lower the heat and simmer, covered, for 30 minutes.
3. Stir in the mushrooms and cook a further 5 minutes.
4. Bring a pan of salted water to the boil and cook the spaghetti. Drain well. On individual plates, pile the spaghetti, spoon over the bolognese sauce and hand freshly grated Parmesan cheese separately.

Noodles in Walnut Sauce

Chinese Fried Rice

200 g (7 oz) LONG-GRAIN RICE
SALT
225 g (8 oz) STREAKY BACON, RINDED
6 EGGS
75 ml (5 tbsp) VEGETABLE OIL
15 ml (1 tbsp) SOY SAUCE
30 ml (2 tbsp) CHOPPED SPRING ONIONS, TO GARNISH

Serves 3–4

1. Bring a pan of salted water to the boil and cook the rice for about 15 minutes, until just tender.

2. Meanwhile, fry the bacon in its own fat until crisp. Drain and cool. Drain the rice and set aside.

3. Beat together the eggs and 1.25 ml ($\frac{1}{4}$ tsp) salt. Heat 45 ml (3 tbsp) of the oil in a frying pan. Pour in the eggs and stir slowly over gentle heat until they leave the sides of the pan. Lower the heat and push the eggs to one side.

4. Add the rice and remaining oil to the pan and stir with a fork until the rice is well coated. Crumble the bacon and stir into the pan with the soy sauce and scrambled eggs and heat through gently. Spoon into a heated serving dish and sprinkle with chopped spring onions.

Photographed opposite

Rice with Peas

45 ml (3 tbsp) OLIVE OIL
1 LARGE ONION, SKINNED AND SLICED
225 g (8 oz) BROWN RICE
600 ml (1 pint) VEGETABLE STOCK OR WATER
450 g (1 lb) SHELLED PEAS
SALT AND FRESHLY GROUND PEPPER
CHOPPED PARSLEY, TO GARNISH

Serves 4

1. Heat the oil in a saucepan. Add the onion and cook for about 10 minutes, until lightly browned. Add the rice and cook for 2–3 minutes, stirring. Add the stock or water and bring to the boil. Lower the heat and simmer, covered, for 40–45 minutes, until the rice is just tender, adding more liquid if necessary.

2. Bring a pan of salted water to the boil and cook the peas for 10–12 minutes, until tender. Drain and stir into the cooked rice. Season well, sprinkle with chopped parsley.

Casseroled Yellow Rice

100 g (4 oz) DRIED APRICOTS, CUT INTO SMALL DICE
700 ml ($1\frac{1}{4}$ pints) BOILING WATER
225 g (8 oz) LONG-GRAIN RICE
2.5 ml ($\frac{1}{2}$ tsp) SALT
75 g (3 oz) ONIONS, SKINNED AND FINELY CHOPPED
25 g (1 oz) SEEDLESS RAISINS
2.5 ml ($\frac{1}{2}$ tsp) TURMERIC

Serves 4

1. Put the apricots into a bowl and pour over the boiling water. Leave to stand for 1 hour.

2. In an ovenproof casserole, combine the rice, salt, onion, raisins and turmeric.

3. Reboil the water and apricots and pour on to the contents of the casserole. Stir before covering and cook in the oven at 180°C (350°F) mark 4 for about 45 minutes until the water is absorbed and the rice tender.

Spanish Rice

KNOB OF BUTTER
4 RASHERS STREAKY BACON, RINDED AND CHOPPED
1 ONION, SKINNED AND CHOPPED
1 GREEN PEPPER, SEEDED AND CHOPPED
225 g (8 oz) LONG-GRAIN RICE
600 ml (1 pint) CANNED TOMATO JUICE
SALT AND FRESHLY GROUND PEPPER

Serves 4

1. Melt the butter in a frying pan and fry the bacon lightly for 2–3 minutes. Add the onion and pepper and fry for about 5 minutes, until soft. Stir in the rice, tomato juice and seasoning, bring to the boil and cover.

2. Lower the heat and simmer gently for 14–15 minutes. Stir lightly with a fork and serve.

Curried Rice

25 g (1 oz) BUTTER
1 ONION, SKINNED AND FINELY CHOPPED
225 g (8 oz) LONG-GRAIN RICE
25–50 g (1–2 oz) CURRANTS OR SEEDLESS RAISINS
2.5 ml ($\frac{1}{2}$ tsp) CURRY POWDER
600 ml (1 pint) CHICKEN OR BEEF STOCK
SALT AND FRESHLY GROUND PEPPER
25 g (1 oz) BLANCHED ALMONDS, SLIVERED

Serves 4

1. Melt the butter in a frying pan and fry the onion for about 5 minutes, until soft. Add the rice and fry for a further 2–3 minutes, stirring all the time.

2. Add the fruit, curry powder, stock and seasoning and bring to the boil. Stir and cover. Lower the heat and simmer gently for 14–15 minutes. Stir in the almonds and serve.

Chinese Fried Rice and Stir-Fried Pork and Vegetables (page 86)

Paella

Vegetable and Egg Risotto

15 ml (1 tbsp) VEGETABLE OIL
1 ONION, SKINNED AND CHOPPED
175 g (6 oz) BROWN RICE
600 ml (1 pint) VEGETABLE STOCK
15 ml (1 tbsp) TAMARI SAUCE
SALT AND FRESHLY GROUND PEPPER
75 g (3 oz) MUSHROOMS, WIPED AND SLICED
175 g (6 oz) MUNG BEANSPROUTS
50 g (2 oz) TOASTED PEANUTS
4 HARD-BOILED EGGS, SHELLED AND ROUGHLY CHOPPED
CHOPPED PARSLEY, TO GARNISH

Serves 4

1. Heat the oil in a large frying pan and gently fry the onion for 5 minutes until soft. Add the rice and cook for a further 1 minute. Stir in the stock and tamari sauce and season well. Cover and simmer gently for 40–45 minutes, until the rice is just tender.

2. Stir the mushrooms into the rice with the beansprouts, nuts and eggs. Stir-fry for 8 minutes, until the mushrooms are just tender and the beansprouts still crisp. Spoon into a heated serving dish and sprinkle with parsley.

Paella

225 g (8 oz) ITALIAN SAUSAGES
45 ml (3 tbsp) OLIVE OIL
4 CHICKEN LEGS, DIVIDED INTO DRUMSTICKS AND THIGHS
1 LARGE GREEN PEPPER, SEEDED AND SLICED
1 GARLIC CLOVE, SKINNED AND CRUSHED
825 g (1 lb 12 oz) CAN TOMATOES
2.5 ml (½ tsp) GROUND CINNAMON
SALT AND FRESHLY GROUND PEPPER
1.25 ml (¼ tsp) SAFFRON (optional)
30 ml (2 tbsp) HOT WATER (optional)
275 g (10 oz) LONG-GRAIN RICE
50 g (2 oz) PIMIENTOS, SLICED
450 lb (1 lb) PRAWNS, SHELLED
275 g (10 oz) FROZEN PEAS, THAWED
12 BOTTLED MUSSELS, DRAINED

Serves 6–8

1. Cook the sausages in a little water in a covered pan for about 5 minutes. Cook uncovered for a further 20 minutes until the sausages are very well browned. Remove them from the pan, leave to cool and then cut into 1 cm (½ inch) slices.

2. Heat the oil in a large, deep frying pan and fry the chicken until well browned on all sides. Add the green pepper and garlic and cook for a further 2 minutes, until the pepper has softened.

3. Stir in the tomatoes with their liquid, the cinnamon and seasonings and bring to the boil. Lower the heat, cover and simmer for 30 minutes or until the chicken is tender, stirring occasionally.

4. Mix the saffron and water together (if using) and add to the dish with the rice and pimientos. Bring to the boil, lower the heat, cover the pan and simmer gently for a further 15 minutes.

5. Stir in the sausage, prawns and peas, and put the mussels on the top. Cover again and simmer for 5–10 minutes until the mussels are heated through, the rice is tender and all of the liquid has been absorbed.

Photographed opposite

Mince with Rice

25 g (1 oz) BUTTER
1 LARGE ONION, CHOPPED
2 STICKS CELERY, TRIMMED AND CHOPPED (optional)
50 g (2 oz) MUSHROOMS, WIPED AND SLICED
450 g (1 lb) FRESH MINCED MEAT
175–225 g (6–8 oz) LONG-GRAIN RICE
425 g (15 oz) CAN TOMATOES, MADE UP TO 900 ml (1½ pints) WITH STOCK OR WATER
SALT AND FRESHLY GROUND PEPPER
PINCH OF DRIED HERBS
½ BAY LEAF

Serves 4

1. Melt the butter in a pan and fry the onion and celery (if using) for 5 minutes, until soft. Stir in the mushrooms then add the meat and fry until lightly browned.

2. Stir the rice into the pan and continue frying for a further few minutes. Pour in the tomatoes and liquid and add the seasoning and herbs. Bring to the boil, cover and simmer gently until the meat is tender, the rice soft and the liquid absorbed.

Risotto alla Milanese

75 g (3 oz) BUTTER
1 ONION, SKINNED AND FINELY CHOPPED
225 g (8 oz) LONG-GRAIN RICE
150 ml (¼ pint) WHITE WINE
600 ml (1 pint) BOILING CHICKEN STOCK
PINCH POWDERED SAFFRON (optional)
SALT AND FRESHLY GROUND PEPPER
30–45 ml (2–3 tbsp) GRATED PARMESAN CHEESE

Serves 4

1. Melt 50 g (2 oz) butter in a pan and add the onion. Fry gently for about 5 minutes until golden.

2. Add the rice and continue frying, stirring constantly, until the rice looks transparent.

3. Pour in the wine and boil rapidly until well reduced. Add the stock, saffron (if using) and seasoning. Cover and cook for 15–20 minutes or until the rice is tender.

4. Add the remaining butter and half the cheese and stir them into the rice with a fork until the cheese melts. Spoon into a heated serving dish and sprinkle with the remaining cheese.

Photographed on page 194

Risotto alla Milanese (page 193) and Osso Buco (page 96)

SALADS

Red Cabbage and Apple Salad

- ½ RED CABBAGE, ABOUT 900 g (2 lb), FINELY SHREDDED
- 3 EATING APPLES, PEELED, CORED AND SLICED
- 1 SMALL GARLIC CLOVE, SKINNED
- 300 ml (½ pint) SALAD OIL
- 150 ml (¼ pint) CIDER VINEGAR
- 60 ml (4 tbsp) NATURAL YOGURT
- SALT AND FRESHLY GROUND PEPPER

Serves 8

1. Blanch the cabbage: put into a pan of boiling water for 2–3 minutes. Drain and cool.
2. Combine the apples with the cabbage in a bowl. Put the rest of the ingredients in a screw-top jar and shake well. Pour at once over the cabbage and toss.
3. Refrigerate the salad covered overnight. Toss again to mix well before serving.

Photographed opposite

Russian Salad

- 1 SMALL CAULIFLOWER, TRIMMED AND BROKEN INTO SMALL FLORETS
- 125 g (4 oz) TURNIPS, PEELED AND DICED
- 125 g (4 oz) CARROTS, PEELED AND DICED
- 225 g (8 oz) POTATOES, PEELED AND DICED
- 125 g (4 oz) SHELLED PEAS
- SALT AND FRESHLY GROUND PEPPER
- 150 ml (¼ pint) MAYONNAISE (see page 210)
- LEMON JUICE
- 1 SMALL COOKED BEETROOT, SKINNED AND DICED
- 2 TOMATOES, SKINNED AND DICED
- 125 g (4 oz) COOKED TONGUE, DICED
- 125 g (4 oz) PRAWNS, PEELED
- 4 GHERKINS, CHOPPED
- 30 ml (2 tbsp) CAPERS
- 6 OLIVES AND 6 ANCHOVIES, TO GARNISH

Serves 4

1. Bring a pan of salted water to the boil and cook the cauliflower for about 8 minutes until tender. Drain, rinse in cold water and drain again. In the same way cook, rinse and drain the turnips, carrots, potatoes and peas.
2. Put a layer of cauliflower in a deep salad bowl and season well. Thin the mayonnaise with a little lemon juice and spread a little over the cauliflower. Layer the turnips, carrots, potatoes, peas, beetroot, tomatoes, tongue and prawns in the same way, ending with a layer of mayonnaise.
3. Sprinkle over the gherkins and capers and garnish with the olives and anchovies.

Red Bean and Chicken Salad

- 45 ml (3 tbsp) WINE VINEGAR
- 90 ml (6 tbsp) OLIVE OIL
- 2.5 ml (½ tsp) DRIED SAGE
- SALT AND FRESHLY GROUND PEPPER
- 1.1 kg (2½ lb) OVEN-READY ROASTING CHICKEN
- 225 g (8 oz) RED KIDNEY BEANS, SOAKED OVERNIGHT AND DRAINED
- 2 CHICKEN STOCK CUBES
- 1.1 litre (2 pints) BOILING WATER
- 1 BAY LEAF
- 100 g (4 oz) SPRING ONIONS, TRIMMED AND CHOPPED
- 198 g (7 oz) CAN CORN NIBLETS, DRAINED

Serves 6

1. Put the vinegar, oil, sage and seasonings to taste into a screw-top jar and shake together. Leave to infuse while cooking the chicken.
2. Put the beans into a pan and cover with water. Bring to the boil and boil for 10 minutes. Drain and put into a deep pan with the whole chicken.
3. Add the crumbled stock cubes and water to the pan with the bay leaf, 15 ml (1 tbsp) salt and pepper. Cover, bring to the boil, lower the heat and simmer for about 1 hour, or until both chicken and beans are tender.
4. Drain and cool the chicken and beans. Use the well-flavoured stock for another dish. Carve off all the meat from the carcass discarding the skin. Chop the meat roughly.
5. Combine the chicken with the spring onions. Combine the beans and corn. Pile the chicken in the centre of a dish with the bean mixture round it. Reshake the dressing and pour over the chicken salad. Chill to serve.

Tuna and Cauliflower

- ABOUT 225 g (8 oz) CAULIFLOWER, TRIMMED AND BROKEN INTO SMALL FLORETS
- 142 g (5 oz) CARTON NATURAL YOGURT
- 15 ml (1 tbsp) SNIPPED CHIVES
- 1.25 ml (¼ tsp) DRY MUSTARD
- 1 SMALL GARLIC CLOVE, SKINNED AND CRUSHED
- 5 ml (1 tsp) LEMON JUICE
- SALT AND FRESHLY GROUND PEPPER
- 198 g (7 oz) CAN TUNA, DRAINED AND FLAKED
- 1 RED EATING APPLE, CORED AND DICED
- LETTUCE LEAVES, TO SERVE

Serves 2

1. Blanch the cauliflower: put into a pan of boiling salted water for 2 minutes. Drain and plunge into cold water. Drain again.
2. In a bowl, combine the yogurt, chives, mustard, garlic, lemon juice and seasonings.
3. Add the cauliflower, tuna and apple to the bowl and fold through.
4. Line two plates with lettuce leaves and arrange the mixed ingredients on top.

Red Cabbage and Apple Salad

Coleslaw (page 201), at the back, and Greek Salad

Greek Salad

2 LARGE TOMATOES, CUT INTO EIGHTHS
1 GREEN PEPPER, SEEDED AND THINLY SLICED
½ CUCUMBER, THICKLY SLICED
50 g (2 oz) BLACK OR STUFFED OLIVES, HALVED AND STONED
225 g (8 oz) FETA CHEESE, DICED
120 ml (8 tbsp) OLIVE OIL
30–45 ml (2–3 tbsp) LEMON JUICE
SALT AND FRESHLY GROUND PEPPER
PITTA BREAD, TO SERVE

Serves 4

1. Arrange the tomatoes, green pepper, cucumber and olives in a salad bowl. Add the cheese, reserving a few dice, for garnish.
2. Pour over the olive oil, followed by the lemon juice. Season well and crumble over the remaining cheese cubes. Serve with pitta bread.

Photographed above

Waldorf Salad

450 g (1 lb) EATING APPLES
LEMON JUICE
5 ml (1 tsp) SUGAR
150 ml (¼ pint) MAYONNAISE (see page 210)
½ HEAD CELERY, TRIMMED AND SLICED
50 g (2 oz) WALNUTS, CHOPPED
1 LETTUCE, TRIMMED AND SEPARATED

Serves 4

1. Core the apples, slice one and dice the rest. Dip the slices in lemon juice to prevent discoloration. Toss the diced apples in 30 ml (2 tbsp) lemon juice, the sugar and 15 ml (1 tbsp) mayonnaise.
2. Just before serving, add the celery, walnuts and remaining mayonnaise and toss together. Line a bowl with the lettuce leaves and spoon in the mixed ingredients.

Photographed on page 200

Cold Beef in Soured Cream

30 ml (2 tbsp) CORN OIL
450 g (1 lb) LEAN RUMP STEAK IN A THIN SLICE, CUT INTO THIN STRIPS
SALT AND FRESHLY GROUND PEPPER
1 ONION, SKINNED AND FINELY CHOPPED
225 g (8 oz) BUTTON MUSHROOMS, WIPED AND THINLY SLICED
5 ml (1 tsp) FRENCH MUSTARD
2.5 ml (½ tsp) DRIED THYME
1 GREEN EATING APPLE, THINLY SLICED
142 ml (5 fl oz) CARTON SOURED CREAM
15 ml (1 tbsp) LEMON JUICE
LETTUCE LEAVES AND SLICES OF TOAST, TO SERVE

Serves 4

1. Heat the oil in a large frying pan. When hot quickly brown steak in a shallow layer, turning occasionally. Don't crowd the pan, the meat should remain pink in the centre.
2. Transfer the beef to a bowl using a slotted spoon. Season with salt and pepper.
3. Reheat the fat remaining in the pan and fry the onion until golden brown. Add the mushrooms, mustard and thyme. Fry over high heat for 1 minute. Add to the beef, cover and leave to cool.
4. Combine the apple with the soured cream and lemon juice in a bowl.
5. To serve, line a shallow dish with crisp lettuce. Combine the contents of the bowls. Adjust the seasoning and pile into centre of the lettuce. Tuck in slices of freshly toasted bread.

Photographed below

Cold Beef in Soured Cream

Waldorf Salad (page 198), at the back, and Salad Niçoise

Coleslaw

WHITE CABBAGE, TRIMMED AND FINELY SHREDDED
1 LARGE CARROT, PEELED AND GRATED
1 LARGE ONION, SKINNED AND FINELY CHOPPED
45 ml (3 tbsp) CHOPPED PARSLEY
STICKS CELERY, TRIMMED AND SLICED
SALT AND FRESHLY GROUND PEPPER
200 ml (7 fl oz) SALAD CREAM
WATERCRESS, TO GARNISH (optional)

Serves 8

1. In a large bowl, combine the cabbage, carrot, onion, parsley and celery, tossing well together.

2. Season the salad cream well, pour over the vegetables and toss until well coated.

3. Cover and chill in the refrigerator for several hours before serving. Garnish with watercress, if wished.

Photographed on page 198

Two-cheese Egg Salad

125 g (4 oz) SHELLED HAZELNUTS
175 g (6 oz) LONG-GRAIN RICE
HARD-BOILED EGGS, SHELLED AND HALVED LENGTHWAYS
75 g (3 oz) DANISH BLUE CHEESE
75 g (3 oz) FULL-FAT SOFT CHEESE
100 ml (4 fl oz) SINGLE CREAM
SALT AND FRESHLY GROUND PEPPER
227 g (8 oz) CAN PINEAPPLE CHUNKS, DRAINED WITH 60 ml (4 tbsp) JUICE RESERVED
15 ml (1 tbsp) WHITE WINE VINEGAR
SMALL BUNCH WATERCRESS

Serves 6

1. Spread the nuts out on a baking sheet and brown in the oven at 180°C (350°F) mark 4 for 15–20 minutes.

2. Bring a pan of salted water to the boil and cook the rice for about 15 minutes, until just tender. Drain well and cool.

3. Put the toasted hazelnuts into a soft tea-towel and rub off the skins. Chop 25 g (1 oz) of them.

4. Scoop out the egg yolks and press them through a sieve into a bowl. Place the egg whites in a bowl of cold water until required.

5. Add the Danish Blue and full-fat soft cheese, the chopped nuts, cream and seasoning to the egg yolks and beat until well mixed.

6. Combine the rice with the pineapple chunks and reserved juice. Stir in the vinegar with the whole hazelnuts, reserving 12 for garnish. Season to taste. Spoon the rice salad into the centre of a serving dish and put watercress sprigs around the edge.

7. Drain the egg whites and pat them dry with absorbent kitchen paper. Spoon the egg and cheese mixture into a piping bag fitted with a 1 cm (½ inch) plain nozzle and pipe the mixture into the centres of the egg whites. Sit the eggs on the watercress and top each with a whole hazelnut.

Salade Niçoise

198 g (7 oz) CAN TUNA FISH, DRAINED AND FLAKED INTO LARGE CHUNKS
225 g (8 oz) TOMATOES, SKINNED AND QUARTERED
50 g (2 oz) BLACK OLIVES, STONED
½ SMALL CUCUMBER, THINLY SLICED
225 g (8 oz) COOKED FRENCH BEANS
2 HARD-BOILED EGGS, SHELLED AND QUARTERED
90 ml (6 tbsp) SALAD OIL
45 ml (3 tbsp) VINEGAR
1 LARGE GARLIC CLOVE, SKINNED AND CRUSHED
SALT AND FRESHLY GROUND PEPPER
15 ml (1 tbsp) CHOPPED PARSLEY
15 ml (1 tbsp) CHOPPED BASIL
8 ANCHOVIES, HALVED
FRENCH BREAD, TO SERVE

Serves 4

1. Arrange the tuna chunks in a salad bowl with the tomatoes, olives, cucumber, beans and egg quarters.

2. Put the oil, vinegar and garlic into a screw-top jar. Add the seasoning and the herbs. Mix well and pour over the salad.

3. Arrange the anchovy fillets in a pattern over the salad and allow to stand for 30 minutes before serving. Serve with French bread.

Photographed opposite

Garden Salad

½ SMALL CAULIFLOWER
1 LARGE ONION, SKINNED AND DICED
1 CUCUMBER, DICED
1 LARGE GREEN PEPPER, SEEDED AND CUT INTO THIN STRIPS
1 LARGE RED PEPPER, SEEDED AND CUT INTO THIN STRIPS
225 g (8 oz) YOUNG SPINACH, TRIMMED AND ROUGHLY CHOPPED
10 ml (2 tsp) SUGAR
5 ml (1 tsp) PAPRIKA
5 ml (1 tsp) THYME
5 ml (1 tsp) CHOPPED PARSLEY
90 ml (6 tbsp) SALAD OIL
45 ml (3 tbsp) VINEGAR
1 LARGE GARLIC CLOVE, SKINNED AND CRUSHED (optional)
SALT AND FRESHLY GROUND PEPPER

Serves 4

1. Soak the cauliflower in salted water for 30 minutes. Wash, drain and break into florets.

2. Combine the prepared vegetables with the sugar, paprika and herbs.

3. Put the oil, vinegar and garlic (if using) into a screw-top jar. Shake well and pour over the salad ingredients.

Spinach and Avocado Salad

Spinach and Avocado Salad

125 g (4 oz) STREAKY BACON, RINDED
45 ml (3 tbsp) SALAD OIL
15 ml (1 tbsp) WHITE WINE VINEGAR
2.5 ml ($\frac{1}{2}$ tsp) DRIED OREGANO
15 ml (1 tbsp) SNIPPED FRESH CHIVES
350 g (12 oz) SPINACH, TRIMMED
125 g (4 oz) CAERPHILLY CHEESE, CUT INTO 1 cm ($\frac{1}{2}$ inch) CUBES
50 g (2 oz) SPRING ONIONS, TRIMMED AND SNIPPED
2 RIPE AVOCADOS, STONES REMOVED, PEELED AND THINLY SLICED

Serves 4

1. Grill the bacon until crisp. Cool and snip into small pieces.

2. Put the oil, vinegar, oregano and chives into a screw-top jar and whisk or shake well together. Put all the salad ingredients in a bowl, pour over the dressing and toss lightly.

Photographed above

Fennel and Watercress Salad

700 g ($1\frac{1}{2}$ lb) FLORENCE FENNEL, TRIMMED AND THINLY SLICED, RESERVING LEAVES, TO GARNISH
LEMON JUICE
SALT AND FRESHLY GROUND PEPPER
90 ml (6 tbsp) OLIVE OIL
45 ml (3 tbsp) WHITE WINE VINEGAR
1 LARGE BUNCH WATERCRESS, TRIMMED, STALKS FINELY CHOPPED

Serves 6

1. Blanch the fennel: put into a pan of boiling salted water with a squeeze of lemon juice, for 2 minutes only. Drain well.

2. In a bowl, mix the oil, vinegar, watercress stalks and seasoning. Add the fennel and stir to coat with dressing. Cover with cling film and refrigerate for several hours. Put the watercress sprigs into a polythene bag and refrigerate.

3. Just before serving, stir in the watercress sprigs and garnish with snipped fennel leaves.

Rice Salad

450 g (1 lb) LONG-GRAIN RICE
TWO 227 g (8 oz) PACKETS FROZEN MIXED VEGETABLES (PEAS, SWEETCORN AND PEPPERS)
90 ml (6 tbsp) SALAD OIL
45 ml (3 tbsp) VINEGAR
1 GARLIC CLOVE, SKINNED AND CRUSHED (optional)
SALT AND FRESHLY GROUND PEPPER
16 STUFFED OLIVES, SLICED (optional)

Serves 8

1. Bring a pan of salted water to the boil and cook the rice for 10 minutes until tender. Drain and rinse in cold water. Drain well and place in a large serving bowl.
2. Cook the frozen vegetables as directed on the packet, drain and rinse in cold water, then drain again and add to the rice. Stir well together.
3. Put the oil, vinegar and garlic (if using) into a screw-top jar. Season well and shake. Pour over the rice mixture and toss well together. Add the olives, if wished.

Lemon-dressed Avocado Salad

½ SMALL CUCUMBER, SKINNED AND DICED
SALT AND FRESHLY GROUND PEPPER
2 RIPE AVOCADOS
150 ml (¼ pint) VEGETABLE OIL
60 ml (4 tbsp) LEMON JUICE
10 ml (2 tsp) CLEAR HONEY
4 STICKS CELERY, TRIMMED AND THINLY SLICED
50 g (2 oz) SALTED PEANUTS
PAPRIKA PEPPER, TO GARNISH

Serves 6

1. Sprinkle the cucumber with salt to draw out the juices and leave for 20 minutes. Dry on absorbent kitchen paper.
2. Peel, stone and chunkily slice the avocados.
3. Whisk the oil, lemon, honey and seasonings together and toss with the cucumber, celery, avocados and peanuts. Pile into a serving dish. Serve immediately dusted with paprika pepper.

Whole Potato Salad

700 g (1½ lb) NEW POTATOES, SCRUBBED
90 ml (6 tbsp) SALAD OIL
45 ml (3 tbsp) VINEGAR
1 GARLIC CLOVE, SKINNED AND CRUSHED (optional)
SALT AND FRESHLY GROUND PEPPER
CHOPPED PARSLEY OR SNIPPED CHIVES, TO GARNISH

Serves 4–6

1. Cook the potatoes in boiling salted water for 10–15 minutes until tender. Drain and, while still warm, remove the skins. Put the potatoes into a serving dish.
2. Put the oil, vinegar and garlic (if using) into a screw-top jar. Season well and shake. Pour over the potatoes while still warm and leave to cool for 1–2 hours. Serve sprinkled with parsley or chives.

Mixed Salad

175 g (6 oz) FROZEN GREEN BEANS
SALT AND FRESHLY GROUND PEPPER
90 ml (6 tbsp) SALAD OIL
45 ml (3 tbsp) VINEGAR
1 GARLIC CLOVE, SKINNED AND CRUSHED
1 SMALL GREEN PEPPER, SEEDED AND CHOPPED
4 TOMATOES, QUARTERED
1 SMALL ONION, SKINNED AND SLICED
8 ANCHOVIES (optional)
8 BLACK OLIVES

Serves 8

1. Put the beans into a pan of boiling salted water. Bring to the boil, simmer for 2–3 minutes. Drain and set aside to cool.
2. Make the dressing: put the oil, vinegar and garlic into a screw-top jar. Season and shake.
3. Combine all the ingredients with the cold beans in a salad bowl, pour over the dressing and serve at once.

Mozzarella Salad

90 ml (6 tbsp) SALAD OIL
45 ml (3 tbsp) VINEGAR
SALT AND FRESHLY GROUND PEPPER
2 RIPE AVOCADOS
175 g (6 oz) MOZZARELLA CHEESE, THINLY SLICED
4 TOMATOES, THINLY SLICED
CHOPPED PARSLEY AND MINT, TO GARNISH

Serves 4

1. Put the oil and vinegar into a screw-top jar. Season and shake well.
2. Halve the avocados and remove the stones. Peel and cut into slices. Pour the dressing over the avocados. Stir to coat thoroughly and prevent discoloration.
3. Arrange slices of Mozzarella, tomato and avocado on four individual serving plates. Spoon over the dressing and sprinkle with chopped herbs.

Italian Tomato and Egg Salad

6 HARD-BOILED EGGS, SHELLED AND SLICED
6 TOMATOES, SKINNED AND HALVED
49 g (1¾ oz) CAN ANCHOVIES, EACH HALVED
50 g (2 oz) STUFFED OLIVES, SLICED
90 ml (6 tbsp) SALAD OIL
45 ml (3 tbsp) VINEGAR
SALT AND FRESHLY GROUND PEPPER
10 ml (2 tsp) TOMATO PUREE
CHOPPED PARSLEY, TO GARNISH

Serves 6

1. Arrange the egg slices on a platter. Lay the tomatoes on top with two pieces of anchovy across each tomato to make a cross. Garnish the tomato halves with olive slices and sprinkle the rest over the egg.
2. Mix the oil and vinegar in a jug. Season well and stir in the tomato purée. Pour over the salad ingredients and garnish with a little parsley.

Cheese and Chicory Salad

100 g (4 oz) CHEDDAR CHEESE, CUBED
2 LARGE HEADS CHICORY, TRIMMED AND COARSELY CHOPPED
1 GREEN PEPPER, SEEDED AND CHOPPED
2 STICKS CELERY, TRIMMED AND CHOPPED
100 g (4 oz) RADISHES, TRIMMED AND SLICED
30 ml (2 tbsp) BEEF STOCK
SALT AND FRESHLY GROUND PEPPER
90 ml (6 tbsp) VEGETABLE OIL
45 ml (3 tbsp) WHITE WINE VINEGAR
5–10 ml (1–2 tsp) SOFT BROWN SUGAR
1 SMALL GARLIC CLOVE, SKINNED AND CRUSHED
100 g (4 oz) WALNUT HALVES

Serves 4

1. Put the cheese cubes in a salad bowl with the chicory. Add the pepper, celery and radishes and mix together.

2. Put the stock, seasonings, oil, vinegar, sugar and garlic into a screw-top jar and shake well to combine. Pour over the salad and stir in the walnuts.

Photographed right

Tomato Salad with Basil

700 g ($1\frac{1}{2}$ lb) RIPE TOMATOES, SKINNED AND THINLY SLICED
135 ml (9 tbsp) OLIVE OIL
45 ml (3 tbsp) WINE VINEGAR
1 SMALL GARLIC CLOVE, SKINNED AND CRUSHED
30 ml (2 tbsp) CHOPPED BASIL
SALT AND FRESHLY GROUND PEPPER

Serves 6

1. Arrange the tomatoes on six individual serving plates.

2. Put the oil, vinegar, garlic, basil and seasoning in a screw-top jar and shake well. Spoon over the tomatoes.

3. Cover the plates tightly with cling film and chill for about 2 hours.

Salad Kebabs

5 cm (2 inch) PIECE CUCUMBER, SLICED INTO FOUR 1 cm ($\frac{1}{2}$ inch) RINGS
4 SMALL TOMATOES, CUT INTO EIGHTHS
116 g (4 oz) PACKET SLICED SHOULDER OF HAM, SLICED INTO 1 cm ($\frac{1}{2}$ inch) STRIPS
8 SILVERSKIN COCKTAIL ONIONS
BUTTERED PITTA BREAD, TO SERVE

Serves 4

1. Cut each cucumber ring into four wedges.

2. Thread alternate pieces of tomato and cucumber on to eight wooden skewers, lacing the ham strips in between. Finish each stick with an onion.

3. To serve the salad kebabs, plunge them into the pitta pockets and gently ease away the sticks.

Cheese and Chicory Salad

Slimmer's Platter

4 STUFFED GREEN OLIVES, RINSED AND ROUGHLY CHOPPED
113.3 g (4 oz) CARTON COTTAGE CHEESE
5 ml (1 tsp) HORSERADISH RELISH
SALT AND FRESHLY GROUND PEPPER
1 WEDGE OF LETTUCE HEART
1 PEACH, SKINNED AND QUARTERED
6 GRAPES, SKINNED AND HALVED

Serves 1

1. Combine the olives with the cottage cheese and the horseradish. Season well.

2. Arrange the lettuce on a plate with the cottage cheese mixture alongside, surrounded by the peach. Scatter the grape halves on top.

Mixed Bean Salad

275 g (10 oz) MIXED DRIED BEANS (BLACK EYE BEANS AND HARICOTS), SOAKED OVERNIGHT AND DRAINED
60 ml (4 tbsp) SALAD OIL
30 ml (2 tbsp) VINEGAR
SALT AND FRESHLY GROUND PEPPER
1 GARLIC CLOVE, SKINNED AND CRUSHED
2.5 ml ($\frac{1}{2}$ tsp) GROUND CORIANDER
50 g (2 oz) ONIONS, SKINNED AND FINELY SLICED

Serves 6

1. Put the beans into a pan and cover with water. Bring to the boil, then lower the heat and simmer for about 1 hour, or until tender.

2. Drain the beans and put them into a large bowl.

3. Put the oil, vinegar, garlic (if using) with the seasoning and coriander into a screw-top jar and shake well. Pour over the beans while they are still warm, toss well, and leave to cool.

4. Toss the onion with the beans, adjust the seasoning and chill before serving.

Watercress, Sweet Pepper and Apple Salad

100 ml (4 fl oz) SALAD OIL
FINELY GRATED RIND AND JUICE OF 1 LEMON
2.5 ml ($\frac{1}{2}$ tsp) CASTER SUGAR
SALT AND FRESHLY GROUND PEPPER
175 g (6 oz) GREEN PEPPER, SEEDED AND THINLY SLICED
2 CRISP GREEN EATING APPLES, CORED AND THINLY SLICED
2 BUNCHES WATERCRESS, TRIMMED

Serves 4

1. Put the oil, lemon rind and juice, sugar and seasonings into a bowl and mix well. Add the green pepper and apple and toss.

2. Just before serving add the watercress and turn until lightly glistening.

Oriental Chicken Salad

Oriental Chicken Salad

1.4 kg (3 lb) OVEN-READY CHICKEN
1 SMALL CARROT, PEELED AND SLICED
1 SMALL ONION, SKINNED AND SLICED
1 BAY LEAF
6 WHOLE BLACK PEPPERCORNS
TWO 142 g (5 oz) CARTONS NATURAL YOGURT
5 ml (1 tsp) GROUND PAPRIKA
5 ml (1 tsp) GROUND CORIANDER
1 LARGE GARLIC CLOVE, SKINNED AND CRUSHED
30 ml (2 tbsp) LEMON JUICE
SALT AND FRESHLY GROUND PEPPER
1 RED PEPPER, SEEDED AND SLICED
225 g (8 oz) FRESH BEANSPROUTS
125 g (4 oz) STONED DATES, HALVED
CORIANDER LEAVES, TO GARNISH

Serves 6

1. Put the chicken into a large pan with just enough water to cover. Add the carrot, onion, bay leaf and peppercorns and poach until tender—about 50 minutes. Remove the chicken and shred the flesh, discarding skin and bone.

2. Mix the yogurt, spices, garlic, and lemon juice and stir in the still warm chicken. Season to taste. Cool.

3. Stir the vegetables and fruit into the cool chicken mixture. Cover and chill well before serving garnished with coriander leaves.

Photographed above

;moky Avocado and ;rapefruit Salad

25 g (8 oz) SMOKED CHEESE, CUT INTO THIN STRIPS
GRAPEFRUIT, PEELED, DIVIDED INTO SEGMENTS AND SET SIDE IN A BOWL TO RETAIN THE JUICES
42 ml (5 fl oz) CARTON SOURED CREAM
ALT AND FRESHLY GROUND PEPPER
LARGE RIPE AVOCADOS
5 g (1 oz) SALTED CASHEW NUTS
APRIKA PEPPER, TO GARNISH
ETTUCE LEAVES
ERB OATCAKES, TO SERVE (see page 265)

erves 6

. Mix the cheese with the grapefruit, grapefruit juices, oured cream and seasoning.
. Halve the avocados, remove the stones and pile the alad ingredients into the centre of each one.
. Sprinkle the cashew nuts over the avocados and ust lightly with paprika. Serve on lettuce leaves on ndividual plates.

'hotographed below

Avocado and Red Bean Salad

30 ml (2 tbsp) LEMON JUICE
60 ml (4 tbsp) VEGETABLE OIL
10 ml (2 tsp) FRENCH MUSTARD
SALT AND FRESHLY GROUND PEPPER
1.25 ml ($\frac{1}{4}$ tsp) CASTER SUGAR
2 RIPE AVOCADOS
432 g ($15\frac{1}{4}$ oz) CAN RED KIDNEY BEANS, DRAINED
SHREDDED LETTUCE
FRENCH BREAD, TO SERVE

Serves 6

1. Put the lemon juice, oil, mustard, seasoning and sugar into a bowl and whisk well together.
2. Halve the avocados and remove the stones. Skin and slice into small pieces. Immediately stir the avocado gently through the drsssing until well coated.
3. Stir the beans gently into the avocado mixture. Cover tightly with cling film and refrigerate for 2 hours.
4. Give the salad a gentle stir. Arrange on small plates lined with shredded lettuce. Serve with French bread.

;moky Avocado and Grapefruit Salad

Crisp Lettuce with Orange

Crisp Lettuce with Orange

1 LARGE CRISP LETTUCE, TRIMMED AND CUT INTO 8 WEDGES
½ BUNCH WATERCRESS, TRIMMED
2 LARGE ORANGES, PEELED, THINLY SLICED AND SET ASIDE IN A BOWL TO RETAIN THE JUICES
ABOUT 75 ml (5 tbsp) SALAD OIL
2 SLICES WHITE BREAD, CRUSTS REMOVED, CUT INTO 1 cm (½ inch) SQUARES
SALT AND FRESHLY GROUND PEPPER
60 ml (4 tbsp) WHITE WINE VINEGAR
2.5 ml (½ tsp) CASTER SUGAR

Serves 8

1. Arrange the lettuce, watercress and orange slices in a serving bowl. Cover and chill.

2. Heat a little oil, about 15 ml (1 tbsp), in a frying pan and fry the bread until crisp and golden. Drain well and sprinkle with salt.

3. Whisk 60 ml (4 tbsp) oil, the vinegar, sugar and seasoning into the orange juice. Pour over the salad and add the fried bread squares just before serving.

Photographed above

Chilled Cauliflower with Lemon Dressing

450 g (1 lb) CAULIFLOWER, TRIMMED AND BROKEN INTO SMALL FLORETS
FINELY GRATED RIND OF ½ LEMON
45 ml (3 tbsp) LEMON JUICE
120 ml (8 tbsp) VEGETABLE OIL
SALT AND FRESHLY GROUND PEPPER
1.25 ml (¼ tsp) DRIED OREGANO OR MARJORAM
1 SMALL GREEN PEPPER, SEEDED AND CHOPPED
1 CANNED PIMIENTO, CHOPPED
1 GARLIC CLOVE, SKINNED

Serves 4

1. Cook the cauliflower in 2.5 cm (1 inch) of boiling salted water for about 3 minutes. Drain, rinse in cold water and drain again. Turn the cauliflower into a serving dish.

2. Put the remaining ingredients into a screw-top jar, shake well together and pour the dressing over the cauliflower. Leave at room temperature for 2–3 hours. Remove the garlic clove before serving.

SAUCES & STUFFINGS

Classic Mayonnaise

1 EGG YOLK
2.5 ml (½ tsp) MUSTARD POWDER
2.5 ml (½ tsp) SALT
1.25 ml (¼ tsp) FRESHLY GROUND PEPPER
2.5 ml (½ tsp) SUGAR
ABOUT 150 ml (¼ pint) SALAD OIL
15 ml (1 tbsp) WHITE VINEGAR OR LEMON JUICE

Makes about 150 ml (¼ pint)

1. Put the egg yolk into a bowl with the seasonings and sugar. Mix thoroughly, then add the oil drop by drop, stirring briskly with a wooden spoon the whole time or using a whisk, until the sauce is thick and smooth. If it becomes too thick add a little of the vinegar.

2. When all the oil has been added, add the vinegar gradually and mix thoroughly.

Note: Should the sauce curdle during the making process, put another egg yolk into a bowl and add the curdled sauce very gradually, in the same way as the oil is added to the original egg yolk.

Bread Sauce

Use as an accompaniment to roast chicken, turkey or pheasant.

2 CLOVES
1 ONION, SKINNED
1 SMALL BAY LEAF
450 ml (¾ pint) MILK
75 g (3 oz) FRESH WHITE BREADCRUMBS
SALT AND FRESHLY GROUND WHITE PEPPER
15 g (½ oz) BUTTER

Makes enough for 6 servings

1. Stick the cloves into the onion and place in a small heavy-based pan with the bay leaf and the milk to cover.

2. Bring slowly to the boil, remove from the heat, cover and leave to infuse for 10 minutes, then remove the onion and bay leaf.

3. Add the breadcrumbs and seasoning, return to the heat and simmer gently, covered, for 10–15 minutes, stirring occasionally. Stir in the butter.

Tomato Sauce

30 ml (2 tbsp) VEGETABLE OIL
1 ONION, SKINNED AND CHOPPED
1 GARLIC CLOVE, SKINNED AND CRUSHED
TWO 425 g (15 oz) CANS TOMATO JUICE
141 g (5 oz) CAN TOMATO PUREE
10 ml (2 tsp) BROWN SUGAR
30 ml (2 tbsp) CHOPPED PARSLEY
5 ml (1 tsp) DRIED OREGANO
5 ml (1 tsp) SALT
PINCH OF PEPPER
1 BAY LEAF

Makes about 900 ml (1½ pints)

1. Heat the oil in a large saucepan, add the onion and garlic and fry for 10 minutes, stirring frequently.

2. Add the remaining ingredients and bring the mixture to the boil. Lower the heat, partially cover and cook for 30 minutes. Discard the bay leaf.

Barbecue Sauce

Use as an accompaniment to chicken, sausages, hamburgers or chops.

50 g (2 oz) BUTTER
1 LARGE ONION, SKINNED AND CHOPPED
5 ml (1 tsp) TOMATO PUREE
30 ml (2 tbsp) VINEGAR
30 ml (2 tbsp) DEMERARA SUGAR
10 ml (2 tsp) MUSTARD POWDER
30 ml (2 tbsp) WORCESTERSHIRE SAUCE
150 ml (¼ pint) WATER

Makes enough for 4 servings

1. Melt the butter in a saucepan and fry the onion for 5 minutes, until soft. Stir in the tomato purée and continue cooking for a further 3 minutes.

2. Blend together the remaining ingredients until smooth and stir in the onion mixture. Return to the pan and simmer uncovered for a further 10 minutes.

Tartare Sauce

Serve with fried fish.

150 ml (¼ pint) MAYONNAISE (see left)
5 ml (1 tsp) SNIPPED CHIVES
10 ml (2 tsp) CHOPPED PARSLEY
10 ml (2 tsp) CHOPPED CAPERS
10 ml (2 tsp) CHOPPED GHERKINS
15 ml (1 tbsp) LEMON JUICE

Makes 200 ml (7 fl oz)

1. Make the mayonnaise and add the herbs, capers and gherkins. Stir in the lemon juice and mix well.

2. Leave the sauce for at least 1 hour before serving so that the flavours have a chance to blend.

Mustard Sauce

Mustard Sauce

Use for carrots, celery hearts, herring, mackerel, cheese, ham and bacon dishes.

40 g ($1\frac{1}{2}$ oz) BUTTER
45 ml (3 tbsp) PLAIN FLOUR
450 ml ($\frac{3}{4}$ pint) MILK
30 ml (2 tbsp) MUSTARD POWDER
20 ml (4 tsp) MALT VINEGAR
SALT AND FRESHLY GROUND PEPPER
30 ml (2 tbsp) SINGLE CREAM (optional)

Makes 450 ml ($\frac{3}{4}$ pint)

1. Melt the butter in a saucepan. Add the flour and cook over low heat, stirring, for 2 minutes.

2. Remove from the heat and gradually stir in the milk. Return to the heat and bring to the boil slowly. Continue to cook, stirring until the sauce thickens. Simmer for a further 2–3 minutes.

3. Blend the mustard powder with the vinegar and whisk into the sauce, season. Stir in the fresh cream (if using). Reheat but do not boil.

Photographed above

Mild Curry Sauce

Mild Curry Sauce

Use for marrow, cabbage wedges, hard-boiled eggs or combining with pieces of cooked fish, chicken or meat.

50 g (2 oz) BUTTER
1 ONION, SKINNED AND FINELY CHOPPED
15–20 ml (3–4 tsp) MILD CURRY POWDER
45 ml (3 tbsp) PLAIN FLOUR
450 ml (¾ pint) MILK, OR HALF STOCK AND HALF MILK
30 ml (2 tbsp) MANGO OR APPLE CHUTNEY
SALT AND FRESHLY GROUND PEPPER

Makes 450 ml (¾ pint)

1. Melt the butter in a pan and fry the onion until golden.
2. Stir in the curry powder and cook for 3–4 minutes. Add the flour and cook for 2–3 minutes, stirring.
3. Remove from the heat and gradually stir in the milk. Return to the heat and bring to the boil slowly. Continue to cook, stirring, until the sauce thickens. Simmer for a further 2–3 minutes.
4. Add the chutney and season well. Reheat to serving temperature.

Photographed above

Horseradish Cream

Serve with trout or mackerel.

30 ml (2 tbsp) GRATED FRESH HORSERADISH
10 ml (2 tsp) LEMON JUICE
10 ml (2 tsp) SUGAR
PINCH MUSTARD POWDER (optional)
150 ml (¼ pint) DOUBLE CREAM

Makes 225 ml (8 fl oz)

1. Mix the horseradish with the lemon juice, sugar and pinch of mustard.
2. Whip the cream lightly, then fold in the horseradish mixture.

Sharp Gooseberry Sauce

Serve with baked or grilled mackerel.

225 g (8 oz) GOOSEBERRIES, TOPPED AND TAILED
25 g (1 oz) BUTTER
30–60 ml (2–4 tbsp) SUGAR

Makes 300 ml (½ pint)

1. Stew the fruit in as little water as possible, until soft and pulped, stirring occasionally.
2. Purée the mixture in a blender or rub it through a sieve until smooth.
3. Stir in the butter and sugar to taste and heat through.

Butterscotch Sauce

A topping for vanilla ice cream.

25 g (1 oz) BUTTER
30 ml (2 tbsp) SOFT BROWN SUGAR
15 ml (1 tbsp) GOLDEN SYRUP
45 ml (3 tbsp) CHOPPED NUTS
SQUEEZE OF LEMON JUICE (optional)

Makes about 100 ml (4 fl oz)

1. Warm the butter, sugar and syrup in a saucepan until well blended.
2. Boil for 1 minute and stir in the nuts and lemon juice. Serve at once.

Photographed below

Butterscotch Sauce

Chestnut Stuffing

Use with chicken or turkey.

450 g (1 lb) FRESH CHESTNUTS OR 225 g (8 oz) CANNED WHOLE UNSWEETENED CHESTNUTS, DRAINED
25 g (1 oz) BUTTER
225 g (8 oz) ONIONS, SKINNED AND CHOPPED
350 g (12 oz) FRESH BROWN BREADCRUMBS
75 g (3 oz) SHREDDED SUET
45 ml (3 tbsp) CREAMED HORSERADISH
5 ml (1 tsp) LEMON JUICE
SALT AND FRESHLY GROUND PEPPER

Serves 8

1. If using fresh chestnuts, make a small cut along the flat side of each. Bake in a 220°C (425°F) mark 7 oven for 10 minutes, or until the skins crack. Peel when cooled. Simmer the chestnuts in salted water for 20 minutes or until tender. Drain and chop roughly.

2. Melt the butter in a frying pan and gently fry the onion until soft but not coloured.

3. Remove from the heat, toss in the chopped chestnuts, breadcrumbs, suet, horseradish, lemon juice and seasonings.

4. Either continue to fry slowly on top of the cooker, stirring occasionally for 15–20 minutes, or spoon into an ovenproof dish, cover and bake at 200°C (400°F) mark 6 for 30–35 minutes. Uncover and bake for a further 15 minutes.

Rice Stuffing

50 g (2 oz) BROWN RICE
2 CHICKEN LIVERS, CHOPPED
1 SMALL ONION, SKINNED AND CHOPPED
50 g (2 oz) SEEDLESS RAISINS
50 g (2 oz) BLANCHED ALMONDS, CHOPPED
30 ml (2 tbsp) CHOPPED PARSLEY
25 g (1 oz) BUTTER, MELTED
SALT AND FRESHLY GROUND PEPPER
1 EGG, BEATEN

Makes enough to stuff one 2 kg (4½ lb) chicken; one 1 kg (2½ lb) marrow or a large fish

1. Bring a pan of salted water to the boil and cook the rice for about 45 minutes until tender. Drain well and cool.

2. Mix the cooled rice with all the other ingredients, binding them well with the egg.

Herb Stuffing

40 g (1½ oz) BUTTER
1 LARGE ONION, SKINNED AND CHOPPED
75 g (3 oz) FRESH BREADCRUMBS
30 ml (2 tbsp) CHOPPED FRESH PARSLEY
SALT AND FRESHLY GROUND PEPPER

Makes enough to stuff one 1.8–2.3 kg (4–5 lb) chicken

1. Melt the butter in a frying pan and fry the onion until softened. Stir in the remaining ingredients and mix thoroughly.

Mushroom Stuffing

Use to stuff a goose or turkey.

25 g (1 oz) BUTTER OR MARGARINE
100 g (4 oz) MUSHROOMS, WIPED AND CHOPPED
1 SMALL ONION, SKINNED AND CHOPPED
15 ml (1 tbsp) CHOPPED PARSLEY
SALT AND FRESHLY GROUND PEPPER
100 g (4 oz) FRESH WHITE BREADCRUMBS
BEATEN EGG, TO BIND

Makes enough for a 2.3 kg (5 lb) bird

1. Melt the butter in a pan and lightly fry the mushrooms and onion for 2–3 minutes until soft but not coloured.

2. Add the parsley, seasoning and breadcrumbs and bind with a little beaten egg.

Note: The mixture may also be used to stuff tomatoes or green peppers, but for this purpose the amount of breadcrumbs should be reduced to 50 g (2 oz).

Nut Stuffing

50 g (2 oz) BUTTER
2 SMALL ONIONS, SKINNED AND FINELY CHOPPED
100 g (4 oz) MUSHROOMS, WIPED AND FINELY CHOPPED
50 g (2 oz) SHELLED WALNUTS, FINELY CHOPPED
45 ml (3 tbsp) SHELLED CASHEW NUTS, FINELY CHOPPED
6 BRAZIL NUTS, SHELLED, FINELY CHOPPED
PINCH OF DRIED MIXED HERBS
15 ml (1 tbsp) CHOPPED PARSLEY
175 g (6 oz) FRESH WHITE BREADCRUMBS
1 EGG, SIZE 2, BEATEN
GIBLET STOCK (optional)
SALT AND FRESHLY GROUND PEPPER

Makes enough for a 4–4.5 kg (9–10 lb) turkey

1. Melt the butter in a saucepan and gently fry the onion for 5 minutes, add the mushrooms and gently fry for a further 5 minutes.

2. Mix the chopped nuts, mixed herbs, parsley and breadcrumbs with the mushroom mixture. Bind with the beaten egg and moisten with a little stock if necessary. Season to taste.

Apple and Celery Stuffing

Use with duck or pork.

25 g (1 oz) BUTTER
50 g (2 oz) BACON, RINDED AND CHOPPED
2 ONIONS, SKINNED AND CHOPPED
2 STICKS CELERY, TRIMMED AND CHOPPED
4 COOKING APPLES, PEELED, CORED AND SLICED
75 g (3 oz) FRESH WHITE BREADCRUMBS
30 ml (2 tbsp) CHOPPED PARSLEY
SUGAR, TO TASTE
SALT AND FRESHLY GROUND PEPPER

Makes enough for a 2 kg (4½ lb) duck

1. Melt the butter in a pan and fry the bacon for 2–3 minutes until golden brown. Remove from the pan with a slotted spoon.
2. Fry the onions and celery for 5 minutes and remove from the pan with a slotted spoon.
3. Fry the apples for 2–3 minutes, until soft. Mix all the ingredients together.

Bacon or Ham Stuffing

Use as a stuffing for vegetables such as tomatoes, small marrows, peppers or poultry.

15 ml (1 tbsp) DRIPPING
½ SMALL ONION, SKINNED AND CHOPPED
2 MUSHROOMS, WIPED AND CHOPPED
50–75 g (2–3 oz) COOKED BACON OR HAM, CHOPPED
25 g (1 oz) FRESH WHITE BREADCRUMBS
SALT AND FRESHLY GROUND PEPPER
LITTLE DRY MUSTARD
FEW DROPS OF WORCESTERSHIRE SAUCE
BEATEN EGG OR MILK, TO BIND

Makes enough for a 1.4 kg (3 lb) chicken

1. Melt the dripping in a pan and lightly fry the onion for 1–2 minutes. Add the mushrooms and bacon or ham and fry until the onion is soft but not coloured.
2. Remove from the heat and add the crumbs, seasonings and sauce and bind with beaten egg or milk.

Corn and Bacon Stuffing

50 g (2 oz) BUTTER
100 g (4 oz) STREAKY BACON RASHERS, RINDED AND CHOPPED
1 SMALL ONION, SKINNED AND CHOPPED
326 g (11½ oz) CAN SWEETCORN KERNELS, DRAINED
½ SMALL GREEN PEPPER, SEEDED AND FINELY CHOPPED
100 g (4 oz) FRESH WHITE BREADCRUMBS
30 ml (2 tbsp) CHOPPED PARSLEY
SALT AND FRESHLY GROUND PEPPER
1 EGG, SIZE 6, BEATEN

Makes enough for a 4.5–5.4 kg (10–12 lb) turkey

1. Melt the butter in a pan and gently fry the bacon and onion together for a few minutes.
2. Add the sweetcorn to the pan with the green peppers. Cook for a few more minutes.
3. Remove from the heat. Stir in the breadcrumbs, parsley and seasoning and mix well. Add enough of the beaten egg to bind the mixture.

Apricot and Ginger Stuffing

100 g (4 oz) FRESH WHITE BREADCRUMBS
50 g (2 oz) SHREDDED SUET
225 g (8 oz) CANNED APRICOT HALVES, DRAINED AND FINELY CHOPPED, OR 100 g (4 oz) DRIED APRICOTS, SOAKED OVERNIGHT IN WATER, DRAINED AND FINELY CHOPPED
4 PIECES STEM GINGER, FINELY CHOPPED
1 EGG, SIZE 2, BEATEN
SALT AND FRESHLY GROUND PEPPER

Makes enough for a 1.8 kg (4 lb) duck; double the quantities for a goose

1. Mix the breadcrumbs with the suet and add the apricots and ginger.
2. Bind with the egg and season to taste.

Sage and Onion Stuffing

2 LARGE ONIONS, SKINNED AND CHOPPED
25 g (1 oz) BUTTER
SALT AND FRESHLY GROUND PEPPER
100 g (4 oz) FRESH WHITE BREADCRUMBS
10 ml (2 tsp) DRIED SAGE

Makes enough for a 1.8 kg (4 lb) chicken or duck; double the quantities for a goose

1. Put the onions in a pan and cover with cold water. Bring to the boil and cook for about 10 minutes.
2. Drain and mix with the other ingredients.

Mint and Rosemary Stuffing

50 g (2 oz) BUTTER OR MARGARINE
2 ONIONS, SKINNED AND FINELY CHOPPED
2 CELERY STICKS, TRIMMED AND CHOPPED
225 g (8 oz) FRESH WHITE OR WHOLEMEAL BREADCRUMBS
30 ml (2 tbsp) CHOPPED FRESH MINT
10 ml (2 tsp) CHOPPED FRESH ROSEMARY
SALT AND FRESHLY GROUND PEPPER
1 EGG, BEATEN

Makes enough for a 4.5–5.4 kg (10–12 lb) turkey

1. Melt the fat in a saucepan, add the onion and celery and cook for 5 minutes until soft.
2. Add the remaining ingredients and bind together with the beaten egg.

Mushroom Stuffing (page 214), shown here with roast poussins

DESSERTS

All Seasons Fruit Salad Pie

450 g (1 lb) DRIED MIXED FRUITS (PRUNES, PEARS, PEACHES, APRICOTS, APPLE RINGS), SOAKED OVERNIGHT AND DRAINED, RESERVING 90 ml (6 tbsp) LIQUID
75 g (3 oz) SUGAR
200 g (7 oz) PLAIN FLOUR
PINCH OF SALT
150 g (5 oz) BUTTER OR LARD, DICED
30 ml (2 tbsp) LEMON JUICE
ABOUT 105 ml (7 tbsp) WATER
BEATEN EGG WHITE, TO GLAZE
CASTER SUGAR, TO DUST
30 ml (2 tbsp) ORANGE-FLAVOURED LIQUEUR
142 ml (5 fl oz) CARTON DOUBLE CREAM

Serves 6

1. Layer the fruit in a 1.1 litre (2 pint) pie dish with the sugar and the reserved liquid. Place a pie funnel in the middle.
2. Sift the flour and salt into a bowl and stir in the fat.
3. Mix with the lemon juice and just enough cold water to make a firm dough.
4. On a lightly floured surface, roll to a strip three times as long as it is wide. Fold the bottom third up and the top third down and turn through 90°. Seal the edges. Continue to roll and fold in this way four times altogether. Chill, covered, for 30 minutes.
5. On a lightly floured surface, roll out the pastry and cover the pie. Glaze with egg white and dust with caster sugar. Bake at 220°C (425°F) mark 7 for 25 minutes, then cover with foil and continue to bake at 190°C (375°F) mark 5 for about 20 minutes.
6. Pour the liqueur then the cream through the funnel.

Photographed opposite

Gingered Pears

50 g (2 oz) BUTTER
2.5 ml (½ tsp) GROUND GINGER
700 g (1½ lb) FIRM DESSERT PEARS, PEELED, QUARTERED AND CORED
15 ml (1 tbsp) GOLDEN SYRUP
30 ml (2 tbsp) GINGER WINE
1 PIECE STEM GINGER, SLICED

Serves 4

1. Melt the butter in a frying pan and add the ground ginger.
2. Add the pears and cook gently on both sides for about 8 minutes or until pears are tender.
3. Stir in syrup and ginger wine and stir thoroughly until well blended. Bubble the mixture for a few minutes until of a syrupy consistency.
4. Stir through the slices of stem ginger. Serve immediately.

Greengage Coconut Sponge

15 ml (1 tbsp) CLEAR HONEY
225 g (8 oz) GREENGAGES, HALVED AND STONED
75 g (3 oz) BUTTER OR MARGARINE
75 g (3 oz) CASTER SUGAR
1 EGG, BEATEN
125 g (4 oz) SELF-RAISING FLOUR
25 g (1 oz) DESICCATED COCONUT
MILK, TO MIX

Serves 4–6

1. Grease a 1.1 litre (2 pint) pudding basin and spoon the honey into the base.
2. Put the greengages, cut side down, over the base and sides of the pudding basin.
3. Cream together the fat and sugar. Add the egg a little at a time, beating after each addition. Lightly beat in the flour with the coconut and enough milk to mix to a dropping consistency.
4. Spoon the mixture over the fruit in the basin and cover with a layer of greased greaseproof paper and foil.
5. Put into a steamer and steam over boiling water for about 2 hours. Turn out and serve.

Honey Lemon Surprise Pudding

225 g (8 oz) SELF-RAISING FLOUR
SALT
100 g (4 oz) SHREDDED SUET
100 g (4 oz) FRESH WHITE BREADCRUMBS
50 g (2 oz) SOFT BROWN SUGAR
350 g (12 oz) CLEAR HONEY
1 LARGE, RIPE, THIN-SKINNED LEMON
BUTTER, FOR GREASING
POURING CREAM OR CUSTARD, FOR SERVING

Serves 6

1. Sift the flour with a pinch of salt into a large bowl. Add the suet and sufficient cold water to give a soft dough. Knead lightly.
2. Grease a 1.1 litre (2 pint) pudding basin. On a lightly floured surface, roll out the dough. Use two-thirds to line the basin.
3. Mix the crumbs and sugar together and spoon into the basin with the honey, placing the whole lemon in the centre.
4. Cover with the remaining pastry, sealing the edges well. Cover with buttered greaseproof paper and foil, which has been pleated to allow the pudding to rise. Secure with string. Put into a steamer over boiling water, cover and steam for 4 hours or until the lemon is quite soft. Test through the suet crust with a fine skewer. Turn out and serve at once.
5. Serve with pouring cream or custard.

All Seasons Fruit Salad Pie

Walnut Waffles

Chocolate Orange Sponge Pudding

150 g (5 oz) SELF-RAISING FLOUR
45 ml (3 tbsp) COCOA POWDER
1 ORANGE, RIND FINELY GRATED; FLESH THINLY SLICED
100 g (4 oz) BLOCK MARGARINE
100 g (4 oz) CASTER SUGAR
2 EGGS, BEATEN
MILK, TO MIX

Serves 4

1. Sift the flour and cocoa into a bowl and add the orange rind.
2. Grease a 1.1 litre (2 pint) pudding basin and line the base with the orange slices.
3. Cream the margarine and sugar thoroughly and beat in the eggs a little at a time.
4. Lightly beat in the flour mixture adding enough milk to give a dropping consistency.
5. Turn the mixture into the prepared basin and cover with greased greaseproof paper and foil. Put into a steamer over boiling water. Cover and steam for 2 hours. Turn out and serve at once.

Walnut Waffles

225 g (8 oz) PLAIN FLOUR
15 ml (1 tbsp) BAKING POWDER
30 ml (2 tbsp) CASTER SUGAR
5 ml (1 tsp) SALT
5 ml (1 tsp) GROUND GINGER
3 EGGS, SEPARATED
300 ml ($\frac{1}{2}$ pint) MILK
60 ml (4 tbsp) BUTTER, MELTED
50 g (2 oz) WALNUTS, CHOPPED
OIL, FOR BRUSHING
GOLDEN SYRUP, TO SERVE

Makes 10

1. Sift the first five ingredients into a bowl. Whisk in the egg yolks, milk and melted butter. Add the walnuts.
2. Just before cooking, stiffly whisk the egg whites and gently fold into the batter.
3. Heat a little oil in a 7.5 × 10 cm (3 × 4 inch) waffle iron. Spoon in a little batter and cook for about 1 minute on each side. Keep hot. Repeat until all the batter is used up. Serve hot with golden syrup.

Photographed above

Cider-poached Whole Apples

6 SMALL BRAMLEY APPLES, CORED
50 g (2 oz) DEMERARA SUGAR
200 ml (7 fl oz) SWEET CIDER
25 g (1 oz) UNSALTED BUTTER
1 SMALL CINNAMON STICK
POURING CREAM, TO SERVE (optional)

Serves 6
1. Slit the skin of the apples around the middle with a sharp knife and arrange the apples in a shallow flameproof casserole.
2. Sprinkle over the sugar and pour over the cider. Dot with the butter and add the cinnamon stick.
3. Cover with a lid and simmer very gently for 15–20 minutes, until the apples are tender. Serve hot with pouring cream, if wished.

Plum Upside-down Pudding

30 ml (2 tbsp) DEMERARA SUGAR
25 g (1 oz) WHOLE UNBLANCHED ALMONDS
350 g (12 oz) RED PLUMS, HALVED AND STONED
100 g (4 oz) SOFT-TUB MARGARINE
100 g (4 oz) CASTER SUGAR
2 EGGS
100 g (4 oz) SELF-RAISING FLOUR
50 g (2 oz) GROUND ALMONDS
2.5 ml ($\frac{1}{2}$ tsp) ALMOND ESSENCE

Serves 4–6
1. Thoroughly grease an 18 cm (7 inch) square cake tin and sprinkle the base with the demerara sugar.
2. Put a whole almond in the cavity of each plum half and place each half, face down, in the base of the tin.
3. Put all the remaining ingredients into a bowl and beat well until light and smooth.
4. Turn the creamed mixture into the tin and smooth the surface.
5. Bake at 190°C (375°F) mark 5 for about 1 hour until well risen and golden brown.

Rhubarb and Orange Compote

450 g (1 lb) FRESH RHUBARB, TRIMMED AND THICKLY SLICED
4 ORANGES, PEELED AND SEGMENTED
45 ml (3 tbsp) GOLDEN SYRUP
1.25 ml ($\frac{1}{4}$ tsp) MIXED SPICE

Serves 4
1. Put the rhubarb into a 1.1 litre (2 pint) ovenproof dish or pudding basin and add the orange segments.
2. Spoon over the golden syrup and spice and stir to combine.
3. Cover with foil and put into a steamer over boiling water. Cover and steam for 35–40 minutes, until the rhubarb is tender.

Flambé Bananas

50 g (2 oz) BUTTER
FINELY GRATED RIND OF 1 SMALL ORANGE AND 30 ml (2 tbsp) JUICE
5 ml (1 tsp) GROUND MIXED SPICE
6 BANANAS, PEELED AND QUARTERED
15 ml (1 tbsp) DARK SOFT BROWN SUGAR
15 ml (1 tbsp) BRANDY
15 ml (1 tbsp) ORANGE LIQUEUR

Serves 4
1. Melt the butter in a frying pan and add the orange rind.
2. Stir in the mixed spice and add the bananas. Cook until softened and lightly browned, turning during cooking.
3. Stir in the sugar and dissolve in the butter. Flame in the brandy and liqueur and add the orange juice. Shake the pan gently to mix and serve immediately.

Rhubarb Crunch

450 g (1 lb) RHUBARB, TRIMMED AND CUT IN CHUNKS
25 g (1 oz) SUGAR
45 ml (3 tbsp) WATER
60 ml (4 tbsp) GOLDEN SYRUP
50 g (2 oz) MARGARINE
50 g (2 oz) PORRIDGE OATS
50 g (2 oz) CORNFLAKES
FINELY GRATED RIND OF 1 LEMON

Serves 4
1. Put the rhubarb into an ovenproof dish with the sugar and water.
2. In a pan, gently warm the syrup and margarine. Stir in the porridge oats and cornflakes with the lemon rind.
3. Spoon the mixture over the rhubarb and bake at 190°C (375°F) mark 5 for 30–40 minutes, or until crisp. Cover if necessary. Serve warm.

Banana Apricot Puffs

212 g ($7\frac{1}{2}$ oz) PACKET FROZEN PUFF PASTRY, THAWED
2 FIRM BANANAS
60 ml (4 tbsp) APRICOT JAM
15 ml (1 tbsp) LEMON JUICE
MILK, FOR GLAZING
SUGAR, FOR DREDGING

Serves 4
1. On a lightly floured surface, roll out the pastry very thinly into a large square. Cut into four small squares.
2. Peel and slice the bananas and combine with the jam and lemon juice.
3. Dampen the edges of the pastry, divide the bananas between the pastry squares and fold the pastry into triangles. Seal well and 'knock up' the edges.
4. Brush with milk, dredge with sugar and place on a dampened baking sheet. Bake until puffed and golden, about 15 minutes.

Plum and Apple Double Crust Pie

225 g (8 oz) SELF-RAISING FLOUR
PINCH OF SALT
150 g (5 oz) BUTTER OR MARGARINE, CUT INTO SMALL PIECES
45–60 ml (3–4 tbsp) WATER
5 ml (1 tsp) GROUND CINNAMON
15 ml (1 tbsp) CORNFLOUR
450 g (1 lb) RED PLUMS, HALVED AND STONED
450 g (1 lb) COOKING APPLES, PEELED, CORED AND SLICED
100 g (4 oz) SOFT BROWN SUGAR
MILK AND DEMERARA SUGAR, FOR GLAZING

Serves 6

1. Sift the flour and salt into a bowl. Rub in the fat until the mixture resembles fine breadcrumbs. Add enough cold water to bind to a firm dough.
2. On a lightly floured surface, roll out half the pastry and use to line a 22 cm ($8\frac{1}{2}$ inch) diameter deep pie plate.
3. Mix the cinnamon and cornflour and toss the plums and apples in the mixture. Turn into the pastry-lined dish. Sprinkle over the soft brown sugar.
4. Roll out the remaining pastry and use to cover the dish, sealing the edges. Glaze with milk and sprinkle lightly with demerara sugar.
5. Place on a baking sheet and bake at 200°C (400°F) mark 6 for 30 minutes, then lower to 180°C (350°F) mark 4 for a further 25–30 minutes.

Sweet Cheese Pie

225 g (8 oz) COTTAGE CHEESE, SIEVED
100 g (4 oz) CASTER SUGAR; PLUS EXTRA, TO GLAZE
50 g (2 oz) BUTTER, SOFTENED
2 EGGS, BEATEN
100 g (4 oz) PLAIN FLOUR
45 ml (3 tbsp) MILK
GRATED RIND OF 1 LEMON
376 g ($13\frac{1}{4}$ oz) CAN CRUSHED PINEAPPLE, DRAINED
312 g (13 oz) PACKET FROZEN PUFF PASTRY, THAWED
BEATEN EGG WHITE, TO GLAZE

Serves 6

1. Beat the cottage cheese into the sugar and softened butter. Gradually beat in the eggs.
2. Sift the flour and fold into the cottage cheese mixture with the milk. Stir in the lemon rind and crushed pineapple.
3. On a lightly floured board, roll out two-thirds of the pastry and use to line a 1.1 litre (2 pint) pie dish. Spoon in the cheese filling.
4. Roll out the remaining pastry and any trimmings and cut into thin strips. Use to make a lattice top for the pie, leaving no filling showing.
5. Glaze with beaten egg white and dust with caster sugar. Bake at 220°C (425°F) mark 7 for about 35 minutes, or until the pastry is risen and golden and the filling set. Cover if the pie starts to overbrown. Serve warm.

Old-fashioned Rice Pudding

75 g (3 oz) PUDDING (SHORT-GRAIN) RICE
900 ml ($1\frac{1}{2}$ pints) MILK
1 BAY LEAF
75 g (3 oz) CASTER SUGAR
A DASH OF FRESHLY GRATED NUTMEG
KNOB OF BUTTER

Serves 4

1. Grease a 1.4 litre ($2\frac{1}{2}$ pint) shallow ovenproof pie dish and put the first four ingredients into it. Add a little grated nutmeg and stir gently to mix.
2. Dot the surface of the pudding with the butter.
3. Stand the dish on a baking sheet and bake at 170°C (325°F) mark 3 for about $2\frac{1}{2}$ hours, or until most of the milk has been absorbed and a brown skin has formed on top of the pudding.

Photographed opposite

Deep-dish Apricot Streusel

225 g (8 oz) DRIED APRICOTS, SOAKED OVERNIGHT AND DRAINED
175 g (6 oz) PLAIN FLOUR
PINCH OF SALT
40 g ($1\frac{1}{2}$ oz) MARGARINE, CUT INTO SMALL PIECES
40 g ($1\frac{1}{2}$ oz) LARD, CUT INTO SMALL PIECES
ABOUT 30 ml (2 tbsp) WATER
100 g (4 oz) BUTTER
FINELY GRATED RIND AND JUICE OF 1 LEMON
50 g (2 oz) CASTER SUGAR
2.5 ml ($\frac{1}{2}$ tsp) GROUND CINNAMON
2 EGGS, BEATEN
50 g (2 oz) WHOLEMEAL FLOUR
50 g (2 oz) ROLLED OATS
50 g (2 oz) DEMERARA SUGAR
POURING CUSTARD OR CLOTTED CREAM, TO SERVE

Serves 6

1. Put the apricots into a pan and cover with water. Bring to the boil and simmer for about 1 hour, or until tender.
2. Sift the flour and salt into a bowl and rub in the fat until the mixture resembles fine breadcrumbs. Mix in just enough water to make a firm dough.
3. Roll out on a lightly floured surface and use to line a 1.1 litre (2 pint) pie dish. Bake blind with beans and foil for 20 minutes.
4. Drain the apricots and liquidise them or push through a sieve. Add 50 g (2 oz) butter and the lemon rind and juice. Turn into a bowl and stir in the caster sugar, cinnamon, and beaten eggs. Pour into the pie dish.
5. Combine the wholemeal flour and oats and cut and rub in the remaining butter. Stir in the demerara sugar and sprinkle the mixture over the apricot filling.
6. Bake at 200°C (400°F) mark 6 for 25–30 minutes, or until the topping is lightly browned. Serve warm with pouring custard or clotted cream.

Old-fashioned Rice Pudding

Orange Layer Pudding

Serves 6

- 50 g (2 oz) MARGARINE
- FINELY GRATED RIND OF 2 ORANGES
- 50 g (2 oz) SOFT BROWN SUGAR
- 2 EGGS, SEPARATED
- 200 ml (7 fl oz) MILK
- 60 ml (4 tbsp) FRESH ORANGE JUICE
- 30 ml (2 tbsp) LEMON JUICE
- 50 g (2 oz) SELF-RAISING FLOUR
- CASTER SUGAR, TO DECORATE

1. Cream the margarine, orange rind and sugar. Beat in the egg yolks, one by one. Add the milk, orange and lemon juice then sift in the flour. Beat again well.

2. Whisk the egg whites until standing in stiff peaks and fold into the creamed mixture.

3. Lightly grease a 1.3 litre ($2\frac{1}{4}$ pint) soufflé dish. Cover with buttered foil and put into a steamer over boiling water. Cover and steam for about 45 minutes. The pudding should be firm to the touch but have a custard-like layer at the bottom.

4. Serve immediately, sprinkled with caster sugar.

Apricot and Ginger Upside-down Pudding

Golden Pudding

30 ml (2 tbsp) GOLDEN SYRUP
75 g (3 oz) SELF-RAISING FLOUR
75 g (3 oz) FRESH WHITE BREADCRUMBS
75 g (3 oz) SHREDDED SUET
PINCH OF SALT
50 g (2 oz) CASTER SUGAR
FINELY GRATED RIND OF ½ LEMON
ABOUT 150 ml (¼ pint) MILK

Serves 4

1. Grease a 900 ml (1½ pint) basin and spoon the syrup into it.

2. In a bowl, combine the flour with the breadcrumbs, suet, salt, sugar and lemon rind.

3. Stir enough milk into the mixture to make a soft dropping consistency.

4. Turn the mixture into the basin and cover with greased greaseproof paper and foil. Put into a steamer over boiling water. Cover and steam for about 1½ hours. Turn out and serve hot.

Rich Grape Bread-and-butter Pudding

2 EGGS, BEATEN
284 ml (10 fl oz) CARTON SINGLE CREAM
FEW DROPS ALMOND ESSENCE
175 g (6 oz) GREEN GRAPES, HALVED, SKINNED AND SEEDED
4 THIN SLICES WHITE BREAD AND BUTTER, CRUSTS REMOVED, CUT INTO FINGERS
ABOUT 30 ml (2 tbsp) CASTER SUGAR
BUTTER
DEMERARA SUGAR, TO DECORATE

Serves 4

1. Beat the eggs with the cream and essence.

2. Lightly grease a 900 ml (1½ pint) soufflé dish. Layer the grapes, egg mixture, bread and butter and sugar in the dish. Cover with greased foil and put into a steamer over boiling water. Cover and steam for about 30 minutes or until just set.

3. Scatter demerara sugar over and serve hot.

Apricot and Ginger Upside-down Pudding

- 30 ml (4 tbsp) LONG-GRAIN RICE
- 300 ml (½ pint) MILK
- 150 g (5 oz) BUTTER
- 30 ml (2 tbsp) GOLDEN SYRUP
- 75 g (3 oz) DEMERARA SUGAR
- 411 g (14½ oz) CAN APRICOT HALVES, DRAINED
- 125 g (4 oz) SOFT BROWN SUGAR
- 2 EGGS, SEPARATED
- 75 g (3 oz) SELF-RAISING FLOUR
- 15 ml (3 tsp) GROUND GINGER
- SINGLE CREAM, TO SERVE

Serves 6

1. Put the rice and milk into a pan and bring to the boil. Lower the heat and simmer, covered, for about 25 minutes, or until tender and the milk is absorbed. Cool.
2. Base-line an 18 cm (7 inch) square tin. Melt 25 g (1 oz) butter with the syrup and demerara sugar and spoon into the tin. Arrange the apricots on the top.
3. Whisk the remaining butter until soft, gradually beat in the soft brown sugar, egg yolks and cooled rice mixture.
4. Sift the flour and ginger together and gently fold into the rice mixture. Whisk the egg whites until stiff then fold into the mixture.
5. Spoon into the tin and bake in the oven at 180°C (350°F) mark 4 for about 55 minutes. Turn out and serve hot with the cream.

Photographed opposite

Rich Custard Sponge

- EGGS, BEATEN
- 142 ml (5 fl oz) CARTON DOUBLE CREAM
- 50 g (2 oz) CASTER SUGAR
- 2.5 ml (½ tsp) VANILLA FLAVOURING
- 450 ml (¾ pint) MILK
- 100 g (4 oz) TRIFLE SPONGES
- 15 ml (1 tbsp) CURRANTS
- 15 ml (1 tbsp) SULTANAS
- 15 ml (1 tbsp) RAISINS
- 2.5 ml (½ tsp) FRESHLY GRATED NUTMEG

Serves 6

1. Put the eggs, double cream, sugar and vanilla flavouring into a bowl. Heat the milk in a saucepan. Just before boiling, pour on to the egg mixture.
2. Dip the sponges into the custard and use to line the sides only of a 1.1 litre (2 pint) ovenproof dish.
3. Place the dried fruit in the bottom of the dish and pour the rest of the custard over.
4. Sprinkle with nutmeg and bake in the oven at 150°C (300°F) mark 2 for about 1 hour until lightly set.

Steamed Apple Charlotte

- 225 g (8 oz) FRUIT MALT LOAF, THINLY SLICED
- 75 g (3 oz) BUTTER OR MARGARINE, MELTED
- 700 g (1½ lb) COOKING APPLES, PEELED, CORED AND THINLY SLICED
- 100 g (4 oz) FULL-FAT CREAM CHEESE
- 50 g (2 oz) SOFT BROWN SUGAR
- 2.5 ml (½ tsp) FRESHLY GRATED NUTMEG
- 30 ml (2 tbsp) LEMON JUICE
- 45 ml (3 tbsp) WATER

Serves 6

1. Dip one side of each slice of malt loaf in the melted butter. Use two-thirds to line the bottom and sides of a 1.4 litre (2½ pint) soufflé or other straight-sided ovenproof dish, butter side out.
2. Layer the apples in the dish with cream cheese, sugar, nutmeg, lemon juice and water. Top with the remaining malt loaf, butter side up.
3. Cover the dish with greased foil. Put into a steamer over boiling water, cover and steam for about 2 hours. Serve piping hot.

Spiced Pancakes

- 50 g (2 oz) BUTTER OR MARGARINE
- 50 g (2 oz) SOFT BROWN SUGAR
- FINELY GRATED RIND OF 1 LEMON
- 2.5 ml (½ tsp) GROUND MIXED SPICE
- 2 EGGS
- 50 g (2 oz) PLAIN FLOUR
- 300 ml (½ pint) MILK, WARMED
- CASTER SUGAR
- 45 ml (3 tbsp) LEMON CURD, WARMED

Serves 4

1. Cream the butter with the sugar. Beat in the lemon rind and the spice.
2. Beat the eggs and add gradually to the mixture with half the flour, still beating. Stir in rest of flour with the milk—it may look curdled but this doesn't matter.
3. Grease eight 10 cm (4 inch) shallow Yorkshire-type patty tins or ovenproof saucers and pour the batter into them. Bake at 190°C (375°F) mark 5 for about 20 minutes, or until risen and just set.
4. Loosen around the edges, turn out on to sugared paper. Spread at once with warm lemon curd, fold over in half-moons and serve.

Banana Chiffon Pie

10 ml (2 tsp) POWDERED GELATINE
30 ml (2 tbsp) WATER
100 g (4 oz) DIGESTIVE BISCUITS, CRUSHED
50 g (2 oz) GINGER BISCUITS, CRUSHED
75 g (3 oz) BUTTER OR BLOCK MARGARINE, MELTED
275 g (10 oz) RIPE BANANAS, PEELED
40 g (1½ oz) SOFT BROWN SUGAR
THINLY PARED RIND OF A THIN-SKINNED LEMON
45 ml (3 tbsp) LEMON JUICE
1 EGG WHITE
142 ml (5 fl oz) CARTON DOUBLE CREAM
50 g (2 oz) CHOPPED WALNUTS

Serves 4–6

1. Soak the gelatine in the water in a bowl over hot water.
2. Turn the biscuit crumbs into a bowl and stir in the melted fat until thoroughly mixed. Press the mixture into an 18 cm (7 inch) loose-bottomed flan tin. Chill until set.
3. Blend the bananas, sugar, lemon rind and juice to a purée.
4. Add the dissolved gelatine to the banana mixture and blend again for another second.
5. Lightly whisk the egg white until standing in stiff peaks and gently fold in the banana mixture. Turn into the prepared tin and refrigerate.
6. Lightly whip the cream. Remove the flan ring and decorate the pie with cream and walnuts.

Honeyed Gooseberry Fool

450 g (1 lb) GOOSEBERRIES, TOPPED AND TAILED
90 ml (6 tbsp) THICK HONEY
150 ml (¼ pint) WATER; PLUS 30 ml (2 tbsp)
10 ml (2 tsp) POWDERED GELATINE
GREEN FOOD COLOURING (optional)
150 g (5 oz) CARTON HAZELNUT YOGURT

Serves 4

1. Cook the gooseberries gently with the honey in 150 ml (¼ pint) water in a covered pan until soft.
2. Meanwhile, soak the gelatine in the remaining water in a bowl over hot water.
3. While still warm, purée the fruit and juices with the soaked gelatine in a blender. Sieve to remove all the seeds, add a drop of food colouring (if wished) to tint a pale green and then cool.
4. Fold the yogurt through the cooled fruit purée. Turn into four individual glass dishes, refrigerate to set.

Aromatic Fruit Salad

3 LARGE ORANGES
7.5 ml (1½ tsp) CLEAR HONEY
PINCH OF ALLSPICE
15 ml (1 tbsp) WATER
24 GRAPES, HALVED AND SEEDED
1 EATING APPLE, CORED AND CHOPPED
8 DRIED APRICOTS, CHOPPED
25 g (1 oz) PRESSED DATES, CHOPPED
FLAKED ALMONDS, TO DECORATE

Serves 4

1. Pare the rind from one orange; squeeze the juice from two oranges. Peel the third and chop up the flesh. Cut the pared rind into matchstick strips and simmer for 5 minutes in the honey, allspice and water. Cool.
2. Combine all the fruit, add the orange juice and rind and leave to soak to allow the apricots to soften a little.
3. Sprinkle with flaked almonds before serving.

Pineapple Cheesecake

75 g (3 oz) BUTTER
175 g (6 oz) PLAIN CHOCOLATE WHOLEWHEAT BISCUITS, ROUGHLY CRUSHED
225 g (8 oz) COTTAGE CHEESE
100 g (4 oz) FULL-FAT SOFT CHEESE
PARED RIND AND JUICE OF 1 LARGE LEMON
142 ml (5 fl oz) CARTON SOURED CREAM
3 EGGS, SEPARATED
50 g (2 oz) CASTER SUGAR
15 ml (3 tsp) GELATINE
45 ml (3 tbsp) WATER
TWO 432 g (14½ oz) CANS SLICED PINEAPPLE, DRAINED WITH JUICE RESERVED
60 ml (4 tbsp) SIEVED APRICOT JAM

Serves 10

1. Melt the butter in a pan and stir in the biscuits. Press the crumb mixture into a 23 cm (9 inch) spring-release cake tin and refrigerate to set.
2. Place the cottage and full-fat soft cheeses, lemon rind, 45 ml (3 tbsp) lemon juice and the soured cream in a blender and work until smooth.
3. Whisk the egg yolks and sugar until thick. Soak the gelatine in the water in a small bowl. Dissolve by standing the bowl in a pan of simmering water. Whisk into the egg yolks with the cheese mixture.
4. Roughly chop three-quarters of the pineapple. Whisk the egg whites until stiff and fold into the setting cheese mixture with the chopped pineapple. Pour into the biscuit crust and refrigerate.
5. Carefully remove the sides of the cake tin then, using a fish slice, lift and slide the cheesecake off the base on to a serving plate.
6. Decorate with the reserved pineapple. Pour the reserved juices into a pan and add the jam. Boil to reduce to a thick glaze. Cool and spoon over the pineapple.

Photographed opposite

Pineapple Cheesecake

Gooseberry Charlotte

450 g (1 lb) GOOSEBERRIES, TOPPED AND TAILED
90 ml (6 tbsp) WATER
75 g (3 oz) CASTER SUGAR
10 ml (2 tsp) GELATINE
300 ml ($\frac{1}{2}$ pint) MILK
2 EGG YOLKS
284 ml (10 fl oz) CARTON DOUBLE CREAM
20 LANGUE DE CHATS BISCUITS

Serves 6

1. Put the gooseberries into a small saucepan with 60 ml (4 tbsp) water. Cover the pan and simmer until the fruit softens to a pulpy consistency. Purée in a blender, then sieve to remove the pips. Stir in 50 g (2 oz) of the sugar.
2. Spoon the remaining water into a small bowl and sprinkle the gelatine over the surface. Allow the gelatine to soak until it has become spongy.
3. Warm the milk in a pan. Beat the egg yolks with the remaining sugar until light in colour and add the milk, stirring until evenly blended. Return to the pan and cook over a low heat, stirring all the time, until the custard thickens sufficiently to lightly coat the back of the spoon—do not boil. Remove from the heat and add the soaked gelatine. Stir until dissolved.
4. Pour the custard into a large bowl and mix in the gooseberry purée, leave to cool. Whip the cream until softly stiff. When the gooseberry mixture is cold, but not set, stir in half the cream.
5. Butter and base-line a 15 cm (6 inch) soufflé type non-metal straight sided dish and pour in the gooseberry mixture. Refrigerate to set. When firm turn out on to a flat serving plate.
6. Spread a thin covering of the remaining cream around the edge of the charlotte and spoon the rest into a piping bag fitted with a 1 cm ($\frac{1}{2}$ inch) star vegetable nozzle. Pipe the cream around the top edge. Just before serving, arrange the langue de chats carefully around the outside.

Photographed right

Iced Orange Sabayon

6 EGG YOLKS
175 g (6 oz) DEMERARA SUGAR
90 ml (6 tbsp) ORANGE LIQUEUR
200 ml (7 fl oz) UNSWEETENED ORANGE JUICE
WALNUT HALVES, TO DECORATE

Serves 6

1. At least a day ahead, beat the egg yolks and sugar together until well mixed. Stir in the orange liqueur and orange juice.
2. Pour into a heavy-based saucepan. Stir over a low heat until the mixture just coats the back of the spoon. Do not boil.
3. Pour into six individual soufflé dishes or ramekins and cool. Freeze until firm then wrap in cling film and return to the freezer.
4. Serve straight from the freezer, decorated with walnut halves.

Gooseberry Charlotte

Strawberry Vacherin

3 EGG WHITES
175 g (6 oz) CASTER SUGAR
75 g (3 oz) TOASTED GROUND HAZELNUTS
284 ml (10 fl oz) CARTON DOUBLE CREAM
ICING SUGAR
450 g (1 lb) FRESH STRAWBERRIES

Serves 6

1. Draw two 20 cm (8 inch) circles on non-stick paper. Divide one into six wedge shapes.

2. To make the meringues, whisk the egg whites until stiff. Gradually whisk in the sugar, keeping the mixture stiff. Fold in the ground nuts.

3. Pipe a good half of the mixture on to the plain circle, using a 1 cm ($\frac{1}{2}$ inch) plain nozzle. Pipe the remaining mixture into six separated triangles within the circle area on the other sheet of paper, allowing room between them for spreading.

4. Bake in the oven at 190°C (375°F) mark 5 for 30–35 minutes or until crisp and golden. Cool, then peel off the paper.

5. To complete the vacherin, stiffly whip the cream with icing sugar to taste. Slice the strawberries, reserving one whole and six slices for the decoration. Fold the remaining strawberries into half the cream and pile on to the meringue circle. Place the wedges on top. Decorate with the rest of the whipped cream. Just before serving, dust with icing sugar and add the reserved strawberries.

Photographed on the cover

Strawberry and Almond Japonais

75 g (3 oz) BLANCHED ALMONDS, FINELY CHOPPED
1 (size 2) EGG WHITE
100 g (4 oz) ICING SUGAR
FINELY GRATED RIND AND JUICE OF 1 LARGE ORANGE
284 ml (10 fl oz) CARTON WHIPPING CREAM
350 g (12 oz) SMALL STRAWBERRIES, HULLED
2.5 ml ($\frac{1}{2}$ tsp) ARROWROOT
15 ml (1 tbsp) BRANDY
CASTER SUGAR, TO TASTE

Serves 6

1. Blend the almonds, egg white, icing sugar and orange rind slowly until well mixed.

2. Line two baking sheets with non-stick paper and spoon out the mixture into six rounds. Spread them out slightly, spacing them well apart. Bake at 180°C (350°F) mark 4 for 20–25 minutes, or until crisp. Cool on a wire rack.

3. Lightly whip the cream and spread a ring of it around the edges of each japonais. Arrange the hulled strawberries in the centre.

4. In a pan, blend the arrowroot with the orange juice and brandy, bring to the boil and cook until clear, stirring. Sweeten to taste and brush over the strawberries.

Crème Brulée

Gooseberry Whip

350 g (12 oz) FROZEN GOOSEBERRIES
½ LEMON JELLY TABLET, BROKEN UP
170 g (6 oz) CAN EVAPORATED MILK
A LITTLE GREEN FOOD COLOURING

Serves 4

1. Put the gooseberries in a pan with a drop of water and cook gently until soft. Pass through a sieve and while still hot add the jelly. Stir until dissolved. Leave to cool but not set.

2. Whisk the evaporated milk until really thick and fold through the gooseberry purée with a little green colouring. Spoon into glasses, chill and serve.

Strawberries with Raspberry Sauce

1.8 kg (4 lb) SMALL STRAWBERRIES, HULLED
900 g (2 lb) RASPBERRIES, HULLED
100 g (4 oz) ICING SUGAR, SIFTED

Serves 20 buffet portions

1. Put the strawberries into a large serving bowl.

2. Purée the raspberries in a blender until just smooth and run through a nylon sieve to remove pips.

3. Whisk in the icing sugar and pour over the strawberries. Chill well before serving.

Crème Brûlée

600 ml (1 pint) WHIPPING CREAM
4 EGG YOLKS
75 g (3 oz) CASTER SUGAR
5 ml (1 tsp) VANILLA FLAVOURING

Serves 6

1. Put the cream into the top of a double saucepan or in a bowl over a pan of hot water and heat gently—but do not boil.

2. Meanwhile, put the egg yolks, 50 g (2 oz) of the caster sugar and the vanilla flavouring into a bowl and beat thoroughly. Add the cream and mix well together.

3. Pour the mixture into six individual ramekin dishes and place in a roasting tin containing sufficient water to come halfway up the sides of the dishes. Bake in the oven at 150°C (300°F) mark 2 for about 1 hour or until set. Remove from the roasting tin and leave until cold.

4. Chill in the refrigerator for several hours, preferably overnight. Sprinkle the top of each dish with the remaining sugar and put under a hot grill until the sugar turns to caramel. Chill for 2–3 hours before serving.

Photographed opposite

Pineapple Brulée

2 CANNED PINEAPPLE RINGS, SHREDDED INTO SMALL PIECES
25 g (1 oz) PLAIN SPONGE CAKE OR TRIFLE SPONGES, DICED
1 EGG, PLUS 1 EGG YOLK
142 ml (5 fl oz) CARTON DOUBLE CREAM
75 ml (5 tbsp) MILK
30 ml (2 tbsp) DEMERARA SUGAR

Serves 4

1. Divide the pineapple and sponge cake pieces between four 150 ml (¼ pint) ramekins or small soufflé dishes.

2. Beat the egg and yolk with the cream and milk and pour into the dishes. Stand in a roasting tin, with water halfway up the sides and bake at 170°C (325°F) mark 3 for 30–35 minutes, or until just set.

3. Cool thoroughly and chill well, sprinkle with sugar and glaze under a very hot grill. Chill again to serve.

Apple Flapjack

900 g (2 lb) COOKING APPLES, PEELED, CORED AND SLICED
65 g (2½ oz) SUGAR
150 g (5 oz) BUTTER
60 ml (4 tbsp) GOLDEN SYRUP
225 g (8 oz) ROLLED OATS
1.25 ml (¼ tsp) SALT
5 ml (1 tsp) GROUND GINGER
ICING SUGAR, TO DECORATE

Serves 6

1. Simmer the apples gently in a covered pan with 40 g (1½ oz) sugar, but no liquid, until pulpy. Cool slightly.

2. Butter and base-line an 18 cm (7 inch) round loose-bottomed cake tin.

3. Heat the remaining sugar with the butter and syrup, until dissolved. Stir in the oats, salt and ginger.

4. Before it cools, line the base and sides of the tin with three-quarters of the flapjack mixture—up to 2.5 cm (1 inch) from the rim.

5. Pour the apple pulp into the centre, cover with the remaining mixture, pressing it down lightly.

6. Bake in the oven at 190°C (375°F) mark 5 for 35 minutes. Cool for 10 minutes before loosening the edges and turning out. Serve dredged with icing sugar.

Tangerine Melon Mousse

10 ml (2 tsp) GELATINE
75 ml (5 tbsp) WATER
225 g (8 oz) TANGERINES, RINDS FINELY GRATED
225 g (8 oz) MELON FLESH
25 g (1 oz) SKIMMED MILK POWDER
30 ml (2 tbsp) WATER
1 EGG WHITE
SUGAR, TO TASTE

Serves 4

1. Soak the gelatine in 30 ml (2 tbsp) water over a pan of hot water.

2. Purée half the tangerines and half the melon in a blender with dissolved gelatine, tangerine rind, milk powder and the rest of the water.

3. Turn into a bowl and leave until it begins to thicken.

4. Whisk the egg white and fold into the tangerine mixture. Add a little sugar, to taste. Spoon into individual glasses and chill. Before serving, chop the remaining tangerines and melon and use to decorate.

Banana and Honey Ice-cream

50 g (2 oz) HAZELNUTS
450 g (1 lb) BANANAS
142 ml (5 fl oz) CARTON DOUBLE CREAM
150 g (5 oz) CARTON NATURAL YOGURT
JUICE OF 1 LARGE LEMON
75 ml (5 tbsp) THICK HONEY
2 EGG WHITES

Serves 8

1. Spread the hazelnuts out on a baking sheet and brown in the oven at 180°C (350°F) mark 4 for 15–20 minutes. Put in a tea-towel and rub off the skins. Chop.

2. Peel and mash the bananas in a large bowl. Add the cream, yogurt, lemon juice, honey and hazelnuts. Beat well to combine.

3. Turn into a rigid plastic container—not too deep. Cover and half freeze to the mushy stage.

4. Whisk the egg whites until stiff, fold into the banana mixture and return to the freezer.

5. Transfer to the refrigerator 1 hour before serving.

Honey Mousse

3 EGGS, SEPARATED
100 g (4 oz) CASTER SUGAR
FINELY GRATED RIND OF 2 LEMONS
90 ml (6 tbsp) LEMON JUICE
10 ml (2 tsp) GELATINE
284 ml (10 fl oz) CARTON WHIPPING CREAM
30 ml (2 tbsp) CLEAR HONEY
CHOPPED PISTACHIO NUTS OR COARSELY GRATED CHOCOLATE, TO DECORATE

Serves 6

1. Whisk together the egg yolks, sugar and lemon rind until thick, add 45 ml (3 tbsp) lemon juice and place over a pan of simmering water until thick and mousse-like. Remove from the heat and whisk occasionally until cold.
2. Soak the gelatine in the remaining lemon juice in a small bowl. Place the bowl over a pan of hot water and stir until dissolved.
3. Whip the cream until standing in soft peaks. Whisk the egg whites until stiff. Fold half the cream into the mousse with the gelatine, honey and whisked egg whites. Turn into a 1.1 litre (2 pint) glass bowl.
4. Decorate with the remaining whipped cream and chopped pistachio nuts.

Strawberry Ginger Crisps

50 g (2 oz) GOLDEN SYRUP
50 g (2 oz) CASTER SUGAR
50 g (2 oz) BUTTER
50 g (2 oz) PLAIN FLOUR
2.5 ml ($\frac{1}{2}$ tsp) GROUND GINGER
FINELY GRATED RIND OF $\frac{1}{2}$ LEMON
5 ml (1 tsp) BRANDY
284 ml (10 fl oz) CARTON WHIPPING CREAM
225 g (8 oz) STRAWBERRIES, HULLED, 4 RESERVED WHOLE, THE REST SLICED

Serves 4

1. Line two baking sheets with non-stick paper. Warm the syrup, sugar and butter together in a pan until dissolved. Sift the flour and ginger together and stir into the pan.
2. Add the lemon rind to the pan and stir into the mixture with the brandy.
3. Place twelve 15 ml (1 tbsp) amounts of the mixture on to the baking sheets, allowing them plenty of room to spread.
4. Bake in the oven at 180°C (350°F) mark 4 for 8–10 minutes, until golden. Cool slightly then slide off the paper on to wire racks.
5. Whip the cream until stiff and use to sandwich together three ginger crisps along with slices of strawberries. Repeat twice.
6. Chill the ginger crisps for at least 1 hour and decorate just before serving.

Kiwi Trifle

1 LARGE JAM SWISS ROLL
75 ml (3 fl oz) MEDIUM SHERRY
6 KIWI FRUIT, PEELED AND SLICED
100 g (4 oz) MACAROONS, BROKEN
3 EGG WHITES
125 g (4 oz) CASTER SUGAR
150 ml ($\frac{1}{4}$ pint) DRY WHITE VERMOUTH
30 ml (2 tbsp) BRANDY
15 ml (1 tbsp) LEMON JUICE
284 ml (10 fl oz) CARTON DOUBLE CREAM
WHIPPED CREAM, RATAFIAS AND SLICES OF KIWI FRUIT, TO DECORATE

Serves 8

1. Slice the Swiss roll and arrange in a large trifle bowl. Moisten with some sherry. Place the kiwi fruit over the Swiss roll with broken macaroons.
2. Whisk the egg whites until stiff, then gradually beat in the sugar until firm and glossy. Pour in the vermouth, brandy and lemon juice and gently fold through the meringue.
3. Whip the cream until standing in soft peaks and fold through the meringue mixture.
4. Pour the cream mixture over the Swiss roll and fruit, cover and refrigerate for about 2 hours. Just before serving, decorate with whipped cream, ratafias and slices of kiwi fruit.

Photographed opposite

Lemon Prune Mousse

225 g (8 oz) DRIED PRUNES, SOAKED OVERNIGHT AND DRAINED
PARED RIND OF 1 LEMON
10 ml (2 tsp) POWDERED GELATINE
45 ml (3 tbsp) LEMON JUICE, STRAINED
30 ml (2 tbsp) THICK HONEY
142 ml (5 fl oz) CARTON DOUBLE CREAM
1 EGG WHITE
FLAKED ALMONDS

Serves 4–6

1. Put the prunes into a pan, cover with water and bring to the boil. Add the lemon rind and simmer until the prunes are tender, about 20 minutes.
2. Soak the gelatine in a small bowl with the lemon juice over a pan of hot water.
3. Drain the prunes, reserving 150 ml ($\frac{1}{4}$ pint) cooking liquid. While still hot, stone the prunes and place the flesh in a blender with the reserved juice, dissolved gelatine and honey. Blend until smooth. Turn into a bowl to cool.
4. Lightly whip the cream and whisk the egg white until standing in stiff peaks. As the prune mixture begins to set, fold in the cream then the egg white. Turn the mousse into a glass serving bowl, refrigerate until set. Decorate with flaked almonds.

Kiwi Trifle

Citrus Apple Flan

Citrus Apple Flan

175 g (6 oz) PLAIN FLOUR
PINCH OF SALT
175 g (6 oz) BUTTER, SOFTENED
75 g (3 oz) CASTER SUGAR
3 EGG YOLKS
900 g (2 lb) COOKING APPLES, PEELED, CORED AND ROUGHLY CHOPPED
3 THIN-SKINNED ORANGES, RINDS FINELY GRATED AND THE FLESH THINLY SLICED
45 ml (3 tbsp) GRANULATED SUGAR
60 ml (4 tbsp) THICK-CUT ORANGE MARMALADE
15 ml (1 tbsp) WATER
WHIPPING OR SINGLE CREAM, TO SERVE

Serves 6

1. Sift the flour and salt on to a work surface. Make a well in the centre and place in it 125 g (4 oz) butter, the caster sugar and egg yolks. Work the ingredients together with the fingertips of one hand until smooth. Gradually draw in the flour, with the help of a palette knife. Knead lightly until smooth. Chill, covered, for 30 minutes.

2. Roll out the pastry on a lightly floured surface and use to line a 20 cm (8 inch) flan ring. Bake blind, with foil and beans, in the oven at 200°C (400°F) mark 6 for 10–15 minutes. Remove the foil and beans and leave to cool.

3. Put the apples into a pan with the orange rind, remaining butter, sugar and half the marmalade. Cover and cook gently for about 15 minutes, until the fruit is soft. Open-boil to a thick pulp, stirring frequently. Cool.

4. Fill the flan case with the apple purée and arrange the orange slices on top.

5. Heat the remaining marmalade with the water and sieve the marmalade. Brush over the orange slices. Serve cold with the cream.

Photographed above

Rhubarb Orange Fool

1 ORANGE
900 g (2 lb) RHUBARB, TRIMMED AND CUT INTO 2.5 cm (1 inch) LENGTHS
75 ml (5 tbsp) REDCURRANT JELLY
30 ml (2 tbsp) THICK HONEY
142 ml (5 fl oz) CARTON DOUBLE CREAM
SPONGE FINGERS, TO SERVE

Serves 6

1. Pare a few strips of rind off the orange using a potato peeler. Slice each one into *very* thin strips and blanch: put into a pan of boiling water for 2 minutes. Drain and dry with absorbent kitchen paper and keep covered until required.
2. Put the rhubarb into a saucepan with 90 ml (6 tbsp) strained orange juice, the redcurrant jelly and honey.
3. Cover tightly and simmer gently until the fruit is soft and pulpy. Stir occasionally to prevent the rhubarb sticking to the pan. Cool slightly, then rub through a sieve or purée in a blender. Pour into a large bowl and leave to cool.
4. Whip the cream until standing in soft peaks and fold through the cold fruit purée. Spoon into individual glass dishes, cover and chill well. Decorate with shredded rind. Serve with sponge fingers.

Photographed below

Blancmange

60 ml (4 tbsp) CORNFLOUR
568 ml (1 pint) MILK
STRIP OF LEMON RIND
45 ml (3 tbsp) SUGAR

Serves 4

1. Blend the cornflour to a smooth paste with 30 ml (2 tbsp) of the milk.
2. Boil the remaining milk with the lemon rind and strain it on to the blended mixture, stirring well.
3. Return the mixture to the pan and bring to the boil, stirring all the time, until the mixture thickens and cook for a further 3 minutes. Add sugar to taste.
4. Dampen a 600 ml (1 pint) jelly mould and pour the mixture into it. Leave for several hours until set. Turn out to serve with fresh fruit.

VARIATIONS

Chocolate Omit the lemon rind and add 50 g (2 oz) melted chocolate to the cooked mixture.
Coffee Omit the lemon rind and add 15–30 ml (1–2 tbsp) coffee essence.
Orange Substitute the lemon rind with 5 ml (1 tsp) grated orange rind.
Honey Use 15 ml (1 tbsp) honey instead of the caster sugar.

Rhubarb Orange Fool

English Trifle

568 ml (1 pint) MILK
$\frac{1}{2}$ VANILLA POD
2 EGGS, PLUS 2 EGG YOLKS
30 ml (2 tbsp) CASTER SUGAR
BOX OF 8 TRIFLE SPONGES
175 g (6 oz) RASPBERRY OR STRAWBERRY JAM
100 g (4 oz) MACAROONS, LIGHTLY CRUSHED
100 ml (4 fl oz) MEDIUM SHERRY
40 g ($1\frac{1}{2}$ oz) FLAKED ALMONDS
284 ml (10 fl oz) CARTON DOUBLE CREAM
50 g (2 oz) GLACE CHERRIES, TO DECORATE

Serves 6

1. Put the milk and the vanilla pod into a pan and bring quickly to the boil. Remove from the heat. Cover the pan and leave to infuse for 20 minutes.
2. Beat together the eggs, egg yolks and sugar and strain on the milk. Cook over a gentle heat, without boiling, stirring all the time until the custard thickens slightly. Pour into a bowl; lightly sprinkle the surface with sugar and cool.
3. Spread the trifle sponges with jam, cut up and place in a 2 litre ($3\frac{1}{2}$ pint) shallow serving dish with the macaroons. Spoon over the sherry and leave for 2 hours. Pour over the cold custard.
4. Put the almonds into the grill pan and toast until golden, about 3 minutes, turning frequently.
5. Whip the cream until standing in soft peaks. Top the custard with half the cream. Put the remaining cream into a piping bag fitted with a 1 cm ($\frac{1}{2}$ inch) star nozzle and pipe on top. Decorate with the almonds and cherries.

Mousse au Chocolat

225 g (8 oz) PLAIN CHOCOLATE, BROKEN INTO PIECES
30 ml (2 tbsp) WATER
15 ml (1 tbsp) RUM
125 g (4 oz) BUTTER
125 g (4 oz) CASTER SUGAR
4 EGGS, SEPARATED
142 ml (5 fl oz) CARTON DOUBLE CREAM
CHOCOLATE CURLS, TO DECORATE

Serves 6

1. Put the chocolate into a bowl with the water and rum. Place over simmering water and stir until smooth. Cool slightly.
2. Whisk together the butter and sugar until pale and fluffy, then beat in the egg yolks one at a time.
3. Add the chocolate to the butter mixture and beat for 5 minutes until light.
4. Whisk the whites until stiff and fold into the chocolate. Pour into a serving dish or individual glasses and chill until set. Whip the cream until stiff and use to decorate the mousse. Finish with chocolate curls.

Photographed opposite

Fresh Fruit Flan

454 g (1 lb) PACKET PUFF PASTRY, THAWED
1 EGG, BEATEN
340 g (12 oz) JAR APRICOT JAM
30 ml (2 tbsp) LEMON JUICE
450 g (1 lb) FRESH STRAWBERRIES
3 KIWI FRUIT, PEELED AND SLICED

Serves 10 buffet portions

1. On a lightly floured surface, roll out three-quarters of the pastry to a 30 cm (12 inch) round. Place on a baking sheet and prick well.
2. Roll out the remaining pastry and using a 7.5 cm (3 inch) fluted cutter, stamp out 12 crescents.
3. Brush the pastry round with beaten egg and arrange the crescents around the edge. Brush these with egg too.
4. Bake the pastry case in the oven at 220°C (425°F) mark 7 for 12 minutes. Prick the base again then lower the heat to 170°C (325°F) mark 3 for a further 10 minutes. Cool.
5. Warm the apricot jam and lemon juice, sieve and return to the pan. Brush a little over the base of the pastry case.
6. Arrange the fruit in wedge shapes in the pastry case radiating outwards from the centre to the pastry crescents.
7. Glaze the fruits and pastry edge with the remaining warm jam.

Coffee Cream Soufflés

15 ml (3 tsp) GELATINE
45 ml (3 tbsp) WATER
3 EGGS, SEPARATED
75 g (3 oz) CASTER SUGAR
45 ml (3 tbsp) COFFEE ESSENCE
142 ml (5 fl oz) CARTON SINGLE CREAM
284 ml (10 fl oz) CARTON WHIPPING CREAM
25 g (1 oz) CHOPPED ALMONDS

Serves 6

1. Prepare six 100 ml (4 fl oz) soufflé dishes, by surrounding them with foil to come 2.5 cm (1 inch) above the top of the dish. Secure with adhesive tape.
2. Dissolve the gelatine in the water in a small bowl over a pan of hot water.
3. In a deep bowl, whisk the egg yolks and sugar together over a pan of hot water until thick. Cool to lukewarm.
4. Add the coffee essence and gelatine to the single cream, whisk into the egg yolk mixture. Leave until beginning to set.
5. Whip the whipping cream until standing in soft peaks. Whisk the egg whites until stiff. Fold the cream and egg whites into the coffee mixture. Turn into the prepared soufflé dishes.
6. Refrigerate until set, remove foil and decorate the edges with almonds.

Mousse au Chocolat

Almond Custard Tarts

Almond Custard Tarts

225 g (8 oz) PLAIN FLOUR
125 g (4 oz) BUTTER, CUT INTO SMALL PIECES
200 ml (7 fl oz) MILK; PLUS ABOUT 45 ml (3 tbsp), TO BIND
50 g (2 oz) FLAKED ALMONDS
2 EGGS
50 g (2 oz) CASTER SUGAR
1.25 ml ($\frac{1}{4}$ tsp) RATAFIA FLAVOURING

Makes 10

1. Sift the flour into a bowl and rub in the butter until the mixture resembles fine breadcrumbs. Bind to a firm dough with about 45 ml (3 tbsp) milk.

2. Butter ten 7.5 cm (3 inch) fluted brioche tins and place on a baking sheet.

3. On a lightly floured surface, roll out the pastry thinly and use to line the tins. Chill for 20 minutes. Bake blind with foil and beans in the oven at 200°C (400°F) mark 6 for 15 minutes. Remove the foil and beans.

4. Put the almonds into the grill pan and toast until golden, about 3 minutes, turning frequently.

5. Whisk together the milk, eggs, caster sugar and ratafia flavouring and pour into the pastry cases. Scatter toasted almonds on top. Lower the oven to 180°C (350°F) mark 4 and bake for a further 15–20 minutes until just set. Leave to cool before serving.

Photographed above

Mocha Roulade

15 ml (1 tbsp) INSTANT COFFEE POWDER
15 ml (1 tbsp) WATER
100 g (4 oz) PLAIN CHOCOLATE, BROKEN INTO PIECES
4 EGGS (size 2), SEPARATED
100 g (4 oz) CASTER SUGAR
284 ml (10 fl oz) CARTON DOUBLE CREAM
175 g (6 oz) WHITE GRAPES, HALVED AND SEEDED

Serves 6–8

1. In a small bowl, blend the coffee to a smooth paste with the water. Put the chocolate into the bowl and melt over simmering water. Cool.

2. Cut a 30 cm (12 inch) square of non-stick paper, fold up 2.5 cm (1 inch) all round. Snip into the corners, secure the edges with paperclips to form a free-standing paper case. Place on a baking sheet.

3. Whisk the yolks and sugar until thick then stir in the cool coffee chocolate. Whisk the egg whites until stiff and fold into the mixture. Spread into the paper case.

4. Bake in the oven at 180°C (350°F) mark 4 for about 15 minutes, until firm. Turn out. Cover with a sheet of greaseproof paper and roll up with the paper inside. Leave to cool on a wire rack, seam side down.

5. Whip the cream until standing in soft peaks. When the cake is cold, unroll and remove the paper. Spread it with whipped cream, reroll and decorate with cream and the grapes.

BAKING

French Bread

15 g ($\frac{1}{2}$ oz) FRESH YEAST OR 10 ml (2 tsp) DRIED
250 ml ($\frac{1}{2}$ pint) TEPID WATER
5 ml (1 tsp) CASTER SUGAR
350 g (14 oz) PLAIN FLOUR
50 g (2 oz) CORNFLOUR
5 ml (1 tsp) SALT
OIL
1 EGG

Makes two 35.5 × 15 cm (14 × 6 inch) loaves

1. Crumble the fresh yeast into a bowl, pour in the tepid water and stir gently until smooth. (For dried yeast, dissolve the sugar in the tepid water then sprinkle the yeast over the surface. Leave to stand in a warm place for about 20 minutes, or until frothy, whisking occasionally.)

2. Sift the flour and cornflour with the salt into a large bowl and stir in the sugar. (If dried yeast is being used the sugar will already be incorporated.) Make a well in the centre of the dry ingredients and pour in the yeast liquid. Using a wooden spoon gradually beat the flour into the well of liquid until a firm dough is formed.

3. Turn the dough out on to a lightly floured surface. Rotate the dough with one hand and with the heel of the other, push and stretch the dough from the centre outwards. Continue kneading this way for about 4 minutes, or until the dough is smooth.

4. Lightly oil a large mixing bowl and put the kneaded dough in it. Cover the bowl with oiled cling film or a damp tea-towel and stand it in a warm, not hot, place for about 1 hour, or until the dough has doubled in size.

5. Halve the dough and knead each piece until just smooth. On a well floured surface roll each piece out to an oblong about 35.5 × 15 cm (14 × 6 inches) leaving the ends rounded off. Carefully roll up the dough from the long side like a Swiss roll. Place the rolls, seam side down, on well floured baking sheets.

6. Using a sharp knife make shallow slashes along the top of the dough at 4 cm (1$\frac{1}{2}$ inches) intervals. Beat the egg with a good pinch of salt and brush over the surface of the loaves.

7. Put the loaves in a warm place, uncovered, until trebled in size, 20–40 minutes. They should feel springy to the touch.

8. Heat the oven to 220°C (425°F) mark 7 and place a roasting tin of hot water in the base. Bake the loaves for 15 minutes then remove the pan of water. Continue baking the loaves for a further 8–10 minutes or until well browned and really crisp. The loaves should sound hollow when tapped. Ease off the baking sheets and cool on wire racks.

Photographed right

French Bread

Basic White Bread

15 g (½ oz) FRESH YEAST OR 10 ml (2 tsp) DRIED
ABOUT 450 ml (16 fl oz) TEPID WATER
750 g (1 lb 10 oz) STRONG PLAIN BREAD FLOUR
10 ml (2 tsp) SALT
KNOB OF LARD

Makes three 450 g (1 lb) loaves or one 900 g (2 lb) and one 450 g (1 lb) loaf

1. Crumble the fresh yeast into a bowl and cream with a little of the water until smooth. (If using dried yeast, reconstitute according to packet directions.) Sift the flour and salt into a large bowl and rub in lard. Stir in the yeast liquid and remaining water to give a soft, manageable but not sticky dough.
2. Knead well on a floured surface until smooth and elastic—at least 10 minutes. Shape into a ball and place in a large, oiled bowl. Stretch oiled cling film over the top of the bowl and leave in a warm place for the dough to double in size, about 40 minutes.
3. Grease a 1.7 litre (3 pint) capacity bread tin and an 850 ml (1½ pint) loaf tin. Knead the dough again for 4–5 minutes. Shape two-thirds into a loaf, and place in the larger prepared tin. Shape the remaining third into a loaf, place in the smaller tin.
4. Cover the tins with oiled cling film and leave to rise again until the dough just reaches the top of the tin—about 40 minutes.
5. Bake at 230°C (450°F) mark 8 for 20–25 minutes, until well browned. Cook for a further 10 minutes at 180°C (350°F) mark 4 or until the loaves sound hollow when tapped. Cool on a wire rack.

Basic Brown Bread

25 g (1 oz) FRESH YEAST OR 15 ml (1 tbsp) DRIED
ABOUT 500 ml (18 fl oz) TEPID WATER
750 g (1 lb 10 oz) BROWN WHEATMEAL BREAD FLOUR
15 ml (1 tbsp) CASTER SUGAR
10 ml (2 tsp) SALT
25 g (1 oz) LARD
1 EGG
BARLEY KERNELS, TO FINISH

Makes three 450 g (1 lb) loaves or one 900 g (2 lb) loaf and one 450 g (1 lb) loaf

1. Crumble the fresh yeast into a bowl and cream with a little of the water until smooth. (If using dried yeast, reconstitute according to packet directions.) Sift the flour, sugar and salt into a large bowl and rub in the lard. Stir in the yeast liquid and remaining water to give a manageable but not sticky dough.
2. Knead well on a floured board until smooth and elastic—at least 10 minutes. Shape into a ball and place in a large, oiled bowl. Stretch oiled cling film over the top of the bowl. Leave in a warm place for the dough to double in size, about 40 minutes.
3. Grease three 850 ml (1½ pint) loaf tins. Knead the dough again for 3–4 minutes. Make into three loaf shapes and place each, seam-side down, in a prepared loaf tin. Cover with oiled cling film and leave to rise until double in size.
4. Beat the egg with a pinch of salt and lightly glaze the loaves. Sprinkle with barley kernels and bake at 230°C (450°F) mark 8 about 20 minutes until well browned. Lower the heat to 180°C (350°F) mark 4 for further 10 minutes, or until the loaves sound hollow when tapped. Remove from the tins and cool.

Basic Enriched White Dough

750 g (1 lb 10 oz) STRONG PLAIN FLOUR
10 ml (2 tsp) CASTER SUGAR
25 g (1 oz) FRESH YEAST OR 15 ml (1 tbsp) DRIED
ABOUT 400 ml (14 fl oz) TEPID MILK
10 ml (2 tsp) SALT
75 g (3 oz) BUTTER
1 EGG, BEATEN

Makes three 450 g (1 lb) loaves or one 900 g (2 lb) and one 450 g (1 lb) loaf

1. Sift 200 g (7 oz) flour with the sugar into a large bowl. Crumble in the fresh yeast, make a well in the centre and gradually work in the tepid milk. (If using dried yeast, reconstitute according to packet directions.) Cover the bowl with oiled cling film and leave in a warm place until frothy—about 30 minutes.
2. Sift together the remaining flour and salt and rub in the butter. Stir the egg into the frothing yeast mixture with the dry ingredients. Mix well to a soft but manageable dough, adding a little more flour if the dough is too sticky.
3. Turn on to a floured surface and knead until smooth and elastic—at least 10 minutes. Shape into a ball and put into a clean, oiled bowl. Stretch oiled cling film over the top of the bowl and leave in warm place until the dough has doubled in size. Knead again for 4–5 minutes.
4. Use to make a Honey Nut Stick; Fruited Butterscotch Ring and a Horseradish Crown on page 246.

Sage and Onion Salad Loaf

½ QUANTITY BASIC WHITE BREAD DOUGH (see top left, Steps 1 and 2) MADE UP WITH 21 g (¾ oz) PACKET DRIED ONION SAUCE MIX ADDED TO THE FLOUR AND THE TEPID WATER INCREASED BY ABOUT 15 ml (1 tbsp)
50 g (2 oz) SAGE DERBY CHEESE, FINELY GRATED
1 BEATEN EGG, TO GLAZE

Makes one loaf

1. Grease and base-line a 19 cm (7½ inch) round sandwich tin. Knead the dough again and roll out to a round 35 cm (14 inches) wide. Place in the prepared tin with the edges overlapping the sides of the tin. Heap the cheese in the centre.
2. Fold in the excess dough, drawing it up and over the filling, and pleating into loose, even folds.
3. Cover with oiled cling film and leave in a warm place to rise.
4. Emphasise the folds with a floured finger and brush with beaten egg. Bake at 230°C (450°F) mark 8 for 20 minutes until browned. Lower the oven to 190°C (375°F) mark 5 and bake for about a further 15 minutes. Cool on a wire rack.

)atmeal Coburg

QUANTITY BASIC WHITE BREAD DOUGH (see opposite age, Steps 1 and 2) MADE USING 250 g ($9\frac{1}{2}$ oz) MEDIUM ATMEAL IN PLACE OF THE SAME AMOUNT OF STRONG LAIN FLOUR WITH ONLY 400 ml (14 fl oz) TEPID WATER

ATMEAL, TO FINISH

lakes one loaf

. Grease a baking sheet. Knead the dough again, hape into a large ball and flatten slightly. Place on the aking sheet.

. With a sharp knife, cut a deep cross in the top of the)af. Cover with oiled cling film and leave until doubled ı size.

. Brush with water and scatter with oatmeal. Bake at 30°C (450°F) mark 8 for 20 minutes until browned, ıen lower the oven to 190°C (375°F) mark 5 for about) minutes until the loaf sounds hollow when tapped. ool on a wire rack.

)range Ginger Knot

QUANTITY BASIC WHITE BREAD DOUGH (see opposite age, Steps 1 and 2) MADE UP WITH 10 ml (2 tsp) GROUND INGER, 25 g (1 oz) CHOPPED STEM GINGER, 25 g (1 oz) ASTER SUGAR AND FINELY GRATED RIND OF 1 ORANGE DDED TO THE DRY INGREDIENTS AND THE YEAST REAMED WITH 45 ml (3 tbsp) WARMED BLACK TREACLE ND THE JUICE OF 1 ORANGE MADE UP TO 225 ml (8 fl oz) 'ITH TEPID WATER

BEATEN EGG, TO GLAZE

INGER SYRUP FROM JAR

lakes one loaf

Grease a baking sheet. Knead the dough again, ıvide into eight pieces and roll into oblong sausage ıapes. Tie into knots and place seven in a circle on the ıking sheet with the eighth knot in the centre. Press ›gether for a compact round loaf.

Cover with oiled cling film and leave to rise.

Brush with beaten egg and bake at 230°C (450°F) ark 8 for 20 minutes until golden. Lower the oven to)0°C (375°F) mark 5 for about 15 minutes. Brush with .nger syrup while warm and cool on a wire rack.

;olden Cornmeal Loaves

QUANTITY BASIC WHITE BREAD DOUGH (see opposite ıge, Steps 1 and 2) MADE USING 350 g (13 oz) CORN OR AIZE MEAL IN PLACE OF THE SAME AMOUNT OF STRONG LAIN BREAD FLOUR AND 100 g (4 oz) SOFT LIGHT BROWN JGAR ADDED TO THE DRY INGREDIENTS WITH ONLY)0 ml (14 fl oz) TEPID WATER

)RNMEAL, TO FINISH

lakes two loaves

Grease a 1.7 litre (3 pint) loaf tin. Knead the dough gain and set one-third aside. Using the larger piece, ıke off one-third and make into six golf-ball sized ieces. Shape the rest into a loaf and place in the repared tin. Top with the six pieces, cover with oiled ing film and leave to rise.

Grease an 850 ml ($1\frac{1}{2}$ pint) loaf tin. Shape the other piece of dough into a similar, smaller loaf and place in the prepared tin. Cover and leave to rise.

3. Brush the loaves with water and scatter corn or maize meal over the tops. Bake at 230°C (450°F) mark 8 for 20 minutes until brown and risen. Lower the oven to 190°C (375°F) mark 5 for about 15 minutes. Cool on a wire rack.

Anchovy Wheatmeal Curl

$\frac{1}{2}$ QUANTITY BASIC BROWN BREAD DOUGH (see opposite page, Steps 1 and 2)

50 g (2 oz) CAN ANCHOVY FILLETS

A LITTLE MILK

75 g (3 oz) BUTTER, SOFTENED

FRESHLY GROUND BLACK PEPPER

Makes one loaf

1. Grease and base-line a 19 cm ($7\frac{1}{2}$ inch) round cake tin.

2. Prepare the anchovy butter: soak the anchovies in milk for 10 minutes to remove the salt. Drain. Pound the anchovies, butter and black pepper together and push the mixture through a sieve. Keep covered at cool room temperature.

3. Knead the dough again and roll out to a 30 cm (12 inch) square.

4. Spread the anchovy butter all over the dough and roll up from either side so that the two rolls meet in the centre. Cut across into eight pieces.

5. Place the rolls, cut side down, in the prepared tin.

6. Cover with oiled cling film and leave to rise in a warm place for about 25 minutes, or until double in size.

7. Bake at 230°C (450°F) mark 8 for about 20 minutes. Turn out of the tin and cool on a wire rack.

Almond Filled Coffee Bread

$\frac{1}{2}$ QUANTITY BASIC BROWN BREAD DOUGH (see opposite page, Steps 1 and 2)

175 g (6 oz) ALMOND PASTE

1 EGG, BEATEN

25 g (1 oz) FLAKED ALMONDS

125 g (4 oz) ICING SUGAR, SIFTED

30 ml (2 tbsp) LEMON JUICE

Makes one loaf

1. Grease a baking sheet. Knead the dough again and roll out to a 30 cm (12 inch) square. Cut into nine equal-sized squares.

2. Roll the almond paste into nine balls, flatten slightly and place one in the centre of each dough square.

3. Fold the corners of each square of dough over the almond paste and press down well to secure.

4. Place close together in three rows on the baking sheet. Cover with oiled cling film and leave in a warm place to double in size.

5. Brush with beaten egg, sprinkle with almonds and bake at 230°C (450°F) mark 8 for 15–20 minutes. Slide on to a wire rack and cool a little.

6. Mix the icing sugar in a bowl with the lemon juice and sufficient water to give a pouring consistency. Drizzle over the still warm bread. Eat while warm.

Hot Cross Buns

- 450 g (1 lb) STRONG PLAIN FLOUR
- 25 g (1 oz) FRESH YEAST OR 15 ml (1 tbsp) DRIED
- 5 ml (1 tsp) CASTER SUGAR; PLUS 50 g (2 oz)
- 150 ml ($\frac{1}{4}$ pint) MILK AND 75 ml (5 tbsp) WATER, MIXED
- 50 g (2 oz) BUTTER
- 1 EGG, BEATEN
- 5 ml (1 tsp) SALT
- 5 ml (1 tsp) MIXED SPICE
- 5 ml (1 tsp) GROUND CINNAMON
- 2.5 ml ($\frac{1}{2}$ tsp) FRESHLY GRATED NUTMEG
- 75 g (3 oz) CURRANTS
- 30 ml (2 tbsp) MIXED PEEL, CHOPPED
- 50 g (2 oz) PLAIN FLOUR
- 25 g (1 oz) BUTTER
- 60 ml (4 tbsp) MILK AND WATER, MIXED, TO GLAZE
- 45 ml (3 tbsp) CASTER SUGAR, TO GLAZE

Makes 12

1. Sift 125 g (4 oz) flour into a large bowl and crumble in the fresh yeast. (Or, sprinkle in the dried yeast with 5 ml (1 tsp) caster sugar.) Warm the milk and water mixture to blood heat. Make a well in the centre of the flour and pour in the liquid. Gradually fold in the flour. Leave to stand in a warm place for about 20 minutes, or until frothy.

2. Meanwhile, melt the butter and leave to cool but not set. With a wooden spoon beat the butter and egg into the yeast mixture. Sift in the remaining flour, salt and spices, and add 50 g (2 oz) caster sugar, the currants and mixed peel. Stir well. The dough may seem rather wet but on kneading it will become more manageable.

3. Turn the dough out on to a well floured surface and sprinkle flour over the dough. Knead by rotating the dough with one hand and with the heel of the other pushing and stretching it from the centre outwards. Do not knead any loose dry bits of dough back into it. Knead, sprinkling with flour as necessary, until soft, smooth and elastic—at least 5 minutes.

4. Put the dough into a large, lightly oiled bowl. Cover loosely with oiled cling film or a damp tea-towel and leave to rise in a warm, not hot, place for about 1$\frac{1}{2}$ hours, or until it has doubled in size.

5. Turn the risen dough out on to a lightly floured surface. Knead lightly to knock out the air and divide into 12 pieces. Knead each into a round by bringing the edges into the centre and pressing them lightly together with the fingertips. Rotate each piece of dough and knead lightly.

6. Put the buns, well apart, smooth side up, on floured baking sheets and flatten lightly with the heel of the hand. With a sharp knife lightly mark a cross on the surface of each. Cover loosely with oiled cling film and leave in a warm place for about 40 minutes, or until they have doubled in size.

7. Make the pastry: sift the flour into a bowl. Add the butter and rub in until the mixture resembles fine breadcrumbs. Mix in just enough water to form a firm dough. Roll out on a lightly floured surface to an oblong about 15 × 9 cm (6 × 3$\frac{1}{2}$ inches). Cut 24 narrow pastry strips crossways and brush lightly with water. Uncover the risen buns and place two pastry strips across the marks of each bun. Press on gently.

8. Bake the buns in 220°C (425°F) mark 7 oven for 10 minutes. Lower the heat to 190°C (375°F) mark 5 and bake for a further 8–10 minutes. When cooked they should be golden brown and just firm to the touch.

9. Warm the milk, water and sugar. Brush twice over the hot buns on the baking sheets. Cool on a wire rack.

Photographed opposite

Granary Tea Cake

- 100 g (4 oz) BUTTER
- 250 ml (9 fl oz) MILK
- 750 g (1 lb 10 oz) GRANARY MEAL
- 10 ml (2 tsp) SALT
- 25 g (1 oz) FRESH YEAST OR 15 ml (1 tbsp) DRIED
- 2 EGGS (size 2), BEATEN
- 50 g (2 oz) CURRANTS
- 25 g (1 oz) CHOPPED MIXED PEEL
- BEATEN EGG
- BARLEY KERNELS, TO FINISH

Makes 2 loaves

1. In a pan, melt the butter in the milk and cool.

2. Mix the granary meal and salt. Cream the fresh yeast with a little cool milk. (If using dried yeast reconstitute according to packet directions.)

3. Make a well in centre of the dry ingredients, add the yeast and the remaining milk and eggs. Mix to soft dough with the currants and mixed peel.

4. Knead for 10 minutes, put into a greased bowl, cover with oiled cling film and leave until doubled in size.

5. Grease two baking sheets. Knead the dough again and divide into 16 pieces. Shape into flat ovals. Arrange on the baking sheets, in overlapping rings of eight buns each. Cover with oiled cling film and leave until doubled in size.

6. Brush with beaten egg, scatter with barley kernels and bake at 200°C (400°F) mark 6 for about 25 minutes. Cool on a wire rack.

Zigzag Baton

- 566 g (1 lb 4 oz) PACKET WHITE OR BROWN BREAD MIX
- 45 ml (3 tbsp) WATER
- MILK, TO GLAZE

Makes 1

1. Make up the bread mix, adding the extra water according to packet instructions. Leave to rise in a bowl rather than a bread tin. Grease a baking sheet.

2. Turn the dough out on to a lightly floured board and knead for a few minutes. Using both hands roll into a sausage shape about 40 cm (16 inches) long. Put on to the prepared baking sheet.

3. With a pair of sharp scissors held at a 30° angle to the top surface of the dough, make V-shaped cuts about three-quarters of the way through the dough at 5 cm (2 inch) intervals. Pull each cut section out to alternate sides to give a zigzag appearance. Leave to rise again until twice the size.

4. Brush with milk and bake at 230°C (450°F) mark 8 for about 30 minutes. Cool on a wire rack. To serve, wrap in foil and refresh in the oven.

Hot Cross Buns

Mustard Flower Pots

½ QUANTITY BASIC BROWN BREAD DOUGH (see page 242, Steps 1 and 2) MADE UP WITH 50 g (2 oz) CHOPPED WALNUTS ADDED TO THE DRY INGREDIENTS AND BLENDING 30 ml (2 tbsp) DIJON MUSTARD WITH THE WATER

1 EGG, BEATEN

BARLEY FLAKES, TO FINISH

Makes 2 loaves

1. Thoroughly grease two clean earthenware flower-pots, 700 ml (1¼ pint).

2. Knead the dough again, divide in half and shape each piece to fit a flowerpot.

3. Slash the top of each loaf with a sharp knife. Cover with oiled cling film and stand the pots on a baking sheet. Leave to rise in a warm place until the dough just fills the pots. Emphasise the slash marks again.

4. Brush the surface of each with egg, sprinkle with barley flakes and bake at 220°C (425°F) mark 7 for about 35 minutes, covering lightly with foil if necessary. Ease out of the pots and cool on a wire rack.

Honey Nut Stick

½ QUANTITY BASIC ENRICHED WHITE DOUGH (see page 242, Steps 1 and 2)

90 ml (6 tbsp) CRUNCHY PEANUT BUTTER

60 ml (4 tbsp) THICK HONEY

1 EGG, BEATEN

SESAME SEEDS, TO FINISH

CLEAR HONEY, TO GLAZE

Makes one loaf

1. Roll out the prepared dough to a rectangle 33 × 23 cm (13 × 9 inches). Spread with peanut butter leaving 2.5 cm (1 inch) dough round the edges. Spread honey on top.

2. Grease a baking sheet. Roll the dough up like a Swiss roll from the long edge. Place on the baking sheet and scissor snip to make deep diagonal slashes at 5 cm (2 inch) intervals along the loaf. Open out the leaves of dough slightly.

3. Cover with oiled cling film and leave in a warm place until doubled in size.

4. Brush with egg and scatter over sesame seeds.

5. Bake at 220°C (425°F) mark 7 for 25–30 minutes until browned and risen. Brush with clear honey while still warm. Cool on a wire rack.

Horseradish Crown

½ QUANTITY BASIC ENRICHED WHITE DOUGH (see page 242, Steps 1 and 2) MADE UP WITH 45 ml (3 tbsp) HORSERADISH SAUCE BLENDED WITH THE MILK

35 g (1¼ oz) JAR BEEF SPREAD

1 BEATEN EGG, TO GLAZE

PORRIDGE WHEATMEAL, TO FINISH

Makes one loaf

1. Divide the prepared dough into eight equal pieces.

2. Flatten seven of the pieces and place a knob of beef spread in the middle of each. Bring the edges together and knead gently into a bun.

3. Grease and base-line a 19 cm (7½ inch) round deep cake tin and arrange the buns in the tin with one bun in the centre.

4. Divide the remaining piece of dough into five small balls and arrange round the centre bun. With a well-floured finger make a deep hole in the centre.

5. Cover with oiled cling film and leave to rise until doubled in size.

6. Brush with beaten egg and scatter over the porridge wheatmeal. Bake at 230°C (450°F) mark 8 for 20 minutes, than at 190°C (375°F) mark 5 for about a further 15 minutes. Turn out and cool on a wire rack.

Fruited Butterscotch Ring

½ QUANTITY BASIC ENRICHED WHITE DOUGH (see page 242, Steps 1 and 2)

50 g (2 oz) BUTTER

50 g (2 oz) SOFT LIGHT BROWN SUGAR

30 ml (2 tbsp) GOLDEN SYRUP

50 g (2 oz) CURRANTS

Makes one loaf

1. Shape the prepared dough into about 36 small balls. Grease and base-line a 1.7 litre (3 pint) angel cake tin or plain ring mould.

2. Melt the butter, sugar and golden syrup together in a pan and bring to the boil. Pour into the base of the prepared tin and sprinkle over half the currants.

3. Arrange the balls of dough in loose layers in the tin, sprinkling with the rest of the currants.

4. Cover with oiled cling film and leave to rise until the dough almost reaches the top of the tin.

5. Place the tin on a baking sheet and bake at 220°C (425°F) mark 7 for about 40 minutes.

6. Turn out and cool completely on a wire rack before slicing, or pull apart to eat while still warm.

Home Made Rye

50 g (2 oz) BUTTER

300 ml (11 fl oz) MILK

25 g (1 oz) FRESH YEAST OR 15 ml (1 tbsp) DRIED

5 ml (1 tsp) BROWN SUGAR

150 ml (¼ pint) WARM WATER

60 ml (4 tbsp) BLACK TREACLE

1 EGG

500 g (19 oz) RYE FLOUR

30 ml (2 tbsp) CARAWAY SEEDS

250 g (9 oz) WHOLEWHEAT FLOUR

20 ml (4 tsp) SALT

1 EGG, BEATEN, TO GLAZE

Makes one loaf

1. In a pan, melt the butter in the milk and cool. Cream the fresh yeast with a little water. (If using dried yeast,

reconstitute according to packet directions, using the brown sugar.) Mix the milk and water together with the treacle, brown sugar (if not already used) and the egg.
2. Mix together 250 g (9 oz) rye flour and the caraway seeds. Add the yeast liquid and beat until smooth. Cover with oiled cling film and leave for 30 minutes, until doubled in size.
3. Beat in the rest of flour and salt. Knead for at least 10 minutes. Leave to rise and knead again.
4. Grease and base-line a 19 cm (7½ inch) round tin. Shape the dough into a round and press into the tin. Cover with oiled cling film and leave until doubled in size.
5. Glaze with beaten egg and bake at 200°C (400°F) mark 6 for about 45 minutes. Cool on a wire rack.

Barley Wholewheat Twist

- 225 g (8 oz) BARLEY FLOUR
- 175 g (6 oz) STRONG PLAIN FLOUR
- 10 ml (2 tsp) SALT
- 225 g (8 oz) WHOLEWHEAT FLOUR
- 50 g (2 oz) WHEATGERM
- 50 g (2 oz) BUTTER
- 450 ml (17 fl oz) MILK AND WATER MIXED
- 25 g (1 oz) FRESH YEAST OR 15 ml (1 tbsp) DRIED
- 1 EGG, BEATEN, TO GLAZE
- WHEATGERM, TO FINISH

Makes one loaf
1. Mix the barley flour with 125 g (4 oz) strong plain flour and 5 ml (1 tsp) salt. In another bowl, mix the wholewheat flour, remaining strong plain flour, wheatgerm and remaining salt.
2. In a pan, melt the butter in the milk and water and cool. Cream the fresh yeast with a little cooled liquid. If using dried yeast reconstitute according to packet directions.) Add the remaining liquid.
3. Divide the liquid equally between the bowls of flour, mix each to a soft dough and knead. Leave until double in size.
4. Grease a baking sheet. Knead the dough again. Halve each piece of dough, roll into 30 cm (12 inch) lengths. Twist one of each together, repeat with the other pair. Place both twists on the baking sheet to form a single loaf. Cover with oiled cling film and leave to rise until double in size.
5. Brush with egg, scatter with wheatgerm and bake at 200°C (400°F) mark 6 for about 40 minutes. Cool on a wire rack.

Poppyseed Rolls

- 450 g (1 lb) STRONG PLAIN FLOUR
- 45 ml (3 tbsp) POPPYSEEDS
- 5 ml (1 tsp) SALT
- 5 ml (1 tsp) SUGAR
- 15 g (½ oz) FRESH YEAST OR 7.5 ml (1½ tsp) DRIED YEAST AND A PINCH OF SUGAR
- 325 ml (11 fl oz) WARM MILK
- BEATEN EGG AND MILK, TO GLAZE

Makes 8
1. Mix the flour, 30 ml (2 tbsp) poppyseeds, salt and sugar together.
2. Cream the fresh yeast with a little of the measured milk. Add the remaining milk. If using dried yeast, sprinkle it with the sugar into a little of the milk and leave in a warm place for 15 minutes until frothy. Add the remaining milk.
3. Pour the yeast mixture into the dry ingredients. Mix well to form a firm dough.
4. Knead the dough for at least 10 minutes. Place in an oiled bowl; cover with a clean tea-towel and leave to rise for about 1–1½ hours or until doubled in size.
5. Knead again for 5 minutes. Divide the dough into 24 pieces. Shape each piece into a ball. On a floured baking sheet, place the dough balls in triangular groups of three.
6. Leave the dough triangles to rise in a warm place for 10 minutes. Glaze with a mixture of beaten egg and milk. Sprinkle with the remaining poppyseeds.
7. Bake in the oven at 200°C (400°F) mark 6 for about 20 minutes. Cool on a wire rack.

Scottish Baps

- 450 g (1 lb) STRONG PLAIN FLOUR
- 5 ml (1 tsp) SALT
- 5 ml (1 tsp) CASTER SUGAR
- 50 g (2 oz) LARD
- 15 g (½ oz) FRESH YEAST OR 7.5 ml (1½ tsp) DRIED YEAST AND A PINCH OF SUGAR
- 325 ml (11 fl oz) WARM MILK AND WATER MIXED
- MILK, TO GLAZE

Makes 12
1. Mix together the flour, salt and sugar. Rub in the lard.
2. Cream the fresh yeast with a little of the measured liquid. Add the remaining liquid. If using dried yeast, sprinkle it with the sugar into a little of the measured liquid and leave in a warm place for 15 minutes until frothy. Add the remaining liquid.
3. Pour the yeast liquid on to the dry ingredients. Mix well to form a firm dough. Knead well for at least 10 minutes. Place in an oiled bowl and cover with a clean tea-towel. Leave to rise in a warm place for about 1 hour or until doubled in size.
4. Knead again for 5 minutes. Divide the dough into 12 equal pieces. Shape each piece into a ball and then roll out to a round about 7.5 cm (3 inch) in diameter and 5 mm (¼ inch) thick.
5. Place on a floured baking sheet, brush with milk and dust with flour. Leave to rise further in a warm place for 10 minutes.
6. Bake in the oven at 200°C (400°F) mark 6 for 20–25 minutes. Cool on a wire rack. Dust with more flour.

Spiced Honey Madeira

100 g (4 oz) BUTTER
45 ml (3 tbsp) THICK HONEY
2 EGGS, BEATEN
175 g (6 oz) SELF-RAISING FLOUR
10 ml (2 tsp) GROUND GINGER
PINCH OF SALT
50 g (2 oz) ICING SUGAR
ABOUT 15 ml (1 tbsp) LEMON JUICE

Serves 4–6

1. Grease and line a 750 ml (1¼ pint) loaf tin. Cream the butter and honey together until well blended, beat in the eggs, little by little. Sift the flour with the ginger and salt and fold into the creamed mixture.
2. Turn into the prepared tin and bake at 180°C (350°F) mark 4 for about 40 minutes.
3. Meanwhile, make a glacé icing: sift the icing sugar into a bowl and mix with the lemon juice.
4. Turn the cake out of tin on to a wire rack and, while hot, cover with the glacé icing.

Cinnamon Sponge Drops with Cream

4 EGGS, SEPARATED, PLUS 1 EGG YOLK
75 ml (5 tbsp) CASTER SUGAR
60 ml (4 tbsp) PLAIN FLOUR
60 ml (4 tbsp) CORNFLOUR
40 g (1½ oz) BUTTER, MELTED
ICING SUGAR AND GROUND CINNAMON, TO DUST
284 ml (10 fl oz) CARTON DOUBLE CREAM

Makes 16

1. Line two baking sheets with non-stick paper and pencil out four 10 cm (4 inch) circles on each. Reverse the paper.
2. In a deep bowl, whisk the egg yolks with half the sugar until really thick. Sift the flours and fold them in then gently stir in the cool, still liquid butter.
3. Whisk the egg whites until stiff then fold in the remaining sugar. Fold through the egg yolk mixture.
4. Spread out half the mixture into the marked circles. Sift together a little icing sugar and cinnamon and use to dust the mixture.
5. Bake at 220°C (425°F) mark 7 for about 8 minutes. Ease off the paper and at once fold each sponge drop in half and place in a damp tea-towel until cold. Cook the rest of the sponge mixture in the same way.
6. Whip the cream and fill the sponge drops. They can be kept covered in a cool place for several hours.

Fruit Brazil Butter Cake

175 g (6 oz) BUTTER
175 g (6 oz) CASTER SUGAR
3 EGGS (size 2), BEATEN
50 g (2 oz) CANDIED LEMON PEEL, FINELY CHOPPED
125 g (4 oz) DRIED APRICOTS, CUT INTO SMALL PIECES
125 g (4 oz) SULTANAS
125 g (4 oz) BRAZIL NUTS, ROUGHLY CHOPPED
125 g (4 oz) PLAIN FLOUR
125 g (4 oz) SELF-RAISING FLOUR
APRICOT JAM, SIEVED AND MELTED
225 g (8 oz) BOUGHT MARZIPAN, ROLLED OUT AND BRAZIL NUTS, TO DECORATE

Serves 6–8

1. Line a 1.7 litre (3 pint) loaf tin with buttered greaseproof paper.
2. Whisk the butter and sugar together in a bowl until pale and fluffy. Gradually add the eggs, beating all the time.
3. Mix the lemon peel, apricots, sultanas and nuts together.
4. Sift the plain and self-raising flours and fold into the whisked mixture, then add the fruit and nuts. Spoon into the prepared tin.
5. Bake in the oven at 180°C (350°F) mark 4 for about 1¼ hours (cover if the top starts to overbrown). Cool a little then turn out on to a wire rack.
6. Brush the top of the cake with apricot glaze, then cover with marzipan. Crimp the edges and cut a diamond pattern. Place a sliced nut in each square. Grill the cake until evenly browned.

Photographed opposite

Moist Lemon Syrup Cake

125 g (4 oz) BUTTER OR BLOCK MARGARINE
75 g (3 oz) SOFT BROWN SUGAR
75 g (3 oz) CASTER SUGAR
FINELY GRATED RIND AND JUICE OF 2 LEMONS
2 EGGS (size 2)
175 g (6 oz) SELF-RAISING FLOUR
1.25 ml (¼ tsp) SALT
125 g (4 oz) ICING SUGAR

Serves 6–8

1. Grease a 1.1 litre (2 pint) loaf tin and dust with flour.
2. Cream together the fat, soft brown and caster sugars until pale and fluffy. Add the lemon rind, then beat in the eggs one at a time. Fold in the flour and salt.
3. Turn the mixture into the prepared tin and bake in the oven at 180°C (350°F) mark 4 for 50–60 minutes. Turn on to a wire rack.
4. Beat the lemon juice into the icing sugar. While the cake is still hot, prick all over with a fine skewer and brush evenly all over with the lemon mixture. Repeat until all the glaze is absorbed. Leave until cold.

Fruit Brazil Butter Cake

Walnut Coffee Cake

4 EGGS (size 2)
175 g (6 oz) SOFT DARK BROWN SUGAR
FINELY GRATED RIND OF 1 LEMON
125 g (4 oz) PLAIN FLOUR
150 g (5 oz) WALNUT PIECES, CHOPPED
275 g (10 oz) ICING SUGAR, SIFTED
150 g (5 oz) BUTTER, SOFTENED
45 ml (3 tbsp) COFFEE ESSENCE

Makes a 23 cm (9 inch) cake

1. Grease and base-line a 23 cm (9 inch) round cake tin. Dust with caster sugar and flour.

2. Whisk the eggs, sugar and lemon rind until very thick and mousse-like in appearance.

3. Sift the flour and fold in with 50 g (2 oz) of walnuts.

4. Pour the mixture into the prepared tin and bake at 180°C (350°F) mark 4 for about 40 minutes, or until firm to the touch. Turn out and cool on a wire rack.

5. Gradually beat the sifted icing sugar into the butter until smooth, work in the coffee essence.

6. Split the gâteau in half and sandwich together again with half the buttercream. Spread the remaining buttercream around the sides and press chopped nuts on to the edge. Decorate with a lattice of the remaining chopped nuts.

Marzipan Pineapple Cake

175 g (6 oz) BUTTER
150 g (5 oz) SOFT LIGHT BROWN SUGAR
FINELY GRATED RIND AND JUICE OF 1 LEMON
FINELY GRATED RIND OF 1 ORANGE AND 15 ml (1 tbsp) JUICE
2 EGGS (size 2); PLUS 2 EGG YOLKS
125 g (4 oz) SELF-RAISING FLOUR
50 g (2 oz) CORNFLOUR
PINCH OF SALT
75 g (3 oz) GLACE PINEAPPLE, THINLY SLICED
75 g (3 oz) BOUGHT MARZIPAN, CUT INTO SMALL PIECES
75 g (3 oz) ICING SUGAR

Makes 24 × 20 cm (9½ × 8 inch) cake

1. Grease and line a 24 × 20 cm (9½ × 8 inch) cake or roasting type tin.

2. Cream the butter, add the sugar and continue to cream until light and fluffy. Add the lemon and orange rind.

3. Lightly beat in the whole eggs, yolks, self-raising and cornflour and salt with 15 ml (1 tbsp) each of orange and lemon juice. Fold in the pineapple.

4. Turn into the prepared tin, level the surface and scatter with marzipan. Bake in the oven at 180°C (350°F) mark 4 for about 45 minutes.

5. Meanwhile make a glacé icing: sift the icing sugar into a bowl and mix with any remaining lemon juice and water to a thick spreading consistency.

6. When the cake is baked, turn out on a wire rack. Brush the top at once with glacé icing. Leave to cool.

Chocolate Fudge Cake

325 g (12 oz) PLAIN CHOCOLATE CAKE COVERING
275 g (10 oz) BUTTER
175 g (6 oz) CASTER SUGAR
4 EGGS (size 2), BEATEN
175 g (6 oz) SELF-RAISING FLOUR
50 g (2 oz) GROUND RICE
10 ml (2 tsp) VANILLA FLAVOURING
50 g (2 oz) FLAKED ALMONDS
100 g (4 oz) ICING SUGAR, SIFTED
10–15 ml (2–3 tsp) COFFEE ESSENCE
TOASTED ALMONDS HALF DIPPED IN MELTED CHOCOLATE (optional), TO DECORATE

Serves 6–8

1. Line a 23 cm (9 inch) round cake tin with buttered greaseproof paper.

2. Warm half the cake covering in a bowl over a pan of simmering water.

3. Whisk 225 g (8 oz) butter and caster sugar together in a bowl until pale and fluffy then gradually beat in eggs, keeping the mixture stiff. Lightly beat in the flour with ground rice, vanilla and flaked almonds and the cool, but still liquid, chocolate cake covering.

4. Turn the mixture into the prepared cake tin and bake in the oven at 180°C (350°F) mark 4 for about 1¼ hours. Cool in the tin 30 minutes before turning out.

5. Melt the remaining chocolate cake covering and use to coat the top and sides of the cake.

6. Whisk the remaining butter in a bowl, beat in icing sugar and essence. Spoon into a piping bag fitted with a 1 cm (½ inch) large star nozzle, and pipe around the cake top. Decorate with toasted almonds.

Photographed opposite

Chocolate Blackcurrant Gâteau

50 g (2 oz) PLAIN CHOCOLATE, BROKEN INTO PIECES
30 ml (2 tbsp) WATER; PLUS 150 ml (¼ pint)
2 EGGS
100 g (4 oz) MARGARINE, SOFTENED
100 g (4 oz) CASTER SUGAR
100 g (4 oz) SELF-RAISING FLOUR
225 g (8 oz) BLACKCURRANTS
50 g (2 oz) SUGAR
15 ml (1 tbsp) ARROWROOT
142 ml (5 fl oz) CARTON WHIPPING CREAM

Serves 8–10

1. Put the chocolate into a bowl with 30 ml (2 tbsp) water. Place over simmering water until melted. Cool slightly and pour the liquid chocolate into a blender. Add the next four ingredients, work for a few seconds.

2. Grease and base-line a 22 cm (8½ inch) sandwich tin. Pour in the mixture and bake at 190°C (375°F) mark 5 for about 30 minutes. Turn out and cool on wire rack.

3. Meanwhile, cook the blackcurrants with the sugar and 150 ml (¼ pint) water until soft. Blend the arrowroot with a little water, stir into the blackcurrants and boil until clear. Cool.

4. Split the chocolate cake in half. Whip the cream and fold the cold blackcurrant mixture through it. Use to sandwich the cake.

Chocolate Fudge Cake

Dark Ginger Cake

175 g (6 oz) BLACK TREACLE
40 g ($1\frac{1}{2}$ oz) DEMERARA SUGAR
75 g (3 oz) BUTTER OR BLOCK MARGARINE
175 g (6 oz) PLAIN FLOUR
10 ml (2 tsp) GROUND GINGER
5 ml (1 tsp) MIXED SPICE
2.5 ml ($\frac{1}{2}$ tsp) BICARBONATE OF SODA
2 EGGS, BEATEN
100 ml (4 fl oz) MILK

Makes an 18 cm (7 inch) cake

1. Grease and base-line an 18 cm (7 inch) round deep tin.

2. Gently heat the treacle, sugar and butter until melted and combined.

3. Sift the flour, spices and bicarbonate of soda together into a bowl.

4. Make a well in the centre and pour in the treacle mixture with the eggs and milk. Beat well with a wooden spoon until smooth.

5. Pour into the prepared tin and bake in the oven at 170°C (325°F) mark 3 for about $1\frac{1}{4}$ hours. Turn out on to a wire rack to cool.

Marmalade Spice Cake

Marmalade Spice Cake

175 g (6 oz) BUTTER, SOFTENED
120 ml (8 tbsp) GOLDEN SYRUP
2 EGGS (size 2), BEATEN
150 ml (10 tbsp) MEDIUM-CUT ORANGE MARMALADE, CHOPPED
350 g (12 oz) SELF-RAISING FLOUR
5 ml (1 tsp) BAKING POWDER
5 ml (1 tsp) FRESHLY GRATED NUTMEG
5 ml (1 tsp) GROUND CINNAMON
1.25 ml (¼ tsp) GROUND CLOVES
ABOUT 150 ml (¼ pint) MILK
50 g (2 oz) CORNFLAKES, CRUSHED

Serves 6–8

1. Butter and base-line a 20 cm (8 inch) square cake tin.
2. In a large bowl, beat the butter with 90 ml (6 tbsp) golden syrup until well mixed. Gradually beat in the eggs, keeping the mixture stiff.
3. Stir half the chopped marmalade into the cake mixture. Sift the flour with the baking powder and spices and add to the cake mixture with sufficient milk to make a fairly stiff consistency.
4. Turn the mixture into the prepared tin and level the surface.
5. Mix the cornflakes with the remaining syrup and chopped marmalade. Carefully spread over the cake mixture.
6. Bake in the oven at 180°C (350°F) mark 4 for about 1 hour. Turn out and cool on a wire rack.

Photographed opposite

Orange and Caraway Castles

75 g (3 oz) BUTTER OR BLOCK MARGARINE
50 g (2 oz) CASTER SUGAR
120 ml (8 tbsp) WELL-FLAVOURED MARMALADE
FINELY GRATED RIND OF 1 ORANGE
2 EGGS, BEATEN
125 g (4 oz) SELF-RAISING FLOUR
PINCH OF SALT
2.5–5 ml (½–1 tsp) CARAWAY SEEDS
25 g (1 oz) CORNFLAKES, CRUSHED

Makes 10

1. Grease ten dariole moulds.
2. Cream together the butter and sugar until pale and fluffy. Beat in 30 ml (2 tbsp) marmalade and the orange rind. Gradually beat in the eggs.
3. Sift together the flour and salt and gently fold into the mixture with the caraway seeds.
4. Divide the mixture between the prepared dariole moulds. On a baking sheet, bake at 170°C (325°F) mark 3 for about 25 minutes.
5. Sieve the remaining marmalade, reserving the shreds. Heat the marmalade gently and use to glaze the sides of each cake. Roll in the crushed cornflakes. Decorate with the reserved shreds.

Cherry and Coconut Cake

250 g (9 oz) SELF-RAISING FLOUR
1.25 ml (¼ tsp) SALT
125 g (4 oz) BUTTER OR BLOCK MARGARINE, CUT INTO SMALL PIECES
75 g (3 oz) DESICCATED COCONUT
125 g (4 oz) CASTER SUGAR
125 g (4 oz) GLACE CHERRIES, FINELY CHOPPED
2 EGGS (size 6), BEATEN
225 ml (8 fl oz) MILK
25 g (1 oz) SHREDDED COCONUT

Serves 8

1. Grease and base-line a 1.3 litre (2¼ pint) loaf tin and dust with flour.
2. Sift the flour and salt into a bowl and rub in the fat. Stir in the coconut, sugar and cherries.
3. Whisk together the eggs and milk and beat into the cake mixture.
4. Spoon the mixture into the tin, levelling the top and scatter over the shredded coconut. Bake in the oven at 180°C (350°F) mark 4 for about 1½ hours. Cover with foil after 40 minutes. Turn out on to a wire rack and leave to cool.

Apple Hazelnut Genoese

75 g (3 oz) BUTTER, SOFTENED
3 EGGS
275 g (10 oz) CASTER SUGAR
50 g (2 oz) PLAIN FLOUR
15 ml (1 tbsp) CORNFLOUR
25 g (1 oz) GROUND HAZELNUTS
APPLE JELLY
1 EGG WHITE
PINCH OF SALT
PINCH OF CREAM OF TARTAR
30 ml (2 tbsp) THICK UNSWEETENED APPLE PUREE

Makes a 20 cm (8 inch) cake

1. Grease and base-line two 18 cm (7 inch) straight-sided sandwich tins. Warm the butter until beginning to melt.
2. Whisk the eggs and 100 g (4 oz) caster sugar until very thick. Sift the flour and cornflour and fold in with the hazelnuts, then fold in the cool, but still pouring, butter.
3. Turn into the prepared tins and bake at 180°C (350°F) mark 4 for about 25 minutes. Turn out and cool on a wire rack. When cold, sandwich the layers together with apple jelly.
4. Prepare the frosting: put the egg white, the remaining sugar together with a pinch each of salt and cream of tartar and the apple purée into a deep bowl over a pan of simmering water for at least 7 minutes, until the mixture thickens and holds stiff peaks. Remove from the heat and continue to whisk for 2 minutes.
5. Cover the cake with the frosting, peaking up the surface. Leave for 2–3 hours before serving.

Orange Madeira

175 g (6 oz) BUTTER OR MARGARINE
175 g (6 oz) CASTER SUGAR
3 EGGS, BEATEN
150 g (5 oz) SELF-RAISING FLOUR
100 g (4 oz) PLAIN FLOUR
FINELY GRATED RIND OF 1 ORANGE AND 30 ml (2 tbsp) ORANGE JUICE
25 g (1 oz) CUBE SUGAR, CRUSHED

Makes an 18 cm (7 inch) cake

1. Grease and base-line an 18 cm (7 inch) round deep tin.
2. Cream together the butter and caster sugar until pale and fluffy. Gradually beat in the eggs. Sift the flours together and fold in.
3. Add the orange rind and fold in with the orange juice. Spoon into the prepared tin and smooth the surface with a palette knife. Sprinkle the crushed sugar evenly over the cake surface.
4. Bake in the oven at 170°C (325°F) mark 3 for about $1\frac{1}{4}$ hours, or until firm to the touch. Turn out on to a wire rack to cool.

Orange Glazed Ginger Cake

125 g (4 oz) LARD
125 g (4 oz) CASTER SUGAR
1 EGG, BEATEN
275 g (10 oz) PLAIN FLOUR
7.5 ml ($1\frac{1}{2}$ tsp) BICARBONATE OF SODA
2.5 ml ($\frac{1}{2}$ tsp) SALT
5 ml (1 tsp) GROUND CINNAMON
5 ml (1 tsp) GROUND GINGER
175 g (6 oz) GOLDEN SYRUP
175 g (6 oz) BLACK TREACLE
225 ml (8 fl oz) WATER
PARED RIND AND JUICE OF 1 ORANGE
175 g (6 oz) ICING SUGAR

Makes a 23 cm (9 inch) cake

1. Grease and line a 23 cm (9 inch) round cake tin.
2. Cream the lard with the sugar. Beat in the egg, followed by the flour, bicarbonate of soda, salt and spices.
3. Warm together the golden syrup and black treacle with the water. Bring to the boil and stir into the mixture, beating all the time until completely incorporated.
4. Turn into the prepared tin. Bake in the oven at 180°C (350°F) mark 4 for about 50 minutes. Allow to cool in the tin before turning out on to a wire rack.
5. Cut the orange rind into needle shreds. Cover with water and boil until tender, about 10 minutes. Drain well.
6. Make a glacé icing: sift the icing sugar into a bowl and mix with 30 ml (2 tbsp) orange juice. Stir in the needle shreds. Evenly coat the top of the cake, allowing the icing to fall down the sides. Leave to set.

Soured Cream Coffee Cake

125 g (4 oz) BUTTER OR BLOCK MARGARINE
200 g (7 oz) CASTER SUGAR
2 EGGS, BEATEN
TWO 142 g (5 fl oz) CARTONS SOURED CREAM
5 ml (1 tsp) VANILLA ESSENCE
175 g (6 oz) SELF-RAISING FLOUR
5 ml (1 tsp) BICARBONATE OF SODA
75 g (3 oz) WALNUT PIECES, ROUGHLY CHOPPED

Makes an 18 cm (7 inch) square cake

1. Grease and line an 18 cm (7 inch) square, 2.3 litre (4 pint) deep baking tin.
2. Beat the butter until soft and creamy and gradually beat in the sugar. Creaming takes longer than usual due to the high proportion of sugar.
3. Beat in the eggs, soured cream and vanilla essence, a little at a time.
4. Sift the flour and bicarbonate of soda together and beat lightly into the creamed mixture with 50 g (2 oz) of the walnuts.
5. Turn into the prepared tin and bake at 180°C (350°F) mark 4 for about 55 minutes. Halfway through cooking time scatter over the rest of the nuts without removing the cake from the oven.
6. Allow to cool a little in the tin. Ease out and serve warm in thick slices.

Victoria Sandwich Cake

175 g (6 oz) BUTTER
175 g (6 oz) CASTER SUGAR
3 EGGS, BEATEN
175 g (6 oz) SELF-RAISING FLOUR
30 ml (2 tbsp) JAM
CASTER SUGAR, TO DREDGE

Serves 6–8

1. Butter two 18 cm (7 inch) sandwich tins and line the base of each with a round of buttered greaseproof paper.
2. Beat the butter and sugar together until pale and fluffy. Add the eggs a little at a time, beating well after each addition. Fold in half the flour, using a metal spoon, then fold in the rest.
3. Place half the mixture in each tin and level with a knife. Bake in the oven at 190°C (375°F) mark 5 for about 20 minutes, until they are well risen, firm to the touch and beginning to shrink away from the sides of the tins. Turn out and cool on a wire rack.
4. When the cakes are cool, sandwich them together with jam and sprinkle the top with caster sugar.

VARIATION: COFFEE
Add 10 ml (2 tsp) instant coffee powder, dissolved in a little warm water, to the butter and sugar with the egg. Or use 10 ml (2 tsp) coffee essence.

Photographed opposite

Victoria Sandwich Cake

Frosted Chocolate Cake

125 g (4 oz) PLAIN FLOUR
30 ml (2 tbsp) CORNFLOUR
7.5 ml (1½ tsp) BAKING POWDER
45 ml (3 tbsp) COCOA POWDER
2 EGGS, SEPARATED
125 g (4 oz) SOFT DARK BROWN SUGAR
100 ml (4 fl oz) CORN OIL
100 ml (4 fl oz) WATER; PLUS 10 ml (2 tsp)
125 g (4 oz) PLAIN DESSERT CHOCOLATE, BROKEN INTO PIECES
25 g (1 oz) BUTTER

Makes a 20 cm (8 inch) cake

1. Grease and base-line a deep 20 cm (8 inch) round cake tin.
2. Sift the flours, baking powder and cocoa well together.
3. Whisk the egg yolks, sugar, oil and 100 ml (4 fl oz) water until thoroughly mixed.
4. Stir the oil mixture into the dry ingredients and beat well until smooth.
5. Stiffly whisk the egg whites and fold into the mixture. Pour into the prepared tin.
6. Bake at once at 180°C (350°F) mark 4 for about 45 minutes. Turn out on to a wire rack and cool.
7. Melt the chocolate and butter with 10 ml (2 tsp) water in a small bowl over a pan of simmering water. Cool until beginning to set.
8. Spread the chocolate over the cake and ridge with a blunt edged knife.

Fruit Crusted Cider Cake

45 ml (3 tbsp) GOLDEN SYRUP
150 g (5 oz) BUTTER OR BLOCK MARGARINE
350 g (12 oz) COOKING APPLES, PEELED, CORED AND FINELY CHOPPED
45 ml (3 tbsp) MINCEMEAT
50 g (2 oz) CORNFLAKES, CRUSHED
125 g (4 oz) CASTER SUGAR
2 EGGS, BEATEN
125 g (4 oz) SELF-RAISING FLOUR
45 ml (3 tbsp) DRY CIDER

Makes 12 bars

1. Foil-line a 35.5 × 11.5 cm (14 × 4½ inch) shallow rectangular tart frame and grease well.
2. Melt the syrup and 25 g (1 oz) butter gently together in a saucepan and stir in the apple, mincemeat and cornflakes.
3. Cream together the remaining butter and sugar until pale and fluffy and gradually beat in the eggs.
4. Sift the flour and fold into the mixture, then add the cider. Spoon into the prepared tin and smooth over the surface with a palette knife. Spread the syrup topping evenly over the cake surface.
5. Bake at 170°C (325°F) mark 3 for about 45–50 minutes, or until firm to the touch. Cool still in the metal frame, then cut into bars for serving.

Date and Spice Cake

175 g (6 oz) STONED DATES, FINELY CHOPPED
45 ml (3 tbsp) BOILING WATER
FINELY GRATED RIND OF 1 ORANGE AND 45 ml (3 tbsp) JUICE
175 g (6 oz) BUTTER OR BLOCK MARGARINE
175 g (6 oz) CASTER SUGAR
3 EGGS, BEATEN
5 ml (1 tsp) GROUND MIXED SPICE
5 ml (1 tsp) GROUND GINGER
200 g (7 oz) SELF-RAISING FLOUR

Serves 6–8

1. Put the dates into a small bowl. Pour over the boiling water and add the orange rind and juice. Leave aside for a few hours, preferably overnight.
2. Grease a 1.4 litre (2½ pint) ring mould.
3. Cream the butter and sugar until pale and fluffy and beat in the eggs, a little at a time.
4. Sift the spices and flour together and fold into the creamed mixture with the date mixture. Spoon into the prepared ring mould and level the surface.
5. Bake in the oven at 170°C (325°F) mark 3 for 40–45 minutes, or until firm to the touch. Turn out carefully on to a wire rack.

Frosted Coconut Cake

50 g (2 oz) SHELLED HAZELNUTS
225 g (8 oz) BUTTER OR BLOCK MARGARINE
225 g (8 oz) CASTER SUGAR
5 EGGS
2.5 ml (½ tsp) VANILLA ESSENCE
125 g (4 oz) PLAIN FLOUR
125 g (4 oz) SELF-RAISING FLOUR
40 g (1½ oz) DESICCATED COCONUT
75 g (3 oz) ICING SUGAR, SIFTED
SHREDDED COCONUT

Makes a 20 cm (8 inch) cake

1. Grease and base-line a 20 cm (8 inch) base measurement spring-release cake tin.
2. Spread the hazelnuts out on a baking sheet and brown in the oven at 180°C (350°F) mark 4 for 15–20 minutes. Put into a soft tea-towel and rub off the skins. Finely chop.
3. Cream the fat and sugar until light and fluffy. Whisk 4 whole eggs and 1 yolk together and gradually beat into the creamed mixture with 2.5 ml (½ tsp) vanilla essence.
4. Fold in the flours, 25 g (1 oz) desiccated coconut, and half the nuts.
5. Turn into tin and bake at 180°C (350°F) mark 4 for 45 minutes.
6. Meanwhile, prepare a meringue topping. Whisk the egg white until stiff and gradually whisk in the icing sugar, keeping the mixture stiff. Fold in the remaining desiccated coconut and hazelnuts.
7. Spoon the meringue topping on to the partially baked cake and scatter with shredded coconut.
8. Return to the oven for 20–30 minutes or until a skewer comes out of cake clean. Cover lightly after 15 minutes.

Lemon Swiss Roll

3 EGGS (size 2)
100 g (4 oz) CASTER SUGAR
100 g (4 oz) PLAIN FLOUR
142 ml (5 fl oz) CARTON DOUBLE CREAM
about 275 g (10 oz) LEMON CURD
100 g (4 oz) ICING SUGAR
20 ml (4 tsp) WATER

Makes a 33 cm (13 inch) roll

1. Grease and base-line a 33 × 23 × 1.5 cm (13 × 9 × ½ inch) Swiss roll tin. Dust out with a little caster sugar and flour.
2. Whisk the eggs and sugar, preferably with an electric hand mixer, until really thick. Sift the flour over the surface and fold gently through the egg mixture.
3. Turn into the prepared tin and level the surface. Bake at 200°C (400°F) mark 6 for 10–12 minutes, or until firm to the touch and shrunk a little from the sides of the tin.
4. Turn out on to a sheet of sugared greaseproof paper and roll up with the paper inside. Cool on a wire rack.
5. Whip the cream until it just holds its shape. Unroll the Swiss roll and spread with three-quarters of the lemon curd. Top with cream. Roll up again and place on a serving plate.
6. Make the glacé icing: sift the icing sugar into a bowl and add the water. Spoon down the Swiss roll. Straight away, using the point of a teaspoon, place rough lines of lemon curd across the icing and pull a skewer through to form a feather pattern.

Balmoral Almond Cake

175 g (6 oz) BUTTER OR BLOCK MARGARINE
125 g (4 oz) CASTER SUGAR
ALMOND ESSENCE
2 EGGS, BEATEN
50 g (2 oz) GROUND ALMONDS
125 g (4 oz) SELF-RAISING FLOUR
30 ml (2 tbsp) MILK
125 g (4 oz) ICING SUGAR, SIFTED

Makes a 25 cm (10 inch) cake

1. Grease a 25 cm (10 inch) long, 900 ml (1½ pint) ribbed Balmoral cake tin, or use a 16 × 11.5 cm (6½ × 4¼ inch) top measurement loaf tin.
2. Cream together 125 g (4 oz) fat and the caster sugar until light and fluffy. Add a few drops of almond essence. Beat in the eggs a little at a time. Fold in the ground almonds and flour with the milk.
3. Spoon into the prepared tin and bake in the oven at 170°C (325°F) mark 3 for 45–50 minutes, or until firm to the touch.
4. Turn out on to a wire rack to cool. Cream the remaining fat and icing sugar together and flavour with a little almond essence. Use to decorate the top of the cake.

Pineapple Griestorte

3 EGGS, SEPARATED
125 g (4 oz) CASTER SUGAR
376 g (13¼ oz) CAN PINEAPPLE PIECES, DRAINED, WITH JUICE RESERVED
75 g (3 oz) SEMOLINA
142 ml (5 fl oz) CARTON WHIPPING CREAM
150 g (5 oz) ICING SUGAR

Makes a 20 cm (8 inch) cake

1. Grease and base-line a 20 cm (8 inch) round cake tin.
2. Whisk together the egg yolks and sugar until pale and really thick.
3. Stir 30 ml (2 tbsp) pineapple juice and the semolina into the egg mixture.
4. Stiffly whisk the egg whites and gently fold in.
5. Turn into the prepared tin and bake at 180°C (350°F) mark 4 for about 40 minutes. Turn out on to a wire rack to cool.
6. Roughly chop the pineapple pieces. Split the cake in half and fill with cream and pineapple.
7. Make a glacé icing: sift the icing sugar into a bowl and add just enough of the reserved pineapple juice, about 20 ml (4 tsp), to give a very thin covering for the cake. Spread over the cake surface with a palette knife.

Rich Chocolate Ring

75 g (3 oz) HAZELNUTS
125 g (4½ oz) BUTTER
150 g (5 oz) CASTER SUGAR
5 EGGS, SEPARATED
225 g (8 oz) PLAIN DESSERT CHOCOLATE
60 ml (4 tbsp) DRIED BROWN BREADCRUMBS
40 g (1 oz) PLAIN FLOUR
30 ml (2 tbsp) WATER
50 g (2 oz) MILK CHOCOLATE

Serves 8

1. Grease a 1.7 litre (3 pint) ring mould and dust the tin with flour.
2. Spread the hazelnuts out on a baking sheet and brown in the oven at 180°C (350°F) mark 4 for 15–20 minutes. Put into a soft tea-towel and rub off the skins, then grind the nuts.
3. Beat together 100 g (3½ oz) butter with the caster sugar until light and fluffy. Gradually beat in the egg yolks.
4. Melt 75 g (3½ oz) plain chocolate in a small bowl over simmering water. Cool until tepid and beat into the egg mixture. Gently stir in the hazelnuts, breadcrumbs and flour.
5. Whisk the egg whites stiffly and fold into mixture. Turn into the prepared tin. Bake at 200°C (400°F) mark 6 for 30–35 minutes. Cool on a wire rack.
6. Melt the remaining plain chocolate with 30 ml (2 tbsp) water and the rest of butter in a bowl over simmering water. Cool to a thick spreading consistency and spread over the cake.
7. Melt the milk chocolate and drizzle chocolate over the cake.

Toddy Cake

Marbled Chocolate Cake

50 g (2 oz) PLAIN DESSERT CHOCOLATE, BROKEN INTO PIECES
5 ml (1 tsp) VANILLA ESSENCE
15 ml (1 tbsp) WATER
225 g (8 oz) BUTTER
225 g (8 oz) CASTER SUGAR
4 EGGS (size 2)
225 g (8 oz) PLAIN FLOUR
10 ml (2 tsp) BAKING POWDER
2.5 ml ($\frac{1}{2}$ tsp) SALT
50 g (2 oz) GROUND ALMONDS
30 ml (2 tbsp) MILK

Serves 8

1. Grease a 1.7 litre (3 pint) ring mould.
2. Melt the chocolate with the vanilla essence and water in a small bowl over a pan of simmering water. Leave to cool.
3. Cream together the butter and sugar until pale and fluffy. Beat in the eggs one at a time.
4. Sift the flour, baking powder and salt together and fold into the creamed mixture with the ground almonds. Stir in the milk.
5. Spoon half the mixture evenly into the base of the prepared tin.
6. Stir the cooled but still soft chocolate into the remaining mixture. Spoon into the tin. Draw a knife through the mixture in a spiral and level the surface.
7. Bake in the oven at 180°C (350°F) mark 4 for about 55 minutes. Turn out on to a wire rack to cool.

Toddy Cake

225 g (8 oz) BUTTER
175 g (6 oz) SOFT BROWN SUGAR
FINELY GRATED RIND OF 1 LEMON AND 15 ml (1 tbsp) LEMON JUICE
3 EGGS, BEATEN
175 g (6 oz) SELF-RAISING FLOUR, SIFTED
60 ml (4 tbsp) WHISKY
30 ml (2 tbsp) THICK HONEY
175 g (6 oz) ICING SUGAR, SIFTED
A FEW WALNUT HALVES

Serves 6–8

1. Butter and base-line two 18 cm (7 inch) straight-sided sandwich tins.
2. Whisk 175 g (6 oz) butter, add the sugar and lemon rind. Continue to whisk until pale and fluffy. Gradually beat in the eggs, keeping the mixture stiff.
3. Fold in half the sifted flour, then the whisky and the remaining flour. Spoon into the prepared tins.
4. Bake in the oven at 190°C (375°F) mark 5 for 20–25 minutes. Turn out and cool on a wire rack.
5. Whisk the remaining butter with the honey and gradually work in the icing sugar and the lemon juice.
6. Sandwich the cake together with half the butter-cream and swirl the rest over the top. Decorate with walnuts.

Photographed opposite

Apricot and Cinnamon Cake

225 g (8 oz) SELF-RAISING FLOUR
10 ml (2 tsp) GROUND CINNAMON
125 g (4 oz) BUTTER OR BLOCK MARGARINE, CUT INTO SMALL PIECES
150 g (5 oz) SOFT BROWN SUGAR
125–175 g (4–6 oz) DRIED APRICOTS, CHOPPED
15 ml (1 tbsp) CLEAR HONEY
45 ml (3 tbsp) MILK
2 EGGS, BEATEN
CLEAR HONEY, TO GLAZE

Makes an 18 cm (7 inch) cake

1. Grease and base-line an 18 cm (7 inch), 2 litre ($3\frac{1}{2}$ pint) round deep-sided cake tin.
2. Sift the flour and cinnamon into a bowl and rub in the fat until the mixture resembles fine breadcrumbs.
3. Stir in the sugar and apricots. Mix the honey and milk together and add to dry ingredients with the eggs. Mix well together and spoon into the prepared tin.
4. Bake in the oven at 170°C (325°F) mark 3 for about 1 hour 20 minutes, or until firm to the touch. Cool slightly and turn out on to a wire rack.
5. While still warm, brush the top of the cake with the clear honey. Repeat while cooling.

Honey Frosted Carrot Cake

225 g (8 oz) SELF RAISING FLOUR
10 ml (2 tsp) BAKING POWDER
10 ml (2 tsp) GROUND CINNAMON
150 g (5 oz) SOFT LIGHT BROWN SUGAR
25 g (1 oz) BRAN BUDS
225 g (8 oz) CARROTS, PEELED AND COARSELY GRATED
2 EGGS
45 ml (3 tbsp) CLEAR HONEY
150 ml ($\frac{1}{4}$ pint) CORN OIL
1 EGG WHITE (size 6)
75 g (3 oz) CASTER SUGAR
PINCH OF SALT
15 ml (1 tbsp) WATER
PINCH OF CREAM OF TARTAR

Makes a 20 cm (8 inch) cake

1. Grease and base-line a 20 cm (8 inch) round cake tin.
2. Mix together the flour, baking powder, cinnamon, sugar and Bran Buds. Add the carrot.
3. Beat together the eggs, 30 ml (2 tbsp) honey and the oil. Stir into the dry ingredients, beating well as the mixture loosens.
4. Spoon into the prepared tin and bake at 180°C (350°F) mark 4 for about 50 minutes. Turn out on to a wire rack to cool.
5. Make the frosting: put the egg white, sugar, salt, water and cream of tartar into a bowl over a pan of simmering water and whisk for at least 7 minutes until the mixture thickens and stands in peaks. Remove from the heat and continue whisking for 2 minutes. Stir in the remaining honey and swirl over the cake at once.

Caramel Banana Torte

Caramel Banana Torte

50 g (2 oz) FLAKED ALMONDS
175 g (6 oz) SELF-RAISING FLOUR
1.25 ml (¼ tsp) BAKING POWDER
1.25 ml (¼ tsp) BICARBONATE OF SODA
50 g (2 oz) BUTTER
150 g (5 oz) CASTER SUGAR
350 g (12 oz) RIPE BANANAS
2.5 ml (½ tsp) FRESHLY GRATED NUTMEG
45 ml (3 tbsp) MILK
1 EGG
75 g (3 oz) SUGAR
175 g (6 oz) FULL-FAT CREAM CHEESE
30 ml (2 tbsp) LEMON JUICE
30 ml (2 tbsp) ICING SUGAR, SIFTED

Serves 8

1. Grease and base-line a 20 cm (8 inch) round cake tin. Put the almonds into the grill pan and toast until golden, about 3 minutes, turning frequently.
2. Sift the flour, baking powder and bicarbonate of soda into a bowl and rub in the fat. Stir in the caster sugar.
3. Peel half the bananas, mash and then beat with the grated nutmeg, milk and egg. Stir into the dry ingredients and spoon into the prepared tin. Level the surface.
4. Bake at 180°C (350°F) mark 4 for about 40 minutes. Cool in the tin for 5 minutes. Turn out on to a wire rack and leave until cold.
5. Split the cake. Caramelise the sugar in a small pan. Immediately pour over the top surface of the split cake, spreading with an oiled knife. Mark the caramel into eight portions.
6. Beat together the cream cheese, lemon juice and icing sugar. Peel and chop the remaining bananas and sandwich the cakes with half the cream cheese and the banana. Spread a little cream cheese around the sides and cover with the toasted almonds. Decorate the top with the remaining cream cheese.

Photographed opposite

Coffee Praline Gâteau

225 g (9 oz) CASTER SUGAR
75 g (3 oz) BLANCHED ALMONDS
250 g (9 oz) UNSALTED BUTTER
3 EGGS
75 g (3 oz) PLAIN FLOUR
2 EGG YOLKS
60 ml (4 tbsp) WATER
15 ml (1 tbsp) COFFEE ESSENCE
ICING SUGAR, SIFTED, TO DUST

Makes a 20 cm (8 inch) cake

1. Prepare the praline: heat 75 g (3 oz) sugar with the nuts until the sugar caramelises. Turn out on to an oiled baking sheet and cool. When cold, grind the nuts.
2. Melt 75 g (3 oz) butter. Cool. Grease and base-line a 20 cm (8 inch) round cake tin. Dust out with a little sugar and flour.
3. Whisk the whole eggs with 75 g (3 oz) sugar until really thick. Lightly fold in the sifted flour with 60 ml (4 tbsp) praline followed by the cool, but still flowing, butter.
4. Turn into prepared tin and bake at 180°C (350°F) mark 4 for about 25 minutes, or until light golden brown and the cake has shrunk away a little from the tin. Turn out on to a wire rack to cool.
5. Meanwhile, make the butter frosting: beat the egg yolks in a deep bowl. Put the remaining sugar with the water into a pan over low heat and dissolve the sugar without boiling. Then bring to the boil and boil steadily for 2–3 minutes to reach 107°C (225°F) on a sugar thermometer. Pour the syrup on to the yolks in a steady stream, whisking constantly. Continue whisking until thick and cold.
6. Cream the remaining butter until pale and fluffy and beat in the egg syrup. Beat in the coffee essence and half the remaining praline.
7. Split the cake and sandwich sparingly with the butter frosting. Spread a little more round the edges and press praline on this. Pipe the rest of the frosting in whirls on the top. Dust with icing sugar.

Lemon Seed Cake

175 g (6 oz) BLOCK MARGARINE OR BUTTER
175 g (6 oz) SOFT BROWN SUGAR
FINELY GRATED RIND OF 2 LARGE LEMONS
60 ml (4 tbsp) LEMON JUICE
3 EGGS, SEPARATED
250 g (9 oz) SELF-RAISING FLOUR
10 ml (2 tsp) CARAWAY SEEDS
150 g (5 oz) BUTTER
175 g (6 oz) SUGAR
ICING SUGAR, SIFTED, TO DUST

Makes an 18 cm (7 inch) cake

1. Grease and base-line an 18 cm (7 inch) round cake tin.
2. Cream together the fat, brown sugar and half the finely grated lemon rind, until pale and fluffy.
3. Gradually beat in the egg yolks, then stir in the flour, caraway seeds and 45 ml (3 tbsp) lemon juice.
4. Stiffly whisk the egg whites and fold into the mixture. Turn into the prepared tin and bake in the oven at 180°C (350°F) mark 4 for about 1 hour. Turn on to a wire rack to cool.
5. Prepare the butter icing: cream the butter until of spreading consistency. Gradually beat in the sugar and 15 ml (1 tbsp) lemon juice. Beat in the remaining lemon rind.
6. Use the lemon butter icing to completely coat the cake and then swirl using a small palette knife. Dust lightly with sifted icing sugar. Best eaten the next day.

Choux Cream Puffs

175 g (6 oz) BUTTER, CUT INTO SMALL PIECES
450 ml ($\frac{3}{4}$ pint) WATER; PLUS 600 ml (1 pint)
200 g ($7\frac{1}{2}$ oz) PLAIN FLOUR
6 EGGS, BEATEN
900 ml ($1\frac{1}{2}$ pints) WHIPPING CREAM
ICING SUGAR, SIFTED, TO DUST
450 g (1 lb) PLAIN DESSERT CHOCOLATE, BROKEN INTO PIECES
75 g (3 oz) CASTER SUGAR

Serves 20 buffet portions

1. Put the butter into a saucepan with 450 ml ($\frac{3}{4}$ pint) water. Heat gently until the butter melts then bring to a fast boil.
2. Immediately remove from the heat and sift in the flour. Beat until the mixture peels away from the pan. Cool.
3. Gradually beat in the eggs, keeping the mixture stiff.
4. Grease baking sheets. Spoon the mixture into a piping bag fitted with a plain nozzle and pipe into 40 rings on to the baking sheets, allowing room to spread.
5. Bake at 200°C (400°F) mark 6 for about 30 minutes, or until well risen and crisp. Split open and cool on wire racks.
6. Whip the cream and fill the buns. Dust with icing sugar and chill for 1 hour.
7. Meanwhile, make the chocolate sauce: put the chocolate into a bowl with the 600 ml (1 pint) water and the caster sugar. Place over simmering water and stir until smooth. Simmer gently in the open pan until the sauce reduces and thickens slightly. Serve separately.

Cherry Scones

225 g (8 oz) SELF-RAISING FLOUR
50 g (2 oz) BUTTER, CUT INTO SMALL PIECES
25 g (1 oz) CASTER SUGAR
50 g (2 oz) GLACE CHERRIES, ROUGHLY CHOPPED
25 g (1 oz) CRUNCHY WHEATGERM
ABOUT 150 ml ($\frac{1}{4}$ pint) MILK

Makes about 14

1. Sift the flour into a bowl and rub in the butter until the mixture resembles fine breadcrumbs. Stir in the caster sugar.
2. Stir the cherries into the flour mixture until evenly distributed then add the wheatgerm.
3. Mix to a soft dough with about 150 ml ($\frac{1}{4}$ pint) milk, kneading lightly until just smooth.
4. Roll out the dough on a lightly floured work surface to about a 2 cm ($\frac{3}{4}$ inch) thickness. Stamp out crescent shapes using a 6.5 cm ($2\frac{1}{2}$ inch) fluted cutter, kneading and rerolling the dough until it is all used up.
5. Place the scones on a preheated baking sheet, brush the tops with milk and bake in the oven at 230°C (450°F) mark 8 for 10–12 minutes. Cool on a wire rack.
6. Serve immediately, split and spread with butter.

Photographed opposite

Streusel Apple Flan

150 g (5 oz) PLAIN FLOUR
PINCH OF SALT
5 ml (1 tsp) CASTER SUGAR
75 g (3 oz) MARGARINE, CUT INTO SMALL PIECES
45 ml (3 tbsp) MARMALADE
1 LARGE COOKING APPLE, 350 g (12 oz), PEELED AND CORED
50 g (2 oz) BUTTER
50 g (2 oz) SUGAR
100 g (4 oz) FRESH BREADCRUMBS
GRATED RIND OF 1 ORANGE
1.25 ml ($\frac{1}{4}$ tsp) GROUND CINNAMON

Serves 4

1. Make the pastry: sift the flour and salt into a bowl, add the caster sugar and rub in the margarine until the mixture resembles fine breadcrumbs. Add just enough water to form a firm dough.
2. Roll out the dough on a lightly floured surface and use to line an 18 cm (7 inch) flan ring placed on a baking sheet. Spread the marmalade over the base of the flan.
3. Slice the apple thinly and evenly into the flan case.
4. Melt the butter in a pan, stir in the sugar, breadcrumbs and orange rind, mixing well. Spread this over the apple pressing it down lightly. Sprinkle with cinnamon. Bake at 200°C (400°F) mark 6 for about 25 minutes, or until cooked through.

Apple Almond Pie

50 g (2 oz) PUDDING RICE
450 ml ($\frac{3}{4}$ pint) MILK
100 g (4 oz) CASTER SUGAR
175 g (6 oz) PLAIN FLOUR
100 g (4 oz) BUTTER OR BLOCK MARGARINE
75 g (3 oz) GROUND ALMONDS
1 EGG, BEATEN
700 g ($1\frac{1}{2}$ lb) COOKING APPLES, PEELED, CORED AND SLICED
60 ml (4 tbsp) CIDER
CREAMY MILK AND CASTER SUGAR, TO GLAZE

Serves 6

1. Put the rice and milk into a pan with 25 g (1 oz) sugar and bring to the boil, stirring. Simmer for about 15 minutes, or until the rice is tender. Spoon over the base of a 1.1 litre (2 pint) pie dish.
2. Make the pastry: sift the flour into a bowl and rub in the butter. Stir in 50 g (2 oz) each of ground almonds and sugar and bind with the egg to a soft dough. Leave to chill for 45 minutes.
3. Spread the apple slices over the rice. Mix together the remaining sugar and ground almonds and sprinkle over the apples with the cider.
4. Roll out the pastry on a lightly floured surface, handling it as carefully as possible, and cover the pie dish. Brush with milk and sprinkle with caster sugar.
5. Bake at 180°C (350°F) mark 4 for 25 minutes, then cover with foil and return to the oven for a further 35–40 minutes.

Cherry Scones

Almond and Hazelnut Barquettes

125 g (4 oz) PLAIN FLOUR	
25 g (1 oz) ICING SUGAR; PLUS 60 ml (4 tbsp)	
50 g (2 oz) BUTTER	
1 EGG, SEPARATED; PLUS 1 EGG WHITE	
75 g (3 oz) HAZELNUTS	
25 g (1 oz) GROUND ALMONDS	
15 ml (1 tbsp) CASTER SUGAR	
5 ml (1 tsp) WATER	

Makes 8

1. Sift together the flour and 25 g (1 oz) icing sugar. Rub in the butter. Add the egg yolk and bind to a smooth paste adding 15 ml (1 tbsp) water if necessary. Chill for 20 minutes then use the mixture to line eight boat moulds about 11.5 cm ($4\frac{1}{2}$ inches) in length.

2. Spread the hazelnuts out on a baking sheet and brown in the oven at 180°C (350°F) mark 4 for 15–20 minutes. Allow to cool, then finely chop, leaving the skins on. Mix with the ground almonds.

3. Lightly beat one egg white with the caster sugar until frothy. Beat in the nut mixture together with the water.

4. Spoon a little of the mixture into each lined mould. Bake at 190°C (375°F) mark 5 for 15–20 minutes.

5. For the frosting: sift the remaining icing sugar and beat with just enough egg white to give a coating consistency. Thinly coat each of the barquettes with the icing.

6. Return to the oven for about 5 minutes, or until a pale golden colour.

Grantham Gingerbreads

Grantham Gingerbreads

100 g (4 oz) BUTTER
350 g (12 oz) CASTER SUGAR
1 EGG, BEATEN
250 g (9 oz) SELF-RAISING FLOUR
5 ml (1 tsp) GROUND GINGER

Makes 30

1. Whisk the butter and sugar together in a bowl until pale and fluffy. Gradually beat in the egg.

2. Sift the flour and ginger into the mixture and work in with a fork until it forms a fairly firm dough.

3. Grease baking sheets. Roll the dough into small balls about the size of a walnut and put them on the baking sheets, spaced apart.

4. Bake in the oven at 150°C (300°F) mark 2 for 40–45 minutes until crisp, well risen, hollow and very lightly browned.

Photographed above

Honey Crunch Cookies

100 g (4 oz) BUTTER OR BLOCK MARGARINE
FINELY GRATED RIND OF 1 LEMON
50 g (2 oz) CASTER SUGAR
30 ml (2 tbsp) THICK HONEY
1 EGG YOLK
175 g (6 oz) SELF-RAISING FLOUR

Makes 18–24

1. Cream the fat with the lemon rind and the sugar until light. Add the honey and egg yolk and beat well.

2. Sift the flour and add to the mixture to form a soft dough.

3. Grease baking sheets and put the mixture on them, spaced well apart, in small heaps. Flatten well with a wet fork keeping biscuits round.

4. Bake at 180°C (350°F) mark 4 for 12–15 minutes, until golden brown. Allow to cool for a few minutes on the sheets, remove with a palette knife on to wire racks.

Nut Butter Biscuits

0 g (2 oz) BUTTER
5 g (1 oz) CASTER SUGAR
5 g (3 oz) PLAIN FLOUR
5 g (1 oz) MIXED NUTS: ALMONDS, WALNUTS, HAZELNUTS, INELY CHOPPED
50 g (5 oz) ICING SUGAR
OFFEE ESSENCE, FOR FROSTING (optional)

Makes about 12

. Beat the butter until soft and creamy. Add the caster ugar and beat again.
. Use a fork to stir the flour and the nuts into the reamed mixture.
. Turn the dough out on to a lightly floured surface nd knead lightly into a ball. Roll out thinly between heets of non-stick paper and stamp out 12 rounds using plain or fluted 6.5 cm ($2\frac{1}{2}$ inch) cutter. Reroll trimmings s needed.
. Grease two baking sheets and transfer the rounds o them. Bake in the oven at 170°C (325°F) mark 3 or 20–25 minutes, until slightly coloured. Cool on a ire rack.

Herb Oatcakes

5 g (1 oz) LARD
5 ml (3 fl oz) WATER
25 g (8 oz) MEDIUM OATMEAL
.5 ml ($\frac{1}{2}$ tsp) DRIED SAGE
.25 ml ($\frac{1}{4}$ tsp) BICARBONATE OF SODA
.25 ml ($\frac{1}{4}$ tsp) SALT

Makes 8

. Melt the lard in a pan with the water. Cool.
. Mix the oatmeal, sage, bicarbonate of soda and salt. tir in the cooled lard. Mix to a moist dough adding a ittle more water if needed.
. Pat the dough out on an ungreased baking sheet to a 0 cm (8 inch) round. Roll lightly over the surface to latten it. Flute edges.
. Bake at 180°C (350°F) mark 4 for about 40 minutes.
. Cut into eight wedges while still warm. Allow to firm p slightly before cooling on a rack.

Cheese Sticks

00 g (4 oz) PLAIN FLOUR
INCH OF SALT
0 g (2 oz) BUTTER OR BLOCK MARGARINE, CUT INTO MALL PIECES
0 g (2 oz) MATURE CHEDDAR CHEESE, GRATED
EGG, BEATEN
ARMESAN CHEESE, TO SPRINKLE

Makes 96

. Sift the flour and salt in a bowl. Rub in the fat until he mixture resembles fine breadcrumbs.
. Add the cheese and bind the mixture together with a little beaten egg. Knead lightly to give a smooth dough.
3. Roll out on a lightly floured surface to an oblong 25 × 15 cm (10 × 6 inches). Brush with beaten egg and sprinkle liberally with Parmesan cheese. Press the Parmesan lightly into the egg.
4. Cut into sticks 6 cm × 5 mm ($2\frac{1}{2} \times \frac{1}{4}$ inches) and place on baking sheets. Bake in the oven at 200°C (400°F) mark 6 for about 10 minutes, or until golden brown. Transfer to a wire rack to cool.

Date and Oatmeal Muffins

75 g (3 oz) SELF-RAISING FLOUR
125 g (4 oz) MEDIUM OATMEAL
2.5 ml ($\frac{1}{2}$ tsp) BAKING POWDER
2.5 ml ($\frac{1}{2}$ tsp) BICARBONATE OF SODA
1.25 ml ($\frac{1}{4}$ tsp) SALT
50 g (2 oz) CASTER SUGAR
50 g (2 oz) STONED DATES, CHOPPED
15 ml (1 tbsp) GOLDEN SYRUP
15 g ($\frac{1}{2}$ oz) BUTTER OR MARGARINE
150 ml ($\frac{1}{4}$ pint) MILK

Makes 8

1. Grease eight 10 cm (4 inch) Yorkshire pudding tins.
2. Stir together the dry ingredients, with the dates. Heat the syrup and butter together and stir in the milk.
3. Pour the milk mixture into the dry ingredients stirring all the time.
4. Fill the Yorkshire pudding tins one-third full of mixture. Bake at 200°C (400°F) mark 6 for 15–20 minutes. Eat warm, split and buttered.

Cheese and Date Triangles

50 g (2 oz) PLAIN FLOUR
15 ml (1 tbsp) BAKING POWDER
PINCH OF SALT
175 g (6 oz) WHOLEMEAL FLOUR
50 g (2 oz) BUTTER OR MARGARINE
MILK
125 g (4 oz) FULL-FAT CREAM CHEESE
25 g (1 oz) STONED DATES, CHOPPED
SALT AND FRESHLY GROUND PEPPER
BUTTER OR MARGARINE, FOR SPREADING

Makes 6

1. Grease a baking sheet. Sift the plain flour, baking powder and salt into a large bowl and stir in the wholemeal flour. Rub in the fat and add sufficient milk to give a soft but manageable dough.
2. Knead the dough lightly and roll out on a lightly floured surface to a 15 cm (6 inch) round. Divide into six triangles and mark the tops into a lattice with the back of a knife. Place on the baking sheet.
3. Brush the tops with milk and bake at 230°C (450°F) mark 8 for about 15 minutes. Cool on a wire rack.
4. Blend the cream cheese and dates together with seasoning to taste.
5. Halve the scones, spread with butter or margarine and fill generously with the date cheese spread. Replace the tops.

Animal Butter Biscuits

Animal Butter Biscuits

225 g (8 oz) BUTTER
125 g (4 oz) CASTER SUGAR
275 g (10 oz) PLAIN FLOUR
50 g (2 oz) FINE SEMOLINA
CURRANTS, COCKTAIL STICKS
100 g (4 oz) ICING SUGAR, SIFTED
15 ml (1 tbsp) WARM WATER
12 SMALL APPLES

Makes about 12

1. Beat the butter well in a bowl, then work in the sugar. Stir in the flour and semolina and knead.
2. Roll out on a lightly floured work surface, half at a time, to a 5 mm ($\frac{1}{4}$ inch) thickness. Stamp out animal shapes. If the mixture sticks to the surface, roll out between pieces of non-stick paper.
3. Lift the shapes on to baking sheets and press currants into the heads for eyes. Slide cocktail sticks into the bodies of the animals from the base.
4. Bake in the oven at 180°C (350°F) mark 4 for 15–20 minutes. Cool on wire racks.
5. Make the glacé icing: put the icing sugar into a bowl and gradually add the water, beating well until the icing is smooth and will coat the back of the spoon.
6. Pipe on the children's names with icing. Make a hole in the tops of the apples and push in biscuit sticks.

Photographed above

Peanut Crunchies

125 g (4 oz) BUTTER OR BLOCK MARGARINE
125 g (4 oz) LIGHT SOFT BROWN SUGAR
45 ml (3 tbsp) SMOOTH PEANUT BUTTER
225 g (8 oz) PLAIN FLOUR
2.5 ml ($\frac{1}{2}$ tsp) BICARBONATE OF SODA
2.5 ml ($\frac{1}{2}$ tsp) CREAM OF TARTAR
30 ml (2 tbsp) WATER
1 BEATEN EGG, TO GLAZE
25 g (1 oz) SALTED PEANUTS

Makes about 24

1. Beat the fat in a bowl until creamy. Add the sugar and peanut butter and beat again until light and fluffy.
2. Sift in the flour, bicarbonate of soda and cream of tartar, using a fork to work the dry ingredients into the fat with the water to form a soft mixture. Chill covered for 20 minutes.
3. Turn out the dough on to a lightly floured surface, knead into a ball and roll out fairly thinly. Stamp out about 24 biscuits using a 5 cm (2 inch) cutter. Reknead the trimmings as necessary.
4. Grease a baking sheet and put the biscuits on it, brush with beaten egg and press a few peanuts into the centre of each to decorate. Bake in the oven at 190°C (375°F) mark 5 for about 20 minutes. Transfer to a wire rack to cool.

JAMS & JELLIES

JAMS & JELLIES

Preparing the jars

The jars used for jam must be clean and free from flaws and they must be warmed in a low oven, to prevent cracking, before the jam is put in.

Testing for a set

Jams, jellies and marmalades should be boiled until they reach 105°C (221°F) to obtain a perfect set. Clip the thermometer to the side of the pan when you begin cooking, making sure it does not touch the bottom, and read off the temperature at eye level.

If you have no thermometer, use one or both of the following tests. Remove the pan from the heat during each test to prevent overboiling.

1. Spoon a little jam on to a chilled saucer or plate, allow it to cool, then push a finger across the surface. If the jam is ready to set, the surface will wrinkle.
2. Remove some jam with a wooden spoon. Let it cool slightly, then allow it to drop back into the pan. If the jam is ready the drops will run together along the lower edge of the spoon to form large flakes.

Potting and covering

As soon as a set has been reached, pour the jam into the jars, filling right to the necks. The only exceptions are strawberry and other whole-fruit jams and also marmalades—these should be allowed to cool for at least 15 minutes before being potted (stir before putting into jars), to prevent the fruit rising in the pots. Wipe the outside and rims of the pots and cover the jam while still very hot with a waxed disc, wax side down, making sure it lies flat. Either cover immediately with a dampened Cellophane round, or leave the jam until quite cold before doing this. Label the jar and store in a cool, dark place.

Yield

It is not practical to state the exact yield in jelly recipes because the ripeness of the fruit and the time allowed for dripping both affect the quantity of juice obtained.

Whole Strawberry Jam

1.25 kg ($2\frac{1}{2}$ lb) SMALL STRAWBERRIES, HULLED
45 ml (3 tbsp) LEMON JUICE
1.5 kg (3 lb) SUGAR
KNOB OF BUTTER
227 ml (8 fl oz) BOTTLE OF COMMERCIAL PECTIN

Makes about 2.5 kg (5 lb)

1. Have ready five 450 g (1 lb) jars (see Preparing the jars, left).
2. Put the strawberries into a preserving pan with the lemon juice and sugar. Leave to stand for 1 hour, stirring occasionally.
3. Heat the mixture slowly, stirring, until the sugar has dissolved, then add a small knob of butter to reduce the foaming. Bring to the boil and boil rapidly for 4 minutes, stirring occasionally.
4. Remove the pan from the heat and stir in the pectin. Cool for at least 20 minutes to prevent the fruit rising in the jars, then pot (see Potting and covering, left).

Photographed opposite

Blackberry and Apple Jelly

1 kg (2 lb) COOKING APPLES, UNPEELED AND UNCORED, CUT INTO THICK CHUNKS
2 kg (4 lb) BLACKBERRIES
1.2 litres (2 pints) WATER
SUGAR

See Yield (left)

1. Have jam jars ready (see Preparing the jars, left).
2. Put the apples and blackberries into a preserving pan with the water and simmer gently for about 1 hour until the fruit is really soft and pulpy. Stir from time to time to prevent sticking.
3. Spoon the fruit pulp into a jelly bag or cloth attached to the legs of an upturned stool, and leave to strain into a large bowl for at least 12 hours.
4. Discard the pulp remaining in the jelly bag. Measure the extract and return it to the pan with 500 g (1 lb) sugar for each 600 ml (1 pint) extract. Heat gently, stirring, until the sugar has dissolved, then boil rapidly for about 10 minutes.
5. Test for a set (see left) and, when setting point is reached, remove from the heat and skim off any scum with a slotted spoon. Pot (see Potting and covering, left).

Whole Strawberry Jam

Apricot Jam

Apricot Jam

1.8 kg (4 lb) APRICOTS, HALVED AND STONED, 10 STONES RESERVED
450 ml (¾ pint) WATER
45 ml (3 tbsp) LEMON JUICE
1.8 kg (4 lb) SUGAR

Makes about 2.7 kg (6 lb)

1. Have ready six 450 g (1 lb) jam jars (see Preparing the jars, page 268).
2. Using nutcrackers, carefully crack the outer shell of the apricot stones and reserve the kernels. Blanch the kernels: put into boiling water for 1 minute. Drain and discard the skins.
3. Lightly grease the bottom of a preserving pan with a little butter. Put the apricot halves, the kernels, water and lemon juice into the pan. Simmer gently, until the fruit softens—about 20 minutes, stirring occasionally.
4. Meanwhile, put the sugar into an ovenproof dish in the bottom of the oven to warm. This will help the sugar to dissolve more quickly when added to the apricots. Remove the fruit from the heat and stir in the sugar using a wooden spoon. Stir gently until all traces of sugar have dissolved, returning the pan to a very low heat if necessary. Do not boil until the sugar has dissolved.
5. When the sugar has completely dissolved, bring the contents of the pan to a good rolling boil. Continue boiling for about 15 minutes, stirring occasionally to prevent sticking and burning.
6. When the jam resembles a thick syrup, check the temperature, or test for a set (see page 268).
7. Using a metal spoon, remove the scum from the surface of the jam. Leave to cool slightly in the pan, until a skin forms on top—about 20 minutes. The jam thickens slightly, preventing the apricot kernels from floating to the surface. Stir the jam and pot (see Potting and covering, page 268).

Photographed left

Lemon Honey Curd

FINELY GRATED RIND OF 4 LEMONS AND ABOUT 180 ml (12 tbsp) JUICE
5 EGGS, BEATEN
100 g (4 oz) BUTTER
225 g (8 oz) THICK HONEY
50 g (2 oz) CASTER SUGAR

Makes about 900 g (2 lb)

1. Have ready four 227 g (8 oz) jars (see Preparing the jars, page 268).
2. Put all the ingredients into the top of a double boiler.
3. Place over a pan of simmering water and stir until the sugar has dissolved and the curd thickens enough to coat the back of a wooden spoon, stirring constantly. This will take from 10–20 minutes. Do not allow the curd to boil or it will curdle.
4. Pot (see Potting and covering, page 268) and store in a cool place, preferably the refrigerator. It will keep about one month.

Three-fruit Marmalade

4 RIPE LEMONS, HALVED
2 SWEET ORANGES, HALVED
2 GRAPEFRUITS
3.6 litres (6 pints) WATER
3 kg (6 lb) SUGAR

Makes about 5 kg (10 lb)

1. Have ready ten 450 g (1 lb) jars (see Preparing the jars, page 268).

2. The fruit should weigh a total of about 1.5 kg (3 lb). Squeeze the juice and pips out of the lemons and oranges. Peel the grapefruit and remove any pith and stringy parts from the flesh. Tie the pith, stringy parts and pips from all the fruits in a piece of muslin.

3. Thinly cut the peel of all the fruits and chop the grapefruit flesh roughly. Put the peel, flesh, juice, water and muslin bag into a preserving pan. Simmer gently for 1–1½ hours until the peel is really soft and the contents of the pan are reduced by half.

4. Remove the muslin bag from the pan, squeezing well and allowing the juice to run back into the pan. Add the sugar, stirring until dissolved, then boil rapidly for 15–20 minutes. Test for a set (see page 268) and, when setting point is reached, remove from the heat and skim off any scum with a slotted spoon. Leave the marmalade to stand for 15 minutes, then stir to distribute the peel. Pot (see Potting and covering, page 268).

Seville Orange Marmalade

1.5 kg (3 lb) SEVILLE ORANGES, HALVED
JUICE OF 2 LEMONS
3.6 litres (6 pints) WATER
3 kg (6 lb) SUGAR

Makes about 5 kg (10 lb)

1. Have ready ten 450 g (1 lb) jars (see Preparing the jars, page 268).

2. Squeeze the juice and pips out of the oranges. Tie the pips, and any extra membrane that has come away during squeezing, in a piece of muslin.

3. Slice the orange peel thinly or thickly, as preferred, and put it into a preserving pan with the fruit juices, water and the muslin bag. Simmer gently for about 2 hours until the peel is really soft and the liquid reduced by about half.

4. Remove the muslin bag, squeezing it well and allowing the juice to run back into the pan. Add the sugar, stirring until it has dissolved, then boil the mixture rapidly for about 15 minutes. Test for a set (see page 268) and, when setting point is reached, remove from the heat and skim off any scum with a slotted spoon. Pot (see Potting and covering, page 268).

Melon and Ginger Jam

2 kg (4 lb) [PREPARED WEIGHT] HONEYDEW MELON, SEEDED, SKINNED AND DICED
2 kg (4 lb) SUGAR
25 g (1 oz) ROOT GINGER, PEELED AND CRUSHED
THINLY PARED RIND AND JUICE OF 3 LEMONS
KNOB OF BUTTER

Makes about 2.5 kg (5 lb)

1. Have ready five 450 g (1 lb) jars (see Preparing the jars, page 268).

2. Put the melon into a bowl, sprinkle with about 500 g (1 lb) of the sugar and leave to stand overnight.

3. Tie the crushed ginger in a piece of muslin with the lemon rind. Put into a preserving pan with the melon and lemon juice. Simmer gently for 30 minutes, then remove from the heat and add the rest of the sugar. Stir until the sugar has dissolved, add a knob of butter and boil gently for about 30 minutes until the melon looks transparent.

4. Test for a set (see page 268) and, when setting point is reached, remove from the heat, discard the muslin bag and skim off any scum with a slotted spoon. Pot (see Potting and covering, page 268).

Redcurrant Jelly

1.5 kg (3 lb) REDCURRANTS
600 ml (1 pint) WATER
SUGAR

See Yield (page 268)

1. Have jam jars ready (see Preparing the jars, page 268).

2. There is no need to remove the currants from their stalks. Put them into a preserving pan with the water and simmer gently for about 30 minutes until the fruit is soft and pulpy. Stir from time to time to prevent sticking.

3. Spoon the fruit pulp into a jelly bag or cloth attached to the legs of an upturned stool, and leave to strain into a bowl for at least 12 hours.

4. Discard the pulp remaining in the jelly bag. Measure the extract and return it to the pan with 500 g (1 lb) sugar for each 600 ml (1 pint) extract. Heat gently, stirring, until the sugar has dissolved, then boil rapidly for about 15 minutes.

5. Test for a set (see page 268) and, when setting point is reached, remove from the heat and skim off any scum with a slotted spoon. Pot (see Potting and covering, page 268).

DRINKS

Egg Nog

1 PART RUM, PORT OR SHERRY
1 BARSPOON BRANDY OR LIQUEUR
1 BARSPOON SUGAR SYRUP
1 EGG
3 PARTS MILK OR SINGLE CREAM
FRESHLY GRATED NUTMEG

1. Mix all the ingredients together except the nutmeg and shake them.
2. Strain into a goblet and sprinkle with nutmeg.

Daiquiri

4 PARTS WHITE RUM
1 PART LIME JUICE
DASH SUGAR SYRUP

1. Put all the ingredients together and shake them.

Dry Martini

2 PARTS GIN
2 PARTS DRY VERMOUTH
1 GREEN OLIVE, TO SERVE

1. Combine the gin and vermouth. Stir and serve with a green olive.

Sweet Martini

2 PARTS GIN
1 PART SWEET VERMOUTH
DASH ORANGE BITTERS (optional)
MARASCHINO CHERRY, TO SERVE

1. Combine the gin and vermouth, adding the orange bitters, if wished. Stir and serve with a cherry.

Punch

3 ORANGES
CLOVES
2 LEMONS
1.1 litres (2 pints) WATER
6 BOTTLES RED BORDEAUX WINE
1 BOTTLE PORT
200 ml (7 fl oz) BRANDY
75 ml (3 fl oz) ORANGE LIQUEUR
STICKS OF CINNAMON

Makes about 50 servings
1. Stud 1 orange with cloves and roast it in the oven at 180°C (350°F) mark 4 for 30 minutes.
2. Slice the remaining fruit and put it with the water into a large preserving pan. Bring almost to the boil and stir in the other ingredients. Bring back almost to boiling and transfer the punch to a large bowl.
3. Serve hot, with the clove-studded orange floating in it.

Hot Honey Toddy

1 BOTTLE MEDIUM WHITE WINE
THINLY PARED RIND AND JUICE OF 1 LEMON
30 ml (2 tbsp) CLEAR HONEY
FEW PIECES OF BLADE MACE
5 cm (2 inch) CINNAMON STICK
60 ml (4 tbsp) BRANDY

Makes 6–8 glasses
1. Heat the wine with the lemon rind and juice, honey and flavourings to just below boiling point. Remove from the heat, cover and leave to infuse for 1 hour.
2. Reheat the punch but do not boil. Strain into a warmed jug. Add the brandy and serve immediately, running the punch into the glasses over the back of a spoon to prevent them cracking.

Cassis

Cassis, drunk with chilled dry white wine, is known as kir. Put a dash of cassis and a twist of lemon rind into a wine glass and fill with white wine.

500 g (1 lb) BLACKCURRANTS, STRIGGED AND CRUSHED
600 ml (1 pint) GIN OR BRANDY
SUGAR

Makes 850 ml ($1\frac{1}{2}$ pints)
1. Put the blackcurrants with the gin or brandy into screw-topped jars, then screw down tightly. Leave in a dark place for about 2 months.
2. Strain, then add 175 g (6 oz) sugar to each 600 ml (1 pint) liquid. Pour into a jug, cover and leave for 2 days, stirring at intervals to dissolve the sugar. Strain through muslin. Bottle and store for 6 months.
Photographed opposite

Kir with Cassis

Brandy Alexander and Everton Blue

Everton Blue

¼ GLASS OF GIN
¼ GLASS OF BLUE CURAÇAO
¼ GLASS OF CREME DE BANANE
¼ GLASS OF SINGLE CREAM
LEMON JUICE
GRENADINE

Makes 1

1. Shake all the ingredients except the grenadine and strain into a champagne glass.

2. Add a dash of grenadine so that the drink is blue at the top and red at the bottom.

Photographed opposite

Brandy Alexander

⅓ GLASS OF BRANDY
⅓ GLASS OF CREME DE CACAO
⅓ GLASS OF SINGLE CREAM

Makes 1

1. Shake and strain into a cocktail glass.

Photographed opposite

Manhattan

2 PARTS RYE WHISKEY
1 PART SWEET VERMOUTH
DASH ANGOSTURA BITTERS
MARASCHINO CHERRY, TO SERVE

1. Combine the rye whiskey, vermouth and bitters. Stir and serve with a cherry.

Hot Rumour

1 ORANGE
12 CLOVES
1 BOTTLE RED WINE
45 ml (3 tbsp) DEMERARA RUM
30 ml (2 tbsp) DEMERARA SUGAR

Makes about 900 ml (1½ pints)

1. Stick the orange with the cloves and roast it in the oven at 180°C (350°F) mark 4 for 30 minutes.

2. Heat the wine to just below boiling point and add the rum and sugar. Float the orange on the top and simmer for a further few minutes.

3. Remove the orange and serve the hot drink in punch glasses.

Bloody Mary

1 PART VODKA
2 DASHES WORCESTERSHIRE SAUCE
CELERY SALT
4 PARTS TOMATO JUICE
1 BARSPOON LEMON JUICE
ICE CUBES
TABASCO SAUCE AND FRESHLY GROUND PEPPER
SLICE OF LEMON, TO DECORATE (optional)

1. Mix the vodka, Worcestershire sauce and celery salt in a bowl.

2. Pour the tomato and lemon juice into a jug and stir in the vodka mixture. Add ice and stir again adding Tabasco sauce and pepper to taste. Decorate, if wished, with a slice of lemon.

Grasshopper

⅓ GLASS CREME DE MENTHE
⅓ GLASS CREME DE CACAO
⅓ GLASS SINGLE CREAM

Makes 1

1. Shake all the ingredients and strain into a glass.

Irish Coffee

30 ml (2 tbsp) IRISH WHISKEY
10 ml (2 tsp) DEMERARA SUGAR
1 WINEGLASS HOT STRONG BLACK COFFEE
15–30 ml (1–2 tbsp) DOUBLE CREAM

Makes 1

1. Stir the whiskey and sugar into the hot coffee.

2. Float the cream on top by pouring over the back of a warm spoon. Do not stir.

Pina Colada

65 ml (2½ fl oz) PINEAPPLE JUICE
40 ml (1½ fl oz) BACARDI RUM
25 g (1 oz) CREAMED COCONUT
DASH OF ORANGE-FLAVOURED LIQUEUR
CRUSHED ICE
MARASCHINO CHERRIES AND PINEAPPLE SLICES, TO DECORATE

Makes 1

1. Shake the pineapple juice, rum, coconut and orange liqueur together for 2–3 minutes.

2. Serve poured over crushed ice and decorate with cherries and pineapple slices.

Pippin Cold Punch

Pippin Cold Punch

2 oranges, roughly chopped
300 ml (½ pint) Calvados
100 ml (4 fl oz) orange-flavoured liqueur
large block of ice
600 ml (1 pint) orange juice or cold tea
three 1 litre (1¾ pints) bottles medium cider
apple and orange slices, to decorate

Makes 2 litres (3½ pints)

1. Steep the oranges in the Calvados and orange-flavoured liqueur for 3–4 hours.
2. Put the ice block into a punch bowl and strain the Calvados mixture over it. Add the orange juice or tea and the cider. Decorate with apple and orange slices.

Photographed opposite

Hot Spiced Cider

1 litre (2 pints) cider
100 g (4 oz) sugar
12 whole cloves
4 sticks cinnamon about 5 cm (2 inches) long
8 whole allspice

Makes about 1.2 litres (2–2¼ pints)

1. Put all the ingredients in a saucepan and heat until the sugar has dissolved. Strain the cider into tumblers.

Negroni

2–3 ice cubes
1 part Campari
1 part sweet vermouth
2 parts gin
slice of orange
soda water

1. Put the ice cubes in a tumbler and pour over them the Campari, vermouth and gin. Float the slice of orange on top then top up with soda water to taste.

Whisky Sour

juice of ½ lemon
5 ml (1 tsp) sugar
1 measure whisky
cracked ice

Makes 1

1. Mix together the lemon juice, sugar and whisky and shake well with the cracked ice. Serve in a whisky tumbler.

Brandy Cocktail

1 part brandy
1 part French vermouth
crushed ice
lemon rind curl
maraschino cherry

1. Shake the brandy and vermouth with some crushed ice in a shaker. Pour into a glass and serve with a curl of lemon rind and a cherry.

Honeysuckle Cup

1 bottle medium white wine
15 ml (1 tbsp) clear honey (optional)
25 ml (1½ tbsp) Benedictine
150 ml (¼ pint) brandy
750 ml (25 fl oz) fizzy lemonade
2 lemons, sliced
1 peach, sliced
crushed ice

Makes about 1.4 litres (2½ pints)

1. Mix the wine, honey (if used), Bénédictine, brandy and lemonade and pour over the fruit and ice in a bowl. Leave to stand for a 1 hour before serving.

Rum Punch

1.7 litres (3 pints) cold water
450 g (1 lb) sugar
thinly pared rind and juice of 1 lemon
thinly pared rind of 1 orange and juice of 4 oranges
300 ml (½ pint) strong tea
300–600 ml (½–1 pint) rum

Makes about 3 litres (5–5¼ pints)

1. Put the water and sugar in a pan with the rinds of the lemon and 1 orange. Stir until the sugar is dissolved, bring to the boil and boil for 5 minutes.
2. Remove the pan from the heat and add the juice of the lemon and all the oranges, the tea and the rum.
3. Strain and serve hot or cold.

June Cup

1 bottle Beaujolais, chilled
20 ml (4 tsp) brandy
a few strawberries, hulled and sliced
1 litre (2 pints) fizzy lemonade, chilled

Makes about 2 litres (3½ pints)

1. Pour the Beaujolais and brandy over the strawberries and leave in a cool place for at least 30 minutes.
2. Just before serving, add the lemonade.

Home-made ginger beer

To start the ginger beer 'plant'.

50 g (2 oz) FRESH BAKER'S YEAST
30 ml (2 tbsp) CASTER SUGAR
30 ml (2 tbsp) GROUND GINGER
300 ml ($\frac{1}{2}$ pint) WATER

1. Blend the yeast and sugar until they cream and form a liquid. Add the ground ginger and the water, stir well and place the mixture in a covered jar with a loose-fitting lid.
2. *Each day:* Add 5 ml (1 tsp) ground ginger and 5 ml (1 tsp) caster sugar to the 'plant' and stir well.
3. *After 10 days:* Dissolve 500 g (18 oz) caster sugar in 900 ml ($1\frac{1}{2}$ pints) water, bring to the boil and cool slightly. Add the strained juice of 2 lemons.
4. Strain the prepared ginger beer 'plant' through fine muslin and add the strained liquid to the sugar and lemon juice, together with 3.4 litres (6 pints) water.
5. Stir well and bottle at once in strong, screw-topped bottles (as used for cider or beer). Store in a cool place (this is essential) and use as required.

To make more ginger beer
Halve the 'plant' (the sediment left on the muslin) and place in two separate jars. Add 300 ml ($\frac{1}{2}$ pint) water, 10 ml (2 tsp) ground ginger and 10 ml (2 tsp) caster sugar to each jar; stir and continue to feed daily as above for 10 days; proceed as before.

Lemon Barley Water

50 g (2 oz) PEARL BARLEY
600 ml (1 pint) WATER
50 g (2 oz) SUGAR
JUICE OF 2 LEMONS, STRAINED

Makes about 600 ml (1 pint)
1. Put the barley into a saucepan, just cover with cold water and bring to the boil. Strain off the water and rinse the barley under cold running water. Return it to the saucepan, add the 600 ml (1 pint) water, bring to the boil again, cover and simmer for 1 hour.
2. Strain the liquid into a jug or bowl, add the sugar and cool.
3. When the mixture is cold, add the lemon juice. Use as required; it will keep indefinitely in the refrigerator.

Orange and Grapefruit Squash

900 g (2 lb) SUGAR
900 ml ($1\frac{1}{2}$ pints) WATER
20 ml (4 tsp) TARTARIC ACID
FINELY GRATED RIND AND JUICE OF 2 LARGE ORANGES
FINELY GRATED RIND AND JUICE OF 1 GRAPEFRUIT

Makes about 1.3 litres ($2\frac{1}{4}$ pints)
1. Put the sugar and water into a pan and stir over a gentle heat until the sugar has dissolved. Bring this sugar syrup to the boil and simmer for 10 minutes.
2. Put the tartaric acid and the orange and grapefruit rinds in a large bowl or jug, pour on the syrup and leave to stand overnight.
3. Add the fruit juice, strain and bottle. Serve diluted with water or soda water.

'Still' Lemonade

THINLY PEELED RIND AND JUICE OF 3 LEMONS
175 g (6 oz) SUGAR
900 ml ($1\frac{1}{2}$ pints) BOILING WATER

Makes about 1.1 litres (2 pints)
1. Put the lemon rind and sugar into a large jug and pour on the boiling water. Cover and leave to cool, stirring occasionally.
2. Add the juice of the lemons and strain the lemonade. Serve chilled.

Ice Cream Soda

1 GLASS SODA WATER
15 ml (1 tbsp) ICE CREAM

Makes 1
1. Whisk the soda water and ice cream together with a rotary whisk until frothy or blend them at maximum speed for 1 minute in blender. Pour into a large glass and serve at once.

Bitter Lemon

2 UNPEELED LEMONS OR 3 LEMONS, WITH RIND REMOVED, CUT INTO PIECES
600 ml (1 pint) WATER
100 g (4 oz) SUGAR

Makes about 900 ml ($1\frac{1}{2}$ pints)
1. Put the lemon pieces into a saucepan with the water and bring to the boil. Lower the heat and simmer gently for 10–15 minutes, until the fruit is soft.
2. Add the sugar and stir to dissolve it. Remove from the heat, cover and leave to cool. Strain before using. Serve with soda water and/or gin.

Orangeade

2 ORANGES, RINDS THINLY PARED AND RESERVED
1 LEMON, RIND THINLY PARED AND RESERVED
50 g (2 oz) SUGAR
600 ml (1 pint) BOILING WATER

Makes about 900 ml ($1\frac{1}{2}$ pints)
1. Remove all white pith from the fruit. Put the rinds and sugar into a bowl and pour the boiling water over. Leave to cool, stirring occasionally.
2. Squeeze out the juice from the oranges and the lemon. Strain the cooled liquid and add the fruit juices.

INDEX

Aduki Bean and Beef Cake, 57
All-in-One Egg Supper, 152
All Seasons Fruit Salad Pie, 218
Almond
and Hazelnut Barquettes, 263
and Strawberry Japonais, 229
Apple Pie, 262
Balmoral Cake, 257
Custard Tarts, 238
Filled Coffee Bread, 243
Amandine, Broccoli, 171
Anchovy
and Egg Crispy Fries, 155
Egg Appetiser, 19
Wheatmeal Curl, 243
Animal Butter Biscuits, 266
Appetiser
Anchovy Egg, 19
Avocado, 12
Bean, Lemony, 8
Apple
Almond Pie, 262
and Blackberry Jelly, 268
and Celery Stuffing, 215
and Lemon Lamb, 76
and Plum Double Crust Pie, 222
and Red Cabbage Salad, 196
Charlotte, Steamed, 225
Cider-poached Whole Apples, 221
Flan, Citrus, 234
Flan, Streusel, 262
Flapjack, 231
Hazelnut Genoese, 253
Watercress, Sweet Pepper and Apple Salad, 205
Apricot
and Cinnamon Cake, 259
and Ginger Stuffing, 215
and Ginger Upside-down Pudding, 225
Jam, 271
Puffs, Banana, 221
Streusel, Deep-dish, 222
Aromatic Fruit Salad, 226
Asparagus and Bacon Quiche, 90
Aspic, Braised Beef in, 66
Au Gratin, Courgettes, 158
Aubergine
and Lamb Moussaka, 74
Cheesey-stuffed, 140
Avocado
and Red Bean Salad, 207
and Spinach Salad, 202
Appetiser, 12
Salad, Lemon-dressed, 203
Smoky, and Grapefruit Salad, 207

Bacon, 88–91
and Asparagus Quiche, 90
and Corn Stuffing, 215
and Egg Pilaff, 151
and Fried Liver, 128
and Kidney Roly Poly, 119
and Mince Pie, 61
Blintzes, 90
Flan, Curried, 90
in Cider, 88
Liver and Bacon Chops, 128
Peanut Glazed Bacon Hock, 88
Stew, Midweek, 90
Stuffing, 215
Baked
Cider Baked Rabbit with Cabbage, 114
Drumsticks with Peanuts, 98
Eggs, 151
Fillets with Lemon Sauce, 41
Liver with Dumplings, 124
Tuna-stuffed Potatoes, 146
Bakes, Tuna Rice, 12
Balmoral Almond Cake, 257
Banana
and Honey Ice-Cream, 231
Apricot Puffs, 221
Chiffon Pie, 226
Flambé, 221
Torte, Caramel, 261

Baps, Scottish, 247
Barbecue Sauce, 210
Barbecued Beef and Beans, 66
Barley
and Chicken Broth, 105
Lemon Barley Water, 280
stuffed Mackerel, 42
Wholemeal Twist, 247
Barquettes, Almond and Hazelnut, 263
Basic
Brown Bread, 242
Enriched White Dough, 242
White Bread, 242
Baton Zigzag, 244
Batter, Kidneys in, 120
Beans
Aduki, and Beef Bake, 57
and Barbecued Beef, 66
and Pork Patties, 86
and Vegetable Stew, 138
Appetiser, Lemony (flageolets), 8
Broad, in Parsley Sauce, 176
Butter, and Fish Pie, 44
Creamed, 171
Cannellini and Chicken Soup, 25
Kidney, and Tomato Flan, 145
Mixed Salad, 205
Red, and Avocado Salad, 207
Sprouts and Mushrooms, Stir-fried, 170
White, Soup, 22
with Sauerkraut and Frankfurters, 134
Beef, 54–67 (*see also* Steak)
and Potato Braise, 56
Bake and Aduki Bean, 57
Barbecued and Beans, 66
Beefburgers, 58
Beefy Macaroni Bake, 65
Boeuf Bourguignonne, 55
Braised, in Aspic, 66
Brisket in Red Wine, 67
with Lentils, 61
Brewers' Braise, 56
Brown Stew with Doughboys, 64
Calcutta Curry, 57
Carbonade of, 57
Casserole, Four-in-one, 67
Chilli, with Beans, 58
Chunky, with Celery, 64
Cold, in Soured Cream, 199
Cottage Pie, 55
in Wine, 59
Mince and Bacon Pie, 61
Mince in a Crust, 67
Olives, 62
Oriental Meatballs, 60
Peasant-style Roulades, 61
Pot-au-feu, 64
Roast, 62
Spicy Meatballs, 64
Beefburgers, 58
beer, Home-made ginger, 280
Biscuits, 248–266
Animal Butter, 266
Honey Crunch Cookies, 264
Nut Butter, 265
Peanut Crunchies, 266
Bitter Lemon, 280
Blackberry and Apple Jelly, 268
Blackcurrant Gâteau, Chocolate, 250
Blanquette d'Agneau, 68
Blintzes, Bacon, 90
Bloody Mary, 277
Blue Cheese
Dip, 12
Rarebits, 157
Boeuf Bourguinonne, 55
Boiled Ox Tongue, 130
Bortsch, 26
Braise
Beef and Potato, 56
Brewers', 56
Braised
Beef in Aspic, 66
Beef with Lentils, 61

Brisket with Red Wine, 66
Celery, 167
Brandy
Alexander, 277
Cocktail, 279
Bread, 240–247
Almond Filled Coffee, 243
Anchovy Wheatmeal Curl, 243
and Butter Pudding, Rich Grape, 224
Barley Wholewheat Twist, 247
Basic, Brown, 242
Enriched White Dough, 242
White, 242
French, 240
Fruited Butterscotch Ring, 246
Golden Cornmeal Loaves, 243
Granary Tea Cake, 244
Home Made Rye, 246
Honey Nut Stick, 246
Horseradish Crown, 246
Hot Cross Buns, 244
Mustard Flower Pots, 246
Oatmeal Coburg, 243
Orange Ginger Knot, 243
Poppyseed Rolls, 247
Sage and Onion Salad Loaf, 242
Sauce, 210
Scottish Baps, 247
Zigzag Baton, 247
Breakfast in a Pan, 154
Broccoli Amandine, 171
Broth
Chicken and Barley, 105
Chicken and Macaroni, 30
Kidney and Celery, 118
Mushroom and Rice, 30
Brown
Bread, Basic, 242
Stew with Doughboys, 64
Brûlée
Crème, 231
Pineapple, 231
Brussels
Creamed, 168
Sprouts and Potato Purée, 28
Buns, Hot Cross, 244
Burgers, Millet and Nut, 146
Butter
Bean and Fish Pie, 44
Biscuits, Animal, 266
Buttermilk Soup, Cauliflower, 28
Butterscotch Sauce, 213

Cabbage
and Hazelnut Croquettes, 167
Savoury Spring, 178
Stir-fried, with Caraway, 164
Whole Stuffed, 143
with Cider Baked Rabbit, 114
Cakes, 248–266
Almond and Hazelnut Barquettes, 263
Apple Hazelnut Genoese, 253
Apricot and Cinnamon, 259
Balmoral Almond, 257
Caramel Banana Torte, 261
Cheese and Date Triangles, 265
Cherry and Coconut, 259
Cherry Scones, 262
Chocolate Blackcurrant Gâteau, 250
Chocolate Fudge, 250
Choux Cream Puffs, 262
Cinnamon Sponge Drops with Cream, 248
Coffee Praline Gâteau, 261
Dark Ginger, 251
Date and Oatmeal Muffins, 265
Date and Spice, 256
Frosted Chocolate, 256
Frosted Coconut, 256
Fruit Brazil Butter, 248
Fruit Crusted Cider, 256
Greengage Coconut Sponge, 231
Honey Frosted Carrot, 259
Lemon Seed, 261
Marbled Chocolate Cake, 259

Cakes (*contd*)
Marmalade Spice, 253
Marzipan Pineapple, 250
Moist Lemon Syrup, 248
Orange Caraway Castles, 253
Orange Glazed Ginger, 254
Orange Madeira, 255
Pineapple Griestorte, 257
Soured Cream Coffee, 255
Spicy Honey Madeira, 248
Streusel Apple Flan, 262
Toddy, 259
Victoria Sandwich, 254
Walnut Coffee, 250
Calcutta Curry, 57
Cannellini and Chicken Soup, 25
Caramel Banana Torte, 261
Caramelled Gammon, 88
Caraway
and Orange Castles, 253
Dumplings, with Veal Goulash, 96
Carbonade of Beef, 57
Cardamon and Carrot Soup, 30
Carrot
and Cardamon Soup, 30
and Onion with Parsnip Sauce, 174
and Watercress Soup, 25
Cake, Honey Frosted, 259
Vichy, 176
Casserole
Beef, Four-in-one, 66
Lambs' Hearts in a, 131
Liver and Sausage, 124
Minted Lamb, 73
of Rolled Stuffed Veal, 96
Red Pepper and Pasta, 188
Spring Pork, 86
Casseroled Lamb with Aubergine, 72
Cassis, 274
Cassoulet, 78
Cauliflower
and Celery Pie, 145
and Tuna Salad, 196
Buttermilk Soup, 28
Chilled, with Lemon Dressing, 208
Fritters, 164
Spicy, Medley, 168
Celery
and Cauliflower Pie, 145
and Cheese Potage, 28
and Kidney Broth, 118
and Stilton Soup, 25
Braised, 167
Lentil, Ragout, 174
Mousse, Hot Blue Cheese and, 156
stuffed Pork Shoulder, 78
Charlotte
Gooseberry, 228
Steamed Apple, 225
Cheese, 156–162
and Celery Potage, 28
and Chicory Salad, 204
and Corn Soufflé, 157
and Date Triangles, 265
and Onion Pie, 143
and Tomato Fries, 143
Blue, Dip, (with variation), 12
Blue, Rarebits, 157
Cheesey-stuffed Aubergines, 140
Corn Dip, 12
Cottage, and Ham Cocottes, 91
Courgettes au Gratin, 158
Fondue, 160
Grandma's, Pudding, 157
Herby, Dip, 12
Hot Blue, and Celery Mousse, 156
Macaroni, 156
Palmiers, 11
Sticks, 265
Stilton, Savoury Eggs with, 15
Sweet, Pie, 222
Two-cheese Egg Salad, 201
Cheesecake
Pineapple, 226
Savoury, 226
Cherry
and Coconut Cake, 253
Scones, 262
Chestnut Stuffing, 214
Chicken, 98–107
and Apricot Pasta, 184
and Barley Broth, 105
and Cannellini Soup, 25
and Leek Pudding, 102
and Macaroni Broth, 30
and Red Bean Salad, 196
and Sweetcorn Potato Cakes, 107
Baked Drumsticks with Peanuts, 98
Bird in a Pot, 101
Chinese, 98
Coronation, 99
Curried, Envelopes, 101
Curried, Pilaff, 98
Honey Barbecued, 101
Hotpot, 106
Liver and Orange Skewers, 129
Liver Sauté, 129
Liver Toasties, 19
Livers Aloha, 124
Oriental, Salad, 206
Pâté, 20
Poached, with Horseradish Sauce, 101
Roast, 107
Scalloped, with Potatoes, 98
with Lemon and Almonds, 104
with Tarragon Sauce, 102
Chicory and Cheese Salad, 204
Chilled Cauliflower with Lemon Dressing, 208
Chilli
Beef with Beans, 58
Pizza Fingers, 145
Chinese
Chicken, 98
Fried Rice, 190
style Egg Drop Soup, 151
Chocolate
Blackcurrant Gâteau, 231
Frosted Cake, 256
Fudge Cake, 250
Marbled Cake, 259
Mousse au Chocolat, 236
Orange Sponge Pudding, 220
Rich Ring, 257
Chops, Liver and Bacon, 128
Choux Cream Puffs, 262
Chowder, Smoked Haddock, 50
Chunky Beef with Celery, 64
Cider
Baked Rabbit with Cabbage, 114
Cake, Fruit Crusted, 256
Hot Spiced, 279
poached Whole Apples, 221
Pork Sauté, 85
Cinnamon
and Apricot Cake, 259
Sponge Drops with Cream, 248
Citrus Apple Flan, 234
Coburg, Oatmeal, 243
Cocktail
Brandy, 279
Halibut, 19
Prawn, 12
Coconut
and Cherry Cake, 253
Cake, Frosted, 256
Cod
and Cucumber Mornay, 47
Roe Patties, 37
Smoked, Patties, 37
Steak with Mushrooms and Spinach, 52
with Coriander in Cream, 41
Coffee
Cream Soufflés, 236
Irish, 277
Praline Gâteau, 261
Walnut Coffee Cake, 250
Coley, Golden Glazed, 50
Compote, Rhubarb and Orange, 221
Cookies, Honey Crunch, 264
Corn
and Bacon Stuffing, 215
and Cheese Soufflé, 157
and Leek Slaw, 176
and Pork Pan Supper, 86
Dip, 12
filled Tomatoes, Hot, 164
Corn Dip, 12
Cornmeal, Golden, Loaves, 243
Coronation Chicken, 99
Cottage Cheese and Ham Cocottes, 91
Cottage Pie, 55
Courgette
and Potato Savoury, 168
au Gratin, 158
Provençale, 172
with Walnuts and Sage, 170
Cream
Choux Puffs, 262
of Onion Soup, 30
of Parsley Soup, 22
Creamed
Brussels, 168
Butter Beans, 171
Crème Brûlée, 231
Crêpes, Curried Haddock, 42
Crisp Lettuce with Orange Salad, 208
Crispy Fish Dumplings, 50
Croquettes
Bacon and Egg, 152
Cabbage and Hazelnut, 167
Fish, 37
Croûtes, Egg and Spinach, 151
Crumble, Cheshire Lamb, 70
Cucumber
and Cod Mornay, 47
Tzaziki, 19
Curd, Lemon Honey, 271
Curried
Bacon Flan, 90
Chicken Envelopes, 101
Chicken Pilaff, 98
Egg and Potato Slice, 153
Egg Deckers, 153
Haddock Crêpes, 42
Parsnip Soup, 25
Pasta Soup, 28
Rice, 190
Seafood Pasta, 183
Curry
Calcutta, 57
Prawn, 38
Sauce, Mild, 212
Custard
Sponge, Rich, 225
Tarts, Almond, 238

Daiquiri, 274
Dark Ginger Cake, 251
Date
and Cheese Triangles, 265
and Oatmeal Muffins, 265
and Spice Cake, 256
Deckers, Curried Egg, 153
Deep-dish Apricot Streusel, 222
Deep-fried Fish Fillets, 37
Desserts, Cold, 226–238
Almond Custard Tarts, 238
Aromatic Fruit Salad, 226
Banana and Honey Ice-cream, 231
Banana Chiffon Pie, 226
Blancmange, 235
Chocolate Blackcurrant Gâteau, 231
Citrus Apple Flan, 234
Coffee Cream Soufflés, 236
Crème Brûlée, 231
English Trifle, 236
Fresh Fruit Flan, 236
Gooseberry Charlotte, 228
Gooseberry Whip, 230
Honey Mousse, 232
Honeyed Gooseberry Fool, 226
Iced Orange Sabayon, 228
Kiwi Trifle, 232
Lemon Prune Mousse, 232

Desserts (*contd*)
Mocha Roulade, 238
Mousse au Chocolat, 236
Pineapple Brûlée, 231
Pineapple Cheesecake, 226
Rhubarb Orange Fool, 235
Strawberry and Almond Japanois, 229
Strawberry Ginger Crisps, 232
Strawberry Vacherin, 229
Strawberries with Raspberry Sauce, 230
Tangerine Melon Mousse, 231
Desserts, Hot, 218–225
All Seasons Fruit Salad Pie, 218
Apple Flapjack, 218
Apricot and Ginger Upside-down Pudding, 225
Banana Apricot Puffs, 221
Chocolate Orange Sponge Pudding, 220
Cider-poached Whole Apples, 221
Deep-dish Apricot Streusel, 222
Flambé Bananas, 221
Gingered Pears, 218
Golden Pudding, 224
Honey Lemon Surprise Pudding, 218
Old-fashioned Rice Pudding, 222
Orange Layer Pudding, 223
Plum and Apple Double Crust Pie, 222
Plum Upside-down Pudding, 221
Rhubarb and Orange Compote, 221
Rhubarb Crunch, 221
Rich Custard Sponge, 225
Rich Grape Bread-and-Butter Pudding, 224
Spiced Pancakes, 225
Steamed Apple Charlotte, 225
Sweet Cheese Pie, 222
Walnut Waffles, 220
Dip
Blue Cheese, 12
Corn, 12
Herby Cheese, 12
Dough, Basic Enriched White, 242
Drinks, 274–280
Bitter Lemon, 280
Bloody Mary, 277
Brandy Alexander, 277
Brandy Cocktail, 279
Cassis, 274
Daiquiri, 274
Dry Martini, 274
Egg Nog, 274
Everton Blue, 277
Grasshopper, 277
Home-made ginger beer, 280
Honeysuckle Cup, 279
Hot Honey Toddy, 274
Hot Rumour, 277
Hot Spiced Cider, 279
Ice Cream Soda, 280
Irish Coffee, 277
June Cup, 279
Lemon Barley Water, 280
Manhattan, 277
Negroni, 279
Orange and Grapefruit Squash, 280
Orangeade, 280
Pina Colada, 277
Pippin Cold Punch, 279
Punch, 274
Rum Punch, 279
'Still' Lemonade, 280
Sweet Martini, 274
Whisky Sour, 279
Drumsticks, Baked with Peanuts, 98
Duck and Game, 116–117
Duckling
Ratatouille, 116
with Raisin Rice Stuffing, 116
Dumplings
Crispy Fish, 50
with Baked Liver, 124
Dry Martini, 274

Eastern
Casserole of Lamb, 73
Spiced Liver, 127
Eggs, 148–155
All-in-one Supper, 152
and Anchovy Crispy Fries, 155
and Bacon Croquettes, 152
and Bacon Pilaff, 157
and Spinach Croûtes, 151
and Tomato Gratin, 152
Appetiser, Anchovy, 19
Arnold Bennett Omelette, 34
Baked, 151
Baked with Mushrooms, 151
Breakfast in a Pan, 154
Chinese Style, Drop Soup, 151
Curried, and Potato Slice, 153
Deckers, Curried, 153
Egg Nog, 274
Fricassée, 148
Omelette in a Roll, 148
Omelette Niçoise, 154
Poached, with Cucumber and Coriander Sauce, 155
Salad, and Italian Tomato, 203
Savoury with Stilton, 15
Spanish-style Omelette, 154
Stuffed, Mayonnaise, 153
Tarragon Buttered, on Pasta, 152
English Trifle, 236
Escalopes, Turkey with Hazelnut Cream Sauce, 110

Fennel and Watercress Salad, 202
Fish, 34–52 (*see also* Cod, Haddock, etc)
and Butter Bean Pie, 44
Dumplings, Crispy, 50
en Papillote, 45
Fillets, Baked with Lemon Sauce, 41
Fillets, Deep-fried, 37
Hot Pot, Summer, 52
Quenelles, 48
Fisherman's Hot Pot, 47
Flambé, Bananas, 221
Flan
Apple Streusel, 262
Citrus Apple, 234
Curried Bacon, 90
Fresh Fruit, 236
Kidney Bean and Tomato, 145
Tomato and Onion, 139
Flapjack, Apple, 218
Flower Pots, Mustard, 246
Fondant Potatoes, 176
Fondue, Cheese, 160
Fool
Honeyed Gooseberry, 226
Rhubarb Orange, 235
Frankfurter
and Beans with Sauerkraut, 134
Ratatouille, 132
French Bread, 240
Fresh Fruit Flan, 236
Fricassée
Egg, 148
of Veal, 92
Fried Liver and Bacon, 128
Fritters
Cauliflower, 164
Sweetcorn, 176
Frosted
Chocolate Cake, 256
Coconut Cake, 256
Fruit
Cake, Brazil Butter, 248
Cake, Crusted Cider, 256
Flan, Fresh, 236
Salad, Aromatic, 226
Salad Pie, All Seasons, 218
Fruited Butterscotch Ring, 246

Game and Duck, 116–117
Gammon
Caramelled, 88
Roast, 88
Garden Salad, 201
Gâteau, Chocolate Blackcurrant, 250
Ginger
and Apricot Stuffing, 215
and Apricot Upside-down Pudding, 225
and Melon Jam, 272
beer, Home-made, 280
Cake, Dark, 251
Cake, Orange Glazed, 254
Crisps, Strawberry, 232
Gingerbread, Grantham, 264
Gingered Pears, 218
Golden
Coley, Glazed, 50
Cornmeal Loaves, 243
Pudding, 224
Vegetable Soup, 24
Gooseberry
Charlotte, 228
Fool, Honeyed, 226
Sauce, 213
Whip, 230
Goujons
Liver, with Orange Sauce, 127
of Liver, 126
Goulash, 58
Veal, with Caraway Dumplings, 96
Granary Tea Cake, 244
Grandma's Cheese Pudding, 157
Grantham Gingerbreads, 264
Grapefruit
and Orange Squash, 280
Grilled, 12
Salad, Smoky Avocado and, 207
Grasshopper, 277
Gratin, Egg and Tomato, 152
Greek Salad, 198
Greengage Coconut Sponge, 218
Greens, Stir-fried, 170
Grilled
Grapefruit, 12
Herrings, 48

Haddock
and Mushroom Puffs, 42
au Gratin, 50
Curried, Crêpes, 42
Kedgeree, 38
Savoury, Crumble, 52
Seafood Scallops, 16
Smoked, Chowder, 50
Halibut
Cocktail, 19
Marinated Steaks, 52
Ham
Cocottes, Cottage Cheese and, 91
Stuffing, 215
Hazelnut
and Almond Barquettes, 263
and Cabbage Croquettes, 167
Genoese, Apple, 253
Hearts
Lambs', in a Casserole, 131
Ragout of Ox, with Lemon, 130
Herb
Oatcakes, 214
Stuffing, 265
Herby Cheese Dip, 12
Home-made ginger beer, 280
Home-made Rye, 246
Honey
and Banana Ice-cream, 231
Barbecued Chicken, 101
Crunch Cookies, 264
Frosted Carrot Cake, 259
Lemon Surprise Pudding, 218
Mousse, 232
Nut Stick, 246
Honeyed Gooseberry Fool, 226
Honeysuckle Cup, 279
Horseradish
Cream, 212
Crown, 246
Hot
and Sour Soup, 26
Blue Cheese and Celery Mousse, 156
Corn-filled Tomatoes, 164

Hot (*contd*)
Cross Buns, 244
Desserts, *see* Desserts, Hot
Honey Toddy, 274
Rumour, 277
Savoury Soufflé, 152
Spiced Cider, 279
Hot Pot
Fisherman's, 47
Lamb and Cider, 73
Summer Fish, 52
Hungarian Veal, 95

Ice Cream
Banana and Honey, 231
Soda, 280
Iced Orange Sabayon, 228
Individual Yorkshire Puddings, 62
Irish
Coffee, 277
Stew, 69

Jams, 268–272
Apricot, 271
Lemon Honey Curd, 271
Melon and Ginger, 272
potting and covering, 268
preparing jars for, 268
Seville Orange Marmalade, 272
testing for set, 208
Three-fruit Marmalade, 272
Whole Strawberry Jam, 268
Jellies, 268–272
Blackberry and Apple, 268
Redcurrant, 272
Jumbo Stuffed Tomatoes, 15
June Cup, 279

Kebabs
Lamb and Apricot, 71
Salad, 204
Kedgeree, Haddock, 38
Kidney, 118–123
à la Crème, 118
and Bacon Roly Poly, 119
and Celery Broth, 118
and Mushroom Pie with Lemon, 118
and Pasta Soup, 121
and Steak Pudding, 54
and Veal Deep Dish Pie, 95
in Batter, 120
in Sherry Sauce, 123
Sautéed, 118
Kiev, Veal, 95
Kiwi Trifle, 232

Lamb, 68–77
and Apricot Kebabs, 71
and Cider Hotpot, 73
and Maître d'Hôtel Butter, 72
and Spinach au Gratin, 74
Apple and Lemon, 76
Aubergine Moussaka, 74
Blanquette d'Agneau, 68
Casserole, Minted, 73
Casseroled, with Aubergine, 72
Cassoulet, 78
Crumble, Cheshire, 70
Cutlets, Marinaded, with Rosemary, 68
Eastern Casserole of, 73
Fillet of, with Black Beans, 68
Hearts in a Casserole, 131
in Tomato Sauce, 77
Irish Stew, 69
Piquant, with Rosemary, 76
Pot Roast with Bean Stuffing, 74
Savoury, and Mushrooms, 69
Shoulder of, Stuffed with Apricots, 71
Sweet and Sour, with Pasta, 70
Tikka Kebab, 76
Tongues Portugaise, 131
with Fennel, 73
with Orange Sauce, 68
Lancashire Tripe and Onions, 131
Lasagne al Forno, 186

Layered Potatoes and Swedes, 170
Leeks
and Chicken Pudding, 102
and Corn Slaw, 176
and Split Pea Soup, 25
in Cheese Sauce, 160
with Crumbed Pork, 82
with Potato Topped Liver, 126
Lemon
Barley Water, 280
dressed Avocado Salad, 203
Honey Curd, 271
Moist Syrup Cake, 248
Prune Mousse, 232
Seed Cake, 261
Swiss Roll, 257
Lemonade, 'Still', 280
Lemony Bean Appetiser, 8
Lentil
and Swede Purée, 30
Celery Ragout, 174
Lettuce
Crisp, with Orange Salad, 208
Liver, 124–129
and Bacon Chops, 128
and Sausage Casserole, 124
and Sausage Ragout, 129
Baked, with Dumplings, 124
Chicken, Aloha, 124
Chicken, Pâté, 20
Chicken, Sautée, 129
Chicken, Toasties, 19
Eastern Spiced, 127
Fried, with Bacon, 128
Goujons of, 126
Goujons with Orange Sauce, 127
in Stroganoff Sauce, 128
Jardinière, 127
Mexican, 126
Potato Topped, with Leeks, 126
Potted, Pop-ins, 124
Quick-fried, with Red Beans, 128
Rumaki, 129
Skewers, Chicken and Orange, 129
stuffed Cannelloni, 127
with Rice in Tomato Sauce, 126
Loaf, Sage and Onion Salad, 242

Macaroni
and Cheese Broth, 30
Cheese, 156
Mackerel
Barley-stuffed, 42
Fillets, Stuffed, 48
Smoked, Mousse, 8
Smothered, 42
Madeira, Orange, 254
Manhattan, 277
Marbled Chocolate Cake, 259
Marinaded Lamb Cutlets with Rosemary, 68
Marinated Halibut Steaks, 52
Marmalade
Seville Orange, 272
Spice Cake, 253
Three-fruit, 272
Martini
Dry, 274
Sweet, 274
Marzipan Pineapple Cake, 250
Mayonnaise
Classic, 210
Stuffed Egg, 153
Meatballs
Oriental, 60
Spicy, 64
Melon
and Ginger Jam, 272
Seafood Salad, 8
Tangerine Mousse, 231
Meunière Sweetbreads, 130
Mexican Liver, 126
Midweek Bacon Stew, 90
Mild Curry Sauce, 212
Millet and Nut Burgers, 146

Mince
and Bacon Pie, 61
in a Crust, 67
with Rice, 108
Mini Heroes, 132
Mint and Rosemary Stuffing, 215
Minted
Lamb Casserole, 73
Pear Vinaigrette, 19
Mixed
Bean Salad, 203
Glazed Vegetables, 168
Salad, 203
Mocha Roulade, 238
Moist Lemon Syrup Cake, 248
Mornay, Cod and Cucumber, 47
Moussaka, Lamb and Aubergine, 74
Mousse
au Chocolat, 236
Honey, 232
Hot Blue Cheese and Celery, 156
Lemon Prune, 232
Smoked Mackerel, 8
Tangerine Melon, 231
Mozzarella Salad, 203
Muffins, Date and Oatmeal, 265
Mulligatawny Soup, 22
Mushrooms
and Kidney Pie with Lemon, 118
and Peas, 172
and Rice Broth, 30
Puffs, and Haddock, 42
Soup, Hot and Sour, 26
Stir-fried, and Beansprouts, 170
Stuffed, 15
Stuffing, 214
Sweet Pickled, 15
with Baked Eggs, 151
with Pork, 82
Mussel Bisque, 29
Mustard Sauce, 211

Negroni, 279
Niçoise, Omelette, 154
Noodles in Walnut Sauce, 188
Nut
and Millet Burgers, 146
Butter Biscuits, 265
Stuffing, 214

Oatcakes, Herb, 265
Oatmeal
and Date Muffins, 265
Coburg, 243
Offal, 130–131
Boiled Ox Tongue, 130
Lambs' Hearts in a Casserole, 131
Lambs' Tongues Portugaise, 131
Lancashire Tripe and Onions, 131
Oxtail Paprika, 130
Ragout of Ox Heart with Lemon, 130
Sweetbreads in Mushrooms and Cream, 131
Sweetbreads Meunière, 130
Okra and Apple with Veal, 94
Old-fashioned Rice Pudding, 222
Omelette
Arnold Bennett, 34
in a Roll, 148
Niçoise, 154
Spanish-style, 154
Onions
and Carrot with Parsnip Sauce, 174
and Cheese Pie, 143
and Sage Stuffing, 215
and Tomato Flan, 139
and Tomato Salad, 11
Cream of Onion Soup, 30
Pizza Pie, 140
Spread, 11
Orange
and Caraway Castles, 253
and Chicken Liver Skewers, 129
and Grapefruit Squash, 280
and Rhubarb Compote, 221

Orange (*contd*)
and Spinach Soup, 24
Ginger Knot, 243
Glazed Ginger Cake, 254
Glazed Spare Ribs, 84
Layer Pudding, 223
Madeira, 254
Rhubarb Fool, 235
Sabayon, Iced, 228
Salad with Crisp Lettuce, 208
Orangeade, 280
Oriental
Chicken Salad, 206
Meatballs, 60–61
Osso Buco, 96
Oven-fried Potato Balls, 164
Ox
Heart Ragout with Lemon, 138
Tongue, Boiled, 130
Oxtail Paprika, 130

Paella, 193
Palmiers, Cheese, 11
Pan Pizza, 136
Pancakes
Bacon Blintzes, 90
Spiced, 225
Paprika, Oxtail, 130
Parcelled Pork, 80
Parsley Soup, Cream of, 22
Parsnip
Curried, Soup, 25
Sauce, with Onion and Carrot, 174
Souffléed, 170
Partridge, with Grapes, 117
Pasta, 180–189
and Frankfurter Scramble, 184
and Kidney Soup, 121
Bake, 180
Chicken Apricot, 184
Curried, Seafood, 183
Curried, Soup, 28
Lasagne al Forno, 186
Red Pepper and, Casserole, 188
Salami Antipasta, 8
Sausage Rolls, 188
Spaghetti alla Carbonara, 167
Spinach and Ham Cannelloni, 183
Tarragon Buttered Eggs on, 152
Tuna and, in Soured Cream, 183
Vegetable Lasagne, 184
with Broccoli, 184
with Kidney Sauce, 180
with Peas and Ham in Cream Sauce, 183
Pâté, 20
Patties
Bean and Pork, 86
Cod Roe, with Corn Sauce, 47
Smoked Cod, 37
Peanut
Crunches, 266
Drumsticks Baked with, 98
Glazed Bacon Hock, 88
Pear, Minted Vinaigrette, 19
Peas
and Mushrooms, 172
Gingered, 218
Soup, Shropshire, 32
with Rice, 192
Peasant-style Roulades, 61
Pease Pudding, 176
Penny Pinchers' Pizza, 143
Pepper
Red, and Pasta Casserole, 188
Soup, Speedy Tomato and, 32
Peppered Lamb Stew, 76
Pork with Fruit, 80
Pheasant with Cranberries, 117
Pickled Popover, 132
Pie
Apple Almond, 262
Banana Chiffon, 226
Celery and Cauliflower, 145
Cottage, 55
Fruit Salad, All Seasons, 218
Kidney and Mushroom, with Lemon, 118
Mince and Bacon, 116
Onion and Cheese, 143
Onion, Pizza, 140
Pigeon, 116
Plum and Apple Double Crust, 222
Poacher's, 114
Rabbit and Forcemeat, 114
Sausage Double-crust, 132
Sweet Cheese, 222
Veal and Kidney Deep Dish, 95
Pigeon
Pie, 116
with Prunes, 117
Wood, in Beer, 117
Pilaff, Curried Chicken, 98
Pina Colada, 277
Pineapple
Brûlée, 231
Cheesecake, 226
Griestorte, 257
Marzipan Cake, 250
Pippin Cold Punch, 279
Piquant Lamb with Rosemary, 76
Pizza
Chilli, Fingers, 145
Onion Pie, 140
Pan, 136
Penny Pinchers', 143
Quick, 138
Plum
and Apple Double Crust Pie, 222
Upside-down Pudding, 221
Poached
Chicken with Horseradish Cream Sauce, 101
Eggs with Cucumber and Coriander Sauce, 155
Poacher's Pie, 114
Pop-ins, Potted Liver, 124
Popovers, Pickle, 132
Poppyseed Rolls, 247
Pork, 78–87
and Apple Loaf, 80
and Apricot Parcels, 78
and Bean Patties, 86
and Corn Pan Supper, 86
and Vegetables, Stir-fried, 86
Casserole, Spring, 86
Cassoulet, 78
Chops, Baked Stuffed, 80
Crumbled, with Leeks, 82
Parcelled, 80
Peppered, with Fruit, 80
Sauté, Cider, 85
Shoulder, Celery-stuffed, 78
Spare Ribs, Orange-glazed, 84
Spiced, with Dumplings, 78
Stuffed, Sage and Bacon, 81
Tenderloins, Rolled, 84
with Mushrooms, 82
with Tomato and Barley, 81
Portugaise Lambs' Tongues, 131
Portuguese Skate, 47
Pot-au-feu, 64
Pot Roast Chicken with Horseradish Cream Sauce, 101
Potato
and Brussels Sprouts Purée, 28
and Courgette Savoury, 168
and Swede, Layered, 170
Balls, Oven-fried, 164
Cakes, Chicken and Sweetcorn, 107
Fondant, 176
Liver Topped with, and Leeks, 126
Sauté, 172
Slice, Curried Egg and, 153
Spinach Wedges, 172
Tuna-stuffed Baked, 146
Whole, Salad, 203
with Scalloped Chicken, 98
Potted Liver Pop-ins, 124
Prawn
Cocktail, 12
Curry, 38
Stir-fried, 38
Prune, Lemon Mousse, 232
Pudding
Apricot and Ginger Upside-down, 225
Chicken and Leek, 102
Chocolate Orange Sponge, 220
Golden, 224
Grandma's Cheese, 157
Honey Lemon Surprise, 218
Individual Yorkshire, 62
Old-fashioned Rice, 222
Orange Layer, 223
Pease, 176
Plum Upside-down, 221
Rich Grape Bread-and-Butter, 224
Steak and Kidney, 54
Punch
Pippin Cold, 279
Rum, 279
Purée
Brussels Sprouts and Potato, 28
Swede and Lentil, 30

Quenelles, 48
Quiche, Asparagus and Bacon, 90
Quick
Fried Liver with Red Beans, 128
Pizza, 138

Rabbit, 114–115
and Forcemeat Pie, 114
Cider Baked, with Cabbage, 114
Poacher's Pie, 114
Ragout
Lentil Celery, 174
Liver and Sausage, 129
of Ox Heart with Lemon, 130
of Veal, 95
Turkey, with Savoury Scones, 113
Rarebits, Blue Cheese, 157
Raspberry Sauce with Strawberries, 230
Ratatouille, 175
Duckling, 116
Frankfurter, 132
Red
Bean and Chicken Salad, 196
Cabbage and Apple Salad, 196
Cabbage and Sausage Soup, 22
Pepper and Pasta Casserole, 188
Redcurrant Jelly, 272
Rhubarb
and Orange Compote, 221
Crunch, 221
Orange Fool, 235
Rice, 190–194
and Mushroom Broth, 30
Bakes, Tuna, 12
Chinese Fried, 190
Curried, 190
Mince with, 193
Paella, 193
Pudding, Old-fashioned, 222
Risotto alla Milanese, 193
Salad, 203
Spanish, 190
Stuffing, 214
Vegetable and Egg Risotto, 193
with Liver in Tomato Sauce, 126
with Peas, 190
Yellow, Casseroled, 190
Rich
Chocolate Ring, 257
Custard Sponge, 225
Grape Bread-and-Butter Pudding, 224
Risotto alla Milanese, 193
Roast
Beef, 62
Chicken,107
Gammon, 88
Rolled Pork Tenderloins, 84
Rolls
Poppyseed, 247
Sausage Pasta, 188
Roly Poly, Kidney and Bacon, 119

Rosemary and Mint Stuffing, 215
Roulades
  Mocha, 238
  Peasant-style, 61
  Spinach and Lentil, 136
Rum
  Punch, 279
  Rumaki, 129
Russian Salad, 196
Rye, Home Made, 246

Sabayon, Iced Orange, 228
Sage
  and Bacon Stuffed Pork, 81
  and Onion Salad Loaf, 242
  and Onion Stuffing, 215
  and Walnuts with Courgettes, 170
Salad
  Fruit, Aromatic, 226
  Onion and Tomato, 11
  Seafood, Melon, 8
Salads, 196–208
  Avocado and Red Bean, 207
  Cheese and Chicory, 204
  Chilled Cauliflower with Lemon Dressing, 208
  Cold Beef in Soured Cream, 199
  Coleslaw, 201
  Crisp Lettuce with Orange, 208
  Fennel and Watercress, 202
  Garden, 201
  Greek, 198
  Italian Tomato and Egg, 203
  Kebabs, 204
  Lemon-dressed Avocado, 203
  Mixed, 203
  Mixed Bean, 205
  Mozzarella, 203
  Oriental Chicken, 206
  Red Bean and Chicken, 196
  Red Cabbage and Apple, 196
  Rice, 203
  Russian, 196
  Salade Niçoise, 201
  Slimmer's Platter, 205
  Smoky Avocado and Grapefruit, 207
  Spinach and Avocado, 202
  Tomato, with Basil, 204
  Tuna and Cauliflower, 196
  Two-cheese Egg, 201
  Waldorf, 198
  Watercress, Sweet Pepper and Apple, 205
  Whole Potato, 202
Salami
  Antipasta, 8
  Mini Heroes, 130
Sandwich, Victoria Cake, 254
Sardine
  Fresh, with Herbs, 34
  Savouries, 16
Sauces, 210–213
  Barbecue, 210
  Bread, 210
  Butterscotch, 213
  Classic Mayonnaise, 210
  Horseradish Cream, 213
  Mild Curry, 212
  Mustard, 211
  Sharp Gooseberry, 213
  Tartare, 210
  Tomato, 210
Sauerkraut, with Beans and Frankfurters, 134
Sausage
  and Liver Casserole, 124
  and Red Cabbage, 22
  Double-crust Pie, 132
  Frankfurter Ratatouille, 132
  Frankfurters with Beans and Sauerkraut, 134
  Mini Heroes, 132
  Pasta Rolls, 188
  Ragout, Liver and, 129
  Toad in the Hole, 132
  Yorkshires with Onion Sauce, 135
Sauté
  Chicken Liver, 129
  Cider Pork, 85
  Potatoes, 172
Sautéed Kidneys, 118
Savouries, Sardine, 16
Savoury
  Cheesecake, 162
  Eggs with Stilton, 15
  Haddock Crumble, 52
  Lamb and Mushrooms, 69
  Potato and Courgette, 168
  Scones with Turkey Ragout, 113
  Soufflé, Hot, 154
  Spring Cabbage, 178
Scalloped Chicken with Potatoes, 98
Scallops, Seafood, 16
Scones, Cherry, 262
Scottish Baps, 247
Seafood
  Melon Salad, 8
  Scallops, 16
Seville Orange Marmalade, 272
Sharp Gooseberry Sauce, 213
Shoulder of Lamb Stuffed with Apricots, 71
Shropshire Pea Soup, 32
Skate Portuguese, 47
Slaw, Leek and Corn, 176
Smoked
  Cod Patties, 37
  Haddock Chowder, 50
  Mackerel Mousse, 8
Smoky Avocado and Grapefruit Salad, 207
Smothered Mackerel, 42
Soda, Ice Cream, 280
Soufflé
  Cheese and Corn, 157
  Coffee Cream, 236
  Hot Savoury, 154
  Parsnip, 170
Soups, 22–33
  Bortsch, 26
  Brussels Sprouts and Potato Purée, 28
  Cannellini and Chicken, 25
  Carrot and Cardamon, 30
  Cauliflower Buttermilk, 28
  Celery and Stilton, 25
  Cheese and Celery Potage, 28
  Chicken and Macaroni Broth, 30
  Chinese-style Egg Drop, 151
  Cream of Onion, 30
  Cream of Parsley, 22
  Curried Parsnip, 25
  Curried Pasta, 28
  Golden Vegetable, 24
  Hot and Sour, 26
  Kidney and Pasta, 121
  Leek and Split Pea, 25
  Mulligatawny, 22
  Mushroom and Rice, 30
  Mussel Bisque, 29
  Red Cabbage and Sausage, 22
  Shropshire Pea, 32
  Speedy Tomato and Pepper, 32
  Spinach and Lamb au Gratin, 74
  Spinach and Orange, 24
  Swede and Lentil Purée, 30
  Watercress and Carrot, 25
  White Bean, 22
Sour and Hot Soup, 26
Soured Cream Coffee Cake, 254
Spaghetti
  alla Carbonara, 187
  Bolognaise, 188
  Napoletana, 180
Spanish
  Rice, 190
  style Omelette, 154
Spare Ribs, Orange-glazed, 84
Speedy Tomato and Pepper Soup, 32
Spice
  and Dale Cake, 253
  Marmalade Cake, 253
Spiced
  Honey Madeira Cake, 248
  Onions, 11
  Pancakes, 225
  Pork with Dumplings, 78
Spicy
  Cauliflower Medley, 168
  Meatballs, 64
Spinach
  and Avocado Salad, 202
  and Ham Cannelloni, 183
  and Lamb au Gratin, 74
  and Lentil Roulade, 136
  and Orange Soup, 24
  Potato Wedges, 144
  with Nutmeg, 178
Split Pea and Leek Soup, 25
Sponge
  Cinnamon, Drops with Cream, 248
  Greengage Coconut, 231
  Rich Custard, 225
Spring
  Cabbage, Savoury, 178
  Pork Casserole, 86
Starters, 8–20
Steak
  and Kidney Pudding, 54
  Cannelloni au Gratin, 57
  Carbonade of Beef, 57
  Chilli Beef with Beans, 58
  Goulash, 58
  Pepperbag, 62
  Pie, 66
  Pudding, 54
  with Cream Sauce, 60
Steamed Apple Charlotte, 225
Stew
  Bacon, Midweek, 90
  Bean and Vegetable, 138
  Irish, 69
  Peppered Lamb, 76
'Still' Lemonade, 280
Stilton
  and Celery Soup, 25
  Eggs, Savoury with, 15
Stir-fried
  Cabbage with Caraway, 164
  Greens, 170
  Mushrooms and Bean Sprouts, 170
  Pork and Vegetable, 86
  Prawns, 38
Strawberry
  and Almond Japonais, 229
  Ginger Crisps, 232
  Vacharin, 229
  Whole Jam, 268
  with Raspberry Sauce, 230
Streusel
  Apple Flan, 262
  Apricot, Deep Dish, 222
Stroganoff Sauce, Liver in, 128
Stuffed
  Casserole of Rolled Veal, 96
  Cheesey Aubergines, 140
  Egg Mayonnaise, 153
  Liver, Cannelloni, 127
  Mackerel Fillets, 48
  Mushrooms, 15
  Shoulder of Lamb with Apricots, 71
  Tomatoes, Jumbo, 15
  Tuna Potatoes, Baked, 146
  Whole Cabbage, 43
Stuffings, 214–216
  Apple and Celery, 215
  Apricot and Ginger, 215
  Bacon or Ham, 215
  Chestnut, 214
  Corn and Bacon, 215
  Herb, 214
  Mint and Rosemary, 215
  Mushroom, 214
  Nut, 214
  Rice, 214
  Sage and Onion, 215
Summer Fish Hot Pot, 52

Swede
  and Lentil Purée, 30
  and Potatoes, Layered, 170
Sweet
  and Sour Lamb with Pasta, 70
  Cheese Pie, 222
  Pepper, Watercress and Apple Salad, 205
  Pickled Mushrooms, 15
Sweetbreads
  in Mushrooms and Cream, 131
  Meunière, 130
Sweetcorn
  and Chicken Potato Cakes, 107
  Fritters, 176
Swiss Roll, Lemon, 257

Tangerine Melon Mousse, 231
Tarragon Buttered Eggs on Pasta, 152
Tartare Sauce, 210
Tarts, Almond Custard, 238
Tea Cake, Granary, 244
Three-fruit Marmalade, 272
Toad in the Hole (with variation), 132
Toasties, Chicken Liver, 19
Toddy
  Cake, 259
  Hot Honey, 274
Tomato
  and Cheese Fries, 143
  and Egg Gratin, 152
  and Kidney Bean Flan, 145
  and Onion Flan, 139
  and Onion Salad, 11
  Hot Corn-filled, 164
  Italian, and Egg Salad, 203
  Jumbo, Stuffed, 15
  Salad with Basil, 204
  Sauce, 210
Tongues
  Lambs', Portugaise, 131
  Ox, Boiled, 130
Torte
  Caramel Banana, 261
Tortellini Bake, 180
Trifle
  English, 236
  Kiwi, 232
Tripe and Onions, Lancashire, 131
Trout in Cream, 38
Tuna
  and Cauliflower Salad, 196
  and Pasta in Soured Cream, 183
  Rice Bakes, 12
  stuffed Potatoes, Baked, 146
Turkey, 108–113
  Escalopes with Hazelnut Cream Sauce, 110
  in Spiced Yogurt, 108
  Ragout with Savoury Scones, 113
  'Sirloin', 112
Two-cheese Egg Salad, 201
Tzaziki (Cucumber), 19

Vacharin, Strawberry, 229
Veal, 92–95
  and Kidney Deep Dish Pie, 95
  Casserole of Rolled Stuffed, 96
  Fricassée of, 92
  Goulash with Caraway Dumplings, 96
  Hungarian, 95
  Kiev, 95
  Ragout of, 95
  with Okra and Apple, 94
Vegetable Dishes, 136–146
Vegetables, 164–178
  and Bean Stew, 138
  and Egg Risotto, 193
  Carrots, Vichy, 176
  Curried Parsnip Soup, 25
  Golden, Soup, 24
  Lasagne, 184
  Lemony Bean Appetiser, 8
  Mixed Glazed, 168
  Mushrooms, Stuffed, 15
  Okra and Apple with Veal, 94
  Onion and Tomato Salad, 11
  Onions, Spiced, 11
  Pot, 136
  Spinach and Orange Soup, 24
  Stir-fried Pork and, 86
  Tomato and Onion Flan, 139
Vichy Carrots, 176
Victoria Sandwich Cake, 254
Vinaigrette, Minted Pear, 19

Waffles, Walnut, 220
Waldorf Salad, 198
Walnut
  Coffee Cake, 250
  Waffles, 220
Walnuts and Sage with Courgettes, 170
Watercress
  and Carrot Soup, 25
  and Fennel Salad, 202
  Sweet Pepper and Apple Salad, 205
Wheatmeal, Anchovy Curl (Loaf), 203
Whip, Gooseberry, 230
Whisky Sour, 279
White
  Bean Soup, 22
  Bread, Basic, 242
  Dough, Enriched Basic, 242
Whole
  Potato Salad, 203
  Stuffed Cabbage, 143
Wholewheat, Barley Twist, 247
Wood Pigeon in Beer, 117

Yogurt, Spiced, Turkey in, 108
Yorkshire Puddings, Individual, 62
Yorkshires, Sausage, with Onion Sauce, 135

Zigzag Baton, 244